Skiing and S
in North America

written and researched by

Tam Leach, Stephen Timblin,
and Christian Williams

with additional contributions by
Alf Alderson

NEW YORK • LONDON • DELHI
www.roughguides.com

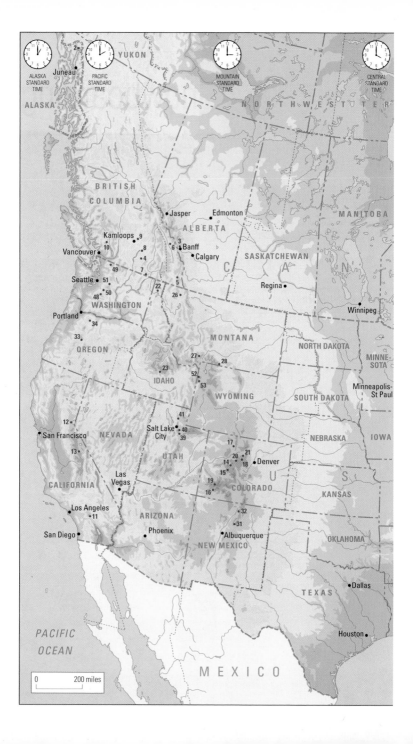

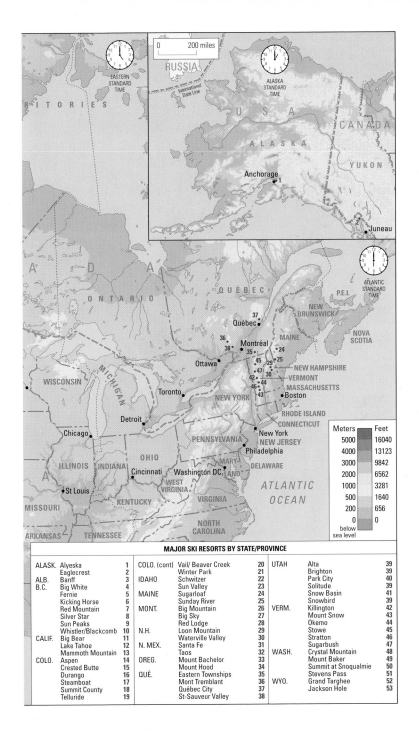

ATLANTIC STANDARD TIME

ALASKA STANDARD TIME

EASTERN STANDARD TIME

Meters	Feet
5000	16040
4000	13123
3000	9842
2000	6562
1000	3281
500	1640
200	656
0	0
below sea level	

0   200 miles

MAJOR SKI RESORTS BY STATE/PROVINCE

ALASK.	Alyeska	1	COLO. (cont)	Vail/ Beaver Creek	20	UTAH	Alta	39
	Eaglecrest	2		Winter Park	21		Brighton	39
ALB.	Banff	3	IDAHO	Schwitzer	22		Park City	40
B.C.	Big White	4		Sun Valley	23		Solitude	39
	Fernie	5	MAINE	Sugarloaf	24		Snow Basin	41
	Kicking Horse	6		Sunday River	25		Snowbird	39
	Red Mountain	7	MONT.	Big Mountain	26	VERM.	Killington	42
	Silver Star	8		Big Sky	27		Mount Snow	43
	Sun Peaks	9		Red Lodge	28		Okemo	44
	Whistler/Blackcomb	10	N.H.	Loon Mountain	29		Stowe	45
CALIF.	Big Bear	11		Waterville Valley	30		Stratton	46
	Lake Tahoe	12	N. MEX.	Santa Fe	31		Sugarbush	47
	Mammoth Mountain	13		Taos	32	WASH.	Crystal Mountain	48
COLO.	Aspen	14	OREG.	Mount Bachelor	33		Mount Baker	49
	Crested Butte	15		Mount Hood	34		Summit at Snoqualmie	50
	Durango	16	QUÉ.	Eastern Townships	35		Stevens Pass	51
	Steamboat	17		Mont Tremblant	36	WYO.	Grand Targhee	52
	Summit County	18		Québec City	37		Jackson Hole	53
	Telluride	19		St-Sauveur Valley	38			

Skiing and Snowboarding
in North America

North America offers some of the best skiing and snowboarding on the planet. From Alaska to Maine, New Mexico to Québec, more than 400 resorts are scattered across the continent; collectively they receive some 75 million ski visits each year. Ranging in style from destination resorts and corporate mega-mountains to day-use mom-and-pop hills, some located just outside major urban areas, they address the needs of every level of skier and every conceivable type of vacationer.

Distinctions go well past the types of resort on offer. **Snow quality**, for example, varies dramatically between regions; however, the resorts often meticulously groom their primary runs, and extensive snowmaking is prevalent at all but the smallest resorts. **Lodges**, both on and off the slopes, range from tiny, dilapidated cabins to enormous stone edifices filled with roaring fireplaces; all by and large maintain reliably high standards of service and quality, as do the resorts' attendant ski schools and facilities. Below the slopes, the **mountain towns** and **base areas** differ considerably in character. Some, like Aspen or Telluride in Colorado, are century-old mining towns that have been converted into attractive bases for skiers. Others, like Colorado's Vail or Squaw Valley in California, are modern, massive, and functional – though some resorts designed from scratch aren't

v

necessarily soulless, as proved by Tremblant in Québec and Whistler in British Columbia.

While it can be hard, and sometimes counterproductive, to generalize, important differences exist between the North American skiing and boarding scene and those elsewhere in the world. Curiously, on a continent specializing in gigantic proportions, even major North American ski resorts will feel relatively small in size in comparison to their sprawling European counterparts. In many areas, particularly in the US and Canadian Rockies, this is compensated by the proximity of resorts to one another – making multiple resorts an easy day-trip from one another. The character of the ski areas is also substantially different from those elsewhere, with most set at least in part below treeline and so generally consisting of a series of synthetic trails cut through wooded slopes. Many of these can be extremely similar and feel conspicuously artificial, sometimes even monotonous. But this is more than offset by the abundance of fantastic **tree-skiing** in many areas – as well as the high quality of **terrain parks** and **pipes** that cover at least one run at

> **The western half of the continent is where the finest alpine terrain is found**

nearly every resort. Similarly, while **backcountry skiing** around North American resorts is frequently discouraged or forbidden, the presence of off-piste terrain within resort boundaries – maintained to neutralize avalanche danger – makes the availability of relatively safe expert runs here an absolute highlight. A final, more superficial, difference is in the **grading system**. Green circles denote beginner runs; blue squares intermediate; black and double black diamonds advanced and expert runs respectively.

Where to go

This is obviously the million-dollar question, with so much at your disposal and so many considerations to take into account. You might consider heading for deep powder stashes in the Rockies, relaxed cruising and carving in the East, heliskiing in Alaska, or spring riding in the Sierra Nevadas and Cascades. You may be looking for the most proximate ski hill for a day-long getaway, or an area which provides something new to tackle each day of an extended vacation.

The first decision likely involves location. While North American resorts differ enormously, there are several **distinct geographical regions** where ski areas share similar characteristics, as reflected in the chapter arrangement of this book. We cover the US first, east to west, then go back and do the same with Canada; note, though, that you

> **An overriding factor in your choice of resort should be your own abilities**

can smoothly cross borders between the two, if you want to ski a bit of both countries on a longer trip. The western half of the continent is where the finest alpine terrain is found, with the lion's share of top-notch ski areas dotted north to south along the hulking Rocky Mountains, which extend from Canada all the way down to the Southwest USA. These tend to have the lightest snow, largest acreage, and the most visitors; they often are

typically the most expensive as well. Further west, closer to the Pacific, the snow becomes wetter and heavier, the terrain often more challenging.

Snowfall is as important as natural terrain in terms of deciding where to go. In general, storms are heaviest on the West Coast as the Sierra Nevada and Cascade ranges form natural blockades that snatch the full force of precipitation off the Pacific Ocean. The dense, moist snow that results doesn't just fall, it dumps (three to six feet in a single day is not unusual), but more often than not it's overly heavy with texture more akin to oat-

The origins of skiing and snowboarding in North America

Thought to have been first invented by Scandinavians – archeologists in Sweden found short wide skis estimated to be 4500 years old – skiing was brought to North America by their descendants in the 1800s. It was in California's Sierra Nevadas that immigrant gold miners began to use 12-foot solid oak skis and a pole for propulsion. But commercialized downhill skiing on the continent was more or less born in Sun Valley, Idaho, which opened its first lifts in 1936, copying successful initiatives in Europe. North America can claim credit for inventing snowboarding, a sport first inspired by the popularity of the "snurfer" – a plank with a rope tied to the nose developed in the 1960s. Snowboards resembling their present form began to appear in the 1970s, thanks in large part to the efforts of one of the sport's most renowned architects, Jake Burton; he debuted his innovations at Vermont's Stratton Mountain in 1977. Since then the sport has spread far and wide; though a handful of resorts maintain a ban on snowboarding, riders now make up an estimated 25–30 percent of North American resortgoers, and at many resorts boarders have an equal, if not greater, presence than their skiing counterparts.

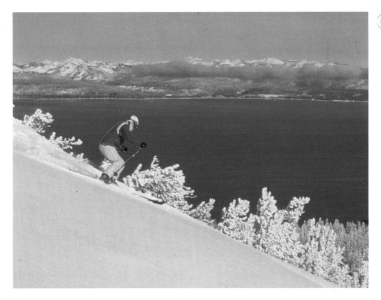

meal than powder. As the storms follow the jet stream east, past the Nevada desert and over the Great Salt Lake, storms blitz the resorts of Utah. Though the snow is not quite as deep as on the West Coast, Utah's powder is generally regarded as the best on the continent: light, dry, and fluffy. The snow that falls in neighboring Colorado and Wyoming comes a close second. North of the US Rockies, into the Canadian part of the range, colder temperatures ensure snow coverage and quality preserves longer. On the other end of the Rockies, New Mexico receives snow with largely the same characteristics, though it gets fewer annual inches. Lacking the high altitudes of their western counterparts, New England and Québec pale in comparison: limited snow fall, ice, and the telltale yellow patches of artificially blown snow are prevalent here.

> **Utah's powder is generally regarded as the best – light, dry, and fluffy**

Weather conditions for each region are further explained within the introductions to each region and within each resort's individual account. Note that while the statistics in the "**Mountain info**" boxes are useful means of comparing resorts at-a-glance, the figures should be interpreted with a grain of salt. Statistics can paint a false picture, particularly when resorts in different regions are compared: local climates cause markedly different snow conditions; acreage sizes can be deceptive when a resort's skiable terrain is poorly utilized or bland; and elevation may be unimportant if storm systems pass frequently, as is the case with resorts in the Pacific Northwest.

An overriding factor in your choice of resort should be your own **abilities**, which is why we've broken down resort mountains into beginner, intermediate, and expert sections. Be skeptical when viewing the resort's self-created **terrain breakdown** as ski areas will skew percentages in order to seem more diverse than they really are.

Further considerations such as your **budget**, the size of your group, what **accommodation** you'll need, whether extensive **off-slope activities** are important, what type of **ski town** is nearby, and numerous other factors should all be taken into account before you set out. We've done our best to detail such determining factors in each resort write-up, and provide some means for comparison in the chapter introductions.

When to go

As important as where to go – if not more – is deciding **when to go**. Try to avoid peak times when prices are hiked and runs teem with skiers; see p.35 for details on holiday periods to avoid as well as the individual resorts for specifics on special events that pack in the crowds.

Nailing down specific **seasons** is tricky as opening and closing dates vary significantly between regions and even between resorts in the same area. The Northeast, with its mild autumns and warmer springs, usually has the shortest seasons. Resorts in the Rockies open as early as October and tend

Terrain parks

As recently as the early 1990s most resorts regarded terrain parks as little more than holding pens, a way to keep upstart snowboarders separate from the sedate skiing majority. Nowadays young freestyle skiers are almost as prevalent as riders, and the caliber of a resort's jumps, jibs, and pipes is a real selling point. Most major resorts offer a halfpipe, sometimes two, and at least a handful of kickers and rails; the best cater to a range of skill levels, from mini terrain gardens for kids to huge huckers and towering super-pipes for the daring. Standards are particularly high in California, a state with a long history of skateboarding and surfing. Icy conditions in the Northeast don't make for the softest landings, but the region is regarded as home to the best pipes. A few pointers: don't jump before checking out all the landings, which can vary from day to day; don't jump until the person before you has reappeared on the other side of the landing; and don't snowplow slowly down the middle of the halfpipe – everyone will silently (or quite vocally) curse you for making them wait.

to close by mid-April, when crowds are dwindling anyway. By contrast, many West Coast resorts – often frequented by locals rather than international visitors on vacation – have the customer base to stay open as long as there is snow. Larger Tahoe ski areas often operate lifts through the end of May, Mammoth maintains its parks through July (conditions permitting), and Mount Hood's Timberline and portions of Whistler-Blackcomb stay open virtually all year long. Alaska is best avoided during the dark, cold months from December to early February. By March, however, the days are galloping in length towards the 24-hour daylight of midsummer, perfect for spring skiing well into the evening hours.

The traditional start at most resorts is around Thanksgiving, the fourth Thursday in November, even if it's only a few patchy, icy runs. Conditions begin to hit their prime closer to Christmas, and the high season is more or less in effect from mid-January through early March. April, with its longer, sunnier days, can bring granular "corn snow" that offers decent riding in the morning but turns unbearably mushy by lunchtime.

18

Rough Guide favorites

Whether during one ski trip or an entire season, it's not feasible to experience all a particular region, much less the entire continent, has to offer. What follows is a series of lists meant to help you narrow your choices down, if you're looking for places that stand out in specific categories. That might mean the best slopes for experts to tackle, or the top hot springs in which to soak your tired body. Each category lists the top seven suggestions, arranged in alphabetical order; one resort in each list is illustrated by a photo, with a page reference to take you straight into the guide where you can find out more.

Overall

Alta/Snowbird, UT pp.262 & 286 ▶
Aspen, CO p.133
Banff, AB p.461
Jackson Hole, WY p.237
Squaw Valley, CA p.347
Vail, CO p.192
Whistler, BC p.497

Snow quality

Alta/Snowbird, UT pp.262 & 286
Fernie, BC p.482 ▶
Grand Targhee, WY p.231
Marmot Basin, AB p.491
Solitude/Brighton, UT pp.291 & 267
Steamboat, CO p.177
Wolf Creek, CO p.251

Most scenic

Alyeska, AK p.400
Homewood, CA p.412
Jackson Hole, WY p.237
Kicking Horse, BC p.476
Lake Louise, AB p.471 ▶
Le Massif, Québec p.450
Telluride, CO p.168

For beginners

Aspen Buttermilk/
Snowmass, CO p.137
Boreal, CA p.411
Copper, CO p.144
◀ **Marmot Basin, AB p.491**
Smuggler's Notch, VT p.104
Stoneham, Québec p.448
Sun Peaks, BC p.519

For intermediates

Big White, BC p.513
Copper, CO p.144
Grand Targhee, WY p.231
Heavenly, CA p.358 ▶
Mount Bachelor, OR p.368
Sun Peaks, BC p.519
Durango, CO p.157

For experts

Alta/Snowbird, UT
pp.262 & 286
Fernie, BC p.482
◀ **Jackson Hole, WY p.237**
Kicking Horse, BC p.476
Red Mountain, BC p.486
Silverton, CO p.250
Squaw Valley, CA p.347

Least crowded

Family-friendly

Terrain parks

Off-slope activities

Cheap eats

Bill Peyton's, Lake Louise, AB p.475
The Fire Sign Cafe, Tahoe City,
CA p.338
Gone Bakery, Whistler, BC p.508 ▶
The Happy Cooker, Georgetown,
CO p.167
Lone Star Taqueria, Salt Lake City,
UT p.261
The Slogar, Crested Butte, CO p.155
Sprouts, South Lake Tahoe, CA p.344

Splurge restaurants

◀ ***Allred's*, Telluride, CO p.174**
Antares, Steamboat, CO p.182
Hemingway's, Killington, VT, p.51
Java Sushi, Truckee, CA p.339
Seafood buffet at *Snow Park Lodge*,
Deer Valley, UT p.283
Shallow Shaft, Alta, UT p.267
Sushi Village, Whistler, BC p.509

Party resorts

Banff, AB p.461
Breckenridge, CO p.120
Killington, VT p.45 ▶
Park City, UT p.270
Tremblant, Québec p.426
Vail, CO p.192
Whistler, BC p.497

Mountain towns

Aspen, CO p.133
◀ **Crested Butte, CO p.149**
Jackson Hole, WY p.237
Park City, UT p.270
Rossland, BC p.486
Stowe, VT p.59
Telluride, CO p.168

Backcountry exploration

Halfpipes

Trees

Spas and hot springs

Contents

Using this Rough Guide

We've tried to make this Rough Guide a good read and easy to use. The book is divided into five main sections, and you should be able to find whatever you want in one of them.

Color section

The front color section offers a quick survey of Skiing and Snowboarding in North America. The **introduction** aims to give you an overall feel of the continent's resorts, with suggestions on how best to choose your destinations. We also tell you about general weather and crowd patterns and when the best times to go are. Next, our authors round up their favorite aspects of the resorts and tell you what not to miss – whether it's the best terrain park, most family-friendly place, or overall resort experience. Right after this comes a full **contents** list.

Basics

The Basics section covers all the **pre-departure** nitty-gritty to help you plan your trip. This is where to find out which airlines fly to your destination, what to do about money and insurance, food, public transportation, car rental, ski and snowboard equipment, any special needs you might have – in fact just about every piece of **general practical information** you might need.

Guide

This is the heart of the Rough Guide, divided into user-friendly chapters, each of which covers a specific region and its resorts. Every chapter starts with a list of **highlights** and an **introduction** that helps you to decide where to go. Chapters then move on

to **detailed coverage** of each resort. Introductions to the various towns, resorts, and mountains within each chapter should help you plan your itinerary. After specifics on **arrival**, **information**, and **getting around**, plus a special "**Mountain info**" box with relevant statistics, we tackle **the mountain** itself, covering what's best for **each level of skier**, followed by **ticket**, **lesson**, and **rental** information, **accommodation** options, reviews of places to **eat**, **drink**, and have **fun**, and any **other activities and attractions** worth mentioning. Longer accounts also have a directory of practical **listings**. Finally, each region ends with a wrap-up of the **Best of the Rest** – usually smaller resorts that don't get the full treatment but have something worthwhile to recommend them.

Glossary

The Glossary defines and explains various **skiing and snowboarding terms** used frequently throughout the book, as an aide to beginners and experts alike.

Index + small print

Apart from a **full index**, which includes maps as well as resorts, this section covers publishing information, credits, and acknowledgments, and also has our contact details in case you want to send in updates and corrections to the book – or suggestions as to how we might improve it.

Map and chapter list

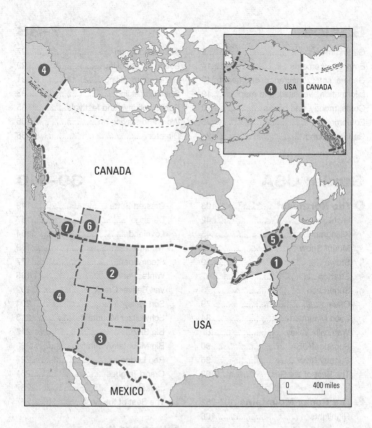

Contents

Guide: Canada

Glossary

Index + small print

Map symbols

maps are listed in the full index using colored text

-----	International boundary	▲	Mountain peak
— ···	State/province boundary	🔆	Mountain range
- - - -	Chapter boundary	⤙	Pass
🔵5	U.S. Interstate highway	🌿	Springs
15	Canadian autoroute	⚡	Ski area
5	U.S. Highway	🎿	Cross country ski area
5	Yellowhead highway	P	Parking
5	State highway	P	Free parking
———	Main road	⊞	Hospital
▬▬	Pedestrianized street	ⓘ	Information office
▥▥▥	Steps	⊠	Post office
------	Path	★	Bus stop/station
———	Trail	⛳	Golf course
- - -	Ferry route	⛪	Monastery
———	Waterway	■	Building
- - -	Chair lifts/gondolas	⬭	Ice rink/stadium
✈	International airport	▦	Park
✈	Domestic airport	▦	Forest
Ⓗ	Heliport	▦	Glacier
⬥	Lodge		

Basics

Basics

Getting there

Alpine resorts spread across North America from Appalachian Maine to California's Sierra Nevada, from Alaska's mighty Chugach Mountains to the southern Rockies of New Mexico, and specific advice on flights to every airport with access to a ski area would comprise a whole guide on its own. For information on the closest airports to a particular resort, see the pertinent review within the guide. Wintertime in North America is typically low season, meaning fares are affordable save for Christmas and New Year's when prices are hiked and seats at a premium. There are exceptions, particularly if you plan on flying into a smaller regional airport closer to a major resort.

You can often cut costs by using a **specialist flight agent** with either a consolidator, who buys up blocks of tickets from the airlines and sells them at a discount, or a **discount agent**, who, in addition to dealing with discounted flights, may also offer special student and youth fares and a range of other travel-related services such as travel insurance and car rentals. Some agents specialize in **charter flights**; they may be cheaper than anything available on a scheduled flight, but departure dates are fixed and withdrawal penalties are high. For some destinations, you may find it cheaper to try a **package deal** from one of the tour operators listed below and then find your own accommodation when you get there.

Booking flights online

Many airlines and discount travel websites offer the opportunity to book tickets online, cutting out the costs of agents and middlemen. Deals can often be found through discount or auction sites as well as through airlines websites.

Online booking agents and general travel sites

ⓦ **travel.yahoo.com** Incorporates Rough Guide material in its coverage of destination countries and cities across the world, with information about places to eat, sleep, and go.

ⓦ **www.cheapflights.com** Bookings from the UK and Ireland only (for US, ⓦ www.cheapflights.com; for Canada, ⓦ www.cheapflights.ca). Flight deals, travel agents, plus links to other travel sites.

ⓦ **www.cheaptickets.com** Discount flight specialists (US only).

ⓦ **www.etn.nl/discount.htm** Consolidator and discount agent Web links, maintained by the non-profit European Travel Network.

ⓦ **www.expedia.com** Discount airfares search engine and daily deals.

ⓦ **www.flyaow.com** Online air travel info and reservations site.

ⓦ **www.gaytravel.com** Gay online travel agent, offering accommodation, tours, and more.

ⓦ **www.geocities.com/thavery2000** List of airline toll-free numbers (from the US) and websites.

ⓦ **www.hotwire.com** Bookings from the US only. Last-minute savings of up to forty percent on regular published fares. Travellers must be at least 18 and there are no refunds, transfers, or changes allowed. Log-in required.

ⓦ **www.lastminute.com** Offers last-minute holiday package and flight-only deals (UK only; for Australia, ⓦ www.lastminute.com.au).

ⓦ **www.priceline.com** Name-your-own-price website that has deals at around forty percent off standard fares. You cannot specify flight times (although you do specify dates) and the tickets are nonrefundable, nontransferable, and nonchangeable (US only; for the UK, ⓦ www.priceline.co.uk).

ⓦ **www.skyauction.com** Bookings from the US only. Auctions tickets and travel packages using a "second bid" scheme. The best strategy is to bid the maximum you're willing to pay, since if you win you'll pay just enough to beat the runner-up regardless of your maximum bid.

ⓦ **www.smilinjack.com/airlines.htm** Lists an up-to-date compilation of airline website addresses.

ⓦ **travelocity.com** Destination guides, hot Web fares, and best deals for car hire, accommodation as well as fares. Provides access to the travel agent system SABRE, the most comprehensive central reservations system in the US.

🕸 **www.travelshop.com.au** Australian website offering discounted flights, packages, insurance, and online bookings.

Flights from the US and Canada

To squeeze the most amount of time on the slopes as possible, you're likely to **fly** if a particular resort is anywhere more than a day's drive away. But even regionally a flight can often work out to your advantage. For example, while the majority of New Yorkers visiting Stowe in northern Vermont arrive via a seven hour car ride, an affordable flight from JFK via Jet Blue to nearby Burlington will land you two extra half-days of skiing time. Such situations exist across the country, and we've listed handy regional airports throughout the guide.

Airlines

Air Canada ☎1-888/247-2262,
🕸www.aircanada.ca
Alaska Airlines ☎1-800/252-7522,
🕸www.alaska-air.com
America West Airlines ☎1-800/235-9292,
🕸www.americawest.com
American Airlines ☎1-800/433-7300,
🕸www.aa.com
American Trans Air ☎1-800/435-9282,
🕸www.ata.com
Continental Airlines domestic ☎1-800/523-3273, international ☎1-800/231-0856,
🕸www.continental.com
Delta Air Lines domestic ☎1-800/221-1212, international ☎1-800/241-4141, 🕸www.delta.com
JetBlue ☎1-800/538-2583, 🕸www.jetblue.com
Northwest/KLM Airlines domestic ☎1-800/225-2525, international ☎1-800/447-4747,
🕸www.nwa.com, 🕸www.klm.com.
Reno Air ☎1-800/433-7300, 🕸www.aa.com. Part of American Airlines.
Southwest Airlines ☎1-800/435-9792,
🕸www.southwest.com
US Airways domestic ☎1-800/428-4322, international ☎1-800/622-1015, 🕸www.usair.com

Discount travel companies

Airtech ☎212/219-7000, 🕸www.airtech.com. Standby seat broker; also deals in consolidator fares and courier flights.

For information on car rental and train and bus travel within the United States and Canada, see "Getting around" beginning on p.24.

Council Travel ☎1-800/2COUNCIL, 🕸www.counciltravel.com. Nationwide organization, specializing in student/budget travel. Flights from the US only. Owned by STA Travel.
SkyLink US ☎1-800/AIR-ONLY or 212/573-8980, Canada ☎1-800/SKY-LINK, 🕸www.skylinkus.com. Consolidator.
STA Travel US ☎1-800/781-4040, Canada 1-888/427-5639, 🕸www.sta-travel.com. Worldwide specialists in independent travel; also student IDs, travel insurance, and car rental.
Student Flights ☎1-800/255-8000 or 480/951-1177, 🕸www.isecard.com. Student/youth fares, student IDs.
TFI Tours ☎1-800/745-8000 or 212/736-1140, 🕸www.lowestairprice.com. Consolidator.
Travac ☎1-800/TRAV-800, 🕸www.thetravelsite.com. Consolidator and charter broker with offices in New York City and Orlando.
Travelers Advantage ☎1-877/259-2691, 🕸www.travelersadvantage.com. Discount travel club; annual membership fee required (currently $1 for 3 months' trial).
Travel Avenue ☎1-800/333-3335, 🕸www.travelavenue.com. Full-service travel agent that offers discounts in the form of rebates.
Travel Cuts Canada ☎1-800/667-2887, US ☎1-866/246-9762, 🕸www.travelcuts.com. Canadian student-travel organization.
Worldtek Travel ☎1-800/243-1723, 🕸www.worldtek.com. Discount travel agency for worldwide travel.

Tour operators

Ami-tour ☎403/932-7224, 🕸www.amitour.com. Tour operator out of Calgary specializing in packages to ski resorts in British Columbia and Alberta, including driving tours taking in several resorts.
Delta Vacations ☎1-800/654-6559, 🕸www.deltavacations.com. Full packages, including car rental and accommodations, offered mainly to resorts in Colorado and Utah.
Gotta Travel ☎905/755-0999 or ☎1-800/465-3034, 🕸www.gottatravel.com. Budget agency with resort trips out to both Western and Eastern Canada, along with many of Vermont's larger resorts.
Holidaze Ski Tours ☎1-800/526-2827 or 732/280-1120, 🕸www.holidaze.com. Packages to

many Western US resorts, along with Whistler and Banff in Canada.

Moguls ☎1-800/666-4857, ⓦwww.moguls.com. Boulder, Colorado, tour operator run by skiing and snowboarding enthusiasts. Packages for all budgets offered for resorts across North America. Heli-skiing trips with several of the top outfits also booked.

Rocky Mountain Tours ☎1-800/525-7547, ⓦwww.skithewest.com. Extensive packages, including car rental and lift tickets, available for most major resorts in the Western US. A good place to look for discounted flights into smaller airports like Jackson (Jackson Hole), Hayden (Steamboat), or Bozeman (Big Sky).

Ski-Can ☎1-888/475-4226, ⓦwww.skican.com. Large and knowledgeable operator with trips to all major Canadian resorts and limited packages to Steamboat, Aspen, and Vail.

Ski-fo ☎1-800/361-1654, ⓦwww.ski-fo.com. Package deals to resorts in eastern Canada and the eastern US, including Tremblant, Killington, and Sugarbush.

Snow Ventures 1-800/845-7157, ⓦwww .snowventures.com. Experienced outfit with budget to deluxe packages to most major western resorts in the US and Canada. Equipment rentals can be booked as part of packages.

Flights from the UK and Ireland

In the US, more than twenty cities are accessed via nonstop flights from the UK and connect with an extensive network of domestic flights. Direct services (which may land once or twice on the way, but are called direct if they keep the same flight number throughout their journey) fly from Britain to nearly every other major US city. The main **Canadian** gateways are Montréal and Toronto, but there are also nonstop flights to Calgary, Edmonton, Ottawa, and Vancouver, and connecting services to a number of other destinations.

One-stop direct flights to destinations beyond the East Coast are often cheaper than nonstop flights. They can even save time, because customs and immigration are cleared on first touchdown into the US rather than the final destination, which may be a busy international gateway. For an idea of flight times, nonstop flights from London to Vancouver take eleven or twelve hours, and approximately seven to Boston.

Airlines

Air Canada UK ☎0870/5247 226, Republic of Ireland ☎01/679 3958, ⓦwww.aircanada.com
Aer Lingus UK ☎0845/084 4444, Republic of Ireland ☎0818/365 000, ⓦwww.aerlingus.ie
American Airlines UK ☎0845/7789 789 or 020/8572 5555, Republic of Ireland ☎01/602 0550, ⓦwww.aa.com
British Airways UK ☎0845/77 333 77, Republic of Ireland ☎1800/626 747, ⓦwww.ba.com
Continental Airlines UK ☎0800/776 464 or 01293/776 464, ⓦwww.continental.com/uk; Republic of Ireland ☎1890/925 252, ⓦwww.continental.com/ie
Delta UK ☎0800/414 767, Republic of Ireland ☎01/407 3165, ⓦwww.delta.com
KLM UK ☎0870/507 4074, ⓦwww.klmuk.com.
United Airlines UK ☎0845/8444 777, ⓦwww.unitedairlines.co.uk
Virgin Atlantic Airways UK ☎01293/747 747, ⓦwww.virgin-atlantic.com

Flight and travel agents

Aran Travel International Republic of Ireland ☎091/562 595, ⓦhomepages.iol.ie/~arantvl /aranmain.htm. Good-value flights to all parts of the world.
CIE Tours International Republic of Ireland ☎01/703 1888, ⓦwww.cietours.ie. General flight and tour agent.
Co-op Travel Care UK ☎0870/112 0099, ⓦwww.travelcareonline.com. Flights and holidays around the world.
Destination Group UK ☎020/7400 7045, ⓦwww .destination-group.com. Good discount airfares.
Flightbookers UK ☎0870/010 7000, ⓦwww.ebookers.com. Low fares and extensive flight selection.
Go Holidays Republic of Ireland ☎01/874 4126, ⓦwww.goholidays.ie. Package tour specialists.
Joe Walsh Tours Republic of Ireland ☎01/676 0991, ⓦwww.joewalshtours.ie. General budget fares agent.
Lee Travel Republic of Ireland ☎021/277 111, ⓦwww.leetravel.ie. Flights and holidays worldwide.
McCarthy's Travel Republic of Ireland ☎021/427 0127, ⓦwww.mccarthystravel.ie. General flight agent.
North South Travel UK ☎ & ℻01245/608 291, ⓦwww.northsouthtravel.co.uk. Friendly travel agency, offering discounted fares worldwide – profits are used to support projects in the developing world, especially the promotion of sustainable tourism.

Premier Travel Northern Ireland ☎028/7126 3333, ⊛www.premiertravel.uk.com. Discount flight specialists.

STA Travel UK ☎0870/1600 599, ⊛www.statravel .co.uk. Worldwide specialists in low-cost flights and tours for students and under-26s, though other customers welcome.

Top Deck UK ☎020/7244 8000, ⊛www .topdecktravel.co.uk. Long-established agent dealing in discount flights.

Trailfinders UK ☎020/7628 7628, ⊛www .trailfinders.co.uk, **Republic of Ireland** ☎01/677 7888, ⊛www.trailfinders.ie. One of the most efficient agents for independent travelers; produce a very useful quarterly magazine worth scrutinizing for round-the-world routes.

Travel Bag UK ☎0870/890 1456, ⊛www.travelbag .co.uk. Discount flights to Australia, New Zealand, USA, and the Far East; official Qantas agent.

Travel Cuts UK ☎020/7255 2082 or 7255 1944, ⊛www.travelcuts.co.uk. Canadian company specializing in budget, student, and youth travel and round-the-world tickets.

usit NOW Republic of Ireland ☎01/602 1600, **Northern Ireland** ☎028/9032 7111, ⊛www.usitnow.ie. Student and youth specialists for flights and trains.

Tour operators

Alpine Answers ☎0208/871 4656, ⊛www .alpineanswers.co.uk. London-based operator with a knowledgeable staff of skiers, specializing in condo and home rental holidays and hotel packages. Good last-minute deals often available on their website.

Exodus UK ☎020/8675 5550, **Republic of Ireland** ☎01/677 1029, ⊛www.exodus.co.uk. Adventure tour operator primarily catering to small groups. While winter trips are limited, there are a few cross-country and snowshoe expeditions around Yellowstone, Denver, or Quebec that could work well in conjunction with a longer downhill skiing trip.

Inghams ☎0208/780 4433, ⊛www.inghams.com. Large and respected tour operator with a long menu of ski trip options, including city stopovers and beginner packages.

Rocky Mountain Holidays ☎0870/366 5442, ⊛www.rockymountain.co.uk. Student and budget-minded operator with trips to resorts in Colorado, Utah, California, and British Columbia. A useful source for information and visas for working at a North American resort.

Ski Independence ☎0870/555 0555, ⊛www .ski-independence.co.uk. Reputable agency with links to more than forty North American resorts. Good

fly-drive packages available, along with trips taking in a few days at a stopover city like Boston or Denver.

Ski Safari ☎01273/223 680, ⊛www.skisafari .com. Operator with package deals for dozens of resorts across North America. Best considered for their "safari" tours offering creative options like a ski-and-sun journey taking in both Whistler and Hawaii.

Thomas Cook UK ☎0870/5666 222, ⊛www .thomascook.co.uk. Long-established one-stop 24-hour travel agency for package holidays or scheduled flights, with bureau de change issuing Thomas Cook travelers' checks, travel insurance, and car rental. Resort package deals available for Banff, Tremblant, Winter Park, and Breckenridge.

Flights from Australia and New Zealand

Other than holiday packages that may be on offer, the best deals from Australasia to North America are available from the travel agents listed on p.13 or from the websites listed on p.9. Should you be planning an extended stay, air passes valid in the continental US and Canada are often available, but note that these must be bought before you go.

Los Angeles is the main North American gateway for flights from Australasia. When they have surplus capacity, airlines frequently offer special fares from Australia to Los Angeles, which can be as low as A$1400 including tax from the eastern states. Otherwise the best you're likely to find are the regular Air New Zealand, Qantas, and United flights to Los Angeles: expect to pay around A$1600 including tax from the eastern states, rising to A$2000 from Western Australia. From New Zealand, ski-season fares from Auckland or Christchurch (add another NZ$150 for Wellington departures) start at around NZ$2150 to LA. There are also flights available direct to San Francisco and Vancouver.

Airlines

Air Canada Australia ☎1300/655 747 or 02/9286 8900, **New Zealand** ☎09/379 3371, ⊛www.aircanada.com

Air New Zealand Australia ☎13 24 76, ⊛www.airnz.com.au, **New Zealand** ☎0800/737 000, ⊛www.airnz.co.nz

America West Airlines Australia ☎02/9267 2138 or 1300/364 757, **New Zealand** ☎0800/866 000, ⊛www.americawest.com

American Airlines Australia ☎1300/130 757,
New Zealand ☎09/309 9159, ⓦwww.aa.com
British Airways Australia ☎1300/767 177, New
Zealand ☎0800/274 847 or 09/356 8690,
ⓦwww.britishairways.com
Continental Airlines Australia ☎1300/361 400,
New Zealand ☎09/308 3350,
ⓦwww.flycontinental.com
Delta Air Lines Australia ☎02/9251 3211, New
Zealand ☎09/379 3370, ⓦwww.delta.com
KLM/Northwest Airlines Australia ☎1300/303
747, ⓦwww.klm.com/au_en, New Zealand
☎09/309 1782, ⓦwww.klm.com/nz_en
Korean Air Australia ☎02/9262 6000, New
Zealand ☎09/914 2000, ⓦwww.koreanair.com.au.
Malaysia Airlines Australia ☎13 26 27, New
Zealand ☎0800/777 747, ⓦwww.malaysiaairlines
.com.my
Philippine Airlines Australia ☎02/9279 2020,
New Zealand ☎09/379 8522, ⓦwww
.philippineairlines.com
Qantas Australia ☎13 13 13, ⓦwww.qantas.com
.au, New Zealand ☎0800/808 767, ⓦwww.qantas
.co.nz
Singapore Airlines Australia ☎13 10 11, New
Zealand ☎0800/808 909, ⓦwww.singaporeair.com
South African Airways Australia ☎02/9223
4402, New Zealand ☎09/309 9132,
ⓦwww.flysaa.com
Swiss Air Australia ☎1300/724 666,
ⓦwww.swiss.com.
United Airlines Australia ☎13 17 77, ⓦwww
.unitedairlines.com.au, New Zealand ☎09/379 3800
or 0800/508 648, ⓦwww.unitedairlines.co.nz
Virgin Atlantic Airways Australia ☎02/9244
2747, New Zealand ☎09/308 3377,
ⓦwww.virgin-atlantic.com

Flight and travel agents

Flight Centre Australia ☎13 31 33 or 02/9235
3522, ⓦwww.flightcentre.com.au, New Zealand

☎0800 243 544 or 09/358 4310, ⓦwww
.flightcentre.co.nz
Holiday Shoppe New Zealand ☎0800/808 480,
ⓦwww.holidayshoppe.co.nz
New Zealand Destinations Unlimited New
Zealand ☎09/414 1685 ⓦwww.holiday.co.nz.
Northern Gateway Australia ☎1800/174 800,
ⓦwww.northerngateway.com.au
Silke's Travel Australia ☎1800 807 860, or
02/8347 2000, ⓦwww.silkes.com.au. Gay and
lesbian specialist travel agent.
STA Travel Australia ☎1300/733 035, ⓦwww
.statravel.com.au, New Zealand ☎0508/782 872,
ⓦwww.statravel.co.nz
Student Uni Travel Australia ☎02/9232 8444,
ⓦwww.sut.com.au, New Zealand ☎09/379 4224,
ⓦwww.sut.co.nz
Trailfinders Australia ☎02/9247 7666,
ⓦwww.trailfinders.com.au

Tour operators

Canada & America Travel Specialists Australia
☎02/9922 4600, ⓦwww.canada-americatravel
.com.au. Wholesalers of Greyhound Ameripasses
along with flight and accommodation deals in North
America.
Ski Max Australia ☎1300/ 136 997, ⓦwww.skimax.com
.au. In collaboration with Quantas, Ski Max has a
long list of moderately priced packages, fly-drive,
and city stopover tours for most major resorts in
western North America.
Snow Bookings Only Australia ☎1800/623 266,
ⓦwww.snowbookingsonly.com.au. Worth a look for
charter flights or larger package deals to Canadian
resorts, including Whistler, Fernie, Banff, Big White,
and Silver Star.
Travelplan Australia ☎02/9958 1888 or 1300/
130 754, ⓦwww.travelplan.com.au. Specializing in
mid-range to deluxe packages to most major
Western resorts in North America. Particularly good
for families or groups.

Entry requirements

For EU, Australian, and New Zealand tourists planning short stays of up to ninety days in the United States or Canada, the only documentation required is a valid passport. Visas are, however, required in all cases for entry into the United States of more than ninety days, and the same usually applies – though there is a little more flexibility – for entry into Canada. Visas are also required for entry into both countries for those planning to work or study there. Slightly different again is the situation regarding US and Canadian nationals crossing into each other's countries.

Entering the US

Visa waiver forms are handed out on incoming planes and are processed during immigration control at your initial point of arrival on US soil. The form requires details of where you are staying on your first night and the date you intend to leave the US. You should be able to prove that you have enough money to support yourself while in the US. Part of the form will be attached to your passport, where it must stay until you leave. The same form also covers entry across the land border with Canada.

Citizens of all other countries should contact their local US embassy or consulate for details on current entry requirements. Even those eligible for the visa waiver scheme *must* apply for a free tourist visa if they intend to stay in the US for more than ninety days; for advice on working or studying in the US, see p.36.

US embassies and consulates elsewhere

Australia

Embassy 21 Moonah Place, Canberra, ACT 2600 ☎02/6214 5600, ⊛www.usis–Australia.gov /embassy
Consulates Melbourne 553 St Kilda Rd, Melbourne, VIC 3004 ☎03/9526 5900, ⊛www .usis-australia.gov/melbourne; **Sydney** 19–29 Martin Place, Sydney, NSW 2000 ☎02/9373 9200, ⊛www.usconsydney.com; **Perth** 16 St George's Terrace, 13th Floor Perth WA 6000 ☎08/9202 1224
Visa hotline ☎1902/941 641 (premium rated, $1.50 per minute)

Canada

Embassy 490 Sussex Drive, Ottawa, ON K1N 148 ☎613/238-5335, ⊛www.usembassycanada.gov
Consulates Calgary 615 Macleod Trail SE, 10th Floor, Calgary, AB T2G 4T8 ☎403/266-8962; **Halifax** Suite 904, Wharf Tower II, 1969 Upper Water St, Halifax, NS B3J 3R7 ☎902/429-2480; **Montreal** 1155 St. Alexandre St, Montréal, PQ H5B 1G1 ☎514/398-9695; **Québec City** 2 Place Terrasse Dufferin, Québec City, PQ G1R 4T9 ☎418/692-2095; **Toronto** 360 University Ave, Toronto, ON M5G 1S4 ☎416/595-1700; **Vancouver** 1095 W Pender St, 21st Floor, Vancouver, BC V6E 2M6 ☎604/685-4311

Ireland

42 Elgin Rd, Ballsbridge, Dublin 4 ☎01/668 8777, ⊛www.usembassy.ie

New Zealand

Embassy 29 Fitzherbert Terrace, Thorndon, Wellington ☎04/462-2000, ⊛www/usembassy .state.gov/wellington
Consulate 3rd Floor, Citibank Building, 23 Customs St, Auckland ☎09/303 2724
Address for visa applications Non-Immigrant Visas, Private Bag 92022, Auckland 1

UK

Embassy 5 Upper Grosvenor St, London W1A 1AE ☎020/7499 9000
Visa hotline ☎0891/200290
Consulates Edinburgh 3 Regent Terrace, Edinburgh EH7 5BW ☎0131/556 8315; **Belfast** Queens House, 14 Queen St, Belfast BT1 6EQ ☎028/9032 8239

Foreign embassies and consulates in the US

Australia

1601 Massachusetts Ave NW, Washington DC 20036 ☎202/797-3000

Canada

Embassy 501 Pennsylvania Ave NW, Washington DC 20001 ☎202/682-1740, ⊛www .canadianembassy.org
Consulates Boston Three Copley Place, Suite 400, Boston MA 02216 ☎617/262-3760; **Chicago** Two Prudential Plaza, 188 North Stetson Ave, Suite 2400, Chicago IL 60601 ☎312/616-1860; **Los Angeles** 558 South Hope St, 9th Floor, Los Angeles CA 90071-2627 ☎213/346-2700; **New York** 1251 Avenue of the Americas, New York, NY 10020-1175 ☎212/596-1793; **San Francisco** 555 Montgomery St, Suite 1288, San Francisco CA 94111 ☎415/834-3180

Ireland

2234 Massachusetts Ave NW, Washington DC 20008 ☎202/462-3939, ⊛www/irelandemb.org

New Zealand

37 Observatory Circle NW, Washington DC 20008 ☎202/328-4800, ⊛www.nzembassy.org

UK

Embassy 3100 Massachusetts Ave NW, Washington DC 20008 ☎202/588-6500, ⊛www.britainusa.com/consular/embassy
Consulates Boston Federal Reserve Plaza, 25th Floor, 600 Atlantic Ave, Boston, MA 022190, ☎617/248–9555; **Chicago** The Wrigley Building, 400 N Michigan Ave, Suite 1306, Chicago, IL 60611 ☎312/970-3800; **Los Angeles** 11766 Wilshire Blvd, Suite 400, Los Angeles, CA 90025 ☎310/477-3322; **New York** 845 3rd Ave, New York, NY 10022 ☎212/745-0200; **San Francisco** 1 Sansome St, Suite 850, San Francisco, CA 94104 ☎415/981-3030; **Houston** Wells Fargo Plaza, 19th Floor, 1000 Louisiana, Suite 1900 Houston, TX 77002 ☎713/659–6270

Entering Canada

All visitors to Canada have to complete a **waiver form**, which you'll be given on the plane or at the US–Canada border. On the form you'll have to give details of where you intend to stay during your trip. If you don't

know, write "touring," but be prepared to give an idea of your schedule and destinations to the immigration officer. Admission is normally granted for a period of up to ninety days and you may be asked to show how much **money** you have: a credit card or $300 cash per week of the proposed visit is usually considered sufficient. Custom officials may also ask to see a return or onward ticket. If they ask where you're staying and you give the name and address of friends, don't be surprised if they call to check. If you plan a longer trip, Canadian immigration officials may permit stays of up to six months. Check with the Canadian High Commission for details before you leave.

Canadian high commissions, consulates, and embassies abroad

Australia and New Zealand

Auckland 9th Floor, Jetset Centre, 44–48 Emily Place, Auckland 1 ☎09/309-8516, ⊛www.dfait -maeci.gc.ca/newzealand/; **Canberra** Commonwealth Avenue, Canberra, ACT 2600 ☎06/270-4000, ⊛www.dfait-maeci.gc.ca/australia/; **Sydney** Level 5, Quay West Building, 111 Harrington St, Sydney, NSW 2000 ☎02/9364-3000; **24-hour visa information and application** ☎02/9364-3050

US

Chicago 2 Prudential Plaza, 180 N Stetson Ave, Suite 2400, Chicago, IL 60601 ☎312/616-1860; **Los Angeles** 550 South Hope St, 9th Floor, Los Angeles, CA 90071-2627 ☎213/346-2700; **New York** 1251 Ave of the Americas, New York, NY 10020-1175 ☎212/596-1628; **Washington DC** 501 Pennsylvania Ave NW, Washington DC 20001 ☎202/682-1740

There are also consulates in Atlanta, Boston, Buffalo, Dallas, Detroit, Minneapolis, Princeton, and Seattle. Check ⊛www.canadianembassy.org for details.

Customs

Customs officials in both Canada and the US will ask for your completed **customs declaration form**, handed out on all incoming flights and border crossings. Officers check whether you're carrying any fresh foods and ask if you've visited a farm in the last month. As well as foods and anything agricultural, it's prohibited to carry into the

US and Canadian travelers

United States and Canadian citizens previously enjoyed the freedom of crossing the border without a passport as long as they were carrying some form of official ID. Technically this still applies to car drivers, but after the events of 9/11 scrutiny at all crossings has become more rigid and at the very least you'll want to bring a photocopy of your birth certificate along with a valid voter registration card. All airlines and major bus companies now insist on both photo identification and proof of citizenship before accepting you as a passenger. In all cases, it's recommended that you take your passport and, if you plan to stay for more than ninety days, a visa. Note that if you cross the border in a car, trunk and passenger compartments are subject to spot searches by the customs personnel of both countries. Remember, too, that both nationalities are legally barred from seeking employment in each other's country.

US any articles from North Korea, Libya, or Cuba, obscene publications, lottery tickets, illegal chocolate, liqueurs or pre-Columbian artifacts. Anyone caught bringing drugs into either country will not only face prosecution but will also be entered in the records as an undesirable and probably denied entry for all time. The **duty-free allowance** if you're over 17 in the US is 200 cigarettes and 100 cigars (*not* Cuban) and, if you're over 21, a liter of spirits. The duty-free allowance in Canada if you're over 19 (18 in Alberta) is 200 cigarettes and 50 cigars plus 1.1 liters of liquor.

Extensions

On entry into the **US**, the date stamped on your passport is the latest you're legally allowed to stay. Leaving a few days later may not matter, especially if you're heading home, but more than a week delay or so can result in a protracted, rather unpleasant interrogation from officials, which may cause you to miss your flight. Overstaying may also cause you to be turned away the next time you try to enter the US. To get an extension

before your time is up, apply at the nearest **US Immigration and Naturalization Service** (INS) office (addresses appear in the Federal Government Offices listings in local telephone directories; ⊛ www.ins.gov).

At every **Canadian** port of entry, the immigration officer decides the length of stay permitted up to a maximum of six months, but not usually more than three. For visits of more than three months, study trips, and stints of temporary employment contact the nearest Canadian embassy, consulate, or high commission for authorization prior to departure. For an extension during your visit, a written application is required with the **Canadian Immigration Centre** several weeks before the expiry of the authorized visit.

In both countries officials will usually assume that you're working illegally if you apply for an extension and it's up to you to convince them otherwise. Do this by providing evidence of ample finances and, if you can, bring along an American or Canadian citizen to vouch for you. You'll also have to explain why you didn't plan for the extra time initially.

General safety, insurance, and health

Statistically, skiing and snowboarding are less dangerous activities than riding a bicycle. Yet minor injuries are common on the mountain and it is vital to have insurance to cover potential medical expenses, as well as to take the necessary precautions to ensure your safety as best you can. Canada has an excellent health service, but it costs nonresidents between $50 and $1000 a day to use. Treatment in the United States is of the highest quality but is prohibitively expensive for the uninsured.

Insurance

Some all-risks home insurance policies may cover your possessions when overseas and many private medical schemes include coverage when abroad. Foreign students will often find that their student health coverage extends during their vacations and for one term beyond the date of last enrolment. After exhausting these possibilities, you might want to contact a specialist travel insurance company, or consider the travel insurance deal we offer (see box below). A typical policy covers the loss of baggage, tickets, and – up to a certain limit – cash or checks, as well as any necessary cancellations or curtailments. Note that per-article limits are typically $400, not enough to cover high-end skis or boards.

Health coverage should cover "hazardous pursuits." Check that skiing and snowboarding are included within that bracket, and if you plan on riding in the backcountry, ensure that the policy includes off-piste ski-

ing (note that, if permitted, the proviso is generally "with a guide"). Specialized ski policies are really only suitable for prepurchased, all-inclusive trips; the extra premium covers the costs of ski passes and rentals, should injury or bad weather curtail your vacation. Seasonal workers should be fine with youth policies, though aspiring professionals should bear in mind that regular insurance policies do not cover injuries that occur during competitions.

Health

On the mountain, **ski patrol** is the equivalent of ☎911, the emergency number for both Canada and the US. If an accident occurs to a companion, cross your skis or place a snowboard in the snow above the injured person, post another person higher up the slope to prevent collisions, and ask a passing rider to call for ski patrol. Typically dressed in red jackets adorned with white crosses, these expert skiers, avalanche specialists, and medical technicians deal with hundreds of injuries annually. Most accident victims will be taken off the mountain in a sled and towed by a patroller. Ski town hospitals are small but are equipped to deal with most skiing and snowboarding injuries. Should you need to see a doctor for a non-emergency, lists can be found in the *Yellow Pages* under "Clinics" or "Physicians and Surgeons." The basic consultation fee is $50–100, payable in advance. Medications aren't cheap; keep all your receipts for later claims on your insurance policy.

Sunburn, dehydration, and hypothermia

Likely health concerns will include **sunburn**, **dehydration**, and **hypothermia**. To prevent the latter, drink plenty of water and keep dry and warm wearing several synthetic or wool layers (see Equipment, p.23). Initial signs of hypothermia include confusion, exhaustion, and numbness. Drinking plenty of water also counteracts the dehydration that results from dry mountain air (many North American resorts are actually located in a high desert environment), lengthy bouts of physical activity, and those daily saunas or hot tubs. Common indications of dehydration are dry, chapped lips – despite the use of sunscreen – regular nosebleeds, and nausea. Sunburn occurs faster at higher altitudes as the effects of the sun are compounded by the reflection of light off snow. Always use plenty of sunscreen and wear high-quality sunglasses or goggles to avoid painful, potentially damaging eye burn.

Altitude sickness

Particularly in the Rockies, where ski mountains top 13,000ft, **altitude sickness** can occur as the body adjusts to taking in less oxygen. (Though there isn't actually less oxygen in the air at higher altitudes, lower barometric pressure means the body absorbs less oxygen.)

Symptoms include headaches, nausea, weakness, and difficulty breathing, though most people won't notice a problem beyond a couple of nights of disturbed sleep. While acclimating, make sure to drink plenty of fluids and avoid overexertion. Ski patrol or the local clinic can alleviate sickness with a small dose of supplemental oxygen, though most symptoms pass within 48 hours. Serious problems brought on by more extreme altitudes are unlikely at the elevations attained in North America, but if symptoms persist or worsen, see a doctor immediately.

Safety

Trail maps in North America carry a version of the skier and snowboarder **Responsibility Code**, a collection of rules endorsed by resorts, ski patrols, and instructors. To experienced riders, these rules are common sense. Beginners need to do their part in making the mountain as safe as possible by following them.

As freestyle skiing and riding rise in popularity, resorts are also increasingly using the "Smart Style" terrain park initiative. Terrain features are marked on the trail map and on posted signs on the mountain with an orange oval.

Other areas highlighted on the trail map are slow or family zones, usually on beginner trails heavily used by passing skier traffic. Banners are posted at the head of the trail, and zones are monitored by ski patrol. If caught, speeding skiers may receive a caution or fine or have their passes revoked.

Make sure to ski with a buddy, watch out for the deep wells that can form around the base of trees, and consider carrying walkie-talkies to stay in touch; cell phone reception is not reliable in the mountains. Should a member of your group become missing, post a message on the bulletin boards located at the bottom of most lifts. Contact ski patrol if you think there's a chance that they could have been involved in an accident.

Helmets

Helmets are increasingly worn by skiers and snowboarders across North America, with most children's ski schools now requiring waivers if a helmet is not worn. Proponents swear by them, citing collisions with rocks and falls in the pipe where the helmet cracked but the head did not. Others point to the fact that helmets are only really effective at speeds of 12mph or lower, and complain that their use encourages a false sense of security and reckless riding.

Responsibility Codes

The Responsibility Code used by resorts in the United States has seven guidelines:

▶ Always stay in control, and be able to stop or avoid other people or objects.

▶ People ahead of you have the right of way. It is your responsibility to avoid them.

▶ You must not stop where you obstruct a trail or are not visible from above.

▶ Whenever starting downhill or merging into a trail, look uphill and yield to others.

▶ Always use devices to help prevent runaway equipment.

▶ Observe all posted signs and warnings. Keep off closed trails and out of closed areas.

▶ Prior to using any lift, you must have the knowledge and ability to load, ride, and unload safely.

Canada's Alpine Responsibility Code is practically identical, but includes the stipulations that:

▶ If you are involved in or witness a collision or accident, you must remain at the scene and identify yourself to the Ski Patrol.

▶ You must not use lifts or terrain if your ability is impaired through use of alcohol or drugs.

Information, websites, and maps

Often the most useful source of information on each resort is its individual website. We've listed resort homepages throughout the guide, and on them you'll be able to gather everything from in-depth directions and the latest ticket prices to last-minute ski and stay packages. While the majority of information found on the sites can be trusted, one should be skeptical of the current conditions listed. It's not an uncommon practice to be overly optimistic in describing snowfall and the latest state of trails. A general rule of thumb is to downgrade trail descriptions by one notch. There are, of course, ski areas reporting honest conditions, but it's undoubtedly better to arrive with lower expectations and be pleasantly surprised than vice versa. Another important source of information is the resort's snow phones, often toll-free numbers with recordings detailing the latest conditions. Again, these numbers are listed throughout the guide, and it pays to maintain a skeptical attitude on conditions.

Useful websites

Besides the homepages of the resorts there's a wide array of useful **websites** for planning a downhill vacation. For a larger resort or town, search the Web for local publications and/or Chamber of Commerce sites if you want to do more research before (or during) your trip. What follows is a short list of nonresort-specific sites dedicated to larger regions or various aspects of skiing and snowboarding. Many of the sites below contain useful **message boards** that are notable for finding everything from ride-shares to equipment deals.

ⓦ **www.avalanche.org** Information on avalanches throughout North America. Links to local avalanche centers are available along with information on safety courses and the latest slides.

ⓦ **www.canadianskipatrol.com** Loaded with details on resorts across Canada, particularly helpful for updates on festivals and special events.

19

ⓦ**www.couloirmag.com** A major source for those who prefer hiking to lifts, this site deals with all aspects of backcountry exploration. Most useful for entertaining articles, gear reviews, and a handy chat room.

ⓦ**www.gorp.com** Attractive site covering outdoor pursuits throughout the world. Skiing and snowboarding are covered, but GORP is best visited for ideas on active day-off pursuits, including snowshoeing and dog-sledding.

ⓦ**www.skicanadamag.com** Scores of recent skiing articles along with equipment and resort reviews.

ⓦ**www.skimag.com** The official site of *Ski* magazine has hundreds of articles and photos archived. Worth a visit for gear reviews, tips on skiing techniques, and updated snow reports complete with forecasts for the week ahead.

ⓦ**www.skimaps.com** Best site for a comprehensive list of trail maps from around the world, even if they are frequently a year or two out of date. Equally enjoyable for checking out the big guns like Whistler and Vail as it is for checking out bite-sized hills like Michigan's Mt. Brighton Ski Area.

ⓦ**www.transworldsnowboarding.com** Site of the top-selling snowboard magazine, filled with news and interviews along with an array of photos and videos. Even though they're often filled with conceited chatter, the various message boards can be a useful source of information as well.

ⓦ**www.travel.yahoo.com** Click on Yahoo's Ski & Snow Guide for consistently updated snow reports for resorts across North America. The Snow Alert option lets you set up emailed notices for the latest snowfalls at your chosen resorts.

Maps

As they're only necessary once on the mountain and because every resort hands out **trail maps** for free at their ticket windows and information desks, there's no reason to attempt purchasing these ahead of time. Should you want a look at the slopes before arriving, downloadable trail maps can be found on the majority of resort homepages. Note that trail maps change from year to year, so make sure you are looking at the latest version. As for larger road and regional maps of the US and Canada, both local tourist centers as well as any of the following map outlets should be able to provide what you're looking for. Rand McNally's *Road Atlas* (US$12), available at bookstores and gas stations virtually everywhere in North America, is your best one-volume source for road-tripping.

Costs, money, and banks

To help plan your ski or snowboard vacation, this book contains price information on all your main costs both in broad terms, for travel, accommodation, and eating, and specifically, for tickets, lessons, and rentals. Prices are given in US or Canadian dollars throughout the guide as appropriate ($), with a label – US$ or Can$ – wherever confusion might arise. General costs outlined in Basics are in US dollars.

Costs

Ticket prices vary dramatically from region to region, budget lodging at one resort might be luxury suite at another, and varying **costs** on food, lessons, rentals, and gear can bring the price of a one-week trip anywhere from $600 to $2000 per individual.

Your biggest single expense is likely to be accommodation (see p.27), with the most basic options being hostel dorm beds in the $15–20 range. Expect to pay around $50 for basic hotel rooms and at least double this for slopeside accommodations. Another major expense is getting around (see p.24), particularly if you decide to rent a car during your vacation; two people sharing can expect to pay $50 each per day. Resort services such as tickets, lessons, and rentals vary tremendously between resorts but can mount to an additional $100 per person per day. Expenses for food and drink

Currency exchange rates

US$1=Can$1.40=UK£.60
Can$1=US$.70=UK£.45
UK£1=US$1.60=Can$2.20
Note: these rates are approximate at
time of publication.

are relatively small in comparison, but if you are keen to live it up a little it's fairly easy to go through at least $40 per day.

Cutting costs

It's difficult to get around the fact that skiing vacations are expensive, but there are several ways to **cut costs**. These come mainly by buying various items together in a package, but planning your vacation outside busy holiday periods can play a large part too.

Ski-packages that bundle accommodation and ticket expenses together typically offer a ten to twenty percent overall discount. Most ski area websites list participating local accommodations and have a central reservation system to take bookings. Only local hostels or motels in distant towns are generally more economical than these packages.

If possible avoid staying in a resort around Christmas and early January, or on public holiday weekends. The off-season doesn't necessarily mean poor conditions; many ski areas receive dependable snow as early as mid-November and some of the best snowfalls, especially in central Colorado, occur in late March and early April. Early and late season passes are terrific value, and last-minute specials are easy to acquire.

If you can get there cheaply, visiting **Canada** is particularly recommended. Conditions are generally excellent and the currently weak Canadian dollar makes almost everything – and certainly accommodation and tickets – cheaper than equivalent US resorts.

Youth and student discounts

Youth/student ID cards pay for themselves quickly, particularly in cutting travel costs, and some ski areas offer discounts on passes for college students. Full-time students are eligible for the International Student ID Card (ISIC, @www.isiccard.com), which enti-

tles the bearer to special air, rail, and bus fares and discounts at museums, theaters and other attractions. For Americans there's also a health benefit, providing up to $3000 in emergency medical coverage and $100 a day for sixty days in the hospital, plus a 24-hour hotline to call in the event of a medical, legal, or financial emergency. The card costs $22 in the USA; C$16 in Canada; AUS$16.50 in Australia; NZ$21 in New Zealand; £6 in the UK; and EU$12.70 in the Republic of Ireland.

Those 26 or younger qualify for the **International Youth Travel Card**, which costs US$22/£7 and carries the same benefits. Teachers should purchase the **International Teacher Card**, offering similar discounts for US$22, Can$16, AUS$16.50, and NZ$21. All cards are available in the US from Council Travel, STA, and Travel Cuts and in Canada from Hostelling International; in Australia and New Zealand from STA or Campus Travel; and in the UK from STA. A university photo ID might provide some discounts but is not as easily recognizable as the ISIC cards.

Money

Upheaval in world markets causes constant fluctuation in the **value** of both the Canadian and US dollar. In recent years, and in relation to the US dollar, one Canadian dollar has been worth between 75¢ and 85¢; one Australian dollar worth around 55¢ and one New Zealand dollar between 40¢ and 50¢; one pound sterling typically buys $1.55 to $1.65.

US currency comes in denominations of $1, $5, $10, $20, $50, and $100. One dollar is made up of 100 cents, with coins of 1 cent (a penny), 5 cents (a nickel), 10 cents (a dime), and 25 cents (a quarter). Quarters are handy for all vending machines, parking meters, and telephones. You may also come across the newly introduced dollar coin but are unlikely to see a rare 50¢ coin.

The **Canadian dollar**, also made up of 100 cents, is issued in 5¢ (nickel), 10¢ (dime), 25¢ (quarter) and $1 and $2 coins. The one-dollar coin is universally known as a "loonie" after the loon, a bird on one of its faces, and the two-dollar occasionally referred to as a "twoonie." Paper currency comes in $5, $10, $20, $50, $100, $500 and $1000 denominations. US dollars are also widely accepted on a one-for-one basis, but given the exchange rate between them, it's clearly in your interest to acquire Canadian currency.

Cash and travelers' checks

The most straightforward way of accessing your funds is to draw **cash** from **automatic teller machines** (ATMs), located not just in banks but also in many gas stations, supermarkets, and convenience stores. Most bank cards are linked to one of the major international networks like Plus or Cirrus.

Major banks in larger cities will change foreign currency and foreign currency travelers' checks, but in general it's far better to have your **travelers' checks** in US dollars. The most recognized kinds are American Express and Thomas Cook, widely available from travel agencies and banks in most countries. The usual fee for travelers' check sales is one or two percent, though this may be waived if you buy the checks through a bank where you have an account. Make sure to keep the purchase agreement and a record of check serial numbers safe and separate from the checks themselves. In the event that checks are lost or stolen, the issuing company will expect you to report the loss immediately to their office. Most companies can replace lost or stolen checks within 24 hours. For American Express contact ☎1-800/221-7282; for Thomas Cook ☎1-800/223-7373.

Credit and debit cards

Mastercard, Visa, and American Express are accepted just about everywhere. Remember that all cash advances are treated as loans, with interest accruing daily from the date of withdrawal; there may be a transaction fee on top of this. However, you may be able to make withdrawals from **ATMs** in the US or Canada using your debit card, which is not liable to interest payments, and the flat transaction fee is usually nominal. Make sure you have a personal identification number (PIN) that's designed to work overseas.

Somewhere between travelers' checks and credit cards is Visa TravelMoney, a disposable prepaid debit card with a PIN that works in all ATMs that take Visa cards. Load up your account with funds before leaving home and when they run out, simply throw the card away. You can buy up to nine cards to access the same funds – useful for couples or families traveling together – and it's a good idea to buy at least one extra as a back-up in case of loss or theft. There is also a 24-hour toll-free customer assistance number ☎1-800/847-2399. The card is available in most countries from branches of Thomas Cook and Citicorp. For more information, check the Visa TravelMoney website at ⊛www.usa.visa.com/personal/cards/visa_travel_money.html.

Wiring money

Having money wired from home using one of the companies listed below is never convenient or cheap and should only be considered as a last resort. It's possible to have money wired directly from a bank in your home country to a North American bank, although this is somewhat less reliable because it involves two separate institutions. If you go this route, your home bank will need the address of the branch bank where you want to pick up the money and the address and telex number of the receiving country's head office, which will act as the clearing house. Money wired this way normally takes two working days to arrive and costs around $40 per transaction.

Money-wiring companies

Thomas Cook US ☎1-800/287-7362, Canada ☎1-888/823-4732, Great Britain ☎01733/318 922, Northern Ireland ☎028/9055 0030, Republic of Ireland ☎01/677 1721, ⊛www.thomascook.com **Travelers Express MoneyGram** US ☎1-800/955-7777, Canada ☎1-800/933-3278, UK ☎0800/018 0104, Republic of Ireland ☎1850/205 800, Australia ☎1800/230 100, New Zealand ☎0800/262 263, ⊛www.moneygram.com **Western Union** US and Canada ☎1-800/325-6000, Australia ☎1800/501 500, New Zealand ☎0800/270 000, UK ☎0800/833 833, Republic of Ireland ☎1800/395 395, ⊛www.westernunion.com

Equipment

Renting equipment is a quick way to add $15–40 to the price of a ski day, but for beginners and infrequent visitors to the mountains it is generally the most practical option. Make sure that whatever equipment you end up using fits properly. Incorrectly sized boots that seemed comfortable when you tried them on become hideously painful once on the slopes, while skis or boards that are too long, short, or stiff for the novice make the learning process that much harder. If you ride at least a couple of weeks a year, buying gear is cheaper than renting.

What to rent

Resorts charge a premium on their **rentals**, yet often have a limited and overused inventory. Expect to pay from $20 per day for a basic ski package (note that shaped skis are the norm these days, replacing the traditional straight ski with a more ergonomic, easy-to-turn mode) and $30 plus for a snowboard and boots. Aside from an expensive, high-end **demo** selection, resort rental equipment is typically purchased from just one or two manufacturers, from a range specifically designed to be used as rental gear – lower cost products that are more durable but less performance driven. This is particularly true of snowboard rentals. Boots are often soft and mushy, and boards are tailored to the complete novice. A few resorts only have boards with **step-in bindings** available, an easy-in, easy-out system that works well for beginners but has lost favor with experienced riders and is incompatible with the more commonly sold strap-in system. Independent ski or snowboard stores usually maintain an excellent selection of up-to-date, quality gear with rates a few dollars less per day than at the resorts. Multi-day rentals are cheaper, and seasonal rentals may be available (starting at around $150). Inexpensive alternatives are rental-specific stores, which are in competition for the casual, novice skier. Rates are rock bottom, starting at under $10 for basic skis and around $20 for a snowboard package, but equipment is typically low-end and has often been experienced a few years of abuse. Telemark skis are increasingly available, as are snowshoes and, less often, cross-country (or Nordic) skis. Off the mountain, visit the local Nordic center or climbing, hiking, and wilderness specialist for the best selection. A credit card and often a driver's license or passport are necessary when renting; cash is rarely accepted since a hefty deposit is required. Advance online rentals are increasingly encouraged by resorts and larger stores, allowing them to guarantee gear will be available, and saves you up to 20 percent per day. Book as early as possible for maximum savings. A few possibilities are ⑩www.rentskis.com, a reservation system used by larger stores and many of the Rocky Mountain and west coast resorts; Colorado- and Utah-based ski chain Christy Sports (⑩www.christysports.com); and Intrawest-owned Breeze/MAX (⑩www.breezeski.com), which you can find pretty much anywhere.

Large ski shops often rent clothes, helmets, and more occasionally gloves and goggles.

What to buy

Eyewear and **sunscreen** are priorities: high-altitude rays and the reflective properties of snow can cause severe eye damage and sunburn if appropriate precautions are not taken. Pack sunscreen with at least a factor 30 and buy a decent set of goggles – more practical than sunglasses – as they protect your eyes from sun, snow, and wind. Most goggles have some type of ventilation system to prevent steam up. Use mittens with removable fleece liners. The best gloves have a soft patch on the thumbs for nose-wiping comfort (known as a snot pad or rag) and a plastic ridge used to wipe excess snow off the outside of goggles. Heavyweight wool socks are not ideal; ski- or snowboard-specific socks are padded over the hard-working shin and ankle areas, with less material in the toes to allow better heat transfer around your feet. Bring a wool hat and consider a neck gator. Similar to a scarf neck, gators keep snow from getting into your jacket should you take a tumble in powder and can be pulled up over the face on long, windy chairlift rides.

With clothing, layering is key. Avoid cotton as it retains water, staying damp and cold on the skin after exposure to snow or sweat. Pack at least one set of thermal underwear and cover with any old wool or fleece sweater and the best waterproof and breathable pants you can afford. Some pants come with highly resistant GORE-TEX® patches on the butt and knees, particularly useful for beginners. Fleece pants are a welcome extra on cold days. Buying a pair of quality, well-fitted boots is a more important first investment than skis or a board; the essential interface between your muscles and the snow, they need to be broken in to suit each individual. Clothes, eyewear, and equipment cost less in North America than Europe, Australia, and elsewhere; unfortunately, you may not find exactly what you want after the pre-Christmas drain on stock. The hectic annual turnover has its advantages, as spring is a great time to find bargains.

Baggage

Skis or a snowboard can be carried as one piece of the two-piece baggage allowance on international flights, providing that your bag weighs under 70lb. Unfortunately, not all check-in staff are familiar with this stipulation; complain to the airline if charged. Internal flights within North America may incur an excess fee, particularly if traveling on small aircraft; this is typically $85–125.

Getting around

Unless you intend to zero in on one resort for the duration of your trip, having your own vehicle is the best option for any downhill vacation. This provides you with more flexibility in choosing your resort, a greater choice of places to conveniently stay and eat – which can help cut costs – and an easy place to stow and transport cumbersome equipment. The primary downside of private transportation is the need to deal with often tricky and usually tiring winter driving conditions, not to mention finding parking in some crowded resort areas. Rail and bus services are frequently the best option for budget-conscious solo travelers making only a few stops or traveling for a long period of time with lengthy stays at each stop. Trains and buses, however, will only take you between major cities and regional towns, rarely to the resorts themselves. Private shuttle buses, available at most transportation hubs, provide the best way to get to individual ski resorts and occasionally provide services between nearby resorts. Details of all public transportation options, along with any necessary route-finding information for drivers, are listed in the *Arrrival, information, and getting around* section for each major resort.

By car

Those in possession of a US, UK, Canadian, Australian, or New Zealand driver's license can legally drive in both the US and Canada. In the US **speed limits** vary between 65 and 75mph on large interstates, with lower limits of 35–45 mph applying to roads in commercial areas and a limit of 20mph near schools when children are present. In Canada the maximum speed limit is 100kph on major highways, 80kph on rural highways, and 50kph or less in urban areas. Fuel prices

Winter driving

Winter driving is likely to be the most perilous activity you will do on a ski or snowboarding holiday and it pays to be prepared. Basic equipment should include an ice scraper for clearing windshields and, in areas of high snowfall, a shovel for clearing away built-up snow. Snow tires are essential and should suffice for general highway driving and ascending ski area roads since both are regularly cleared. On more remote roads it is often advisable and sometimes required to carry chains.

If you're unaccustomed to driving in icy **conditions**, it's best to avoid driving during snowstorms. Keep yourself informed on road and weather conditions, using resort websites, snow lines, and numbers listed in each resort account. En route you can also check at local tourist offices or at a gas station.

Even with the best precautions, you may find yourself sliding on an icy road or stuck in deep snow. If you start to skid in a car without an antilock brake system (ABS), release the brakes immediately, repeatedly reapplying them until the car is under control. In ABS-equipped cars this process should occur automatically. In anticipation of getting stuck or breaking down, it's worth packing warm clothes, blankets, food, and water. Having a mobile phone can also be reassuring, and potentially a lifesaver. If you are stuck in deep snow don't leave the engine running to keep warm in order to avoid carbon monoxide poisoning.

vary tremendously around North America and can cost anywhere between $1.15 and $2.50 a gallon (3.8 liters).

Both Canadian and US law require that any alcohol be carried unopened in the trunk of the car. It's illegal to make a U-turn anywhere where an unbroken line runs down the middle of a road. At junctions in some states and provinces it's legal to turn right on a red light if there is no traffic approaching from the left. At crossroads with multiple stop signs ("Arrêt" in Quebec), all traffic must stop before proceeding in order of arrival. Traffic in both directions must stop if a school bus is stationary with its flashing lights on, as this means children are getting on or off. In the US, Driving Under the Influence (DUI) is a very serious offense and the police are entitled to administer various breath, saliva, and urine tests. If considered intoxicated, you'll be locked up until sober and receive fines of several hundred dollars, or in extreme – or repeat – cases, face incarceration for thirty days or longer. Drunk driving is treated in a similar way in Canada as police need no excuse to stop you, and if you are over the limit your keys, license, and car will be impounded and you may end up in jail for a few days. In either country, if the police flag you down, don't get out of the car or reach into the glove compartment

unless requested to do so. Officers are wary of motorists with weapons, so sit still with your hands on the wheel and be polite.

Car rental

Car rentals are available for anyone over 21 holding a license for over a year. A credit card is necessary as rental agencies (listed on p.26) rarely accept cash deposits. All rental cars in North America have automatic transmission and most companies allow travel between the US–Canadian border, but be sure to confirm this in advance with your rental company.

Advance **booking** usually ensures the best rates. Most companies have some leeway in their charges to help them beat their competitors, so it's worth haggling. Discounts are often available with membership to a motoring organization or ownership of a certain type of credit card or frequent-flyer card. If you are taking a transatlantic flight, you might be able to secure a fly-drive package or at least a discounted rate with a partner company of your airline. **Rental rates** are charged by the day or week and can vary dramatically between agencies and different parts of the country. A typical rate is $60 per day and $300 per week. Those under 25 can expect to pay a surcharge. Be sure to check the small print on advertised prices as they rarely include taxes and surcharges. Clarify any additional costs in advance to avoid nasty surprises on pick-up or drop-off. Check whether the rate includes unlimited mileage and what the insurance costs will be.

Collision Damage Waiver (CDW) – sometimes called Liability Damage Waiver or Physical Damage Waiver – is generally not included in rental charges but is strongly recommended. It covers any damage to the vehicle that occurs while in your possession, from scratches to full collisions, regardless of who is at fault. North American car-owners are likely to be covered for CDW by their own vehicle insurance already, and some credit card companies extend coverage to anyone using their card. CDW insurance typically costs an additional $10–15 per day.

Be sure to check your **third-party liability**. Standard policies cover the first $15,000 of a claim against you. This is rarely enough and companies advise taking out extra insurance, usually a further $10 per day, to indemnify drivers up to $2,000,000.

When renting a car for **winter driving** rent either a four-wheel drive (4WD) – usually an extra $10 a day – or a car equipped with snow tires and ABS. Larger companies, particularly those listed below, can often supply ski and snowboard racks if requested. In the event of a breakdown, call the emergency assistance number printed on your rental contract. If not carrying your own, you might consider renting a mobile phone from the car rental agency for a nominal amount.

Car rental agencies

Alamo ☎1-800/522-9696, ⌨www.alamo.com
Avis US ☎1-800/331-1084, Canada ☎1-800 /272-5871, ⌨www.avis.com
Budget ☎1-800/527-0700, ⌨www .budgetrentacar.com
Dollar ☎1-800/800-4000, ⌨www.dollar.com
Enterprise Rent-a-Car ☎1-800/325-8007, ⌨www.enterprise.com
Europcar ☎1-877/940 6900, ⌨www.europcar.com
Hertz US ☎1-800/654-3001, Canada ☎1-800 /263-0600, ⌨www.hertz.com
Holiday Autos ☎1-800/422-7737, ⌨www.holidayautos.com
National ☎1-800/227-7368, ⌨www.nationalcar.com
Thrifty ☎1-800/367-2277, ⌨www.thrifty.com

Hitchhiking

Although practiced regularly in more remote areas, hitchhiking in the US or Canada is generally a bad idea. Common sense is your most valuable asset in judging situations, and women should never hitch alone.

Motoring organizations

In North America

AAA ☎1-800/AAA-HELP, ⌨www.aaa.com. Each state has its own club – check the phone book for local address and phone number.
CAA ☎613/247-0117, ⌨www.caa.ca. Each region has its own club – check the phone book for local address and phone number.

In the UK and Ireland

AA UK ☎0870/600 0371, ⌨www.theaa.com
AA Ireland Dublin ☎01/617 9988, ⌨www.aaireland.ie
RAC UK ☎0800/550 055, ⌨www.rac.co.uk

In Australia and New Zealand

AAA Australia ☎02/6247 7311, ⌨www.aaa.asn.au
New Zealand AA New Zealand ☎09/377 4660, ⌨www.nzaa.co.nz

By bus

Greyhound (☎1-800/229-9424, ⌨www .greyhound.com in the US; ☎1-800/661-8747, ⌨www.greyhound.ca in Canada) links all major cities and many smaller towns and connects with the services of some smaller regional bus companies. Reservations are not essential but recommended; if they are full you'll just need to wait for the next bus. If you intend to travel extensively or exclusively by bus, consider buying a Greyhound Ameripass, offering unlimited travel within a set time limit. A seven-day pass costs $200; thirty days $399; and passes up to sixty days are available. Children travel half price, and there are discounts for North American students and seniors.

In Canada, bus services are run by the Moose Network (☎604/944-3007 or 1-888 /388-4881 in Western Canada; ☎905/853-

4762 or 1-888/816-8873 in Eastern Canada ⓦwww.moosenetwork.com) between British Columbia's resorts and the main ski areas in Quebec. One of their week-long trips in Quebec costs CDN$400; three days in the west start at CDN$200.

By rail

Both the American **Amtrak** (ⓣ1-800/USA-RAIL, ⓦwww.amtrak.com) and Canadian **VIA Rail** (Toronto ⓣ416/366-8411, rest of Canada ⓣ1-888/VIA-RAIL, US (via Amtrak; ⓣ1-800/USA-RAIL, ⓦwww.viarail.ca), offer reliable train service across the continent. Stops in most mountainous areas are limited and few stations offer direct access to mountain towns or resorts; the train is really just an alternative to flying. For skiers heading to the Rockies or the Sierra Nevadas, the *Californian Zephyr* leaves Chicago for Kansas City then heads to Denver and Salt Lake City – stopping at Winter Park (see p.185) and Glenwood Springs (see p.135) en route – before continuing to the southern Californian coast. In Canada, VIA Rail connects Toronto, Winnipeg, and Saskatoon with Jasper and Whistler with its **Snow Train** (ⓣ1-800/561-8630 ⓦwww.snowtraintojasper.com. Ski packages are offered that split time between Whistler and Marmot Basin; and, using bus transfers, VIA Rail can also include stays in Banff.

The costs of rail travel are similar to flying, with one-way cross-country fares around $285. If you are traveling round-trip you can take advantage of Explore America fares, which allow three stopovers within a 45-day period. Amtrak rail passes are worthwhile if traveling more broadly; a fifteen-day pass costs $200 in the winter months; a thirty-day pass is $270.

By plane

Airports throughout North America connect major cities with smaller, local airports. Reservations are not essential but recommended. For more information on regional flights see Getting There, p.9.

Accommodation

Accommodation standards in North American ski resorts are generally high, and costs inevitably form a significant proportion of expenses for any trip. During regular season, it's tough to find a room in a resort for under $70, even at small motels well past their prime. Prices are particularly steep over holiday periods, when rooms get booked months in advance. Most ski resorts maintain their own booking system (normally available through a toll-free number and via the resort website). This may be the central reservation agency for the entire area – a job often handled by the local Chamber of Commerce – or may simply deal in resort-owned properties; we have indicated which in the text.

Cheaper lodgings exist in **adjacent towns**, particularly in areas popular with summer visitors, where budget motels proliferate and basic rooms can start as low as $30 per night. Rates are only a little higher at similar establishments on the outskirts of large cities, an option in some regions for those willing to commute to the slopes each day (and forgo any ski town atmosphere). Canadian ski towns usually offer dormitory accommodations, but hostels in American resorts are scarce – and prices, normally $18–30, are seldom much cheaper than sharing a motel room or low-end B&B.

In nearly all cases, accommodation **rates** work on a sliding scale. Prices jump significantly on weekends, and sky-high premiums are charged over the two-week period covering Christmas and New Year, on Martin Luther King and Presidents' Day weekends,

Accommodation price codes

Accommodation has been price-coded according to the cost of the least expensive double room available midweek during regular ski season. Expect weekend rates to be some $20–60 more expensive. Price codes do not include lodging taxes, which vary not just by state but by town and ski area and may add (in the most extreme cases) as much as 25 percent to the rate. Six to twelve percent is a bit closer to average.

❶ up to US$40/up to Can$55
❷ US$40-60/Can$55-80
❸ US$60-90/Can$80-120
❹ US$90-120/Can$120-160
❺ US$120-150/Can$160-200

❻ US$150-180/Can$200-240
❼ US$180-240/Can$240-320
❽ US$240-300/Can$320-400
❾ US$300+/Can$400+

and for the duration of Spring Break (see p.35 for more on these holiday periods). Rates drop prior to the third week in December and from April onwards.

Motels and hotels

Luxury **hotels** are common in North American ski resorts, from intimate New England inns and Victorian redbrick townhouses to modern concrete edifices – the latter often constructed with giant logs and river rock fireplaces in an attempt to add a rustic mountain touch. A few **all-inclusive ski lodges** charge weekly rates for all accommodation, meals, and occasionally lift tickets and lessons too. Ski town **motels** are not as cheap as their highway counterparts, but still represent value for money over hotel accommodation. Two queen beds per room is the norm in most chains – along with cable TV, phones, and en-suite bathrooms – reducing costs for those sharing. Some places allow a third single bed for around $10 on top of the price, and most include an extended continental breakfast – typically a bland buffet of hot and cold cereals, breads, juice, and coffee.

Bed and breakfasts

Bed-and-breakfasts often represent the best-value deals in the mountains, particularly for couples. Many conform to the stereotypical American B&B template: romantic, restored Victorian mansions, filled with lace and antiques. Converted ranches and log cabins are also common, usually out in the meadows or woods a few miles from the resorts. Most B&Bs have no more than

ten bedrooms, but occasionally larger inns advertise themselves as bed-and-breakfasts – and while some of these are as well-appointed as their more intimate counterparts, particularly in New England, others are really just remodeled motels. True B&Bs offer huge (often gourmet) breakfasts and après snacks – which may be home-made cookies and hot drinks, or appetizers, cheese, and wine. Prices vary from $70 to $300 per night; most double-occupancy rooms fall between $85 and $150.

Condominiums

Best for families and large groups, **condominiums** offer full kitchens and living areas in addition to a place to sleep. Guests typically have access to a communal indoor or outdoor hot tub and, occasionally, a pool. Condos range from rather shabby, cramped apartments to spacious two-story townhomes, and inside you might find as much variety. Most property management companies post photographs on their websites, at least of the exteriors. **Condo-hotels** are a collection of suites within a large hotel-style building that offer all the amenities associated with a hotel: fitness center, pool, hot tubs, one or more restaurants, front desk and concierge services. Many of the newer condo-hotels are grand slopeside properties affiliated with the ski area.

Rates for condominiums can work out at less than $30 per person per night at the lower end of the scale. Cleaning and linen charges can add over $100 to your bill. Maximum occupancy figures for rentals refer to the number of bed spaces available (including pull-out beds), but agencies will seldom check up on the numbers unless the occupants get rowdy. Parking spaces are usually limited, particularly in apartment-style complexes.

Cabins and vacation homes

As with condominiums, vacation homes – **ski cabins** as they're often called – come in all shapes and sizes, ranging from rustic A-framed wooden cottages to new log mansions with private outdoor hot tubs, game rooms, and large garages. **Cabin resorts** are groups of little wooden cottages, often dating from before the 1950s and once used as fishing cabins or rustic summer retreats. Most are still fairly basic but have been cozily refurbished. Rates for ski cabins are much the same as condos.

Hostels

There are only a handful of hostels in ski resorts across North America, none of which require hostel membership – though a few do charge members a dollar or so less. Specific details are listed for each resort where relevant. Some maintain traditional hostel curfews and require the completion of daily chores; those that do insist on the use

of sheet sleeping bags rent them for a minimal fee. Winter is a quiet time for most hostels – particularly midweek – but during this period entire hostels may sporadically be rented out to private groups, so book as far in advance as possible.

Hostels.com (🖥 www.hostels.com) is a useful Web-based resource for all North American hostels, with up-to-date listings and contact information.

Camping and RVs

Most official **campgrounds** in the mountains are closed during the winter, as they tend to be blanketed in snow. If that doesn't put you off, contact the local Forest Service, as winter camping may be permitted in some areas. A few commercial campgrounds in each region are open for **motor homes**, and many resorts permit RVs overnight in their free lots – though you should always call to enquire in advance and check before you park. Motor homes can be rented in major cities across North America and, as winter is the off-season for RV companies, rates are at their lowest then. Expect to pay $400–900 for the week. Local companies usually offer better rates than national giants like Cruise America (☎ 800/327-7799, 🖥 www.cruiseamerica.com).

Eating and drinking

North America doesn't have the reputation of France or Switzerland for fine mountain dining. Self-service cafeterias are the norm at resorts, fine really, as lunch – the meal you're most likely to be eating on-mountain – is simply a means to an end, with the priority to refuel fast and get back on the mountain. Fortunately, most ski towns boast a wider variety of eating options, and there you'll find the requisite burger and steakhouse joints, sushi, fondue, Mexican standards, even the occasional gourmet restaurant, and plenty of spots serving up vegetarian choices. Most resorts have a few bars and spots for après-ski, but the best of those too can typically be found in the closest ski town.

Meals and costs

On-mountain dining is notoriously over-priced, because the resort has you hostage; $10 for a very simple lunch is the norm, a

few times that for dinner. Prices for off-mountain meals generally depend on the number of choices available and whether or not the resort area is an upscale or trendy one – it's too large a continent to do much generalizing. Fortunately, despite remote mountain locations, ingredients are generally high quality: salads are crisp and filled with interesting veggies, while the fish for sushi is flown in regularly.

Ski town **breakfasts** come big and cheap. If you don't want to sit down to load up on eggs or pancakes at a café or diner, opt for a pastry, bagel, or breakfast burrito-to-go from a multitude of bakeries, bagelries, and the like. Resort cafeterias at the base of the ski area typically serve breakfast from around 7am, but the food is rarely exciting and usually pricey, while the espresso – if they have it – is poor.

Lunch is the time to brown bag it. Take a sandwich or an energy bar (just remember to keep energy bars in an inside pocket so that they don't freeze and become jaw breakers; sandwiches might be better off in a locker) and stop for a hot chocolate or soda when energy runs low. On-mountain cafeterias are typically food-court style, with hamburger grills, a baked potato bar, salads, pizza, and vaguely Mexican- and Chinese-influenced dishes.

Dinner will be the main meal of the day, and the most expensive; we've attempted to unearth some of the better-value local spots, along with places worthy of splashing out. Grills and brewpubs are ubiquitous, with steakhouses prominent in cattle ranching regions. Authentic Mexican food can be found in the little taquerias patronized by the Latino communities that are the service backbone of the resorts. Italian cooking ranges from inexpensive pizza and pasta to pricey regional specialties. French cuisine is likewise upscale; German, Swiss, and Austrian restaurants are geared to those who secretly wish they were in the Alps. Chinese food is everywhere, but often Americanized and bland. Excellent sushi is found in almost every major resort town – again at a price.

Après-ski

Eating during **après** is one way of eating for less; quite substantial snacks are served at many restaurants from around 3pm. Bars may offer this too; it's a good way to fill up even if you're not drinking. In ski towns like Aspen and Crested Butte, some of the more expensive places offer bar menus at night: food is practically the same as what is being served at the tables, but at half the price and with a better view.

Self-catering

Even skiers not staying in condominiums can avoid eating out for every meal; most hotels have refrigerators and coffee machines, and some have kitchenettes. All but the smallest ski towns are home to a small health-food shop and at least one large regional supermarket. Most of the supermarkets don't close until 9 or 10pm (except on Sundays, when some shut by late afternoon). In the more populated areas, 24-hour opening is the norm.

Drinking

For many skiers, apres-ski – typically from 3 to 5 or 6pm, the equivalent of an early happy hour and coinciding with the end of the ski day – is the start of **drinking** time, with food and drink specials on offer. Bars also often have nighttime special deals early in the week, when the crowd is much more oriented to locals than the visitors who flock to the resorts on weekends. The usual assortment of dusty saloons and sleek brewpubs can be found in mountain towns; the latter offer handcrafted beers in the form of crisp pilsners, wheat beers, and stout on tap, at prices only marginally above domestics like Budweiser, Coors, and Miller.

To buy or consume alcohol in the US you need to be 21 with valid identification even if you look much older. In Canada, 18 is the legal drinking age in Québec, and 19 in Alberta and British Columbia. Each state and quite often each town has different laws regarding what type of alcohol can be sold where and when. At most resorts, bars generally stay open until 2am.

It's important to note that **intoxication** occurs quicker at higher altitudes, especially during your first few days on-mountain. See the section on altitude sickness (p.18) and be sure to keep hydrated while riding.

Backcountry skiing

While we have offered suggestions for backcountry explorations throughout the guide, some of the information is deliberately vague: the number of fatalities from avalanches and other backcountry hazards has grown exponentially with the huge increase in backcountry traffic over the past decade. Even if you already have experience out of bounds, it's still best to consult local guides, US Forest Service rangers, ski patrol, or specialist backcountry stores for insider information. If it's your first time off-piste consider using a professional guide or joining a snowcat or helitrip, and be sure to take an avalanche course.

Boundary rules

Each state and province has different laws and Forest Service regulations pertaining to ski area **boundaries**, and each ski area applies those laws more or less formally. At some resorts, crossing the ropes is illegal at all times, in all places – violators will have their passes pulled, and possibly face criminal charges. Others, particularly in California and the Northwest, maintain "open-boundary" policies; skiers may leave the resort provided an area is not specifically closed. There are open gates along the perimeter where riders may exit the area legally and exercise their right to travel on National Forest land. These are usually tucked away, well out of sight of the casual skier, and are often not marked on the trail map. Backcountry riders are not the responsibility of the ski area. If there's an accident or one becomes lost, local law enforcement will typically conduct the search-and-rescue at a substantial financial expense to the victim.

Avalanches

Avalanches do not typically "just happen," but are, to an extent, predictable; in many fatal cases, the victim, or member of the victim's party, did something to trigger the slide. The gradient and shape of a slope, recent weather and snowfall patterns, and geographical position (in the northern hemisphere, eighty percent of avalanches occur on north-facing slopes) can all be used to assess slide potential. Hands-on avalanche courses are highly recommended for all advanced riders and essential for those

planning backcountry forays without a guide. Knowledge of first aid is also important and courses are available throughout North America, offered by local colleges, resort ski patrols, backcountry guide schools, and outdoor sporting goods stores, including national giants like REI (Recreational Equipment, Inc).

Other than taking an avalanche course and riding with a guide, a few common sense rules apply to travel in the backcountry; many are also applicable when riding off-piste in a resort: never ride alone; carry an energy bar or other high-energy food; drink regularly to avoid dehydration. Wear a transceiver in potential avalanche terrain, and know how to use it – transceivers, or "peeps," send out radio signals that can be used to locate the wearer if buried. The path of an avalanche can be hundreds of feet wide, and speed of discovery is the key factor in saving a victim's life. Should the worst happen, attempt to stay on top of the snow by "swimming." Once it slows down, cup your hands in front of your face to create an airpocket. Try not to panic; dribble, and observe the path of your spit to ascertain which way is up before attempting to dig yourself out.

Other hazards

Pay attention to your surroundings. Hidden rocks, logs, and creekbeds are accidents waiting to happen; uneven snow is a clue to their presence. Tree wells are common in the below-timberline terrain found in North America, particularly during epic powder years. These potential traps are deep holes in the snowpack surrounding the trunks of larger trees, where the umbrella-like shelter of overhanging branches prevents the snow from compacting. They are typically only visible when it's too late, and riders caught in a tree well are likely to suffocate if not rescued almost immediately. Overhanging cornices are dangerous from both above and below, as the lip can break off with little warning. Approach with caution, and never hang around on top of a cornice in a group. Always check the local weather report before setting out, as poor conditions add a significant element of risk.

Backcountry resources

We've listed avalanche hotline numbers and backcountry guiding services specific to each region throughout the guide, but there are many useful resources online to help with pre-trip planning. The best avalanche courses are held in the field; three levels of proficiency can be taken.

Avalanche websites

American Avalanche Association ⊛www .avalanche.org. National organization of avalanche professionals, including forecasters, researchers, and ski patrollers. The website links to state-specific avalanche centers.

Canadian Avalanche Association and Centre ⊛www.avalanche.ca. Website of Canada's national avalanche association and center. The site has links to classes, statistics, and weather reports; updated reports are available toll-free at ☏800/667-1105.

Colorado Avalanche Information Center ⊛http://geosurvey.state.co.us/avalanche. Online home of the avalanche forecasting and education center for Colorado. Among the advice and statistics are listings of avalanche courses throughout the state and useful links to regional forecasting centers around the US.

CyberSpace Avalanche Center ⊛www.csac.org and ⊛www.casc.org/Canada. Maintains comprehensive websites for the US and Canada. Bulletin boards offer local advice and the online store maintains a huge inventory of safety equipment, books, and videos.

Forest Service National Avalanche Center ⊛www.avalanche.org/%nac/. Most useful for its links to Forest Service avalanche centers across the US.

Utah Avalanche Center ⊛www.avalanche.com. Essential for anyone planning a backcountry trip in the state. Contains an extensive list of local phone numbers and contact information.

Avalanche courses

The American Avalanche Institute, PO Box 308, Wilson, WY 83014 ☏307/733-3315, ⊛www .avalanchecourse.com. Teaching avalanche awareness since 1974. Level I to III courses are now held in ten states. Costs for a Level I course are $170–180.

The American Institute for Avalanche Research and Training ⊛www.avtraining.org. The Institute trains instructors for guide schools around the US and maintains links to these schools on their website.

Other useful resources

Backcountry Magazine ⊛www.backcountry magazine.com. The online version of this info-packed glossy contains a wealth of information, from longer features to course listings, avalanche news, and gear reviews.

Couloir Online ⊛www.coulouirmag.com First magazine in the US dedicated to backcountry riding maintains extensive online archives covering critiques of resort's backcountry policies to advice on how to use an avalanche transceiver.

Specialist skiing

Certain resorts cater more to specific groups than others (snowboarders, families, etc), but if you have special needs to be taken care of, chances are any resort will meet them.

Families and children

Ski schools emphasize play over heavy-handed instruction. Young, enthusiastic teachers couldn't care less about perfect form, except as a method to make skiing or snowboarding easier, for their young charges. Nearly all mountains have some areas geared toward adolescents: children's trail maps highlight the frontier forts, teepees, "mines," and "caves" that are dotted around dedicated beginner areas. Gently rolling "pinball" trails are cut through flat glades especially for kids. Smaller beginners use easy step-on, step-off "magic carpets" instead of drag or chairlifts, located right by the children's center so that tired skiers can take a break indoors.

Typically the larger resorts offer the most extensive **childcare facilities**, with children-only dining areas and indoor play areas for different age groups. Rates at these areas range from $80 to $100 for a full day of lessons, lunch, play, and equipment rentals. Prices are half that for a package at one of the smaller resorts.

Snowboarding is not typically taught in group lessons to children under 7, though there is some debate as to whether this is more to do with the development of a child's coordination than a lack of miniature equipment. Only a few of the larger resorts offer separate lessons for older teenagers (try Aspen or Steamboat); admission to children's ski school typically stops between the ages of 12 to 14. Note that helmets are now required (and can be rented) for kids signed up for lessons, unless parents sign a waiver releasing liability.

Smaller resorts typically sell cut-rate children's tickets, and kids under 5 or 6 ski free at many major ski areas. Arapahoe Basin, Big Sky, Brighton, Crystal Mountain, Steamboat, and a number of the Tahoe resorts (including Squaw) are among those offering excellent deals for the under-12. "Kids ski and stay free" packages are often available if booked through the resort.

Seniors

Discounts for **seniors** kick in anywhere between the age of 55 and 65, with many resorts offering free tickets to those 70 and over. Enquire at the ticket window, as this deal is rarely posted.

Resources

The 70+ Ski Club 1633 Albany St, Schenectady, NY 12304 ☎518/346-5505; $10 dues per annum. Organizes trips, prints newsletters biannually, and produces a yearly updated list of ski areas that give discounts or free tickets to the over-70s.
Elderhostel ☎978/323-4141 or 877/426-2167, ⊕www.elderhostel.org. Not-for-profit organization formed in 1975, dedicated to arranging all-inclusive, educational vacations for the over-55s. Week-long programs are arranged in resorts across North America, with fees averaging $600.
Over The Hill Gang 1820 W Colorado Ave, Colorado Springs, CO 80904 ☎719/389-0022, ⊕www.skiersover50.com. Open to skiers and snowboarders over 50 ($75 annual dues), this club organizes group ski days throughout Colorado; members receive discounts of up to 35 percent at nearly 100 resorts across North America.

Women

Over the past decade, both non-profit organizations and the participant-hungry ski industry have been making a concerted effort to introduce more **women** to skiing and snowboarding. Ski areas of every size offer women-only programs, ski and snowboard clinics taught by local female pros, and the annual "Take Your Daughter to the Snow Week," in which resorts participate in a scheme to give two-for-one tickets to families with daughters in tow.

Resources

Babes in the Backcountry Breckenridge ☎970/453-4060, ⊛www.babesinthebackcountry .com. Experienced outdoorswomen who teach backcountry skills for skiers and snowboarders, offer telemark clinics, run hut trips and organize avalanche courses. Classes are held in Colorado, Utah, and California and prices range from $40 for a half-day lesson to over $500 for multiday trips.
High Cascade ☎800/334-4272, ⊛www.highcascade.com. Runs women-only snowboard camps during the winter and spring, Camps are held at Mt Hood Meadows and Mt Bachelor, Oregon and cost $895 for four nights accommodation, three days coaching, lift passes, and all meals.

Gay and lesbian

Small ski town communities are used to a constant influx of out-of-towners and generally possess a laissez-faire attitude toward **gay travelers**, though in more rural areas couples may find it in their interest to postpone displays of affection. Such precautions would be laughed at, however, during the gay ski weeks held each year across the continent.

Aspen's is the most famous, running for over two decades and hosted by the Aspen Gay and Lesbian Community Fund non-profit (☎970/925-9249, ⊛www.gayskiweek .com). It is held in late January and attended by over 3500 participants, and off-slope activities include tea dances and club nights, comedy shows, a film festival, gallery openings, cocktail receptions, and dinners. Proceeds from the week are donated to charity. Altitude, (☎604/899-6209 or 888 /258-4883, ⊛www.outontheslopes.com), held at Whistler in early February, is a popular week-long event that attracts a clubby, younger crowd. Smaller events include Lake Tahoe Winter Fest, a ski week sponsored by the Nevada Gay and Lesbian Visitors Bureau (☎877/777-4950, ⊛www.laketahoewinterfest .com), and the Utah Gay and Lesbian Ski Week (☎877/429-6368, ⊛www.communityvisions .org/SKIING/).

Resources

COSA Colorado ☎303/355-5029, http://members .tde.com/cosa. Has a snowboarding offshoot, OutBoard(⊛www.outboard.org).

EZ Ryders New York ⓔezrydersnyc@yahoo.com, ⊛www.ezryders.netj
Outryders New England ⓔinfo@outryders.org, ⊛www.outryders.org
SAGA North California ☎415/995-2772, ⊛www.saganorth.com. Based in San Francisco, this group organizes weekend trips to Tahoe, social get-togethers, and learn-to-ski and snowboard events. Offshoots exist in LA (☎310/281-6761, ⊛www.sagala.org) and San Diego (☎619/695-8107, ⊛www.sagasd.com).
Skibuddies Seattle ☎206/568-4030, ⊛www.skibuddies.org
Ski Out Portland ⓔinfo@skiout.org, ⊛www.skiout.org

Skiers with disabilities

Skiers with mobility problems, visual impairments, or other physical difficulties are likely to find Canada and the US more in tune with their needs than anywhere else in the world, both on and off the slopes. Well over a hundred resorts have **adaptive skiing programs** and equipment rental to accommodate a wide range of physical and mental disabilities, including visual impairment. Most also offer discounts on lift tickets. All public buildings must be wheelchair-accessible and have suitable toilets; hotels constructed within the past decade must have rooms (and bathrooms) accessible to wheelchair users.

Resources

British Ski Club for the Disabled ☎01494 /433211, ⊛www.bscd.org.uk. Offers advice on everything from insurance to technique, and organizes group skiing holidays to North American resorts.
Canadian Association for Disabled Skiers ☎250/427-7712, ⊛www.disabledskiing.ca. National organization with links to programs and local groups across the provinces.
Disabled Snowsports New Zealand ⓔinfo@disabledskiing.org.nz, ⊛www .disabledskiing.org.nz. Online resource for skiers based in New Zealand.
Disabled Sports USA ☎301/217-0960, ⊛www .dsusa.org. Useful national resource with links to adaptive programs and ski teams across the country.
Disabled Wintersport Australia ☎02/6495 2082, ⊛www.disabledwintersport.com.au. National organization providing contacts and travel advice for Australian skiers.
National Sports Center for the Disabled ☎970/726-1540, ⊛www.nscd.org. Located in

Winter Park, this respected center has been critical to the development of adaptive programs across North America; a wide range of day classes and vacations are offered.

Ski for Light ☎612/827-3232, ⊛www.sfl.org. National organization that organizes Nordic (cross-country) skiing for the visually and mobility impaired.

Public holidays and festivals

On the public holidays listed below, shops, banks, and offices are likely to be closed and both accommodation prices and visitors at resorts are likely to reach peak numbers. If thoughts of long lines and inflated prices are intolerable, plan around these breaks by heading for a smaller, less renowned ski area or by visiting the atypical major resort where lines are unheard of at anytime.

The first major holiday of the ski season is the United State's **Thanksgiving**, held on the fourth Thursday of November. (Canada also celebrates Thanksgiving, but it's held in October before resorts have opened.) Many resorts use this extra-long weekend as an opening date, and early-season deals abound. Cheap package or not, it's often the case that only a minimal percentage of trails will be open, and even those may be littered with dangerous rock and ice patches. Avoid planning a Thanksgiving getaway until the very last moment, when conditions can be confirmed and plans canceled if need be.

The **Christmas** (Dec 25) to **New Year's Day** (Jan 1) holiday period a month later is when most resorts begin running at full speed. As with Thanksgiving, conditions can be somewhat of a gamble. One thing you can count on are long lines at both chairlifts and local restaurants.

There are very few major holidays during the heart of the ski season. In the US, the two long-weekend breaks to look out for are **Martin Luther King Jr's Birthday** (occurs on the third Monday in January) and **Presidents' Day** (on the third Monday in February). During these times crowds at many resorts – particularly those within driving distance of large cities – can be overwhelming. Both holidays typically lead to larger crowds in Canada as well, with US vacationers using them as bookends to longer breaks.

A final holiday period to watch out for in both the US and Canada is **Spring Break**, a week to two-week vacation given to students of all ages in late February or anytime through March. As Spring Break periods differ from region to region (and even from school to school), it's impossible to pinpoint a specific week to be cautious of. If worried about possible overcrowding at a particular ski area, contact the resort itself or the local tourist office for more information.

In addition to these holidays, virtually every resort has a varied menu of individual **festivals** and smaller events held throughout the season. Few are large enough to consider avoiding a ski area for fear of crowds, partially because the biggest are typically held over spring when the slopes are less crowded anyway. Any festival or event large enough to plan a trip around – either to visit or to miss – has been detailed throughout the guide.

Ski season public holidays

Fourth Thurs in Nov Thanksgiving Day (US only)
December 25 Christmas Day
December 26 Boxing Day (Can only)
Jan 1 New Year's Day
Third Mon in Jan Martin Luther King Jr's Birthday (US only)
Third Mon in Feb Presidents' Day (US only)
Good Friday two days before Easter Sunday
Easter Sunday usually March/April

Work and staying on

Ski resorts and all the attendant businesses surrounding them rely heavily on temporary workers – Vail, for example, hires as many as 15,000 workers between its four Colorado ski areas (Vail, Beaver Creek, Breckenridge, and Keystone). Recruitment starts in late October/early November, and legal residents or those with work authorization who show up in town during that period should have no problems finding work on the mountain or in surrounding hotels, restaurants, or ski shops. January is another good time to find work, as some of those initially hired will have left, disillusioned by low wages (expect $6–10 an hour) and less time on the mountain than they had hoped.

International workers

International workers are an important resource for most larger ski areas in the States, who typically employ those with either J-1 or H-2B visas. J-1 status is issued to students on an Exchange Visitor Program, set up through a work and travel program such as International Exchange Programs (see opposite). Applicants must be full-time students or recent graduates. The J-1 is usually issued for the four-month period immediately following the end of the university year, with an extra month tacked on afterwards for travel. This visa works best for students from the southern hemisphere, whose summer break syncs up with the North American ski season.

Ski areas like the J-1, because the student's work and travel program takes on the role of sponsor and deals with all the immigration paperwork and costs. Some of the larger resorts send reps down to the southern hemisphere to recruit potential J-1s at student job fairs (Mammoth); others encourage online application from those on J-1 programs (Winter Park), or simply ask that the student turn up during the fall recruitment period for a walk-in interview, J-1 in hand (Vail). With no job guaranteed, this latter option may seem daunting, but if you've shown the initiative it takes to get into the country legally, any large resort's Human Resources department will likely be happy to find you work.

Unless you want to work at a snowboarding or skiing summer camp at Mt Hood (see p.379), J-1s are of no use to most European

students, whose university break falls well outside the North American ski season. One option is the H-2B status, a temporary specialist visa open to nonstudents. Applicants must be sponsored by the employer, so while some resorts will hire H-2Bs for more menial jobs (lift operators, line cooks, cashiers), others are only prepared to expend the energy on ski or snowboard instructors, who typically need certification at the equivalent of PSIA (Professional Ski Instructors of America) Level 1, and a year's experience. Applications for H-2B visas are taken as early as May, and competition can be stiff.

Employment in Canada is easier for Brits under the age of 30, who, like Australians, New Zealanders, and South Africans, can apply for a year-long work visa through BUNAC or one of its worldwide affiliates (see opposite). With the necessary paperwork in hand, it's simply a case of showing up at a resort during the fall recruitment period; walk-in interviews are the preferred method of hiring. Another avenue for British jobseekers are the UK ski tour operators. Hiring starts in the summer, and competition is steep for the few positions available in Canada and the US.

Illegal work is not quite as easy to find as it used to be, now that governments of both countries have introduced high fines for companies caught employing anyone without a social security (US) or social insurance (Canada) number, identification that proves you're part of the legal workforce. It does exist in larger ski resorts but is likely to be of the less visible, poorly paid kind. Most legal jobs at the resorts invariably come with a pass attached, while many local businesses will subsidize passes in the quest to attract staff for the season.

In all instances, applicants should have sufficient funds to cover their first month in the resort. Paychecks are typically issued every two weeks, but may be initially deferred for a month. Deposits and/or a month's rent up-front are required to sign a lease on an apartment or condo. Accommodation is not cheap in North American resort areas, with rates comparable to those in the large cities, averaging $500 for a private room in a shared apartment. Employee housing is limited and not particularly cheap; expect to pay upwards of $250 per month for dorm accommodation. Once in town, most visitor centers have useful Relocation Guides designed for newcomers to the region; some even have specific handbooks for seasonal workers.

Job listings and work programs

Numerous third-party recruitment websites now exist for ski industry jobs, including @www.resortjobs.com, @www.natives.co.uk, @www.coolworks.com, @www.jobsinparadise .com and @www.skiingthenet.com. However, the most direct resources for job-hunters are the official websites of the resorts (or tour operators) themselves. Links to these are posted on @www.skicentral.com and @www .payaway.co.uk. Two of the largest employers in North America are found at @www .skijob1.com, the hub for all Vail resorts ski areas, and @www.wework2play.com, which covers the many Intrawest-owned ski areas and resort villages across the continent.

Organizations

BUNAC (British Universities' North America Club), ☎020/7251-3742, @www.bunac.org. Though British students cannot take advantage of the Work America program run by this long-standing student work–travel organization, those aiming for a career in ski area, restaurant, or hotel management may find internship positions through BUNAC's OPT USA program. Also runs the Work Canada and Gap Canada programs for the UK. Contacts to work programs for other students of other nationalities are listed on BUNAC's website.

CCUSA ☎415/339-2728 or 800/999-CAMP (US); ☎02/9223 3366 (Aus); ☎09/573-7813 (NZ); ☎021/425-7100 (SA; other country-specific numbers listed on the website); @www.ccusa.com. International work–study program used by many resorts to recruit students on the J-1 visa.

InterExchange ☎212/924-0446, @www .interexchange.org. US-based work–travel organization specializing in the J-1 visa, open to international students of many nationalities.

The International Academy ☎02920/672500 or freephone 07000/123SKI, @www .international-academy.com. UK-based organization offering pricey seven- or twelve-week ski instructor courses in Canada and the US, primarily aimed at gap-year students. Courses start at £4890; half-board lodging, flights, ski pass, and instructor training are included in the cost, but visa expenses and insurance are not.

International Exchange Programs ☎03/9329 3866, @www.iep.org.au (Australia); ☎09/366-6255, @www.iepnz.co.nz (New Zealand). BUNAC partner in Australasia, popular with ski resorts as a third-party organizer for the J-1 visa. Also arranges work authorization for Canada, valid for up to a year.

SASTS ☎021/418-3794, @www.sasts.org.za. South African equivalent to BUNAC or IEP, which runs a specific Ski USA program in addition to arranging general J-1 and Canadian work authorization status.

Directory

Addresses In general, roads in the US and Canada are laid out on a grid system, creating "blocks" of buildings. The first one or two digits of a specific address refer to the block, which will be numbered in sequence from a central point, usually downtown. For example, 620 S Cedar Ave will be six blocks south of downtown. It is crucial, therefore, to take note of components such as "NW" or "SE" in addresses; 3620 SW King St will be a very long way indeed from 3620 NE King St.

Cigarettes and smoking Smoking is generally frowned upon – though many US and Canadian citizens still smoke and cigarettes are easily found in convenience stores and quite often bars. Restaurants are usually divided into nonsmoking and smoking sections (though several states, including California, have banned smoking indoors entirely) and smoking is forbidden on public transportation and flights.

Electricity 110V AC.

ID Should be carried at all times. Two pieces will suffice, one of which should have a photo: a passport and credit card(s) are your best bets. Not having your license with you while driving may be cause for arrest.

Measurements and sizes In the US, distances are in inches, feet, yards, and miles, and weights in ounces, pounds, and tons. American pints and gallons are about four-fifths of imperial ones. Clothing sizes are four figures less what they would be in the UK – a British women's size 12 is a US size 8 – while British shoe sizes are 1/2 below

American ones for women, and one size below for men. Canada officially uses the metric system, though many people still use the imperial system. Distances are in kilometers; temperatures in degrees Celsius; and foodstuffs, gas, and drink are sold in grams, kilograms, or liters. A few important conversions to know: 1 mile = 1.609 kilometers; 1 foot = 0.3048 meters.

Temperatures Given in Fahrenheit in the US, in Celsius (or Centigrade) in Canada. To convert between the two: Centigrade = (Fahrenheit - 32) x $5/9$; Fahrenheit = Centigrade x $9/5 + 32$.

Time zones The continental US spreads over four different time zones, plus one each in Alaska and Hawaii, while Canada divides into six, most of which overlap with the US. For the purposes of this book, the ones to know are the **Eastern** time zone (EST), taking in Quebec and the Northeast US, 5hrs behind Greenwich Mean Time; **Mountain** (MST) covering Alberta, the Rocky Mountains, and most of the Southwest, 2hrs behind EST; and **Pacific** (PST), with all the West Coast states and much of British Columbia clocking in 3hrs behind EST. **Alaska** is 2hrs behind the Pacific zone.

Tipping Expected for all bar and restaurant service at a rate between fifteen to twenty percent or so on the bill (unless the service is utterly abominable). About the same amount should be added to taxi fares. A hotel porter who has lugged your suitcases up several flights of stairs should receive $3 to $5.

Guide:
USA

USA

The Northeast

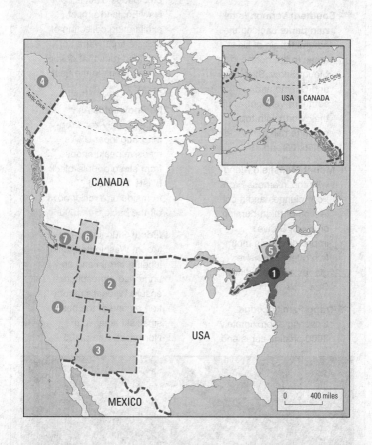

chapter 1 # Highlights

✳ **Tuesdays at Killington** An overcrowded headache on weekends, New England's largest resort is transformed midweek and perfect for riders of all abilities. See p.45

✳ **Southern Vermont's terrain parks** Lacking the natural terrain of ski areas to the north, Mount Snow, Stratton and Okemo and in southern Vermont all up their worth with top-notch terrain parks. See pp.55, 69 and 79

✳ **Mount Mansfield** Along with the infamous Front Four plunges and a collection of thigh-burning cruisers, Stowe's impressive main mountain offers extensive glades and freeriding. See p.59

✳ **Trapp Family Lodge** Covering approximately 3000 pristine acres and owned by the family that inspired *The Sound of Music*, this Tyrolean lodge is Stowe's finest overnight option. See p.65

✳ **Castlerock** Sugarbush's precipitous peak is home New England's most exhilarating collection of trails, a tight warren of treelined runs that define expert skiing in the East. See p.73

✳ **The Snowfields** An expert's-only zone topping Sugarloaf USA's massive peak; choose from steep double-black blasts down the frontside or a rocky bowl off the back. See p.90

✳ **Wildcat** Stunning views of Mount Washington, challenging terrain and an unhurried atmosphere ensure Wildcat's reputation as one of the best small ski areas in the Northeast. See p.105

The Northeast

S maller and generally less technically adventurous than their western counterparts, the ski resorts of the **Northeast** were once the glamour destinations of American skiing. But with the rise of affordable air travel in the 1970s, alpine enthusiasts east of the Mississippi began to travel in droves to the Rocky Mountains and beyond. That's not to say that eastern resorts are hurting for customers, as the heavily populated Atlantic seaboard continues to supply a steady stream of dedicated visitors; however, rare is the visitor nowadays who comes from outside the region for an extended vacation.

Because most visitors come to the region's slopes for a few days instead of a week-long trip, dramatic crowding can be a problem on weekends. If you happen to be visiting for a week or more consider taking Saturday off to avoid long lift lines and other annoyances. Of course this also means that many resorts feel like deserted ghost towns during the weekdays, with practically the whole mountain yours to explore.

There's no getting over that the skiing is different here, from navigating the tight networks of alleys that snake down tree-lined slopes to dealing with the sometimes off-putting snow conditions. While stunning powder days do occur, you're more likely to spend your day sliding across patches of bullet-proof ice. This typically results in a reliance by the resorts on snow-making and grooming operations, as well as special attention to improving upon their natural terrain by maintaining excellent freestyle parks. Still, while steep chutes and massive cliffdrops may be all but non-existent, there are enough true double black plunges to humble even the finest expert riders.

Overall, **Vermont** offers the best skiing in the region. The rolling Green Mountains

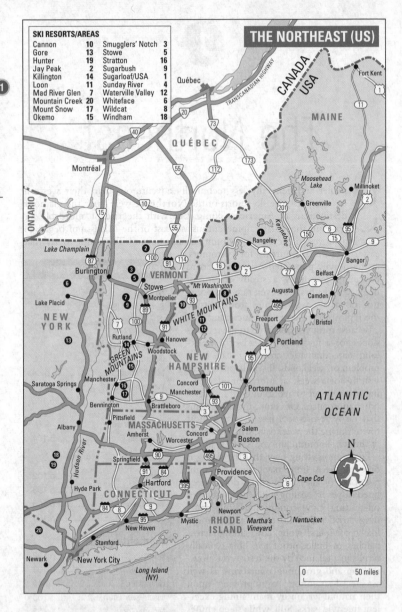

SKI RESORTS/AREAS

Cannon	10	Smugglers' Notch	3
Gore	13	Stowe	5
Hunter	19	Stratton	16
Jay Peak	2	Sugarbush	9
Killington	14	Sugarloaf/USA	1
Loon	11	Sunday River	4
Mad River Glen	7	Waterville Valley	12
Mountain Creek	20	Whiteface	6
Mount Snow	17	Wildcat	8
Okemo	15	Windham	18

THE NORTHEAST (US)

contain at their southernmost extremities **Mount Snow**, with **Stratton** and smaller **Bromley** located near the town of Manchester around a half-hour drive north on Route 100. Keep heading north on Route 100 and you'll find the big names in Vermont skiing, like **Killington**, the largest ski area in the region with 1182 acres of terrain, and eventually **Stowe**, both a town and impressive resort that together make the finest one-stop destination in the state.

A few smaller resorts are further on, including **Jay Peak**, close to the Canadian border and the snowiest resort out east.

Resorts in **New Hampshire** are dotted across the White Mountains, many within a short drive of breathtaking Mount Washington, the northeast's tallest peak (6288ft) – though no resorts reach close to that altitude. What the spots – including **Loon**, **Waterville Valley**, **Cannon**, and **Wildcat** – do share with the peak are tempestuous weather patterns and some extended steeps to go along with relatively accessible locations. Accessibility is the major drawback to the two best resorts in **Maine**: **Sugarloaf** and **Sunday River**. Both are large and varied enough to warrant an extended visit, but for some the temptation to fly out West or save several hours drive time by visiting more southerly resorts is too hard to pass up.

New York is home to dozens of small resorts, none of which – save perhaps **Whiteface** or **Gore** in the Adirondacks – is worth planning a trip around.

Killington

Even if you don't swallow the hype of the **KILLINGTON** media machine, it's hard to deny the resort its due. They may pump their status as having the longest ski season in the East (based on a few crummy artificial snow runs forced to open a month too early and a month too late), tout the super-extensive lift system (nearly one-fifth of its 32 lifts are surface tows and another fifth are over on nearby Pico Mountain), and gloat over the fact that more visitors come here than any other resort in the region – by a long shot – but in the end it's all unnecessary and only serves to inflate expectations.

The reality is that its ski area is one of the finest in the Northeast, with some long trails worthy of comparison with tops in the West. Already sitting in a substantial snowbelt, the **snowmaking** program here is unparalleled, providing cover during even the most dismal of conditions. And the varied **terrain**, from steep tree runs and perfect mogul fields to extra-long cruisers and well-tended terrain parks, faces in virtually every direction, ensuring conditions are at least decent somewhere on the hill.

During mid-season **weekends and holidays**, the "The Beast of the East," as the resort is sometimes known, rears its ugly head with visitors swarming to the slopes. Already notoriously difficult to negotiate, the resort's tangled web of trails fills with skiers torpedoing out of control at trail crossings and poseur boarders mysteriously

Mountain info

Phone ☎802/422-3333
Snow phone ☎802/422-3261
Website ⊛www.killington.com
Price $59 midweek, $64 weekend
Operating times Late Nov to May; Mon–Fri 9am–4pm, Sat–Sun 8am–4pm
No. of lifts 31, including 2 gondolas and 6 towropes
Base elevation 1165′
Summit elevation 4241′
Vertical drop 3050′
No. of trails 200
Acreage 1182
Beginner 30%
Intermediate 39%
Expert 31%
Average snowfall 250″
Snowmaking Yes (750 acres)
Night skiing No
Nursery facilities The Friendly Penguin, 6 weeks to 6 years, reservations needed ☎1-800 /621-6687

camping out at the most inopportune locations. The overcrowding leads to slopes turning to ice more quickly and long waits at chairlifts; be sure to keep an eye on your gear as well when down at the bottom as thefts aren't uncommon.

True, the area's already happening **party scene** reaches a fevered pitch during these busy times, but that's little consolation for the headache that often proceeds a night out. Slowly inching closer to the Vegas Strip than a Vermont village, five-mile long **Killington Road** is lined with everything a resort without a central base needs – restaurants, bars, rental shops, and accommodation. It certainly makes things easy to find, but it's far from any notion of quaint Vermont.

Arrival, orientation, and getting around

While the majority of visitors arrive by **car** – the resort is around three hours from Boston and five from New York City – the Killington region has dependable air and rail links. The tiny Rutland State Airport offers daily **flights** from Boston via USAirways Express, while flights from further afield call in at the Burlington Airport, a two-hour drive to the north. Airlines servicing Burlington include American, United, Northwest, Continental, and JetBlue (see p.10 in Basics for contact information). By **train**, Amtrak's *Ethan Allen Express* route runs a daily afternoon service from New York City to Rutland, via Albany, with a connecting bus service to the slopes. If you'd rather **rent a car** when arriving in Rutland, local options include Thrifty, 279 S Main St (☏802/773-5901), and Enterprise, 144 Woodstock Ave (☏802/773-0855); both run pick-ups at the train station.

Killington has an efficient **regional bus service**, known simply as The Bus (☏802/773-3244 ext 62, ⓦwww.thebus.com; $1). The red-and-white buses run regular services from as far off as Rutland and all five of its Killington routes end at the Snowshed Lodge area. Almost every accommodation within ten miles of the slopes is serviced by The Bus, meaning it's a good way to avoid the hassle of early-morning parking. The handiest routes are the Red #7 to Rutland (8am–9pm) and the evening Black #6 service with frequent stops up and down Killington Road (5.30pm–2am).

As for **orientation**, Killington has a half-dozen **base areas** to choose from. The first turn-off on Route 4 when driving in from Rutland is for tiny Pico Mountain. A few miles beyond lies the entry to **Killington Road**, which snakes its way up to the Snowshed, Ram's Head, and Killington base areas. Past the turn-off for Killington Road, Route 4 continues another couple of miles to the Skyeship Base Area station, along with the turn-off to East Mountain Road and the Bear Mountain base area. All of these bases sell lift tickets, so mid-week simply head to the closest or the one accessing your favorite mountain area. On busy weekends avoid both the Snowshed and Ram's Head areas, and instead head (if you've got a prepurchased pass) to the **Snowdon Quad**, which opens a few minutes earlier than other lifts and is accessible from the Killington Base Area parking lot.

The mountain

Before hopping aboard a lift, the first thing you'll want to do is pick a time and a place to meet with your skiing partners because you're going to get split up. The web of trails can be confusing and one wrong turn is all it takes to end up at a completely different base area than intended. Use the resort's friendly ski

ambassadors, who can help get you oriented and will direct you to the best current conditions in the sprawling ski area.

The resort's tallest point is **Mount Killington** at 4241ft, from which it's possible to spot Stowe's Mount Mansfield and New York's Whiteface on a clear day. Areas to the left of the peak include **The Canyon**, laced with steep double blacks, and the progressively easier zones of **Snowdon** and **Ram's Head**. To the right facing down from the peak, trails lead to **Skye Peak**, the ski area's most confusing intersection, where trails dive off in several divergent directions, and **Bear Mountain**, a favorite of advanced skiers that's home to iconic mogul run Outer Limits. Far below is the Skyeship Base Station on Route 4, reached via a pair of long, unexciting runs that account for an extra 1000ft in Killington's misleadingly large vertical drop.

Though several mogul-filled runs and impressive glades are dotted about the entire ski area, the majority are best suited for **intermediates**, many of whom will feel comfortable on Killington's single black diamonds as well. If you're here for an extended stay, take busy **Saturdays off** or at least head to nearby **Pico**, a few miles away on Route 4 (see box overleaf). If that's not an option, at least save yourself the hassle of returning to the longer lines by sticking to lifts that don't directly lead to a base area, like the Snowdon, Superstar, and Canyon quads.

Beginner

With three lifts running during the busiest periods, the flat and wide **Snowshed Slope** appears ideal for beginners to practice linking turns on. But during busier periods it quickly becomes inundated with riders skipping out on the parallel terrain-park and others flying through at breakneck speeds on their way to the base. After conquering Snowshed, you're best off heading for the wide cruisers at **Ram's Head**, a short walk away. Greens spread across the rest of the ski area, but many cut uncomfortably across steeper slopes. Others, especially **Juggernaut** on the resort's far west side, look enticing on the map but have too many flat spots to be much more than an unintended workout unless conditions are perfect.

Intermediate

With every lift at the resort featuring at least one blue route, intermediates are the best served group at Killington. Regardless, blue runners need to pay close attention to where they are going; one wrong turn could leave you stranded above a bumpy and icy black slope with no way out but down. For a warm-up try the black diamond-free **Ram's Head** area, with wide blues perfect for carving. Also here is **Squeeze Play**, a top spot for confident intermediates to begin exploring glades with trees spaced out at comfortable distances. One lift over, **Snowdon** features several worthy blues and a tighter tree zone known as **Low Rider**. On the opposite side of Killington Peak, both Skye Peak and Bear Mountain are home to more notable blues, including super-wide **Needle's Eye** at the former and more challenging **Bear Claw**, with a nice steep shot in the middle, at the latter.

Expert

Experts will want to spend most of their time in either **The Canyon** area or on **Bear Mountain**. The Canyon, accessed by the Canyon Quad, is split down its steep middle by **Double Dipper**, a wide highway with double blacks lining both sides. Bear Mountain offers the most advanced terrain, including the long

Pico

Until the long-promised links built between Killington's main ski area and **Pico** (pronounced Pike-oh), the resort's policy of adding Pico's statistics to the overall mix makes little sense as it is an entirely separate mountain. You can ride on a Killington ticket – passes for Pico are $15 cheaper – but it's highly unlikely that you'd visit both ski areas in the same day. On weekends and during busy periods, consider hitting up Pico's 200 acres of predominantly intermediate terrain in order to escape the crowds at Killington's main mountain a few miles east on Route 4.

While there are considerably fewer than 48 separate **trails** as pitched by the resort – Upper Pike, Mid-Pike, and Lower-Pike are, for example, one continuous trail, not three – the seven **lifts** here make getting about a breeze. From the summit of Pico Peak (3967ft), half-a-dozen narrow runs, including the two toughest, Giant Killer and Summit Glades, shoot down the fall line some 500ft before the ski area opens up to flatter, wide-open cruisers. Experts could become bored quickly here – several of the blacks are closer to blues – but intermediates will find most of the mountain enjoyable and confident beginners will be able to sharpen their skills on some flatter runs off the Golden Express and Knome's Knoll chairs.

Outer Limits mogul run with its steep vertical of knee-busting bumps. Nearby runs include typically ungroomed **Wildfire** and the unmissable double diamond **Devil's Fiddle**, a wide-open steep that gives a thrilling flash of Rocky Mountain-style skiing.

The rest of the best challenging terrain is found in the trees. **Julio**, accessed via Escapade or Launch Pad from Killington Peak, is for aggressive experts who revel in exploring tight tree lines littered with rocks and even some small cliff jumps. Tree-skiers will also want to explore the unmarked **Toilet Bowl**, the steep tree-choked slope on the Snowdon side of Royal Flush that's a local favorite on powder mornings. If you're up for some short **hikes** both the top of Killington Peak and the area atop Ram's Head are accessible, with the reward being thrilling lines and possible face shots anytime after a recent storm.

Freestyle

Killington's main **terrain park** – known as The Beach – is unfortunately located on the Snowshed Slope, the resort's busiest area. Enough snow is pumped into the park to allow for two long lines littered with progressively bigger jumps, along with some rails and a long fun box. The park gets overall high marks, but if the snow is sluggish you can forget about launching off the bigger jumps as the overall pitch is flat. The **half-pipe**, a quality superpipe with 15ft walls, is groomed regularly and located above the K-1 Express Gondola. The main complaint here is that there's no towrope, meaning a hike back up after each run.

Lift tickets, lessons, and rentals

Day passes at Killington run $59 midweek, $64 on weekends, with savings of a few dollars per day on extended day passes. Juniors (6–12) and seniors pay $37/$40, young adults (13–18) $54/$58. Having to teach probably more beginning skiers than any other East Coast resort, Killington's **ski school** (☎802/422-6837) gets good grades for both patience and experience. During busy periods, however, the Snowshed and Ram's Head learner areas get far too overrun for comfort. Never-ever packages include rentals, beginner's pass, and morning lessons for $75, more advanced group lessons from $35 a session, and private lessons beginning at $85 an hour. It's generally best to arrive with skis or board in hand: boarders should stop in at Darkside Snowboards (℡802/422-8600) near the top of the access road, while skiers should try the Basin Ski Shop (℡802/422-3234, ⓦwww.basinski.com). Both carry top-flight gear at reasonable rates.

Accommodation

While there is a wealth of **accommodation** options around Killington, very few are slopeside. Most are strung along the long main access road, but many of the most affordable, and often more personable, options are on Route 4 within a few miles of the Killington Road turn-off. **Condominiums** are prevalent as well, and many options are run by the resort itself. It's not impossible to find a good deal around the resort area, but keep in mind the rates rise on weekends up to 25 percent, even higher during holiday periods.

If you are driving up late at night or looking for the cheapest bed and don't mind the fifteen-mile drive to the slopes, there are several chain options in **Rutland** including *Holiday Inn*, 411 S Main St (℡802/775-4303; ❸), *Econo Lodge*, 238 S Main St (℡802/773-2784; ❷), and *Comfort Inn*, 19 Allen St (℡802/775-2200; ❷).

Condominiums

Killington Resort Villages ℡1-877/458-4637, ⓦwww.killingtonresortvillage.com. The resort's central reservations service, booking for both the *Killington Grand* (see below) and several condominium complexes. The locations of their condos are superb, as most are either trailside or within walking distance of a lift, and the few that aren't are serviced regularly by shuttle buses. Overall quality can be a crapshoot.

Wise Vacations ℡802/773-4202 or 1-800/639-4680, ⓦwww.wisevacations.com. Reputable operator with dozens of properties, from slopeside condos to luxurious private homes sleeping ten or more. One of their finest options is *The Woods*, a high-end two-bedroom condominium complex near the bottom of Killington Road, complete with individual hot tubs, spacious kitchens, and access to an onsite spa and gourmet restaurant.

Hotels, motels, and inns

Comfort Inn 905 Killington Rd ℡1-800/257-8664, ⓦwww.comfortinn.com. Dependable, if soulless, chain hotel located near the bottom of the resort's access road. The motel rooms are spread out in a relatively attractive townhouse style, some with balconies. A very basic continental breakfast offered, and most rooms have cable TV and VCRs. Midweek ❺, weekend ❻

Cortina Inn and Resort 103 Route-4, Killington ℡802/773-3333 or 1-800/451-6108, ⓦwww.cortinainn.com. Full-service, sprawling inn a few miles from Killington Road with nearly 100 individually decorated rooms, including a few family suites with open-hearth wood stoves sleeping up to six. The décor has a slightly dated country feel, but there are welcome touches like a gallery featuring the work of local artists, an indoor pool, and a pair of restaurants (full breakfast included in rates). Sleigh rides and snowshoe hikes are offered directly out back. Midweek ❻, weekend ❼

Econo Lodge 51 Route-4, Mendon ℡802/773-6644 or 1-800/992-9067. The most affordable private rooms close to the slopes are in this budget motel, three miles from Pico and ten from Killington Road. Rooms are rather shabby, but still good value, especially the efficiencies sleeping up to four. Amenities include a small hot tub, simple continental breakfast and game room with pool and ping-pong tables. Midweek ❸, weekend ❹, efficiencies ❸, ❺

Inn at Long Trail Route 4 at Sherburn Pass, between Pico and Killington Road ℡1-800/325-2540, ⓦwww.innatlongtrail.com. Reputed to be the state's oldest public ski lodge, this inn boasts a communal vibe that's rare around these increasingly commercial parts. Wood dominates the interior, from hardwood floors and raw tree trunk supports to a massive redwood hot tub. The standard rooms and suites are small and their individual amenities sparse (no TV or phones), but the spacious common areas and on-site restaurant along with *McGrath's Irish Pub* (see p.52) ensure you only need your room for sleep and not hanging out. Weekend rates include both breakfast and dinner. Midweek ❸, weekend ❺

The Killington Grand Snowshed base area ℡1-800/897-6665, ⓦwww.killington.com. If you're looking for a spot within walking distance of the lifts, this 200-room hotel and conference center is,

save for condos, your only option. The common areas are inviting, with large fireplaces, and the outdoor heated pool adds a decadent touch. Rooms, studios, and the 1–3-bedroom suites are comfortable, but you're really paying for the convenience factor. Midweek ❼, weekend ❾
Mountain Sports Inn 813 Killington Rd ☎802/422-3315 or 1-800/422-3315, ⊛www .mountainsportsinn.com. Feeling a bit like a high-end private home, this thirty-room inn on the access road caters to skiers and boarders who want hearty cooked breakfasts and a hot tub to soak in at the end of the day. The plain, impeccably clean rooms all have cable TV and either queen or two double beds, and there are a few suites sleeping up to six with a queen, two doubles, and queen pullout sofa in the living room. Wine and beer served in the evening and there's a tuning room on site. Midweek ❸, weekend ❺
The Summit Killington Road, 1.5 miles from Route 4 ☎802/422-3535 or 1-800/635-6343, ⊛www .summitlodgevermont.com. This throwback lodge, whose mascots are two St Bernards lolling about, is the type of place where families feel comfortable enough to mingle in their pajamas at breakfast. The old-time atmosphere is present in the rooms as well, which feature hand-hewn wooden

walls, quilt bedspreads, and rocking chairs. Stone fireplaces keep the common areas toasty, and a quality onsite restaurant and friendly pub add to the *Summit*'s charm. Midweek ❺, weekend ❼
Turn of River Lodge Route 4 ☎802/422-3766 or 1-800/782-9867, ⊛www.turnofriverlodge.com. The cheapest beds near the slopes are housed in this handsome stone-and-wood hostel-like lodge some three miles east of Killington Road, half that from the Skyeship Gondola. A great value, with bunks in dorms ranging from six to twelve beds, along with basic private rooms, some of which share bathrooms. There's a common area with fireplace and TV, tuning room, and a small kitchen area with microwave. The Bus stops right out front. Midweek dorm $25, weekend $30; midweek room ❷, weekend ❹
Val Roc Motel 8006 Route-4 ☎1-800/238-8762, ⊛www.valroc.com. Though the Killington Road turn-off is six miles away, this plain but clean motel is less than a half-mile from the Skyeship Gondola's base. The rooms either have two double beds or a double, single, and pull-out couch and several have microwaves, fridges, and coffeemakers. Other extras include a simple continental breakfast, outdoor hot tub, and a small game room with a pool table. Midweek ❸, weekend ❹

Eating

Even though dozens of **restaurants** line Killington Road, there is little variety, especially if you want something a bit exotic. At least no chain fast-food emporiums scar the landscape, with the closest clustered on Rutland's Main Street a twenty-minute drive away. If here for more than a few nights, consider driving to nearby **Woodstock**, a quaint Vermont village a half-hour east on Route 4 that's home to a small but creative dining scene.

On-mountain the resort's restaurants are average, and bringing along a packed lunch is recommended. All base areas contain basic cafeterias, while both the Snowshed and Killington lodges contain a *Sushi Yoshi* (see below) and bland pubs. Killington Peak and Bear Mountain hold the best options of the bunch, with the former offering towering views across much of Vermont and the latter spring BBQs on a deck looking straight out at Upper Limit's mega-mogul field. For a quick on-mountain lunch and a convenient meeting point, consider *Raul's Burritos*, a tiny shack at the top of the Skyeship Gondola's first drop-off.

If **self-catering**, the Killington Market (daily 6.30am–11pm; ☎802/422-7736) on the access road has small meat, produce, and dairy sections along with a deli and beer/wine selections. Cheaper supplies can be found in Rutland, where large supermarkets line South Main Street (Route 7).

Casey's Caboose Killington Road ☎802/422-3795. A decent spot for families, this nonsmoking restaurant prides itself on a large kids' menu and its collection of train memorabilia. Offerings range from pub grub to prime rib, pasta, and veal dishes (all around the $20 mark). The small bar is packed for the free wings during happy hour (3–6pm) and

for the $2 Box Car Baskets – model trains loaded with wings or chicken fingers – after 9pm.
The Chinese Gourmet and Sushi Yoshi Killington Road ☎802/422-4241. About midway up Killington Road – look for the metallic green Dragon out front – countless centuries of cuisine unite under one roof at this unpretentious restaurant.

Though the Chinese menu is extensive, a combo of raw fish – complete sushi dinners start at $20 – and warm sake are the main draw.

Crazy Mountain Killington Road ☎802/422-2113. About a mile up Killington's access road sits this small café with mismatched tables, espresso-based coffees, and simple breakfasts. Fresh-baked goods include bagels, muffins, and sugary cinnamon rolls, while heartier egg sandwiches ($3–5) and Belgian waffles ($6) are also served. Consider grabbing a pannini sandwich for a quality take-out lunch.

The Garlic Killington Road ☎802/422-5055. The scent of garlic hangs heavy in the air at this attractive Italian eatery. Like most restaurants on Killington Road, wood dominates the décor – unlike most others, it's creatively matched with stylish light fixtures and castle-like mounds of melted wax topped with votive candles. Pastas include a spicy *puttanesca* ($14) and a seafood linguini loaded with shrimp, calamari, and clams ($21), while entrees range from grilled ahi tuna ($18) to veal scaloppini ($18). Save room for the six-layer chocolate cake, tiramisu, or blueberry cheesecake.

Grist Mill Killington Road ☎802/422-3970. Popular après-ski spot (see overleaf) that's also worth a look for dinner. Families and pleasantly buzzed skiers tuck into basic, dependable ribs ($18), steaks ($16–18), and daily fish specials.

Hemingway's 4988 Route 4, between junctions 100N and 100S ☎802/422-3886. *Hemingway's* is not only the finest restaurant within shouting distance of the ski area, but also one of the finest in New England. Romantic and expensive, the rotating menu includes hand-rolled rabbit tortellini, followed by sliced duck served with a confit of duck strudel. Price-fixed, expect to pay $50–65 per person depending on the night's choices, not including alcohol. Dinner only from 6pm, closed most Mondays. Reservations essential.

Pizza Jerks Killington Road ☎802/422-4111. Popular and bright pizzeria located a little over a mile up Killington Road from Route 4. There's plenty of room – and draft beer – available should you choose to dine in, though take-out and free delivery are also available.

Ppeppers Killington Road ☎802/422-3177. A welcome break from the area's rustic décor, *Ppeppers* is a fun 1950's styled black-and-white checkered diner with large vinyl booths and walls lined with local skiing photos. As it's the last big breakfast option before the slopes, be prepared for a wait on weekend mornings to sample filling omelettes ($6) or French toast stuffed with cream cheese and covered in strawberries. Later in the day enjoy huge chicken and pasta dishes for under $15. Open daily 7am–11pm.

Ralphie's Pizza Killington Road, just past the Grist Mill ☎802/422-2345. Small pizzeria with a short, vegetarian, and kosher menu where even the "meat" toppings are soy-based. A large cheese pie runs $14, while the house salad loaded with veggies costs $8. Though mainly take-out and delivery, there is also a tiny eat in area. Open 4pm until late.

The Wobbly Barn Killington Road ☎802/422-6171. Hidden a floor below the bar area (see p.52) is a rustic steakhouse, famed for its huge soup, salad, and bread bar ($10). Carnivores are well served with an excellent prime rib ($20) and filet mignon ($23). Tuesday is wild game night, featuring venison, elk, and buffalo; friday is seafood; and Sunday's specialty is BBQ.

Nightlife and entertainment

Killington is known as New England's hardest partying ski town. Lacking a main village center, the main après-ski and nightlife options are dotted along Killington Road, with a few located on Route 4 meaning a taxi, shuttle bus, or designated driver will probably be part of your evening plans. Competition for the après-ski crowd is fierce, and freebies are customary; those on a budget can get by on skipping dinner and surviving on the free wings, nachos and other bar munchies offered nightly during early-evening **happy hours**.

Other evening options are scarce in the immediate vicinity, but Rutland has the Plaza Movieplex (☎802/775-5500) on Merchants Row, while the Paramount Theater at 38 Center St (☎802/775-0903) hosts Broadway plays along with the occasional comedic or dance performance. On the opposite end of the cultural scale, the huge Rutland Bowlerama **bowling alley** is at 158 South Main St (Route 7); call ahead to make sure it's not a league night (☎802/773-7707).

Grist Mill Killington Road ☎ 802/422-3970. Toward the bottom of the access road sits this friendly establishment, built around a massive antique mill wheel. The large bar area inside hosts a popular après-ski scene, with a thirty-something crowd taking advantage of $2 pint specials and the infamous Goombay Smash, a lethal rum-and-juice concoction served up in a mason jar. The bar serves your average pub grub, with a heaping pile of nachos running $8.

McGrath's Irish Pub *Long Trail Inn*, Route 4 at Sherburn Pass, between Pico and Killington Road ☎ 1-800/325-2540. A perfect antidote to the more raucous establishments on Killington Road, this warm and friendly pub claims to sell more pints of Guinness than anyone in the state. Built around a massive boulder jutting through the north wall, the bar is coated in Irish paraphernalia and has a tasty pub menu that includes Guinness stew ($7) and shepherd's pie ($7). Live Irish music played on weekend evenings.

The Nightspot Killington Road ☎ 802/422-9885. The closest Killington comes to a big-city nightclub is this dark, multiroom spot attracting a younger crowd. On a good night, you'll dance to DJ-spun hip-hop and house. On a bad night you'll flee from hoards of cocky patrons with fake IDs and fake gold chains. The *Outback* pizzeria in back serves decent wood-fired pizzas, with an all-you-can-eat buffet ($7) on Monday nights.

The Pickle Barrel Killington Road ☎ 802/422-3035. Along with the *Wobbly Barn*, this rambunctious concert hall, opened in 1971, is the reason Killington regularly wins top party honors in the East. Relatively big-name bands regularly headline the main stage, though crowds tend to fill the hall regardless of who is playing. Open mainly Thurs–Sun, other days during holiday weeks. Free happy hour buffet on Saturdays only (4–6pm). Cover varies.

The Wobbly Barn Killington Road ☎ 802/422-6171, ⊛ www.wobblybarn.com. The sawdust covered floor of this three-story barn quickly fills with singles grooving to live bands blaring anything from reggae to country. Two bands play every day. Happy hour starts at 4pm and features a free nachos bar. Cover charge varies.

Other activities and attractions

Without a central village area to explore, you'll need a car to pursue most **off-slope activities**. If there's a decent amount of snow on the ground, consider Killington Snowmobile Tours (☎ 802/422-2121, ⊛ www.snowmobilevermont .com), who offer both a **snowmobile** tour of the mountain area ($60) as well as a more isolated romp through the woods ($100). An alternative is **cross-country skiing** at the 50km-plus Mountain Meadows Nordic ski area (☎ 802 /775-7077, ⊛ www.xcskiing.net), located on Thundering Brook Road off Route 4 due east of the Killington Road entrance; adults can expect to pay around $35 for a full day pass and rentals.

To escape the cold, there's a small **climbing wall** in Rutland's Green Mountain Rock Climbing Center, 223 Woodward Ave (☎ 802/773-3343, ⊛ www.home.aol.com.gmrcc), and a **health spa** in The Woods condo complex off Killington Road (☎ 802/422-3139; massages $65 an hour; herbal body wrap).

Listings

Internet Virtual Café, 1307 Killington Rd (above *Pizza Jerks*) ☎ 802/422-2304. Daily 11am–10pm; $15 an hour for access.
Pharmacy Hannaford supermarket, 241 S Main St (Route 7), Rutland. Pharmacy hours Mon–Fri 9am–9pm, Sat 9am–7pm, Sun 9am–6pm.
Post office 2046 Route 4, Mon–Fri 8am–4.30pm, Sat 8am–10pm.

Mount Snow

Popular with families and freestylers, **Mount Snow**'s best attribute is its location. It's the southernmost Vermont resort, so Boston and New York residents can leave work on a Friday and arrive slopeside in time for a late dinner or, if traffic is bad, a nightcap. This certainly isn't a secret, and while midweek often finds Mount Snow deserted, Saturday and Sundays (and holidays, of course) are given over to weekend visitors en masse. Likewise, the resort's smallish base area and the friendly, if unexciting, business area strung along Route 100 to the south swell to capacity on weekends.

On the slopes, Mount Snow's 750 total acres of skiable **terrain** make it the second largest resort in Vermont, behind Killington. The advantage here is that the slopes are easy to negotiate: everything, save for **Haystack** a few miles to the south (see box on p.55), spills down logically from a central peak at 3600ft. The downfall is the remarkable uniformity to much of the terrain; while the rolling cruisers are a blast, and the **freestyling** some of New England's best, intermediate run after intermediate run can get a bit repetitive and make the total area feel smaller than it is.

Mountain info

Phone ☎802/464-3333
Snow phone ☎802/464-2151
Website ⊛www.mountsnow.com
Price $52 midweek, $62 weekend
Operating times Dec to mid-April; Mon–Fri 9am–4pm, Sat–Sun 8am–4pm (Haystack weekends/holidays only 8am–4pm)
No. of lifts 23, including 5 surface tows
Base elevation 1900′
Summit elevation 3600′
Vertical drop 1700′
No. of trails 145
Acreage 750
Beginner 22%
Intermediate 49%
Expert 29%
Average snowfall 160″
Snowmaking Yes (475 acres)
Night skiing No
Nursery facilities Yes, 6 weeks to 6 years; reservations required on ☎1-800/889-4411

Mount Snow's other problem, ironically, is its lack of **snow**. Though tall enough to collect good-size dumps when storms roll by, the resort averages a meager 160 inches of snowfall per year, a fair amount less than even its competitors just an hour or so to the north. Even with a collection of snowguns working overtime, conditions can be less than ideal.

Arrival, information, and getting around

With the closest public transportation stop-off located twenty miles away in Brattleboro, the only viable option for getting to Mount Snow is by **car**. Located directly off Route 100 in southern Vermont, the resort is approximately a four-hour drive from New York City and two-and-a-half hours from Boston. On Friday evenings, expect to add up to another hour.

Surrounding the resort, **West Dover**, is basically a string of inns, restaurants, and small shops stretching for miles south of the resort on Route 100. It has no definable center, so you'll need to head south of the slopes ten miles to **Wilmington**, at the junction of Route 100 N and Route 9, to enjoy a tiny but still pleasant village setting. Though arriving via car is pretty much a necessity, the area does have a reliable and free **public bus network**. It is known as the Moover (☎802/464-8487, ⊛www.moover.com), and most routes on the black-and-white cow theme buses cover the West Dover and Wilmington area from 8am to 5pm.

The mountain

Mainly flat, with plenty of long rolling runs, Mount Snow is tailor-made for intermediates. The mountain's eastern-facing front face, split between the broad **Main Face** and skinnier **Carinthia** due south, presents dozens of blue cruisers, several stretching from peak to base. Most of these trails roll across enough undulations and past enough glades to keep the skiing interesting. The front face is also where freestylers run laps on a pair of **superb terrain parks**. To the left of the Main Face is **North Face**, a challenging expert area with a half-dozen blazed trails, a good steep pitch, and some ample-sized glades. In the opposite direction off the summit's mini-maze of frosted pines lies the ski area's final "face," smaller **Sunbrook**, a sunny, southern-facing collection of even more blue runs along with Beartrap, a seriously sculpted mogul run.

With 23 **lifts**, including several surface lifts servicing the base area's bunny slopes, traveling from face to face is a snap. Lift lines, nonexistent midweek, can be an annoyance on weekends. To avoid the worst of them, stick to the slightly slower three-person chairs like Ego Alley, Sundance, and Summit Local.

Beginners

Though there isn't a whole lot of green on the trail map, most competent beginners should have few problems tackling many of the ski area's blue runs. If it's your first time out, hit the collection of magic carpets, towropes, and short-chairlifts that access the bunny slopes at the resort's base. Outside of the base, most of the greens cut across the slopes, including **Long John,** which works its way back and forth across the mountain's Main Face from summit to base. When feeling confident, step up to the blues of **Carinthia,** staying away from the jumps on Inferno and El Diablo, or **Big and Little Dipper** over in Sunbrook. Should the weekend crowds make you feel skittish, consider heading to **Haystack**, where you'll find a handful of isolated long greens.

Intermediate

Well over seventy percent of the mountain is open to intermediates, making Mount Snow one of New England's top such resorts. Typically less crowded and more sunny in the morning, Sunbrook is a good place to warm up, stretching out on the wide curves on **Big Dipper** and **Thanks Walt** among others. From here, head to Carinthia to try **Titanium** and **Nitro**, speedy and nearly pencil-straight blues lined under the Nitro Express quad. After reaching your top speed, move to Main Face and tackle **Sundance**, wide as a football field and a great trail to practice turns – just watch out for the series of stomach-churning dips midway through. One trail over, the serpentine **One More Time** is a joy to session, peppered with enough rolls to practice minor airs along with the option of diving in and out of **The Boonies** glades to the left. When it's time to give your ego a check, cut over to the North Face to try your luck on some true black diamonds.

Expert

Expert skiers and boarders will find most of the best runs on **North Face**. Should you arrive during a storm, head here first before the powder gets stomped out. Otherwise tread carefully early morning as the sun might not yet have had a chance to thaw the icy-hard slopes. Highlights here include **Fallen Timber**, a smooth blast that lets you test the limits of comfortable speeds, and **Ripcord**, a super-steep mogul run rightfully considered to be the resort's

Haystack

Similar to its sister resort Killington – both mountains are owned by the American Skiing Company – Mount Snow has an unattached peak, **Haystack**, whose stats are tabulated into the resort's overall tally. Haystack and Mount Snow were once connected by catwalk and locals still tend to lump them together as one mountain. Currently only open on weekends and holidays, Haystack attracts locals avoiding the crowds just up the road. Though small, it has some quality runs, especially the black-diamond **Witches** peak – including Wizard, Merlin, and Gandolf trails and the Enchanted Forest and Warlock's Woods **glades** abutting them. Newbies will appreciate the lack of crowds when linking turns on the greens and mellow blues here, especially **Outcast**, a green hugging the resort boundary for nearly two miles. A bonus to the weekend-only status is that it's possible to find **fresh snow** on Saturday mornings days after a storm.

toughest trail. Unless you're into challenging yourself on the resort's terrain parks, the rest of Mount Snow's expert terrain can be found in the **trees**. If conditions are right, a half-day can be spent choosing lines in North Face's **The Trials** and **Epiphany** glades, and over in the Main Face's **Fantastiks**, a good powder stash spot as it tends to collect windblown snow. On weekends, steeps-lovers will want to hitch a ride to test the terrain on **Haystack's Witches** peak (see box above).

Freestyle

In 1992, Mount Snow opened **Uno Blanco Gulcho**, winning the hearts of boarders with what was then one of the East Coast's longest and most intense terrain parks. They've since upped the ante with **Inferno**, on the slopes of Carinthia, the park that played host to the X-Games in 2000. The bottom line is that jibbers and jumpers have a wealth of rails, boxes, and progressively bigger jumps to ride, the absolute biggest being located at the bottom of Inferno. Mount Snow has also long been a favorite of pipe riders. The resort tries to have two **halfpipes** up and running if conditions allow, but at the very least count on a well-groomed superpipe to ride.

Lift tickets, lessons, and rentals

Lift ticket prices are on par with other resorts in Vermont. Adults pay $61 on weekends and holidays and $52 mid-week. There are small savings on multi-day passes, while kids and seniors save 25 percent off the standard pass price. Tickets for Haystack (see box above) cost $43 for adults, $30 for kids/seniors. The **ski school** (☎1–800/889–4411) offers a list of classes, starting at $35 for a morning group lesson. As for **renting gear**, the shops in the resort's main base lodge – Backside Snowboards for riders, Mountain Snow Sports for skiers – both supply decent set-ups for $35 a day. Arrive as early as possible on weekends to avoid waits.

Accommodation

There are plenty of **accommodation** options around Mount Snow, though within the base area choices are limited to the resort's 200-room *Grand Summit*, the 100-room *Snow Lake Lodge*, and a handful of condo complexes (☎1–800/451–4211). Most of the area's beds are in the inns and lodges along Route 100 to the south, with a few more on Route 9. Rates rise substantially on weekends, so book as far ahead as possible at these times. Midweek you should have no trouble getting a bed. Be sure to ask about extra charges before booking regardless of the day; adding a 15 percent service charge to the quote is a common practice here.

Andirons Lodge Route 100 N, West Dover ☎802 /464-2114 or 1-800/445-7669, ⓦwww.andirons .com. Just under two miles from the slopes, this relatively nondescript lodge is connected to a dependable restaurant and bar, the *Billiard Sanctuary*. Though not flashy, the fifty-plus rooms are at least clean and there are plenty of amenities including an indoor pool, hot tub, and sauna. A handful of rooms have two doubles and a single bed, fitting five in a pinch. Weekday ❹, weekend ❺

Grand Summit Hotel slopeside ☎1-800/451-4211, ⓦwww.mountsnow.com. The impersonal and sterile *Grand Summit* is a behemoth, home to rental shops, a deli, restaurant, and a full-service spa. It's also well located, only steps from several chairlifts. Though nothing to crow about, accommodations – which range from standard hotel rooms to three-room suites with kitchens – are clean and perfectly functional, with thoughtful touches like stereo systems, hampers for wet gear, and VCRs. Midweek ❻, weekend ❼

The Gray Ghost Inn 290 Route 100, West Dover ☎802/464-2474 or 1-800/745-3615, ⓦwww.grayghostinn.com. Named after a fishing lure, not an alleged in-house ghost, this popular 26-room B&B fills up well in advance on weekends. Within a mile from the slopes, the rooms are all en-suite and the friendly vibe spreads to the comfortable common areas, outdoor hot tub and sauna, and delicious breakfasts. The proprietor's black lab runs about freely, so being a dog-lover is a plus. Midweek ❸, weekend ❺

The Hermitage Coldbrook Rd ☎802/464-3511, ⓦwww.hermitageinn.com. Located on the road to Haystack, this charming country inn is housed in a

farmhouse dating back to the eighteenth century. All of the individually decorated rooms include working fireplaces, VCRs, and private bathrooms, and rates include breakfast and dinner, the latter served in a glorious dining room (see review opposite). Over thirty miles of groomed cross-country ski/snowshoe trails available free for guests right out the front door. The inn also runs the simpler *Brookbound* B&B ($70) a mile away. ❼

Old Red Mill Inn Route 100, Wilmington ☎802 /464-3700 or 1-877/733-6455, ⓦwww.oldredmill .com. Due north of the junction of routes 9 and 100 and some nine miles south of the slopes, this former sawmill offers some of the cheapest, if creaky and basic, rooms in the area. The tavern downstairs makes for a pleasant escape. Full breakfast served on weekends. Midweek ❸, weekend ❹

Snow Lake Lodge slopeside ☎1-800/451-4211, ⓦwww.mountsnow.com. This lodge is pretty much unremarkable in every way save for its decent location within walking distance of the *Snow Barn* bar. Most of the motel-style rooms have double beds, though suites with king-size beds are available as well. While still within the base area, most guest choose to ride the free shuttle the 400 yards to and from the slopes. Midweek ❹, weekend ❻

Viking Inn East Main St, Wilmington ☎802/464-5608 or 1-800/722-4427, ⓦwww.vikingmotel.net. Located a half-mile east of the turn-off to Mount Snow, this Wilmington motel may not have the most advantageous address in town, but it's handy for those on a budget or if everything else is booked up. Midweek ❸, weekend ❹

Eating, drinking, and entertainment

Most **restaurants** can be found either on Route 100 south of the slopes or on Wilmington's small downtown strip; reservations are recommended for the finer establishments. **On-mountain** options are largely uninspired; you're best off packing a lunch, though failing that both the base area and *Summit Lodge* at the peak have cafeterias. Wilmington has a Shaws **supermarket** on East Main Street.

During the week, the region's **bars** are typically low-key, though drink specials and free snacks may help draw you in. On weekends, however, Bostonians and New Yorkers looking to let off steam fill the bars to capacity, especially the *Snow Barn* and *The Silo*. For a calmer evening out, the Mountain Park Plaza, three miles south of the slopes on Route 100, contains the small Mountain Park **cinema** (☎802/464-6447), which shows Hollywood flicks for $5.

Restaurants and cafés

Café Tannery Route 100, West Dover. Three miles south of Mount Snow, this friendly café is best for its light fare, including a tasty peanut noodle salad with chicken ($9) and a portobello burger ($9). More filling meals include peppercorn steak ($20), good homemade meatloaf ($16), and pasta primavera ($14).

Dot's Restaurant 3 Main St, Wilmington ☎802 /464-7284. The local favorite for hearty breakfasts, *Dot's* has everything from omelettes to fruit-filled pancakes. Later in the day try the fiery chili or diner staples like meatloaf ($10), fried chicken ($11), and fish and chips ($11). Recommended. Daily 5.30am–8pm (9pm on Fri and Sat).

Fennessey's Route 100, West Dover ☎802/464-6111. Connected to the more rambunctious *Deacon's Den* (see below), this relaxed, mid-price restaurant serves dependable entrees like veal *saltimbocca*, lamb chops, and swordfish steaks (all near the $20 mark). Save room for the Vermont apple pie.

First Wok Mountain Park Plaza, Route 100, West Dover ☎802/464-5861. Their claim as the best Chinese food in the area is tempered because they're the *only* Chinese restaurant in the area. Worth it, however, if you're craving non-Yankee cuisine or seeing a movie at the nearby theater. Best dishes include the tangerine chicken ($13) and tofu with vegetables in garlic sauce ($13).

Giuseppes South Main St, Wilmington ☎802/464-2022. Low-key pizzeria across from Wilmington's library that's ideal for those on a tight budget. A large pizza starts at $10, while plates of pasta with garlic bread go for $6. Take out, but no delivery. Closed Tues.

The Hermitage Coldbrook Rd ☎802/464-3511. The dining room of this country inn near Haystack (see review opposite) is decorated with dozens of wooden decoy ducks and hand-carved birds. The creative menu includes starters like homemade venison sausage ($9) and escargot ($9), followed by local game dishes, trout florentine, and various steaks (all around $25). The wine list regularly wins awards from *Wine Spectator* magazine; no surprise considering there's a 40,000-bottle wine cellar downstairs.

Poncho's Wreck South Main St, Wilmington ☎802/464-9320. Locally renowned eatery known equally for its décor – a cornucopia of bizarre trinkets – and wide-ranging menu. Besides serving the best Mexican grub in the region, *Poncho's* menu includes king crab legs, baby back ribs, and gut-busting steaks in the $15–20 range, best washed down with killer margaritas. Dinner nightly 4–10pm, with early-bird specials 4–6pm.

Two Tannery Road 2 Tannery Rd, West Dover ☎802/464-2707. Competes with the *Hermitage* for the finest dining establishment in the area. Housed in the one-time retreat of Teddy Roosevelt's clan, it has a continental menu featuring several nightly fresh fish specials, along with standards like steak *au poivre*. Expect to pay around $100 for two, including drinks. Less expensive eats can be had in the attached tavern, which offers a simpler menu in the $10–15 range.

Bars

Billiard Sanctuary *Andirons Lodge*, Route 100 N, West Dover ☎802/464-9975. This classy poolhall, decorated in dark wood tones, makes for a comfortable place to relive the day's activities. The six tables rent for $12 an hour, and there's live music most weekend nights. Daily 4pm–2am; no cover.

Deacon's Den Route 100, West Dover ☎802/464-9361. Located two miles south of the resort entrance, this roadhouse has been a local watering hole for nearly three decades. The funky bar area is strewn with all manner of ephemera, from old baseball pennants and gas pumps to dusty banjos, and there are several beers on tap to sip on while taking it all in. The pub grub menu is extensive, and there's a pool table and a few arcade games.

The Silo Route 100, West Dover ☎802/464-2553, www.silorestaurant.com. Popular bar/restaurant complex only a few hundred yards south of Mount Snow's access road. During the week, specials like 10-cent wings and $1 drafts pull folks in, but such gimmicks are unneeded on weekends. A family-friendly dining area is located in the 100-year-old hay barn attached to the silo. Food served until 1am.

Snow Barn Mount Snow entrance ☎802/464-1100 ext 4693, ⓦ www.snowbarn.com. Relatively quiet during the week and all the better for it, this large bar on the fringe of the base area erupts on weekends, when a younger crowd pounds local microbrews and dances to live rock and reggae music.

Other activities and attractions

Mount Snow is more of a weekend getaway than a holiday destination, so the odds you'll be taking part in a major off-slope activity are rather slim. Should you have a hankering, there are several options, best of which is **cross–country**

△ Snowboarder on rail, Okemo, VT

skiing through the idyllic Green Mountains on *The Hermitage* inn's 30km of groomed trails. Located on the access road to Haystack, the inn rents out both skis and snowshoes for $15, and charges the same to use their trails. Other possibilities are a **snowmobile** tour with High Country Snowmobile (☎802/464-2108, ⓦwww.high-country-tours.com), a **sleigh ride** at nearby Adams Farm (☎802/464-3762), or a visit to the *Grand Summit's* slopeside **spa** (☎802/464-6606).

Listings

Internet Available free at the Wilmington library; see below.

Library 16 South Main St, Wilmington (due south of the Hwy 9 and Route 100 N junction). Hours vary, so call ahead on ☎802/464-8557.

Pharmacy Rite Aid pharmacy, East Main St, Wilmington Mon–Sat 9am–9pm, Sun 9am–5pm.

Post office Mountain Park Plaza, Route 100, West Dover, Mon–Fri 7.30am–4.30pm, Sat 9.30–11.30am.

Stowe

Stowe, more than any other New England resort, embodies the ideals of tradition. Seventy years ago the first skiable trail was cut on rocky **Mount Mansfield**, the ski area's majestic main mountain and the tallest in Vermont. By 1940 the longest chairlift in the United States at that time operated along with the country's first ski patrol outfit. Much has evolved since then, but much has stayed the same, with narrow, winding runs remaining the hallmark of the ski area's in-bounds terrain and miles of forested slopes making up Stowe's accessible, outstanding backcountry. Snowfall, too, has remained relatively consistent over the years, thanks in part to nearby Lake Champlain.

Some seven miles below the resort lies the quintessentially Vermont **village of Stowe**, with a picturesque, white-steepled church and historic center lined with clapboard nineteenth-century buildings. The village has retained its New England charm, while the seven-mile long **Mountain Road** (Route 108) separating the ski area and town has borne the brunt of development, with the region's restaurants and accommodations. This means a good deal of off-slope time is spent driving the access road and not in the village itself. Fortunately, enough natural spaces have been left along its route to keep things pleasant and peaceful. Indeed, a five-mile long recreational path that weaves alongside the road is sce-

Mountain info

Phone ☎802/253-3000 or 1-800/253-4754

Snow phone ☎802/253-3600

Website ⓦwww.stowe.com

Price $60

Operating times Nov–April; Mon–Fri 8am–4pm, Sat–Sun 7:30am–4pm; night skiing Thurs–Sun 5–9pm

No. of lifts 11, including 3 surface tows

Base elevation 1280´

Summit elevation 4395´

Vertical drop 2360´

No. of trails 48

Acreage 480 acres

Beginner 16%

Intermediate 59%

Expert 25%

Average snowfall 260″

Snowmaking Yes, 400 acres

Night skiing Yes, Thurs–Sat 5–9pm

Nursery facilities 6 weeks to 6 years ☎802/253-3000; reservations required

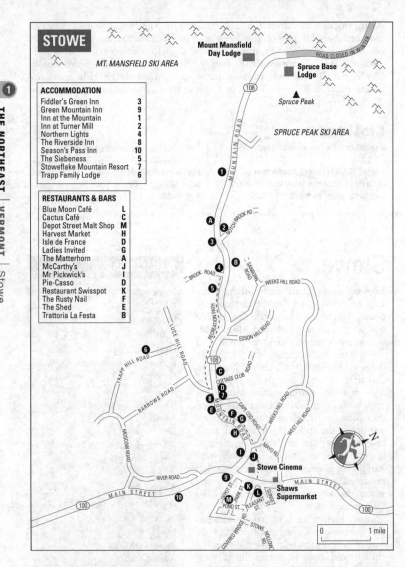

STOWE

MT. MANSFIELD SKI AREA

Mount Mansfield
Day Lodge

ROAD CLOSED IN WINTER

Spruce Base
Lodge

108

Spruce Peak

SPRUCE PEAK SKI AREA

ACCOMMODATION

Fiddler's Green Inn	3
Green Mountain Inn	9
Inn at the Mountain	1
Inn at Turner Mill	2
Northern Lights	4
The Riverside Inn	8
Season's Pass Inn	10
The Siebeness	5
Stoweflake Mountain Resort	7
Trapp Family Lodge	6

RESTAURANTS & BARS

Blue Moon Café	L
Cactus Café	C
Depot Street Malt Shop	M
Harvest Market	H
Isle de France	D
Ladies Invited	G
The Matterhorn	A
McCarthy's	J
Mr Pickwick's	I
Pie-Casso	D
Restaurant Swisspot	K
The Rusty Nail	F
The Shed	E
Trattoria La Festa	B

MOUNTAIN ROAD

NITCH BROOK RD

SANBORN ROAD

WEEKS HILL ROAD

BROOK ROAD

RECREATION PATH

EDSON HILL ROAD

LUCE HILL ROAD

TRAPP HILL ROAD

BARROWS ROAD

MOSCOW ROAD

108

COTTAGE CLUB RD

CAPE COD ROAD

WEEKS HILL ROAD

WEST HILL ROAD

MAYO RD

RIVER ROAD

MAIN STREET

100

DEPOT ST

PARK ST

POND ST

COVERED BRIDGE RD

PLEASANT ST

STOWE HOLLOW RD

SUNSET ST

Stowe Cinema

Shaws
Supermarket

MAIN STREET

100

N

0   1 mile

nic enough to draw out cross-country and snowshoe enthusiasts despite the 150km of wooded Nordic skiing trails that await in the surrounding area.

As with the village of Stowe, the **resort's base area** has managed to retain its traditional flavor, though in this case it's not quite a success story. Save for the *Inn at the Mountain*, located a mile below the main base, there's no slope-side lodging to be had. Until a proposed base "hamlet" gets built, overall slope-side amenities will remain as is, sparse with a few cafeterias and rental shops and little else.

Some visitors complain of a Yankee **attitude** that can be as cold as the winter winds. Though it may be true that locals don't suffer fools gladly, the antidote to any provincial venom is easy – don't be a fool. If the black-diamond trails of the Front Four look too steep to attempt, they probably are. And if you're not ready to head off-piste, don't. Few things anger regulars more than a "zamboni," an inexperienced skier or boarder sliding through the backcountry leaving a wide swathe of destroyed lines in their wake.

Arrival, information, and getting around

Located in north-central Vermont a fifteen-minute **drive** from I-89's exit 10, Stowe is an easy ride from Montreal (2.5 hours), Boston (3.5 hours), and New York City (6 hours). With **Burlington International Airport** located forty minutes away, many visitors choose to fly. Continental, United, and US Airways all have routes through Burlington from several major US cities, and JetBlue runs daily flights from New York City's JFK for as little as $40 one-way (see p.10 for contact details). **Car rental** options at the airport include Avis (☎802/864-0411), Hertz (☎802/864-7409), and National (☎802/864-7441), and many area hotels offer free transfers. Arriving by **train** is another option, with Amtrak's *Vermonter* line calling in at the Waterbury-Stowe station daily.

Orienting yourself at Stowe is simple, with the small historic village separated from the ski area by the seven-mile long Mountain Road (also known as Route 108). In the village, the Stowe Area Association at 51 Main St provides **information** along with an accommodation booking service. (☎1-877/467-8693, ⊛www.gostowe.com). As for **getting around**, a car is your best bet. The Stowe Village Mountain Shuttle **trolley** (daily 8am–10pm; $1; ☎802/253-7585) runs routes on the access road, though waits of up to 45 minutes outside of peak hours are not unheard of.

The mountain

Stowe's ski area has considerably more **trails** than its official tally. Known colloquially as the **Front 48**, the official blazed trails webbed across Mount Mansfield (4395ft) and Spruce Peak (3390ft) are – with some remarkable exceptions – the high-quality stomping grounds of beginner to advanced-intermediates. Off-piste are dozens if not hundreds of hike-to and traversable lines that cement Stowe's reputation as one of the finest advanced free-riding resort in the East. Trying to finagle the names or locations of these unmarked trails from regulars can be a nearly impossible task, but learning the lay of the in-bounds territory is not. Most of the runs across both peaks are pleasingly curvaceous and lengthy with few confusing intersections, making getting lost or split up within the resort's official boundaries difficult.

Broad and tall with a rocky, bald peak, **Mount Mansfield** holds a wonderfully diverse array of terrain. To break down the peak, study the mountain's profile on the trail map, looking for the outline of a face that appears along its long ridge. Beneath the **Nose** of this face spill more than half of the resort's blazed trails, including the fabled **Front Four**, a collection of true blacks that can be downright terrifying (and often closed) when conditions aren't prime. Under the **Lip** of Mount Mansfield are the runs accessed via the resort's eight-person **Gondola**, including the peak-to-base Perry Merrill and Gondolier blues open for **night-skiing** Thursday through Saturday. Below the mountain's most prominent facial feature and tallest point, the **Chin,** is an expanse of off-piste State Forest that hides a seemingly infinite collection of lines. As none of the lifts on Mount Mansfield reaches the summit, the entire stretch from the Forehead to the Adam's Apple remains **hike-to** terrain for backcountry explorers.

The mellower **Spruce Peak** is unconnected to Mount Mansfield for now though a lift linking the two is planned. As the base for the resort's ski school, its lower slopes clog during busier periods with wobbly-kneed newbies navigating down wide-open treeless greens. Up above, there's a web of winding blue trails that are frequently empty, though a lack of snowmaking abilities means conditions can be dicey. From the backside of Spruce, an unofficial trail can be used to connect to **Smugglers Notch** (see p.104), but the path is ungroomed and unpatrolled and should only be attempted with a local guide and a plan for getting back. Besides a lack of snowmaking, Spruce's other main fault is agonizingly slow lifts, especially the peak-reaching Big Spruce Double, known locally as Big Pig.

One thing to keep in mind when visiting is Stowe's **early opening hours**, 8am on weekdays and 7.30am on weekends and holidays. On a good powder day, folks line up at least a half-hour early, and if you arrive too late in the morning you may be hunting for stashes.

Beginner

Beginners at Stowe will spend most of their time on the resort's far edges, either on the wide greens toward the base of **Spruce Peak** or weaving down the narrow greens accessed via the **Toll House double** on the ski area's opposite end. The former is home to the ski school and several short lifts, and the latter area on the resort's eastern end is the place to head once you can link turns. The half-dozen trails here are used solely by beginners (save for day's end when guests of the lift-side *Inn at the Mountain* or the nearby condos head back home). The final must-ride green, and the lone way first-timers can get near the top, is the peak-to-base **Toll Road** green, the resort's longest trail at almost four miles in length.

Intermediate

Even though Stowe's backcountry terrain is strictly off-limits to those not completely comfortable on black diamond runs, intermediates have little to be bummed about here. In-bounds, every lift accesses at least one blue trail, meaning the entire stretch is open to exploration. Isolated from Mount Mansfield and somewhat of a pain to traverse from, Spruce Peak nonetheless has three fine top-to-bottom blues – **Smugglers**, **Main Street**, and **Sterling** – that are under-visited and worth sessioning when there's been a recent natural snowfall. On Mount Mansfield, the two finest blues are the wide thigh-burners **Perry Merrill** and **Gondolier** under the gondola. Further east are around a dozen blues accessed via the ForRunner, Lookout, and Mountain chairs, including the black-to-blue **Nosedive**, a Stowe classic since the 1930s. While it used to have seven steep turns, the three that remain will still have you testing the fit of your boots; it's the perfect step before moving on to the ski area's more advanced runs.

Expert

In-bounds, expert skiing at Stowe is defined by the **Front 4**, a pod of steep and bumpy black diamond trails lined underneath the ForRunner quad. The easiest of the bunch is **Liftline**, typically groomed and flattening considerably after an initial steep plunge. Next up is **National**, around the same steepness but more bumpy. The final two trails, **Starr** and **Goat**, are hair-raising by any scale and should only be attempted when conditions warrant – though the resort tends to close them down when it hasn't snowed, there are times when both narrow shots are little more than blue-iced bumps. Before considering an off-piste adventure, test your preparedness with the **Lookout Glades** and **Tres Amigos Glades** accessed via the Lookout or ForRunner chairs.

To experience the best of Stowe's **backcountry terrain**, you have two options. The first is to **hike** up from the top of either ForRunner or the Gondola to reach Mount Mansfield's ridgeline. Between the Nose and the Chin is a massive cliffband, and getting disoriented is far easier than it seems so don't go it alone. The reward, however, is an arctic-like ecosystem with several steep chutes. The second option is to head for the massive forest beneath the Chin to hunt down areas such as **Hellbrook** and **Angel Food**. Look for the path diving into the woods to your left a short way down Chinclip from the Gondola drop-off. While the lines closest to Chinclip make their way back to the Gondola Base Area, many end at the snow-covered Mountain Road (Route 108), closed to traffic during the winter, and thus necessitating a hike back to the base area.

Freestyle

Despite snowboard-giant Burton being headquartered in nearby Burlington, Stowe's purpose-built **freestyle terrain** is only decent. Marked improvements have been made in recent years, but with fewer snowguns zeroed in on terrain parks and the pipe than the competition, much depends on the weather. The main terrain park, **Tyro**, has two lines, snow permitting, along with a smallish selection of rails and fun boxes. A few runs west, North Slope is home to a **superpipe**, which demands a hike back up or a long lap up the Mountain Triple chair to get back. Toward the base of the Gondola, there's a **snowdeck park** that offers cheap rentals. Cliffs and logslides abound in the **backcountry**, so consider skipping the parks to hunt them down should you have both the skills and a local guide to show you the way.

Lift tickets, lessons, and rentals

Lift tickets at Stowe cost $63 per day during the weekends, a few dollars less midweek. Junior and senior riders save $20 and extended 2- to 7-day tickets offer reasonable savings. The well-regarded **ski school** offers a wide range of courses for ages 3 and up, with rates starting at $35 for a group lesson to $300 for a full day of one-on-one schooling. The resort utilizes the Learn-to-Ride program for newbie boarders (see p.534 for more on this system) and features a range of Burton rentals for around $30 per day, with basic ski packages costing around the same price. Should you want higher quality gear, the Stowe Toys and Burton demo centers by the base of the ForRunner quad rent out the latest equipment, including telemark skis and snowblades, in packages running around $40 per day. Note that if you're also taking a lesson, you can get a complete all-day rental for only $15. Pinnacle Ski (home to Snowboard Addic as well) toward the top end of the Mountain Road (℡802/253-7222, ⓦwww .pinnacleskisports.com) rents out a wide range of quality demo gear for around $35 per day.

Accommodation

The region's wide selection of quaint **inns** adds to Stowe's ambience. Finding a comfortable place to sleep in the $125–175 per night range is simple, while the luxurious *Green Mountain Inn* and *Trapp Family Lodge* cover the high end of the scale. But thanks in part to the indefinite closing of the slopeside *Mount*

Mansfield Hostel, Stowe has a severe shortage of budget beds. Until the proposed Spruce Base Area village is built, there is also very little slopeside lodging. **Condos** are less prevalent at Stowe than other Vermont resorts, though both the resort itself (see *Inn at the Mountain* below) and All Seasons Rentals (☎802 /253-7353 or 1-800/547-8693, ⊛www.stowerentals.com) have rentals.

Those looking for an adventurous overnight experience can try renting out the *Stone Hut*, atop the mountain. Built in 1936, this former warming hut has room for up to a dozen and is rented out for $110 a night by Vermont State Parks (☎802/253-4010, ⊛www.vtstateparks.com) via a lottery system beginning each April for the upcoming ski season. With all heat and cooking revolving around a sole wood stove, you need to be prepared to rough it somewhat.

Fiddler's Green Inn 4859 Mountain Rd ☎802/253-8124 or 1-800/882-5346, ⊛www .fiddlersgreeninn.com. This bright-yellow no-non-sense B&B toward the top end of the access road offers seven en-suite rooms along with one bunkroom, the latter usually saved for older children of visiting families. The atmosphere is very friendly and a delicious fully cooked breakfast is served daily around a large communal table. ❹

Green Mountain Inn Main St ☎802/253-7301 or 1-800/253-7302, ⊛www.greenmountaininn.com. Recently expanded to 100 rooms, this historic inn has been standing in the heart of Stowe village since 1833. Inside is a pleasing mix of old and new, with both fire-warmed libraries and a heated outdoor pool and health club. Accommodations range from larger-than-average size hotel rooms up to individual townhouses, all suitably decorated with antique flourishes and four-poster beds. Midweek ❺, weekend ❻

Inn at the Mountain ☎802/253-3000 or 1-800 /253-4754, ⊛www.stowe.com. Resort-owned and the sole slopeside accommodation at Stowe, this inn lacks the warmth and personality found at other area accommodations. The double chair up from the inn is torturously slow, but the location is still prime and should you choose one of the frequent mid-week ski-and-stay deals the slightly sterile rooms should suffice. There are also several one- to three-bedroom condos available for rent nearby. Guests of both the *Inn* and condos receive free access to Stowe's cross-country trails. Inn midweek ❺, weekend ❻; condos midweek ❼, weekend ❽

Inn at Turner Mill 56 Turner Mill Lane ☎802 /253-2062 or 1-800/992-0016, ⊛www.turnermill .com. Just off the Mountain Road a stone's throw from the entrance to Stowe Resort, this good-value inn spreading over nine acres offers comfortable and original accommodations in one- to four-bed-room suites, many of which include full kitchens and fireplaces. While all rooms have a rustic feel, each accommodation is en-suite with TVs and

telephones. The owners, who built many of the inn's beds and chairs, are a font of information on local ice climbing and Nordic skiing and offer free use of snowshoes. Recommended. One bedroom ❹, with kitchen ❺

Northern Lights 4441 Mountain Rd ☎802/253-8541 or 1-800/448-4554, ⊛www.stowelodge.com. A favorite with large groups, the laid-back *Northern Lights* is an Austrian lodge on the outside and all-American motel on the inside. One of the better values in the area, it has fifty rooms in total, made up mostly of standard motel-like rooms with king beds or two doubles, though a handful of effi-ciency apartments and a few budget "munchkin rooms" with a bed and little else are also avail-able. Extras include a basic full cooked breakfast, massive game room with pool table, ping pong and air hockey, large-screen TV room with a movie library, and an indoor pool, sauna, and hot tub. Midweek ❹, weekend ❺

The Riverside Inn 1965 Mountain Rd ☎802/253-4217 or 1-800/966-4217, ⊛www.rivinn.com. While this establishment has seen better days, it is one of the cheapest options on the mountain road. The main house has ten rooms, while a motel-like strip out back holds six more. Rooms are basic, but most include TV, VCR, and private bathroom. If booked far enough in advance, a group of up to 22 can rent out the entire main house. Amenities include a pool table, karaoke machine, and living room fireplace. Midweek ❷, weekend ❹

Season's Pass Inn 613 South Main St ☎802 /253-7244 or 1-800/441-4575, ⊛www .seasonspass.com. No-frills motel located a few hundred yards south of the main village area. Though rooms are rather sparse, rates are about as cheap as they get hereabouts. All rooms have TVs, there's an indoor pool, and a free continental breakfast is offered daily. Midweek ❸, weekend ❹

The Siebeness 3681 Mountain Rd ☎802/253-8942 or 1-800/426-9001, ⊛www.siebeness.com. This romantic B&B on a rather isolated stretch of the access road offers a small selection of antique-filled rooms centered around deluxe four-poster or canopied beds. Full gourmet breakfasts served daily, and the innkeeper can light a fire by the outdoor hot tub. No children and no smoking. ➎

Stoweflake Mountain Resort 1746 Mountain Rd ☎802/253-7355 or 1-800/253-2232, ⓦwww.stoweflake.com. Full-service resort with some 150 rooms, making it one of Stowe's largest accommodation options. While the accommodations, ranging from average-sized hotel rooms to townhouses, are comfortable and the on-site eateries are respectable, the overall vibe is too staid to justify the price. There is an on-site spa, complete with indoor pool, racquetball court,

steam room, and several treatment rooms. Midweek ➎, weekend ➐

Trapp Family Lodge 700 Trapp Hill Rd ☎802/253-8511 or 1-800/826-7000. Stowe's most beloved resort, the *Trapp Family Lodge* – still owned by the family that inspired *The Sound of Music* – seems transported straight from the Alps. Located on 2800 acres of rolling hills a short drive south of the Mountain Road, both the Main Lodge and Lower Lodge are decked out in Tyrolean style, with some 120 exceedingly comfortable and elegant rooms between them. Besides the fine dining and a superb on-site Nordic center (see p.67), sing-alongs and fire-lit common rooms go a long way toward keeping up the ambience. ➑

Eating, drinking, and entertainment

With more three- and four-star restaurants than any other ski town in New England, hunting down a good place to **eat** in Stowe is a snap. Just as pleasing is the fact that no fast-food chains plague the area, with the sole *McDonalds* closing in 2002 reputedly due to a lack of customers. Unfortunately, **on-mountain** dining is nowhere near as inspired. Save for fancy lunches at the mountain-top *Cliff House*, the cafeteria food served elsewhere is bland, and you're best off grabbing a sandwich or snacks on the drive in. If self-catering, there's a large Shaw's supermarket about a mile north of village on Route 100 (Sun–Thurs 7am–9pm; Fri–Sat 7am–11pm).

Stowe's **nightlife** scene is limited. For a night out, many locals head west to Burlington, and *The Matterhorn* and less frequently *The Rusty Nail* can get a bit rowdy on weekends. Beyond that, a handful of bars and taverns are spread about, fine for a group drink but little more. The Stowe Cinema 3-Plex (☎802/253-4678) on Mountain Road plays first-run flicks.

Cafés and restaurants

Blue Moon Café 35 School St ☎802/253-7007. Colorful village café that boasts one of Stowe's most original menus. The Asian-inspired continental cuisine changes frequently, but entrees may include such pairings as sweet and sour braised rabbit ($22) or banana leaf steamed halibut Thai coconut curry ($20). A vegetarian entrée offered nightly. Dinner only, reservations recommended.

Cactus Café 2160 Mountain Rd ☎802/253-7770. Good and fairly priced Southwestern cuisine served in a warm and friendly adobe-esque interior. Entrees, including fine seafood specials, average $10–15, and the homemade jalepeño pepper appetizer will have you re-evaluating their lowly pub-grub status. Fantastic margaritas as well.

Depot Street Malt Shop 57 Depot St ☎802/253-4269. Downtown diner with a cliched though still cozy 1950s theme. There are no rollerskating waitresses, but you can still get burgers, cheese steaks, and grilled cheeses for around $5–6. Try

the fountain treats, ranging from thick chocolate milkshakes to a tart lime rickey.

Harvest Market 1031 Mountain Rd ☎802/253-3800. Gourmet market that's worth checking out in the morning for fresh pastries and espresso coffees, and also for take-out gourmet sandwiches for lunch. Full take-out meals also available if self-catering. Daily from 7am.

Isle de France 1899 Mountain Rd ☎802/253-7751. One of Stowe's finest high-end restaurants has been serving authentic French cuisine for 25 years. Expect to pay around $100 for two, including a bottle of wine and tip. If the formal dining room, modeled after the Ritz Carlton in Paris, is too elegant, a more relaxed attached bistro serves standards like strip steak for $15–20. Dinner only; closed Mondays.

The Matterhorn 4969 Mountain Rd ☎802/253-8198. Though a bar first (see overleaf), the *Matterhorn* deserves a food mention for its sushi bar – the sole place to suck down raw fish in the region.

McCarthy's Mountain Rd, next door to Stowe Cinema ☎802/253-8626. A short distance off Main Street up the Mountain Road sits this unassuming eatery, dishing out perhaps Stowe's best breakfast. Best or not, it's certainly one of the most affordable, with omelettes, *huevos rancheros*, and apple pancakes all served for $5 or less. Daily 6:30am–3pm.

Mr Pickwick's *Ye Olde England Inne*, 433 Mountain Rd ☎802/253-7558. English theme restaurant decorated in heavy wood tones. Standards such as bangers and mash ($15) and beef wellington ($25) appear, but the various game dishes (including pheasant, wild boar, and caribou) are most memorable. Worth a visit for the bar alone, featuring over 100 beers, 40 single malt whiskeys, and a massive wine list.

Pie-Casso 1880 Mountain Rd ☎802/253-4411. A basic but dependable pizzeria with the best pies on the Mountain Road, available for eat-in, take-out and delivery. The wide list of toppings includes eggplant, shrimp, and strangely falafel, and the menu also includes a short list of salads of subs. Beer available if eating in.

Restaurant Swisspot Main St ☎802/253-4622. Hard to miss on Stowe village's main drag, this is the top stop should your ski vacation needs include a fondue dinner. The rest of the menu ranges from bratwurst ($12) to grilled tuna ($18), but the cheese or beef fondue averaging $15 per person is best.

Trattoria La Festa 4080 Mountain Rd ☎802/253-8480. A truly festive Italian restaurant where you can nurse a post-feast bottle of wine without feeling rushed. Serving what the owners deem "Italian soul food," top choices include seafood-loaded *spaghetti pescatore* ($17) and a decadent sirloin stuffed with prosciutto and mozzarella ($21). Closed Sundays.

Bars and clubs

Ladies Invited 1056 Mountain Rd ☎802/253-9077. Relaxed and friendly establishment on the mountain road that's the closest you'll get to a dive bar. The music leans toward the Dead and reggae and among the many animal heads adorning the walls are two of the largest moose heads you'll ever see, peering over a slightly beat-up pool table.

The Matterhorn 4969 Mountain Rd ☎802/253-8198. Sectioned off with a martini bar, game room, and decent-sized stage and dance floor, the *Matterhorn* is Stowe's most popular après-ski and nightlife venue. Relatively quiet midweek, it gets packed from Thursday through Sunday when live bands take the stage at 9pm. The larger-than-average pub-grub selection includes pizzas, salads, and even a sushi bar.

The Rusty Nail The Mountain Rd ☎802/253-6245. Restaurant and nightlcub about a mile from the village that's worth visiting on weekends when the occasional decent rock or funk band takes to the small stage.

The Shed 1859 Mountain Rd ☎802/253-4364. Good home-brewed beers – including the very fine Smugglers Stout – served in a barn-like bar that's an annex to a much larger restaurant. In the early evening the overall vibe is very casual, with tired-out skiers downing mugs of brew. There's a wide range of pub grub, with frequent specials like $3 pints and 30-cent wings. Later in the evening the crowd can get noisy, and food is served until midnight.

Other activities and attractions

A major reason that Stowe is one of New England's finest destination resorts is the wide array of **off-slope activities** available. With one of the largest trail networks in the country, Stowe's most obvious secondary activities – and primary ones for many visitors – are **cross-country skiing** and **snowshoe trekking** (see opposite for details). Other winter options include **dogsledding** (*Eden Mountain Lodge* ☎802/635-9070), **snowmobiling** (Stowe Snowmobile Tours ☎802/253-6221), **ice-climbing** (Mountain Sport & Bike Shop ☎802 /253-7919), and **sleigh rides** (*Trapp Family Lodge* ☎802/253-8511; *Stowehof Inn* ☎802/253-9722).

Indoor choices are nearly as prevalent. The village is worth strolling for a close-up look at its picturesque buildings and attractive if slightly overpriced antique shops. Also in town is the **Vermont Ski Museum** at 1 South Main St (Mon & Wed–Sun 10am–6pm; ⓦwww.vermontskimuseum.org), worth a quick peek for the antique ski-lifts and ski gear on display. **The Swimming Hole**, 75 Weeks Hill Rd ($10; ☎802/253-9229), is an indoor pool/gym complex open to the public, though the best **spa** in the region is at the *Stoweflake Resort* (☎802/253-7355; see p.65), which charges $20 per day for nonguests not including treatments.

Cross-country skiing and snowshoeing

Stowe is one of the rare downhill resorts that also attracts **Nordic skiers** for extended stays. The groomed network of trails exceeds 150km and is connected via four main touring centers – the *Trapp Family Lodge*, Stowe Resort, *Edson Hill Manor*, and *Stoweflake Resort*. The two centers with the best access to the best range of trails are Stowe Resort (☎802/253-3000) and the *Trapp Family Lodge* (☎802/253-8511); expect to pay $15 for a trail pass and $20 for rentals at either, and both offer a wide range of lessons.

    Snowshoe trekking is another popular diversion. The Nordic centers at both the resort and *Trapp Family Lodge* rent out gear for $15 and can point out the best local trails. Also worthwhile is a snowshoe **tour** with Umiak Outdoor Outfitters, 849 South Main St (☎802/253-2317, ⓦwww.umiak.com), which offers a moonlight jaunt through the woods ($40, including snacks) and a popular trip around the nearby Ben & Jerry's ice-cream factory that also includes a tour of the facilities ($12).

    To stock up on any Nordic, telemark, or snowshoe **equipment**, try the Mountain Sport & Bike Shop at 580 Mountain Rd (☎802/253-7919); the store also organizes backcountry expeditions.

Listings

Internet Free access available at both the Stowe Visitor Center, 51 Main St, and the Octagon Café on top of the mountain itself by ForRunner Quad drop-off point.
Library Helen Day Art Center, School Street (Mon, Wed & Fri 9:30am–5:30pm; Tues & Thurs 2–7pm; Sat 10am–3pm).

Pharmacy Heritage Drugs, 1878 Mountain Rd (Mon–Fri 9am–6pm, Sat 10am–3pm, close Sun; ☎802/253-2544).
Post office 105 Depot St (Mon–Fri 7–5pm, Sat 9am–noon, closed Sun).

Stratton

Southern Vermont's **STRATTON** boasts the dubious distinction of having the highest priced lift ticket in the region. It might not be readily apparent what you're paying for at first glance; indeed, prices have shot up more in an attempt to thin out the massive weekend crowds that plague competing resorts than for any other reason. Whether or not the plan is working is arguable – crowds still seem out of hand during busy periods – but the scheme has attracted a more refined, some might say snobbish, bunch than the average East Coast ski area. Stratton's prototypical New England trails, narrow, tree-lined, and flat on the whole, also work to draw less out-of-control skiers, who at least get some bang for their buck with impressive grooming and snowmaking programs and the most efficient lift system in the East.

    A point that seems somewhat at odds with the ski area's blue-blooded reputation is that Stratton is also the best **freestyle** resort in the East, with half-a-dozen terrain parks and one of the country's top half-pipes. As now told with near mythical reverence, snowboard pioneer Jake Burton tested some of the first ever boards here on night-rides in the early 1980s, and today the resort continues to promote the sport as the regular host of the **US Open** snowboarding championships in March.

It's during these championships that Stratton comes most alive, with revelers flocking to watch the jib jam, superpipe, and slopestyle competitions before crowding into area bars. Things are far more family-oriented the rest of the year. The Intrawest resort group – which includes Whistler and Mammoth – has pumped millions of dollars into upgrading both the slopes and the base, which is supposed to mimic a quaint Vermont village but looks more like an overblown dollhouse. Regardless, it's undeniably convenient, with a respectable range of restaurants, bars, rental shops, and nearby accommodation. Should you opt for a genuine Vermont town, **Manchester** is twenty miles away and full of historic inns, fine restaurants, and scores of popular, if unsightly, outlet shops.

Arrival and orientation

There are no practical mass transit options nearby, meaning most visitors arrive by **car**. Located off Route 30 in southern Vermont, Stratton is nearly three hours by car from Boston and just over four from New York City. The closest airport is in Albany, one and a half hours drive away. Orienting yourself with the resort is simple as there are only two base areas, **Stratton Village** and the much smaller **Sun Bowl Lodge**. The former is home to the resort's Intrawest-designed village as well as nearly all of the amenities, while the latter is worth using only on weekends when the main area's parking lots are full. Outside of the resort, the main hub of activity is **Manchester**, a large town twenty miles to the west.

The mountain

With the finest **lift** system in the East and all of the trails spilling down from one rounded peak, Stratton's slopes are easy to navigate. Most trails are relatively simple, with few steeps and a **grooming program** that turns runs into wall-to-wall carpet; if you're a fan of smooth cruisers you'll be well served here. Only the **terrain parks** might raise the hairs on the back of your neck. As the lone base-to-peak lift at the mountain, the supposed twelve-person **gondola** (a dozen small children might be able to comfortably squeeze in) is where lines most often form. Typically less crowded is the wind-protected Sun Bowl on the ski area's eastern side, complete with a pair of high-speed six-person chairs. Should crowds anywhere get unmanageable, follow the locals to nearby **Bromley** (see p.102).

Mountain info

Phone ☎802/297-2200 or 1-800/787-2886

Snow phone ☎802/297-4211

Website ⊛www.stratton.com

Price $72 weekend, $60 midweek

Operating times Late Nov to early April; daily 8:30am–4pm

No. of lifts 16, including 5 surface lifts

Base elevation 1872′

Summit elevation 3875′

Vertical drop 2003′

Number of trails 90

Acreage 585

Beginner 42%

Intermediate 31%

Expert 27%

Average snowfall 180″

Snowmaking Yes (500 acres)

Night skiing No

Nursery facilities Yes, six weeks to four years; reservation required ☎1-800/787-2886

Beginner

Thanks to a superb ski school, impeccable grooming and a hefty selection of trails, Stratton is one of New England's best beginner hills. Adventurous newcomers should have little problem finding isolated green runs if willing to leave the confines of the beginner's area. This zone, located directly above the base area, is a heavily used, large web of greens occupied by the ski school and those still not confident enough to leave the main base lodge behind. High above, from the Gondola drop-off, beginners can work their way down from peak-to-base on several greens, including **West Meadow** and **Wanderer,** hugging the resort's western boundary. On the resort's opposite edge are a collection of more worthwhile trails, including **Lower Middlebrook** and **Churchill Downs,** flat but still cut in the classic East Coast style.

Intermediate

As most of the single black diamond runs here would be rated blue elsewhere and the others are so well groomed that most obstacles are obliterated, everything save for the terrain parks and double blacks is manageable for confident intermediates. Still, except for the Sun Bowl Base Area, blue riders will want to stick toward the top end of the mountain to avoid mixing with the flat learning areas toward the main base. Good runs to warm up on include the resort's widest run, **Sunrise Supertrail,** and pencil-thin **Gentle Ben,** both in the Sun Bowl. Once you're ready to move up the ranking system, try **Upper Kinderbrook,** a winding ego-boosting black that would be rated green out West, and then **Upper Middlebrook,** also in the Sun Bowl and markedly steeper. Tackle these and you're ready for **Liftline,** a speedy black that shoots straight underneath the Snow Bowl quad, and **North America** and **Upper Tamarack** by Ursa Express, both of which curve and whoosh past Stratton's thick forests.

Expert

While there are a few double black diamonds spread across the top of the mountain, expert skiers and riders looking for thrills should head for the trees or terrain parks. The best collection of expert trails spread underneath the Ursa Express and Shoot Star six-person chairs toward the Sun Bowl end of the hill, including **Bear Down** and **Grizzly Bear,** the two toughest blazed trails on the mountain but still not incredibly challenging. The woods, including **Moon Dance** and **Diamond in the Rough,** will have most skiers feeling dared, especially if conditions are icy. The best bump run is **World Cup,** on the opposite end of the ski area, though it's a bit too short to get much of a groove going.

Freestyle

Stratton has deep roots in the freestyle scene. Its first halfpipe was built back during snowboarding's infancy in 1983, and three years later the resort was one of the first in the country to offer lessons to boarders. The resort remains firmly committed to freestylers, and once enough snow has fallen (or has been blown) six separate parks are jammed into the ski area's 585 acres of terrain. While the location of some of the parks changes yearly, consistent areas include **Lower East Meadow,** a naturally sculpted run peppered with stomach-dropping rollers its entire length, and **East Byrnside,** an East Coast classic, home to large jumps and a favorite of both local and visiting pro riders. Next to the latter, **Suntanner** hosts a wide array of rails and fun boxes, as well as a massive

400ft-long **superpipe** that's one of the best on the continent. Two chairs from the base area ensure quick laps of both Suntanner and East Byrnside in all but the most busy of conditions.

Lift tickets, lessons, and rentals

Stratton has the highest priced **lift tickets** in the East, with prices ranging from midweek lows of around $60 to $72 for a Saturday/holiday pass. Juniors and seniors save $10–20 per day, depending on their age. There are decent savings on extended passes, but purchasing the discount-giving **Express Card** ($75–100 depending on when purchased) often works out to be a better deal as it cuts Thursday passes down to $15 and gives cheaper weekend rates as well. More competitively priced is the **Stratton Ski School** (☏1-800/787-2886), with comprehensive programs for all abilities, including Burton's Learn-to-Ride program for newbie boarders (see p.534 for information on this system) and a wide array of kids programs. Two-hour group lessons begin at $35, while private lessons start at $75 per hour. If at all possible take your first lesson midweek, when you'll have more elbow room to learn.

For **rentals**, the resort's Village Rental Shop (☏802/297-4099) has basic ski and board packages starting at $30, with high-end set-ups running closer to $40. Elsewhere, boarders should stop in at the superb Syd & Dusty's (☏802/297-4323) in the village, while skiers will want to call in at nearby Stratton Sports (☏802/297-4330); both stores offer the latest in top demos and offer overnight tune-ups.

Accommodation

Accommodation in Manchester is more affordable, but the long drive to the slopes might make you cough up that extra few dollars to stay slopeside. Another option is one of the more rurally located inns between the resort and town. Stratton runs all of the slopeside accommodations; while their standard rates are generally overpriced, great ski-and-stay packages are frequently offered, especially midweek.

Stratton Village and around

Alpenrose Inn Winhall Rd, Bondville ☏802/297-2750 or 1-877/206-9343, ⓦwww.alpen-rose.com. Located on a back road ten minutes from the slopes, this pleasant family-run inn has sledding, cross-country skiing, and ice-skating available in the woods out its back door. The basic but comfortable rooms have private bathrooms and attractive quilt bedspreads, and there are several common areas with fireplaces and games. Cooked breakfasts are served daily around a Kachelofen, a ceramic wood-burning oven. A full apartment above the garage sleeping six is also available. Midweek ❹, weekend ❺

Jamaica House Hotel Route 30, Jamaica ☏802/874-4149, ⓦwww.jamaicahousehotel.com. South on Route 30 in tiny Jamaica, this eclectic hotel has several economically priced, attractive rooms in a hostel-like environment. Yoga classes and massages offered onsite. Midweek ❷, weekend ❸

Liftline Lodge Stratton Base ☏1-800/787-2776, ⓦwww.stratton.com. Only a short walk from the lifts, this resort-run lodge is best for those willing to sacrifice deluxe comforts for affordable slopeside lodging. Built in the 1960s and looking like it, rooms have large bathrooms and TVs, and the onsite *Café on the Corner* (see opposite) is a powerful morning draw. Great packages, especially midweek, often available. Midweek ❺, weekend ❻

Long Trail House Stratton Base ☏1-800/787-2776, ⓦwww.stratton.com. Opened in 1999, *Long Trail* offers comfortable though slightly cramped one-bedroom condos a short walk from the lifts in sprawling colonial-styled buildings. Amenities include several hot tubs and a heated outdoor pool. If you really want to live it up, a deluxe five-bedroom/five-bathroom penthouse is rented out for $1000–2500 a night. Midweek ❼, weekend ❽.

Stratton Condominiums Stratton Base ☏1-800/787-2776, ⓦwww.stratton.com. The resort manages five separate condo complexes, ranging from one to four bedrooms all with fireplaces. Couples or small groups will want to look into one-bedroom at Obertal, while up to eight can stay in the three-bedroom units of the centrally located Village Watch. Styles Brook and Vantage Point require shuttling to and from the slopes. Midweek ⑧, weekend ⑨

Stratton Mountain Inn Stratton Base ☎1-800/787-2776, ⓦwww.stratton.com. A 125-room, full-service hotel located a short shuttle ride or long hike from the slopes. Rooms either have two queen beds or a queen and pull-out sofa, and extras include heated pool, sauna, and a hot tub. Service can be exceedingly slow, and the onsite restaurants are far from inspiring. Midweek ⑤, weekend ⑦

Stratton Village Lodge Stratton Base ☎1-800/787-2776, ⓦwww.stratton.com. Right in the middle of the village, this attractive lodge offers both contemporary hotel rooms and two-story lofts. Amenities are a bit sparse although guests can access the *Stratton Mountain Inn's* pool a shuttle ride away. Midweek ⑤, weekend ⑦

Manchester

The Equinox Route 7A ☎1-888/367-7625, ⓦwww.equinoxresort.com. At the base of Mount Equinox

sits this majestic, full-service resort dating back more than a hundred years. Definitely not for ski bums, the elegantly appointed rooms and worthy onsite restaurants (including the *Marsh Tavern;* see p.72) may make you not want to leave its creature comforts. The wide list of activities available include a full-service spa, snowshoeing on 2300 acres, a Range Rover off-road driving school, and even a falconry school. Midweek ⑦, weekend ⑥

Manchester Highlands Inn 216 Highlands Ave ⓦ802/362-4565 or 1-800/743-4565, ⓦwww.highlandsinn.com. One of Manchester's several fine inns, the *Highlands* is housed in a beautiful Victorian perched on a hill a couple of blocks above Depot Street. The fifteen guestrooms are decorated with lace and antiques, and the basement is a giant game room and drinking den. Gourmet breakfasts served daily, as are afternoon snacks. Midweek ⑤, weekend ⑥

Skylight Lodge Route 11/30 ☎802/362-2566. Simple accommodation for a simple price, this classic ski lodge is no-frills but not without charm. Rooms accommodate one to four bunks and are best for those looking to ski hard all day and bed down early. Rates, per person, include breakfast. ①

Eating, drinking, and entertainment

The base village and Manchester combine to give Stratton one of the better **dining** scenes in Vermont. Except during the US Open snowboarding championships, only *Grizzly's* and *The Green Door* manage to keep the **après-ski** scene buzzing through the early evening. The closest **movie theater** is the Village Picture Shows (☎802/362-4771), located in the Manchester Shopping Center in town on Routes 11/30.

If **self-catering**, Stratton Provisions in the village center (☎802/297-9850) sells supplies at marked-up prices. Should you have the time and means, you're better off heading to the Shaw's supermarket on Hwy-7 in Manchester (Mon–Sat 7am–11pm, Sunday 7am–9pm).

Stratton Village and around

Blue Moon Café Stratton Village ☎802/297-2093. Delicious sweet and savory crepes ($5–9), served along with frittatas, soups, and sandwiches, from 7am to 6pm daily. A loft bar upstairs opens for fondue and wine après-ski on weekends.

Café on the Corner *Liftline Lodge* ☎802/297-6141. The best mountainside breakfasts are served in this sunny café, across from the entrance to the village strip. Try the spicy *chorizo con huevos* ($8) or Belgian Foster ($8), a dangerously sweet waffles and bananas Foster concoction. Daily 7am–noon.

Mulberry Street Stratton Village ☎802/297-3065. At the entrance to Stratton Village, this

generic Italian eatery dishes up pastas and a few Italian entrees, all best bypassed in favor of the relatively inexpensive pizzas. An attached martini and cigar bar attracts a slightly upscale crowd for a subdued après-ski.

Mulligans Stratton Village ☎802/297-9293. Popular if uninspiring dinner spot (lunch served weekends only) in the village center, serving large platters of standard fare in a simple, tavern-like environment. Nightly specials such as New England lobster bake ($12) augment a hefty menu of burgers, steaks, and seafood platters. The après-ski scene can get buzzing thanks to ten-cent wings at the bar, though the rowdiest head downstairs to the *Green Door* (see p.72). No smoking.

Out Back at Winhall River Route 30 South, Bondville ⊕ 802/297-3663. Located a quarter mile south of Stratton's access road, the *Out Back*'s airy dining room, hung with local watercolors and quilts, makes for a refreshing break from the resort village. Entrees, all in the $15–20 range, include a paper-thin veal *picatta* and grilled salmon topped with asparagus and a vermouth cream sauce. A favorite of locals, the attached pub serves cheaper but no less tasty meals and has a pool table and eight brews on tap. Reservations recommended for the dining room on weekends.

Manchester and around

Al Ducci's 133 Elm St and Highland Ave ⊕ 802/362-4499. This authentic Italian grocer, located a block off Depot Street, is Manchester's finest stop for sandwiches to go. Mon–Sat 7.30am–6pm, Sun 9am–4pm.

The Marsh Tavern *The Equinox*, Route 7A ⊕ 802/362-4700. As good an excuse as any to tour this magnificent hotel, the tartan-lined *Marsh Tavern*, which dates back to 1769, serves up fancy pub grub in a warm environment. A warm fire, top-shelf whiskeys, and occasional live music add to the ambiance.

Mika's *Avalanche Motor Lodge*, Routes 11/30 ⊕ 802/362-8100. The region's sole sushi restaurant is attached to a motel in between Stratton and Manchester. The décor inside is all Asian kitsch and the menu is extensive, ranging from tuna rolls ($6) to beef teriyaki ($17). Chinese food on offer as well.

Mistral's Toll Gate Rd ⊕ 802/362-1779. With an intimate riverside setting just off Route 11/30 to Manchester, this handsome restaurant is best for a romantic night out. The French menu, which rotates regularly and may include such spectacular mains as roast duck with pears and juniper berries ($25) or a stuffed *chateaubriand béarnaise* for two ($64), is matched by an award-winning wine list.

The Sirloin Saloon Routes 11/30 ⊕ 802/362-2600. This basic, fairly priced downtown steakhouse dishes out dependable cuts of meat that should please any carnivore. Lighter options include a large salad bar and some fish dishes.

Up For Breakfast 4935 Main St ⊕ 802/362-4204. If staying in Manchester make it a point to breakfast at this popular café. The fabulous morning meals – from basic omelettes to sourdough French toast stuffed with lingonberry cream cheese – are well worth the long waits.

Bars and clubs

Candeleros 5103 Main St, Manchester ⊕ 802/362-0836. Follow the lead of locals and stick to the cantina portion of this downtown Mexican restaurant. Arrive with a designated driver or taxi number in hand, as the margaritas, made with one of two dozen tequilas on offer, are potent and addictive.

The Foggy Goggle Route 30 South, Bondville ⊕ 802/297-1300. This club, located at the foot of Stratton's access road, hosts touring bands of often dubious quality and what they claim to be "the best DJs in the region." Apparently, Vermont's top disk jockeys prefer spinning a mix of Top-40 and bubblegum trance, so be forewarned if heading out for a night of dancing. If you're planning on partying nonstop, consider renting a room in the attached motel. Cover $5–15.

The Green Door Pub Stratton Village ⊕ 802/297-2093. Located below *Mulligans* in the village, this is Stratton's best and rowdiest bar – though to be sure the competition's not all that stiff. It attracts an even mix of locals and first-timers who come to play pool or foosball or hear the occasional live band.

Grizzly's Stratton Village. Large and popular second floor après-ski bar in the main base lodge. Along with daily drink specials, a large deck, occasional live music, and surprisingly good wood oven pizzas keep the post-slope glow alight. Open late on weekends so diehards can stay glued to their barstools in sweaty ski gear for longer than should be humanly possible.

Other activities and attractions

The most popular off-slope activity is **outlet shopping** in Manchester, the best of which are J Crew, Timberland, Movado, and Versace. More active pastimes include cross-country skiing and snowshoe trekking at the resort's own **Nordic center** (⊕ 802/297-4114), split between more advanced loops by the Sun Bowl Lodge and flatter trails at the Country Club off the main access road; trail fees and rentals both cost around $15. If looking for a day in a **spa**, both the village-based Stratton Sports Center (⊕ 802/297-4230) and the more luxurious Avanyu spa in Manchester's *Equinox* resort (⊕ 1-800/362-4747) offer a full range of massage treatments.

Sugarbush

As unlikely as it seems nowadays, north-central Vermont's rustic and under-visited **Sugarbush** was the trendy stomping grounds of New England's upper crust back in the 1960s. The local community might tell them not to bother to come back, but neither did it have much love for the American Skiing Company (ASC), which ran the resort until a group of local investors bought it a few years ago.

To their credit, ASC did much to improve the resort's sinking infrastructure after taking over in 1994, but the company's vision never gelled with locals, and after several projects, including a slopeside lodge, were howled down, the company shelved their plans and a palpable sense of neglect took over. It remains to be seen if annual numbers will increase with new ownership in place – Killington to the south receives at least twice as many skiers per year – but visitors should be the lucky recipients of the new upbeat attitude. Base area amenities, save for some condos and a few restaurants, are still basic, but the heavily wooded slopes tell a different story. Already home to some of Vermont's most exciting terrain – including **Castlerock**, a stellar constellation of expert runs – Sugarbush has well-placed new lifts and more

Mountain info

Phone ☎1-800/537-8427
Snow phone ☎802/583-7669
Website ⊛www.sugarbush.com
Price $48 midweek, $57 weekend
Operating times Early Dec to late April Mon–Fri 9am–4pm, Sat–Sun 8:30am–4pm
No. of lifts 17, including 4 surface tows
Base elevation 1535′
Summit elevation 4135′
Vertical drop 2650′
Number of trails 115
Acreage 435
Beginner 18%
Intermediate 39%
Expert 43%
Average snowfall 260″
Snowmaking Yes, 285 acres
Night skiing No
Nursery facilities Sugarbush Day School, six weeks or older; reservations required on ☎802 /583-6717

intense grooming, which have only strengthened the allegiances of a loyal following. It's hard, after all, not to feel love for a resort that decides to eschew modern resort practices by replacing an old and creaky double chair with another double chair (instead of a high-speed quad) in the name of tradition.

As with Stowe to the north, the 'Bush can be unbearably cold and even dangerously icy. And while it is based by the quaint villages of **Warren** and **Waitsfield**, those looking for a ski-then-party scene will find the valley's pace too slow and nightlife options too few. But with run after superb run matched by affordably priced lift tickets and dependable snowfall, it shouldn't be long before Sugarbush, glamorous or not, wins back the hearts of visiting skiers and snowboarders.

Arrival, information, and getting around

Sugarbush is tucked away in north-central Vermont's Mad River Valley, off Route 100 midway between Stowe to the north and Killington to the south. Virtually all its visitors arrive by car; the drive takes around three hours from Montreal, three and a half from Boston and five and a half from New York City. The closest **airport** is 45 minutes away in Burlington and the closest **train** station, in Waterbury, is a 25-minute drive away; for details on both, including rental car options, see the arrival information in the Stowe account on p.61.

The resort itself is located between the relatively unspoiled towns of Warren and larger Waitsfield, both ideal examples of New England villages complete with covered bridges and general stores. As the resort's bare base holds few amenities, the region's accommodation, eating, and drinking options are spread across the valley, with the largest grouping on the Sugarbush Access Road and around Waitsfield village, off the junction of routes 100 and 17. Just beyond Waitsfield lies the neighboring resort of **Mad River Glen**, p.103. Though a car is certainly the easiest way to get around, the valley does have a **public transportation** system in the form of the free Mad-Bus (℡802/496-7433, Ⓦwww.madriver.com/madbus). Several of the routes run only on weekends and peak weekdays, but the two most useful – one connecting North and South peaks every thirty minutes, the other heading to Waitsfield every sixty minutes – run daily from 8.30am to 6pm.

The mountain

Sugarbush likes to claim its skiable terrain spreads across six peaks, though it's much easier (and makes more sense) to think of it in terms of a **South Peak** and **North Peak**. The resort's original ski area, larger South Peak contains North Lynx, Castlerock, Lincoln, and Gadd peaks. Home to the main base and ski school, it is where you'll find the majority of expert terrain as well as a dedicated beginner's zone. North Peak, added in the late Seventies, holds the resort's tallest point, Mount Ellen (4135ft), as well as much shorter Inverness, and is laced with somewhat wider cruiser runs, a few steep plunges, and the main terrain park and half-pipe. A new lift has shortened the trip up to Mount Ellen's peak from 45 minutes to fewer than twenty, and should you want to pocket fifteen thousand feet of vertical drop before lunch all that's stopping you is conditioning.

While neither base has much in terms of facilities, North Peak is nearly barren, with only the Mount Ellen Lodge's tiny cafeteria. Connecting the two base areas, the Slide Brook quad traverses high above a wide expanse of forest known as the **Wild Slide** in under fifteen minutes. In cold weather, consider taking the shuttle bus back and forth instead as frostbite can be a serious concern. Locals in the know head off-piste to poach lines in the Wild Slide, but this shouldn't be attempted without a guide, lest you choose the wrong line.

There are a few nasty flat spots spread across the in-bounds terrain as well. Keep your speed and you should make it through them all. The one major annoyance here that you can do little about is the **weather**. Layering completely should help you combat the oft-arctic temps, but high winds frequently shut down lifts, especially Heaven's Gate and Slide Brook, so be prepared to work around these closures.

Beginner

Sugarbush's never-ever zone, with the saccharine-sweet name of **Family Adventureland**, is located to the right of South Peak's base. Though not especially large, it does have a double chair and towrope here and a lack of crowds makes learning relatively stress-free. There's very little beginner's terrain on South Peak outside of this slow-ski zone; when ready head for North Peak's collection of green runs, suitable for confident beginners though intermediates and experts can appreciate them as well. Try **Walt's Trail**, which narrowly curves its way through a grove of birch trees from the top of the Inverness quad.

Intermediate

Sugarbush's cruisers won't instantly boost the egos of intermediates, but spend a few days attacking the twisting tree-lined blues and you can't help but improve your skills. On South Peak, the best runs, including **Domino** and **Jester**, are off the Super Bravo quad. After warming up on these, take the Valley House double and follow the ultrawide **Snowball** to **Moonshine**, which dips off with some quick turns before steering into a steeper area dotted with trees every ten yards or so. For more challenges, follow Snowball again but continue on to **Eden**; rated black, it's a perfect spot to learn how to ski the trees. Over on North Peak, several long cruisers will steal any energy you have left, even after resting on the shuttle or long lift ride over and the two-stage lift up to Mount Ellen's peak. From the top, **Rim Run** to **Cruiser** to **Straight Shot** takes several miles to cover the resort's 2650ft of vertical drop.

Expert

Mount Ellen has some worthwhile black runs spilling down its peak, but you'll first have to tire of South Peak's bounty of excellent expert runs before heading over to sample them. The undoubted star of South Peak and the resort itself is **Castlerock**, a warren of tight trails that follow the steep, natural contours of its peak. Lines often form at the base of the long double chair leading up the Rock, and with limited snowmaking and grooming the runs are typically bumped out and can be sketchy in poor conditions, but that's overshadowed by the originality and challenge of the terrain. The gnarliest trail is **Liftline**, shooting straight down over rocky terrain that includes a long drop where skiers come close to smacking into lift riders on the way up. **Rumble** next door is a narrow double diamond tunnel through the trees, while single blacks **Castlerock Run** and **Middle Earth** are perhaps the most enjoyable, with variable pitches and sharp turns. The blue **Troll Road** weaves across all these, but is accessed only by blacks.

Beyond the Rock, dozens more blacks await, including **Paradise**, **Ripcord**, and the intense peak-to-base **Organgrinder** accessed via the Heaven's Gate triple chair, another top experts lift. Thanks to split grooming on these steep plunges, bump enthusiasts can chug down the moguls while others can smoothly swoop down the opposite halves. Further south are the more worthwhile blacks, including **Stein's Run**, a bumped-out double black that's the longest sustained steep on the hill.

Freestyle

It's true that more attention has been paid to freestyle features at the resort in recent years, but freeriding still rules at the Bush. Save for a few beginners' bumps and a miniature halfpipe on South Peak, North Peak is where the action is. The **Adrenaline Zone** terrain and rail park stretches nearly the entire length of the Green Mountain express quad and has a decent collection of tabletops, ramps, and rails. There's normally at least one massive jump open for the resort's freestyle team, and the steep pitch of the slope means major airs are attainable if you have skills to match. The Adrenaline Zone ends at the **halfpipe**, which the resort grooms irregularly. Should you only want to ride the pipe, a $10 halfpipe (hike-up only) pass is available.

Lift tickets, lessons, and rentals

Markedly cheaper than its Vermont competition, **lift tickets** at Sugarbush cost $48 midweek and $57 on weekends. Juniors (7–12) and seniors are charged

$35/37, while young adults (13–18) pay $42/49. If you plan on visiting often, the $42 **Sugarcard** entitles you to $42 lift tickets throughout the season except on Saturdays. The resort's **ski school** (☎1-888/651-4827) has a range of beginner and intermediate programs, starting with $35 group morning and afternoon sessions. An array of special programs, including snowboard camps and private lessons with extreme skier John Egan, are detailed in full on the resort's website. As for rentals, the **Alpine Options** (☎1-888/888-9131) shops located both on the access road and in the main base area can set up both skiers and boarders with rental and demo packages at affordable rates.

Accommodation

With the only slopeside options being a few of the resort's own condo complexes, the valley's forty-odd accommodation choices all draw a healthy though rarely excessive number of visitors come the weekend. Midweek it clears out and prices fall accordingly. There are no chain options in the valley, and the majority of inns, lodges, and B&Bs exude heaps of New England personality. The drawback is that they fall into the mid-to-upper price range, charging $90–120 midweek, $110–150 come the weekend. The most affordable option for those in small groups is undoubtedly a **condominium**, the majority of which are conveniently spread around the main base area.

Hotels, lodges, and inns

Inn at the Mad River Barn 2849 Millbrook Rd (Route 17) ☎802/496-3310 or 1-800/631-0466, ⊛www.madriverbarn.com. Located between Sugarbush's North Peak and the Mad River Glen ski area, this inn is run by Betsy Pratt, former owner of Mad River Glen and still a dominant personality in the valley. Snowboarders may choose to bed elsewhere (or be forced to listen to Pratt complain about the evil done by them) but skiers and families will revel in the communal ski lodge vibe including large common areas and group dining. Rooms are ample, clean, and comfortable, with a few sleeping six. A cooked breakfast is included in the rates, and inexpensive dinners are available to guests nightly. Midweek ❸, weekend ❹
John Egan's Big World Lodge Route 100 ☎802/496-5557, ⊛www.bigworldvermont.com. More notable for the attached pub/restaurant, this low-slung motel by the entrance to Sugarbush's access road has some of the cheapest rates around. While clean and with mini-fridges, the wood-paneled walls and muted tones in the twelve rooms are slightly depressing. Eight of the rooms have a queen bed and tiny loft with two singles crammed in and thus allow four guests to crash on a relative budget ($15 per night, per person for third and fourth guests). Midweek ❸, weekend ❹
The Pitcher Inn 275 Main St, Warren ☎802/496-6350 or 1-888/496-6350, ⊛www.pitcherinn.com. Controversial when first opened – many locals feared the high-end plan could begin wiping out the valley's more relaxed vibe – *The Pitcher Inn* has comfortably established itself atop the region's

accommodation hierarchy. Traditional in appearance, the white clapboard inn with wide porches and a gabled-roof has eleven rooms, each creatively decorated to match a chapter in Vermont's history. It's nowhere near as overdone as one might guess, and choices like the School room, complete with full chalkboard, are a delight, as are the onsite restaurant (see p.78) and nearby spa (see p.78). ❾
Sugar Lodge Sugarbush Access Rd ☎802/583-3300 or 1-800/982-3465, ⊛www.sugarlodge.com. A good value with great ski-and-stay packages, this lodge a half-mile from the main base has twenty-plus plain but clean and above-average size hotel-style rooms, most with two double beds (which four can squeeze in if desired). All rooms have TV, phones, and private bath, and one suite is available with full kitchen and a futon in the living area. Extras include an onsite laundry, continental breakfasts, and an outdoor hot tub with views of Lincoln Peak. Midweek ❸, weekend ❹
Sugarbush Inn 2405 Sugarbush Access Rd ☎1-800/537-8427, ⊛www.sugarbush.com. Impersonal and overpriced when compared to neighboring accommodations, the resort-owned 45-room *Sugarbush Inn* is at least convenient, with two onsite restaurants and a good location under a mile from the slopes. It's also the only true full-service hotel in the area, and if you're more a fan of efficiency and speed than the idiosyncratic nature of country inns, this should be your first choice. Midweek ❻, weekend ❼
The Sugartree Inn Sugarbush Access Rd ☎802/583-3211 or 1-800/666-8907, ⊛www.sugartree.com. English and Vermont styles collide in this

nine bedroom B&B, conveniently located en-route to the main base area. Best for those seeking a quiet environment, the nine colorful though slightly chintzy en-suite bedrooms range from tiny to spacious, with three holding canopied beds. A delicious breakfast is included in the rate. Midweek ❹, weekend ❺

Tucker Hill Inn Route 17, Waitsfield ☎802/496-3983 or 1-800/543-7841, ⒲www.tuckerhill.com. This handsome and recently renovated country inn en route to Mad River Glen is located on a fourteen-acre parcel with cross-country trails out the back door. While the majority of rooms hover around $100–150, a few of the rooms above its pub go for as low as $60 midweek, perhaps the best deal in the region. Midweek ❸, weekend ❹

Condominiums

The Bridges Family Resort Sugarbush Access Rd ☎802/583-2922 or 1-800/453-2922,

⒲www.bridgesresort.com. This large, well-run complex, a five-minute shuttle ride from the slopes, has a hundred one- to three- bedroom units, all privately owned and individually decorated. All come with kitchens and fireplaces and access to indoor tennis courts, indoor pool, and an outdoor hot tub. A one bedroom starting at $165 midweek skyrockets to $430 come the weekend.

Sugarbush Resort Condominiums ☎1-800/537-8427, ⒲www.sugarbush.com. The resort manages several separate condominium complexes along with two large clusters of townhouses, all within walking or quick shuttle distance of the lifts. Prices vary from as low as $150 per weekend night for a one-bedroom condo to around $600 for a four-bedroom townhouse, but ski-and-stay packages can make this the most economical option. Guests receive access to the Sugarbush Health and Athletic Club (see p.78).

Eating and drinking

The region is not lined end to end with **restaurants**, but there are still several quality options in every price range sprinkled below the base area and in nearby Waitsfield. The only choice in tiny Warren is *The Pitcher Inn*, well worth a visit if you've got the cash. For **snacks**, a quick egg sandwich or a complete take-out lunch from the Paradise Deli halfway up the main access road (Sun–Thurs 7am–10pm, Fri–Sat 7am–11pm) is recommended over the generally sub par cafeterias. For more substantial offerings, Mehuron's **supermarket** on Route 100 in Waitsfield has a fine selection of groceries along with wines and liquors (Mon–Sat 8.30am–5pm, Sun 8am–6pm).

As far as **nightlife** options are concerned, the region only gets really rocking during the busier holiday times. Still, those looking for a friendly tavern or two to visit are well served, and live music isn't hard to find on weekends. The local **cinema**, Mad River Flicks, is on Carroll Road just off Route 100 in Waitsfield (☎802/496-4200).

Cafés and restaurants

American Flatbread Restaurant Lareau Farm Country Inn, Route 100, Waitsfield ☎802/496-8856, ⒲www.americanflatbread.com. A bakery during the week, *American Flatbread* transforms its rustic workspace, anchored by a primitive wood-fired earthen oven, into a restaurant on Friday and Saturday evenings. Lines stretch out the door for the listed menu: salad ($4) and an array of delicious flatbread pizzas ($10–15) made with natural, organic products. Recommended. Friday and Saturday 5.30–9.30pm only, no reservations taken.
Bridge Street Bakery Bridge St, Waitsfield ☎802/496-0077. Next to Waitsfield's picturesque covered bridge, this cozy bakery specializes in fresh-baked, chewy bagels and croissants. Later in the day you can opt for soup, sandwiches, or the all-you-can-eat salad bar ($6). Mon, Wed–Sun 7am–7pm.

Chez Henri Sugarbush Village ☎802/583-2600. This amiable French bistro by the base area's covered bridge has been a firm favorite since 1964. Open daily from 11.30am, *Chez Henri* is as popular for European-styled full meals in between morning and afternoon sessions as it is for longer evening feasts. The lunch menu includes cheese fondue, French onion soup, and steak frites, while dinners run the gamut from roasted duck and rack of lamb to a fine bouillabaisse. Expect to pay around $15 per person at lunch, twice that for dinner, not including drinks.
Hyde Away Inn Route 17, Waitsfield ☎802/496-2322. An unpretentious, local favorite serving classic New England cuisine – cheddar-stuffed meatloaf, maple chicken, and BBQ pork chops – at affordable prices. The attached tavern has cheaper pub grub (also served in the dining room)

and a fireplace around which to relive the day's activities.

Pepper's 3180 German Flats Rd ☎ 802/583-2202. Located on the road connecting South and North Peaks, this breakfast-only café/lodge offers the best morning meals in the area. Options range from a bowl of oatmeal ($2) to eggs Florentine ($8), with plenty between.

The Pitcher Inn 275 Main St, Warren ☎ 802/496-6350. The fanciest lodging option in the region is also home to the most upscale restaurant. The menu is far more adventurous than the traditional dining room would lead you to believe, with eclectic combinations such as jalapeño-roasted duckling and grilled wahoo with lemon-mint risotto. Expect to pay around $100 per couple, including a selection from the large wine list. Open from 6pm, closed Tuesday. Reservations recommended.

Taverns and bars

Blue Tooth Sugarbush Access Rd ☎ 802/583-2656. Recently purchased by the resort, the region's largest tavern/nightclub attracts mainly tourists for après-ski featuring free soup and popcorn. Skip the food on offer and focus instead on the brews and the live bands that play on most weekends. Should things be slow, there's a pool table and pinball machine to while away the time. Open from 3pm daily.

John Egan's Big World Tavern Route 100 ☎ 802/496-3033. Owned by renowned extreme skier John Egan, this popular tavern by the foot of the access road is decorated with posters of other notorious skiers. The menu stretches well beyond average pub fare with plenty of wood-grilled meats and fish, Hungarian goulash, and some vegetarian options. There's also an extensive beer and single malt selection.

Mad Mountain Tavern Junction of Route 17 and Route 100, Waitsfield ☎ 802/496-2562. This rough around the edges watering hole is a top spot to rub elbows with the locals and sample one (or more) of the nearly twenty microbrews on tap. Live bands frequently play on weekends.

Other activities and attractions

There isn't a wealth of off-slope activities to be found in the valley. The best active option is **cross-country skiing** and **snowshoe trekking** at Ole's (☎ 802/496-3430, ⊛ www.olesxc.com), reached via Airport Road a short distance north of Sugarbush Access Road on Route 100. A pass for the 45km of groomed trails costs $13, while ski rentals run $16. Snowshoes cost $16 per day, and can be used on both the Nordic trails and on over ten miles of untouched forest routes. Indoors, the **Sugarbush Health and Racquet Club** by the base of Lincoln Mountain (☎ 802/583-6700; $13 entry fee for nonresort guests) has a workout room, indoor pool and hot tubs, three indoor tennis courts, and a climbing wall that costs $12 a day including equipment. Massages are also offered, but the best **spa** in the region is the Alta Spa (☎ 802/496-2582), located across from *The Pitcher Inn* on Warren's short Main Street. Both Warren and Waitsfield also have enough antique shops and country stores to satisfy **shoppers** for a half-day or so.

Listings

Pharmacy The Drugstore, next to Mehuron's in the Village Square Shopping Mall in Waitsfield off Route 100 (Mon–Sat 8.30–500, Sun 9am–1pm; ☎ 802/496-2345).

Okemo

In many ways **Okemo** epitomizes how to build a successful New England ski resort; no other ski area in the region – and perhaps even the country – manages to squeeze as much out of its mountain as **Okemo**. Its owners, Tim and Diane Mueller, spent the last twenty years transforming what was just an average hill in central Vermont's Green Mountains into one of the region's most successful resorts, beloved mainly by families but also attracting a faithful freestyle set.

The secret to the Muellers' success is no mystery. Okemo's **grooming** program is the best in the East, with wall-to-wall corduroy across the slopes. The **snowmaking** system covering 95 percent of skiable terrain is impeccable as is the overall quality of **service**, with one of the friendliest mountain staffs around and scores of family programs. And with the recent introduction of **Jackson Gore**, 150 acres of skiable terrain along with a tidy base village to follow in the near future, crowds have even more room to spread out across.

Of course the owners wouldn't need to go to such lengths were the mountain not pancake flat. While beginners and intermediates will revel on the silky-smooth cruisers, experts searching for **challenging terrain** will have very little, if any, luck finding it. Some formidable terrain has been created with the addition of several **terrain parks** and a **world-class half-pipe**, but those craving steep thrills should head elsewhere.

Even once the Jackson Gore master-plan base village is complete, most amenities will still be in **Ludlow**, spread out less than a mile below the slopes. It's not a particularly quaint town, though it's convenient as most everything is stretched along the mile-long Main Street (Route 103).

Mountain info

Phone ☎802/228-4041
Snow phone ☎802/228-5222
Website ⊛www.okemo.com
Price $57 midweek, $62 weekend
Operating times Mid-Nov to mid-April; Mon–Fri 9am–4pm, Sat–Sun 8am–4pm
No. of lifts 16, including 5 surface tows
Base elevation 1194'
Summit elevation 3344'
Vertical drop 2150'
Number of trails 106
Acreage 560
Beginner 25%
Intermediate 50%
Expert 25%
Average snowfall 200"
Snowmaking Yes (530 acres)
Night skiing No
Nursery facilities Penguin Playground, ☎802/228-1780 reservations required

Arrival, information, and getting around

Located in south-central Vermont, Okemo sees the vast majority of its visitors arrive by **car**. Expect the trip to take around three hours from Boston, and five from New York City. **Trains** are another option, with Amtrak's *Ethan Allen Express* route running a daily afternoon service from New York City to Rutland 25 miles away, with a connecting bus service to the slopes.

Outside of **Ludlow**, **Proctorsville**, a smaller town five minutes drive east on Route 103, contains a few more eating and overnight options. Though a car is basically a necessity, a free **shuttle** runs regular routes in Ludlow and Proctorsville (7am–6pm) on weekends and holidays; stops are at local inns.

The mountain

It took years of court battles, but with the 2002–03 season's addition of **Jackson Gore** – argued to be a black bear habitat by environmentalists – Okemo now can claim two legitimate peaks. **Okemo Mountain Peak** (3344ft) still has the majority of runs, including a southern face home to a dozen or so runs that warm up nicely in the morning sun. The front face is dominated by peak-to-base blue cruisers, along with several terrain parks and an excellent superpipe. Smaller and shorter, Jackson Gore (2725ft) contains a dozen trails, some slightly steeper than those on Okemo's main face. Across the entire ski area, the consistently smooth grooming will have you zipping at high speeds in all but the iciest conditions.

The biggest layout headache is the wide condo-lined **beginner area** at the main base area. To escape this patch, you first have to ride one of two quad chairs to the bunny slope's top end. By 10am on weekends, this portion of the mountain is a logjam of frustrated families and ski school classes; do yourself a favor by arriving early and hightailing it out of here, returning only when the day is done. Beyond here, the **lift system** is efficient, though lines do tend to form at the Northstar express quad in the ski area's center. The least crowded zones are furthest from base areas, and early on weekend mornings it's often possible to get a full two hours of peaceful riding off either the South Face or Solitude express quads before the hordes catch up.

Beginner

Despite the claustrophobically crowded nature of some of the bunny slopes, Okemo does have its advantages. The summit-to-base **Mountain Road**, over four miles long, is the most curvaceous and enjoyable green. With the overall **flatness** of the ski area and the smooth grooming, most beginners will also feel perfectly comfortable on Okemo's blues. Try **Sidewinder** or **Jolly Green Giant**, both wide intermediate trails that allow plenty of room for turns.

Intermediate

The intermediate runs here are remarkably consistent, quite long and loaded with enough rollers and turns to keep things interesting. Still, by the end of the day the blues pretty much blend together, and there are only a few runs that standout from the herd. These include speedy **Upper** and **Lower World Cup**, and **Sapphire** and **Dreamweaver**, the last two offering dips and lips that'll keep your eyes wide open and your stomach dropping. On weekends stick to the runs with the fewest crowds, often those on the slopes of South Face and Jackson Gore.

Expert

Unless experts visit the terrain parks, their scariest moments might be swinging precipitously on a chairlift during a forceful summit wind gust. Most of the black runs are really blues, although the moguls on **Sel's Choice** and **Upper Nor'Easter** are challenging. The glade runs over on the south face – **Double Diamond** and **Outrage** – are best at high speeds, and Jackson Gore has some fifty more acres of trees to explore. Nothing to brag about, the steepest runs are on South Face and Jackson Gore, including **Quantum Leap,** down below the liftline of the latter.

Freestyle

One of Okemo's strongest aspects is its freestyle terrain. There are two regularly groomed **halfpipes**, one average (Pipe Down) and the other (The Super Pipe) one of the country's best, with walls up to 20ft tall and several snowguns ensuring that conditions remain at least decent, albeit icy, throughout the year. A towrope leads back to the top, cutting out lift waits and hikes. Next to the superpipe and also accessed via the towrope is The Zone, laced with several rails, spines, and jumps and only one of several **terrain parks** located across the ski area. Snow permitting, the resort builds up to five separate parks, ranging from beginner's bumps to the massive tabletops located in Nor'Easter down the mountain front face. The glades are also littered with logslides, well worth sessioning if you can find their locations.

Lift tickets, lessons, and rentals

Adult **lift tickets** cost $57 midweek, $62 on weekends. Young adults (13–18) and seniors save $10, juniors (7–12) save $20, and kids 6 and under ski free. Note that for the first hour of each day, lifts are open free of charge so you can test out the conditions before buying a pass.

The resort's **ski school** has a very good reputation, and the consistently groomed runs make for perfect trails on which to learn, provided the crowds aren't overwhelming. There are several programs, starting at $35 for a two-hour group lesson. Newbie snowboarders should try the Burton Learn-to-Ride program (see p.534), costing $100 for a full day including two lessons, lower mountain ticket, and special board rental. As for **rentals**, the resort has reliable skis (Salomon and Elan) and boards (Burton, Salomon, and Sims), but to avoid weekend crowds head to Ludlow's Northern Ski Works, 10 Main St (☎802/228-3344), and Darkside Snowboards, across from the resort's main entrance (☎802/228-5444).

Accommodation

Ludlow's main drag is home to several inns and **motels**, and the entire Okemo Valley has more than enough lodges, B&Bs, and inns to handle even the busiest of periods. Slopeside it's all **condominiums**, many run by the resort itself. As with other mountains in the region, except during holiday periods you should have no problem finding midweek deals and accommodation, even on arrival. On weekends always book as far ahead as possible and don't expect any great deals, as rates jump twenty to forty percent.

Condominiums

Okemo Mountain Resort Properties ☎1-800/786-5366, ✆www.okemo.com. The resort manages five separate condo complexes, and all save for one (the four-bedroom Okemo Village unit) are directly on the slopes. The Solitude Village complex is tops, with an attached sports center and indoor/outdoor pool, though all are comfortable and reliably clean. Rates start as low as $100 a night midweek for the one-bedroom Okemo Mountain Lodge units.
Okemo Mountain Vacation Center ☎1-800/829-8205, ✆www.okemovacations.com. Independent booking agent with condominiums and homes slopeside and throughout the surrounding area.

Hotels, motels, and inns

All Seasons Motel 112 Main St, Ludlow ☎802/228-8100 or 1-888/228-8100, ✆www.virtualvermont.com/allseasons. Though the rooms in this two-story motel have a dated Seventies feel, the location is hard to beat as Ludlow's downtown restaurants and bars are all within walking distance. All rooms have small fridges and Cable TV, and a handful of efficiency suites are also available. Midweek ❸ weekend ❻
Andrie Rose Inn 13 Pleasant St, Ludlow ☎802/228-4846 or 1-800/223-4846, ✆www.andrieroseinn.com. A classic New England inn in an 1830s home a block off Ludlow's Main Street. The antique-filled main lodge houses nine guest

rooms, while adjacent guesthouses are home to larger suites, including two-bedroom family units with full kitchen. Full cooked breakfasts are included if staying in the main lodge. Midweek ❺, weekend ❻

Best Western Ludlow Colonial Motel 93 Main St, Ludlow ☎802/228-8188, ⊛www .bestwesternludlow.com. This buttercup-yellow complex at the end of Ludlow's main drag contains a wide array of overnight options, from standard rooms and suites to a small collection of apartment condos. Standard rooms all have two queen beds, fridges, coffeemakers, and tubs in bathrooms. There's a laundromat and a small exercise room. Midweek ❹, weekend ❺

The Castle Inn Junction of Routes 103 & 131, Proctorsville ☎1-800/438-7908 or 802/226-7688, ⊛www.thecastle-vt.com. For couples on a splurge, any of the ten antique-rich guestrooms in this romantic stone mansion perched high above Proctorsville will delight. The common areas are loaded with original early twentieth-century touches including drawn plaster ceilings and hand-

carved paneling. The onsite restaurant is one of the area's best (see below for a review). Midweek ❻, weekend ❼

Combes Family Inn 953 East Lake Rd, Ludlow ☎802/228-8799 or 1-800/822-8799, ⊛www .combsfamilyinn.com. Located in a former farmhouse some three miles from the slopes, this inn is tailormade for families. A few of the eleven rooms are larger family suites, and the communal scene is relaxed, unpretentious, and fun with a game-filled common room and a sledding hill nearby. Cooked country breakfasts served daily and three-course dinners can be added for $15 per adult, $8 per child. Midweek ❺, weekend ❻

Timber Inn Motel Route 103 ☎802/228-8666, ⊛www.timberinnmotel.com. Clean and popular motel, located in a slightly isolated spot off the Black River a little over a mile from the slopes. The simple cedar and pine walls add a rustic feel, though amenities like hot tub, sauna, and cable TV help keep things from feeling too backwoods. A two-bedroom apartment with full kitchen fitting up to six is also available. Midweek ❸, weekend ❹

Eating, drinking, and entertainment

With dozens of **restaurants** to choose from, you shouldn't have a problem finding a place to eat in the Valley. Make reservations on weekends, as the area's best choices tend to fill up fast. **On-mountain** there are several decent cafeterias, but consider picking up a sandwich down at *Mac's Delicatessen* (see opposite). For a sit-down lunch, head to *Gables* at the base of the Solitude express chair, where crabcakes, chicken clubs, and burgers cost around $10.

As far as **nightlife** is concerned, nearby Killington attracts most of the buzz. The main base area's *Loft* tavern is the top après-ski spot. The **closest** movie theater is the Ellis Theater (☎802/885-2929), fifteen curvy miles to the east in Springfield, which is why both video rental stores on Main Street are packed on weekend evenings.

If **self-catering**, it's worth the short drive to Singletons' Store on Route 131 in Proctorsville (☎802/226-7666), an eclectic grocery selling smoked meats, wines, and liquor side-by-side with hunting gear and ammo.

Restaurants and cafés

Andrie Rose Inn 13 Pleasant St, Ludlow ☎802/ 228-4846. If you can get a table, the award-winning four-course meals served are unforgettable. Entrees include curry-roasted cod with tomatoes and roast peppers and seared sea scallops with garlic sundried tomato pesto. Expensive, but worth the splurge. Friday and Saturday evenings only; reservations essential.

Café at deLIGHT 145 Main St, Ludlow ☎802/228-2150. This unassuming café dishes up the town's best breakfasts. Good-value meals include two eggs, homefries, and coffee for $3.25 and a stack of blueberry pancakes for $5.

The Castle Junction of Routes 103 & 131, Proctorsville ☎802/226-7361. Housed in a former governor's mansion that doubles as an inn (see above), this is the fanciest and most expensive restaurant in the region. Dishes may include beef Wellington ($49) and Vermont venison medallions sautéed in Vidalia onions ($47). Private fireside dining available by reservation.

Goodman's American Pie 106 Main St, Ludlow ☎802/228-4271. Thin-crust, wood-oven pizzas ($15 for a large) served in a low-key setting. While pizza options abound (you can choose from five different sauces and nearly twenty toppings) the salad menu is sparse and no beer is served. More traditional pies are served across the street at *Wicked Good Pizza* (☎802/228-4131), who deliver up to 9pm.

Mac's Delicatessen Route 103, Ludlow ☎802/228-7810. Directly next to Okemo's access road is the best deli in town, with inventive sandwiches that are perfect for packing up and taking onto the mountain. The "Saga Blues" (turkey, blue cheese, and honey mustard) and the "Eggplant Wosie" (eggplant, provolone, and pesto mayo) are both tops. Also worth a quick stop for egg sandwiches and muffins at breakfast. Daily 7.30am–6pm.

Old Town Farm Inn 665 Route 10, Chester ☎802/875-2346. Surprising as it may seem, this country B&B serves up authentic Japanese cuisine to go along with its rustic charm. The owner, a sixth-generation chef from Honshu, Japan, has created a menu that stretches well beyond delicious sushi rolls, including a house specialty of grilled freshwater eel ($20), steamed bamboo wrapped salmon ($16), and several worthwhile beef dishes. Recommended. Wed–Sun 5–10pm, reservations required.

A State of Bean Okemo Marketplace Plaza, Route 103, Ludlow ☎802/228-2326. A colorful coffee-house, filled with couches on which to enjoy one of several flavored coffees or espresso-based drinks. Simple breakfasts and lunches are served.

Tacos Tacos Lamere Square Plaza, Main St, Ludlow ☎802/228-7899. Small and informal Mexican joint serving decent burritos and tacos perfect for those on a budget. Takeout available, often required on busy nights when the four tables inside are taken.

Bars

Black River Brewing Company 2588 Route 103, Proctorsville ☎802/228-3100. A friendly and casual brewpub worth the drive east of Ludlow. There's a large fireplace, booth and bar seating, and a substantial menu with a good cheddar ale soup ($7), bangers and mash ($11), fish and chips ($11), and lots more. At least four freshly brewed beers on tap at any given time. Open Mon–Fri 4pm–close, Sat–Sun noon–close.

Christopher's Sports and Spirits 145 Main St, Ludlow ☎802/228-7822. A dive basement bar that entertains with cheap drinks, a couple of pool tables, video games, and a jukebox full of classic rock.

The Loft Main base area ☎802/228-5638. The top on-mountain après-ski spot, housed in a small and often packed three-floor barn just below the main unloading area. Advertises itself as the "home of warm beer, lousy food, and grumpy owner," but the pub grub is dependable and cold beer flows from fifteen taps. The top floor holds a small arcade room for the kids.

Other activities and attractions

Though pleasant, Ludlow is not interesting enough to explore on a day off; better to head either to **Woodstock** or **Manchester**, 45 minutes away, for a look at an attractive Vermont village. If sticking to the snow, the Okemo Valley Nordic Center (☎802/228-1396) is located a mile from the slopes off of Route 103 and has nearly 30km of attractive **cross-country skiing** trails and another 10km dedicated to **snowshoe hikes**. A trail pass costs $17, as do rentals. **Snowmobiling** is another option – check with Okemo Snowmobile Tours (☎1-800/FAT-TRACK, ⓦ www.snowmobilevermont.com) – and for skaters a small indoor **skatepark** in the Rampage teen center is open most nights (☎802/228-2400).

Listings

Internet Available at the Fletcher Library (see below).

Library Fletcher Memorial Library, 88 Main St, Ludlow (Mon & Wed 10am–7.30pm, Tues, Thurs & Fri 10am–5pm, Sat 10am–1pm, Sun closed).

Pharmacy Brooks Pharmacy, 211 Main St next to Shaw's supermarket (9am–5.30pm, Sat 9am–2pm, closed Sun).

Post office 198 Main St (Mon–Fri 8.30am–5pm, Sat 8.30–10.30am).

Loon Mountain

Reliable snowmaking, immaculate grooming, and a convenient location easily accessible from Boston have made **Loon** New Hampshire's most popular ski area. On weekends this can be an obvious problem, and during the busiest winter periods you may want to consider visiting nearby Cannon or Wildcat further afield. At other times, come to Loon to sample the state's widest mix of terrain, including an enjoyable collection of carpeted cruising runs and freestyle features to go along with a sprinkling of never-ever trails and a few advanced steep shots both in and out of the woods.

Another advantage that Loon has over the local competition is the quality of off-slope amenities. The nearby towns of **North Woodstock** and **Lincoln**, on opposite sides of I-93 from each other, offer an array of accommodation and restaurants that's cosmopolitan by the Granite State's standards. But is Loon worth visiting over Vermont's larger slopes or Maine's main two mountains? Frankly no, as it's easy enough to sample everything Loon has to offer in less than a day. Still, if the thought of adding another hour or two to a family road-trip or an early morning getaway is too much to bear, you can't go too wrong here.

Mountain info

Phone ☎603/745-8111
Snow phone ☎603/745-8100
Website ⊛www.loonmtn.com
Price $49 weekdays, $54 weekends
Operating times Dec–March; Mon–Fri 8:30am–3:45pm, Sat–Sun 8am–3:45pm
No. of lifts 10, including a gondola and three surface tows
Base elevation 950´
Summit elevation 3050´
Vertical drop 2100´
Number of trails 44
Acreage 275
Beginner 16%
Intermediate 64%
Expert 20%
Average snowfall 121˝
Snowmaking Yes (270 acres)
Night skiing No
Nursery facilities Yes, 6 weeks to 6 years; reservations on ☎603/745-8111

Arrival and getting around

Sandwiched between I-93 and the western end of the scenic Kancamagus Highway, Loon is an easy two-hour **car** ride from the Boston area, four from Montreal, and six from New York City. The resort is located a few miles east of I-93's exit 32. In between lies **Lincoln's** somewhat ungainly commercial strip, Main Street/Route 112. Directly west of the interstate exit is the more pleasant **North Woodstock**, though the small strip here contains a fraction of what's found on Lincoln's main drag. Having a car is not an absolute necessity as some area accommodations have links with a **shuttle** service, but you'd be better off with your own wheels.

The mountain

The straightforward layout and efficient lift system make the slopes a breeze to negotiate. A four-person gondola effectively divides the mountain in half, leading up to **Summit Lodge**. From here, the upper third of the mountain is home to the trails with the most personality, including a few greens for beginners, and they bend and weave pleasingly while cutting across the fall line. To the left and right of Summit are a dozen or so long blues running down the slopes, testament to the fact that intermediates are the best looked-after group at Loon. Never-evers can head to a small dedicated area on the resort's western edge, while experts will spend most of their time on **North Peak**, at the opposite end. Here a triple chair accesses a pair of long, steep, and partially bumped black diamond runs, some decent trees shots, and Sunset, a curving blue that leads back toward the mountain's center. There are also five marked gladed areas worth exploring if it has snowed recently; as very little of the resort's artificial snow gets blown into the trees, these tree zones can be extremely icy and treacherous during all-too-frequent snow droughts.

Loon runs neck and neck with Waterville Valley for best **terrain park** in the state. The park stretches down 1500 vertical feet and is laced with kickers and tabletops of various sizes along with a worthy collection of rails. Smaller jumps are sprinkled across the slopes in less intimidating "pocket parks," and toward the base there's a decent **halfpipe**.

Lift tickets, lessons, and rentals

Compared to neighboring resorts at Loon **lift tickets** aren't cheap. During weekdays adult passes cost $49 per day, on weekends and holidays passes rise to $54. Young adults (13–17) pay $42/$48, while juniors (6–12) are charged $32/$36. Seniors pay only $15 except on Saturdays, when prices jump to the full $54. If you plan on visiting more than a week over the course of the season, consider the Threedom Pass, detailed in the Waterville Valley account on p.88. Lessons through Loon's snowsports program begin at $33 for a group session, with ticket/rental/lesson packages beginning around $100. The resort offers a full range of **rentals**, but you'll save money and get better gear by trying the equipment shops on Lincoln's main drag. A good stop for both boarders and skiers is Lahout's (☎603/745-6970), which claims to be the oldest existing ski shop in the country.

Accommodation

Along with its location, a major draw for visitors to Loon is the area's selection of reasonably priced **accommodation**. Everyone from couples on a quick overnight getaway to large families on an extended vacation should have little trouble finding a suitable if unglamorous place to stay in Lincoln or North Woodstock. For slopeside accommodation the sole option is the pricey *Mountain Club on Loon*. You'll need to make reservations well in advance for weekends and holiday stays.

The Beacon Route 3, off I-93's Exit 3, North Woodstock ☎603/745-8118 or 1-800/258-8934, ⓦwww.beaconresort.com. This sprawling complex with over 130 rooms offers perfectly comfortable if slightly dated motel rooms and one- to three-bedroom cabins, often rented out via affordable package deals. Amenities include an indoor pool complex with hot tub, game room, and on-site restaurant. Midweek ❸, weekend ❹

Comfort Inn Main St (Route 112), Lincoln ☎603/745-6700 or 1-888/589-8112, ⓦwww.comfortinnloon.com. Sterile and slightly over-priced chain accommodation located right off I-93's exit 32. On top of standard motel rooms, several larger suites with separate bedrooms and fire-places are available. All rooms have a coffeemaker and fridge, and a very basic continental breakfast is served daily. Midweek ❹, weekend ❻

Mountain Club on Loon slopeside, Loon Resort ☎603/745-2244 or 1-800/229-7829, ⓦwww.mtnclubonloon.com. The most expensive lodging in the area is, not coincidentally, the sole slopeside choice as well. Accommodations include traditional hotel rooms with king-size beds, studios with room for up to four, and more spacious two-room family suites sleeping six in a pinch. All guests have access to the onsite fitness center that includes an indoor pool, hot tub and steam room, weight rooms, and racquetball court. There are two worthwhile restaurants on-site. Midweek ❻, weekend ❼

Parker's Motel Route 3, two miles north of I-93's exit 33, Lincoln ☎603/745-8341 or 1-800/766-6835, ☺www.parkersmotel.com. Basic motel located equidistant from Cannon and Loon resorts with the cheapest rates in the region. Along with plain motel units, there are larger family rooms and two-bedroom suites sleeping up to four. A single three-bedroom cottage sleeping up to six starts at $90 per night ($150 on weekends). Midweek ❷, weekend ❸

Woodstock Inn Main St (Route 3), North Woodstock ☎603/745-3951 or 1-800/321-3985, ☺www.woodstockinnnh.com. Even with a pair of restaurants and a brewery on-site (see below), the region's finest B&B maintains a cozy atmosphere. The inn rents out a dozen rooms spread across four separate buildings; most rooms are on the small side, and two share a bathroom. Affordable rates include a fine breakfast in the main house's *Clement Grill*. Midweek ❸, weekend ❹

Eating, drinking, and entertainment

After several years of upgrading the slopeside **restaurants**, there are now seven cafeterias, cafés, and restaurants to choose from. Away from the mountain are dozens more, mainly lining Lincoln and North Woodstock's main streets. While the cuisine on the whole is standard New England surf and turf, prices are reasonable and a few options manage to stand out. As for **drinking**, there's a pair of popular après-ski bars slopeside – the *Paul Bunyan Room* and *Babe's Lounge* – worth a peek once the day is done, but North Woodstock holds your best bets. Another entertainment option is the Lincoln Cinemas (☎603/745-6238) **movie theater** on Main Street (Route 112), with four screens playing the latest Hollywood adventures.

Elvio's Lincoln Square Outlet Mall, Main St (Route 112), Lincoln ☎603/745-8817. Whether you choose takeout or to eat in the plain dining room, *Elvio's* is the place for pizza. A large pie starts at around $10, and salads, subs, and basic pastas are also available.

Gordi's Kancamagus Hwy, between Loon and downtown Lincoln ☎603/745-6635. Dependable albeit basic cuisine served up in an airy, unpretentious dining room with a large salad bar. Try the baked haddock ($13), jerk shrimp ($14), or fresh catch of the day. The attached bar, loaded with all manner of ski paraphernalia (two owners are former Olympians), is a popular après-ski spot for its free eats and a friendly scene.

Sunny Day Diner Route 3 and Connector Rd, Lincoln ☎603/745-4833. The area's most creative restaurant, located about a mile north of downtown North Woodstock, is housed in a restored 1950s dining car with plenty of shiny chrome paired up with red vinyl booths and stools. Fantastic breakfasts include banana bread French toast ($6) and smoked salmon omelettes ($7), while the shifting evening menu typically includes fresh fish, steak, and diner standbys like meatloaf and open-faced sandwiches. Save room as well for the killer homemade deserts. Recommended. Breakfast and lunch daily 7am–2pm, dinner Fri–Sat 4.30–8pm only; closed Tues.

Truants Tavern Main St (Route 3), North Woodstock. Packed on weekends, this tavern features slightly better food than the *Woodstock Station* across the street. The pub grub consists mainly of burgers and sandwiches in the $6–8 range, though more adventurous plates such as veal dijonaise ($15) and broiled salmon ($14) are available after 4pm daily. A foosball table and decent beer selection provide the entertainment.

White Mt Bagel Main St (Route 112), Lincoln ☎603/745-8576. Open daily from 6.30am, this small shop is a perfect pit stop for a bagel with cream cheese or an egg sandwich while driving in to Loon via I-93. Also worth considering for a takeout lunch.

Woodstock Station and Brewery Main St (Route 3), North Woodstock ☎603/745-3951. A tourist favorite, this multiroom restaurant and brewery located below its eponymous inn has a massive, eclectic menu with nearly 100 items under the $10 mark. Nothing is particularly exciting, but most everything, from Mexican to seafood, is a safe bet. Live music and trivia games keep the bar crowd entertained nightly, while the *Clement Room Grille* upstairs serves more deluxe evening meals. *Clement* is also a top breakfast alternative for tasty eggs benedict should the *Sunny Day Diner* be overrun.

Other activities and attractions

If the weather's nice take a **scenic drive** across the Kancamagus Highway, a thirty-mile winding route through deep woods, past photogenic mountain vistas before ending at the town of Conway. From Conway, it's another thirty miles or so north to reach Mount Washington, New England's tallest peak. More active pursuits include **cross-country skiing** on the resort's own 35km of groomed trails; rentals are expensive at $22 per adult, with trail passes costing a more reasonable $14. There are also miles of well-kept backcountry trails worth tramping in the surrounding state forests.

Listings

Bookstore Mountain Wanderer, Main St (Route 112), Lincoln ⌖603/745-2707.
Internet Free at the Lincoln Library (see below).
Library Lincoln Public Library, Church St, Lincoln Mon–Fri noon–8pm, Sat 10am–noon.

Pharmacy Rite Aid, Main St (Route 112), Lincoln. Mon–Sat 8am–9pm (⌖603/745-5660)
Post office Lincoln Center North, Main Street (Route 112), Lincoln; Mon–Fri 8am–5pm, Sat 8am–noon.

Waterville Valley

Waterville Valley lacks the endearing, rustic atmosphere that saturates resorts throughout the rest of New Hampshire. That's because it was thrown up, including its condos and village, virtually overnight back in the 1960s. Today it's a self-contained community (there are only around 250 year-round residents) where upwards of 6000 day-trippers and vacationers flock on weekends, attracted by affordable lift tickets and an accessible location. The slopes themselves are less of a draw. Although more World Cup events have been held here than any other Eastern resort, the terrain is bland overall and can't compare with the challenges found at larger resorts in Vermont or Maine – or even local spots like Loon, Cannon, or Wildcat further to the north. The lack of exciting runs doesn't seem to faze the majority of visitors, tempted by the self-contained nature of the resort and also by good package deals that help smooth out the rough spots of planning a family trip. Don't be lulled, however, into thinking that the resort area is expansive or even all that pleasing. The small village, located over a mile drive away from the slopes, is basically an overblown condo complex with a handful of storefront shops. Nonetheless, with most everything centrally located, the layout does compliment a family getaway.

Arrival and getting around

One of Waterville Valley's greatest assets is its proximity to Boston, only two hours away by **car.** From other major cities, the ride is markedly longer – four hours from Montreal, six from New York City – and better ski resorts can be reached more quickly. If you fly to the region, use Boston's Logan Airport or the closer but less accessible Manchester airport seventy miles away. The resort's well-signed **village** sits on a flat parcel of land off Route 49 just over ten miles from the major interstate I-93. The base of the ski area is a mile away from the village, but frequent free **shuttles** ply the route, so leaving your car village-side if staying here is best. On weekends the parking lots by the ski area fill fast, so arrive early to avoid a long walk to the slopes if day-tripping.

① The mountain

Waterville Valley's **ski area** shares many of the same qualities that make its village attractive to families. With all runs leading back to a single base area, the slopes are easily negotiated and getting split up is rarely a worry. Cut wide and without swooping turns, the majority of runs are the opposite of classic New England-style trails. Like the village, the terrain lacks the excitement and personality that give many northeastern mountains their edge. If your interests lie toward challenging or even original runs, you're best off heading elsewhere.

All of the resort's trails spill down the 4004ft tall **Mount Tecumseh**, flat on the whole but with consistent fall lines that allow for speedy giant-slalom type runs. Most of the difficult runs that do exist follow the fallline down the center of the slope, including **True Grit** and **Bobby's Run**, short and decently steep mogul runs that are the resort's only doubleblacks. Surrounding these from the peak to the base and from boundary to boundary are a dozen or so solid cruising blues. Though there are no green trails on the upper half of the mountain, many of the blues are wide enough to be handled by all but the greenest of green riders. There are two bite-sized, never-ever areas directly by the base area, isolated enough to keep hotshots from zipping through and disrupting the learning process.

When it comes to **freestyle** options, the resort has a respectable array of features including an in-ground halfpipe, a dozen rails and fun boxes, and a large quarter-pipe.

Mountain info

Phone ☎603/236-8311 or 1-800/468-2553

Snow phone ☎603/236-4144

Website ⊛www.waterville.com

Price $39 weekday and weekend/$51 holiday

Operating times Dec–March; Mon–Fri 9am–4pm, Sat–Sun 8am–4pm

No. of lifts 12, including 2 surface lifts

Base elevation 1984′

Summit elevation 4004′

Vertical drop 2020′

Number of trails 52

Acreage 225

Beginner 20%

Intermediate 60%

Expert 20%

Average snowfall 135″

Snowmaking Yes (225 acres)

Night skiing No

Nursery facilities Yes, 6 months to 4 years; reservations required on ☎603/468-2553

Lift tickets, lessons, and rentals

Throughout most of the season, **lift tickets** at Waterville Valley are reasonably priced at $39 per adult, $29 for teens and college students, and $19 for seniors and youths (6-12). During holiday periods, rates rise to $47, $37, and $23 respectively. If planning on skiing in New Hampshire regularly, consider looking into the resort's **Threedom Passes**, usable at nearby Loon and smaller Cranmore to the north; the most popular "Anytime Limited Pass" is good every day save for ten holiday blockouts ($350 for adults, $270 teens and college students, $240 for seniors/youths); the **ski school** is affordable, with lesson-and-lift-ticket combos starting as low as $45 and lesson/pass/rental combos at $65. **Rentals** in the area are only available at the resort itself, with ski and board packages costing $30 per day. Should you need rentals on the weekend, arrive early or be prepared for an epic wait.

Accommodation

Condominiums are the main **accommodation** option at Waterville Valley, and even the local inns and lodges offer larger one- and two-bedroom units that are all but indistinguishable from a condo or townhouse. As a large percentage of resort visitors are local day-trippers, the 3000 or so beds clustered within a small area are more than enough, though during the busiest vacation periods reserving as far in advance as possible is recommended. Before booking, check with the resort's **central reservation service** (☎1-800/478-2552) and ask about current ski-and-stay packages, which can work out to exceptional savings. All of the following lodgings include access to the White Mountain Athletic Club (see p.90).

Black Bear Lodge Village Rd ☎1-800/349-2327, ⓦwww.black-bear-lodge.com. Favored by families, this all-suite hotel features simple, plainly furnished units sleeping up to six that are basically longer than average hotel rooms with pull-out bunks and a room divider offering the idea of privacy. All rooms have a TV with VCR and small kitchenettes. There's a small indoor/outdoor pool, steam room, and arcade, and kids are kept entertained with nightly G-rated movies in the TV room. Midweek ➎, weekend ➏

Golden Eagle Lodge Snowsbrook Rd ☎1-888/703-2453, ⓦwww.goldeneaglelodge.com. The resort's fanciest full-service accommodation is housed in an elegant structure full of peaks and turrets. Both one- and two-bedroom condominium style suites are offered, all featuring full kitchens, cable TV, and a dining area. Amenities include a heated indoor pool, a pair of hot tubs, and men's and women's saunas. Midweek ➏, weekend ➐

Silver Fox Inn Snowsbrook Rd ☎1-888/236-3699, ⓦwww.silverfoxinn.com. A member of the Best Western chain, the *Silver Fox* has adequate hotel-style accommodation by the Town Square. Nonsmoking throughout, all the rooms come with either a queen bed or two doubles, and a simple continental breakfast is served daily. Midweek ➍, weekend ➎

Snowy Owl Inn Village Rd ☎1-800/766-9969, ⓦwww.snowyowlinn.com. Located steps from the village, this 85-room inn with an attractive lobby complete with three-story fieldstone fireplace draws in everyone, from couples to extended families, with its wide range of room options. Everything from hotel-style units with a queen bed to a two-bedroom fireside suite sleeping eight are available. The loft-style rooms sleeping up to six are particularly good value, going for as little as $130 per night midweek. An indoor octagon-shaped pool and two hot tubs are the featured extras. Midweek ➍, weekend ➎

Valley Inn Tecumseh Rd ☎1-800/343-0969, ⓦwww.valleyinn.com. As with the slightly less formal *Snowy Owl Inn*, this full-service resort features a wide range of options. Parlor suites are attractively decorated and come with a cozy living room area, while master suites sleep four to six and include small kitchenettes. There are also a few smaller economy rooms available, though rates for similar rooms at the *Silver Fox* nearby are slightly cheaper. Extras include a substantial continental breakfast, a large indoor/outdoor pool, and an on-site tavern. Midweek ➍, weekend ➎

Waterville Valley Town Square Village Rd ☎1-888/462-9887, ⓦwww.waterville.com. These plainly decorated but perfectly functional three-bedroom (two-bathroom) condos sit at the heart of the village and are the most conveniently placed condo units. All come with fully equipped kitchens, a pair of TVs and VCR, and are located up a flight of stairs from the village base. Limited smoking units are available. Midweek ➏, weekend ➑

Eating and drinking

With the majority of local options huddled either around the mountain's base or down the road around the village's square, eating out here is nothing if not convenient. This doesn't make up for the fact that choices are largely uninspired. On the **slopes**, you'll find a pair of cafeterias: *Buckets*, which is good for ribs and beers on the weekends, and *Schwendi*, a German restaurant below the summit. The main slopeside après-ski spot – and decent for a burger or salad at lunch – is *T-Bars*, with live music on most weekends. The **village** down below has more options, but not by much, and if you're staying in a condo, self-catering may be your best choice. Affordable spots around the square include sandwiches at the *Jugtown Deli* and sub-par pizzas and pastas at the *Olde Waterville Pizza Company*. For something more substantial, *Diamonds Edge North* (☎603/236-2006) on the square's east side serves up steaks, fish, and some Italian entrees in the $15–20 range.

The finest restaurants are out on Route-49. Above the White Mountain Athletic Club and a five-minute walk from the Town Square, *The Coyote Grill* (☎603/236-4919; reservations recommended) is the best option. The menu includes grilled steaks and seafood, along with creative mains like pan-seared duck breast ($20) and a very fine calamari appetizer ($7). Six miles further on Route 49 toward the interstate is the worthwhile *William Tell* (☎603/726-3618), featuring the likes of Wiener schnitzel ($17) and cheese fondue ($13).

With its family-first agenda, raging nights out don't happen here. The TV-filled *Legends 1291* sports bar off the Town Square is the main **drinking den**.

Other activities and attractions

Cross-country skiing or snowshoe trekking is offered out of the village-based **Nordic center**, which regularly grooms 75km of trails. A trail pass for a day runs $15 per adult, $10 per child, with rentals running around the same price. Lessons are available, as are affordable group tours. The nearby **White Mountain Athletic Club** (☎603/236-8303; free for resort accommodation guests) is another popular option, home to a large indoor pool, several saunas, a couple of indoor tennis courts, and a variety of exercise programs. Other options include **sleigh rides** and **ice-skating** as well as a 4ft mini-skateboard ramp by the base area come the weekend.

Sugarloaf/USA

There are few ski slopes east of the Mississippi that take one's breath away, which is why the turn on Route 27 revealing the first unencumbered view of **Sugarloaf's** peak, the second highest in Maine, has been justifiably dubbed "Oh-My-Gosh Corner." Officially known as Sugarloaf/USA (a Michigan resort owns the rights to Sugarloaf), the ski area sprawls across a massive cone laced with trails that could do double-duty as names for death metal bands: White Nitro, Ignitor, and Misery Whip, to name a few. These trails, along with dozens of others, are celebrated by experts, but intermediates and beginners have plenty of terrain to play on as well. Up at the peak, the **Snowfields** supply the only lift-accessed, above-treeline skiing in the East. But beneath the white-capped summit lie more mogul fields and steep chutes, giant glades and lazy greens, along with a worthwhile terrain park and halfpipe. Plus, with a boundary-to-boundary open-skiing policy and the second best vertical drop in the East (2820ft), there are enough secret spots and extra-long thigh-burning cruisers to fill a week-long vacation – a real anomaly for the region.

The 'Loaf, as it's affectionately known, has a leg up on many Eastern mountains with its base facilities as well, home to an alpine **village** that is truly slopeside, not spread along an access road or located miles away. The village center is not very attractive or large, but has enough amenities for the majority of visitors. Plus with two hotels and nearly a thousand condominiums pleas-

Mountain info

Phone ☎1-800/843-5623

Snow phone ☎207/237-6808

Website ⊛www.sugarloaf.com

Price $53, $54 holidays

Operating times Nov–April;
Daily 8:30am–4pm

No. of lifts 15, including two
surface tows

Base elevation 1417′

Summit elevation 4237′

Vertical drop 2820′

Number of trails 128

Acreage 530 acres

Beginner 24%

Intermediate 28%

Expert 48%

Average snowfall 240″

Snowmaking Yes (490 acres)

Night skiing No

Nursery facilities Yes, 10
weeks to 5 years; reservations
required on ☎207/237-6804

ingly designed to be as unobtrusive as possible, staying within walking distance of the lifts is the norm, not the exception.

Sugarloaf is far from any major city and for some it's hard to argue with the fact that in the time it takes to get here, several hours could have already been spent taking turns on ski areas to the south – or even used to fly out West. Nevertheless, the terrain, **snowfall**, and **thin crowds** found here simply don't exist further south in the East.

Arrival, information, and getting around

Located in western Maine some 75 meandering miles on Route 27 from I-95, the closest major highway, the resort is five hours via **car** from both Boston and Montreal and between seven and eight hours from New York City. The closest major **airport** and **train station** are in Portland, Maine, more than two hours away; from there you can rent a car with Hertz or Avis among others.

Getting situated upon arrival is simple. The small base **village**, a mismatched cluster of half-a-dozen structures built in a variety of styles and materials, is surrounded by block upon block of condo complexes. At the bottom of the resort's mile-long access road, Route 27 heads north seven miles to **Stratton** and **Eustis** five miles beyond, and south to **Kingfield** fifteen miles away. None of these basically one-street towns are overly picturesque, though they're useful for budget accommodation, supplies, and a few extra dining options. A free **shuttle** service operates in the base area daily for those not within walking distance of the village, but to visit the outlying areas a car is necessary.

The mountain

At Sugarloaf, what you see from the approach is basically what you get. While the **ski area** is divided up into several different zones – King Pine, Whiffletree, Timberline, etc – everything is located on one mountain. There are no hidden peaks, only a sliver of a backside and, with all trails leading back to the base, getting lost is not really possible. But don't let these facts lull you into underestimating the ski area. It may only be one mountain but it's a massive one, with exceptionally diverse terrain.

Blazed trails account for 530 **acres** of that terrain, with an excellent collection of expert runs to go along with solid intermediate and beginner options. With an open boundary-to-boundary policy, the resort claims up to 1400 acres of accessible terrain. That's quite a stretch considering much of the area is simply unskiable, but there's no denying that those willing and able to head into the trees have hundreds more acres to explore.

The main complaint lodged about the ski area revolves around the **lift system**. While efficient with four quad chairs and nine double/triple chairs, the sole lift accessing the peak is the Timberline quad climbing the mountain's western shoulder. This means quickly lapping the Snowfields is out of the question, as the only way to get back up to them – save for hiking – is to work your way back around the mountain to the Timberline quad via a series of lifts. Optimists claim this keeps the top runs sparsely populated, but that's little consolation on a powder-day when you lose half an hour of precious time working back up to the peak.

Beginner

Known as an extreme mountain, the 'Loaf nonetheless offers everyone from never-evers to those looking to step up to blues a good amount of available terrain. Congestion is rarely a problem, and several of the best beginner areas are suitably isolated, keeping them the domain of learners and not speed demons taking shortcuts down to the base. The easiest bunny slope and the main learning area is the **Birches**-to-**Snowbrook** trail that runs *below* the village, heading through a tunnel, en-route to several condo complexes. If for some reason this is crowded, avoid the busier greens located toward the mountain center and stick to the edges. The **Whiffletree** area, to the far left looking up the mountain, has several worthwhile runs including some of the ski area's easiest blues. Slightly trickier is the terrain on West Mountain on the ski area's opposite side. Accessed via the Bucksaw double chair, the top green route here is the narrow and curving **Horseshoe**-to-**Lower Glancer** run that works back down to the base.

Intermediate

Though only a quarter of its trails are rated blue, Sugarloaf is still fine for intermediates willing to pick and choose their way across the slopes, so long as wrong turns onto a double-diamond trail are avoided. Cruisers and single blacks suitable for confident intermediates can be accessed off virtually every lift, with the western half of the mountain home to the best selection. The peak-to-base **Tote Road**, one of the resort's oldest runs and its longest at three miles, gives a taste of the winding trails that dominate the resort's landscape. In the same area, both **King's Landing** and **Haymaker** corkscrew down winding fall lines. Nearby the bottom two-thirds of famed **Narrow Gauge** (see "Expert" below), accessible via the Sugarloaf Superquad, is another must-hit trail. On the mountain's eastern side, the under-visited King Pine Bowl supplies more thrills, including **Haul Back** running under the King Pine Triple and **Ramdown**-to-**Springboard**, a pencil-straight combo covering over 2000ft of vertical drop.

Expert

Eight genuine double black diamond trails line up side-by-side like a family portrait on the frontside of Sugarloaf's 4237ft summit. Known as the Snowfields, this collection of runs gives the resort its lofty reputation. One of the Northeast's steepest trails, **White Nitro** screams downhill here blasting midway over a lip caused by the **Spillway Crosscut**. Though certainly perilous, Nitro is groomed regularly, meaning some of its untouched neighbors – including the twisting, mogul-studded **Bubblecuffer**, a powder day favorite – are just as difficult, if not more so. And when conditions permit, the Snowfield's

backside opens to reveal a steep rock-studded bowl only a short hike away. Still, there's plenty more than just the Snowfields. Straight down the center of the mountain, long and steep runs such as **Gondola Line** and **Competition Hill** inspire fierce loyalty among regulars, while **Widowmaker** and **Flume** in the undervisted King Pine Bowl serve as training runs for the US Ski Team. Impressive glades litter the slopes as well, with two of the toughest being **Max Headroom** toward the mountain's center and **Can't Dog**, a larger patch on the mountain's eastern boundary originally cut by locals before being swallowed up by the resort. All experts should ride the twisting peak-to-base **Narrow Gauge**, cut back in the 1950s and the only trail in the East that the ISF (International Ski Federation) has officially rated for all disciplines (Downhill, Super G, Giant Slalom, and Slalom). It's the site of numerous world-class races, and competitors have reached speeds in excess of 90mph on this trail.

Freestyle

The **terrain parks** at Sugarloaf aren't enticing enough to distract much from the freeriding thrills the mountain supplies, but there is a wide mix of jumps and a small array of rails. A beginner's park with a few small jumps and a few rollers is located on Cruiser under the Whiffletree chair. **Stomping Grounds**, the main terrain park, is on the resort's opposite end, reached easiest from the Sugarloaf quad. Progressively bigger jumps are well represented here, and the relative steepness of the slope means that overshooting the biggest tabletop might very well be the main hurdle for confident riders. Groomed several times a week, the **superpipe** located above the Stomping Grounds is most notable for its massive size. At over four hundred feet long and fifty feet wide, it may seem intimidating but is actually easier to handle with more room to land and less extreme wall angles.

Lift tickets, lessons, and rentals

Daily **lift tickets** at Sugarloaf are fairly priced, without the major weekend price jumps that occur at most resorts in New England. Adults pay $53, young adults (13–18) $48, and juniors/seniors $36. Rates over the holidays are only raised a single dollar. Though savings for extended stays are minimal, you can save a few bucks by purchasing tickets online from the resort's website before arriving. Should you plan a regional ski tour, note that extended passes can be used at other American Skiing Co resorts including Sunday River and Killington. Sugarloaf's **ski school** (☎207/237-6924) offers the typical range of classes; sessions begin as low as $25 for a 90-minute group clinic and rise to $65 per hour for private lessons. The ski school is best for kids, with an inventive moose-suited mascot leading sessions that include lunch and indoor activities. The main rental options in the village are the Boardroom Snowboard Shop (☎207/237-6829) and Sugarloaf Ski Shop (☎207/237-5010), both offering packages beginning at $32 per day.

Accommodation

The best **accommodation** options at Sugarloaf are the pair of hotels and massive web of condos in and around the base area. Prices can be high, though the resort offers a variety of cost-cutting, ski-and-stay packages throughout the season. Both Stratton and Kingfield have a handful of **budget** accommodation, worth a look only if affordability is a major concern.

Sugarloaf Village

Grand Summit ☎1-800/843-5623, ⓦwww
.sugarloaf.com. The standard flagship hotel at all
American Ski Co resorts, the slopeside *Grand
Summit* is Sugarloaf's finest full-service accommodation, with several room variations along with
an on-site restaurant and pub, fitness room, indoor
pool, hottub, and sauna. Rooms have cable TV and
VCRs, while suites include a wet bar and
microwave. Larger suites range from one to three
bedrooms with the latter costing as much as $675
per night. Overpriced unless a ski-and-stay package is available. Midweek ⑤, weekend ⑥
Sugarloaf Condominiums ☎1-800/843-5623,
ⓦwww.sugarloaf.com. The vast majority of slopeside accommodations are in the ten or so condominium complexes across the base area. The
spread includes everything from small studios to
massive five-bedroom units. While the resort does-
n't actually own the condos, their central reservation service does the bookings for most and also
hands out passes to the Sugarloaf Sports and
Fitness Club. Midweek ⑥, weekend ⑦
Sugarloaf Inn ☎1-800/843-5623, ⓦwww
.sugarloaf.com. Less glamorous than the *Grand
Summit* due in large part to its 1960s box architecture, the *Sugarloaf Inn* is at least a more affordable place to stay within a short distance of the ski
area. Guests receive access to the *Summit's*
indoor pool. While not slopeside, the inn is connected to the Sawduster double chair that cruises
directly over the village center en-route to the
slopes. Midweek ⑤, weekend ⑥

The outlying areas

Herbert Hotel 246 Main St (Route 27), Kingfield
☎207/265-2000 or 1-888/656-9922, ⓦwww
.herbertgrandhotel.com. Dating back to 1917, this
slightly shabby hotel oozes personality and faded
grandeur. The two dozen rooms range from tiny
doubles with two twin beds to a three-room suite
sleeping six ($160 per night). Rooms have few
decorative flourishes but the oak-paneled lobby is
furnished with a dusty grand piano and several
stuffed beasts. Basic continental breakfast.
Midweek ③, weekend ④
Judson's Sugarloaf Motel Route 27 ☎207/
235-2641, ⓦwww.sugarloafusa.com. Highway-
side motel five miles south of the resort most
notable for its competitive rates and on-site bar,
a locally favored watering hole with eight brews
on tap. Rooms are plain but clean. Midweek ③,
weekend ④
Mountain View Motel Route 27, Stratton
☎207/246-2033. Six miles north of the resort and
a couple of miles south of Stratton's center, the
basic, highway-side *Mountain View* has eight
accommodation options, including a pair of two-
bedroom apartment units sleeping up to six
($125–150 per night). The remaining six options
are motel units, two with kitchenettes, sleeping up
to four. Though far from fancy, all units have small
TVs and fridges. Pets allowed. ③
Three Stanley Avenue Stanley Ave, Kingfield
☎207/265-554, ⓦwww.stanleyavenue.com. This
six-room B&B – half with private bathrooms – has
some of the best rates in the area, with a minimal
midweek-to-weekend price jump and a cooked
breakfast included. Rooms have simple antique
furnishings, though they lack modern amenities
like TV and a private phone. The restaurant next
door is one of the region's finest (see opposite).
Midweek ②, weekend ③

Eating and drinking

There are around a dozen **restaurants** in the base village and a few more
sprinkled along the access road. More choices lie north and south on Route
27, but the drive is only worthwhile when heading out for a fine-dining
splurge or if you're tired of the village offerings. **Nightlife** options are similarly
accessible though scarcer, with the *Widowmaker Lounge* running the après-ski
and live music scenes and *The Bag and Kettle* and *Theo's* serving tasty homebrews. A party resort this is not.

Sugarloaf Groceries (Sun–Thurs 8am–9am, Fri–Sat 8am–10pm) in Village
West has basic supplies, beer, and wine, but those **self-catering** should buy
most items beforehand. If you haven't planned ahead, Mountainside Grocers by
the access road entry has small meat, produces and deli departments (Sun–
Thurs, 8am–8pm, Fri–Sat 8am–10pm).

Sugarloaf Village

The Bag and Kettle Village Center ☎207/237-2451. Impossible to avoid, since virtually everyone who visits or works at the resort ends up at *The Bag's* bar, sampling from a list of fine microbrews like the tasty Trout Ale. Juicy hamburgers are a star attraction, though wood-fired pizzas, chicken sandwiches, and other standards are available along with some kid-friendly platters. Live music later in the evening is common, with Monday's blues and brews night especially popular.

D'Ellies Village West ☎207/237-2490. Relaxed and affordable bakery/deli is the best place for a quick slopeside breakfast, whether it's a sloppy but delicious fried egg on a bagel or fresh-baked muffins and sugar-charged cinnamon buns. Lunch is limited to soups, salads, and deli sandwiches served on fresh baked bread. Daily 8am–5pm.

Double Diamond *Grand Summit* ☎207/237-2222. Hotel steakhouse featuring six different cuts of beef, from *chateaubriand* for two ($44) down to a hand-cut ribeye steak ($17) along with other entrees such as salmon en croute ($19) and wood-fired pork chops ($19). The attached pub (non-smoking until 9pm) can provide a quiet drink should *The Bag & Kettle* be too noisy. Dinner reservations recommended.

Gepetto's Village West ☎207/237-2192. This independently owned village restaurant is a local favorite for both hearty slopeside lunches along with more substantial dinner choices, all served in a casual, plant-filled setting. Early in the day, try the superb crabcake burger ($8), while in the evening pastas ($10–15) or fish specials are your best bet. Tuesday nights entrees are two-for-one.

Theo's Access Road ☎207/237-2211. Named after Theodore Johnsen, America's first ski manufacturer, this brewpub a short drive down from the base area is housed in an airy barn-like space. Locals and visitors mingle over the microbrews, including a root beer for the little ones. The menu includes plenty of fried appetizers along with steaks ($18–20), a scallop and shrimp gumbo ($14), and vegetable stuffed ravioli ($14). Non-smoking. Daily 4–11pm.

Widowmaker Lounge Base Lodge. Resort-owned bar that draws in the largest après-ski scene due to a lift-facing location on the backside of the Base Lodge. Bands play regularly and the large deck is a fine spot for a spring brew.

The outlying areas

One Stanley Avenue Stanley Ave, Kingfield ☎207/265-5541. Chef/owner Dan Davis's restaurant is arguably the finest dining experience in the region. Prices are steep but well worth it for such creative entrees as poached sweetbreads with applejack and chives ($24), venison stroganoff ($21), and dilled lobster on shredded zucchini ($27). Closed Mon, reservations required.

The Porter House Route 27, Eustis ☎207/246-7932. Located a dozen miles north of the resort, this converted, early 1900s country farmhouse also makes a worthwhile dinner destination. Ask for a table near the wood-burning stove and choose from such French-inspired items as homemade pate or the house specialty roast duck, along with steak and local seafood, all in the $8–20 range. There's also a substantial wine list. Open Wed–Sun only, reservations required.

Other activities and attractions

Active groups and families have several worthwhile off-slope options, beginning with the **Sugarloaf Outdoor Center** (Tues–Sat 9am–9pm, Sun–Mon 9am–5pm; ☎207/237-6830) located a mile south of the resort's access road on Route 27. From here, approximately 100km of groomed **cross-country** and **snowshoe** trails spaghetti their way through the woods and up the mountain's lower slopes. Trail fees for the state's largest Nordic network are $16 per adult, $10 for kids and seniors, with ski rentals running $18/$14 respectively. Snowshoe rentals including a trail pass are $20. The center also has an outdoor Olympic-sized **skating rink**, with fees and rentals each costing $5. Between the outdoor center and the access road is the **Antigravity Complex** (☎207/237-5566). It is frequented mainly by the nearby Carrabassett Valley Academy (a school for Olympic hopefuls) and local families, but visitors are welcome to use the facilities, which include a three-story **climbing wall**, **skatepark** with a massive bowl, a huge workout room, trampoline pits, and more. Hours change regularly, so call ahead for details. The final indoor option, located just outside of the village center, is the **Sugarloaf Sports and Fitness**

Club (daily 7am–9pm; free to guests who book accommodation through the resort, and $15 for everyone else). Facilities include an indoor pool, hot tub, steam room, weight room, along with racquetball courts, a small climbing wall, and massage treatments, all at additional costs.

Listings

Library Webster Library, Depot St, Kingfield (☎207/265-2052; hours vary).

Pharmacy The closest full-service pharmacies are in Farmington, a 45-minute drive to the south. In Kingfield, Dr. Smith does offer limited services; call ahead at ☎207/265-5088.

Post office Depot St, Kingfield Mon–Fri 8am–4:30pm; Sat 8am–noon.

Sunday River

Sunday River's greatest selling point is consistency. In a region plagued by poor conditions, the lower average temperatures of this southern Maine resort combined with massive snowmaking and grooming operations ensure that ample snow cover is rarely a problem. A paltry natural snowfall limits powder days, but thanks to row after row of snowguns so are days spent sliding down dirt-streaked trails – a boon to Northeastern enthusiasts resigned to miserable days once inferior conditions set in.

Likewise atypical for a northeastern resort, Sunday River's expansive trail network stretches like pulled taffy across a three-mile long expanse. The resort maintains that the width encompasses "eight mountain peaks," though it's more of an extended bumpy ridge than independent peaks. Regardless, the layout does give the ski area a decidedly novel feel for an East Coast mountain, with dozens of wide trails separated by broad wooded patches spilling straight down the ski area's western and eastern reaches. Toward the center lies a more typical tangle of narrow runs which are no less fun, though typically more crowded.

Due in part to this spread-out nature, the resort lacks a main slopeside center. While there are plans for an alpine village to be built beneath the western Jordan Bowl around the *Jordan Grand* hotel, the majority of the resort's dowdy amenities are currently located on the ski area's opposite end around the *Grand Summit* hotel and White Cap and South Ridge base lodges. Five miles south of the main base area is the logging town of

Bethel, an attractive and isolated country village with better eating, drinking, and lodging options than anything slopeside.

Arrival and getting around

Further south and closer to I-95, Sunday River is less of a chore to reach than Maine's other large resort, Sugarloaf/USA. Still, it's quite a hike, taking approximately three and a half hours from Boston, four from Montreal, and seven from New York City. Portland, an hour and a half away, is the site of the closest **airport** and **train station**. If you do arrive via plane or Amtrak's *Downeaster*, you can rent a car from firms including Hertz (☎1-800/654-3131) and Avis (☎1-800/230-4898).

Upon reaching the area, the short and well-signed Sunday River Road leads into the resort off of Route 2. Somewhat alleviating the base area sprawl is an efficient **public transportation** network, led by frequent and free trolleys linking all of the resort's accommodations and base lodges. The free Mountain Explorer shuttle runs several routes daily (mid-Dec to early April; 6.30am–11pm) from the resort into Bethel.

The mountain

With snowguns blanketing approximately 640 acres of terrain and an army of snowcats heading out nightly, Sunday River does just about all it can to ensure prime conditions. All of the grooming, though, does strip the slopes of some of their challenge and overall personality, and if one carpeted run after another is unappealing, consider Sugarloaf/USA to the north or one of northern Vermont's more rugged resorts.

The busiest portion of the ski area is its center, from **South Ridge** at the bottom to **North Peak** mid-mountain up to **Spruce Peak** at the top. Home to several quality trails, this zone is best visited early and avoided once the crowds congregate come midday. East of here are the progressively steeper **Barker**, **Locke**, and **White Cap** "peaks," where you'll find both the resort's most challenging runs, including the mogul-riddled White Heat, and its best freestyle terrain. On the resort's western side **Aurora**, **Oz**, and **Jordan Bowl** string out side-by-side. Cut with broad trails, all three are worth lapping for their blue cruisers and trickier gladed terrain. The main drawback on this side is finding your way back to the more popular base areas as the only way back out (via the slopes) is either the sometimes closed Quantum Leap traverse chair or Kansas, an aptly named traverse that's both flat and boring.

Each separate zone has a lift reaching its peak, with the larger areas – namely White Cap and South Ridge – containing more lifts toward their base. Efficient during the busiest periods, the resort will close certain lifts during slow times meaning an annoying traverse may be necessary. Working lifts or not, should you find yourself on the wrong end of the resort at day's end, consider taking a few more runs where you are and taking a trolley back to your car or accommodation instead of traversing back.

Beginner

The **South Ridge** zone, located directly above the resort's largest base lodge, is the dedicated beginner's area. It is accessed by three side-by-side lifts, so getting atop the various greens is not a problem. Outside of this permanent "slow zone" the rest of Sunday River's beginner terrain is more difficult to access, with green runs sprinkled across the ski area rather than concentrated in one or two spots. Once you're ready to step it up, the best places to head are either to the Jordan Bowl to run laps on Lollapalooza or to lower White Cap to try out under-visited Moonstruck or even the blue-rated Starlight. Many of the runs outside of the South Ridge beginner's area cross blue and black runs, so take a trail map to avoid any wrong turns and be aware of speeding skiers.

Intermediate

While there aren't too many clusters of blue runs here, every peak has at least a bailout trail, meaning confident intermediates can access the entire mountain. To best appreciate the ski area, intermediates should head out early and hit up Spruce Peak. From here, **Ricky Business** and **American Express** are two of the longest, widest blues on the slopes, worth sessioning until long lines form at the Spruce Peak triple. Beneath these two runs, a half-dozen more blue runs – including steep **3-D** and easy **Escapade** – work their way around the beginner's slow zone from the North Peak Lodge down to the Perfect Turn Express. From the top of this chair, take winding Paradigm into the Aurora Peak area, where **Northern Lights** awaits. Wide and curving from peak to base, it's one of the top cruisers in the East with several bumps for catching minor airs. Further west, Jordan Bowl has two worthwhile cruisers, **Excalibur** and **Rogue Angel**. Get a taste of the resort's black terrain here by tackling the **Lost Princess**, sprinkled with trees as it falls down the center of Oz.

Expert

Every "peak" across Sunday River's ski area accesses decent expert terrain, and similar to intermediates, those looking for challenging terrain are best off picking and choosing their way across the mountain. The toughest runs spill down White Cap on the resort's eastern edge. Plunging directly beneath White Heat quad chair, **White Heat** runs neck and neck with Killington's Outer Limits for best mogul run in the East. Dropping 1200ft down a consistently steep pitch, half the trail is groomed while the other half contains perfectly spaced moguls the entire distance. Less known but equally steep, **Shockwave**, one run over, is even more challenging, with trickier bumps and a double fall line to contend with. **Chutzpah** and **Hardball**, two marked double black tree zones on either side of White Heat, round out White Cap's difficult vertical. Next door, both Locke and Barker offer challenging runs, including **Agony**, a torturously bumpy line directly beneath the Sunday River Express chair, and **Right Stuff**, a groomed single black used by local race teams and a blast to tackle at full speed. Good wooded terrain is accessed via the Oz and Jordan Bowl, including wide-and-fast **Blind Ambition** and tighter **Wizard's Gulch**. Several more worthwhile black runs fall down Oz's lightly wooded face. Be sure the Oz quad is open before venturing over or be prepared for long lines at the Jordan Bowl Express.

Freestyle

After years of constant improvement, Sunday River's freestyle scene can proudly claim a spot a notch below East Coast leaders Stratton, Mount Snow, and Okemo. **Rocking Chair**, the main park located on Barker, begins with a series of rails before splitting into two lines. To the left sits a massive hit with take-offs ranging from difficult to insane, while to the right a more mellow line laced with more rails and some smaller hits awaits. At the bottom of the run both routes end at a large quarter-pipe. Toward the bottom of White Cap,

Starlight is the secondary park tailored for intermediate riders, while **Whoville** minipark on South Ridge has a few small jumps and a funbox to try. Back by Rocking Chair on Barker sits the resort's **Superpipe**, a true monster with walls soaring over twenty feet and regularly cut by the resort's own Zaugg Pipe Monster. For newbies, there's a **minipipe** on South Ridge with slightly more manageable eight-foot walls.

Lift tickets, lessons, and rentals

A few dollars cheaper than at most large Northeastern resorts, midweek lift tickets at Sunday River run $50 for adults, $45 for young adults (13–18), and $32 for juniors/seniors. Rates on weekends and holidays jump about $5 per group. Purchase tickets from the Sunday River website for better discounts. The **ski school** (⊕207/824-5959) offers first-time skier/rider packages (including equipment rental, a limited lift ticket, and a clinic) for $65, while basic group courses start at $30 for an hour-and-a-half class. Private lessons cost $65 per hour, $350 for a full day. If looking for **rental** equipment, five separate Crisports Ski shops dotted across the resort rent basic gear (South Ridge, White Cap, and Barker base lodges along with the *Grand Summit* and *Jordan Grand* hotels). Off the mountain, high-end demo skis can be rented from Jack Frost (⊕207/824-2519), while boarders should head for Pinnacle Snowboard Shop (⊕207/824-6636); both are on Sunday River Road.

Accommodation

Unless money is no concern, skip the two resort-run hotels book ending the ski area in favor of accommodations either on the resort's access roads or in Bethel, a fifteen-minute drive away. Those looking for the **cheapest beds** should check first with the *Snow Cap Inn*'s dormitory; both the *Sunday River Inn* and Bethel's *Chapman Inn* also have dorm beds with full breakfast included in the rates. The resort has several condo complexes for $110–500 per night; check their website or call ⊕1-800/543-2754 for more details.

Slopeside and around

Black Bear Bed and Breakfast 829 Sunday River Rd ⊕207/824-0908 or 1-888/299-5487, ⊛www.bbearbandb.com. A five-minute drive from the slopes, this charming B&B has cross-country ski trails leading out the front door and a half-dozen tastefully appointed en-suite guestrooms. The inn's relaxed vibe is aided by an attic guest lounge complete with a large collection of jazz and folk CDs and several working Victrola phonographs. Full country breakfasts, cooked to order, are included in the rates, and wine and local microbrews are served in the afternoon – best enjoyed after a dip in the outdoor hot tub. Midweek ❹, weekends ❺

Grand Summit White Cap Base ⊕1-800/543-2754, ⊛www.sundayriver.com. Similar to the ASC's other *Grand Summits*; this full-service hotel's strongest point is a superb ski-in/ski-out location. Inside the rooms lack personality, though the array of hotel rooms, studios, and one-bedroom condo units with full kitchens is handy for various-sized parties. Amenities include an outdoor

pool, spa, and a pair of restaurants. Midweek ❻, weekend ❼

Jordan Grand Monkey Brook Rd ⊕1-800/543-2754, ⊛www.sundayriver.com. The better of two full-service hotels run by the resort is located several winding miles from the rest of the resort's hubbub perched beneath the wooded Jordan Bowl area. This isolation is part of the charm, though plans are in the works to use the ski-in/ski-out hotel as an anchor for a future alpine village. Rooms and amenities are basically the same as those at the *Grand Summit* (see above), though some two-bedroom units are available as well. Facilities include a wonderful outdoor pool. Midweek ❻, weekend ❼

Snow Cap Inn South Ridge Base ⊕1-800/543-2754, ⊛www.sundayriver.com. Friendly, resort-run accommodation a few hundred yards from the South Ridge Base Area. The 67 rooms are high-end motel quality, and include two queen beds, TV, and access to a fitness room and outdoor hot tub. An attached dormitory rents beds for $30 per night, but clubs and race teams usually fill the entire space throughout most of the season. Even so, this is where you'll find the only affordable accommodations within walking distance of the lifts, especially on a ski-and-stay package. Midweek ④, weekend ⑥

Sunday River Inn 23 Skiway Rd ℗207/824-2410, ⓦwww.sundayriverinn.com. This popular, family-friendly inn is a real throwback, recalling days when communal ski dorms were the norm. Plainly decorated, accommodations are split between five dorm rooms and nearly twenty private suites, the majority of which have shared bathrooms. Rates include breakfast and dinner served buffet style, as well as free passes to the onsite cross-country ski center (see opposite). Dorm ②, rooms midweek ③, weekend ④

Bethel

Bethel Spa Motel Main St ℗207/824-2989. Dowdy second-floor motel on Bethel's main drag, best for those on a tight budget. All rooms have TV, fridges, and phones. Midweek $50, weekend $65.

Chapman Inn Bethel Common ℗207/824-2657, ⓦwww.chapmaninn.com. Rough around the edges but good value, this inn built in 1865 offers six private rooms (two en-suite) along with over two dozen bunk beds in an attached dormitory. The private rooms in the main building are decorated with antiques, while the dormitory has a more playful feel with a kitchen and recreation room with pool and ping-pong tables. A filling breakfast is included in the rates for both dorm beds and suites. Dorms ②, private room midweek ③, weekend ④

The Inn at the Rostay 186 Mayville Rd (Route 2) ℗207/824-3111 or 1-888/754-0072, ⓦwww .rostay.com. This cheery, highway-side motel situated between the slopes and downtown Bethel has sixteen cozy motel rooms that are an especially good value midweek. All rooms have a microwave and VCR (complimentary movies available in office), and have either two doubles or a queen with pullout couch that can fit four in a pinch. An optional full breakfast can be included for $5 per person. Midweek ③, weekend ④

L'Auberge Inn Mill Hill Rd ℗207/824-2774 or 1-800/760-2774, ⓦwww.laubergecountryinn.com. Housed in a converted carriage house dating from the late 1850s, *L'Auberge* is one of the area's most attractive options. All seven rooms are en-suite and range from spacious double-bed rooms to the Theater Suite, complete with four-poster beds and a sitting room. There's also a self-contained apartment sleeping five ($140). Breakfasts cooked to order daily, and the onsite restaurant is one of the region's finest (see opposite). ④

Eating and drinking

Sunday River is in the midst of upgrading its dour on-mountain dining scene. Except for *Sliders* at the *Jordan Grand,* you're best off heading to the **restaurants** on the access road or in Bethel. The best **supermarket** is the Hannafords on Bethel's Main Street (Mon–Sat 8am–8pm, Sun 9am–6pm). When it comes to **nightlife**, Sunday River is on the quiet side. During après-ski, the resort-run *Shipyard Brewhaus* and *Foggy Google* bars – in the Barker and South Ridge base lodges – can be counted on for a low-key pint or two. Afterward many move on to the *Matterhorn* and *Sunday River Brewing Co* on the access road or to *Suds Pub* in Bethel. If you'd rather catch the latest blockbuster, head to the Casablanca Cinema 4 on Cross Street, Bethel (℗207/824-8248).

Slopeside and around

Matterhorn Sunday River Rd ℗207/824-6271. Friendly and bright restaurant/bar with ski equipment covering the walls, picnic table seating downstairs, and slightly more formal seating upstairs. Top choices on the menu include fiery hot wings and delicious wood-fired pizzas, the best in the region. A pool table, video games, occasional live music, and Glacier Bowls – 60oz cocktails made to share – provide the entertainment. The *Great Grizzly* steakhouse in the same building serves decent steaks and barbecue.

Sliders *Jordan Grand*, Monkey Brook Rd ℗207/824-5100. The finest on-mountain restaurant, housed in an attractive circular room with large windows looking out onto Jordan Bowl. A few light items are available – including grilled fish and chicken sandwiches ($9) – but heavier entrees are Sliders' specialty. Try the roast duck in a maple cranberry sauce ($20) or the broiled swordfish ($18). During spring, the outside deck is the premier spot for a lazy lunch.

Sunday River Brewing Co Sunday River Rd and Route 2 ℗207/824-4253. Less lively than the

Matterhorn but with a larger menu, this brewpub on the corner of the access road fills quickly for dinner. Ask for a table by the massive fieldstone fireplace and choose from entrees ranging from grilled sandwich platters and barbecue meats to a Maine seafood strudel laced with shrimp, scallops, lobster, and crab meat. The Black Bear Porter is the finest of the five microbrews on tap. Live music on Fri and Sat nights, with $1.50 drafts on Wed eves.

Bethel

Bistro L'Auberge Mill Hill Rd ☎207/824-2774. This attractive country inn off the Bethel Commons opens its dining room to the public Thurs–Sat nights only, serving fine continental cuisine. Continually rotating, the menu might include sea bass *provençal* ($20), sautéed veal medallions with thyme ($22), or monkfish wrapped in Parma ham ($20). The appetizers are delicious and the wine list is extensive. Reservations essential.
Crossroads Diner Parkway and Route 2 ☎207 /824-3673. No-frills, local's diner dishing out greasy breakfasts on the cheap; a tall stack of pancakes with coffee runs $4.50. Later in the day, try standards such as fried fish, burgers, and chili dogs.

Java House Lower Main St ☎207/824-0562. Worth a stop should you be in Bethel and be in need of a caffeine wake-up call. Offers a small selection of fresh-baked breads and other assorted treats. Open from 6.30am daily.
Kowloon Village Lower Main St ☎207/824-3707. One of the few ethnic restaurants in the area. Serving up decent but basic Americanized Chinese dishes.
Sudbury Inn Main St ☎207/824-2174. While slightly less adventurous than at the *Bistro L'Auberge* up the road, the meals served here are no less tasty. Top mains include a roasted rack of lamb ($24), beef tournedos ($23), and a cassoulet made with salmon, scallops, and shrimp ($18). Closed Mon. Reservations recommended.
Suds Pub Main St ☎207/824-6558. Located downstairs from the upmarket *Sudbury Inn* (see above), this friendly and occasionally raucous bar with a substantial pub-grub menu should be your first choice for a night out in Bethel. Opens at 4pm daily, giving your group a chance to work their way through the 29 beers on tap. Thurs night is "Hoot Night," an especially lively open-mike session that's been running for some fifteen years.

Other activities and attractions

Save for driving along Maine's bumpy back highways, the sole off-slope activity that could conceivably take up a full day is **cross-country** skiing at the Sunday River Cross-Country Ski Center, 23 Skiway Rd (☎207/824–2410, ⓦwww.sundayriverinn.com). Passes for the 40km of trails cost $15 per adult, $8 per child, while rental equipment runs $16 and $10 respectively. The White Cap Fun Center (Mon–Fri 5–9pm, Sat noon–10pm, Sun noon–5pm; ☎207/824–5969) at the resort offers a range of activities mainly for the younger set, including a **tubing park** and **ice skating**, at reasonable rates. The center also runs a snowskate park, though hours can be limited so call ahead for details. Kids will enjoy the **Big Adventure Center** (☎207/824–0929) on Route 2 in Bethel, which has indoor laser tag along with a climbing wall and gaming arcade.

Listings

Internet The local library and Bethel Chamber of Commerce, 8 Station Place (Mon–Sat 9am–5pm, Sat 9am–noon), both have free access.
Library Broad St, Bethel (☎207/824-2520; hours vary so call ahead).

Pharmacy Rite Aid, Parkway and Route 2, Bethel Mon–Sat 8:30am–9pm, Sun 9am–6pm; ☎207/824-8088.
Post office Sunday River Crossing, Sunday River Rd Mon–Fri 8am–4.15pm, Sat 8.30am–noon.

The Best of the Rest

Bromley, Vermont

Located close to both the southern Vermont town of Manchester and the larger (and more expensive) resort of Stratton, Bromley (adult $46–52, junior $32–35; ☏802/824-5522, ⓦwww.bromley.com) is adored by local families for its unpretentious nature and traditional atmosphere. Spend more than a few days straight here and you may end up knowing everyone's name. The slopes have a nearly complete southern exposure, meaning that Bromley's forty-plus trails are often entirely bathed in sunlight. While not a destination in itself, the ski area's 300 acres are worth trying if visiting Stratton for an extended stay and hoping to escape furious weekend crowds. With the majority of the slopes suitable for beginner and intermediates and an unhurried, family-first environment, it's ideal for those learning to ski and board. Experts will quickly tire of the mainly flat slopes, though there are some decent glades. For accommodation along with eating and drinking recommendations, see the Stratton review beginning on p.67.

Cannon, New Hampshire

Located in Franconia State Park, Cannon (adult $35–45, junior $23–29; ☏603/823-8800 or 1-800/237-9007, ⓦwww.cannonmt.com) was home to the US's first dedicated racing trail cut in 1933 along with the country's first aerial tramway, which began carting sightseers up to the peak's breathtaking vistas five years later. Others may have long since surpassed these achievements, but Cannon's expert edge remains sharp. Even with less than 200 official acres of terrain spread over 45 trails, the resort still manages to supply some of the finest expert thrills in the region, making it the best advanced mountain in New Hampshire. More options are found out of bounds – including the old trails on Mittersill, a defunct ski area next door – if you know where to look or who to ask. Recent growth has doubled the number of green trails, and affordable rates combined with other attractions like a tubing hill and children's day camps keep families satisfied. The eight lifts here include the impressive seventy-person aerial tramway, which may seem somewhat incongruous riding over such a small ski area until you take into account the frostbite-cold winds that blow through regularly. As with other resorts in the White Mountains, you'll want to bundle up properly before hitting the slopes. Franconia, five minutes to the north, supplies the closest accommodation. Ten minutes in the opposite direction, Lincoln and Woodstock have a wider range of amenities to choose from.

Gore, New York

Located a short drive away from the upstate New York town of North Creek, state-run Gore (adult $52, junior $30; ☏518/251-2411 or 1-800/342-1234, ⓦwww.goremountain.com) has spent the last several years quietly notching its way up the East Coast resort chain. Recent improvements across the 300-acre ski area include a heated eight-person gondola, a speedy triple chair, new trails, and updated snowmaking abilities to take advantage of an unquenchable source in the nearby Hudson River. Local hype has it that these new developments will cause the low-key resort to lose its "best-kept secret" tag, but that's unlikely considering big-city Northeasterners can reach many of Vermont's larger resorts – including Killington, Stratton, and Okemo – in the same or less time. But should you be looking for a relatively rustic adventure, you could easily spend two days exploring a selection of blue cruisers stretching up to 2000 vertical feet, a handful of serious double blacks and exhilarating glades up to a mile in length.

Hunter Mountain, New York

Downhillers from New York City often head to the Catskill's Hunter Mountain, one of the closest slopes within easy day-trip reach (adult $50 weekend, $40 midweek; junior $30 weekend, $25 midweek; ☎1-888/486-8376, ⓦwww.huntermtn.com). Midweek, the 240-acre bump in the Catskills is a solid choice, with enough diversity of terrain to warrant the door-to-lift three-hour drive or shuttle bus from the city. While the alleged double black diamond runs will bore most experts quickly, intermediates and beginners have enough trails spread over 1500ft of vertical drop for a full day, and the small terrain park has hits and rails worth at least few sessions. On weekends or holidays, though, the heavily advertised slopes turn into an absolute zoo, with lift waits longer than the runs themselves and dangerously overcrowded trails. Should you only have time for a day-trip, consider somewhat less crowded Windham (see p.105) instead; for freestylers New Jersey's Mountain Creek (see p.104) is the better bet. If planning an overnight trip, the extra hour it takes to reach southern Vermont's resorts is well worth whatever hassle it may bring. From New York City, affordable day-trip bus shuttles are run by, among others, Blades (☎212/477-7350) and Paragon (☎212/255-8036).

Jay Peak, Vermont

Northern Vermont's Jay Peak (adult $53, junior $39; ☎802/988-2611 or 1-800/451-4449, ⓦwww.jaypeakresort.com) isn't located in a snow belt, it's smack in the middle of a 500lb snow girdle. Averaging 350 inches of the wet stuff a year – more than many major Western resorts – this is the only New England ski area where a powder day is the norm. And with dozens of skiable glades, some of which stretch over a mile in length, finding stashes several days after the latest storm is common. Take heed that most of the terrain is serious stuff; while there's enough among the 385 acres for all but the most green beginners to play on for a day, the best-served are those who eat up trees. Tight trees at that, and even when only yards from a blazed trail you should ride with a partner. The major drawback is that the mountain is far from anywhere save Montréal (1hr 30min drive). From Boston the trip is around four hours, seven from New York City. Amtrak calls in daily at St Albans, 45 minutes away, while the closest airport is in Burlington, an hour and a half away in good weather. A lesser problem is a general lack of facilities. The resort runs several condo complexes as well as a pair of affordably priced hotels (from $70 a night; check website for details); a few worthwhile inns are scattered around the area. Restaurants and bars are scarcer still.

Mad River Glen, Vermont

Tucked into the Mad River Valley with neighboring Sugarbush, fiercely independent Mad River Glen (adult $42, senior/junior $30; ☎802/496-3551, ⓦwww.madriverglen.com) attracts a cult-like following. Telltale signs that you've been brainwashed might include a pair of broken ski-poles barely held together with duct-tape, chipped skis, a battered helmet, and a "Mad River Glen: Ski It If You Can" bumper sticker on the back of your unwashed car. This won't include possession of a snowboard, as they were banned here long ago. Shareholders, who make up most of the regulars (this is the only cooperatively owned ski area in America), don't seem bent on changing this anytime soon. There are only 115 blazed acres of terrain, but the resort claims up to 800 more acres of "boundary to boundary" tree skiing. Nearly every inch of it is actively explored by some of the state's top skiers and telemarkers, who revel in the difficult nature of the bumped-out slopes and brag about the minimal snowmaking facilities (average annual fall is 250 inches). Some grooming does take place on the intermediate and beginner runs – on average tougher than blues and greens elsewhere in the state – but the majority of skiing is on natural powder and much of it is accessed by the 40-year-old single chair that creaks its up way to the resort's highest point, Stark's Nest (3637ft). For Mad River Valley practicalities, see the Sugarbush account beginning on p.73. Should you want to learn to telemark, Mad River Glen's ski school is arguably the best choice in the country.

Mountain Creek, New Jersey

Mountain Creek (daily 9am–10pm; adult $50, youth $45; ℡973/827-2000, Ⓦwww.mountaincreek.com) has gained an ever-growing following by dedicating itself to freestyling. Twenty percent of the 200-acre ski area is purpose-built freestyle terrain, allowing the resort to turn what is little more than a series of large hills into a tricked-out snowpark. The five separate terrain parks include a collection of various-sized hits, a full superpipe, and some of the finest rails on the East Coast. Located in Vernon, only sixty miles west of Manhattan, it should come as no surprise that overall the mountain is dreadfully flat and intermediate and expert freeriders will quickly tire of the forty short, narrow trails away from the parks by lunch. Intrawest, Mountain Creek's owner, is building one of their pedestrian villages here, complete with a large hotel, but this shouldn't change the fact that the resort is best for park rats or Manhattanites looking to hit the closest hill post-work. If you've got the time and money for a weekend stay or longer, the larger resorts to the north in Vermont and New Hampshire are a better option.

Smugglers' Notch, Vermont

Only a few miles away from Stowe but a long drive as Route 108 is closed during winter, Smuggler's Notch (adult $54, junior $38; ℡1-800/451-8752, Ⓦwww.smuggs.com) carves out its niche by catering to families. It's not uncommon for households to pack the car and drive several extra hours past competing ski areas to access the superb programs on offer at this northern resort, from a top-notch nursery to award-winning ski school programs. The good news for parents as well as those arriving kid-free is that Smuggs has more to offer than just ego-boosting greens across its seventy trails spreading over three mountain peaks, including a boundary-to-boundary policy of tree skiing and an impressive vertical drop (2610ft). There's also a pair of fine terrain parks and a long superpipe. Still, kids seem to be the happiest of all visitors, entertained by mascots like Mogul Mouse, an indoor FunZone, and even a small petting zoo slopeside. Also located slopeside is an 85-acre village, complete with all the amenities needed for an extended stay. The resort itself manages scores of condos, and a handful of fine restaurants are located within the village.

Whiteface, New York

New York's best all-around ski resort and the only region in the US to host two separate Winter Olympics (1932 and 1980), Whiteface (adult $60, junior $30; ☎518/946-2223, ⓦwww.whiteface.com) remains woefully undervisited. It's not the terrain that keeps enthusiasts away – 3400ft of vertical drop keeps grins pasted on the faces of regulars – but more the bone-chilling temperatures and long drive required to reach the Adirondacks locale, five-plus hours away from New York City by car. Should you make the journey, the narrow 215-acre ski area has more than enough terrain for a hard-charging weekend. Beginners can drift about pretty much anywhere on the lower half of the mountain (where there's also a decent terrain park and halfpipe), while intermediates have a wide selection of blues snaking down from the twin peaks of Whiteface (4386ft) and Little Whiteface (3676ft). Advanced skiers have the best choices, with steep runs like Upper Cloudspin and Upper Skyward and the bumps of Approach on Little Whiteface, not to mention the seriously challenging terrain of The Slides. Nine miles away, Lake Placid has plenty to entertain you, with a rich collections of bookstores, bars, and restaurants on its Main Street, which fronts Mirror Lake (Lake Placid is actually just north of town). There's also the small but absorbing Olympic Museum, and the Olympic ski jump and sled course – open to the public for $40 a ride – just outside town are also worth a visit.

Wildcat, New Hampshire

New Hampshire's Presidential Range is notable for stunning mountain vistas, and Wildcat (adult $42–52, junior $25; ☎603/466-3326 or 1-800/255-6439, ⓦwww.skiwildcat.com) lays claim to some of the finest in the region. Known as an expert hill, a good chunk of the 47 trails plunge narrowly over bumps and through tight glades spilling off a 4062ft high peak. (There are also some superb backcountry options off the backside leading all the way down to tiny Jackson for which you need a local guide.) Fine cruising runs include Lynx, a blast of a blue that bends and weaves its way down the center of the 225-acre ski area. Less confident skiers and riders have fewer worthy options, though the peak-to-base Polecat meanders for nearly three miles and is the longest trail in New Hampshire. There's also a basic terrain park and halfpipe. The main reason Wildcat maintains its status as a local's mountain is not terrain but a lack of slopeside amenities. This is no destination resort, and all you'll find huddled at the base is the basic Bobcat Lodge, home to equipment rentals and a plain pub and cafeteria. The towns of Jackson and Gorham, each around twenty minutes away, have a handful of historic country inns along with less inspiring motels to choose from. The cheapest beds are at the *Hiker's Paradise* bunkhouse, operated by the *Colonial Comfort Inn* in Gorham (☎603-466-2732, ⓦwww.hikersparadise; $15 per person).

Windham, New York

A day is all it takes to explore Windham (adult $50 weekend, $40 midweek; junior $30 weekend, $25 midweek; ☎1-800/754-9463, ⓦwww.skiwindham.com), located just over two hours north of New York City by car. Crowds are an issue on weekends and holidays, though they're rarely, if ever, as ferocious or loutish as at nearby Hunter (see p.103). Windham offers 220 acres of moderately diverse skiing. While the short pitch on The Wall is surprisingly steep, experts will be yawning by lunch. But beginners and intermediates have enough runs to fill a day, and a short halfpipe and decent terrain park keep freestylers happy – as will night riding Thurs–Sun (4–10pm; $22), when both the park and pipe are brightly lit. Cheap weekend getaway packages can be purchased from Windham's website, though if planning an overnight trip the extra hour's drive to Vermont is well worth your time. From New York City, several ski/boards shops – including Blades (℡212/477-7350) and Paragon (℡212/255-8036) – organize affordable day-trip shuttle buses.

The Rocky Mountains

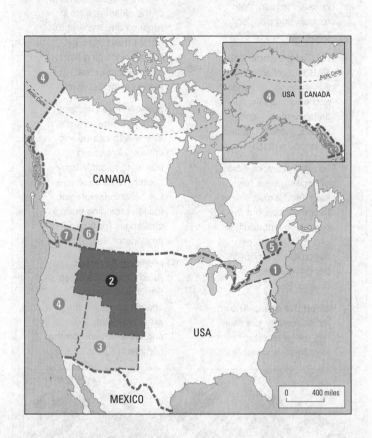

chapter 2

Highlights

✳ **Copper Mountain** Busy with Denverites on weekends, this inexpensive, versatile resort genuinely has something for everyone, from gentle greens and long rolling cruisers to mammoth moguls and powdery back bowls. See p.144

✳ **The Claim Jumper** Rustic B&B that reflects the eccentricities, surprises and personable nature of its hometown – understated, friendly Crested Butte. See p.153

✳ **Riding Mavericks** Acres of aspen groves have long lured expert skiers to Steamboat, but the resort's recent addition of a ridiculously long superpipe (over 550ft) brings freestylers in droves. See p.180

✳ **Vail on the cheap** Known for its wealthy clientele, this mega-resort is home to numerous cheap eats,

lively bars and, of course, some of the best skiing in North America, let alone Colorado. See p.192

✳ **Schmoozing at Sun Valley** A forerunner to Aspen, Sun Valley is one of the oldest resorts in America and the first to attract the rich and famous, including Marilyn Monroe and Ernest Hemingway. See p.204

✳ **Jackson Hole** The complete package for expert riders, with hair-raising chutes, ultra-steep bowls, formidable back-country routes and even the occasional foraging moose providing enough challenges for trips of any length. See p.237

✳ **Freeriding Silverton** Amid Colorado's steep San Juans, just one chairlift accesses the only completely ungroomed resort on the continent. See p.250

2

The Rocky Mountains

S traddling the Continental Divide, that broad backbone of the American West, the resorts of the **Rocky Mountains** are the highest in North America. Reliably blitzed with light and dry snow, and dotted with restored mining towns that appeal to a romantic aesthetic of the Wild West, the region is synonymous with skiing. **Colorado** alone records more skier visits annually than California and Utah combined, while **Idaho**, **Montana**, and **Wyoming** all boast major, if isolated, ski areas.

Southern Idaho's glitzy **Sun Valley** was the original Rocky Mountain destination, wowing guests with the world's first chairlift when the resort debuted in 1936. Lower profile and significantly cheaper, rapidly growing **Schweitzer**, in the north of the state, suffers the same drawback as all the Rocky Mountain resorts outside of Colorado – a remote location. Flights into the small regional airports serving these ski towns are expensive, and the journey can be frustratingly long; however, the inconvenience has its virtue, manifested in nonexistent liftlines. The emptiness is almost eerie during quiet periods in Montana's purpose-built resort of **Big Sky**, some 45 miles south of Bozeman. Though less widely known, the ski areas outside the hip town of **Whitefish** and small frontier settlement of **Red Lodge** (on the edges of Glacier and Yellowstone National Parks, respectively) have more to offer off the slopes. The busiest and most renowned of the northern Rockies resorts is Wyoming's **Jackson Hole**, a breeding ground of vertiginous peaks and chutes. **Grand Targhee**, cut off from the crowds on the western slope of the towering Tetons, is Jackson's low-key neighbor, though the ski area's reputation is growing as tales of its epic powder spread.

The resorts that flank Colorado's major interstate, I-70, west of Denver, provide a much different experience. Though the slopes are relatively uncluttered midweek and the mountainous landscape gratifyingly wild, the ski communities that cluster around here possess a decidedly suburban flair. Skiers speeding up the freeway en route to more renowned resorts often overlook **Loveland**, a mere 71 miles from Denver and the only sizeable ski area on the eastern slope of the Continental Divide. **Winter Park** is tucked over treacherous Berthoud Pass to the north; like Loveland, the family-friendly resort is visited primarily by Denverites, and is much less commercial than its busy **Summit County** neighbors to the west. Of these, small but steep **Arapahoe Basin** is the cheapest and draws a cultlike following; **Copper** is most underrated; **Breckenridge** has a party-town atmosphere; and condo-heavy **Keystone** receives considerably less snow than the 300-plus annual inches that are the Colorado norm.

Vail lies thirty minutes further west along I-70. With acres of open-bowl skiing and miles of intermediate trails, this is the largest ski area in the US, even before the manicured acres of its snooty but satisfyingly steep sister resort

THE ROCKY MOUNTAINS (US)

CANADA

USA

ALBERTA

SASKATCHEWAN

NORTH DAKOTA

SOUTH DAKOTA

MONTANA

WYOMING

IDAHO

OREGON

N

Priest Lake

Schweitzer

Big Mountain

Whitefish

Coeur d'Alene

Flathead Lake

Missoula

BITTERROOT MOUNTAINS

Salmon River

Brundage

McCall

Bogus Basin

Boise

Snake River

Sun Valley

Lincoln

Butte

Great Falls

Missouri River

Missouri River

Bridger Bowl

Bozeman

Big Sky

Big Sky

West Yellowstone

Red Lodge

Yellowstone River

Grand Targhee

Teton Village

Jackson Hole

Jackson

Pocatello

Lander

Bighorn River

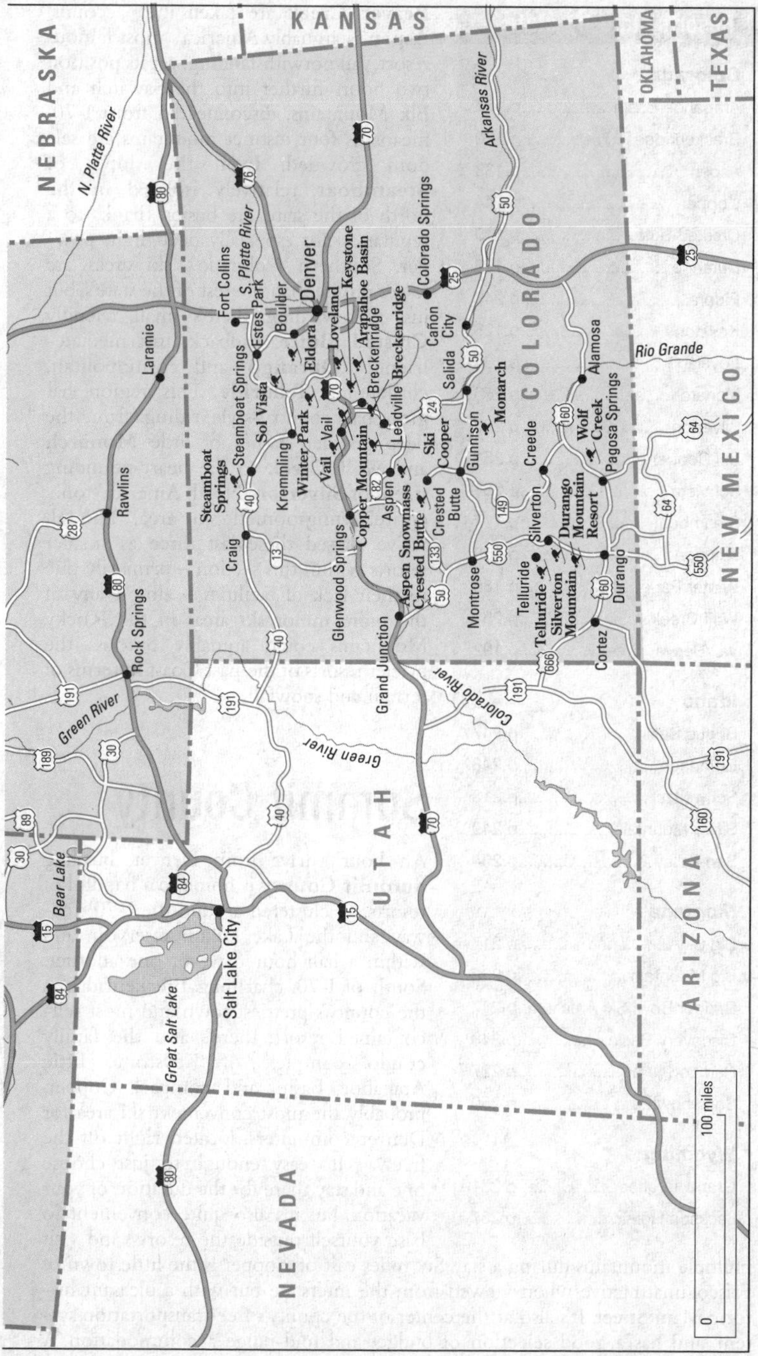
NEBRASKA
KANSAS
OKLAHOMA
TEXAS
COLORADO
NEW MEXICO
UTAH
ARIZONA
NEVADA
N. Platte River
S. Platte River
Arkansas River
Rio Grande
Green River
Colorado River
Bear Lake
Great Salt Lake
Salt Lake City
Denver
Fort Collins
Estes Park
Boulder
Eldora
Loveland
Keystone
Arapahoe Basin
Breckenridge
Colorado Springs
Cañon City
Salida
Monarch
Leadville
Ski Cooper
Gunnison
Crested Butte
Aspen
Aspen Snowmass
Copper Mountain
Vail
Winter Park
Sol Vista
Kremmling
Steamboat Springs
Craig
Glenwood Springs
Grand Junction
Montrose
Telluride
Silverton
Silverton Mountain
Durango Mountain Resort
Durango
Cortez
Creede
Wolf Creek
Pagosa Springs
Alamosa
Laramie
Rawlins
Rock Springs
80
76
70
25
50
24
82
40
13
133
550
149
160
64
287
191
30
189
89
84
15
666
100 miles
0

Beaver Creek are taken into account. **Aspen** is arguably America's most famous resort, Vail notwithstanding, yet its position two hours further into the Sawatch and Elk Mountains, disconnected from I-70, means its four distinct mountains are seldom crowded. Even the slopes of **Steamboat**, relatively isolated in the north of the state, are busier, thanks to a reputation for especially deep, light powder. Southern Colorado's ski areas are lower profile than the rest of the state's, but just as rewarding: there's small, friendly **Crested Butte**; laidback, intermediate-friendly **Durango**, and cosmopolitan, challenging **Telluride**. This region has great backcountry-style riding, from the deep powder stashes of little **Monarch** and **Wolf Creek** to the heart-pounding steeps of **Silverton**, North America's only entirely ungroomed ski area. Though we've classed these last three as smaller resorts within this section – primarily due to their lack of facilities – almost any of the more minor ski areas in the Rocky Mountains could arguably outclass the pricier resorts of the East Coast in terms of terrain and snowfall.

Summit County

An hour's drive from Denver, bustling **Summit County** is home to a handful of resorts, all clustered around the I-70 freeway and the Lake Dillon reservoir, and within a half-hour drive of one another. South of I-70, charming Breckenridge is the county's prettiest town and most self-contained resort; there's also the family condo complex of Keystone, little Arapahoe Basin, and compact Copper, probably the most convenient ski area for Denver commuters, located right off the freeway. It's easy enough to just choose one and stay there for the duration of your vacation, but it's also quite convenient to base yourself outside the resorts, and visit multiple mountains during a stay. Six miles east of Copper is the little town of Frisco, unattractive when viewed from the interstate but with a pleasant historic Main Street. It's also at the center of the county's free transportation system, and has a good selection of budget and mid-range accommodation. A short drive east, the towns of Dillon and Silverthorne squat at the northern end of Lake Dillon, a gray collection of factory stores, strip malls, motels, and condos bisected by the freeway.

Arrival, information, and getting around

Conditions and traffic permitting, the towns and resorts of Summit County are less than two hours from Denver along I-70, on the western side of the Eisenhower Tunnel. Buses run daily from Denver and Denver International Airport (less than $15 each way; see above for this and more expensive shuttle options). Meanwhile, Greyhound calls in at the Frisco transit center, 1010 Meadow Drive (☎970/668-8917), just behind Safeway off I-70, exit 203. The transit center is the hub of the Summit Stage (☎970/668-0999, ⓦwww .co.summit.co.us), a comprehensive **free bus system** serving the county and linking to the free shuttles within each ski resort. Buses run every half-hour during the morning and afternoon ski commute, with hourly service at other times (from 6-6.30am to 1-1.30am). The KAB Express (☎970/496-4200) connects Breckenridge directly to Keystone and Arapahoe Basin, while Vail Resorts Express operates a daily shuttle service from Breckenridge and Keystone to Vail and Beaver Creek, stopping at the Frisco transit center enroute; reservations are required (☎970/469-8245, $12 in advance, $15 walk-on). A large free Park & Ride lot is located next to the transit center.

The Summit County Chamber of Commerce (☎1-800/530-3099, ⓦwww .summitchamber.org) runs two **visitor centers**, one by the factory stores just off I-70 in Silverthorne, at 246 Rainbow Drive (☎970/262-0817), and one in Frisco, at 916 North Summit (daily 9am–5pm; ☎970/668-2051).

Lift tickets and rentals

The cheapest way to ski in Summit County is on a prepurchased **season pass**. The Buddy Pass (from $299) covers Breckenridge, Keystone, and Arapahoe Basin, while the Colorado Pass (from $319) also includes ten days of skiing at Vail and Beaver Creek. Passes must be purchased in-state.

You can typically **rent gear** from an independent outlet near each Summit ski area; these are listed in the relevant sections. An alternative is to rent in Silverthorne, Dillon, or Frisco, where you'll find a rash of rather dated outlets; prices tend to be a little cheaper, and discount lift tickets are usually available. Most locally reputed of the pack is Mountain Sports Outlet, south of 1-70 behind Arby's, Silverthorne (℡970/262-2836), where ski rental packages start at $10, snowboards from $20, and can be prebooked at ⓦwww.rentskis.com. ReCycle Ski and Sport, 842 Summit Blvd, Frisco (℡970/668-5150), is a huge barn of a place selling used skis and boards and with a nice sideline in tuning. At the top end of the spectrum is Wilderness Sports, 400 Main St, Frisco (℡970/668-8804), with two locations in Silverthorne as well; this is the main local backcountry store, with notice boards, great rental rates on regular skis (from $10) and boards ($20), in addition to snowshoes, telemark, and backcountry ski rental.

Accommodation

Silverthorne/Dillon and Frisco make inexpensive alternative bases to the resorts themselves. **Accommodation** in the former is almost all blocky motel lodging and rambling condo complexes, while more pedestrian-friendly Frisco is home to cuter, if a bit old-fashioned lodges, some with dorm-style accommodation. To rent a condo or mountain home in the county, contact Summit County Central Reservations (℡800/365-6365, ⓦwww.centralres.net), who can refer you onto smaller property management companies if necessary, and also book B&Bs or lodges.

Dillon/Silverthorne

Alpen Hütte Lodge-Hostelling 471 Rainbow Drive, Silverthorne ℡970/468-6336, ⓦwww.alpenhutte.com. Tudor-beamed, traditional hostel standing alone in a large parking lot between the creek and factory stores. Facilities include two comfy lounges and a kitchen, private rooms, and clean dorms; a midnight curfew is imposed. Office hours 7am–noon and 4pm–midnight. Dorms $23–29, rooms ❸

Home & Hearth B&B 1518 Rainbow Drive, Dillon ℡970/468-5541, ⓦwww.colorado-bnb.com/hhearth. Relaxed, good-value five-bedroom home on the outskirts of Dillon, warmed by potbellied stoves and offering Nintendo, studio space, and a rustic outdoors tub. One room has four bunks. ❸

The Lodge at Carolina in the Pines 864 E Anemone Trail, Dillon ℡970/262-7500, ⓦwww.carolinainthepines.com. Large, upscale B&B, surrounded by pines and close to Lake Dillon. Décor of the ten rooms ranges from flouncy to backwoods rustic, all stylishly done; amenities include two lounges, outdoor tub, sauna, and extensive

video collection. Popular for weddings; no children under thirteen. ❻–❼

Silver Inn 691 Blue River Pkwy, Silverthorne ℡970/513-0104 or 888/513-0104, silverinn@aol.com. Independent motel lacking in aesthetic charms, but family-run, clean, and affordable, with spacious rooms, fridges, communal microwave, sauna, and hot tub. ❸

Wildernest Silverthorne ℡800/554-2212, ⓦwww.wildernest.com. Stay where the locals live, in a huge condo neighborhood on the hill above Silverthorne. Studios from ❹, two beds from ❻, on holidays prices almost double.

Frisco

Alpine Inn 105 Lusher Ct ℡970/668-3122 or 800/314-3122, alpinein@summit.net. Recently built motel right by I-70, with an indoor heated pool and hot tub, clean rooms, and reasonable rates, right next to the Frisco Transportation Center. ❸

Frisco Lodge 321 Main St ℡970/668-0195 or 800/279-6000, ⓦwww.friscolodge.com. Creaky,

The backcountry

The **backcountry descents** of Summit County are well traveled. Loveland Pass is one of the most famous backcountry areas in the country, with long, powder-drenched runs spilling east and west off the Continental Divide. Easily accessed off Hwy-6 (take the Loveland Pass exit off I-70 or continue east on Hwy-6 past A-Basin), the eastern descents are the most popular; lines plunge off the horseshoe ridgeline into an open bowl crested with cornices, funneling down into tight trees. Less sheltered, longer routes off the southwest side drop all the way down into the A-Basin ski area but require a longer initial hike and are more prone to avalanche. The usual backcountry precautions should be taken.

Almost as popular are the areas reached through the access gates at A-Basin; the tight trees of the Beavers and the open bowl runs down to Montezuma are well known to Basin locals. Breck's gates are used to get to the goods on neighboring peaks in the Ten Mile range; south of town, Forest Service trails lead up to descents off Boreas Pass, Hoosier Pass, and Quandary Peak. Stop in at one of the Wilderness stores (listed in rentals) for local advice, and check out the excellent First Trax site (ⓦwww.firsttrax.com). For avalanche info, check out http://geosurvey.state.co.us /avalanche/.

atmospheric old lodge – the oldest in Summit County – located in the center of town; some rooms share bathrooms. Cooked buffet breakfast and teatime snacks are served in the cluttered lounge; free Web access is included, and the friendly owners have arranged great lift ticket deals with Copper. Shared bath from ❸.
Galena Street Mountain Inn 106 Galena St ☎970/668-3224 or 800/248-9138, ⓦcolorado-bnb.com/galena. This very modern backstreet home is rather different to the average B&B, with fourteen spotless guest rooms (all with VCRs), a café-style dining area, and a bright, contemporary feel throughout. Welcoming hosts proffer cookies and cooked breakfasts; the hot tub is tucked into a conservatory. ❹–❺
Hotel Frisco 308 Main St ☎970/668-5009 or 800/262-1002, ⓦwww.hotelfrisco.com. At the center of Frisco's Victorian Main Street, rooms in this refurbished old townhome are simply furnished; some have their own deck and tub. High-speed Internet access is available in the small library. ❸
Just Bunks 208 Teller St ☎970/668-4757,

ⓦwww.hostels.com/justbunks. Just one bright, clean bunkroom boasting two log-furniture bunks, a modern fireplace, and TV; linens are provided. Use of the owner's kitchen is permitted, and they even throw in free passes to the Frisco Nordic Center. ❸
Snowshoe Motel 521 Main St ☎970/668-3444, ⓦwww.summitcountycolorado.com/snowshoemo-tel/. Squat gray building with very basic but clean rooms. Good rates for the area, though the "continental breakfast" is little more than powdered donuts; kitchenettes available for a few extra bucks. ❷
Woods Inn 205 S 2nd Ave ☎970/668-2255 or 877/664-3777, ⓦwww.woodsinnbandb.com. Just off Main Street, this warm home contains a couple of comfy dorm rooms ($22–28 per bunk) and a few somewhat overpriced doubles above a rather chaotic kitchen and lounge. Next door, the recently built two-story inn building houses twelve simply decorated motel-style rooms and suites, sleeping four to fourteen; some have kitchenettes. All guests may use the hot tub in the pretty pagoda on the lawn. ❹–❾

Eating

Summit County is no culinary hotspot, best for its range of budget and mid-range restaurants, with Frisco's Main Street the most appealing location for those who like to browse a selection of menus before choosing a spot.

Dillon/Silverthorne

Arapahoe Café and Pub 626 Lake Dillon Drive, Dillon ☎970/468-0873. Cute wooden cottage by the marina; the dinner menu verges on traditional fine dining but the place is most popular with the

locals for hearty breakfasts en route to Keystone or A-Basin. Breakfast 7am-2.30pm, lunch 11am–2.30pm, dinner 5–9pm.
Blue Moon Bakery 249 Summit Summit Place Shopping Center, Silverthorne ☎970/468-1472.

Hefty sandwiches, breakfast bagels, and pastries to go, with a small eat-in area for more substantial fodder. 6.30am–2.30pm.

Dillon Dam Brewery 100 Little Dam Rd, Dillon ☎970/262-7777. Regulars of all ages prop up the giant U-shaped bar of this spacious brewpub after a day spent hard at work on the mountains of A-Basin and Keystone. Dam Straight Lager and other beers come direct from shiny vats in the corner, and the alcohol is tempered by an inventive but hearty bar menu. 11.30am–10pm.

Fiesta Jalisco 269 Summit Place Shopping Center, Silverthorne ☎970/468-9552 (also at 224 S Main, Breckenridge ☎970/547-3836). Dark, family-style Mexican restaurant, serving enchiladas, burritos, and combination plates for lunch and dinner; inexpensive.

The Historic Mint 347 Blue River Parkway ☎970/468-5247. Fusty family steakhouse where diners flame-broil their own dinners. Excellent value, with surprisingly tender all-you-can eat steak from $10, and a huge salad bar.

Masatos City Market Center, Hwy-6 ☎970/262-6600. Decent sushi, tempura, and noodles at just slightly inflated prices, though there are $5.95 lunch specials. Mon–Fri 11.30am–2pm, nightly 5–10pm. Reservations recommended.

Sunshine Café Summit Place Shopping Center, Silverthorne ☎970/468-6663. Locals' choice for leisurely breakfasts and brunch, with healthy options and substantial egg platters cheerfully served. Handily located next to Wilderness Sports. 7am–3pm.

Wild Bills Stone Oven Pizza 119 La Bonte St, Dillon ☎970/468-2006. Up in the Dillon marina, this low-key, low-ceilinged pizza place, with its comfy booths, pool table, and weekend band nights, makes a good pit stop en route to the bowling alley up the road. 11.30am–11.30pm.

Frisco

Backcountry Brewery 710 Main St ☎970/668-2337. Giant, two-story brewpub on the corner of Main and Hwy-6, with decent homebrews and a good selection of après appetizers, a pizzeria, and a seriously long salad and potato bar.

Barkley's Margaritagrille 620 Main St ☎970/668-3694. Rib house meets Mexican in Frisco's basement entertainment empire: a sports bar, club, and pizza place are found on the same premises. Don't let that put you off: this family-friendly restaurant offers decent, if not particularly authentic, burritos, fish tacos, and ribs.

The Blue Spruce Inn 20 Main St ☎970/668-5900. Charming blue-painted wooden cottage in operation since 1947, boasting an atmospheric saloon in addition to the dining room. Manages to offer both elegant, eclectic dinners and an inexpensive but inventive bar menu, for which feat it receives heaps of praise from both locals and visitors alike. Reservations recommended. Happy hour 4–6pm, dinner 5–10pm.

Butterhorn Bakery & Café 408 Old Main St ☎970/668-3997. The more grab-it-and-go of Frisco's two excellent breakfast haunts, though there's nothing to stop you lingering over Eggy Bread, skillets, or pancakes, surrounded by racks of heavenly scented cookies, muffins, brownies, and cakes. Sandwiches and homemade soups for lunch. Mon 7.30am–4pm, Wed–Sun 7.30am–5pm.

Log Cabin Café 121 Main St ☎970/668-3947. Mountain Man breakfasts for the hugely hungry include pork chops, grits, and hotcakes, but inexpensive one-egg specials, oatmeal, and single pancakes are also on the menu. Since breakfast is served until 2pm and the little place has a phenomenal reputation, the line out the door is almost a permanent fixture. Additional lunch items include jumbo burgers and salads. Mon–Fri 6am–2pm, Sat–Sun 7am–2pm.

Rocky Mountain Coffee Roasters 285 Main St ☎970/668-3470. According to the sticker on the tip jar, friends don't let friends drink at Starbucks, they leave them a mug behind the counter in this lived-in little store. A good place to pick up breakfast bagels, granola, or a cup of coffee to go. Internet access, too.

Tuscato 307 Main St, Frisco ☎970/668-3644. Faux-rustic traditional Italian, reasonably priced (pasta entrees are $10–15, others a few dollars more) and popular with locals looking to go a little upscale.

Drinking and entertainment

If you're looking for the local party town, head to Breckenridge; otherwise, Frisco has a couple of spots on Main Street popular with locals. The local multiplex is on Hwy-6 in Dillon, with bowling and billiards up the hill in the marina district.

Barkley's West 610 Main St, Frisco ☎970/389-6940. Pool, arcade games, DJs, shows, and pizza by the slice downstairs from Barkely's Margaritagrille.

Moose Jaw 208 Main St, Frisco ☎970/668-3931. Divey, Western-style bar with a limited bar menu but a regular local drinking crowd.

Other activities and attractions

The **Frisco Nordic Center**, 18454 Hwy-9 (☏970/668-0866, ⊛www.colorado .net/~nord/, 9am–4pm daily, trail passes $14, beginner packages from $30), maintains 43km of trails through the White River National Forest, on the shores of Lake Dillon. Rentals (from $14) and tune-ups are available from the comfy log cabin lodge.

There are also **cross-country** trails at the golf course in Silverthorne, 2929 Golden Eagle Rd, and an ice-skating area on the corner of Hamilton Road and Hwy-9 (dawn until dusk, Dec–Feb). More information on these is available from the Silverthorne Rec Center, 430 Rainbow Drive (Mon–Fri 6am–9pm, Sat 7am–9pm, Sun 8am–9pm; pool Mon–Fri 6.30am–8.30pm, Sat–Sun 9am–8.30pm, day pass including classes $8.50; ☏970/262-7372). Though not quite as nice as the center in Breckenridge, it boasts a pool complex with waterslide, indoor track, and racquetball courts, and offers a full roster of fitness and yoga classes.

Arapahoe Basin

Conduct a straw poll of Summit County skiers and a surprising number would name **Arapahoe Basin** (alternately A-Basin or just 'the Basin') as their favorite. Small in acreage but not in stature, this no-frills, five-lift mountain is revered by hardcore skiers and backcountry riders for the steepest in-bounds slopes in Summit County and, more notably, the highest terrain on the continent. Opened with one tow in 1946 – the first in the state – A-Basin was something of a Colorado pioneer. Even now, despite various shifts in ownership, the Basin retains an independence from its partner Vail Resorts. There are no condos or hotels at its base, no store-lined plazas, no extensive network of carefully groomed blues. In bad weather, A-Basin is the toughest Summit County resort to reach, and the slow lifts and stark terrain are exposed to driving winter storms. Offering only the most basic facilities, natural, rocky terrain, and affordable passes, skiing, and skiing hard, takes priority here.

Not that regulars don't know how to have a good time off their skis. Thanks to the impressive elevation and traditionally

Mountain info

Phone ☏970/468-0718 or 888/ARAPAHOE (272-7246)

Snow phone Same as above

Website ⊛www.arapahoebasin.com

Price $47

Operating times Nov–June daily 9am–4pm; Exo and Pal lifts 8.30am Sat, Sun, & holidays

No. of lifts 5

Base elevation 10780′

Summit elevation 13050′

Vertical drop 3978′

No. of trails 66

Acreage 490

Beginner 15%

Intermediate 45%

Expert 40%

Average snowfall 367″

Snowmaking New in 2002/03 (125 acres)

Night skiing No

Nursery facilities Yes, ages 1–3 years, ☏888/272-7246; skiing 4–14, snowboarding 9–14

decent snowfall, the season here typically stretches into June, and summer pre, during, and après-ski on-mountain and in the parking lot is legendary. Though the past decade has witnessed some perturbingly dry seasons, years of should-we-shouldn't-we local negotiations and Forest Service wrangling have finally ended with the installation of snowmaking at the Basin. Purists are not pleased, but a Fourth of July closing date now looks to be a more regular occurrence.

Arrival, information, and getting around

Only 64 miles west of Denver, A-Basin is the closest Summit County resort to towns in Colorado's Front Range, at least when the winding Hwy-6 over Loveland Pass is open. If it's closed, drivers have to double-back onto Hwy-6 from the Silverthorne exit on I-70, and pass Keystone en route. Park in the lower lot, if possible, particularly on sunny days. This is "The Beach," home to Summit County's spring-long tailgating party and just a ski-boot stumble from the lifts. Free shuttle buses from Keystone link A-Basin to the rest of the county via the Summit Stage and KAB Express bus services (see p.113). The journey from Breckenridge or Copper can be a long one, particularly on public transit (up to two hours), but it's viable to combine a day riding at both the Basin and Keystone – particularly if taking advantage of night skiing at the latter. If planning on meeting up with friends, don't rely on cell phones as reception is patchy at best in Summit and is awful at the Basin. Use the message boards at the base of each lift instead.

The mountain

With just five lifts accessing a single open bowl that funnels back to the base area, there is little need for a trail map at A-Basin. Half the mountain is above treeline, but the ski area does offer a few small shots through the pines. Limited intermediate trails and its reputation as a hardcore expert's mountain keep crowds away, though the parking lots fill up on the weekend with Colorado families taking advantage of the lower prices and low-key atmosphere. Of the regulars who flock here, freestyle skiers seem to slightly outnumber snowboarders, the former taking the moguls of the notorious Pallavicini nose in stride. Most advanced riders with backcountry leanings will enjoy the Basin, particularly when the East Wall, a wonderland of cliffs and powder, is open. There are also several popular (and dangerous) backcountry descents in the immediate area accessed from US Forest Service gates; see the box on p.115.

Beginner

Even with the insanely cheap "beginner's lift only" passes available, it's hard to recommend A-Basin to newbies. Never-evers can spend an afternoon pottering on the small meadow under the short Molly Hogan lift, but green runs suited to more experienced beginners are limited, particularly in the case of snowboarders, who will likely get stuck on the mid-mountain flats. Try to stay rider's left off Midway and keep well away from flat-as-a-pancake Wrangler.

Intermediate

Intermediates should avoid A-Basin in poor weather, as they won't be in the protective shelter of the trees, or if they're hoping to have a wealth of runs to choose from. Still, the mountain's blues are wonderful rolling roads, primarily above treeline, and offer the confident intermediate the chance to work on their steeps skills, jumps, and moguls. Signposted "tours" link trails on the mountain – the intermediate route is the **Wee Lena Way**. For access to the summit, choose the faster Lenawee lift over the slow Norway double; both serve the main intermediate area.

Expert

Rusty or less experienced riders will find the blues under Cornice Run more than an opening challenge. A-Basin's blacks are mostly double and ungroomed and the high-caliber skiers who frequent the place soon bump it out. Regulars drive up to the mountain, park in the lot at the foot of **Pallavicini** lift, and lap the precipitous moguls, skinny glades, and alleyways of this outcrop all day. The further you drop off the ridge skier's left from the lift, the tighter the terrain and the longer you have to spend on Pali Wag, a narrow pathway out. If the **East Wall** is open, hike only in designated routes or risk the wrath of ski patrol and other locals. More gentle runs are strung along the East Wall traverse, but for instant gratification look for the lowest gate just above East Gully. See p.115 for local backcountry advice.

Freestyle

There is no artificial terrain at A-Basin; for freeriders, the appeal lies in the many natural rolls, rocks, cliffs, and cornices that can be enjoyed by nearly all abilities. When the East Wall is open, there are plenty of cliff drops; when closed, take your pick of trajectories off the long Cornice Run. For small to mid-sized hips, dips, and bumps, try the blue runs at the top of the mountain. The trees below Midway conceal tight bumpy corridors, while the rugged, rocky terrain of Palli is a playground for those who can handle hucking and landing on bumpy steeps.

Lift tickets, lessons, and rentals

Multi-day Vail **tickets** are valid at A-Basin, though in peak season it makes more sense just to buy an A-Basin ticket ($47) independently, for $20 less. Children's tickets are free with the purchase of a full-price adult ticket, and anyone can ride the bunny slope lift for just $5. Call the ski area for details of current discount ticket promotions offered through select Colorado stores. A-Basin offers the cheapest season passes in Summit County. Available online, the preseason Bonus Pass ($199) includes five days at other Colorado Vail-owned resorts (though only one can be taken at Vail/Beaver Creek), valid any day of the year. Typical season passes ($149) are available year round.

The base area **rental** hut offers great tech telemark rentals ($35), decent and inexpensive ski packages (from $20), but only basic snowboards (strap and step-in bindings, $30). See the Summit County "Lift tickets and rentals" section on p.114 for more suggestions. The ski school (☎970/496-7007) is small and rel-atively inexpensive (two-hour lessons $39, packages from $59), while the High Adventure program offers excellent multiday clinics for experts. From freeski-ing camps to teleskiing lessons and avalanche school, classes are taught by enthusiastic local pros and prices are inexpensive ($30–75 per day).

Practicalities

There is no **lodging** here. For nearby options see pp.114–115, or check the resort's website for package deals with regional hotels, most offering lift-and-lodging packages from $50 per person. Brown-bag lunches are the norm, but the lodge does house a basic **cafeteria** with excellent coffee, a smoothie cart, and the small *6th Alley Bar*. Once the weather heats up, barbecues are held at the midway station every weekend. Festivities are scheduled at The Beach (see p.118) and on-mountain weekly from the end of March, with a huge beach party held over Memorial Day weekend.

Breckenridge

Breckenridge is one of the most visited resorts in the country, more, perhaps, for the sum of its parts than for any great skiing it might offer. Founded in 1859 after the discovery of gold nearby, and developed during the further quest for silver, the symbols of its modern-day prosperity are quite tangible: a picture-postcard Victorian village that supports a sleek and modern resort; a deserved reputation as Colorado's hardest partying ski town; and rambling acres of runs almost guaranteed to boost the egos of even the most nervous intermediate. Add its history of catering to snowboarders, consistently producing one of the world's best terrain parks, the allure of Colorado powder, and an aggressive program of upgrades and expansions to terrain and facilities and it's no surprise that folks from all over the world flock to Breck (as it's known locally).

There are, inevitably, downsides to such success. So many visitors looking for the quintessential ski vacation makes for massive crowding of the slopes and facilities. The village may scream quaint mountain hideaway, but the atmosphere can be decidedly urban, with a younger party crew trawling the streets come nighttime. Then there's the skiing itself. While there is undoubtedly plenty for the once-a-year "expert" skier to enjoy, and a number of hidden powder stashes across the mountain, a lack of thrills and variety does it in. Breck is on the whole disappointingly flat, and even once you get to its upper slopes they're often bleak and icy, suffering from the wind's wrath more than any resort in Summit County.

Mountain info

Phone ☎970/453-5000 or 877/593-5260 (reservations)
Snow phone ☎970/453-6118
Website ⊛www.breckenridge.com
Price $49-65
Operating times Mid-Nov to late April daily 8.30am-4pm
No. of lifts 27, inc 12 surface lifts
Base elevation 9600′
Summit elevation 12998′
Vertical drop 3398′
No. of trails 139
Acreage 2208
Beginner 13%
Intermediate 32%
Expert 55%
Average snowfall 300″
Snowmaking Yes (516 acres)
Night skiing No
Nursery facilities Yes, from 2 months; reservations required on ☎970/453-3258; skiing 3–14, snowboarding 7–14

Arrival, information, and getting around

Of the ski resorts in Summit County, Breck is the furthest from Denver, twenty minutes south of I-70 on Hwy-9. In lieu of a car, "Free Ride" shuttle buses (☎970/547-3140) run through town from 6.30am to midnight, serving the Peak 8 and Beaver Run (Peak 9) base areas, outlying condos, and all stops in

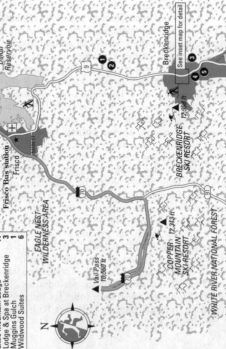
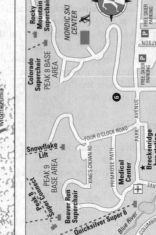

SUMMIT COUNTY & BRECKENRIDGE

ACCOMMODATION

Abbott Placer Inn	9
Allaire Timbers Inn	5
Bed & Breakfasts on North Main	7
Breckenridge Mountain Lodge	8
Breckenridge Wayside Inn	2
The Corral	4
Fireside Inn	10
Little Mountain Lodge	11
Lodge & Spa at Breckenridge	3
Muggins Gulch	1
Wildwood Suites	6

RESTAURANTS

Blue Moose Restaurant	G
Blue River Bistro	E
Breckenridge Brewery	F
Café Alpine	I
Clint's Bakery & Coffee House	C
Downstairs at Eric's	D
Fatty's	J
Mi Casa	A
Rasta Pasta	B
Sushi Breck	H

between. Each of the nine routes operates every twenty to thirty minutes. Pick up a schedule and map from Breckenridge Station on South Park Avenue, the transfer point to free, county-wide Summit Stage buses (see p.113). For more information try the town's **visitor centers** at 317 S Main (daily 9am-5pm; ☎970/453-5579) or at 309 N Main (daily 9am–5pm; ☎970/453-6018, ⓦwww.gobreck.com) in a small wooden hut on the way into town.

Buses stop at the free Miners and Tailings skier lots, located off Watson Avenue. Drivers coming from I-70 and Frisco should take the North Park turnoff on their way into town or risk getting stuck in the traffic endemic to Main Street. Tiger and F-lots are the closest pay lots to the Village at the base of Peak 9, and the lot at the base of Peak 8 fills early.

The mountain

With a long, horizontal strip spanning four peaks of the Ten Mile Range, Breckenridge's layout is a bit odd. Each peak, despite occupying the same ridge, is distinct from the next. They are separated by deep gullies, and getting from one to the next is almost impossible without both traversing and lift hopping. Since Breckenridge lacks a huge vertical drop (contrary to statistics, which are skewed by foot-access-only, double diamond bowls and a couple of winding cat tracks linking the ski area to the town below), peak-to-peak exploration might seem the best way to make the most of the mountain, but traveling from the imaginatively named Peaks 7 to 10 can easily take the better part of an afternoon.

At least the lifts are fast and the trails well marked, though Breck's trail classification statistics are more warped than most and it's best to simply ignore them. This mountain is particularly suited to beginners and intermediates, despite what percentages might say. Only Peaks 7 and 8 offer skiing off their windswept summits, in open bowls that seldom have sufficient snow to justify the hike. The majority of Breckenridge's lift-served terrain is well below treeline. There is, however, expert terrain; it's just of matter of knowing where to find it – on a powder day, that's not hard. If the lower Peak 8 bowls are too windswept, or you just don't fancy the t-bar to get there, head into the gullies between the peaks. Some areas, like the Peak 9 chutes, are marked on the map; other prime spots take a little more looking.

The resort has two main **access points**, one in town at the bottom of Peak 9, the other a free shuttle ride up the hill at the Peak 8 base. In the morning it's a toss-up between opting for the busy QuickSilver lift directly behind the **Village** at Breckenridge condos or lugging up the hill to the **Beaver Run** chair, which is want for heavy traffic until later in the day. Aside from a handful of steep bumps and forested chutes in the back, most of **Peak 9** is fast cruising territory with wide blues that progress into more gently rolling aspen-lined lower slopes. Peak 9 lifts also serve **Peak 10**, almost exclusively an advanced mountain, with its groomed blacks, testing bumps, and steep, windswept glades. **Peak 8** lifts access all Breck's above-treeline double diamond bowls, the resort's celebrated terrain park, and acres of mellow meadows. A long traverse from the top of Peak 8's Rocky Mountain Super Chair leads to the recent **Peak 7** expansion: 165 lift-served acres of gentle glades and long blue cruisers. Mountain orientation tours for intermediates and above depart at 9.30am daily from the bottom of Beaver Run (Peak 9) and the Colorado Super Chair (Peak 8).

Beginner

On-mountain crowds can be intimidating for those of a nervous disposition but, overall, Breckenridge serves as a decent introduction to life on the slopes. Slow-moving surface lifts and flat beginner trails are found at the base of Peaks 8 and 9. Peak 8 has the better views but the tree-lined Peak 9 greens are more sheltered, and are closer to town should you wish to end your day early. Additionally, Peak 9 has a novice snowboarder slope for ski school attendees, complete with minipark. Both snowboarders and skiers should avoid the long, busy cattracks between peaks, particularly on weekends.

Intermediate

Stay off Peak 10 until confident enough to handle icy steeps. That's about all the direction intermediates need, as the mountain belongs to them. There are plenty of cruisers here, and almost every run at Breck seems to have some small lip, mound, or cat track to launch off. The rolling blues off Peak 9 are a little longer than those on Peak 8, but those who traverse across to the new Peak 7 lift will be rewarded with emptier slopes and a shot at powder-filled glades. Short blacks on the front face of Peak 8 are manageable for a confident intermediate in good conditions, as are the blacks in the back bowl off Chair 6.

Expert

The often icy groomed blacks and moguls of Peak 10 are the most consistent choice for traditional alpine skiers, though the trails high on the backside of Peak 8 are also popular. Bump runs in the upper gullies between the peaks are more challenging, but need a fairly deep base of snow. It's the same with the stumpy glades off Peak 10 known as The Burn, which get chunked up fast, and for the Peak 9 chutes. On a calm powder day, clutch the t-bar up into the open bowls of Peaks 7 and 8, but be prepared to hike up to Imperial Bowl or out toward the Peak 7 summit for the best above-treeline goods. Check out p.115 for backcountry advice.

Freestyle

Breckenridge hosted the original Snowboarding World Cup in 1985 and was the quintessential spot for jibbers in the early Nineties, but the resort's reputation dwindled due to its mostly mellow natural terrain. In today's climate of super-pipes, monster rails, and twin-tipped aerial assaults, however, Breck is once again a contender. The Peak 8 park is a monster, with both park and pipe frequently used in contest series such as the Triple Crown. There's a minipark tucked away under C lift on Peak 9, but novice jibbers may find cruising the many small natural bumps and kickers of the mountain just as entertaining. Check the trees for log slides; Peak 9 aspens tend to be a particularly fruitful source.

Lift tickets, lessons and rentals

There are few **ticket** deals unless you purchase your tickets prior to or very early in the season, and even kids' tickets are expensive. Breckenridge multiday tickets are valid at Keystone and Arapahoe Basin, with restricted use at more expensive Vail and Beaver Creek. They can be purchased online (at least fourteen days in advance) for savings of $8 to $20. **Ski school** (℡888/LRN-2SKI) meets at both the Village and Beaver Run areas at the bottom of Peak 9 and at the base of Peak 8. Snowboarders have the option of tuition through the Burton Method Centers located at both peaks. For intermediate, advanced, and

Breck's specialty classes, check the meeting point well in advance, as some advanced classes are restricted to a particular base area or meet mid-mountain. Full-day lessons (from $65) for beginners run in the morning with half-day options (from $55) in the afternoon. Expect to pay $10 more over the holidays. Add $11 to include a lift ticket in the package and roughly another $25 for equipment. Intermediate and advanced half-day lessons (from $55) are available every morning, but are only offered in the afternoons if interest is sufficient. Adaptive programs are run through the excellent Breckenridge Outdoor Education Center (℡970/453-6422, ⊕www.boec.org).

Breckenridge Sports (℡970/453-8318) is the official resort **rental outlet** and has numerous locations in town and on-mountain. Packages are reasonable (from $25 for skis, $30 for boards) and can be booked at a discount online through ⊕www.rentskis.com. Several independent gear shops compete for business in town. For good tuning and quality demos, try Mountain Wave Snowboards, 600 South Park Ave (℡970/453-8305, $25 with multiday discounts) or the respected A Racer's Edge ski shop, 114 N Main (℡970/453-0995 or 1-800/451-5363). Low prices on basic equipment and clothing, goggle, and glove rentals are available at Colorado Ski and Snowboard Rental, 110 Ski Hill Rd (℡970/453-1477 or 1-800/248-1477).

Accommodation

There's a fair range of **accommodation** in Breckenridge, though to find inexpensive motels you'll have to travel twenty minutes north to Frisco or Dillon (see pp.114–115). B&Bs cluster around the old Victorian center, hotels hug the Village slopes, and condo complexes pepper the woods west of Main Street, on the hillside below the ski area. Run by the Chamber of Commerce, Breckenridge Central Reservations (℡877/791-3968, ⊕www.breckvacations.com) handles all bookings. Peak Property (℡970/453-1724 or 800/458-7998, ⊕www.peakproperty.com) is a good source of privately owned condos and homes, most are on the outskirts of town. Currently Vail Resorts has stakes in a number of properties as well, including the rambling *Village at Breckenridge*, exclusive *Thunder Mountain* condos, and ugly but well-appointed *Great Divide Lodge* hotel (℡970/453-4500 or 1-800/321-8444; $190–260), and last-minute deals are often available online. The company also hopes to soon built a great deal more around the newly opened Peak 7, including private homes and the construction of a gondola linking Peaks 7 and 8 to the center of town.

Abbett Placer Inn 205 S French St ℡970/453-6489, ⊕www.abbettplacerbnb.com. Rather musty but inexpensive B&B, with four ensuite rooms and one four-bunk dorm ($39). ❹

Allaire Timbers Inn 9511 S Main St ℡970/453-7530, ⊕www.allairetimbers.com. Large, contemporary log-cabin B&B on the outskirts of town, filled with shiny pine furniture and boasting great views from the outdoor tub, but perhaps a little too slick and impersonal for some. ❻

Bed & Breakfasts on North Main 303 N Main St ℡970/453-2975 or 800/795-2975, ⊕www.breckenridge-inn.com. An elegantly restored Victorian house, romantic little cottage and timber-framed barn, all nestled together between Main St

and the Blue River. Candlelit breakfasts and outdoor tub. ❹

Breckenridge Mountain Lodge 600 S Ridge St ℡453-2333 or 800/525-2224, ⊕www.breckmountainlodge.com. Relatively inexpensive motel close to the slopes and Main Street. The 71 rooms are simply decorated with log-frame queens and bunks. Amenities include outdoor tubs, games room, and dining area. Continental breakfast included. ❸, ski packages from $70pp.

Breckenridge Wayside Inn 165 Tiger Rd ℡970/453-5540 or 800/927-7669, ⊕www.summitnet.com/wayside. Five minutes from town, this is a smaller, less expensive version of *Breckenridge Mountain Lodge*. The welcoming lounge is dominated by Summit County's largest fireplace, the outdoor tub surrounded by meadows. Benefits include complimentary continental breakfast and hot beverages. **❸**

The Corral 700 Broken Lance Drive ☏970/547-9600 or 888/609-9600. Spacious, upscale condo hotel at the south end of Main, with sauna and hot tubs. **❼** for a one bed, up to **❾** for a three bed with hot tub and loft.

Fireside Inn 114 N French St ☏970/453-6456, ⓦwww.firesideinn.com. Run by expat Brits, this ramshackle hostel offers four floral, antique-filled bedrooms, all with private baths, and five rather shabby dorm rooms. Its bustling and homely, and amenities include an indoor tub, Internet access, microwave, and fridge. Dorms $30–38, rooms **❹**

Little Mountain Lodge 98 Sunbeam Drive ☏970/453-1969 or 1-800/468-7707. Stylish and luxurious ten-room B&B in a spacious log home. Each room is minimally decorated, and the public areas include an airy and elegant lounge with a riverrock fireplace, basement rec room with pool table, and secluded outdoor tub. Gourmet break-

fast and evening snacks included. **❻**

Lodge and Spa at Breckenridge 112 Overlook Drive ☏970/453-9300 or 1-800/736-1607, ⓦwww.thelodgeatbreck.com. Perched at the top of a cliff above town, hewn from logs and surrounded by forest, this luxury hotel is also home to an athletic club and spa (including indoor pool and outdoor tubs). Stylish and comfortable rooms, many with private balconies. **❼**

Muggins Gulch 4023 Tiger Rd ☏970/453-7414 or 1-800/275-8304, ⓦwww.mugginsgulch.com. Gorgeous post-and-beam lodge between Frisco and Breck, with three suites and two queen rooms, all with private baths; tasty breakfasts and afternoon snacks too. The Swallow Suite sleeps up to four. **❺** (regular season), **❻** (holidays).

Wildwood Suites 120 Sawmill Rd ☏970/453-0232 or 800/866-0300, ⓦwww.wildwoodsuites.com. Attractive, no-frills condo suites, two blocks from town with end of the day ski-in access from the slopes. Amenities include outdoor tubs, sauna, laundry and free continental breakfast. One-bedroom condo **❺**

Eating

Christmas tree lights along Main Street make a sparkling path through the town's many **restaurants** and **cafés**. Most are reasonably priced as ski resorts go, though nearby Frisco (see p.116) has less expensive options. Reservations are recommended for dinner, though even a guaranteed table won't prevent you from having to wait at Breck's busier restaurants on the weekends. City Market (☏970/453-0818) is on the bus route at the north end of town, while Amazing Grace Natural Foods, 213 Lincoln Ave (☏970/453-1445), is in the center. The **on-mountain** restaurants here are primarily large, pricey food courts. Eat here early if at all, as they become exceedingly crowded. Most fun for kids is the mining–themed *Ten Mile Station*, between Peaks 9 and 10, but you'll be out faster from just-about-affordable *Border Burritos*, downstairs in the lodge at the base of Peak 8.

Blue Moose Restaurant 540 S Main St ☏970/453-7227. Bright and warm breakfast spot close to the village, serving fruit pancakes, oatmeal, and all manner of egg dishes.

Blue River Bistro 305 N Main St ☏970/453-6974. Elegant but easy-going bistro with reasonable prices, down at the north end of Main. Dinner choices include an extensive selection of pastas ($15), in addition to a more meaty selection, and the martini menu rocks out with a whopping 75 variations. 11am–2am.

Breckenridge Brewery S Main St ☏970/453-1550. Brewpub close to the slopes, whose vats produce a range of tasty, nationally – distributed beers. The kitchen turns out a decent grill menu, of

burritos, burgers, and that ilk, and piled-high plates of nachos that preclude the need for an entree.

Café Alpine 106 E Adams Ave ☏970/453-8218. Innovative American fine dining, highly praised and priced but without the snooty pretensions. A different menu is served each night, with an emphasis on the use of seasonal and regional ingredients to create colorful, multiflavored dishes. There's a cheaper tapas bar upstairs as well. Extensive wine list. Dinner and tapas from 5pm nightly.

Clint's Bakery and Coffee House 131 S Main St ☏970/453-1736. Cappuccino and conversation in the front, sandwich counter in the back. Great for to-go breakfasts and brown-bag lunches.

Downstairs at Eric's 111 S Main St ☎970/453-1401. A rambling basement sports bar and family dining room, with burgers, fries, and the like at reasonable prices.

Mi Casa 600 Park Ave ☎970/453-2071. Cavernous, always busy Mexican cantina with a second branch in Keystone, filled with everyone from families to the resort's VIPs. Margaritas are excellent; huge salads, combo plates, and generous fajitas run around $10.

Rasta Pasta 411 S Main St ☎970/453-7467. A Breckenridge institution, this rather scruffy base-ment café turns out spicy spaghettis with a Caribbean twist. Reggae thumps in the background, and prices are only slightly inflated.

Sushi Breck La Cima Mall, 500 S Main St ☎970/453-8338. Great sushi in a bright, airy space in one of Main Street's red-brick malls. Sake-steamed clams, magic mushrooms, and the Peaks 8, 9, and 10 rolls are among the more unusual items on the menu, in addition to a classic sushi menu, a wide selection of vegetarian rolls, and vintage Japanese sakes. Sun–Thurs 3.30pm until 9 or 10pm; Fri–Sat, 3.30–11pm.

Bars and entertainment

Breck is a blast with attractive venues, engaging **bars** and decent **clubs**. If you have too good of a time, there's a free Tipsy Taxi service (☎970/389-7460). Annual **festivals** include the International Snow Sculpting Championships and the long-running Ullr Fest, homage to the Norse god of winter. Plays are performed Thurs–Sat in the little Backstage Theatre, at 121 S Ridge St (☎970/453-0199, ⑩www.backstage.org). The Speakeasy basement screening room is housed in the Colorado Mountain College, 103 S Harris St (☎970/453-3624); check the *Summit Daily News* (⑩www.summitdaily.com) for listings.

Cecilia's 520 S Main, La Cima Mall ☎970/458-2243. Large club with separate dance floor, pool table, and cocktail bar. Take advantage of their two-for-one martini specials on Monday afternoons (3–7pm). DJs most nights along with the occasional live act.

Clancy's Irish Pub 100 N Main St ☎970/453-5431. Rowdy Irish bar that attracts a boisterous, heavy-drinking crowd.

Breckenridge BBQ 301 S Main St ☎970/453-7313. The upstairs bar of this rib-shack makes a quiet spot for a late-evening drink and game of pool.

Brown Hotel 208 N Ridge St ☎970/453-0084. Drinking at this old boarding house is a little like hanging out in somebody's home – somebody just happens to have a bar installed in the parlor, and has installed arcade games in the closet.

Liquid Lounge 520 S Main St ☎970/453-2782. Small space-aged lounge above *Cecilia's*, with chilled-out dance music playing constantly. Take advantage of the booths and pool tables earlier in the week, before the Breckenridge weekend crush.

The St Bernard 103 S Main St ☎970/453-2572. Busy, low-key drinking den, tucked away in the back of the St Bernard restaurant and often over-looked by the louder, party-hard contingent.

Salt Creek Saloon 110 E Lincoln St ☎970/453-4949. In a barn-like space above the Salt Creek restaurant, you'll find lots of men in cowboy hats (and a few women) line dancing.

Sherpa and Yeti's 320 S Main St ☎970/547-9299. Booming basement spot, home to most of the live bands that end up in Breck and hellishly hectic at times.

Other activities and attractions

There's such a wealth of active **off-slope activities** at Breckenridge, from dog sledding to dinner sleigh rides to fly-fishing and snowcat tours, that you're best off stopping in at the Chamber's visitor centers for advice and bookings (☎970/453-6018 or 1-877/864-0868). **Ice skaters** head for the indoor and outdoor rinks at the Stephen C. West Arena, 0189 Boreas Pass Rd (☎970/547-9974, $6 admission, $3 rental, hours vary). If a hockey game is scheduled, try little Maggie Pond in the Village (☎970/453-2000, $6 admission, $6 rentals). Out on the golf course, the Gold Run Nordic Center (daily 9am–4pm, passes $14, rentals from $14, private lessons available; ☎970/547-7889) maintains 14km of groomed trails; if you like more technically diverse trails, try the Nordic Center

△ Purgatory Tower, Durango, CO

on Ski Hill Road (daily 9am–4pm; lesson-and-ski-packages $30; ☎970/453-6855), which grooms 32km of track below Peak 8. There's also a huge number of backcountry ski touring and snowshoe routes in the area, with trailheads south of town around Hoosier and Boreas passes, and the possibility of hut-to-hut touring (see box p.135); call the Dillon Forest Service rangers on ☎970/468-5400 for more info, or stop in at Mountain Outfitters, 112 S Ridge St (☎970/453-2201), for backcountry rentals and route suggestions.

Breck's impressive Rec Center, 0880 Airport Rd (☎970/453-1734, Mon–Fri 6am–10pm, Sat 7am–10pm, Sun 8am–10pm, day pass $10), offers an excellent climbing wall, pilates reformer, spinning bikes, ice rinks, and pool. History buffs can pick up free guides from the visitor centers and explore downtown's National Historic District; pay a visit to the Edwin Carter Museum, located in a log cabin built in 1875 (on the corner of Wellington and Ridge streets, Wed 10am–1pm, Thurs–Fri 1–4pm, admission free); or pan for gold and take an underground tour at the old Country Boy Mine, 592 French Gulch Rd (☎970/453-4405, hours and admission vary according to activity).

Listings

Avalanche hotline ☎970/668-0600.
Bookshops Mountain Java Coffee & Books, 118 S Ridge ☎970/453-1874 or Weber's, 100 S Main St ☎970/453-4723.
Forest Service ☎970/468-5400.
Internet Summit County South Branch Library, 504 Airport Rd, Breckenridge ☎970/453-6098.
Medical Breckenridge Medical Center, 555 S Park

Ave, by the Peak 9 lifts ☎970/453-1010. The nearest hospital is in Frisco.
Pharmacy The Breckenridge Drug Store, 111 Ski Hill Rd ☎970/453-2362.
Police ☎970/453-2941.
Post office 305 S Ridge Rd ☎970/547-0347.
Road conditions ☎303/639-1234 (Colorado), ☎970/668-1090 (Summit County).

Keystone

Mercurial **Keystone** is pitched squarely as a family resort, its all-inclusive nature attracting a condo-seeking crowd eager to mix activities like stargazing and wine-tasting with their daily dose of powder. But this is no gated Beaver Creek; Keystone is both surprisingly affordable and more challenging than its family reputation suggests. Though long intermediate cruisers are abundant, there's also an easily reached web of beginner runs along with some enjoyable expert terrain, including a couple of undervisited back bowls with powder stashes that belie Keystone's poor snow record. The ski area also hosts the only **night skiing** in Summit County, an extensive operation that also floods the park and pipe in light.

The resort itself is not so much a village as a string of seven condominium complexes strung out along Hwy-6 in the steep-sided Snake River Valley. Only two of the villages – **River Run** and **Mountain House** – are slopeside, and both contain a handful of storefront restaurants, rental shops, and the like. River Run is the newest and is where the resort has been focusing much of its amenities attention as of late. Keystone Village is best at night with its restaurant-lined boardwalk curving around a gigantic ice rink, but has begun to show its age in the daylight.

Arrival, information, and getting around

If Loveland Pass is open, drivers from Denver and the Front Range have the option of taking the Hwy-6 exit before the Eisenhower Tunnel and following the scenic and less crowded route over winding Loveland Pass. Most prefer to speed along I-70 (or crawl, in weekend traffic) to Silverthorne, then double-back six miles to the resort. The most convenient **parking** for day skiers is in the free Montezuma lot off Gondola Rd, adjacent to the River Run base area. If you're driving from Silverthorne, keep going past Keystone Village and Mountain House to the last exit before the Loveland Pass turn-off.

Bisected by Hwy-6, Keystone's village sprawl is not conducive to walking. Fortunately, the resort's free **shuttles** run frequently from 7am to 9pm. An on-call shuttle (☎970/496-EASE) is available after hours to outlying areas. Departing from the Mountain House transportation hub, free Summit Stage buses (daily 6am–1.30am; ☎970/668-0999, see p.113) link Keystone to the rest of Summit County via Dillon, Silverthorne, and Frisco. For a direct connection to Breckenridge take the KAB Express (☎970/496-2000, also free). The Vail Resorts Express serves Vail and Beaver Creek (☎970/469-8245, $12 in advance, $15 walk-on), and Keystone shuttle buses run every half-hour to Arapahoe Basin.

The mountain

Keystone's gondola swings up from the River Run Village base to the summit of **Keystone Mountain**, the most prominent of the ski area's three back-to-back peaks. Many visitors don't venture beyond this extensive front face, which is criss-crossed with an efficient lift system. Almost all of the beginner trails, a good variety of blue terrain and the resort's skinny terrain park can be accessed here. With two base areas, it's a busy place littered with "Go Slow" signs, trail crossings, and unsteady groups of novices. Skiers can avoid lines to the gondola by jumping on the speedy Summit Express.

An impressively large area on this front face is lit for **night skiing**, which is included in day tickets. The lights go off at 8pm daily during peak periods, with a limited weekend or Wed–Sat schedule at other times. As well as being the only area with lights, the front face also receives most of the benefit from Keystone's extensive **snowmaking** program. Gunning up the blowers in the fall, Keystone aims to open before Halloween, competing with Loveland and Copper for the earliest Colorado opening date. Unfortunately, Keystone needs its snowguns for more than just an early opening because its annual snowfall trails Breckenridge, Copper, and Vail. Meticulous grooming and a sheltered location keep the worst of the ice away; however, by late afternoon the busy routes back to the **River Run** and **Mountain House** base areas can be treacherous.

The backside of Keystone Mountain offers a taste of what's in store on the remaining two mountains, **North Peak** (11,660ft) and the **Outback** (12,200ft): long blues and blacks, many of the latter laced with moguls throughout. Though you're rarely alone at Keystone, the crowds do thin out the further back you ski from the main face. Even better, seeing as the resort tends to attract more casual skiers and fewer locals, powder days are less of a mad dash and more experienced riders can have their pick of fresh lines throughout the morning hours. Even if it's not a powder day, you'll generally be rewarded for exploring the hike-to areas like the **Outback bowls** or **The Windows**; they're not daring enough to attract much of the local hardcore contingent and generally too out of the way for vacationers.

Beginner

True first-timers might want to take a few short runs using the surface lifts at the flat **Discovery** area by the Mountain House. All others can head straight up the mountain to a wide, gentle meadow of sheltered green runs around the two **Packsaddle** lifts. Though often busy with ski school groups and families, these tame slopes are seldom used by more experienced skiers. Never-evers can also zip up on the gondola from River Run as the summit of Keystone Mountain holds yet another small learning area, complete with a short beginner chairlift. Confident beginners not perturbed by crowds can then tackle **Schoolmarm**, a long, gentle green guiding skiers through the Packsaddle and down to either base. The tired (or nervous) can take the gondola back home.

Intermediate

Keystone is a challenging mountain for intermediates. After warming up on any of the half-dozen or so shorter blues located on the front face, confident intermediates are best off escaping the more crowded beginner zones by heading over to **North Peak** and the **Outback**. The eight or so lengthy blues running down Outback are the quietest, not surprising given the six-mile trek it takes to get there, and many intermediates choose to spend much of the day lapping them on the speedy Outback Express chair. On North Face, only a trio of intermediate cruisers might be shown on the trail map, but many of the blacks here are only slightly tougher than the blues, liberally sprinkled with wide, soft moguls conducive to progression.

Expert

Mogul bashers and downhill carvers will find plenty to do at Keystone. Only the busy front face of Keystone Mountain has little to offer, aside from a couple of short, steep shots that are a blast in powder, and **Last Hoot**, a downhill black surprisingly located below the Packsaddle nursery slopes. It's worth hiking as far as you can be bothered to get fresh powder shots in the two Outback bowls, North and South, though more experienced off-piste skiers may be disappointed by their less than hair-raising pitch and short vertical. Of the two, the southern bowl is less crowded and has the more enjoyable traverse out, but the northern option has a steeper pitched, if shorter, fall line. If heading for the trees, keep in mind that the glades on North Peak are only worth exploring when there's a deep base. The higher altitude tree shots below the Outback bowls are more reliable, though for moguls, the North Face will do you fine. There are also some serious cliffs up on the **Windows**, but this hikeable in-bounds area is rarely open.

Freestyle

Running half the length of the mountain's front face, Keystone's **constructed terrain** and **pipe** are not so intimidating, perfect for junior jibbers and those looking for smaller hits and rails. The park does become more popular at night as riders with day jobs at neighboring resorts head here to play under the floodlights. Ice can be a problem, particularly when poor conditions lead to a base that's almost all artificial snow. A couple of the short black shots on the front face have spots that can be jumped, but Keystone is too well groomed to throw up much natural hucking terrain. The charm of the Outback lies in powder and trees, not drops.

Lift tickets, lessons, and rentals

Tickets are significantly cheaper here in off-peak periods, with few deals available at other times unless you purchase your tickets prior to, or very early in, the season. Current programs include the Perfect 10 pack, available online, and value season pass deals available in-state (see p.114). Keystone multiday tickets are valid at Breckenridge and Arapahoe Basin, with restricted use at more expensive Vail and Beaver Creek, and can be purchased online (at least fourteen days in advance) for savings of $8 to $20.

The brown huts of the Keystone **ski school** (☏800/255-3715) and Keystone Sports **rental outlets** cluster around the Mountain House and River Run lifts. Full- and half-day lessons (from $59/$47, lift and gear not included) for all levels are available at both locations, with beginner night courses offered only at Mountain House. Specialty classes include telemark sessions, women's only workshops (given the cringworthy "Camp Betty" nametag), and multiday clinics with Olympians Steve and Phil Mahre; day packages start at $100. Adequate resort rental packages from $23 for skis, $30 for boards can be booked in advance at ⓦwww.rentskis.com. Quality independent options in River Run include the friendly Polar Revolution board shop (☏970/496-4657) and the custom boot-fitters of Precision Ski (☏970/468-5584).

Accommodation

Accommodation at Keystone ranges from lived-in Seventies-style studios a bus ride from the mountain, to plush, spacious pads right on the slopes. All include access to hot tubs or pools, and can be booked online or through Keystone Central Reservations (☏888/222-9298). Of the seven **condo villages**, the slopeside *River Run* and aging *Keystone Village* are the busiest, with direct access to restaurants and amenities. *Mountain House* condos are best for families who want to be close to the beginner slopes, *Forest* is a good-value, residential-style development in the woods, and *Ski Tip* features secluded, upscale mountain homes. *Aspen Ridge* and *Mountain View* are located on the northern, more exposed side of the highway. The resort only manages two **hotels**, the modern *Inn at Keystone*, well appointed but shaped like a toast rack, and the rather subdued four-star *Keystone Lodge*.

Arapahoe Motel 22859 Hwy-6 ☏970/513-9009, ⓦwww.arapahoemotel.com. Dark but comfortably remodeled motel on the northern side of Hwy-6, within walking distance of the Mountain House

Base Area. Facilities include an indoor hot tub and sauna, plus in-room fridges and microwaves. **❸–❺**

Ski Tip Lodge 764 Montezuma Rd ☎970/496-4950 or 800/742-0905, ⊛www.skitiplodge.com. Renovated in the 1940s to be Colorado's first ski lodge, from a previous incarnation as a turn-of-the-century stagecoach stop. Genuinely rustic yet comfortable, boasting a gourmet restaurant, this alpine-style ten-room B&B is managed by Keystone Resort; guests receive the same activities passport as condo dwellers, and rooms with shared bath are surprisingly reasonable. **❺–❼**

Eating and drinking

Within the major River Run and Keystone village areas, Keystone's collection of **restaurants** have the squeaky clean character of a theme park and are on the whole uninspired (reservations on ☎970/496-4386). You'll find the expensive resort-run establishments atop the mountain itself (*Alpenglow Stube, Der Fondue Chessel*) and cheaper options outside the resort on Hwy-6. As for daytime snacking on the slopes, the on-mountain cafeterias are much like any other resorts; try *La Bontes Cabin*, between Keystone and North peaks, for tasty stews, soups, and wraps. Grocery shopping is limited to the gas station mart on Hwy-6 and a convenience store in River Run; the nearest substantial supermarket is in Dillon.

Out on the golf course, the elegantly rustic *Keystone Ranch* has recently garnered the Zagat award for best restaurant in Colorado; a more intimate gourmet supper is served at the *Ski Tip Lodge*, a restored 1880s stagecoach stop (see accommodation above). Reservations for all Keystone restaurants can be made on ☎970/496-4386, which makes dining out even easier but does nothing to detract from the theme park atmosphere. A welcome contrast is the *Inxpot* (☎970/496-4627), a "fiercely independent" coffee shop, breakfast counter, cocktail bar, and bookstore in the River Run plaza. The place resembles a cozy living room, with a fireplace and tons of deep-stuffed couches; their breakfast muffins make a good start to the day.

Aside from doings at the *Goat Tavern* and the *Snake River Saloon*, Keystone is quiet after dark. The resort tries hard to keep crowds packed into both villages at the end of the day, scheduling après parties, torchlight parades, and the like, but most overnight visitors seem more content to head back to their condos to watch a DVD.

The Goat Tavern 22954 Hwy-6 ☎970/513-YDIG Don't let the roadhouse exterior and dog-eared dining room – or the Pabst Blue Ribbon sign – mislead you; this bar is Keystone's finest purveyor of evening entertainment, from pajama parties to out-of-town bands, and a welcome contrast to the slick restaurants of the village. Daily 11–2am.

Pizza 101 Snowdance Plaza ☎970/262-0200. Tiny pizza joint opposite *The Goat Tavern*, plastered in Polaroids and baking up an interesting menu of pizzas (from $8.50), calzones, and stombolis. Daily from 11am until late.

Snake River Saloon Hwy-6 and Oro Grande Rd ☎970/468-2788. Country rock and dancing takes place at this locals' venue. The resort is trying hard to keep the crowds in the village at the end of the day, scheduling peak-season après parties, weekly evening ice skating sessions, torchlight parades and storytelling, holiday festivals, and annual events such as the Mardi Gras Parade and Tiki Torchlight Snowshoe race.

Other activities and attractions

Almost all **off-slope activities** are included in the free "Mountain Passports" that accompany Keystone lodging packages. These run the gamut from snowshoeing and ice skating (not rentals) to wine tasting and yoga. Clinics for all abilities are also offered on topics including telemark skiing, fly-fishing, learning to tune your board, and figuring out what's wrong with your stance and ski boot. For details on activities elsewhere in Summit County, see p.117.

Aspen

Mountain info – general

Second only to Vail in size, and with an equally outsized reputation, **Aspen Skiing Company** has spent its recent years performing a bit of a balancing act. Once happy to bowl along under the gilded weight of its world-famous standing, ritzy Aspen faced the danger of pigeonholing itself; as the last decade ended, the town had grown increasingly exclusive, having priced out younger and more impecunious skiers and forbidding snowboarding on Aspen Mountain – the resort was in need of an image fix. It began to cater more toward the youth market by becoming the (now perma-

Mountain info – general

Phone ☎970/925-1220 or 800/525-6200

Snow phone ☎970/925-1221 or 888/277-3676

Website ⊛www.aspensnowmass.com

Price $68

Total acreage 4893

Nursery facilities Yes, Snowcubs, based at Snowmass, 8 weeks to 3 years; skiing 3–17, snowboarding 5–17; reservations required, recommended at least one month in advance; ☎877/282-7736

nent) host of the Winter X-Games, and by 2001 snowboarding was allowed on all of Aspen's mountains. The wealthy elite certainly still come, but so does a whole new set of regulars, and a flourishing, permanent community also manages to exist in a parallel world to the expensive visitors' version, vital to help counterbalance the decadent consumerism of its more ostentatious clientele.

Founded back in 1879, the town of Aspen developed slowly, thanks to its remote location, to become one of the world's top silver producers. By the time the silver market crashed fourteen years later, it had acquired tasteful residential palaces, grand hotels, and an opera house. Miners were quick to leave and within a year of the crash only a quarter of the populace remained. In the 1930s, with the population slumped below seven hundred, it was, ironically enough, the anti-poverty WPA program that gave the community the cash to build its **first crude ski lift**. Entrepreneurs seized the opportunity presented by the varied terrain and plentiful snow, along with the know-how of former 10th Mountain Division soldiers stationed at nearby Camp Hale (see p.135), and the first chairlift was dedicated on Aspen Mountain (now known as Ajax) in 1947. Skiing has since spread to three more separate mountains, and the social jet set arrived in force during the 1960s.

Today each of those mountains has emerged with a distinct reputation. **Ajax**, the first peak to be accessed, consists of predominantly expert terrain, while **Aspen Highlands** offers skiers a backcountry-style playground. **Buttermilk** is one of the best mountains to learn on in the state, and the large, family-friendly **Snowmass** is covered in perfectly groomed cruising runs.

The **costs** of enjoying the resort's operations – where customer service is paramount – are indeed high, with tickets, lessons, lodgings, and food exorbitantly priced in peak season, less so in late fall and early spring. The preserved Victorian town is one of the most attractive ski towns anywhere, but it's more economical to base yourself in a neighboring place like Basalt, or even the nearest major town, Glenwood Springs, forty miles away.

Arrival, information, and getting around

Scheduled **flights** land at little Sardy Field (☎970/920-5384, ⊛www.aspenairport.com), three miles from Aspen, while more planes serve Eagle County Airport, seventy miles east along the interstate. There are no mountain passes between

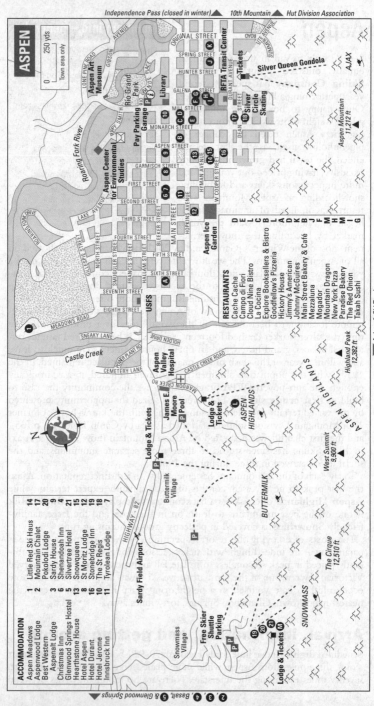

Independence Pass (closed in winter) ▲   10th Mountain ▲ Hut Division Association

ASPEN

0   250 yds

Town area only

Silver Queen Gondola

AJAX

Aspen Mountain
11,212 ft

Silver
Circle
Skating

Aspen Art Museum

Library

Pay Parking
Garage

Rio Grand
Park

Aspen Center for Environmental Studies

Roaring Fork River

Aspen Ice Garden

USFS

Castle Creek

Aspen Valley Hospital

James E. Moore Pool

Lodge & Tickets

ASPEN HIGHLANDS

Highland Peak
12,382 ft

West Summit
9,900 ft

The Cirque
12,510 ft

BUTTERMILK

SNOWMASS

Ashcroft Ski Touring ▶

Lodge & Tickets

Free Skier Shuttle Parking

Snowmass Village

Buttermilk Village

Sardy Field Airport

HIGHWAY 82

RESTAURANTS

Cache Cache	D
Campo di Fiori	E
Cloud Nine Bistro	C
La Cocina	B
Explore Booksellers & Bistro	L
Goodfellow's Pizzeria	A
Hickory House	D
Jimmy's American	K
Johnny McGuires	B
Main Street Bakery & Café	J
Mezzaluna	F
Mogador	M
Mountain Dragon	H
New York Pizza	I
Paradise Bakery	M
The Red Onion	H
Takah Sushi	G

ACCOMMODATION

Aspen Meadows	1
Aspenwood Lodge	2
Best Western	20
Aspenalt Lodge	
Christmas Inn	9
Shenandoah Inn	4
Glenwood Springs Hostel	21
Silvertree Hotel	5
Hearthstone House	13
Snowqueen	15
Hotel Aspen	8
St Moritz Lodge	12
Hotel Durant	16
Stonebridge Inn	19
Hotel Jerome	10
The St Regis	18
Innsbruck Inn	11
Little Red Ski Haus	14
Mountain Chalet	17
Pokolodi Lodge	20
Sardy House	3
Tyrolean Lodge	7

▲ 2, Basalt, 5, 3, 4, & Glenwood Springs

Eagle and Aspen, just the vertical walls and twisting turns of Glenwood Canyon – a scenic drive, but an intimidating one in the snow. Pricey shuttle transfers are available with Colorado Mountain Express (T800/ 525-6363, $62 each way). Flights into Denver are typically much less expensive, but the city is a five-hour journey along I-70, over two mountain passes, and shuttles from DIA cost a whopping $102 each way. For the past couple of years the resort has been offering a flight-and-lift ticket package from Denver in an attempt to lure the city crowds, departing at 8.20am and returning by 8pm ($99, Wwww.aspenskiplane.com). National car-rental agencies serve all three airports, but prices at Eagle and Sardy are at a mountain premium, parking in town can be expensive, and Aspen's efficient bus service and pedestrian-friendly layout precludes the need for a car.

Amtrak and Greyhound call in at the Glenwood Springs station. Roaring Fork Transit Agency (RFTA) buses (T970/925-8484, Wwww.rfta.com) that connect to Aspen from the West Glenwood Mall add another hour or more to the trip. Once in town, RFTA buses are free to skiers, connecting downtown, outlying (free) parking lots, all four mountains, and the airport with frequent service throughout the day. Additionally, buses link Aspen and Snowmass every

10th Mountain Division and its Hut System

Set up during World War II, the **10th Mountain Division** was envisioned as an elite corps for missions against the Nazis in the snow-covered regions of mountainous Europe. America's only winter warfare unit, the men of the Mountain Division returned to became a major force in the development of skiing in the US. Troops were originally stationed at Camp Hale (dubbed Camp Hell) near Vail. Soldiers would strike out into the backcountry with ninety pounds of gear in their rucksacks, skiing on seven-and-a-half-foot long hickory boards at altitudes of over 13,000ft. The first snowmobiles, motorized toboggans, and snowcats were all developed during these exercises. Many of the 10th Division soldiers were themselves expats from Austria and Switzerland, already well-versed in alpine skills, who found themselves drawn to the raw, undeveloped mountains of their adopted country. More than two thousand of them became ski instructors upon returning from the war, and it is claimed that 62 present-day American ski resorts were either founded or originally run by veterans. In Colorado, these included the development of both Aspen and Vail.

The **10th Mountain Division Hut System**, 1280 Ute Ave, Aspen (T970/925-5775, Wwww.huts.org), was also the brainchild of a former 10th Division soldier. The system enables access to hundreds of miles of scenic backcountry mountain trails that sprawl over 34 square miles of National Forest between Leadville, Aspen, and Vail. Well-marked and well-used cross-country trails connect the seventeen huts, with boundless possibility for powder descents on the surrounding slopes. While the paths in are suitable for less experienced skiers, hut-to-hut skiing requires a high level of fitness and winter wilderness skills; flawless map, route-finding, and compass skills are essential, along with avalanche training.

Each of the huts is furnished with basic necessities like wood, a stove, electric lights, and cookware; mattresses up the comfort level of the sleeping quarters. Most sleep around sixteen people. Two of the nicest huts are the *Shrine Mountain Inn* and the Fowler/Hilliard huts. To reserve a place in a hut ($22–35 per person per night) call 10th Mountain Division Hut System, who can also reserve places for the even more remote Alfred A. Braun Hut System, which encompasses six huts between Aspen and Crested Butte. Reservations should be made well in advance for winter and are taken from June 1st for the following season. Paragon Guides (from $990; T970/926-5299, Wwww.paragonguides.com) run fully supported three- to six-day Nordic skiing trips between the huts.

fifteen minutes (6am–2.30am; $3) and serve Basalt, Carbondale, and Glenwood Springs hourly (6am–midnight; $6).

Pick up bus route schedules, discount coupons, and other local information from the **visitor center** at 425 Rio Grande Place (Mon–Fri 9am–5pm; ☎970 /925-1940 or 1-800/262-7736, ⊛www.aspenchamber.org), that is tucked under the Rio Grande parking structure.

The mountains

The four mountains are connected by Hwy-82, with Aspen Mountain rising out of town and Snowmass the last in the chain, nine miles away. All are included on the same ticket and though most visitors zero in on one mountain per day, the resort's efficient shuttles make transfers between them relatively painless. Most opt to ride just one area each day – and usually choose based on their skill level and particular interests - but it would be possible if inefficient to take at least a couple of runs on each. Mountain concierge services ensure that transfers are smooth, and parents have the option of dropping their kid off at the gondola, where a chaperoned bus will take them to one of the flatter hills for their lessons, then return them back to the Aspen gondola at the end of the day. Jibbers should take a couple of warm–up runs with their downhiller friends at Highlands in the morning, then head off for a rail session at Buttermilk in the afternoon.

On-mountain customer service is paramount: ambassadors lead tours daily at each ski area, guest services stock sunscreen, water, and courtesy phones, while coffee and cookies are handed out at the end of the day. You can also sign up for free snowcat rides with the slope groomers after the lifts close, and get first tracks before runs officially open (both available at Aspen Mountain and Snowmass; book in advance with the mountain concierge, ☎970/925-1220).

Ajax

Looming Ajax – accessed by the Silver Queen gondola right out of town – is a mogul-packed monster, known for its awesome steeps, bumps, and pine and aspen trees. There are no runs for **beginners**, and most of the **intermediate** runs here are busy pathways that funnel down through the deep gullies formed by the mountain's three precipitous ridges – Gentlemen's, Bell, and International. The best of the blues are just below the summit and under Ruthie's lift. On a powder day, **experts** should hit the short blacks off the back of the summit for a warm-up. The moguls here tend to be wider and softer than the bumpy, hard wall of double diamonds comprising the lower front face. If conditions are prime, head straight for Trainors, Rayburns, or Bingo Glades, gated areas open only as snow permits. The last of the four areas to be opened to snow-boarders, Aspen's **freestyle park** is only open in spring.

Mountain info – Aspen Mountain (Ajax)

Operating times Mid-Nov to mid-April 9am–4pm
No. of lifts 8, including 1 gondola
Base elevation 7945′
Summit elevation 11212′
Vertical drop 3267′
No. of trails 76
Acreage 673
Beginner 0%
Intermediate 35%
Expert 65%
Average snowfall 300″
Snowmaking Yes (210 acres)
Night skiing No

Aspen Highlands

Highlands is an uncrowded mountain best suited for rugged backcountry enthusiasts. There is, however, terrain for all levels, draped on the mountain in a rather odd lay-out: on the area's front peak (Loge 11,675ft), black trails are at the bottom and the sides, greens in the middle, and blues at the top. Though pleasant, the **beginner** trails are best avoided by the nervous. The learning area sits in the trees atop a steep rise, invisible from the base area, and is served by a chairlift only accessible via a cat track cut across the black runs on the lower face. **Intermediates** are well served by two high-speed quads that access mostly straight shots like Gunbarrel, along with a couple of longer, cruising runs; for your first bumps, try Grandprix. The most tantalizing **expert** terrain is way in the back on Highland peak, a huge bowl of steep powder faces, rocks,

and chutes. Most of the bowl is above timberline but there are glades on the lower flanks. Come prepared to hike: it's a good hour to the 12,382ft summit, though you can drop in earlier along the ridge, or catch a ride on the snow-cat which runs from the top of the Loge Peak lift to the first gate (runs 11am–1pm). Crested by cornices and only opened in its entirety in 2003, the bowl is 45 degrees steep – but then most of Highland's black runs are double diamonds, due to pitch, terrain, or a healthy combination of both. For those who don't feel like hiking, Loge Peak features a huge array of terrain. Explore either flank off the summit for powder stashes in the woods, or head to the short, tight, bumpy drops hidden in the trees on the lower slopes.

Buttermilk

At 420 acres, Buttermilk is the smallest of the four mountains and has one of the worst snowfall records in Colorado (100 inches less than its neighbors). Yet it is also one of the best places in the country to learn to ride, with its long, rolling runs at just the right pitch to encourage progression and build confidence. **Never-evers** start on flats right by the base lodge, then progress to tree-lined trails at the top of the mountain under West Buttermilk lift. The long, rolling, wide-open, blissfully uncrowd-ed cruising runs here also attract **snow-boarders** in droves, and Buttermilk is the center of Aspen's annual Boardfest held in December, during which skiers are banned from this mountain. The epicenter of this festival is Buttermilk's exceptional **rail park**. Though there are some harder runs, experts and advanced intermediates with no interest in rail parks can happily ignore Buttermilk.

Snowmass

Larger than the other three areas combined, and bigger than many single-mountain resorts, Snowmass boasts the longest lift-served vertical drop in the States. It's the most well rounded of Aspen's four mountains, with an extensive network of exquisitely groomed trails. Despite statistics that claim only seven percent of these runs are green, **never-evers** will have few problems on the flat lower slopes, and many mid-mountain blues are easily within the grasp of more confident **beginners**. Snowmass's sheltered, empty trails through the aspen trees on Two Creeks offer a good warm-up for lower **intermediates**. Elk Camp runs are slightly wilder with short,

Mountain info – Snowmass
Operating times Mid-Nov to mid-April 9am–4pm
No. of lifts 20, including 5 surface
Base elevation 8104′
Summit elevation 12,510′
Vertical drop 4406′
No. of trails 83
Acreage 3010
Beginner 7%
Intermediate 55%
Expert 38%
Average snowfall 300″
Snowmaking Yes (180 acres)
Night skiing No

steeper sections, littered with bumps and rollers for high-speed launching. Gentle glades and long gullies are located on Big Burn; advanced intermediates looking for something steeper should try the groomed blacks and mogul runs off Sam's Knob. At midday, one previously closed run is opened for fresh corduroy carving: this is known as the "Noon Groom", and details are posted on the daily grooming reports. Higher up off the ridgeline, the Cirque and Hanging Valley Wall offer **experts** rocky, technical descents, though don't attempt the latter toward the end of the day – the traverse out from the top of High Alpine lift is time-consuming. The best constructed hits in Aspen are arguably in the Trenchtown park at Snowmass, as are a handful of middling to big rails. It's a shame that Snowmass's excellent grooming doesn't extend to its **halfpipe**, which though well proportioned, is only cut a couple of times a week. There are also very basic **beginner parks** and miniparks.

Lift tickets, lessons, and rentals

Lift tickets are expensive and season passes pricey, though you can book multiday passes at least seven days in advance to save up to ten percent or before December to save a few bucks more. In April prices are slashed by around a

---

Independent backcountry options

Aspen Skiing Corp isn't precious about skiers using its lifts to access the backcountry around here. The exit gates off Highlands and Snowmass are well used, while the resort offers a more hand-held experience by way of its phenomenally expensive snowcat trips on the back of Aspen Mountain ($225–300). Aspen Expeditions (☏970/925-7625) and Aspen Alpine Guides (☏970/925-6618) run backcountry trips among the surrounding 14ers (mountains that top 14,000ft), hut-to-hut tours, ski mountaineering, and avalanche classes, while Ute Mountaineer, 308 S Mill St (☏970/925-2849) is the place to rent backcountry gear and get the lowdown on local routes. For details on the 10th Mountain Hut System, see p.135.

third, with last-minute lift-and-lodging packages starting at under $100 per person, a huge discount on regular season prices.

The Aspen **ski school** (☎970/923-1227 or 877/282-7736) has an excellent reputation and, befitting the resort's celebrity stature, is outfitted by Ralph Lauren. It's also exorbitantly expensive – none of the prices quoted here includes lift tickets or rentals, except for the all-inclusive beginners' package ($109). Highlights of the program include snowboard lessons for under-8s ($159), beginner through advanced classes for teens, complete with post-riding socials (ages 13-17, $69), and freeskiing camps for younger skiers (ages 10-19) ($349 for four days). Adults can take off-piste workshops, practice on an indoor skiing simulator ($179), or join intensive workshop camps led by pros like world freestyle champ John Clendenin. Challenge Aspen offers lessons for skiers with disabilities, starting at $75. Lift tickets cost half the regular price and adaptive equipment rental is $20 (☎970/923-0578, ⊛www.challengeaspen.com).

Pro Mountain Sports and D&E Ski and Snowboard (☎970/920-2337) are the well-stocked Aspen Skiing Company **rental** chains. Rates run $18–36 with discounts on multiday rentals or if booked online a week in advance. In town, the low-key Pride Snowboards, 465 N Mill St (☎970/920-9280), offers rentals from $25, while Hamilton Sports, 520 E Durant Ave (☎970/925-1200), has high-end ski demos and is rated for its ski-tuning skills.

Accommodation

Accommodation costs in Aspen are high and compounded by a relative lack of midweek discounts, as weekly vacations here are the norm. But at least the range of possibilities is wide, spanning from hostel beds and 1960s condo suites to glamorous hotels and restored Victorian B&Bs. What all have in common is their sociability, and almost every hotel offers après-ski wine and cheese in addition to large continental breakfasts. The majority can be booked through Aspen and Snowmass Lodging Reservations (☎970/925-9000 or 800/262-7736, ⊛www.aspen4u.com, last-minute deals at ⊛www.stayaspen.com). Snowmass is deservedly popular with families, and the condos there often work out to be the best deals for groups, though the village lacks atmosphere and almost all of the area's restaurants, stores, bars, and clubs are located over in Aspen. There's a limited amount of accommodation at Buttermilk, but with no services in the immediate vicinity, staying here is not recommended.

Given the local dearth of cheap motel rooms – Aspen's old motor lodges have been gussied up and now charge $150–250 a night – you'll need to travel to the nearby towns for such options. The modest spa town of **Glenwood Springs** has plenty of reasonable choices – its hot springs are an attractive bonus – but is a forty-minute drive from the mountains. This makes the mid-priced options in the Victorian railroad town of **Basalt**, sixteen miles from Aspen, more attractive.

Aspen

Aspen Meadows 845 Meadows Rd ☎970/925-4240, ⊛www.aspenmeadows.com. Stylish Bauhaus-influenced complex on the outskirts of town, home to the famed Aspen Institute, a non-profit thinktank. All the elegantly minimal one- and two-bedroom suites have floor-to-ceiling windows and sitting areas, and guests have access to a restaurant, the Hefner Lounge, and a health club with outdoor pool and jacuzzi. ❻–❾

Christmas Inn 232 W Main St ☎970/925-3822 or 1-800/625-5581, ⊛www.christmasinn.com. This cheery red-and-green motel has charming doubles at low rates. Indoor sauna and hot tub; continental breakfast included. ❺

Hearthstone House 134 E Hyman Ave ☎970/925-7632 or 1-888/925-7632, ⊛www .hearthstonehouse.com. Homage to Frank Lloyd Wright, minimalist boutique hotel, and B&B all rolled into one. Guests can relax in the herbal steam room and outdoor jacuzzi or head over to the Aspen Club and Spa – access is included in the room rate. Average ❼, online lift/lodging specials from $76 per person.

Hotel Aspen 110 West Main St ☎970/925-3441 or 1-800/527-7369, ⊛www.hotelaspen.com. Typical of "midrange" Aspen properties, motel-style rooms come with down comforters and robes. Breakfast and après-ski snacks are served in the communal lounge, occupied by older couples who return to Aspen year after year. Amenities include a small heated pool and two tubs. Doubles from ❻, online specials and lift/lodging packages from $100 per person.

Hotel Durant 122 E Durant ☎970/925-8500 or 877/438-7268, ⊛www.durantaspen.com. Two blocks from the gondola, this modern inn is elegantly furnished and has a great outdoor tub. Large continental breakfast and evening appetizers are served in the communal lounge. Standard room ❺

Hotel Jerome 330 E Main St ☎970/920-1000 or 800/331-7213, ⊛www.hoteljerome.com. Ostentatious Victorian palace in the heart of town, an Aspen landmark for over a century, stuffed with floral-patterned antiques and all the amenities you'd expect considering the top-end price. Kings ❾, but spring ski packages from ❽

Innsbruck Inn 233 W Main St ☎970/925-2980, ⊛www.preferredlodging.com. Dated alpine-style lodge on the outside, eclectically sunny on the inside; prices are a little steeper than its motel neighbors on West Main, but the furnishings and amenities are of a much higher quality. Après is served in front of the fire in the plush lounge, and there's an outdoor pool and jacuzzi. Also manages a selection of comfortable cabins, known collectively as L'Auberge d'Aspen. Ski packages from $120 per person in a four-bed room, queens ❼

Little Red Ski Haus 118 E Cooper St ☎970/925-3333 or 866/630-6119, ⊛www.littleredskihaus .net. Recently remodeled, this B&B is more upmarket than the more old-fashioned *Snow Queen* next door, with a graceful music room, stylish bedrooms, and an outdoor tub on the deck. ❼–❾

Mountain Chalet 333 E Durant Ave ☎970/925-7797. Inexpensive for Aspen, this modest mountain lodge offers dorm beds from $35 to $50, along with small private rooms (❹) and one- and two-bedroom suites (❽). Pluses include a gym, pool, tub, and generous continental breakfast.

Sardy House 128 E Main St ☎970/920-2525, ⊛www.sardyhouse.com. With fourteen spacious rooms and six suites, this turreted redbrick Victorian is more luxury inn than true B&B, complete with a pool, sauna, and hot tub. Home to the highly rated and highly priced *Jack's Restaurant*,

which serves breakfast and dinner daily. ❼–❾, ski packages available.

Snow Queen Victorian 124 E Cooper St ☎970/925-8455, ⊠sqlodge@rof.net. The oldest Victorian lodge in town is showing its age with rather faded furnishings, especially in the separate loft apartments. Prices are decent for Aspen, but it's more than you'd pay for comparable quality elsewhere. ❺

St Moritz Lodge 334 W Hyman Ave ☎970/925-3220 or 800/817-2069, ⊛www.stmoritzlodge.com. Economical, though not exactly a bargain, this lodge offers tiny but clean dorm rooms, small lodge rooms, and basic condos. Continental breakfast is included, and there's an outdoor pool and tub, a steam room, communal microwave, and laundry facilities. Discounts are given for extended stays; four sharing get the best deal. Dorm beds $30–44, basic lodge rooms ❸–❻, condos (1–2 beds) ❺

The St Regis 315 E Dean St ☎970/920-3300, ⊛www.stregisaspen.com. Aspen's most opulent lodging, a grand redbrick fortress with enclosed courtyards, endless corridors and fiery sculptures, dark restaurants and drinking dens. Think the Hogwarts of Colorado – you almost expect the stairs to move. Unfortunately, prices are surreal as well. ❾

Tyrolean Lodge 200 W Main St ☎970/925-4595, 888/220-2809, ⊛www.tyroleanlodge.com. Dated building decorated with old skiing paraphernalia. There's no complimentary breakfast or a tub, but it's great value for big groups, as each room has a kitchenette, two queens, and one twin bed. Top floor rooms are the most spacious, though fitting five can be tight; some have fireplaces. ❸–❺

Snowmass

Pokolodi Lodge 25 Daly Lane ☎970/923-4310 or 800/666-4556, ⊛www.pokolodi.com. Motel-style lodging on the slopes. Guests have use of laundry facilities, the outdoor pool, and hot tub. A continental breakfast is included. ❸–❻

Silvertree Hotel Snowmass Village ☎970/923-3520 or 800/837-4255, www.silvertreehotel.com. Large, full-service hotel right on the slopes with little in the way of visual charms but heavy on creature comforts. The health club includes outdoor pools and tubs, sauna, and steam rooms and there's a ski shop onsite.

Stonebridge Inn 300 Carriage Way☎970/923-2420 or 800/213-3214, ⊛www.stonebridgeinn .com. Clubby mountain lodge, cozier than the average Snowmass accommodations, though the bedrooms are nothing special. A decent continental breakfast is included, along with access to the outdoor pool, tubs, and sauna. ❻

Down valley

Aspenwood Lodge 220 Midland Ave, Basalt
970/927-4747 or 800/905-6797, ⓦwww
.aspenwoodlodge.com. Basic, clean suites and
small (one- to two-bed) apartments with kitchens
and livings rooms, plus a handful of motel-style
rooms. One beds ❸, two beds ❺

Best Western Aspenalt Lodge 157 Basalt Center
Circle, Basalt ☎970/927-3191 or 877/379-6476,
ⓦwww.bestwestern.com/aspenaltlodge. Spacious
motel rooms, most with two queen beds.
Continental breakfast is included, and the outdoor
tub overlooks the river. ❸

Glenwood Springs Hostel 1021 Grand Ave,
Glenwood Springs ☎970/945-8545 or 800/9-

HOSTEL, ⓦwww.hostelcolorado.com. Laid-back
hostel with a meditation room, photography dark-
rooms, and shared record collection in addition to
two kitchens. Clean and friendly, though a little
run-down and cramped. Very cheap for a US hostel. Significantly discounted tickets to both Aspen
and Vail available. Dorms from $12, couples
rooms ❶

Shenandoah Inn 600 Frying Pan Rd, Basalt
☎970/927-4991 or 800/804-5520, ⓦwww
.shenandoahinn.com. Comfortable B&B on the
banks of the Frying Pan River with four lodge
rooms, a cozy two-bedroom log cabin, outdoor
tub, and spacious communal areas. Rooms ❹,
cabin ❻

Eating

As expected, many of Aspen's classy **cafés** and **restaurants** are decidedly
upscale; reservations are essential and entrees often top $25. But many also offer
a bar menu featuring only slightly modified versions of entrees at a substantially lower price and usually available to walk-ins. Good budget places also
exist and many of them are local bars serving good, reasonably priced food as
well (see *Bars and entertainment* overleaf). The town's famous *Popcorn Wagon*, 305
S Mill St, serves crepes, gyros, and hot drinks for under $5 and is now much
copied elsewhere. Clark's Market, 300 Puppy Smith St (☎970/925-8046), is
the downtown **grocery**.

Aspen's on-mountain restaurants are a cut above – even the cafeteria-style
lodges are run by respected chefs. Oysters and sushi are served on the outdoor
deck at *Gwyn's* on Aspen Mountain, goat cheese pizza in the warming hut at
the top of Big Burn, and Mongolian barbecue at Buttermilk; meanwhile, *Cloud
Nine* on Aspen Highlands (see below) is the top-rated resort eatery.

Cache Cache 205 S Mill St ☎970/925-3835.
Elegant restaurant decorated in pastel hues serving items like rotisserie chicken with kalamata
olives and capers, an outstanding *osso buco*, and
a duck salad with candied walnuts ($12). The busy
bar serves up smaller, cheaper helpings of excellent food as well. Daily 5.30–10.30pm.

Campo de Fiori 205 S Mill St ☎970/920-7717.
Cramped and noisy bistro with great Italian food.
Particularly good selection of antipasti and unusual
pastas, like the *malfatti* dumplings, complement
the extensive wine menu. Moderate to expensive;
ask for the bar menu to avoid a hefty tab. Daily
5.30–11pm.

Cloud Nine Bistro Aspen Highlands ☎970/923-
8715. Intimate mountaintop cabin that relies more
on just the jawdropping view to justify its high
prices. An inventive prix fixe menu is served
Thursday nights only; reservations are essential,
and diners are transported up the mountain via a
snowcat. *Cloud Nine* is open for lunch daily, with
the homemade soups, salad, and breads of the

Cloud Nine Soupbowl the more budget option.

Explore Booksellers & Bistro 221 E Main St
☎970/925-5336. The nooks and crannies of this
two-story Victorian house are crammed with books
and avid readers. Upstairs, the quaint café offers
creative and moderately priced vegetarian food,
good espresso, and pastries. Daily 10am–10pm.

Goodfellows Pizza Snowmass Village Mall
☎970/923-2299. Not much in terms of surroundings, but great pizzas, sandwiches, and subs. $3 a
slice isn't particularly cheap, but it's an outright
bargain when compared to on-mountain lunch
prices. Daily 11am–9pm.

Hickory House 730 W Main St ☎970/925-2313.
Rib house that turns out the best sit-down breakfasts in town, from buttery waffles to meaty,
southern-style platters that are particularly welcome after a night out in Aspen's bars, and good
value by town standards. 6.30am–10pm.

Il Poggio 73 Elbert Lane, Snowmass ☎970/923-
4292. Bustling, warm Italian joint that's the pick of
the bunch in the unexciting Snowmass dining

scene: good pasta and pizza and decent fresh antipasti, at only moderately expensive prices. 5.30–10pm.

Jimmy's American 205 S Mill St ☎970/925-6020. This grill is classic Aspen: American diner food like burgers and chicken dinners, but cooked with flair served in a pricy cosmopolitan setting. Sit at the bar if you'd like your entree to be under $10; the vantage point for people-watching is better and access to the restaurant's hefty selection of tequilas more direct. 5.30–11.30pm.

Johnny McGuires 730 E Cooper Ave ☎970/920-9255. Neighborhood sub shop that serves huge, healthful sandwiches, accompanied by the deli's much-loved pickles. At around $7, this is one of the best values in town. Open daily.

La Cocina 308 E Hopkins Ave ☎970/925-9714. The New Mexican dishes served in the rustic, homely dining room of this long-time Aspen favorite are made fresh, with no lard but heapings of chile-infused sauce. Prices are moderate and the salsa and chips almost make a meal in themselves – when downed with sufficient quantities of the stellar margaritas. Daily 5–10pm.

Main Street Bakery & Café 201 E Main St ☎970/925-6446. The windows of this little bakery get steamed up early with locals popping in for a quick, wholesome breakfast to go, or downing oatmeal at one of the small tables. Hot sandwiches, soups, and salads are served at lunch. Opens at 7am.

Mezzaluna 624 E Cooper Ave ☎970/925-5882. Noisy, LA-style dining room with a menu of pastas ($14–18) and more expensive "big plate" entrees like ahi tuna and lamb shank. A little overpriced, perhaps, though the wood-fired pizza is a bargain during après ($5), and a less expensive bar menu is served until late, keeping the place constantly busy. Daily from lunch until late.

Mogador 430 E Hyman Ave ☎970/429-1072. Clear garlic soup, black ink leeks, and sherry-poached figs are not classic ski town fare, but then the Mediterranean-inspired *Mogador* is no classic ski town restaurant. As if the regular dining room were not exotic enough, diners are offered the chance to eat at the chef's table – right in the sparkling kitchen. Expensive.

Mountain Dragon Snowmass Village Mall ☎970/923-3576. Not the most inventive Asian restaurant in the world, but worth visiting after a day at Snowmass for the après ski drink specials and free appetizers, served 4–6pm daily.

New York Pizza Hyman Ave Mall ☎970/920-3088. Snowboard stickers line the narrow stairs leading up to Aspen's best-loved little pizza parlor. Slices from $2.75, salads under $10. Open lunch until late.

Paradise Bakery 320 S Galena St ☎970/920-1444, and in the Snowmass Mall, Snowmass. Not really an eat-in sort of bakery, but the best place in town for cookies and coffee. Tasty bargains lurk in their large box of discounted day-old pastries. Daily 6.30am–late.

The Red Onion 420 E Cooper Mall ☎925-9043. In business since 1892, Aspen's oldest bar is also *the* spot in town for burgers, and one of the few places to get a filling dinner for under $10. Can get rowdy during après, 3.30–6pm. Daily 11.30am–10pm, bar until 2am.

Takah Sushi Hyman Ave Mall ☎970/925-8588. Though the sushi here runs $5–6.50 a item, the fish in this alleyway restaurant is so good that the locals eat here as often as they can afford it. Non-sushi fans are also catered to, with a menu that includes pan-Asian dishes like *pad thai* ($18) and Chilean sea bass ($25). Reservations suggested.

Bars and entertainment

Aspen's **nightlife** ranks among the best of any ski town in North America. Exhibiting a distinctly urban flavor, people here eat late and drink later, with bands and DJs kicking off well after 10pm. The town runs a Tipsy Taxi service (☎970/923-5064), free to those who overindulge, at the discretion of their barman. Quiet nights are spent at the three-screen Carmike Cinemas, 625 E Main St (☎970/925-2050), or catching an art house film or show at the splendid Wheeler Opera House (☎970/920-5770), erected during the Victorian silver boom. The Aspen Music Festival, held every summer, presents a winter schedule of classic concerts at the Harris Concert Hall (☎970/925-9042), while the Aspen Santa Fe Ballet performs at the Aspen District Theater (☎970/925-6098). Pick up a copy of the free *Aspen Daily News* for detailed listings.

As a vacation spot of the media elite, the town hosts numerous **festivals** throughout the season; from December's pre-Oscar Academy Screenings and

February's HBO Comedy Week to the oldest and best attended Gay and Lesbian Ski Week in the US (☎970/925-9249, ⦿www.gayskiweek.com). On-mountain events range from celebrity downhills to World Cup qualifiers.

Double Diamond 450 S Galena St ☎970/920-6905. Large basement venue that hosts everything from big-name bands to calendar-girl contests. The place itself is a little dingy; go for a show, not just for a drink.

Elevation 304 E Hopkins Ave ☎970/544-5166. Stylish, warm restaurant that doubles as the town's late-night DJ bar. Has that big-city atmosphere down pat.

Eric's 315 E Hyman Ave ☎970/920-1488. Classy billiards room downstairs in the Mill Street Plaza, linked to both a cigar bar and a bar for nonsmokers. Prices are high for both drinks and pool.

The Grottos 320 S Mill St, ☎970/925-3775. Mountain punk-hippy hangout that sprawls over connecting rooms in the bowels of downtown. Local bands and DJs play five nights a week.

J-Bar *Hotel Jerome*, 330 E Main St ☎970/920-1000. A slightly older crowd congregates along the grand bar in the historic *Hotel Jerome*, an opulent Aspen watering hole since 1889.

Shooter's Saloon 220 S Galena St ☎970/925-4567 This place aims to be rowdy and raucous, from the dance floor to the pool table. Eighties Nights are scheduled frequently.

Whiskey Rocks 515 S Mill St ☎970/544-2485. This stylish, dark lounge bar inside the *St Regis* hotel resembles a scene from a Bret Easton Ellis novel, filled with Aspen's wealthy youth.

Woody Creek Tavern 2 Woody Creek Plaza, River Road, Woody Creek ☎970/923-4585. Notorious thanks to the writings of Hunter S. Thompson, this little bar just north of town is patronized by the rich and famous searching for a fresh lime juice margarita.

Other activities and attractions

Aspen's "Fifth Mountain" is easily its best value, since the 65km of **cross-country** ski trails groomed by the Aspen/Snowmass Nordic Council (⦿www.aspennordic.com) is one of the most extensive free cross-country trail networks in the US. It can be accessed from both the Aspen Cross-Country Center, 308 S Mill St (☎970/544-9246), and the Snowmass Club Cross-Country Center, 239 Snowmass Club Circle (☎970/923-3148), both of which offer equipment and lessons (rentals from $13.50, lessons from $30, tours from $50). Should you tire of these trails you can also explore the 22 miles of groomed trails maintained by Ashcroft Ski Touring Unlimited (☎970/925-1971, trail passes from $10, rentals $20, lessons $45, tours $65), centered on the old ghost town of Ashcroft eleven miles west up Castle Creek Road. Those in search of **backcountry adventure** should contact the 10th Mountain Division Hut Association office in town (see box on p.135). Ute Mountaineers, 308 S Mill St (☎970/925-2849), is a fantastic source of local equipment for cross-country skiers and has **snowshoe** rentals as well.

The **skatepark** next to the Rio Grande Park is small but perfectly formed; locals try it out as often as the weather permits. Othello's, 465 N Mill (☎970/544-8274), the town skateshop, has a small basement miniramp. For ice skating, visit the pretty Silver Circle outdoor rink, 433 E Durant (☎970/925-6360, $6.50, skates $2.50). Yoga, fitness classes, cardio equipment, and 3200ft of indoor climbing wall are located at The Red Brick Gym, 110 E Hallam (☎970/920-5140), an affordable, city-run option among a sea of pricey spas.

Venture down to Glenwood Springs to sink into the sulphurous **mineral waters** at the rather institutional Glenwood Springs Pool, 410 N River St (daily 9am–10pm; $10.25; ☎970/945-6571), purportedly the largest of its kind, or relax in the steam baths of the subterranean Yampa Spa Vapor Caves, 706 E 6th St (daily 9am–9pm; $8.75; ☎970/945-0667), where spa treatments are also on offer. Locals eschew both and head to the river, where the bubbling pools near the I-70 bridge are free.

Listings

Copper

The largest ski area in Summit County, **Copper** spreads across a cascading mountain with suitable terrain for virtually every rider, from blue cruisers and back-bowl freeriders to mogul bashers and nervous 6-year-olds – a wider mix than any of its neighbors.

Despite this – and its reasonable ticket prices and long ski season – the mountain remains markedly underrated. Much of this is due to a notion of it as little more than a ski area with a string of condos attached, not the typical image of a destination resort. Over its thirty years Copper has been known as a commuter mountain, and to a large extent it is; even the resort's employees live elsewhere. Yet there is a sense of community, albeit a daytime one, that caters to families while paying attention to the desires of younger freeriders. Customer service is friendly and there are welcome touches like tool benches at the top of each lift and lots of clean and comfortable public spaces to lounge about in. There is, however, little off-slope variety at Copper, in dining, entertainment, or accommodation, and almost no sign of local life once the lifts have closed. On the whole, families looking to take advantage of extensive kid- and teen-programs along with the good-value ski-and-stay deals offered at Copper's more antiquated condos should base themselves in the resort. Others might rather try the busy and unpretentious community of Frisco (pp.114–115) six miles away and linked to Copper by the county's free bus system.

Mountain info

Phone ☎970/968-2882 or 800/458-8386

Snow phone ☎970/968-2100 or 800/789-7609

Website ⊛www.coppercolorado.com

Price $34–61

Operating times Early Nov to third week in April, Mon–Fri, 9am–4pm; weekends, 8.30am–4pm

No. of lifts 22, including 1 high-speed six-pack and 4 high-speed quads

Base elevation 9712′

Summit elevation 12313′

Vertical drop 2601′

No. of trails 125

Acreage 2450

Beginner 21%

Intermediate 25%

Expert 54% (skewed by back bowls)

Average snowfall 280″

Snowmaking Yes (380 acres)

Night skiing No

Nursery facilities Yes, ☎866/241-1481, from $75 full day; Belly Button Babies and Bakery, Mountain Plaza building, 6 weeks to 4 years, skiing from age 3, snowboarding from 7

Arrival and getting around

Only 75 miles from Denver straight up I-70, Copper nestles right next to the freeway at the crossroads of Summit and Eagle counties, making it just as fast, if not faster, to get to than geographically closer Winter Park, Breck, Keystone, or A-Basin. Copper is twenty miles east of Vail and an hour from Eagle County Airport. Resort Express **shuttles** from DIA cost $52 one way, taking two to three hours to make the trip to Copper. Free Summit Stage buses link the resort with the rest of the county, running 6am–midnight. For more detailed information on getting to and traveling around Summit, see p.113.

The resort base comprises three areas: the East Village, primarily a gateway to more advanced terrain; the new Village at Copper, home to rentals, coffee shops, bars, and most ski and snowboard lessons; and Union Creek, the children's center and beginner ski (but not snowboard) school. If wondering which base to hit first, head to the Village at Copper, the resort's busy hub.

Resort guests can park beside or under their accommodation. Day visitors have the choice of the free Alpine and Corn lots, connected to all bases via a frequent free shuttle (6am–11pm) or four pay lots ($10-15) marginally closer to the slopes.

The mountain

"If there were a mountain that had terrain for skiing, it would be Copper Mountain."
US Forest Service survey, 1972

The front face of the ski area, which neatly spreads over two peaks, is naturally segregated with easier slopes to the west and the toughest terrain to the east, with a rolling graduation between the two. Despite a mostly successful attempt to replicate this division at ground level – experts depart from the East Village, beginner skiers from Union Creek, and everyone else funnels through the central Village at Copper – it soon becomes apparent that things aren't quite that simple. For a start, there's some very good intermediate and expert terrain high on the western boundary. And then there's the valley down the center of the ski area; the ridgelines of Copper and Union peaks funnel down to the Village at Copper in a V with each fork served by a high-speed quad, providing the main access points to the mountain. With a deep rift between the two ridges by the time they reach their respective summits, it's especially important for groups to figure out what peak they're aiming for and exactly which lift they decide to meet at the top of later – crossing between the two involves a run back to base. Ignore the Easy Road catwalk as it's frustratingly flat. On the backside are Copper's four bowls, above the treeline and tucked away from the worst of the weekend crowds.

The nuances of Copper's undulating, ridge-lined terrain are hard to figure out from studying the stylized trail map, shaded to emphasize terrain breakdown but with faded-out geographical features that make on-mountain navigation tricky. It's not just the trail map that breaks with tradition; ski patrol wear mango-orange jackets accented with lime-green crosses. Those wearing green jackets are mountain ambassadors; stop by their yurt next to Solitude Station for free cookies and mountain tours, which depart at 10.30am and 1pm daily.

Beginner

Never-evers should avoid the green runs directly above the Village, as they are crowded thoroughfares that often get icy, particularly late in the day. Instead start out on the quieter, gentler western slopes accessed from the Union Creek base. Magic carpets, tows, and three slow chairlifts serve green-only territory that is very rarely visited by more advanced skiers. Once confident on longer trails, head to the top of American Flyer (or take High Point to the Timberline Express) and try **Roundabout**, a quiet and wide cruiser littered with little berms and rollers, just right for tasting those first few inches of air. (More advanced riders will also enjoy Roundabout, making it a good warm-up or wind-down for mixed-ability groups.) Novice snowboarders should avoid the flat Woodwinds Traverse heading from Timberline Express to the Village as it's a calf-burner even for more experienced riders.

Intermediate

Cautious intermediates may want to warm up on **Roundabout** (see above) to avoid the weekend crowds in the center of the mountain, but if the masses don't bother you head up American Eagle from the Village and follow any of the half-dozen blue trails meandering straight down the fall line. Next head up the Excelerator lift directly above American Eagle (or ride Super Bee from the East Village) to access **Andy's Encore**, a 2400ft vertical cruiser that's a proto-type Copper-blue laced with both flatter ridgeline sections and challenging drops. On the opposite, western boundary, the blue fingers under the Timberline Express are training grounds for powder monkeys, flanked by mellow glades and blessed with small natural hits and stashes of deep snow. When ready to step it up to blacks, head higher up the mountain from here to the **Far West** and **Retreat** trails near Union Meadows; the slightly bumped pistes here are peacefully secluded and shorter in length than the thigh burners on the eastern slopes. Aspiring bowl riders should try easier Copper Bowl first.

Expert

If arriving with passes and gear and looking to session expert terrain all day, consider parking close to the isolated Alpine doublechair on Copper's eastern boundary; this is the most direct route to the forested bumps and cascading powder pockets on the steepest slopes of the front face. Otherwise, start at East Village and ride up Super Bee to its drop-off just above **Resolution Bowl**, a bald crest that shoots behind the front face into tight, cluttered glades and bumped-out trails. Be warned that a more southerly aspect back here can result in patchy conditions. Icier blacks descend back into the East Village, but after lapping Resolution head for Copper's four alpine bowls instead. The chutes and cornices of **Spaulding Bowl** are tempting, but getting back out involves a long descent to the bottom of Resolution. If time is limited or you need to meet up regularly with lower level skiers, ungroomed **Enchanted Forest** or **Union Bowl** will keep you on the front face and funnel you down between the two American lifts back to base. The snow on these two faces is more reliable than in **Copper Bowl** on the backside, but when conditions warrant, head here first to hopefully snag a ride on the first-come, first-served free snowcat that follows the boundary out to the chutes and glades of relatively untouched **Tucker Mountain** one bowl over. On the frontside, the finest glades are **Sail Away** and **17 Glades**, both short but sweet with plenty of stashes. For backcountry advice, see p.115.

Freestyle

Copper's parks and superpipe are well maintained, and just about the only gripe is that the main park, **Loverly**, is surprisingly difficult to reach. Take the slow High Point chair from Union Creek, which lets off directly above the park, or the speedy American Flyer and stay high on the ridgeline until the park entrance is within your sights. The park caters to all abilities with three distinct tabletop and rail lines to follow. Further down the mountain, within full view of the Village plaza, the **Hollywood** hit (plus a couple of warm-up huckers) is heavily used in the spring, with various check-me-out contests playing their part in Intrawest's long menu of such events. For more laid-back options, intermediates can drop into the woods under **American Flyer**, which hide a multitude of mini-jibs. Or try the minipark and gentle rollers on **Roundabout** and the small cornice that builds up above **Timber Ridge**, rider's left off the Sierra lift. Pro huckers can try their luck among the cliffs and gullies of **Copper Bowl**, take the free snowcat to **Tucker Bowl**, or hike out along Union Peak to hit the **Onion Roll**, a giant, natural kicker.

Lift tickets, lessons, and rentals

During the heart of the season, adults tickets don't come cheap ($61), though there are numerous ways to get heavy discounts. Available online, the Copper card ($10) nets savings on food, lessons, and tickets; also watch out for the Four Pass, available from King Soopers grocery stores in December, and good for four tickets for under $100. Later in the year, buy tickets from the supermarket rather than the mountain to save a few bucks. Nonrestricted season passes start at just $250 preseason, not much more once the season begins.

Beginner **ski lessons** meet at Union Creek while all others start at Copper One in the Village. Half-day lessons begin at $50 ($84 including lift ticket and rentals), with an excellent roster of classes from never-ever to all-mountain freeride instruction and terrain park schooling. Special programs include weekly telemark lessons (no rentals available), women-only and, unusually, men-only sessions, catering to all abilities. Copper also maintains great kids and teens programs, full details of which can be found on their website.

The three resort-owned **rental shops** (one at each base lodge) have good rates on beginner ski packages but are fairly expensive for everything else. The resort maintains a high-performance ski store in the village, 9600 FT, but has a limited snowboard inventory. For purchases and demo-quality, inexpensive board rentals, visit Polar Revolution (Tucker Mountain Lodge, ☎970/968-0171). AB Ski and Sport, tucked away in the Snowbridge Square Mall (☎970/968-2908), is better suited to novice skiers and rents outerwear, goggles, and helmets.

Accommodation

Condos are the only **accommodation** at Copper, all either ski-in/ski-out or at most a short walk from the slopes. Standards do vary: deluxe giant timber and stone lodges with access to hot tubs and gyms make up Intrawest's new Village at Copper. Suburban-style townhomes are at the edge of the snow-covered golf course, and though clean the units apparently have been untouched since the 1970s. Studio rooms without kitchens are also offered, usually as annexes of larger condos. The ski area manages most of the property in the resort (☎888/219-2441) and allocates accommodation based on desired size and quality rather than by choice of building; a fifteen percent location fee is charged for specific requests. An alternative is to go through one of two independent property management companies in the resort, Copper Vacations (☎970/968-6840 or 1-800/525-3887, ⊛www.coppervacations.com) or Carbonate Property Management (☎970/968-6854 or 1-800/5-COPPER, ⊛www.carbonate-real-estate.com).

Copper One, *Tucker Mountain Lodge*, *Taylors Crossing*, and *Passage Point* are names to look for if you'd like to stay at modern hotel-style condos in the new Village, while *Copper Springs Lodge* offers similar amenities in the East Village. *Copper Valley*, *Summit House*, and *Telemark Lodge* are among the more basic and cheaper choices on the outskirts of the Village. All ski-and-stay packages booked through the mountain include free parking, access to the Copper Athletic Club, and VIP Beeline tickets, allowing guests to skip lines and use the lifts fifteen minutes early. Packages start at just $69 for lift and lodging, with midweek and family specials usually available.

See pp.114–115 for lodging elsewhere in Summit County.

Eating, drinking, and entertainment

Though a handful of new places opened around Copper's lake in 2003, there's still little serious choice to **eating out**, with most restaurants resort-owned and overpriced. Standards are perfectly fine, but the themeing definitely tires, with the likes of a Russian-style vodka bar competing with an Irish pub and faux-Mexican cantina. For more options or self-catering, your best bets are over in Frisco (see p.116).

With a clientele of day skiers used to bringing their own snacks, on-mountain dining is not a priority. Like the cafeterias at each base area – Grand Hall Market, Jack's, and Union Creek – Solitude Station at the top of American Eagle is a modern food court with typical cafeteria cuisine at the typically overinflated prices. Best bet is to stop by *Frank's*, the hotdog stand for lunch under $5.

Copper management is big on staging **festivals** and **competitions** throughout the year. The annual spring fling draws crowds with big-name bands and a bikini contest, while the season-long Copper Mountain Snowboard Series, closing in on its twentieth year, is the longest running amateur snowboard series in the nation.

The Blue Moose Village Plaza ☎ 970/968-9666. Pizza joint with slopeside après. Sit on the outdoor deck and enjoy $2 slices, drafts, margaritas, and shots. 11am–11pm.

Bongo Billy's Passage Point in the Village ☎ 970/968-0222. Shiny, light branch of the small Colorado coffee shop chain, with decent espresso and baked goods.

Creekside Pizza and Restaurant Snowbridge Square ☎ 970/968-2033. Tucked away across the creek, this cozy spot is the best value in the Village. No ostentatious theming here, just tasty Italian food, sandwiches, and salads. Weekend après includes $1 slices and $2 microbrews. 11am–9pm.

Double Diamond Foxpine Inn, East Village ☎ 970/968-2880. Comfy and worn-in restaurant, family-run and reasonably priced, best known for its $5.95 Friday all-you-can-eat fish fry. 10am–10pm.

Endos Village Plaza ☎ 970/968-3070. Sports bar and grill with salads and entrees big enough to share. Arcade games, pool, and big-screen TVs

more likely to be showing the X-Games than football. Open until (relatively) late, the closest thing to a local hangout. 11am–midnight.

Indian Motorcycle Club Village Plaza ☎ 970/968-2099. Similar to the *Hard Rock Café*, but a more upscale Canadian chain, decorated with motorcycle paraphernalia. The rather pricey evening menu includes plenty of Asian-inspired finger food suitable for après munchies, and entrees that range from steak and sea bass to stir-frys. Deep leather couches and billiard tables by the separate and well-stocked bar – the margaritas go down nicely – make this a relaxing evening haunt for resort guests.

JJ's Rocky Mountain Tavern Copper Station in the East Village, ☎ 970/968-2318. This faux-Western grill at the base of the slopes serves hearty lunches and hosts a longstanding après show with rockin' Moe Dixon (Weds–Sat), catering to the older, more traditional après crowd. 10.30am–10pm.

Other activities and attractions

It doesn't take long to explore this small resort and its handful of family-oriented stores. Copper's Central Reservations (☎888/229-9475 or x4INFO within Copper) might help you find some other diversions, arranging winter catch-and-release fly-fishing on tumbling streams, snowmobiling through the backcountry, or sleigh rides that culminate with dinner in the snowy woods and singsongs around the fire.

Surrounded by the shops and stone buildings of the Village, Westlake is a romantic spot for nighttime ice skating. Located slopeside in East Village, Copper's long tubing lanes have their own tow (Sun–Thurs 11am–7pm, Fri–Sat 11am–8pm; $14 adults, $8 kids). Bring your own cross-country equipment to use the 25km of ungroomed trails that meander through the White River National Forest from Union Creek. The Copper Athletic Club ($10 visitors pass; ☎970/968-2826) offers indoor activities like a swimming pool, tennis court, racquetball, weight room, fitness machines, massage therapy, and spa services.

Listings

Avalanche hotline ☎970/668-0600; Summit County ☎970/668-1090; statewide ☎877-315-7623.
Internet The public library in Frisco has free access.

Medical Copper Medical Center, Bridge End Building ☎970/968-2330.
Pharmacy Copper Medical Center.

Crested Butte

Host of the US extreme skiing and snowboarding championships for the past decade, **Crested Butte** (pronounced "beaut") offers some of the most taxing terrain on the continent. Freeriders from across the region, even across the world, are drawn to the mountain's seemingly vertical runs; it's no surprise that the renaissance of telemark skiing began in the area. Don't let that totally fool you if you're a beginner, though; the lower slopes fan out in a wide web of flat greens, so there is room for groups with mixed abilities.

At the base of the slopes is a bleak resort village adjacent to one of the more unattractive collections of condominiums in North America. Three miles down the road, however, is the town of Crested Butte, a lovingly preserved Victorian mining community, resplendent with gaily painted clapboard homes and stylish restaurants and bars.

Arrival, information, and getting around

A five-hour drive southwest from Denver along mostly two-lane highways, Crested Butte is not the most easily accessible resort in the state – although Colorado's high desert weather patterns mean that the roads are usually dry even during good snow years, except on Hwy-50 over Monarch Pass. Fans would point to the multiple daily flights on United to Gunnison County Airport from Denver; once on the ground, it's thirty minutes to the resort on the Alpine Express Shuttle (☎970/641-5074 or 800/822-4844, $41 round-trip). There's no need to rent a car at the airport unless planning a trip to Monarch (see p.249), Telluride (p.168), or elsewhere. Downtown, almost everything of interest is within a block or two of Elk Avenue, if not on it. The Free Mountain Express shuttle buses serve Crested Butte, Mount Crested Butte, and the outlying condos every fifteen minutes, from 7.15am until midnight, and the inexpensive town taxi (☎970/349-5543) drives the shuttle route past midnight.

If you opt to stay in the small ranching town of Gunnison and drive in for the day, park in the free lots at the intersection of SR135, Gothic Road, and Elk Avenue, beside the visitor center (daily 9am–5pm; ☎970/349-6438 or 800/545-4505, ⊛www.visitcrested butte.com). Take the shuttle up to the ski area. There is also free parking off Snowmass Road in Mount Crested Butte, but it fills fast. Be warned that the speed limit in town is a strictly enforced 15mph.

The mountain

Runs here are often either of the "are you *sure* it's not vertical?" variety or they're flat. Greens are wide and mellow, ideal for absolute beginners, but the majority of blues are a challenge. As for the blacks, Crested Butte has the steepest lift-served terrain in North America; over 42 percent of the ski area is listed as ungroomed, double black diamond. Without persistent autumn storms, however, don't expect the ungroomed terrain to be open consistently before January. In poor years, the Butte's pyramid peak remains out of bounds. Sadly, the resort seems mired in a slough of dry seasons and even the more consistent North Face cliffs, trees, and gullies are more often rocky technical challenges than powder playgrounds. With the ungroomed stuff taken out of the equation, Crested Butte is pretty small. Plans have long been afoot to develop neighboring Snodgrass Peak into Crested Butte North, an almost entirely intermediate mountain. Until then, a week's vacation for a lower intermediate is pushing it. The situation is particularly tough for snowboarders ready to move off the bunny slopes, as there are several unavoidable flat spots that encircle the mountain.

With the exception of these flat tracks, Crested Butte is simple to navigate. Unless staying in a condo accessible from the Gold Link lift area on the backside, everyone ends up riding home under the Keystone quad and congregating outside the Gothic cafeteria. The only real pain is getting back up the mountain from the far side of the North Face bowls. Prepare for a long traverse followed by a three-lift journey.

Mountain info

Phone ☎888/463-6714

Snow phone ☎970/349-2323 or 888/442-8883

Website ⊛www.crestedbutteresort.com

Price $58

Operating times Mid-Dec to early April, 9am–4pm

No. of lifts 14, including 3 surface and 2 Magic Carpet

Base elevation 9375ft

Summit elevation 12162ft

Vertical drop 2775′ lift-served; 3062′ with inbounds hike

No. of trails 85

Acreage 1058

Beginner 15%

Intermediate 44%

Expert 41%

Average snowfall 298″

Snowmaking Yes (300 acres)

Night skiing No

Nursery facilities Yes, Kid's World ☎970/349-2259 or 1-800/600-7349 daycare from 6 months, skiing from 3 years, group snowboarding from 8 years

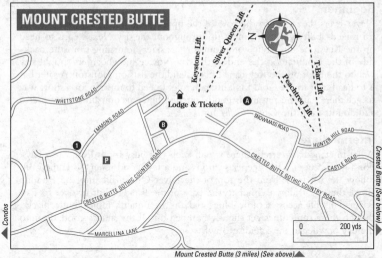

ACCOMMODATION		RESTAURANTS & BARS					
The Claim Jumper	7	Avalanche	B	The Idle Spur	M	Pitas in Paradise	O
Crested Butte Club	4	Baccanale	F	Kochevar's Saloon	E	Princess Wine Bar	H
Crested Butte		Black Whale	G	The Last Steep	L	Ruby Mountain Bakery	N
International Hostel	2	The Brick Oven Pizza	I	Lil's Land & Sea	D	The Slogar	R
Elk Mountain Lodge	3	Butte Bagels	C	Marchitelli's Gourmet		Talk of the Town	M
The Great Escape	5	The Eldo	P	Noodle	Q	Teocali Tamali	K
The Inn at Crested Butte	6	Firehouse Grill	A	The Paradise	J	Timberline	G
The Nordic Inn	1						
Pioneer Cabins	8						

Beginner

Never-evers start close to the base of the upper mountain lifts, making it easy for mixed-ability groups to meet up throughout the day. Next step is to head up the Keystone lift – but watch out for fast skiers returning from the backside of the mountain at the end of the day. Novice snowboarders should stay well to their left off the Keystone lift, to avoid the flats on Houston. A safer bet is to head over to the Gold Link lift; you might need to unstrap for a short way to get there, but the reward is gently pitched blues accompanied by espresso and donuts from the *Camp4Coffee* hut.

Intermediate

What intermediate terrain there is will keep you busy for at least a few days. For a long cruiser with steeper sections and a few good rollers to launch off, follow the cat track from the top of the Silver Queen lift into the Paradise Bowl, then head down either to the base of the Paradise Lift or over to East River. This lift accesses more blues and the mountain's more gentle blacks, though these sometimes get slightly bumped out. If the snow's good, dip into the dry powder in the Paradise Bowl.

Expert

When open, the hike-access only terrain off Silver Queen is a wide expanse of above treeline rocky bowl and couloir riding, dropping down into tiers of aspen glades. Skier's right off Silver Queen is the High Lift t-bar, which places you on top of the infamous Headwall. Hike high for open bowl powder (or, in less than perfect conditions, bumped-out moguls) and rocky cliff bands. Stay low and to skier's left for short, sharp tree runs. Accessed by a poma, the North Face bowls tend to hold powder better than Headwall. Hike up into the trees above the lift to drop a chute into the cliff-strewn upper North Face, to access the far bowls, Spellbound, and Phoenix. Directly underneath the poma are vertiginous glades and forested gullies littered with rocks. It seems to be a point of pride for Butte aficionados that both Headwall and the North Face are served by tricky surface lifts, since these deter novices whose technique for riding sheer slopes involves scraping half the snow off the mountain.

Freestyle

Crested Butte just isn't a jibbers' mountain. With so many cliffs to huck off, manmade terrain isn't a high priority. However, thanks to the involvement of the Crested Butte Academy, a private high school in town for aspiring mountain champs, the pipe here is pretty decent, and there are usually a couple of mid-size hits and rails. One bonus is that the dedicated park/pipe area has its own, albeit slow, lift called Teocall, separate from the rest of the mountain. It's not unusual to see as many telemark skiers in here as skiers and riders. Outside of the park, the loop from the top of Silver Queen lift, through Paradise Bowl and back to the front side, usually throws up a few natural rollers, cat track hits, and the occasional log slide.

Lift tickets, lessons, and rentals

Families do best at Crested Butte in the ticket deal stakes. Kids up to 16 years old pay the same price as their age – so a 5-year-old's ticket would cost $5, a 10-year-old's $10, etc. Lift-and-lodging packages are often announced at the last minute online, while minimal savings are gained by booking multiday tickets at least fourteen days in advance.

Independent backcountry options

Crested Butte's surrounding backcountry consistently gets almost double the amount of snow as the resort. There's plenty of potential for downhill descents and kicker construction in the surrounding hills – along with an extremely high likelihood of avalanches. Fortunately, with a large proportion of Gunnison's Western State graduates headed for careers in the outdoors, the region boasts numerous avalanche and backcountry courses and guides. Crested Butte Mountain Guides (☎970/349-5430, ⓦ www.crestedbutteguides.com) runs avalanche classes throughout the season in conjunction with the AYH hostel, and guides private skiing and snowboarding trips (either on a daily basis or hut and yurt based). One of the simpler excursions in the area can be arranged through the Nordic Center (see p.156) – an overnight trek up to a ski hut in the old ghost town of Gothic. At the opposite end of the scale is the Grand Traverse, an annual "extreme endurance backcountry skiing race" between Crested Butte and its northern neighbor, Aspen.

Regular group **lessons** (expensive at $65) are only scheduled in the morning, but ski school (☎970/349-2252 or 1-800/444-9236) here specializes in technique- and/or terrain-specific workshops ($75), held twice daily. Beginner's lesson-and-lift packages start at $75. The Adaptive Sports Center of Crested Butte (☎1-866/349-2296; ⓦ www.adaptivesports.org) has offered year-round programs since 1987. In winter the schedule includes skiing, snowboarding, cross-country, backcountry trips, snowshoeing, ice skating, dogsledding, and snowmobiling.

The **rental shop** in the Gothic Center is adequate and includes telemark skis, cross-country skis, snowshoes, and helmets in its inventory. Beginner packages are inexpensive, but for anything better you'll pay at least $10 more. For a wider selection of snowboards, head straight for Colorado Boarder (☎970/349-9828) in the slopeside Mountain Mall. The definitive Crested Butte core store, this is the place for tune-ups, gear, and advice on taking a snowmobile out into the backcountry. Close by is Flatiron Sports (☎970/349-6656, ⓦ www.flatironsports.net), the skier's equivalent.

Accommodation

There are few hotels but plenty of condos around the slopes in Mount Crested Butte, with the resort itself (☎888/463-6714; ⓦ www.crestebutteresort.com) the largest property management company in the region. Downtown accommodation is limited but more charming than most on-mountain options, and closer to evening action. There should be no problem finding a room midweek, off-peak. Over holidays, however, even motels thirty miles away in Gunnison flash "no vacancy".

Downtown Crested Butte

The Claim Jumper 704 Whiterock Ave ☎970/349-6471, ⓦ www.visitcrestedbutte.com/claimjumper. Extravagant, higgledy-piggledy B&B whose six rooms are filled with lovingly presented Americana. Jerry, the owner, serves up huge breakfasts, and will even officiate at guests' weddings if asked. Stay in the baseball suite, where memorabilia is behind glass, or the Coca Cola room, with its collection of bottles from around the world. ❹

Crested Butte Club 521 Second St ☎970/349-6655. National Historic Landmark, built in 1886, with eight elegant antique-filled rooms. Breakfast served daily at the lavish mahogany bar. Public areas smell a little of chlorine from the rather tatty spa, though there is a clean, indoor lap pool and tub. Regular rates ❻, midweek discounts may be negotiable depending on state of season. $15 day pass to spa.

Crested Butte International Hostel 615 Teocalli Ave ☎970/349-0588 or 888/389-0588, w www.crestedbuttehostel.com. Built in 1997, this large, friendly hostel is well equipped with an on-site laundromat, river rock fireplace in the lounge, and large dining and kitchen areas. Beds are usually available in winter unless booked out for a group. Ski packages and meal plans are offered, and the hostel hosts a number of outdoor education courses (see backcountry box p.153). $25/27 members/nonmembers; couple's rooms ❸, shared or private bath. No chores, curfew, or lockouts; front desk hours 7.30am–noon, 3–9pm.

Elk Mountain Lodge Second St and Gothic Ave ☎970/349-7533 or 800/374-6521, w www .elkmountainlodge.net. Renovated 1919 miners hotel with a comfy, worn-around-the-edges feel. An inglenook bar, grand piano, indoor hot tub, and library with free Internet access add to the appeal, but it's the friendliness of the staff that really makes the place. An extended continental breakfast is served in the enclosed veranda. Ask for a third-floor room with a balcony. ❸–❹

The Great Escape 329 Whiterock Ave ☎970/349-1131, w www.thegreatescapebnb.com. On a residential street downtown, this intimate, four-room B&B is decorated primarily in the southwestern style, with heated wooden floors, hot tub, and upstairs lounge with great view of the Butte. ❹

The Inn at Crested Butte 510 Whiterock Ave ☎970/349-1225 or 800/949-4828. This seventeen-room ranch-style inn is more relaxed than its brochures suggest. The grandly named "Great Room" feels more like a family lounge, with

games, kids' toys, musical instruments, and Speedy the guinea pig. Bedrooms are modern Scandinavian in décor. There's an outdoor hot tub with wonderful views on the upstairs veranda, and an extended continental breakfast is included in the reasonable prices. Triple occupancy rates ❸, double ❷; minimum stay required over the holidays. Ski packages and handicapped accessible. ❸

Mount Crested Butte

The Nordic Inn 14 Treasury Rd, ☎970/349-5542 or 800/542-7669, w www.nordicinncb.com. A cute, surreal vision of Scandinavia mixed with the style of a 1950s motel – just five minutes' walk from the lifts. Owners Allen and Judy are stalwarts of the Crested Butte community and join guests daily for the extended continental breakfast and around the fireplace in their cozy lobby. The outdoor hot tub has views across the valley. Some rooms have kitchenettes. ❹

Pioneer Cabins 2094 County Rd 740, Cement Creek Rd ☎970/3495517, w www.thepioneer.net. Ten minutes from town, these eight period cabins in the Gunnison National Forest sleep four to six and come with wood stoves or open fireplaces, flannel sheets, fully equipped kitchens, and a heavy dose of wilderness. Communal phone; televisions on request. Of most historical interest are the four built in the 1920s to house skiers from the now-defunct Pioneer ski area. ❸–❹ based on double occupancy; $10 per extra guest, age 5 and under free.

Eating

Dining options in Mount Crested Butte are fairly limited. With the exception of the fondue and raclette at the overplayed *Swiss Chalet*, restaurants here typically offer standard grill fare in uninteresting surroundings, though for $35 ($25 for Colorado residents), the seriously hungry can experience a slice of Club Med, located on the slopes, at their famous dinner buffets.

In town, however, there's an incredible concentration of superb restaurants for such a small, isolated resort; reservations are highly recommended, even during the week. Clarkes, 500 Bellview (☎970/349-6492), is the local **supermarket**, with Mountain Earth Wholefood Grocer, 405 Fourth St (daily 8am–8pm; ☎970/349-5132), good for organic alternatives, fresh fish, herbals, and hot soups and salads at lunch. There are also a couple of places catering to the huge condo contingent with gourmet meals to go – the *Cucina* of Crested Butte, 425 Elk Ave (☎970/349-7174), and *Why Cook?*, Belleview-Majestic Plaza (☎970/349-5858).

At the top of Painter Boy lift, the *Camp4Coffee* is the best on-mountain spot; have real espresso and donuts at noninflated prices. If you've the money and inclination, take an evening sleigh ride (pulled by a snowcat, not reindeer) to the *Paradise Warming House* for four-course posh nosh at 10,000ft. *Rafters* is the base area bar, with the *Gothic Cafeteria* below (☎970/349-2299 or 2260), with large sunny decks right on the slopes and après specials.

Avalanche 433 Eammons Rd, Mount Crested Butte ☎970/349-7195. This worn-around-the-edges grill in the base area has lines out the door at lunch. Huge breakfasts, pizza by the slice, warming chili, burgers and fries from 2pm, and a full bar propped up at all hours by skiers on leave from the slopes; happy hour at 3–7pm is an alternative to resort-run *Rafters*. 7.30am–9pm.

The Brick Oven Pizza 229 Elk Ave, ☎970/349-5044. Reliable pizza and subs in the center of town with free delivery, 5–9pm.

Butte Bagels 218 Maroon Ave, Crested Butte ☎970/349-2707. This ramshackle, brightly painted hut has cream cheese or PB&J bagels for $2, and large filled bagels starting at around $2.50. 7.30am–9pm.

Firehouse Grill 11 Snowmass Rd, Mount Crested Butte ☎970/349-4666. Right off the slopes, this sports bar/grill is owned and operated by local firefighters (many of whom are also on ski patrol and search and rescue), and is open for après and dinner.

The Idle Spur 226 Elk Ave ☎970/349-5026. Home to the Crested Butte Brewery, this huge log-beamed building serves up huge, tasty, but not inexpensive steaks, fish, and fine beers in a large dining room.

The Last Steep 208 Elk Ave ☎970/349-7007. The small entrance leads to a tiny bar and a series of whitewashed rooms, interspersed with colorful fish tanks. Great prices, a friendly atmosphere, and late hours keep the locals coming back for innovative salads, hot sandwiches, and Cajun/Caribbean specials. 11am–late, depending on the crowd.

Lil's Land and Sea 321 Elk Ave ☎970/349-5457. With ingredients flown in from both coasts, the surf n' turf in this elegant, mustard-colored restaurant is fresh and inventive. Try the *ciopinno* seafood stew, or elk medallions with Alaskan king crab legs. Not cheap, though the sushi happy hour at 5.30–6.30pm can be affordable with self-restraint. 5.30pm–9ish, reservations recommended.

Marchitelli's Gourmet Noodle 411 Third St ☎970/349-7401. Italian, not Asian, with the rich scent of hearty pasta sauces tantalizing those waiting for a table. Great food at good prices, with a spaghetti, salad, and bread early-dinner special for four at $19.95, served nightly from 5pm.

The Paradise 303 Elk Ave ☎970/349-6233. Known for filling breakfasts, the *Paradise* is a diner with southwestern/Mexican flavors. Hours vary at the management's discretion.

Pitas in Paradise 214 Elk Ave ☎970/349-0897. Mint-green cabin serving kebabs and lots of veggie options, like falafel, at a low price. Fresh – even the spinning meat looks attractive – and simple, with a dining room to match.

Ruby Mountain Bakery 302 Elk Ave ☎970/349-1291. The place to stop in en route to the mountain to pick up an egg muffin or breakfast burrito to go, or relax with the paper, a coffee, and a pastry. Sandwiches start at $2.95 for a PB&J. 7am–5pm, breakfast served until 11.15am.

The Slogar Second St and Whiterock Ave ☎970/349-5448. Very odd mix, this: Southern-style skillet-fried chicken family dinners, complete with biscuits, gravy, and all the trimmings served in dimly lit, renovated and replicated Victorian surroundings. The centerpiece is an elaborate, carved saloon bar. Odd, but wonderful. $13.45 per adult, ice cream and coffee included. 5–9pm.

Teocali Tamali 311 1/2 Elk Ave ☎970/349-2005. There are a few reasonable Mexican restaurants in town but this bright little spot is fast and fresh. Their burritos were voted "best gut bomb" in town, cost $5, and have fillings like pesto and mahi mahi.

Timberline 201 Elk Ave ☎970/349-9831. Fine dining with a contemporary twist. Splurge on Asian steamed mussels, caribou medallions, or Louisiana gumbo in one of two dining rooms. The ground-floor bistro has stylish terracotta walls, leather booths, and bar stools with cowhide backs; upstairs is less stylish and more expensive. Music on weekends. Entrees $17.50–28.

Bars and entertainment

Locals, college kids from nearby Western State, and visiting crews all gather in much the same spots, and they like to party hard. Few of the bands that play are big name, but there's always a bunch to choose from on the weekend. Bars are all within a block of each other on Elk Avenue; if you don't like one, stumble on. Check the listings in the *Crested Butte Weekly* (free) or *Crested Butte Daily News* (50 cents). The Majestic Theater (Majestic Plaza, ☎970/349-7570) schedules a mixture of blockbusters and indie films on its three screens, while the Crested Butte Center for the Arts, 606 Sixth St (☎970/349-7487), shows special-interest movies and stages plays, readings, and concerts.

Baccanale 209 Elk Ave ☎970/349-5044. Indulge in this stylish Italian restaurant on the cheap during happy hour (4.30–6pm) or stop for a snack and a cocktail. Appetisers are served at the long mirrored bar until 11pm.

Black Whale Third and Elk ☎970/349-0480. Basement bar and restaurant that draws a younger crowd. 3.30pm–midnight; closed Sundays.

The Eldo 215 Elk Ave ☎970/349-6125. Upstairs bar in a long, narrow building whose exterior resembles a set from a Western. Billing itself as a "sunny place for shady people," the *Eldo* hosts the better known acts that come through town. There's a dance floor in back and a balcony over the street

that gets packed during après on sunny spring days.

Kochevar's Saloon 127 Elk Ave ☎970/349-6745. This old brothel still packs them in every night, though these days the attractions are pool tables, drinks specials, free popcorn, and loud music.

Princess Wine Bar 218 Elk Ave ☎970/349-0210. Wine, espresso, and acoustic music in an intimate setting.

Talk of the Town 230 Elk Ave ☎970/349-6809. Old timers prop up the bar downstairs, while the younger crew congregate in the small space upstairs for foosball and pool accompanied by the sounds of local bands and DJs.

Other activities and attractions

Strolling around Elk Avenue's many stores and galleries could easily take up an afternoon, and the period buildings add to the appeal, especially if you don't shop. Gunnison, just south of Crested Butte on Hwy-135, is worth the trip out if you're in a car and have never strolled around the small-town West. On the drive down valley, keep an eye out for the bald eagles that nest in the trees along the East River, drawn to the area by the Roaring Judy Fish Hatchery.

Two blocks off Elk, the friendly staff in the timbered **Nordic Center**, Second Street and Whiterock Avenue (☎970/349-1707), rent cross-country ski packages from $14 and snowshoes at $12 per day. Over 50km of trails are groomed for classic and skate skiing; trail passes are $10, though the town-owned trails through town and up to Mount Crested Butte are free. The staff can offer advice on the extensive backcountry opportunities in the area (see p.153), including an overnight hike up to the Forest Queen Hut in the appropriately named ghost town of Gothic. The hut sleeps eight and has a fully equipped kitchen, with firewood and drinking water provided, though food and bedding must be brought ($12 per person per night). Day and evening snowshoe tours are also offered at the resort (☎970/349-2211). Rent crosscountry and telemark gear from the Troutfitter, 313 Elk Ave (Mon–Sat 9am–6pm, Sun 10am–5pm; ☎970/349-1323); demos are available.

Crested Butte's small **ice rink** is free, located next to the Nordic Center (see above); skates rent for $5 an hour. Go horseback riding at the Powder Ranch (☎970/349-2646) or dogsledding with the Cosmic Cruisers (☎970/641-0529). The visitor's center has leaflets on all the local snowmobile operators. There's also a map available of trailheads in the Gunnison National Forest open for winter activities, including independent snowmobiling, dogsledding, and paragliding.

Listings

Airport Gunnison County Airport ☎970/641-2304.
Avalanche hotline ☎970/349-4022.
Bookshops The Book Store, 327 Elk Ave ☎970/349-0504.
Internet Old Rock Schoolhouse Library, 507 Maroon Ave ☎970/349-6745.

Medical Crested Butte Medical Center, Ore Bucket Building ☎970/349-0321.
Post office 215 Elk Ave ☎970/349-5568.
US Forest Service 9194 Taylor River Rd, Gunnison ☎970/641-4623.

Durango

The ski area formally known as Purgatory is gradually attempting to reinvent itself as **Durango Mountain Resort** (DMR) while maintaining its reputation as an unpretentious and inexpensive alternative to the major Colorado resorts. The small base area recently received a face-lift and new chairlifts and condos are planned, but this modest ski mountain remains decidedly unsophisticated. Tucked into the southwestern corner of Colorado, DMR primarily attracts visitors from Texas and neighboring Southwest states; without the social cachet or facilities of Telluride, the remote area is largely overlooked by skiers from further afield.

The fortunate consequences are short liftlines and uncluttered slopes. All runs are below treeline and there's little in the way of more extreme terrain, but the entire area is naturally terraced, littered with bumps and dips and with trails to suit all levels. Seasonal snowfall varies from epic to average, but – thanks to its location on the southern rim of the Rockies – there are more sunny days here than at any other resort in Colorado. Even in mid-winter, it's typically warm enough for skiers to sit outside in the spruced-up pedestrian plaza of little Purgatory Village.

Most off-slope action occurs in Durango, 25 miles down the Animas valley. Once the railroad hub of the Four Corners region, this comfortable college town is now a summer tourist magnet for bikers, hikers, and history seekers. Its restored redbrick downtown is packed with reasonably priced restaurants and bars, and motels line the highway north of town. Unlike the busier resorts further north, winter is the off-season here, and Durango offers some of the best lodging deals for skiers in the state.

Mountain info	
Phone ☎970/247-9000 or 800/525-0892	
Snow phone ☎970/247-9000	
Website ☸www.durangomountainresort.com	
Price $52	
Operating times Late Nov to first week in April daily 9am–4pm	
No. of lifts 11, including 1 magic carpet and 1 surface for tubing	
Base elevation 8793′	
Summit elevation 10822′	
Vertical drop 2029′	
No. of trails 75	
Acreage 1200	
Beginner 23%	
Intermediate 51%	
Expert 26%	
Average snowfall 260″	
Snowmaking Yes (250 acres)	
Night skiing No	
Nursery facilities Yes, Cub Care (☎970/247-9000, ext 5152), 2 months to 3 years; skiing for 3–12, snowboarding for 8–12	

Arrival, information, and getting around

DMR is an easy three- to four-hour drive from Albuquerque, and seven often snowy ones from Denver. The closest **airport** is little Durango–La Plata County, though cheaper flights are available to Albuquerque, the hub of Southwest Airlines. Car rental companies represented at the Durango Airport and downtown include National (☎970/259-0068) and Dollar (☎970/259-3012). With the resort and town separated by 25 miles, a car is useful if you don't want to rely on the sporadic Mountain TranSport **ski shuttles** ($5 round-trip; ☎970/247-9000). These run along Hwy-550 between Durango and DMR seven times a day, picking up at motels and hotels en route. Many of the downtown hotels also provide a shuttle service to the mountain, while the resort condos run evening trips into town. The Durango LIFT **public bus service** ($1) has a limited daytime service around town, with evening service between north Main and the Durango Mall until around 9.30pm. The Main Avenue red trolley serves the downtown district and is free with tokens from local stores and restaurants. Durango Transportation offers 24-hour taxi and airport shuttle service ($15 one way to town; ☏970/259-4818 or 800/626-2066.)

There are **tourist information** booths on Main Street near the station and at the visitor center, 111 S Camino del Rio (Mon–Fri 8am–5pm; ☏1-800 /525-8855), in a riverside park just off Hwy-160/550 on the east side of town.

The mountain

Don't be intimidated by the short, steep rise of the front face that can be seen from Hwy-550. The fast **Purgatory Village Express** sixpack carries riders over a couple of false summits to a far mellower backside of tree-lined greens, rolling, terraced blues, and powdery, bumped-out blacks, a world away from the groomed, steep, racer-style runs visible from the village. There is, however, an easy way back down to the village; stay to skier's left and ride home on the blues and greens underneath the Twilight lift.

Ideal for intermediates, DMR is perfect for **high-speed cruising**. Though neither huge in acreage nor vertical drop, the sideways-sprawling backside takes time to explore – it's not unusual to find yourself on a run you never knew existed, even after a few days. In general, runs progress in difficulty the further back you go; beginners and cautious intermediates will find it best to stay closer to the front face, under lifts 2 and 3 (chairlifts at DMR are often referred to by number, though all are also named). Be warned that all three backside lifts close at 3.30pm. Snowboarders in particular do not want to be at the top of lift 8 at that time, as they'll end up trudging back along the BD&M Expressway ridge – not an expressway by any stretch of the imagination.

Possibly because of these navigational difficulties, most skiers cluster around the front face or stay in back on the blacks, leaving the terraced blues in the middle section blissfully quiet. These rollercoaster runs of bumps and blind headwalls are suitable for both timid intermediates and more advanced riders – the flat steps are a place to either catch one's breath or catch some air. Though there are "No Jumping" signs on the blind spots, ski patrol is fairly tolerant, particularly on Snag, where building kickers is actually encouraged. Many of the natural rollers are ideal for the wary, since you can see your landing easily and take the hit as big as your speed will allow. There are, however, plenty of blind drops so make sure to use a spotter.

Beginner

Absolute beginners have their own dedicated area squashed in between the freeway and Purgatory Village, a rather grubby and unexciting meadow. Next step is the more interesting **Twilight area**, a collection of winding, tree-lined greens and flat, easy blues. More confident beginners can head straight to the summit on Lift 1. From here, cat tracks curve gently back to the frontside (snowboarders need to stay high to avoid losing their speed), while the gentle Hermosa Parkway leads to Lift 5.

Intermediate

Almost all the blues at DMR are long, wide, and flanked by trees, featuring plenty of diversions on the way down – including natural bumps and rolls, mellow glades, and mini mogul fields. Lower intermediates should start on the more gentle runs under Lifts 2 and 3; those with confidence can work up to the thigh-burning intermediate moguls, wide glades, and gentler blacks underneath Lift 8. In between, **Boogie** and **Peace** are great terraced runs, dotted with patches of easy trees and the odd mogul field left ungroomed down one side of the trail.

Expert

Classic alpine downhills are found on the steep slopes of the front face, terraced by cat tracks and graced with small groves of aspens; try **Styx** first. The best glade riding is on **Paul's Park** under the top of Lift 8. Trees on the rest of the mountain are pretty thick and tight, and jaunts into the woods often end in a walk back to the chairlift. The mountain's few cliff drops can be spotted underneath the lower sections of Lifts 3 and 5. For anything more extreme, or if boredom sets in, consider heading to Silverton or into the backcountry (see box below as the surrounding San Juan range is home to some of the steepest peaks in the country.

Freestyle

DMR's park and pipe are located just below the *Powderhouse* restaurant. It's not bad for a small area, with a selection of kickers and rails from baby on up. Both can be lapped on the creaky, slow Engineer double chair, which runs directly overhead. On busy days, it's often faster to charge around the corner and down to the base area, then head back up the high-speed sixpack.

Lift tickets, lessons, and rentals

DMR is one of the less expensive resorts in Colorado, and **lift ticket** prices are even better value if you plan ahead. Four- and six-ticket packs are available preseason and in January from local grocery stores (try the City Market in Durango), priced at around $25 per ticket. The Total Adventure ticket works well for less-than-hardcore skiers on longer breaks; a day on the mountain can

---

Independent backcountry options

Durango is surrounded by the craggy San Juans, a range respected for its steep slopes and above-timberline skiing. **San Juan Skiing Company** (☏970/259-9671 or 800/208-1780, ⊛www.SanJuanSki.com) **snowcats** operate right off the backside of the resort in the untracked powder of the San Juan National Forest. Daily rates are $175; if you've got the cash, the three-night lodging/cat packages are much better value. **San Juan Snowcat** ($200; ☏719/754-2754, ⊛www.sanjuan-snowcat .com) operates out of Creede, 100 miles to the east. **Silverton**, North America's only wholly ungroomed ski area, is around an hour's drive from DMR, and a less expensive introduction to the backcountry than a snowcat trip (see p.250). Local backcountry spots include Molas and Red Mountain passes, but as avalanche danger is extremely high in this region, solo missions are not advisable. Stop in at Backcountry Experience, 1205 Camino del Rio (☏970/247-5830) downtown, for backcountry advice and mountaineering, climbing, and telemark equipment. Avalanche courses are run by the climbing guides at Southwest Adventures (from $120; ☏970/259-0370 or 800/642-5389, ⊛www.mtnguide.net).

be swapped for one of many alternative activities in the program, from soaking in the hot springs to backcountry touring (See "Other activities and attractions on p.163).

Group **lessons** ($35) are scheduled in the morning and afternoon, with specialty clinics held occasionally throughout the season. Including lift ticket and rentals, the $65 never-ever packages are good value and guarantee success – or free lessons. Based in Purgatory Village, the Adaptive Sports Association (℡970/385-2163, ⊛www.asadurango.org) offers an extensive program to riders with disabilities; lift, lesson, and equipment packages are $80 and should be booked in advance.

Decent **rental options** are available at the base of the slopes. Purgatory Ski Rentals is the resort's fleet store; expert skiers should head to Performance Peak, for new demos and tuning facilities. Bubba's Boards (packages $28; ℡970/259-7377) is the place to rent snowboards. In-town, HassleFree Sports/The Boarding Haus, 2615 North Main Ave (7.30am–7pm; ℡970/259-3874), opens early and offers ski packages from $12 and step-in beginner board packages starting at $20.

Accommodation

There isn't much variety of **accommodation** at the resort itself, with only a few condos on the mountain and a rather shabby *Best Western*. Independently managed condo complexes just a five-minute shuttle ride away include the relatively inexpensive *Needles* (℡970/259-9560) and *Cascade Village*, more upmarket and family oriented (℡970/259-3500 or 800/525-0896).

Because the drive to Durango is an easy one, it's normal for skiers to base themselves in town. The downtown offers some lovingly restored western hotels and B&Bs, while the long strip of mostly ugly motels lining the highway north of town should be kept in mind if price is a factor (rooms can be had there for around $30/night).

Vacation homes close to the resort can be booked through the resort, the Visitor's Center,or Durango Central Reservations (℡800/525-0892 or ℡970/247-8900, ⊛www.durangocentralreservations.com). The Hermosa Meadows Camper Park, 31420 Hwy-550 N #24 (℡970/247-3055 or 800/748-2853), is open year round, with RV spots for $21–30.

Durango Mountain Resort

Apple Orchard Inn 7758 County Rd 203 ℡970/247-0751 or 1-800-426-0751, ⊛www.appleorchardinn.com. Close to Trimble Hot Springs, the simply decorated, crisp white wooden cottages of the Apple Orchard offer more privacy than the average B&B, arranged around the perimeter of a manicured English-style garden. The owners are friendly and flexible, planning breakfast menus according to the guests' wishes and serving up dinner, if it's required. ❸–❹; third person $15 extra, which includes breakfast. **Elkstone Inn** 34940 Hwy-550 N ℡970/385-0488, ⊛www.elkstoneinn.com. On the banks of the Animas, this large cedarwood home has only four guestrooms, but offers spa services such as massage and a peaceful outdoor hot tub. ❹

Logwood B&B 35060 Hwy-550 ℡970/259-4396 or 1-800/369-4082, ⊛www.durango-logwoodinn .com. Beautiful red cedarwood log building, with patchwork quilts on the bed, towering ceilings in the lounge, and mountain views. Each of the eight rooms has its own TV, and there's a rec room with a pool table and exercise bike. ❹–❺ **Purgatory Village Condominium Hotel** #5 Skier Place ℡970/385-2100 or 1-800/693-0175, ⊛www.durangomountainresort.com. The huge discrepancy in prices at this giant, resort-owned condo complex reflects differences in the unit and time of year. Rather shabby luxury, but right on the slopes – and the rooftop hot tubs are really special. The studios are annexes of larger condo suites, and though they do have useful kitchenettes, the dividing walls are thin. ❸–❾

Durango

Days End Motel 2202 Main Ave (Hwy-550) ℡970/259-3311 or 800 242-3297, ⓦwww .daysend.com. Not much to look at but clean and good value, with indoor hot tub, outdoor heated swimming pool, and laundry for the same price as many of the smaller, older motels. Rooms in the new block are larger; some have kitchenettes. Handicapped accessible rooms available. ❶

DoubleTree 150 Fifth St ℡970/259-6580 or 800/222-TREE, ⓦwww.doubletree.com. Best of the chains, this modern hotel downtown has reasonable rates, large rooms and hot tub, sauna, indoor pool, and restaurant. Ski packages are available and a ski shuttle runs to the resort daily. ❸–❻

The Gable House 805 E Fifth Ave ℡970/247-4982, ⓦwww.creativelinks.com/Gablehouse. Roomy B&B that's a living piece of American Victoriana, a Queen Anne home complete with fairytale turret and veranda. Elegant and peaceful, it's located on a quiet residential street downtown. ❹

Iron Horse Inn 5800 N Main Ave ℡970/259-1010 or 800/748-2990, ⓦwww.ironhorseinndurango .com. Family resort by the narrow-gauge railtracks at the north end of town. All suites have lofts with at least one queen and one double bed; some have kitchens. A little dated, perhaps, but with reasonable rates for the space. ❸

Leland House 721 E Second Ave ℡970/385-1920 or 800-664-1920, ⓦwww.Leland-hotel.com. Simple and austere, this sister to the *Rochester* is a fastidiously renovated apartment building, dating from the 1920s. All rooms and suites have kitchens or kitchenettes, though breakfast at the *Rochester* is included. ❺

Rochester Hotel 726 E Second Ave ℡970/385-1920 or 800-664-1920, ⓦwww.rochesterhotel.com. Less self-consciously Victorian than the *Strater*, this 1892 redbrick building feels more like an old family house and has been restored around a Western theme, each room decorated with memorabilia from movies shot in the Durango area. The creaky staircase descends into a comfy dining room, where filling breakfasts and afternoon cookies are served. ❹

Strater Hotel 699 Main Ave ℡970/247-4431 or 800/247-4431, ⓦwww.strater.com. Historic Western hotel with a huge collection of antique furniture and memorabilia, including an elaborate bar (see p.163). ❸–❼

Eating

On and around DMR choices are limited. In a sunny clearing near the top of the Grizzly Lift (#5), *Dante's* has the best location for hanging on the mountain but the food is just average; try *Café de los Pinos* upstairs. Above the terrain park, the *Powderhouse* serves subs and calzones at typically expensive mountain prices; on the beginner's hill is *Columbine Station*, set in an old forester's cabin with open-flame cooking and warming fireplace. *Purgy's* is right on "the beach" at the village base, in an A-frame lodge built in 1966, with martini bar, outdoor grill, and beer "garden" with loungers.

Durango's Main Avenue is lined with **restaurants** catering to all types. North Main is the home of fast food and a large City Market; there's also a City Market downtown in the Town Plaza Shopping Center.

Durango Mountain Resort

Mountain Market and Deli Village Plaza ℡970/247-9000. With a long deli counter and a few bar tables, the deli is not a spot for lingering but a place to purchase inexpensive breakfast burritos, breakfast muffins, and alcohol-to-go. Groceries are overpriced, however, capitalizing on hungry condo guests who forgot to buy in town.

Olde Schoolhouse Café & Saloon 46778 Hwy-550 ℡970/259-2257. Three miles down the road from the resort, opposite the Needles General Store, the *Olde Schoolhouse* serves great pizza, enormous calzones, and locally brewed Ska beer on tap. Though billed as a restaurant, the main room is dominated by the bar, (free) pool table, and local memorabilia.

Village Coffee Company Village Plaza ℡970/247-9000. There's room for just a few tables in this coffee pit stop, but it's nice to find a coffeeshop in a remodeled resort area that hasn't been branded.

Durango

The Buzz House 1019 Main Ave ℡970/385-5831. Cozy, worn-around-the-edges coffeeshop serving breakfast and lunch. Scrambled eggs with tofu served with sides of freshly baked bread and fruit. Mon–Fri 7am–4pm, Sat 8am–4pm.

DSP 600 Main Ave ☏970/385-0420. Decent pizza by the slice, conveniently located downstairs from *The Summit* and within stumbling distance of other downtown bars. Sun–Thurs, 10am–10pm, Fri–Sat 10am–midnight.

Durango Bagel 106 E Fifth St ☏970/385-7297, ⓦwww.durangobagel.com. Bright, simple bagel shop by the steam railway station, with good-value breakfast bagels, cinnamon rolls, and bag lunches to go. 6.30am–3pm daily.

Durango Diner 957 Main Ave ☏970/247-9889. Greasy spoon with green chili that's considered a hangover cure by some. This is the sort of place that gets politely described as having "lots of local color". 6am–2pm daily.

Kachina Kitchen Centennial Center, 325 S Camino del Rio ☏970/247-3536. Inconvenient location east of town, but worth the trip for traditional southwestern fast food at budget prices. Mexican and Native American influences, translating to corn burritos and fry bread tacos. 10am–8pm, closed Sun.

Ken and Sue's East 636 Main Ave ☏970/385-1810. Low-hanging pumpkin-colored lamps and dark wood booths set a stylish tone, and the upscale Asian fusion dishes don't disappoint. The original *Ken and Sue's Place* (937 Main Ave ☏970/259-2616) is a bistro with a spring-fresh touch, and has a more laid-back ambience and home-cooked menu.

Mai Thai 1050 Main Ave ☏970/247-8272. Tiny space with five tables and a handful of counter stools, but the most genuine Asian food in town. The Thai, Indonesian, and Filipino rice dishes, curries, and noodles are also cheap, under $10 for a filling meal. Open 11.30am–8pm Mon to Sat.

Old Tymer's Cafe 1000 Main Ave ☏970/259-2990. Gets the locals' vote for the best burgers in town. Monday night is Burger Night, with huge beef patties on sale for $3.75; on Friday, tacos are just $1.50. 11am–10pm.

Skinny's 1070 Main Ave ☏970/382-2500. Small, popular restaurant that manages to be chic yet relaxed, serving great pastas and Southwest specialties at excellent prices. Mon–Thurs 11.30am–9pm, Fri–Sat 11.30am–10pm, Sun 8am–2pm.

Steaming Bean Coffee Co 915 Main Ave ☏970/385-7500. Large coffeeshop with fresh soups, sandwiches, wraps, and Web access.

Steamworks Brewing Co 801 E Second Ave ☏970/259-9200. Industrial-style brewpub in, unsurprisingly, an old converted steamworks. Decent beer is brewed in the giant vats on show, served with peanuts whose shells end up on the floor. Huge, good-value servings of American classics, from burgers to pastas and large salads; the messy Cajun Boil is a ridiculous amount of food.

Stonehouse Subs 140 E 12th St ☏970/247-4882. This brightly painted wooden house is a little off the main drag downtown, but it's well worth the extra few blocks for their fresh and innovative subs.

Nightlife and entertainment

Beyond hanging out and playing free pool at the *Olde Schoolhouse*, there's not much in the way of **nightlife** near the resort. Durango has a ton of good bars and crawling between them is easy – they're all within a few blocks of each other downtown. There's live music most weekends, with local punk bands and the occasional trance night in addition to the usual rock, blues, and funk offerings. Fort Lewis college runs a theater (☏970/247-7320) and community concert hall (☏970/247-7657), with performing arts series and concerts by the San Juan Symphony staged throughout the winter season (ⓦwww.durangoconcerts .org, ⓦwww.sanjuansymphony.com). Annual events include a midnight run on the Durango & Silverton steam train for New Year; the SnowDown winterfest held annually in late Jan/early Feb; and the terrific Durango Film Festival, held in early March (☏970/259-2291, ⓦwww.durangofilmfestival.com). Durango has two movie theaters: the old-fashioned Gaslight, 102 Fifth St (☏970/247-8133), and Trans-Lux Theaters, next door to the bowling alley in Durango Mall (☏970/247-9799), east of town on Hwy-160/550.

Abbey Theatre 128 E College Drive ☏970/385-1711, ⓦwww.abbeytheatre.com. Basement bar with screenings of indie flicks.

El Rancho Tavern 975 Main Ave ☏970/259-8111.

Jack Dempsey is reputed to have fought his first fight in this long, brick-walled room, which these days is warm and welcoming. With pool tables in the back, murals on the wall, and free popcorn,

The Ranch, as locals call it, is a Durango institution and practically a town meeting place at the end of the night.

Lady Falconburgh's 640 Main Ave ☏970/382-9664, ⊛www.falconburgh.com. Decorated with faux tapestries, tankards, and badly painted heraldic imagery, this is a basement sports bar cum English medieval drinking house. The American grill menu is average; come here for the liquor selection, including 40 single malts, 120 bottled beers, and 20 on tap. Open lunch until late.

San Juan Room 601 E Second Avenue ☏970/382-9880. Spacious upstairs bar/venue with four pool tables, pinball, large seating area, dance floor, and stage. Can be quiet when no band is scheduled, though there are ladies' nights and other weekly specials.

Ska Brewery 545 Turner Drive ☏970/247-5792, ⊛www.skabrewing.com. They like ska. And they brew beer. Good beer, like the Pinstripe Red, sadly only available in the southwest. Visit the ultimate Durango locals in their tasting room. Mon–Fri 4–7pm.

Sky Ute Casino Ignacio ☏970/563-3000. Twenty minutes' drive from town, this tribal casino on the Southern Ute reservation is no Vegas, but draws the crowds, all the same.

Storyville 1150 Main Ave ☏970/259-1475. Though their Southern BBQ, wood-fired pizzas, and calzones are decent, it's the good range of live music that brings the crowds here. There's also a small, separate pool room, with a slightly odd showroom window that puts your game on display to anyone who's passing. Happy hour runs 3–6pm every day; pizza is served until midnight.

Strater Hotel 699 Main Ave ☏970/247-4431. Slightly over-the-top Victorian surroundings. A honky-tonk piano player holds court in the *Diamond Belle Saloon*, while pricey early-evening cocktails are served in the Office "Spiritorium."

The Summit 600 Main Ave ☏970/247-2324. The galleried areas in this small club are made comfy with pool tables and couches. Loads of local bands are showcased on the tiny stage. Daily 4pm–2am.

Other activities and attractions

The resort offers the usual roster of alternative snowy activities: snowmobile trips, dinner sleighrides, tubing hill (Alpine Snowcoaster, open 1–8pm, Thurs–Mon, $5 a ride), and snowshoe tours of the San Juan National Forest. More unusual are the **stargazing** sessions ($49): a snowcat takes would-be astronomers up the mountain to the deck of the *Powderhouse* restaurant, to stare at the heavens through a thirty-inch diameter telescope and drink plenty of hot chocolate. All activities can be booked through the Activities Desk in the Village (☏970/247-9000). In town, the new **recreation center**, 2700 North Main St (Mon–Fri 6am–10pm, Sat 8am–10pm, Sun 10am–6pm; $3.50; ☏970/375-7300), has an indoor track and climbing wall, fitness machines, racketball courts, and indoor pool complex with waterslides and a lap pool. The three tight bowls of Durango's old concrete **skatepark** are, to put it as positively as possible, challenging, though improvements are planned for the near future; the park is by the Animas River downtown, just over the 9th Street bridge. A small indoor park is located in the back of the Shred Shed skateshop, 1150 Main Ave (☏970/259-0913).

Groomed **cross country** is limited: the Nordic Center (☏970/385-2114) opposite the resort has only 16km of groomed trails but offers lessons, inexpensive rentals, and moonlight tours. Trail passes here are $8.50 (lesson packages are included in the Total Adventure Ticket program); there are 10km of free trails out at Vallecito Lake, maintained by the Pine River Valley Nordic Ski Club (☏970/247-1573), but you need your own equipment. After all that activity, **Trimble Hot Springs** (6475 CR 203, just off Hwy-550N; ☏970/247-0212, ⊛www.trimblehotsprings.com), is the place to unwind, an old-fashioned outdoor spa in the suburban ranch land midway between town and resort, with an Olympic-size pool and three natural mineral pools (100°–110°F) surrounded by a tall wooden fence. Massages and other spa treatments available (Sun–Thurs 9am-10pm, Fri–Sat 9am–11pm; day passes $8.50).

Listings

Loveland

Spilling off the Continental Divide, with a base altitude of 10,600ft and the highest chairlift in the world, it's little wonder to see the phrase "In most states, getting this high is a felony" on T-shirts around **Loveland**. But Loveland is more than just altitude. This unpretentious, largely commuter resort 71 miles west of Denver not only averages more snowfall and a longer season than most of its more celebrated Colorado counterparts (a few runs are usually open by Halloween but the record is late September), but has a ski area larger than Crested Butte, Durango, or any of the Aspen mountains except Snowmass.

Yet even with these superlatives, not to mention competitive prices and quality terrain, Loveland remains a relatively undiscovered secret. Base area development is minimal, but down the road are the mining towns of Clear Creek County – Silver Plume, Georgetown, and Idaho Springs – perhaps unappealing from the freeway, but all handy bases full of character with well-preserved Victorians and rustic saloons.

Arrival, information, and getting around

The closest resort to Denver, Loveland is a straight shot up I-70 and located just before the Eisenhower Tunnel – the gateway to Summit County often subject to bottlenecks and closures. Since the ski area is directly off the interstate, a four-wheel-drive is not a necessity, and usually nor are chains. Parking is free at the resort and plentiful in the local towns. For Denver practicalities, see the box on p.113. Working back east along I-70, tiny Silver Plume is 24 miles east of Loveland; quiet

Mountain info	
Phone ☎303/571-5580 or 1-800/736-3754	
Snow phone ☎303/571-5554	
Website ⊛www.skiloveland.com	
Price $23	
Operating times Mid-Oct to late May, Mon–Fri 9am–4pm, Sat & Sun 8.30am–4pm	
No. of lifts 11, including 2 surface lifts	
Base elevation 10600′	
Summit elevation 13010′ (12,700 lift-served)	
Vertical drop 2410′	
No. of trails 65	
Acreage 1265 lift served, plus 100 extra hikeable	
Beginner 25%	
Intermediate 48%	
Expert 27%	
Average snowfall 396″	
Snowmaking Yes (160 acres)	
Night skiing No	
Nursery facilities Yes, from 12 months, ☎303/571-5580 or 1-800/736-3754	

Georgetown 26 miles; Empire 31 miles; and scruffy Idaho Springs, the largest by far, is 42 miles away.

For more information head to the **visitor center** at the west end of Colorado Boulevard (℗303/567-4382 or 1-800/685-7785, Ⓦwww.idahosprings chamber.com) in Idaho Springs.

The mountain

Loveland divides into two neighboring areas: a gentle beginners' mountain in **Loveland Valley**, and **Loveland Basin**, a huge, mostly open bowl that funnels around the freeway and reaches up to the Continental Divide. A free shuttle and a chairlift connect the two.

It's easiest to **navigate** the Basin left to right, using Chair 1 to get up the mountain and traversing across via Chairs 6 and 9. Though barely evident on the trail map, the mountain flattens out at the bottom of Chairs 4 and 6; so take care to carry your speed here. Note that Loveland Basin is notorious for high winds on the often icy uppermost slopes. Be sure to have a neck gator for the chairlift, even it's sunny and warm at the base area.

Beginner

Beginners have their own facilities (ski school, restaurant, bar, rentals) at Loveland Valley, and a surface lift, double chair, and quad accessing wide open greens, curving cat tracks, and three easy blues. Almost the entire Loveland Valley area receives snowmaking, so coverage, even early in the season, is rarely a problem. At Loveland Basin, take slow Chair 2 to Ptarmigan Roost for long, flat greens back to base. Avoid the easy route from Chair 1, as it's a crowded main thoroughfare for better skiers and riders.

Intermediate

Loveland Basin is ideal for intermediates. Most of the groomed trails are tree-lined blues, with open cruisers, corridors, bowls, moguls, and plenty of dips and rollers. Intermediate snowboarders may find the cat tracks back to the base area tiring, so keep your speed.

Expert

There aren't many classic blacks at Loveland, but there is enough decent expert terrain to occupy a day-trip. For bump runs try the blacks around Chair 1. In good snow, the glades off uncrowded Chair 8 are worth sessioning, and this is also the best place to find fresh tracks – particularly if you're prepared to hike out to the boundary or dodge through trees here. Some of the best terrain in the ski area is not accessible via the lifts; explore the steep couloirs and cornices of Porcupine Ridge or head out beyond the ski area to Loveland Pass (see box overleaf).

Freestyle

The park at Loveland is inconsistent but improving, and many freeriders simply prefer to explore around the mountain. Drop below Chair 9 or traverse to skier's left off the top of Chair 2 to access the gully-side dips and kickers on South Chutes and Our Bowl. Or try the area between lifts 4 and 8 which is criss-crossed with cat track launches and where the Sunburst Chutes form a natural pipe. Off of Chair 1 you can look for a few small kickers and log slides tucked away on the side; monster headwalls are near the top of the blacks to skier's right.

Independent backcountry options

Loveland Pass is one of the best-known **backcountry descents** in the US, while Berthoud Pass has long attracted skiers from the eastern flats; for details, see the entries on Summit County (p.115) and Winter Park (p.187), respectively. The guys that run Mount Fun (℡303/567-2996, ⊛www.ski-empiresports.com) operate no-frills snowcat tours for riders who don't care about bringing their own lunch. Just an hour from Denver, the cat traverses the snowy slopes off Jones Pass. Trips leave from Empire Sports, right off exit 234 in Downieville; prices start at $125. If that's outside your budget, head for St Mary's Glacier, popular with backcountry skiers year round – though it's busiest once the ski resorts close, when shovels and sweat turn it into a kicker-filled playground. To get there, take exit 238 off I-70, then head twelve miles on Fall River Road to the old ghost town of Alice, today nothing more than an old schoolhouse and a couple of log cabins.

Lift tickets, lessons, and rentals

Loveland offers several discounted **ticket options**. Buying from a local supermarket or gas station will save a few bucks and season passes are inexpensive ($249). Skiing or Snowboarding **lessons** are available for $74 for a two-and-a-half hour session, lift ticket and rentals; $38 for the lesson only. Absolute beginners get a $13 discount off these prices. The kids' skiing program is particularly good value at $69 for the day, including lunch, lessons, lift pass and rentals. Skiing starts at age 4, riding at 7.

Rentals at the resort are limited, especially for boarders, but prices are reasonable: $25 per day for a snowboard package, $15 for a ski package. The rental hub of Clear Creek County is the truck stop in Downieville, at I-70 exit 234, between Idaho Springs and Georgetown. TBS (℡303/567-9279) is the small local board store while Breeze/Max (℡303/303-629-0111) is a branch of a well-stocked chain. In Idaho Springs, helpful staff at the family-owned tiny Maison De Ski (2804 Colorado Blvd, ℡303/567-2044) have been tuning skis and fitting boots for more than thirty years.

Accommodation

With no accommodation at the ski area, visitors often stay at communities along the Clear Creek Valley. Idaho Springs has the most options, Georgetown has condos dotted around the lake, and the town of Empire has a couple of colorful B&Bs. Loveland's Central Reservations (℡1-800/225-LOVE ⊛www.lovelandreservations.com) offers ski-and-stay packages from $125 per person per night.

Baxter's on the Creek 793 Hwy-103, Idaho Springs ℡303/567-2164, ⊛www.baxtersonthecrk.com. Modern, cozy, creek-side ranch opposite the spooky town cemetery. The personable landlady will spoil you and ply you with huge breakfasts, spiked evening drinks, and delicious rocky road cookies. ❸

Georgetown Mountain Inn 100 Rose St, Georgetown ℡303/569-3201 or 1-800/884-3201. Motel close to the historic downtown district and currently undergoing a facelift; the Colorado rooms now have hand-hewn log furniture and ironwork. Coffee and donut breakfast and use of a hot tub included. ❸

H&H Motor Lodge 2445 Colorado Blvd, Idaho Springs ℡303/567-2838 or 1-800/445-2893; ⊛www.hhlodge.com. One of the most cheerful-looking motels in town with kitchenettes and access to a hot tub and sauna. ❸

Heritage Inn 2622 Colorado Blvd, Idaho Springs ℡303/567-4473, ⊛www.heritageinn.com. Dated but well-run motor lodge with kitsch touches in the décor and many different room permutations. Some rooms include rock fireplaces and in-room jacuzzi tubs for two, and there's a penthouse tower. Rooms on the creek have views of the historic Argo Gold Mine. Indoor pool. ❸

Idaho Springs Motel 2631 Colorado Blvd, Idaho Springs ☏303/567-2242. Basic, clean motel; some rooms come with kitchenettes. ②

Lodge of the Rocky Mountains 1601 Colorado Blvd, Idaho Springs ☏303/567-2839, ⦿www .innkeeperrockies.com. Friendly but rather shabby hostel in a historic lodge that once sheltered Doc Holiday and Wyatt Earp. Beds in four-bed dorm-

rooms: $16; private rooms $40.

The Peck House 83 Sunny Ave, Empire ☏303/ 569-9870, ⦿www.empirehousebb.com. Classic Victorian inn – the oldest operating B&B in Colorado – is one of the area's most upscale options. Rooms are elegant and full of antiques, the cheapest sharing bathrooms. ⑥

Eating and drinking

Gourmet dining is hard to come by in the Clear Creek Valley, but there's a satisfying selection of friendly **restaurants** serving big, inexpensive portions of American favorites. Most cater to day-trippers on their way back to Denver – killing time until traffic east along I-70 clears – so eat early if you want company. The Safeway in Idaho Springs is the main **supermarket** in the Clear Creek Valley, on the same strip as the local fast-food outlets – which includes the decent *Sunrise Donuts*, 2731 Colorado Blvd (☏303/567-4093). Live music is staged sporadically at the local bars; mostly jazz, country, and folk.

Beau Jo's 1517 Miner St, Idaho Springs ☏303/ 567-4376. The first branch of what's now a statewide chain, opened in 1973. Known for its tasty, thick-crust pizza with a huge range of imaginative toppings – even the tofu pizza tastes great – though the plentiful salad bar is also good. Mineshaft ale and other local microbrews are served up in jam jars.

Buffalo Restaurant and Bar 1617 Miner St, Idaho Springs ☏303/567-2729. Buffalo meat – which tastes like beef but it's far leaner – is the star on this menu, served as buffalo black bean chili, buffalo meat pizza, burgers, hot dogs, stew, fajitas, and Buffaloaf. You can also get pizza, salads, and soups in a dining room packed with old mining and pioneering artifacts. A selection of microbrews available.

Grumpys Roadhouse 613 Water St, Silver Plume ☏303/569-3330. Garage turned bar, decorated with memorabilia (including gas tanks), 75-cent pool, peanuts, and popcorn, with live music on Thursdays and sometimes during weekends. The proprietor tries to live up to his name but fails happily.

Happy Cooker 412 Sixth St, Georgetown ☏303/569-3166. Great breakfasts include filling egg dishes and fluffy waffles, and later in the day soups, served with thick slabs of homemade bread. There's also quiche, creative salads, or chunky sandwiches, with great pies for desert.

Java Mountain Roasters 1506 Miner St, Idaho Springs ☏303/567-0304. Ideal breakfast pit stop with coffee-roasting smells in the morning and live music later on.

Red Ram & Rathskeller 606 Sixth St, Georgetown ☏303/569-2300. Neighborhood bar and dependable grill, with huge salads, burgers, ribs, and homemade chili, wings, and potato skins. Busy on weekends, but quiet midweek except in the laid-back basement *Rathskeller*, where the couches and big-screen TV attract local lifties.

Sopp & Truskott 486 Main St, Silver Plume ☏303/ 569-3395. Tiny wholesome bakery tucked away in Silver Plume, open Wed–Sun. When closed, fresh bread is left in the cooler on the stoop.

Tommyknocker Brewery 1401 Miner St, Idaho Springs ☏303/567-2688. Wide selection of microbrews and traditional sodas; après-ski comfort food includes standard grill fare plus stir-fries, "Bowl o' Lumpies" mashed potato and gravy, and chicken-fried elk steak. Inquire about their brewery tours.

Two Brothers Deli 1424 Miner St, Idaho Springs ☏303/567-2439. Though you can eat in, this is the place to stop by to grab a breakfast wrap and huge sandwich to go. Interesting combos for around $5–8 (half sandwiches available), including the all-green veggie mix on sesame semolina bread, and the peanut butter, banana, and marshmallow fluff on sourdough.

Other activities and attractions

Both the visitor center and Ranger's Office (exit 240) in Idaho Springs have trail maps of the many local trails, some of which are good for backcountry **ski touring**. Snowshoes are available from Outback Outfitters (1319 Miner St,

☏303/567-0850) in Idaho Springs and the rental stores listed in the mountain section (on p.166).

The old-fashioned **Indian Springs Resort**, 302 Soda Creek Rd, Idaho Springs (daily 7.30am–10.30pm; ☏303/567-2191, ⓦwww.indianspringsresort .com), is perhaps less impressive than when established in 1869, but its mud baths and geothermal cave pools still attract weary skiers (Mon–Fri $15, weekends and holidays $17); bathing is segregated and nudity permitted. Odor-free mineral springs also feed private indoor and outdoor private tubs ($18/20) and a domed swimming pool ($10/12).

The historic districts of the Clear Creek Valley towns are dotted with antique stores. Particularly diverting is the crammed Antique Shop & Tea House, 456 Main St, Silver Plume (☏303/569-2368). During December the Georgetown Victorian Christmas market is good for craftsy items and general Christmas ambience. For an appreciation of the original economic foundation of the area, try a tour of the now defunct **Phoenix Gold Mine** (☏303/567-0422, ⓦwww .pheonixmine.com) on West Trail Creek Road in Idaho Springs, led by knowledgeable and entertaining former miners.

Listings

Avalanche hotline ☏303/236-9435.
Bookshops Gingerbread Bookstore, 1435 Miner St, Idaho Springs ☏303/567-2304, or Polly Chandler's Bookstore, 505 Rose St, Georgetown ☏303/569-3303.
Internet Idaho Springs Public Library, 219 14th Ave, Idaho Springs ☏303/567-2020.

Medical Acute Injury & Illness Center, 9330 S University Blvd 100, Highlands Ranch, Denver ☏303/683-9393.
Pharmacy Clear Creek Pharmacy Inc, 2325 Miner St, Idaho Springs ☏303/567-2525.
Post office 307 County Road 308, Idaho Springs ☏1-800/275-8777.

Telluride

Surrounded by vast precipitous mountains in Colorado's southwestern corner, the tiny town of **Telluride** is in one of the most picturesque valleys in the Rockies, reminiscent of the Alps in both natural beauty and dramatic terrain.

Settled in the late nineteenth century, colonized by bohemians in the 1960s, and developed as a ski area in the early 1970s, Telluride, in the past decade, has quietly transformed into an opulent winter playground. Drawn to the area for its annual summer film festival, Hollywood celebrities quickly became enamored with the peaceful community, and Telluride was suddenly being touted as the new Aspen or Vail. It's not. There may be many wealthy seasonal residents, patronizing restaurants that are more likely to be found in a cosmopolitan hub than a cozy, mountain village, but the clientele are not here for glitz or shopping. They're here for the spectacular scenery, the town's earthy vibe, and for the chance to spend time on one of the most challenging mountains in North America. With the recent opening of Prospect Bowl Telluride increased its already impressive beginner and early intermediate acreage, and only those who prefer fast cruising will find their choices limited.

Actually, something else that might limit you is the price of a vacation here; the Mountain Village, at the heart of the ski area, is a collection of million-dollar homes, all-inclusive resorts, and condos that might make you think about

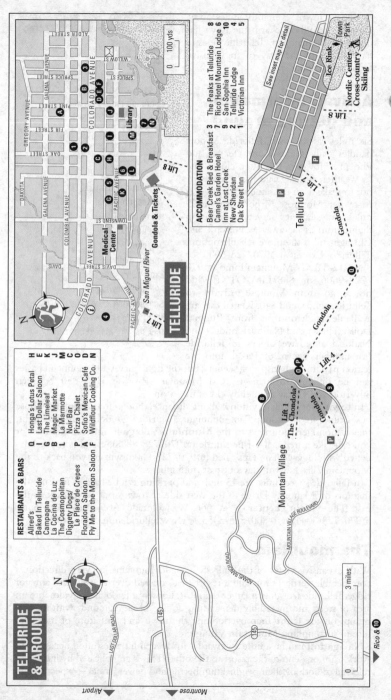

TELLURIDE & AROUND

RESTAURANTS & BARS

Allred's	H
Baked In Telluride	E
Campagna	K
La Cocina de Luz	J
The Cosmopolitan	M
Diggety Dogs/	
Le Place de Crepes	C
Floradora Saloon	O
Fly Me to the Moon Saloon	D
Honga's Lotus Petal	Q
Last Dollar Saloon	I
The Limeleaf	G
Magic Market	B
La Marmotte	L
Noir Bar	P
Pizza Chalet	A
Sofio's Mexican Café	F
Wildflour Cooking Co.	N

TELLURIDE

ACCOMMODATION

Bear Creek Bed & Breakfast	3
Camel's Garden Hotel	7
Inn at Lost Creek	9
New Sheridan	2
Oak Street Inn	1
The Peaks at Telluride	8
Rico Hotel Mountain Lodge	6
San Sophia Inn	10
Telluride Lodge	4
Victorian Inn	5

staying at towns even fifty miles away. Despite the offbeat charm the town has managed to maintain, Telluride doesn't have much in the way of inexpensive accommodation.

Arrival, information, and getting around

Six miles east of town, Telluride Airport handles daily flights from Denver and Phoenix. However, it is often closed due to weather, and luggage has a tendency not to make it on the same small plane as its owner. Montrose Airport may be 65 miles away, but it's served by nonstop flights from as far away as Newark and Chicago and is the more reliable option. Telluride Express (☎970/728-6000 or 888/212-TAXI), Mountain Limo (☎970 /728-9606 or 888/LIM-OTXI), and others go from Montose Airport to Telluride for around $40. Rental cars are available at Montrose from Budget, Dollar, Thrifty, and National. Budget and National also have offices in Telluride (for numbers see p.26). Roads into the

Mountain info

Phone ☎970/728-6900 or 1-866/ 287-5015

Snow phone ☎970/728-7425

Website ⓦwww.tellurideskiresort.com

Operating times Late Nov to early April daily 8.45am–4pm

Price $65

No. of lifts 16, including 1 gondola and 3 surface

Base elevation 8725′

Summit elevation 12260′

Vertical drop 3535′

No. of trails 84

Acreage 1700

Beginner 24%

Intermediate 38%

Expert 38%

Average snowfall 309″

Snowmaking Yes (204 acres)

Night skiing No

Daycare Yes, ☎1-800/801-4832

region pass through inspiring scenery, but the tight curves and mountain passes can be difficult to manage. Red Mountain Pass on Hwy-550 between Silverton and Ouray frequently closes in season.

In **town**, everything is within walking distance, though free Galloping Goose buses run a frequent loop 7am–midnight. Telluride's gondola (7am–midnight; free to nonskiers) journeys to the **Mountain Village** in thirteen minutes, or you can take a free dial-a-ride shuttle (☎970/728-8888), useful if you're burdened with luggage. The Tipsy Taxi (☎970/728-9606) will get you back to the Mountain Village if you stay out past midnight.

In Telluride speed limits are 15 mph and **parking** can be hard to find; use the free lots on Mahoney Drive to the west side of town or at Town Park to the east. The **visitor center** is at 666 W Colorado Ave (daily 9am–5pm; ☎970/728-3041 or 1-800/525-3455, ⓦwww.telluridemm.com).

The mountain

With expansive views of the spiky San Juan Mountains in every direction, a considerable vertical drop, and a resort that's draped over two sides of a major ridge, Telluride feels much larger than it is. Loosely, the ski area divides into an area of steep and incredibly demanding double black diamonds with massive bumps on the **front face** overlooking the town and a mixture of mellower terrain surrounding **Mountain Village**.

Navigation can be a little awkward with several lift rides often necessary to work from one end of the resort to the other. This is complicated by lifts being referred to both by their original numbering and newer names – expect to end up on the wrong chair at least once. The mountain's complexity also extends to the grading of its runs. The usual three categories – green, blue, and black – have been subdivided into single (easier) or double (more advanced) levels of difficulty. This can be useful in finding the right kind of terrain to progress to, but note that many of the grades underrate the difficulty of runs: advanced blues in Telluride could easily be rated as blacks in other resorts. When in doubt, use caution, especially during icy spells.

Beginner

Beginners have a huge practice area below Mountain Village, where the wide, rolling **Meadows** is perfect for learning first turns. From the base of the Meadows, skiers can progress up **Lift 10** to long, slow, entertaining cruisers that weave past the gargantuan homes of Telluride's wealthy. Lift 10 is also the easiest way to get to **Ute Park**, the beginner area in Prospect Bowl. **Snowboarders** should avoid both Ute Park and the flat and long Lift 10 runs and instead, once you can link turns comfortably on the Meadows, loop the mellow blues under Lift 4 – avoiding Boomerang and Cake Walk – which flatten out halfway down.

Intermediate

Intermediates will find few long cruisers at Telluride and progression onto the tough blacks is difficult, but at least the presence of moguls on even gentler slopes makes it a great place to build up bump skills. Even if you don't enjoy bumps, honing your skill here is useful training for tight couloirs and trees. Start on the easier blues under **Lift 4** by the Mountain Village or take Lift 9 to the lower part of **See Forever**. At nearly three miles long it's the best cruiser on the mountain (its upper part is simply a long, flat cat track), named for its panoramic views over the San Juans. Work back to the **Palmyra 5** for short powder and mellow mogul runs and head to the blue rollercoaster dips, bumps, and simple glade of **Prospect Bowl** under the Prospect 12 chair. Be sure to hold your speed until you've figured the area out; it's much easier than it looks on the map, with some tricky flat spots. On the **front face**, there's a choice of the exceptionally hard blue Lookout or a winding cat track; unless you want to work on steeps or feel a compulsion to ski the entire mountain, skip both.

Expert

Telluride is the place to be humbled when you've become complacent in your abilities. Runs like the incredibly steep **Plunge** and **Spiral Staircase**, both dotted with massive moguls, will give even the most advanced riders problems. Less confident experts should take comfort in Telluride's split grooming of many mogul runs; with half the piste flattened and the other half left to bump, you should be able to find a suitable way down. Scanning bump runs from the lifts is also helpful; most have tighter moguls down the center and easier lines at their edges.

Gold Hill is a freerider's dream with steeps, chutes, cliffs, trees, and a powder-trap run-out back to the base. The rest of the Prospect Bowl development isn't of much interest to experts, though a few short blacks, hikeable from Prospect Lift 12, often contain untouched powder stashes.

For **tree runs** try the mellow and widely spaced front face glades. For tighter trees and short bump runs, drop in almost anywhere off the **See Forever** cat track onto the Mountain Village side – accessible from the Apex 6 or Gold Hill 14.

Freestyle

For a resort where many snowboarders prefer moguls to pipes, the **Surge Air Garden terrain park** is surprisingly well developed, and getting better. Small hits and rails sit alongside larger jumps, making it ideal for progressing. There's not much in the way of giant tabletops, but the large rail garden has a mailbox, minirails, and an adequate pipe. Outside the park, the glades on the front face make natural playgrounds and the East and West Drains both are pipe-like gullies.

Lift tickets, lessons, and rentals

Lift tickets are pricey ($65) and few deals are available. If you don't qualify for the college season pass ($189), lift-and-lodging packages are invariably your best bet for discounts.

In high season, classes at Telluride's **ski school** (☎970/728-7507 or 1-800 /801-4832) are only available in full-day format, making it a little pricey ($80). Beginner lift, lesson, and rental packages start at $95. Women's weekends and weekend telemark clinics are also available. The Telluride Adaptive Ski Program (TASP) (☎970/728-7537, ⊛www.skitasp.org), located in the base of the Mountain Village gondola, offers skiers with special needs equipment rentals, ski buddy and guide services, half-price lift tickets, and full lesson/lift ticket/equipment programs.

Rental gear in Telluride is generally expensive. Telluride Sports is the main outlet, with six locations around town and in the Mountain Village. Even basic ski packages are pricey, and the least expensive snowboard package is a step-in – if you want straps, it'll cost $42. Snowshoes, cross-country skis, and clothing

The backcountry

The jagged peaks of the San Juans are a magnet for **backcountry** purists, who claim the region's above-treeline slopes are akin to off-peak descents in the Alps. Open bowls sweep off the backside of the ski area. When in the resort, pay attention to warnings and ropes as tempting powder fields end abruptly above sheer cliffs. The resort maintains backcountry access gates, and there are amazing backcountry opportunities off Palmyra Peak and in the surrounding San Juans.

Due to steep inclines and fluctuating temperatures, the snowpack here is one of the most unstable in the country. Don't even think about going out-of-bounds unless you're experienced, fully equipped, and with a local guide; avalanche classes are also a good idea.

Five backcountry huts operated by the **San Juan Hut System** (☎970/626-3033, ⊛www.sanjuanhuts.com) are dotted along the Mount Sneffels Range. These sleep up to eight in bunks, cost $25 per person per night, and link Telluride, Ridgway, and Ouray. The huts are about six miles apart and linked by easy cross-country ski trails suitable for intermediates. Above the trails, acres of open powder descents beckon.

In the business for twenty years, **Helitrax**, 121 W Colorado Ave (☎970/728-8377 or 866/435-4754, ⊛www.helitrax.net), is the only heli-skiing outfit in Colorado, and one of only a handful in the US not based in Alaska. Clients lean toward the wealthy older skier demographic, though Helitrax' rates – $650 for five runs – are actually on the cheap side. A-Stars depart mid-mountain at the resort, so should poor weather delay take-off, riders can take a few sheltered runs in the trees while they wait to hit up the fresh goods nearby. Helitrax also picks up clients from **Dunton Hot Springs**, PO Box 818, Dolores, CO 81323 (☎970/882-4800, ⊛www.duntonhotsprings.com). Just over an hour's drive from Telluride, this nineteenth-century ghost town has been restored into a luxurious rustic retreat (⑨), complete with saloon, library, bank, and a bathhouse fed by natural springs.

are also available to rent. Paragon (☎970/728-4525, ⊛www.paragontelluride
.com) is the local's favorite, with stores at 213 W Colorado Ave, 236 S Oak St,
and in the Granita Building in Mountain Village. They also rent snowshoes and
Nordic skis. Easy Rider, 101 W Colorado Ave (☎1-800/433-9733, ⊛www
.ezriders.com), a snowboard and skate shop, has board demos as rentals. For
packages, Slopestyle (☎970/728-9889 or 1-888/RIDE-321, ⊛www.slopestyle
.com), at 236 W Colorado Ave and in the Franz Klammer Lodge in the
Mountain Village, is your best bet.

Accommodation

Finding somewhere reasonable to stay in Telluride is nearly always a struggle,
particularly if you're not after the condo accommodation that the town has
eagerly bred over the last decade or so. The best bet is to book as far ahead as
possible. Telluride Central Reservations (☎970/728-6157 or 1-866/287-5015)
can help secure a bed in advance, though their prices are a little above walk-in
rates. If looking for condo accommodation – the best deal if in a group – try
contacting Telluride Resort Accommodations (☎970/728-6621 or 1-800/
538-7754); a two-bedroom, four-person condo works out around $170 and up
a night during the ski season. If you stay out of town at Rico, Ridgway, or
Ouray, you sacrifice convenience for price. At the very least you'll be making
a fifty-mile roundtrip journey each day on roads that are winding and often icy.

Telluride

Bear Creek Bed & Breakfast 221 E Colorado Ave
☎970/728-6681 or 1-800/338-7064, ⊛www
.bearcreektelluride.com. Located on the upper
floors of a modern building on Telluride's main
street, each of the nine rooms is en-suite and has
simple, modern décor. Amenities include a cedar
sauna, steam room, and a rooftop hot tub. ❹

Camel's Garden Hotel 310 S Fir St ☎970/728-
9300 or 1-888/772-2635, ⊛www.camelsgarden
.com. Minimalist modernism right beside the base
of the gondola, with oversized baths, fireplaces,
large outdoor hot tub, and a choice of hotel rooms,
suites, or condos. Rather meager continental
breakfasts included. ❽

New Sheridan Hotel 231 W Colorado Ave ☎970/
728-4351 or 1-800/200-1891, ⊛www.newsheridan
.com. Built in 1895 to replace the original wood
structure, this "new" hotel is almost as old as the
town itself and a much loved landmark. Only some
rooms have private baths, but all guests have use
of the exercise room and the rooftop hot tubs with
views of the gondola, slopes, and San Juan peaks.
Drinks and Web access are available in the cozy
library. The staff is friendly and it's great value for
money. ❹

Oak Street Inn 134 North Oak St ☎970/728-
3383. Hostel that's appealing on the outside but
somewhat decrepit within. The shared bathrooms,
TV lounge, and bunk-bedded rooms are reminiscent of a shabby college dorm. Still, there's a sauna,

it's centrally located, and six can share a room for
$107; at under $18 per person, by far the cheapest deal in Telluride. Two-person rooms cost $58.

San Sophia Inn 330 W Pacific Ave ☎970/728-
3001 or 1-800/537-4781, ⊛www.sansophia.com.
Large upscale B&B with all brass beds and quilts
and serving a huge gourmet breakfast buffet
(available to nonguests for $15) and great après-
ski snacks. Expensive, but the amenable owners
offer good deals during quiet periods. Hot tub. ❻

Telluride Lodge 747 W Pacific Ave ☎970/728-
4400 or 1-888/728-1950, ⊛www.telluridelodge
.com. Large, attractive complex of townhome-style
condos on the eastern edge of town, right by the
base of Lift 7; amenities include two indoor tubs
and laundry facilities. ❼

Victorian Inn 401 W Pacific Ave ☎970/728-6601
or 1-800/611-9893, ⊛www.tellurideinn.com. Motel
lodging with a Victorian veneer that's overpriced
yet inexpensive by local standards. Sauna and hot
tub available; muffins and coffee for breakfast. ❹

Telluride Mountain Village

Inn at Lost Creek 119 Lost Creek Lane
☎970/728-5678 or 1-888/601-5678. Boutique
luxury in the heart of the Mountain Village. No
room is the same, but included are fireplaces,
deluxe kitchenettes with dining tables, TVs, video
and CD libraries, and washer-dryers. There are two
rooftop hot tubs. Lodging-and lift-packages offered
online. ❽

The Peaks at Telluride 136 Country Club Drive ☎970/729-6800 or 1-800/789-2220. Large resort and spa development where you can ski in, ski out and avail yourself of over fifty different spa treatments. The extensive fitness center includes pools and hot tubs, tennis courts, racquetball, and a even climbing wall. ❽

Out of town
Rico Hotel Mountain Lodge Rico ☎970/967-3000. Packages start at $60 per person in the lodge, which has a hot tub, fireplaces in some of the rooms, and laundry facilities. ❹

St Elmo Hotel 426 Main St, Ouray ☎970/325-4951, ⓦwww.stelmohotel.com. Luxurious B&B located on the main drag and home to its own venerable, high-class restaurant. Inside, it's a harmonious combination of polished wood and brass, period furnishings, and stained glass, and all rooms are finely decorated and en suite. Outdoor hot tub as well. ❹

Super 8 Motel Ridgway ☎970/626-5444 or 1-800/368-5444. Dependable chain motel with incredible views of the San Juans, indoor pool, sauna, and hot tub. ❸

Eating

With no fast-food places in town and a plethora of resident hotshot chefs, Telluride offers many opportunities to **eat** well. The restaurants are stylishly comfortable so that haute cuisine and fine wines collide with customers in jeans and fleece. But be warned, food is often pricey and reservations are always recommended.

On-mountain, *Guiseppe's* is a little hut at the top of Lift 9 serving moderately priced soups and hot chocolate in cramped but warm surroundings with amazing views. The giant *Gorrono Ranch* looks like a mining theme park and has a huge deck that's perfect for spring barbecues and people-watching. In Mountain Village, the best budget options are the hot dog and crepe stalls or *Mesa Quesa* quesadillas and the *Mesa Coffee Cottage*. **Groceries** can be bought in town at the Village Market, corner of Fir and Pacific (daily 7.30am–9pm; ☎970/728-4566) or Clarks Market & Deli, 700 W Colorado (☎970/728-3124), out on the west side.

Telluride
Allred's Gondola Station, St Sophia ☎970/728-7474. Unbeatable location at the top of the gondola above the town, with food to match the views. From gourmet takes on continental classics like the beef *carpaccio* with truffle oil, to more tropical creations, such as the red snapper with vanilla-poached crab and mango, the menu is sublime; even the dessert section is tough to choose from. If you can't afford dinner, stop in on the gondola ride back to town and sink into the deep leather couches in front of the fire for serious après snacks. Après from 3pm, dinner from 5.30pm.
Baked In Telluride 127 S Fir St ☎970/728-4705. One of the most affordable options in town, where good muffins and pastries are served early on, while pizza slices and huge portions of the hearty specials are served throughout the day. Try the fine inexpensive bagel sandwich.
Campagna 435 W Pacific Ave ☎970/728-6190. The ambience of a Tuscan home has been recreated in Telluride. Tiny and intimate, the little wooden house has been awarded the highest Zagat ratings in the state for its food – traditional, nourishing dishes

straight from the Tuscan countryside. 6pm–close.
The Cosmopolitan 300 W San Juan ☎970/728-1292, ⓦwww.cosmotelluride.com. The *Cosmo* is elegant yet relaxed, with a well-stocked cellar and friendly sommelier. The chef mixes local ingredients like elk and trout with flavors from around the world to produce upscale bistro dishes like ginger-braised ribs and barbecued salmon. Expensive.
Floradora Saloon 103 West Colorado Ave ☎970/728-3888. Serving fine food in an Old West saloon atmosphere, this busy restaurant is named after two of the town's most popular Victorian call girls. Food runs from teriyaki-glazed salmon and wild mushroom pasta to standard Mexican and burger favorites, and there's a fine salad bar as well.
Honga's Lotus Petal 133 S Oak St ☎970/728-5234. Variety of good Asian dishes with reasonable prices served in stylishly detailed surroundings; deep red and pale green walls, Japanese china, and a quiet tea room with floor seating. The range of food represented here spans Japanese, Korean, Thai, and Indonesian to Chinese; entrees from around $12. Dinner only; reserve a table or wait for a seat in the bar area.

La Cocina de Luz 123 E Colorado Ave ☎970/
728-9355. Some of the best-value meals in
Telluride, conscientiously prepared from fresh
organic ingredients. Join the line in the tiny space
for burritos, tacos, and inventive daily specials.
Mon–Sat 9am–9pm.

La Marmotte 150 W San Juan ☎970/728-6232,
ⓦwww.lamarmotte.com. Run by a French couple
since 1987, this cozy two-story converted ice-
house resembles a Michelin-starred French country restaurant. Dishes include filet de boeuf and
coquilles Saint Jaques. The epitome of restrained,
cultured money in Telluride.

The Limeleaf SwedeFinn Hall, 472 W Pacific
☎970/728-2085, ⓦwww.limeleaf.com. Fresh Thai
and Asian-fusion dishes served in the brightly
painted basement restaurant and upstairs bar-
cum-lounge. Join the locals between 4 and 6pm
for a huge choose-your-own meat n' veg stir-fry at
happy hour prices ($7 instead of $12).

Magic Market 225 S Pine ☎970/728-8789.
Organic salads and healthy rice n' noodle hot dishes as well as sandwiches offered, making it ideal
for a quicker, cheaper lunch or early dinner.

Sofio's Mexican Café 110 E Colorado Ave
☎970/728-4882. Not at the level of La Cocina but
this faux-Mexican-themed place is tops for big
breakfasts; a surprisingly varied menu includes
huge Belgian waffles, pancakes, omelettes, and
fresh fruit juices and smoothies.

The Steaming Bean 221 W Colorado Ave
☎970/728-0793. Slightly bohemian local coffee
shop and webcafé. Daily 7am–7pm.

Wildflour Cooking Co 250 W San Juan
☎970/728-8887. At the base of the gondola in
town, this shiny upscale bakery lures in even
locals for savory stuffed croissants, among other
treats. Daily 8am–8pm.

Telluride Mountain Village

Diggity Dogs/Le Place de Crepes 300 W
Colorado Ave ☎970/728-5033. Next to the
Courthouse in town, in the Mountain Village Plaza.
Telluride's hot dog and crepe stalls offer a cheap,
quality lunch. Both sweet and savory crepes are
available, as are tofu dogs.

Pizza Chalet 562 Mountain Village Blvd
☎970/728-7499. This warm, basic Italian café is
the Mountain Village "budget" option, with slices
from $2.50; salads and hot sandwiches are
around $6.

Out of town

Bon Ton 426 Main St, Ouray ☎970/325-4951.
Accomplished northern Italian food served up in
the St Elmo Hotel's atmospheric red-brick basement. The great Sunday brunch is an unmissable
deal; otherwise it's an expensive choice.

True Grit Café 123 N Lena, Ridgway ☎970/626-
5739. One of the small number of places to eat in
town, serving burgers and sandwiches amidst
stacks of John Wayne memorabilia – his movie
True Grit was filmed around these parts back in
the late 1960s.

Drinking and entertainment

If it's after 9pm and snowing, **nightlife** in town is decidedly muted. Telluride
does have its raucous moments, particularly when a good band passes through
town, but in general the numerous restaurants take center stage as the evening
attraction. Many have stylish bars and après menus; the laid-back Limeleaf (see
above) even has a stage, with regular DJ and band nights. Additionally, the cultural momentum of Telluride's summer **festivals** lasts through the winter, with
art classes, a local choral society, Ciné Club, writing and craft guilds, theater and
dance companies, and chamber orchestra. Many events take place in the
Sheridan Opera House, 110 N Oak (☎970/728-6363 ⓦwww.sheridanopera-
house.com), a restored vaudeville theater. The Nugget Theater, 207 W
Colorado Ave (☎970/728-3030), shows Indie flicks and blockbusters. See the
local Daily Planet newspaper for listings.

Fly Me to the Moon Saloon 132 E Colorado Ave
☎970/728-6666. Noisy and boisterous basement
punk-rock dive with cockeyed pool table, arcade
games, stage, and dance floor. Bands appear
almost nightly; shows usually start late.

Last Dollar Saloon 100 E Colorado Ave ☎970
/728-4800. Better-known as the Buck, this is
Telluride's gritty, smoky, and loud spit-and-sawdust
place. Good selection of local beers; 11.30am–late.

New Sheridan Bar and Pool Hall 225 W
Colorado Ave ☎970/728-3911. Shoot pool with
the ghost of Butch Cassidy in the Victorian film-set
surroundings of the Sheridan's billiard room. The
main bar is busy from early afternoon.

Noir Bar 123 S Oak ☎970/728-TUNA. Step down into this dark, stylish space beneath the Blue Point Grill. Ritzy cocktail menu, plus a good chance of a decent DJ and a late-night crowd.

Smugglers Brewpub and Grille San Juan and Pine ☎970/728-0919. Lively evening hangout with a decent menu of bar food and some good local microbrews.

Other activities and attractions

Cross-country skiers visiting town are also well served around both the town and the Mountain Village by the 40km of free tracks maintained by the **Telluride Nordic Center** (☎970/728-1144), located at the east end of Town Park, who also offer affordable rentals. Intermediate and advanced trails lead from the top of Lift 10 on the mountain to the ghost town of Alta.

The fairytale Faraway Ranch (☎970/728-9386) runs crosscountry and snow-shoeing tours and lessons on their groomers and in the Uncompahgre National Forest. But the best deal for snowshoers are the free nature walks offered by the local Forest Service; you need to rent snowshoes in advance.

Other tours offered locally include dogsledding with Winter Moon Sled Dog tours (☎970/729-0058); snowmobiling with Telluride Snowmobile Adventures (☎970/728-4475), who take riders to the ghost town of Alta or Dunton Hot Springs; and horseback riding with Ride With Roudy (☎970/728-9611). Sleigh rides, snowbiking, tubing, ballooning, paragliding, ice climbing, fly fishing, and trips to Ouray Hot Springs are also available and can be booked through Telluride Visitor Services (☎970/728-4431 or 1-888/288-7360). In town, the Nordic Center (see above) rents **ice skates** for use on the Town Park's rink, which stays open into the night for skating, hockey, and broomball.

Telluride's main indoor sports facility is the **Golden Door Spa** in the Mountain Village *Wyndham Peaks Hotel* (daily entrance fee of $40; ☎970/728-2590, ⓦwww.thepeaksresort.com/spa). The spa here is rated among the world's best; with steam rooms, saunas and mineral tubs, a rock wall, indoor/outdoor pool and waterslide, bike spinning room, pilates and yoga studios, fitness machines, juice and oxygen bars, and vast luxurious locker rooms.

Listings

Avalanche hotline ☎970/247-8187.
Bookshops Bookworks, 191 S Pine ☎970/728-0700.
Internet Wilkinson Public Library, 100 W Pacific Ave ☎970/728-4519, ⓦwww.telluride.lib.co.us (Mon–Thurs, 10am–8pm, Fri–Sat 10am–6pm, Sun noon–5pm).

Medical Telluride Medical Center, 500 W Pacific, ☎970/728-3848.
Pharmacy Sunshine Pharmacy, 236 W Colorado Ave, ☎970/728-3601.
Post office 101 E Colorado Ave ☎970/728-3900.

Steamboat

Having produced the most winter Olympians of any town in the country (54 at last count), **Steamboat** grandly calls itself "Ski Town USA." This is not the only moniker the resort has trademarked; "champagne powder" is the term they coined to refer to the light quality of snow that falls in this northwest Colorado corner. Such brochure-like fodder is usually easy to dismiss, but the truth is Steamboat commands attention as one of the top all-around winter sports destinations in the region. The glorious groves of aspen across Steamboat's five peaks make for a scenic setting when cruising run after run; the fact that this is one of the larger resorts in Colorado means there's little repetition and crowding isn't so bad; and a massive superpipe ensures that freeriders get in on the fun too.

Around the base of the ski area, concrete condos and a handful of restaurants make up Steamboat Village, perhaps best bypassed in favor of the town proper, Steamboat Springs, a small, red-brick settlement a couple of miles to the north. While other Victorian Colorado ski towns grew through silver or gold, in the early 1900s more beef cattle were transported out of Steamboat than from any other place in the US, making the Western feel of the place a bit more authentic and unpretentious than most. Though skiing and tourism took over as the town's prominent business once lifts were installed on Mount Werner in 1963, Steamboat retains its strong sense of community, and is a worthy place for a wander when the slopes close down.

Mountain info

Phone Central Reservations ☏ 970 /879-0740 or 877/237-2628

Snow phone ☏ 970/879-7300

Website ⊛ www.steamboat.com

Price $49–64; lower mountain-only tickets up to $20 less

Operating times Late Nov to mid-April 8.30am–3.30pm

No. of lifts 20, including 1 gondola (plus 5 magic carpets)

Base elevation 6900′

Summit elevation 10568′

Vertical drop 3668′

No of trails 142

Acreage 2939

Beginner 13%

Intermediate 56%

Expert 31%

Average snowfall 311″

Snowmaking Yes (438 acres)

Night skiing No

Nursery facilities Yes, 6 months to 6 years; from $81 full day at Kids' Vacation Center, ☏ 970/871-5375 or 800/299-5017

Arrival, information, and getting around

Steamboat's Yampa Valley Regional Airport is 22 miles north of town in Hayden and is served by American, Continental, Northwest, and United Airlines. Expect to pay $44 for round-trip shuttle service to your accommodation with Alpine Taxi (☏ 970/879-8294 or 800/343-7433, ⊛ www.alpinetaxi .com). With a group, it's usually cheaper to fly into Denver and rent a car.

Many visitors **drive** into Steamboat. In dry weather the journey from Denver is three easy hours. In bad weather, the going gets tough after Kremmling, a dusty hunting town midway between Dillon and Steamboat. Once on Hwy-40, the road climbs up winding Rabbit Ears Pass, often snowbound and slippery. Occasionally the pass is closed, requiring a looping detour via CO-134 and 131; alternatively, take CO-131 directly from I-70 in the Vail Valley. Once you have safely arrived, two pay lots are available close to the slopes off Gondola Square, with a free shuttle-served lot closer to Hwy-40 on Mount Werner Road. Parking downtown is generally not a problem, though spots

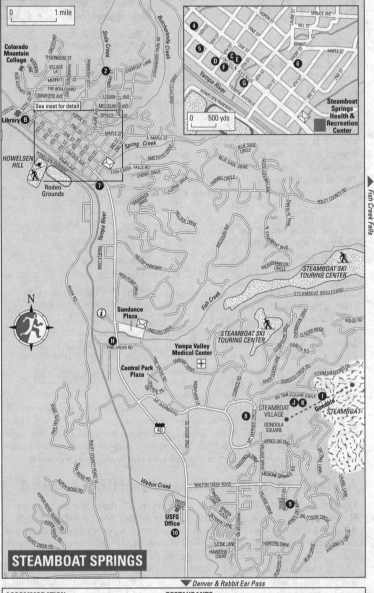

Strawberry Park Hot Springs (7 miles)

Fish Creek Falls

Yampa Valley Airport & Clark

Denver & Rabbit Ear Pass

STEAMBOAT SPRINGS

ACCOMMODATION

The BunkHouse Lodge	10
The Home Ranch	3
Hotel Bristol	5
Inn at Steamboat	9
Mariposa Bed & Breakfast	2
Nordic Lodge	4
Rabbit Ears Motel	7
Steamboat Bed & Breakfast	6
Steamboat Grand	8
Strawberry Hot Springs	1

RESTAURANTS

Antares	D	Johnny B. Good's	E
Boomerang's	F	Tapas Lounge	I
Café Diva	K	The Shack Café	C
Creekside Café & Grill	B	Soda Creek Pizza Co.	H
The Home Ranch	A	Winona's	G
Jitters	J		

right on Lincoln Avenue, the town's main street, can be scarce. Greyhound **buses** stop at Central Park Plaza, between the town and mountain village.

Despite the four miles between downtown and Steamboat's mountain village, **getting around** on the free buses operated by Steamboat Springs Transit (℡970/879-3717) is easy as long as you have a copy of the widely available schedule. Five color-coded routes connect the Gondola Transit Center with downtown and the surrounding condos and motels, running from around 6.30am to 2am daily. A limited regional service connects the service towns of Milner, Hayden, and Craig to Steamboat ($1–3.50). The Chamber Resort Association's **visitor center** is on the way into downtown, opposite the Sundance Plaza at 1255 Lincoln Ave (Mon–Fri, 8am–5pm, Sat 10am–3pm; ℡970/879-0880, ⊛www.steamboatchamber.com).

The mountain

From the ticket offices and ski shops of Gondola Square, the gondola swings up over Christie Peak to Thunderhead Peak, crossing the mountain's lower step. **Christie Peak** is home to Steamboat's terrain park and pipe and to a meadow of beginner lifts and trails. Those planning to only ride here can take either of the Christie lifts to access the same area, thus avoiding the gondola crowds.

Above the gondola, left to right on the trail map, are the steep, tree-filled bowls of **Mount Werner**, the wide open runs and evergreens of **Storm Peak**, and the aspen glades and long cruisers on **Sunshine**. On the back is **Morningside Park**, a short shot of piney glades and powder. A fair amount of crossing from lift to lift is required to navigate from peak to peak, though very little traversing is necessary on your way up the mountain. Coming down is a different story, particularly to skier's right of the mountain; BC Ski Way and Right-O-Way resemble flat, busy highways come late afternoon, and can be a real pain for novice snowboarders and those intimidated by crowds.

Beginner

The base of the mountain is dedicated to never-evers with five magic carpets and three short chairlifts. This wide slope is gently pitched and treeless, but surrounded by buildings and criss-crossed with lift towers and other skiers; it's not the most attractive or quiet place to learn. Take Christie lift to access more interesting greens that wind their way back through the trees to base – novice snowboarders may have problems on the Right-O-Way traverse out – or work up and over to the Sunshine lift and start linking turns on the easy blues below.

Intermediate

Steamboat rewards those averse to repetition with ribbons of blues rolling off every lift. Keep an eye on the trail markings, as it's easy to stray onto the blacks. Head over to Sunshine peak if you want relatively quiet slopes to warm up on. The varied terrain includes **Tomahawk**, a wide, rollercoaster cruiser straddling the resort boundary and a couple of mellow shots through aspens, the quintessential Steamboat experience tamed down for tree virgins. On powder days, head over the hill into Morningside Park, a cascading valley of evergreens where the blacks are fairly short and flat enough in places to be a potential snowboard trap. Once you can handle the fluffy stuff here, take **Buddy's Run** off Storm Peak to the Big Meadow for your first taste of backcountry-style bowl riding, then drop into Longhorn for a meaty bump and mini-hit workout.

Expert

Black bump runs and glades of trees are scattered across the mountain, with short but steep shots off almost every lift. The wide open slope below **Storm Peak** is the best starting point for experts used to more traditional blacks, while the largest concentration of Steamboat's aspens lies between the Priest Creek and Sunshine chairs. If it's a powder day, get over here early. For evergreens and steep chutes, drop into Christmas Tree bowl off the Mount Werner ridge. Take the Morningside Park lift and hike up to the metal weather tower for access to the best powder stashes and cliff drops on the mountain. The Morningside slopes, though short, host a couple of smaller drops, while on the front side, right next to the boundary, the East Face hides more challenging hucking terrain. Keep your speed on the Last Chance traverse out of that area, before dropping into the bumps, hits, and boardercross-style turns in the aspens under the Pony Express.

Freestyle

Named for the notorious California wave, **Mavericks** is a true superpipe – always ridiculously long (around 550ft), expertly groomed, and blessed with a bowled-out corner/quarterpipe/hip at its base. It has its own lift, Bashor, which also serves the terrain park, recently expanded with new rails and a whopping sound system. Outside the park the cascading slopes of Steamboat are covered in natural terrain features: explore every patch of trees, watch for little hits arcing back onto almost every slope, and keep an eye out for fallen aspens.

Lift tickets, lessons, and rentals

There are few lift pass deals at Steamboat, but the resort can be economical for families on a long stay, as kids ski and rent gear for free when their parents ski or rent for five days or more. At $24 for a full day ($66 with beginner lift ticket), **lessons** for beginners are inexpensive, especially for those with their own gear. Half-day lessons for intermediates and above start at $53. The ski school (☎800/299-5017) also offers more expensive bump clinics, women's seminars, pipe sessions, and the opportunity to get first tracks an hour before the upper

Independent backcountry options

The guides of **Steamboat Powder Cat/Blue Sky West**, 1724 Mt Werner Circle (☎970/871-4260 or 800/288-0543), ride on 10,000 acres of aspen-, spruce-, and fir-strewn slopes a short drive from the ski area. With plenty of terrain to explore and a catered lunch stop at an attractive cabin in the woods, this is backcountry skiing at its least threatening. Strong riders should opt for the more challenging Level III expeditions to Soda Mountain. Use of powder skis and boards is included in the price ($288 weekdays, $299 weekends, with low-season rates $100 less). Full-moon descents ($150) and nonskiing scenic tours ($125) in the twelve-person Bombardier cats are also offered. Reserve well in advance.

Rocky Mountain Ventures (☎970/870-8440, ⊛www.verticalgrip.com) guides backcountry riding, snowshoeing, and ice-climbing. Experienced skiers planning on self-guided explorations into the backcountry can pick up maps and information from the USFS ranger office at 925 Weiss Drive (Mon–Fri 8am–5pm, ☎970/879-1870). One of the most popular areas is Rabbit Ears Pass, which segregates snowmobiles to the east, cross-country skiers and snowshoers to the west. Buffalo Pass is another often-used spot. For avalanche classes, check out the schedule at the Colorado Mountain College campus in town.

lifts open. Private adaptive skiing clinics cost $40 for two hours, equipment available but not included. Mountain tours for experienced riders depart from the top of the gondola daily at 10.30am. Nonskiers can ride the gondola for $18, though the upper lodge isn't a particularly great spot to hang out.

Close to the gondola in the Mountain Village, the local branch of Powdertools (☎970/879-1645) is the snowboarder's alternative to the resort-owned Ride Sports/Steamboat Ski Rentals. To purchase **gear** try The Click in the Central Park Plaza (☎970/879-5861). Midway between the town and the mountain Ski Haus, 1450 S Lincoln Ave (☎970/879-0385), has great prices on a wide variety of ski rentals, from basic shaped ($19.50) to telemark ($24.50) and cross-country ($15), as well as inexpensive Burton board rentals.

Accommodation

A huge swathe of **condos** surround the ski area, from convenient slopeside suites to suburban-style homes. A few expensive hotels are available in the Mountain Village with a handful of smaller inns, motels, and B&Bs dotted throughout downtown. Thanks to the efficient free bus system, choice of location simply boils down to price and aesthetic preference. A more remote alternative is to stay in one of the many ranches in the surrounding area.

Steamboat Resorts (☎800/525-5502, ⊛www.steamboatresorts.com) is the largest property management company in town and your best resource for choosing condos. Most properties provide outdoor tubs, ski shuttles, and laundry services. Steamboat Central Reservations (☎800/922-2722, ⊛www.steamboat.com) is best for ski packages, with last-minute lift-and-lodging deals for around $80–100 per person, per night.

The BunkHouse Lodge 3155 S Lincoln Ave ☎970/871-9121 or 877/245-6343, ⊛www.steamboatbunkhouse.com. This new, wood-beamed motel, located between Hwy-40 and the Yampa River on the outskirts of town, includes amenities like mini-fridges, outdoor tub, ski lockers, and continental breakfast served in the spacious lounge. ❸

The Home Ranch 54880 RCR 129, Clark ☎970/879-1780, ⊛www.homeranch.com. Genuine ranch elegance 17 miles north of Steamboat in the Elk River Valley. Along with a four-star restaurant, indoor equestrian center, and 20km of cross-country trails are six handsome cabins and six snug lodge rooms, some with vaulted ceilings, all elegantly appointed. Cabins ❾; lodge rooms ❽

Hotel Bristol 917 Lincoln Ave ☎970/879-3083 or 800/851-0872, ⊛www.steamboathotelbristol.com. Twenty-two small but stylish rooms in an old red-brick building conveniently located in the center of town. The peculiarly located indoor hot tub overlooks the main street; additional bonuses include foosball and complimentary Internet access, ski shuttle, and a continental breakfast. ❹

Inn at Steamboat 3070 Columbine Drive ☎970/879-2600 or 800/872-2601, ⊛www.inn-at-steamboat.com. Inexpensive hotel amid the sea of condos surrounding the ski area, with the friendly if slightly worn air of a much-used ski lodge. All bedrooms have recently been remodeled in knotty pine and leather. Heated outdoor pool, sauna, laundry, pool table, generous continental breakfasts, complimentary hot drinks, and evening socials. From ❸

Mariposa Bed & Breakfast 855 Grand St ☎970/879-1467 or 800/578-1467, ⊛www.mariposabandb.homestead.com. Intimate, Southwestern-style home with only three guest bedrooms, within walking distance of Lincoln. Breakfast consists of excellent coffee, fresh smoothies, and home-baked muffins and pastries. Sneak one away to enjoy later in the garden sunroom. ❹

Nordic Lodge 1036 Lincoln Ave ☎970/879-0531, ⊛www.rockymountainfun.com/nordiclodge.html. Rather grim and boxy exterior, but the relatively inexpensive rooms are clean and comfy, if a bit worn. Outdoor tub available. ❸

Rabbit Ears Motel 201 Lincoln Ave, ☎970/879-1150 or 800/828-7702, ⊛www.rabbitearsmotel.com. Though the distinctive motel sign may be the most visually appealing aspect of this otherwise basic motel, rooms are clean and well appointed (most have microwaves and fridges) and conveniently situated on the eastern edge of town, across from the mineral pool and fitness center complex. ❸

Steamboat Bed & Breakfast 442 Pine St ☏970/879-5724 or 877/335-4321, ⓦwww .steamboatb-b.com. Two blocks from Lincoln, this large Victorian is a quintessential B&B, tastefully antique-strewn, with seven crisp, simple rooms and a cheery dining room below. Conservatory, outdoor deck, and hot tub; hearty cooked breakfasts. Recommended. ⑥

Steamboat Grand 2300 Mt Werner Circle, ☏970/ 871-5050 or 877/269-2628, ⓦwww .steamboatgrand.com. The resort's flagship condo-hotel, mammoth in size, within walking distance of the mountain. Suites come with full kitchens, while hotel-style rooms are spacious and comfy. The large fitness center has saunas, steam rooms, and a heated outdoor pool with two huge hot tubs. Restaurants are rather overrated, though meals in *The Cabin* and *Chaps* are of a high quality. ⑧

Eating

Steamboat isn't really a great dining town. There are, however, a few gems among the bland steakhouses and faux-Mexican cantinas, mostly downtown, off the Lincoln strip. Fast food and supermarkets are located between downtown and the slopes. Far more expensive, the Market on the Mountain, 2500 Village Drive (☏970/879-2965), has a good deli section, while the upscale Steamboat Meat & Seafood Co, 1030 Yampa Ave (☏970/879-3504), sells homemade pasta and fresh seafood flown in daily.

On-mountain, the little *Four Points Hut* below Storm Peak is the best hot chocolate and chili pit stop. At the top of the gondola, the massive lodge houses a bustling cafeteria and *Hazie's*, the resort's pricey restaurant (☏970/871-5150, lunch daily, dinner Thurs–Sat, reservations recommended).

402 Lincoln Ave This giant wooden barn holds three takeout counters, *Asian Pursuasion* (☏970/ 879-3060), *Brookie's Deli and Kitchen* (☏970/879-3060), and *Azteca Taqueria*, (☏970/870-9980), where you can get the best-value food – Thai and Vietnamese noodles, thick sandwiches, and burritos – in Steamboat.

Antares 57 1/2 8th St ☏970/879-9939. Called "new world cuisine," dishes subtly blend tastes from the five continents, so you might have Thai prawns as an appetizer, and Indian curry to follow. The warm, opulent, split-level setting feels almost colonial, belying the cold outside. Expensive but low key, with a comfy bar and live jazz on Friday and Saturday nights. From 5.30pm.

Boomerang's 50 8th St ☏970/879-3131. Grill your own meat at this entry of a local mini-chain; cuts are good quality and under $20. 3–10pm, dinner from 4pm.

Café Diva Torian Plum Plaza, Mountain Village ☏970/871-0508. Intimate, slopeside fine dining, despite the unpromising exterior. Food is predominantly French-American, with Asian influences most obvious in the appetizers. Prepared using the freshest ingredients, the presentation is impeccable. Expensive, but worth it. From 5pm.

Creekside Café and Grill 131 11th St, ☏970/ 879- 4925. Quiet breakfast and lunch option, tucked away from the main strip and mostly patronized by locals. Full, fresh breakfast menu includes multiple eggs benedict and pancake and

waffle variations with plenty of fresh fruit. Lunch is based around sandwiches and salads; dinner features inventive pastas. Live local music on Friday nights. Tues–Sun 7am–2pm, dinner served Wed–Sat 5–9.30pm.

The Home Ranch 54880 RCR 129, Clark ☏970/ 879-1780. One of only two prestigious Relais & Chateaux-recognized restaurants in Colorado, 18 miles up the road from Steamboat in the beautiful Elk River Valley. If you can afford the $65 price tag on whatever the gourmet chef has rustled up that day for the five-course dinner, you can probably afford to stay here too (see p.181), More affordable is the filling buffet lunch ($25), which includes use of the property's cross-country trails (20km).

Jitters 2245 Gondola Square ☏970/879-2158. Convenient for coffee and pastries, with slightly overpriced breakfast goods to go. 7.30am–7.30pm.

Johnny B. Good's 738 Lincoln Ave ☏970/870-8400. Friendly Fifties diner, run by devoted skiers, with shakes, sandwiches, burgers, and meatloaf dinners. Most entrees are under $10. Can be packed with families. 7am–9pm.

The Shack Café 740 Lincoln Ave ☏970/879-9975. Steamboat's quintessential greasy spoon, doling out huge breakfasts since 1969 in murky surroundings. Bloody Marys are on the menu, along with massive egg scrambles and plenty of meaty choices. Mon–Fri 6am–2pm, Sat–Sun 6.30am–2pm.

Strawberry Park Hot Springs

A 4WD is necessary to access the magical **Strawberry Hot Springs**, hidden away in a National Forest valley seven miles from Steamboat. (Shuttle service is available from town.) Hot spring water flows down into rocky pools carved out of the icy-cold creek; masseurs work in stone hobbit-style cottages perched on the hillside. The pools are open until midnight, with nude bathing a popular evening activity. Picturesque accommodation is available on the grounds, though the experience is akin to winter camping – linens are not provided, showering is done in the bath-house, and bare futons, a gas fireplace, charcoal grill, and gas lamp comprise the amenities. Luxury comes in the form of a converted caboose, complete with bedding, bathroom, and solar lights.

Soda Creek Pizza Co US 40 and Pine Grove ☎970/871-1111. Fancy pizza delivered, reasonably priced and accompanied by decent salads and Ben & Jerry's ice cream. Also offers take & bake pizzas. No dine in. Sun–Thurs 11am–10pm, Fri–Sat 11am–11pm.

Tapas Lounge Thunderhead Lodge, Ski Time Square ☎970/879-9232. Affordable tapas, substantial enough to fill you up after two or three plates. A busy spot during après, the *Lounge* is

served by the same kitchen as the more pricey *Mediterranean Grill* downstairs, 3pm–9/10pm.
Winona's 617 Lincoln Ave ☎970/879-2483. Warm bakery with all the breakfast favorites, plus homemade granola, cinnamon buns, muffins, and scones. Lunch is an extensive selection of well-stuffed wraps, salads, and sandwiches, hot and cold. Expect a line out the door, even during the week. Mon–Sat breakfast 7–11am, lunch 11am–3pm, Sun 7am–1pm, breakfast only. $5–10.

Bars and entertainment

Despite being home to a college campus, Steamboat is surprisingly mellow most nights. The handful of **bars** are well patronized, with local DJs and/or bands scheduled on weekends. For information on local events, check the calendar on the Steamboat Chamber's website (Ⓦ www.steamboatchamber.com) or pick up a copy of the free daily *Steamboat Today* or the weekly *Pilot*. Movies are screened at the Carmike Chief Plaza 4 (☎970/879-0181) and Time Square Cinema in the Mountain Village (☎970/879-3530). Most notable of the resort's annual on-mountain **festivities** are the Cowboy Downhill, a ski race finished on horseback, and February's long-running Winter Carnival, when truckloads of snow are dumped on Lincoln Avenue.

Level'z and Lupo's 1860 Ski Times Square ☎970/870-9090. It's not saying much, but this is Steamboat's premier club, typically the place in town to host any big-name band or DJ touring the Colorado resorts. The dance floor is on the third level; a so-called "extreme sports bar," filled with games, and and Internet café are below. Free pool and $2 drinks from 3.30 to 7pm.
Slopeside Grill Slopeside on the Torian Plum Plaza ☎970/879-2916. The pasta and wood-fired pizzas served inside this slopeside wooden shed are pretty tasty (entrees around $10) and food is served until midnight, but it's the giant outdoor bar made of ice that draws the crowds. Look for the deckchairs as you ride down the hill.
Steamboat Brewery & Tavern 5th St and Lincoln Ave, ☎970/879-2233. Award-winning brewery in

the center of town, where the beers are tasty (try the amber) and the hearty microbrewery-style menu more inventive than most, and Internet access is free.
Tugboat Ski Times Square ☎970/879-7070. Traditional après-ski watering hole in a barn-like building, with rock, funk, and blues from 9.30pm, when there's usually a small cover charge. Open until 1am.
Wolf's Den Tavern 703 Lincoln Ave ☎970/871-0008. Formerly known as the *Cellar Lounge*, this is the spot to catch a little-known live band, a dive bar where Steamboat's young and restless hang out. Cover charge varies from a couple of bucks to ten, depending on who's on stage; entry is often free early in the week and before 9 or 10pm.

Other activities and attractions

Besides the typical sleigh rides, horseback riding, snowmobile trips, snowshoe tours (for all contact Steamboat Lake Outfitters; ☎970/879-4404, ⊛www .steamboatoutfitters.com) and ice climbing, fly fishing, dogsledding, balloon trips, and glider flights (arranged through the visitor center or Central Reservations), Steamboat boasts **off-slope activities** unique to the area. Throw a car into a 360° turn on ice at the Bridgestone Winter Driving School (☎970/ 879-6104, ⊛www.winterdrive.com, from $145), the only one of its kind in the US. Cut entirely out of snow, the ten-corner track is used to train Colorado police, truckers, and those who'd rather get into a skid than learn to get out of one.

You'll find a heated outdoor pool and three mineral tubs at the slightly shabby **Steamboat Springs Health and Rec**, 136 Lincoln Ave (☎970/879-1828); Strawberry Hot Springs is a better alternative (see overleaf). The center also houses fitness machines and runs a schedule of yoga and exercise classes daily (Mon–Fri 5.30am–10pm, Sat–Sun 8am–10pm; $7.50 to swim, $15 for pools and fitness center, suits available to rent). For an **indoor activity** try Vertical Grip climbing gym, 1475 S Lincoln (Mon–Fri noon–6pm, Sat–Sun 1-9pm; $15 including gear; ☎970/879-5421).

Steamboat Ski Touring Center (☎970/879-8180) has 30km of trails on the golf course in the hills below the resort. Passes start at $12, rentals from $9, lesson packages from $30. For an easy and free snowshoe trek, hike up to Fish Creek Falls, north on 3rd Avenue from Lincoln. At the base of Hahn's Peak, 29 miles north of town, 30km of groomed trails wind through Steamboat Lake State Park (☎970/879-3922, trail fee $4 per vehicle). Nearby, out of the *Thunderbird Café*, the Mountain Recreation Company (daily 8am–4pm; ☎970/ 871-1495, ⊛www.mountainrec.com) rents cross-country skis and snowshoes and runs catered full-day tours of the area.

Listings

Howelsen Hill

Ski jumping was introduced to Steamboat by Carl Howelsen, a Norwegian Barnum and Bailey circus star known as the "flying Norseman" who showed up in the ranching community around 1914 and almost immediately began to teach the local kids how to throw themselves off wooden platforms. On the south side of the Yampa River downtown, **Howelsen Hill** (☎970/879-8499) is the oldest continually operating ski area in the US, with five ski jumps cut right into the steep-sided mountain. Night skiing tickets cost $15, $5 after 5pm. Weekly alpine races and public ski jumping nights are held for experienced adrenaline junkies ($10, call ☎970/879-0695, ext.112 for details). Howelsen is also the training ground of the **Steamboat Springs Winter Sports Club** (⊛www.sswsc.org), founded by the flying Norseman in 1915 and the oldest ski club west of the Mississippi.

Winter Park

Winter Park, the oldest continuously operating resort in the US, first opened its lifts in 1944 as a municipal facility – a winter park for Denver, located 67 miles away. It was originally developed as a family-oriented mountain, an image it's never quite shaken, though today it's better known for its expert terrain. Over time regional competition has grown drastically, yet Winter Park has had continued success by being modest and good value – particularly for season pass-holders – and through offering plenty of terrain for every type of skier and boarder. Refreshingly this includes skiers with disabilities, and Winter Park is home to the National Sports Center for the Disabled (☎970/726-1540 ⊛www.nscd.org), the continent's largest such center. It provides low-cost lessons and special adaptive equipment for 2500 people a year, and trains serious competitors for its Disabled Ski Team.

Off the slopes, however, there is less choice. Despite the ongoing development in Winter Park's **slopeside village**, the resort is not much more than a modest collection of condominiums. And the eponymous **town** of Winter Park, two miles north along Hwy-40, is little more than a sprawling agglomeration of ski lodges, outfitters, and shopping malls. A further five miles north along Hwy-40 is the even more utilitarian **Fraser**, home for most locals. Though neither is exciting, between them the two towns provide services of a standard and variety that suffice to make the resort a low-key competitor for the far busier Summit County ski areas.

Arrival, information, and getting around

Winter Park is reached from Denver via I-70 and then Hwy-40 (take exit 232), a treacherous and often painfully slow road over the Berthoud Pass which ensures the total journey time is rarely under two hours. See box on Denver, p.113 for directions and car rental information; for up-to-date **local road conditions** call ☎303/639-1000. **Parking** at the resort is easy, with both base areas offering free parking, though lots close to the Winter Park base charge.

Public transport from Denver to Winter Park is provided by Greyhound ($10 one way), by Amtrak ($25 one way) on the *California Zephyr* to Fraser, and by Home James **shuttles** from Denver International Airport (☎303/726-5060 or 1-800/359-7503, ⊛www.homejamestransportation.com; $42 one way). The **Winter Park Ski Train** (reservations required ☎303/296-4754, ⊛www.skitrain.com; $45; 2hr) operates round trips from Denver every Saturday and Sunday – with additional trips over Christmas and on Fridays from early

February – leaving at 7.15am and starting back at 4.15pm. Tickets are available only on a day return basis. Train, bus, and shuttle services from Denver can all be booked through Winter Park Central Reservations (☎970/726-5587 or 1-800/979-0332, ⓦ www.winterparkresort.com).

An excellent network of free **local shuttle buses** renders cars unnecessary connecting Fraser, Winter Park, and most local accommodations with the resort every ten to fifteen minutes using bus stops marked by blue circle signs. Free buses also take passengers from restaurants and bars to the doorstep of their accommodation on Friday and Saturday nights until 2am. The **Winter Park Visitor Center** (daily 8am–5pm, ☎970/726-4118 or 1-800/903-7275, ⓦ www.winterpark-info.com) is located at the junction of Hwy-40 with Vasquez Road.

The mountain

Orientation in Winter Park's topographically complex ski area is difficult, so it's worth spending time poring over the trail map in advance. The area divides into five interconnected zones; two base areas sit below eponymous mountains, while a less accessible bowl, cirque, and ridge lie tucked out of sight behind these.

The resort's main base area is below its namesake; **Winter Park mountain** rises up from the main base area and is the convenient home for much of the resort's beginner and easier intermediate terrain as well as its halfpipe and terrain parks. Overshadowing it is larger and more rugged **Mary Jane mountain**, whose, steep long runs – up to 4.5 miles long – are sprinkled with steep, narrow, bumpy ridges harboring some of the best mogul runs in Colorado. Mary Jane is also the gateway to reaching the fluffy snows of the high-alpine **Parsenn Bowl**, which rises to 12,060ft, making it a magnet for deep powder. Only via lifts into the Parsenn Bowl can you reach the adjacent **Vasquez Cirque**, whose undeveloped, ungroomed off-piste challenges include cornices and rock outcrops. Leaving this cirque, you arrive at the third major peak, the uncrowded **Vasquez Ridge**, a gateway to more backcountry and several quiet maintained runs. From Vasquez Ridge you can return to either Mary Jane mountain or Winter Park mountain.

Beginner

Winter Park has an excellent ski school and an enclosed 200-acre beginner zone – **Discovery Park** – where flat open spaces, short tree-lined runs, and gently winding cat tracks beckon. Confident beginners should progress to the ridge between Winter Park mountain and Mary Jane. Here you'll find long, green cruisers underneath the High Lonesome Express and to the base of Vasquez Ridge. Unless comfortable in heavy traffic, avoid the busy Cranmer Cutoff back from this area to the base of Winter Park and stick to the slow cat tracks further down the mountain.

Intermediate

There are easy blues off every peak and ridge except the Vasquez Cirque. The classic on **Winter Park** is Cranmer, a wide, rolling cruiser popular with advanced carvers as well as intermediates. For less busy blues, head to the Pioneer lift on **Vasquez Ridge**, where a few short blacks are suitable for better intermediates. On **Mary Jane** stay under the Sunnyside lift and dip into easy glades on a gentle pitch through Wildwood and Bellmar bowls. Elsewhere on Mary Jane, as well as on the front face of Winter Park mountain, there are

The backcountry

Until a couple of years ago, **Berthoud Pass** was a fully fledged if underrated ski area; opened in 1937, it was the first resort in Colorado. Then finances crashed, and today this powder-rich spot operates as a 1700-acre snowcat park. Cough up $225 ($195 in the off-season) and a world of open glades, steeps, and bowls is yours; hiking is the cheaper alternative. Park in the Berthoud lot, fifteen miles up from Winter Park, then ride back down into the valley toward the road. On powder days, Hwy-40 is lined with stoked riders hitching back up to the top of the pass. Berthoud Powder Guides (93475 US Hwy-40, ☏970/726-0287 or 800/SKI-BERT, ⊛www .berthoudpowderguides.com) also offer avalanche Level I and II classes, starting at $200 for a two-day course.

either steeper blues or bump runs that have been groomed on one side. In the exposed **Parsenn Bowl** short gentle powder fields and easy glades are an ideal introduction to off-piste riding.

Expert

Winter Park's two biggest expert playgrounds are on Mary Jane and in Vasquez Cirque. The latter is exceptional but hard to access, with each run ending in a long green to the base, requiring three different lifts to get back to the summit. If you do decide to session Vasquez try the drops off the exposed cliffs and couloirs of Alphabet and Shadow Chutes or hike to the cornices that span from the double black diamond **South Headwall** to **Jellyroll**, a slightly mellower pitch that leads into the trees. For great tree runs, try Backside **Parsenn** on the opposite side of the valley.

Many experts prefer to focus on the convenient runs of **Mary Jane**; Riflesight Notch under the **Summit Express** is littered with hidden cliffs and tempting rocks, and the gladed Pine Cliffs and Sluicebox provide excellent freeriding options. Under the **Sunnyside** lift try Awe, Baldy's, and Jeff's Chute, all short but sweet double diamonds with a cliff band running through their center.

Freestyle

Winter Park is gradually improving its **freestyle** terrain, but the number and size of jumps here are limited and more snow-dependent than in a park-proud resort like Breckenridge. The halfpipe is excellent, however, and kept lively by tunes blasted from an adjacent yurt. Terrain parks are usually built just above the Snoasis lodge and so easily sessioned using either the Outrigger or Eskimo Express chairs. For natural hits search the trees on Mary Jane for pinball-type gullies and fallen logs.

Lift tickets, lessons, and rentals

Beginners can ride the Galloping Goose chair on Mary Jane for $5, but in general lift tickets here are comparable with neighboring Summit resorts. Half-day tickets can be taken in the morning or afternoon. Best value is the Rocky Mountain Super Pass (from $319 bought preseason). It also permits season-long access to Copper Mountain (see p.144).

The ski school is excellent, with a huge range of levels and clinics to choose from. Half-day group lessons start at $40, with full-day specialty clinics (moguls are a favorite) from $60. Multiday camps are offered for bump skiers, tele-markers, and women. The Children's Center serves kids from age 3 to 15.

There's no shortage of places to **rent** ski and snowboard gear in Winter Park. The resort's rental facilities (℡1-800/979-0328) are located in West Portal, close to the main base area, and at Mary Jane. Basic packages (starting at around $20) include decent equipment, though for performance gear, outlets in town have the edge. Ski Depot Sports, which has four small branches in the area in addition to their downtown store (℡970/726-8055 or 1-800/525-6484, ⓦwww.skidepot.com), has excellent up-to-date ski packages, a more limited selection of snowboards, good boot fitting and tuning services, and some of the best prices in town. Alternatives include Christy Sports, 78930 Hwy-40, (℡970/726-8873, ⓦwww.christysports.com), located in Cooper Creek Square; their discount outlet across the road; Powdertools, 78786 Hwy-40, downtown Winter Park (℡970/726-1151, ⓦwww.powdertools.com), Christy's snowboard store, with packages from $22 per day; and the good-value Valley Board, Bike, and Ski off Hwy 40, Fraser (℡970/726-8882 or 1-800/544-2431). Note that many local condo hotels and ski lodges have their own ski shops.

Accommodation

A number of new slopeside options are under construction, but for now there's only limited **accommodation** in the resort, leaving most visitors reliant on motels and modern ski lodges in town. Many of these are unusual in that they offer packages that include breakfast and dinner – a more common practice in Europe. Dotted around the valley are a selection of upscale B&Bs. Winter Park Central Reservations (℡970/726-5587 or 1-800/979-0332, ⓦwww .skiwinterpark.com) can arrange lodging in every available style of accommodation and offer a variety of flexible ski packages. If you are looking for a condo in the area also try Winter Park Adventures (℡970/726-5701 or 1-800/ 525-2466, ⓦwww.winterparkadventures.com), which can organize units from $60 per night for two-night minimum stays.

Beaver Village Lodge 79303 Hwy-40 ℡970/726-5741 or 800/666-0281, ⓦwww.beavervillage .com. Large A-frame ski lodge on the resort side of Winter Park town, with small, basic rooms sleeping one to six. Buffet breakfast and dinner included in the rates, served in a school-style dining room. Popular with large groups and some UK tour operators. Facilities include bar, jacuzzi and sauna, pool table, arcade games, laundry, and ski shop. Snowmobiling and sleigh rides also available. Good multiday packages and kids' rates; from $30 per person per night in a six-bed room to $90 peak single.

Devil's Thumb Ranch Country Road 83 ℡970/726-8231, ⓦwww.devilsthumbranch.com. Rustic lodge and private cabins oozing Rocky Mountain charm on the slopes of the Continental Divide, fifteen minutes down valley from Winter Park. Rooms range from simple lodge rooms with shared baths up to four-bedroom cabins. Rates include use of sauna and jacuzzi, a continental breakfast, and cheese and wine tasting. The restaurant is renowned for its fine dining, and there's extensive cross-country skiing from the door. ❹

Iron Horse Resort 257 Winter Park Drive, Winter Park ℡970/726-8851 or 1-800/621-8190, ⓦwww.ironhorse-resort.com. Old-school condo hotel with worn-in furnishings and a maze of zigzag corridors accessible from the slopes via a flat cat track. Units range from studios to two-bed to three premium suites with full kitchens and sun decks. The indoor/outdoor pool, hot tubs, and weight room are a bit basic, but continental breakfast and après-ski are included and kids eat free in the dining room, making it economical for families and groups. ❻

Olympia Motor Lodge 78572 Hwy-40, Winter Park ℡970/726-8843 or 1-800/548-1992. This standard though comfortable downtown motel has rooms with queen beds, some with kitchenettes. ❹

The Outpost 687 County Rd 517 ℡970/726-5346 or 1-800/430-4538, ⓦwww.outpost-colorado .com. Relaxed country ranch tucked away in the pastures just north of Fraser; secluded yet not too far from town. Large, comfy lobby and dining area with open fireplace and separate upstairs lounge, with microwave, snacks, video library, and resident spaniels. Choose from antique-furnished rooms in the main house or in the quieter adults-only annex next to the atrium hot tub. **❺**

Snow Mountain Ranch 1344 County Rd 53 ☎970/ 887-2152 or 303/443-4743, groups 1-800/777- 9622, @www.ymcarockies.org. Simple cabins, vacation homes, and lodge accommodation dotted around a forested 5100 acres, location of the Nordic Center (see "Other activities," overleaf), seven miles north of Fraser along Hwy-40. Extensive facilities include a sports center with indoor pool, basket-ball, roller skating, climbing wall and outdoor ice rink, restaurants, and library. Good group rates. **❸**

TimberHouse Ski Lodge Off Winter Park Drive ☎970/726-5477 or 1-800/843-3502, @www .timberhouseskilodge.com. Traditional ski lodge with genuine alpine atmosphere, built in the 1940s in the woods above the Winter Park base area, and with access to the slopes. Rustic common rooms are bedecked with wood carvings and focus on a huge fireplace. All rooms are unique and range from six-person dorms ($48) to modern doubles with private bath; the older section of the lodge is cozier, and attic rooms offer the most privacy. Amenities include a sauna, and a huge wooden barrel hot tub. Gigantic breakfasts, dinner, and afternoon tea are included. **❹**

Viking Lodge Cooper Creek Square, Winter Park ☎970/726-8885 or 1-800/421-4013, @www .skiwp.com. Clean and well-maintained downtown ski lodge, usually the cheapest deal in town. Rooms are basic, though some have kitchens. Coffee and a continental breakfast are included, and facilities include a game room, whirlpool, and sauna. **❸**

The Vintage Hotel 100 Winter Park Drive ☎970/ 726-8801, @www.vintagehotel.com. Condo-hotel with faded elegance just feet from the ski area, where accommodations range from small hotel rooms without kitchens to three-bedroom condos with full kitchens. Facilities include a game room, a lounge, hot tubs, a sauna, and a courtesy shuttle to town. **❹**

Whistle Stop Bed & Breakfast 178 Fraser Ave, Fraser ☎970/726-8767 or 888/829-2632, @www.winterparkbandb.com. Small, modern B&B on a residential street by the Amtrak station in Fraser. The least expensive in the area, it's run by attentive Texans who bake an endless supply of cookies and offer advice on just about everything and prepare huge Southwestern breakfasts. **❹**

Zephyr Mountain Lodge The Village at Winter Park ☎970/726-8400 or 877/754-8400, @www.zephyrmountainlodge.com. Mammoth slopeside development and the keystone of the new Village at Winter Park development. Offered are one-, two- and three-bedroom condos all sporting luxury rustic-chic décor and priced to match – at least by local standards. **❽**

Eating

Winter Park may lack the selection of **restaurants** present in Summit County or Vail, but overall the range is sufficient. There's little in the resort village, so most restaurants and bars (several do good food – see "Drinking" overleaf) are in town, in plazas and strip malls right beside Hwy-40. Fraser is the best place for groceries, with the choice of Safeway or the Great Mother Market, Hwy-40 and Kings Crossing, Winter Park (☎970/726-4704), a huge health food store.

   Base area dining options at Winter Park mountain include standard bar fare in the Zephyr and Winter Park Mountain lodges, and the inexpensive utilitar-ian West Portal food court. In the latter you can get a full breakfast or bagels and great coffee as well as inexpensive burgers and fries, pasta specials for under $5, and a salad bar. **On-mountain**, the *Sunspot Lodge* at the top of Winter Park mountain has a sundeck with great views but high prices.

Arpeggios 78785 Hwy-40, Winter Park ☎970/ 726-5402. Wonderfully authentic but pricey north-ern Italian fare downtown. The excellent Chicken Fantasia comes with a creamy sauce, nuts, and grapes tossed in with pasta. Reservations recom-mended.

Carlos and Maria's Copper Creek Square, Winter Park ☎970/726-9674. Reliably good, inexpensive Mexican restaurant with low-cost margaritas during the daily happy hour from 3.30 to 6pm.

Carvers Behind Copper Creek Square, Winter Park ☎970/726-8202. Sun-filled, low-ceilinged bakery with historic prints and ancient skis on the walls. Serves a large variety of reasonably priced big breakfasts and some good sandwiches for lunch and is a good place to stock up on picnic items.

Fontenot's Cajun Café Park Plaza, Hwy-40, Winter Park ☎970/726-4021. Squeezed into a strip mall, this is a good option to escape the usual ski town menus, southern-style; choose from items like gumbo, jambalaya, and fish dishes.

Gasthaus Eichler 78786 Hwy-40, Winter Park ☎970/726-5133. Austrian and German specialties (around $20) like schnitzel, *sauerbraten*, or bratwurst with sauerkraut are served with a gourmet twist in this quaint upscale alpine ski lodge downtown. Reservations recommended.

Hernando's Pizza Pub 78199 Hwy-40, Winter Park ☎970/726-5409. A comfortable, roomy spot with exceptionally good pizza (try the garlic pie base) and an invitation to decorate a dollar and add it to the 5000-plus already on the walls.

La Taqueria Park Place, Winter Park ☎970/726-0280. Inexpensive, little place with a few bar tables serving standard Tex-Mex, including super burritos big enough for two at $7.50.

Lodge at Sunspot Winter Park Resort ☎970/726-1446. Gondola cars are attached to the *Zephyr Express* to shuttle gourmands to the top of Winter Park mountain for views over the Continental Divide and a four-course gourmet dinner. Offerings include fresh trout, local lamb, and various wild game options – expect to pay at least $40 per person. Reservations advised. Open Thurs–Sat.

Pepe Osaka's 78727 Hwy-40 ☎970/726-0455. Bringing sushi, sake, and Thai food to town and operating in a subterranean space beneath *Rudi's Deli*. Those fearful of raw fish are kept happy with a selection of inventive pastas, stir-frys, and salads.

The Ranch House Restaurant Country Rd 83 ☎970/726-8231. Traditional and expensive fine dining in an elegant log cabin at this old homestead at Devil's Thumb Ranch (see p.188).

Rudi's Deli Park Plaza, downtown Winter Park ☎970/726-8955. Huge, tasty deli sandwiches, served with chips, coleslaw, or pasta salad. Homemade breads, soups and chili, and loads of veggie options on the "Herbivore board." Take out or eat in their small fast-food style space. Half sandwiches from $3.25, whole from $4.59.

The Shed 78672 Hwy-40, downtown Winter Park ☎970/726-9912. Impressive selection of margaritas and the food is fantastic, if expensive. Their "creative southwestern cuisine" includes such mixed breeds as chicken baklava, tortilla cashew salmon, Cajun chimichangas, and fajitas from veggie ($10) to lobster and mango ($25). Huge salads for under $10.

Drinking and entertainment

Laid-back and limited to a few spots, nightlife in Winter Park is mostly driven by the locals, so expect to recognize faces after a couple of nights. Drinking kicks off at Winter Park resort, but peters out early, leaving places along the main drag in Winter Park and Fraser the best option for a late night out. An alternative to spending evenings in bars is to head to the small Silver Screen Cinema (☎970/726–5390) next to Buckets (see below).

Buckets 78415 Hwy-40, Winter Park ☎970/726-3026. Odd combination of basement laundromat, arcade, and bar that's become a popular hangout for locals. Live music on Monday nights and karaoke on weekends.

Crooked Creek Saloon & Eatery 401 Zerex Ave, Fraser ☎970/726-5727. Occasionally wild and gritty locals' bar, serving Mexican and standard American bar food and plenty of beer; summed up by its slogan "Eat 'til it hurts, drink 'til it feels better!" – yet with a good kids' menu. Live music weekly.

Deno's 78911 Hwy-40, Winter Park ☎970/726-5332. Sports bar serving unexpectedly good food – including pasta ($10), steaks, and spicy Cajun

seafood – plus a hundred or so varieties of beer.

The Hideaway Park Place Center, Hwy-40, Winter Park ☎970/726-1081. Winter Park's closest approximation of a club with a large wooden dance floor with an antler chandelier as the centerpiece. The hip-hop and drum 'n' bass nights (Weds–Fri) blow hot and cold, but the basement bar below, with pool, air hockey, arcade games, and worn-in comfy couches and chairs is much more predictable.

Winter Park Pub 78260 Hwy-40, Winter Park ☎970/726-4929. Sports bar run by a diehard Green Bay Packers fan; widely referred to as simply "the Pub," and the place to be for free pizza during Monday night football.

Other activities and attractions

Cross–country skiers consider the 150–odd miles of cross-country trails in the area, which include plenty of good backcountry options, one of the best networks in the state. Down the valley from the downhill area is the cross-country center **Devil's Thumb Ranch**, 3530 County Rd 83, Tabernash (☎970/726-8231 or 1-800/933-4339, ⓦwww.devilsthumbranch.com), where nearly 100 kilometers of groomed trails fan out into the forest from a central meadow. To get there, drive west from Winter Park to the town of Fraser and turn right onto County Road 83. Tickets are $12 for adults, and lessons and equipment rental are also available for all levels. Another option is the Snow Mountain Ranch YMCA Nordic Center (☎970/887-2152 ext. 4173, ⓦwww.ymcarockies.org), which maintains 100km of trails. Trail passes ($12) are available from the rental shop. Learn-to-ski packages with lessons, rentals, and pass cost $32.

The resort's **Tour Center** (☎970/726-1616) arranges snowshoe explorations of Winter Park's lower slopes and snowcat, moonlit snowmobile, and sleigh rides. Trips are run according to demand and weather conditions. A greater variety of guided trips are offered elsewhere locally and these include **snowmobile** trips up to the Continental Divide, **sleigh rides**, and **dog sledding**. All three are offered by Grand Adventures (☎970/726-9247 or 1-800/726-9247, ⓦwww.grandadventures.com) based in the Beaver Village Lodge. You can snowmobile on a one-hour tour with Trailblazers in Fraser (☎970/726-8452; $35), or around a 25-mile course with Mountain Madness (☎970/726-4529; $35 per hour), just north of town. The forty-strong team at Dog Sled Rides of Winter Park (Kings Crossing Road, downtown Winter Park, ☎970/726-8326, ⓦwww.dogsledrides.com/winterpark) is best for mushing through the forest. For **sleigh rides**, contact Jim's Sleigh Rides (☎970/726-0944), who tow up to twenty guests per sleigh ($18 per person) along the Fraser River, or Devil's Thumb Outfitters (☎970/726-1099, ⓦwww.devilsthumboutfitters.com), who also offer horseback rides.

Other popular evening activities are sliding down the **Tubing Hill** at Fraser (Mon, Wed, Fri 4–10pm, Sat–Sun and holidays 10am–10pm, $12 per hour), half a mile behind the Safeway store, and **ice-skating** at the outdoor Fraser Ice Rink, 601 Zerex Ave (☎970/726-8882). For a relaxing soak head to the **Hot Sulphur Springs Resort and Spa** (☎970/725-3306, 8am–10pm, $14.50 per day; spa treatments, towels, and robes extra, ⓦwww.hotsulphursprings.com) – a scenic thirty-minute drive along Hwy-40 north – passing freight trains whistle at the bathers in the sulfurous outdoor mineral pools; private pools available.

Listings

Avalanche hotline ☎303/371-1080.
Internet Buckets, 78415 Hwy-40 ☎970/726-3026, charges 10 cents per minute.
Medical 7-Mile Medical Clinic, Winter Park Resort ☎970/726-8066.

Pharmacy Fraser Drug Store, 535 Zerex St ☎970/726-1000.
Police Grand County ☎970/726-3343.
Post office 78490 Hwy-40 ☎1-800/275-8777.

Vail/Beaver Creek

These days it's very fashionable to denounce **Vail**. Long the darling of reader polls conducted by glossy ski magazines, the largest ski area in the US occasionally receives raw treatment from journalists, who dub it one of the most boring places to ski on earth. Less harsh critics merely call it flat and bland, thrill-seekers lament the lack of stomach-churning steeps, and no one can say anything redeemable about the frustratingly long liftlines. Even the corporate culture that the resort's parent company has instilled takes quite a beating. But the truth is you'd have to spend quite a while navigating the long cruisers, immense back bowls, stashed-away log slides, and well-maintained terrain parks to get bored – it's not the people's favorite for nothing.

Conceived in the late Fifties by World War II vets Pete Seibert and Earl Eaton, opened in 1962, and incorporated in 1966, Vail Resorts has created a virtual monopoly in central Colorado (owning Beaver Creek, Breckenridge, and Keystone as well), allowing them to charge top dollar for tickets and on-mountain food. This doesn't put off hordes of young skiers – seasonal vagrants, college students, weekenders flying in from either coast, employees at the Summit resorts – who join a wealthy clientele to ski some of the best slopes on the continent and create a decent nighttime buzz for the area.

Mountain info

Phone ☎970/476-5601 or 800/427-8308

Snow phone ☎970/476-4888

Website ⊛www.vail.com

Price $71 peak, off peak $49

Operating times Mid-Nov to third week in April daily 8.30am–4pm

No. of lifts 33, including 1 gondola and 9 surface lifts

Base elevation 8120′

Summit elevation 11570′

Vertical drop 3450′

No. of trails 193

Acreage 5289

Beginner 18%

Intermediate 29%

Expert 53%

Average snowfall 334″

Snowmaking Yes (390 acres)

Night skiing No (Night tubing, biking, ice skating on mountain until 9pm)

Nursery facilities Yes, Small World Play School, from 2 months to 6 years, in Golden Peak children's center only, reservations required (☎970/479-3285); skiing 3–14, snowboarding 7–14

Such popularity breeds a bit of a sprawl, and with superstores and modestly priced lodging options a bus ride down valley in the worker's annex of **West Vail**, picturesque **Minturn**, or the sprawling workaday communities of **Avon** and **Edwards**, the mountain corridor of Eagle County has the feel of an elongated college town. If this fails to appeal, you can go for the condos of **Vail Village**; you might not like its mock-Tyrolean architecture or purpose-built nature, but it's highly convenient, pedestrian-friendly, and has a surprisingly organic nature to it.

Beaver Creek, fifteen miles down valley, is the most closely linked of the Vail Resorts group, and their shared single-day ticket is priced a few dollars higher than one at Keystone or Breckenridge. The mountain makes an excellent complement to Vail, featuring the long double diamond downhills and steep trees that its neighbor lacks, in addition to acres of family-friendly terrain. Trails are more sheltered and the slopes less crowded, while the ambience of the resort and its base settlements (Bachelor Gulch and Arrowhead) are less brash and more exclusive: escalators whisk skiers from town plaza to the slopes, and ambassadors hand out cookies at the end of the ski day; members' clubs are de rigueur; and the customer is king.

 The Reliable Airline

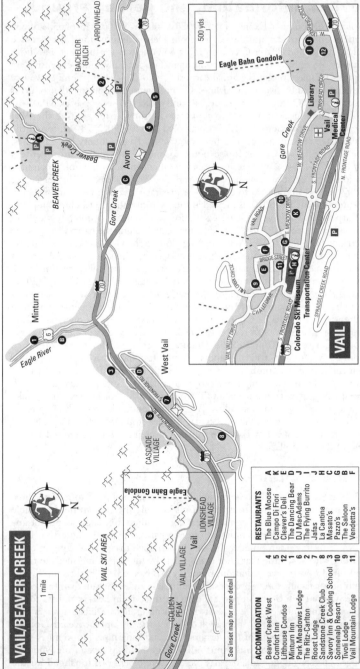

VAIL/BEAVER CREEK

▲ Edwards & Eagle County Airport

▲ Vail Nordic Center, East Vail & Denver

VAIL

Eagle Bahn Gondola

Gore Creek

Vail Medical Center

Library

Colorado Ski Museum
Transportation Center

BRIDGE STREET

W. MEADOW DRIVE

E. MEADOW DRIVE

VAIL ROAD

S. FRONTAGE ROAD

N. FRONTAGE ROAD

CHALET ROAD

VAIL VALLEY DRIVE

MILL CREEK CIRCLE

LIONSHEAD CIRCLE

SPRADDLE CREEK ROAD

70

0   500 yds

N

Minturn

Eagle River

West Vail

Avon

Beaver Creek

BEAVER CREEK

BACHELOR GULCH

ARROWHEAD

Gore Creek

S FRONTAGE ROAD

N FRONTAGE ROAD

CASCADE VILLAGE

VAIL VILLAGE

LIONSHEAD VILLAGE

Vail

Golden Peak

VAIL SKI AREA

Gore Creek

Eagle Bahn Gondola

See inset map for more detail

N

0   1 mile

70

ACCOMMODATION

Beaver Creek West	4
Comfort Inn	5
Lifthouse Condos	12
Minturn Inn	1
Park Meadows Lodge	6
The Ritz-Carlton	2
Roost Lodge	7
Sandstone Creek Club	3
Savory Inn & Cooking School	8
Sonnenalp Resort	10
Tivoli Lodge	9
Vail Mountain Lodge	11

RESTAURANTS

The Blue Moose	A
Campo Di Fiori	K
Cleaver's Deli	E
The Dancing Bear	D
DJ MacAdams	J
The Flying Burrito	I
Jafas	J
La Cantina	H
Masato's	C
Pazzo's	G
The Saloon	B
Vendetta's	F

Arrival, information, and getting around

Colorado Mountain Express (☎970/926-9800 or 1-800/525-6363, ⓦwww
.cmex.com) provides shuttle service from Denver International Airport (see
p.113) to Vail and Beaver Creek, charging $62 one way for the three-plus hour
journey along busy I-70. More convenient but generally more expensive are
flights to Eagle County Regional Airport (☎970/524-9490), 35 miles west of
Vail and served by five major airlines. Ground transportation to either resort is
just $2 on ECO buses, shuttles are $40, and a taxi will set you back $100.

Greyhound buses from Denver (from $30 round-trip) stop at the **Vail
Transportation Center**, 31 S Frontage Rd (☎970/479-2178), on top of the
Vail Village parking garage. The best resource for Eagle County bus schedules,
the Transportation Center is also home to one of Vail's two **visitor centers**
(☎970/479-1394, ⓦwww.visitvailvalley.com), where you can book accommodation, pick up local newspapers, or surf the Web for free; the other center
(☎970/479-1385) is next to the Lionshead garage. Beaver Creek's Information
Center (☎970/845-9090) is located at the western entrance to the town plaza.

Purportedly the largest free transportation service in the country, Town of Vail
buses (6am–2am; ☎970/477-3456) run regularly along the narrow seven-mile
corridor from East to West Vail, stopping close to the Golden Peak, Vail Village,
Lionshead, and Cascade Village lifts. Bus service between and around Avon and
Beaver Creek is complimentary and the two areas are linked to Vail by an
extensive network of resort and county shuttles ($2–3 each way). ECO
(6am–2am; $2; ☎970/323-3520), the Eagle Valley transport system, serves all
outlying areas including Minturn, Leadville (for Ski Cooper, see p.250),
Edwards, and the Eagle County airport. Vail Resorts Express operates a daily
shuttle service from both resorts to Breckenridge and Keystone ($12, reserva-
tions required; ☎970/469-8245). Despite the cost ($13 for 6–24 hours, free
from 5pm–3am and if staying under 60 minutes), most drivers use Vail's convenient Village or Lionshead garages on South Frontage Road right of I-70,
exit 176. On the weekend, it pays to turn up late; once the structures are full,
free parking is permitted on South Frontage Road. For Beaver Creek, take
I-70 exit 167 for Avon and follow Avon Road one mile south through town
to the gated reception center. Regular shuttles stop at the free East Lot and
from the West Lot below Bachelor Gulch. Covered pay lots are located at each
end of the town plaza.

Vail mountain

It's useful to think of this vast mountain in threes. You'll need to refer to three
trail maps: one for the front face, of which only the bottom third is visible
from the village, with its beginner areas, long cruisers, tree shots, upper mountain cliff-drops, and lower-mountain terrain parks; one for the notorious Back
Bowls, a mostly ungroomed, gully-filled open bowl that's challenging in powder but with very little that's not manageable by the upper intermediate rider;
and one for Vail's latest addition, Blue Sky Basin, a tamed "backcountry" area
with north-facing, forested slopes that suffer less under the sun than the sometimes soupy Back Bowls opposite. There are three main **access points** to the
slopes, strung out along the base of the front face, all with lifts that carry riders to mid-mountain. To the east is the low rise of aspen-covered **Golden
Peak**, permanent home of the terrain parks and superpipe. Ten minutes walk
into the center of town, lifts from **Vail Village** head up toward the Mid-Vail
lodge. Vail's speedy gondola departs the concrete blocks of **Lionshead** for the

Eagle's Nest lodge. Three lodges punctuate the ridgeline between front face and back bowls: Two Elk, Patrol Headquarters, and Wildwood.

In terms of terrain, it makes little difference where newcomers start their day. Vail's 33 lifts (which locals confusingly refer to by either number or name, depending on the lift itself; thus Vista Bahn is generally Vista Bahn, but Avanti is always Chair 2) and many well-cut traverses make it fairly easy, if somewhat time-consuming and disorienting at first, to crisscross the upper mountain. Just be sure to factor in distances if arranging a meeting place; eastern Two Elk is at least thirty minutes' skiing from western Wildwood. Of Vail's **bowls**, Game Creek, off the front face, can be reached in the shortest time, then Sun Down and Sun Up. Getting to Siberia Bowl involves a serious trek, with a hefty traverse out. **Blue Sky Basin** is best accessed from the Teacup or China Bowl; though the area's mellow glades, cliff bands and cornices are complimented by a couple of meandering blue trails, just getting there and back involves the better part of an afternoon, on routes that involve substantial catwalk traversing. Useful three hour **mountain tours** for intermediate and advanced riders depart daily at 9.30am from the Lionshead and Vail Village base areas; Blue Sky Basin tours meet at Patrol Headquarters at 10am.

At the end of the day, should you find yourself below Two Elk lodge in the Northeast bowl, consider downloading on Chair 6 (Riva Bahn). The valley behind Golden Peak is far deeper than it looks on the map, and though the always-crowded upper North Face catwalk is rideable, lower Brisk Walk is painful, even for skiers; "brisk" doesn't come into it, but "walk" is certainly apt. The easiest route home is under the gondola to Lionshead. Avoid the 3.30pm skier traffic by stopping at the Eagle's Nest to grab a drink or mess about at Adventure Ridge, then download later on the gondola, which runs until 9pm and is quietly magical at night, with the lights of Vail twinkling below.

Beginner

It's possible to locate a green trail off every lift on the front face. Never-evers can start right in town, on **Gopher Hill** at the bottom of Golden Peak, or head up Lionshead gondola to enjoy the views and sheltered beginner terrain next to **Eagle's Nest**. Both areas have slow-moving beginner lifts. Step up to the wide, tree-lined slopes below Two Elk Lodge, at the top of the mountain, which are relatively uncrowded and steep enough for both snowboarders and skiers to build confidence. Avoid the tedious and busy catwalk back to town by taking the Northwoods lift to Mid-Vail or downloading on Riva Bahn.

Intermediate

Try a few bumps, hit up a mellow glade, or attempt a short black on Mid Vail **Bowl's** fantastically varied terrain. Liftlines here can be long, but you can avoid the wait at Vista Bahn by taking Chair 1 to Chair 2, working your way to the long, wide, cruisers and air-inducing rollers of tree-lined runs underneath the gondola. Near the base are gentle aspen glades with widely spaced trees perfect for off-piste virgins. For more bowl skiing, the groomed runs of **Game Creek** are easiest, progressing to the powder fields of **China Bowl**, though none is beyond the reach of a confident intermediate.

Expert

After a recent storm, head to one of the Back Bowls where even skiers lacking in powder experience should pick up a pair of fat skis and give it a shot – this is the perfect place to learn. If conditions are less than perfect, however, these exposed slopes can become choppy and tedious. Try **Game Creek**, where the snow usually holds better. On the front face are the tight evergreens of Northeast bowl and the terraced aspens under Vista Bahn Express, often closed in dry years. Classic downhill blacks include International and Pepi's, both of which are patchy in warm weather and descend in full view of the gallery outside *Amigos* in Vail Village. For bumps try Mid Vail **Bowl** and the steeps under Northwoods or the overgraded double diamonds on the far eastern boundary. Hardcore downhillers and backcountry aficionados may want to forgo Vail altogether for the steeper slopes of Beaver Creek.

Freestyle

Once a focal point of the snowboard scene in the US, and still home to a number of pros, the superpipe, tabletops, and hips on Golden Peak are consistently well maintained, if not quite up to Breckenridge standards. Better for experienced riders than beginners, the fairly standard mid-park rail garden includes a number of large rainbows and curves. Locals are devoted to the fine art of logslide construction; most are well-hidden, but a few are located under the gondola and rider's right off the Northwoods lift, above the natural halfpipe and jibs of Hairbag Alley. Under Northwoods and neighboring Chair 4 exist serious cliff drops with tight landings in the trees, while rock faces from small to mid-size jut out on the exposed ridges between the back bowls. A decent cornice builds up under the Skyline Express in Blue Sky next to a sketchy but tempting scree field and above a gentle gully of natural dips and hips. On the route back to Lionshead, launch off the many rollers under the gondola before ducking into the pinball turns and logs of Cheetah Gully.

Lift tickets, lessons, and rentals

Day **tickets** for Vail and Beaver Creek are the most expensive of the Vail Resorts and among the highest in the nation. With few local deals, the cheapest way to ski here is to purchase a season pass or Colorado Pass (which includes Vail's Summit County resorts) preseason. Day lift ticket prices are significantly cheaper early and late season, and purchasing online can save $8 for day passes and over $30 on multiday tickets (which can be used at all Vail Resorts).

Independent backcountry options

A couple of well-known **backcountry spots** are accessible through access gates on opposite ends of the Vail ski area ridgeline. To the east of Siberia Bowl are the cliffs of the East Vail chutes, which shouldn't be attempted without a guide and avalanche gear. To the west of Game Creek is the misnamed Minturn Mile, a much longer stretch that leads through glades and aspen forest to the town of Minturn. A popular party route in the spring, this is one of the very few backcountry sojourns where an expert rider needn't worry excessively about the caliber of her escort, though there are a couple of tricky spots, especially in poor conditions. For further forays into the surrounding White River National Forest, contact Paragon Guides (℗970/926-5299 or 877/926-5299, ⊛www.paragonguides.com), who take expert skiers into the backcountry and lead multiday touring trips using the 10th Mountain Division huts (see p.135). Access untouched terrain off Ptarmigan Pass with Vail Snowcat Skiing (℗970/476-7677 or 800/480-9104, ⊛www.vailtransportation.com); rates are around $275, include lunch, and are suitable for advanced intermediates. Snowcat riding is also available nearby at little Ski Cooper (see p.250).

Like Aspen, Vail has an excellent **ski school** (8am-4.30pm; ☎970/476-3239 or 800/475-4543, at Golden Peak and Lionshead bases), with more than 850 highly credentialed staff members from around the world. Fees can reach $95 for a half-day lift and lesson in peak season. For groups of five or six, it's actually cheaper to hire a private instructor than sign up for group classes. One of a handful of US resorts to host the expensive but successful Burton Learn-to-Ride program (see p.534), the school also offers teen sessions, specialized breakthrough clinics, and women's programs hosted by local and visiting pros. There are children's centers at both Lionshead and Golden Peak, as well as on-mountain kids' zones and evening programs at the Adventure Ridge activity center, located at the top of the gondola. Vail's adaptive program (☎970/479-3264) is particularly good value for those with their own equipment, as a five-day ticket is only $99; equipment rental is only available as part of a lesson.

Park at Lionshead if you need to pick up **rental gear**. Kenny's Double Diamond (☎970/476-5500) is a respected name throughout the skiing world, a traditional skier's domain with an excellent boot-fitting service and knowledgeable staff. Pick up a coupon from the visitor center for a 25-percent discount on ski packages ($32). Vail Snowboard Supply (☎970/479-4434) and core basement dwellers One Track Mind (☎970/476-1397), both in Lionshead, are part of the resort-owned Vail Sports chain (☎970/476-9457); book in advance at ⓦwww.rentskis.com to save a few bucks on the $30 and up charged-for boards. Other branches of Vail Sports rent skis or beginner snowboards only. On-mountain demos are available from the Mid Vail ski center and the Burton Super Center.

Beaver Creek

Spared the crowds of Summit County or Vail, the forested slopes of Beaver Creek seem wilder than those of its corporate cousins, despite impeccable grooming and the luxury of the village below. The resort might draw a wealthy clientele, but the mountain itself boasts a small scene of riders seeking technical steeps along with terrain park hits. And while Beaver Creek might be expensive, it's not unwelcoming; free hot chocolate, cookies, and resort postcards (mailed free of charge, too) are all offered in the village at the end of the ski day.

Prime beginner runs are located on the flat summit of towering **Beaver Creek Mountain**, one of three steep-sided peaks rising sharply from the narrow valley floor. **Beaver Creek West** is predominantly an intermediate hill, and the wide open dish of McCoy Park cross-country center atop the mountain provides spectacular views of the Gore Range. Only rocky **Grouse Mountain** is as forbidding as its lower slopes suggest: the trail map might mark a couple of runs blue, but just the perilous outlook at the summit is enough to shake the confidence of all but the most competent skiers.

One disadvantage of the ski area's steep pitches are the dense shadows cast across the lower slopes, causing icy conditions, particularly on the front face above the village. And Beaver Creek is no Vail when it comes to variety of intermediate runs, though blues here are long and well distributed around the ski area, making it a resort well suited to those who like to explore rather than run lifts all day. If you need some guidance, take advantage of the complimentary tours that depart from the top of the Centennial Express Lift Chair at 10am daily.

Beginner

Beginners learn right by the village at the base of the front face, with two surface lifts and two slow double chairs serving bunny slopes and a mini-terrain park. When ready, head up the mountain to the more extensive beginner terrain at the summit. What looks like a precipitous face is, in reality, a wide open meadow, gently rolling and dotted with trees, complete with jaw-dropping views across the Gore Range. Snowboarders should either tackle the gentler blues like **Latigo** and **Gold Dust** on rider's right of the front face or download on the Centennial Express. The trails and tree-lined catwalks around **Bachelor Gulch** are excellent for building confidence, but novice snowboarders may find the flat traverse from Beaver Creek village via the Strawberry Park lift frustrating. Take the Elkhorn lift, which cuts in lower down, or avoid the catwalks altogether by riding the free shuttle directly to Bachelor base.

Mountain info

Phone ☎970/845-9090 or 1-800/427-8308
Snow phone ☎1-800/427-8308
Website ⓦwww.beavercreek.com
Price $71 peak season, from $49 off-peak
Operating times Late Nov to mid-April daily 8.30am–3.30/4pm
No. of lifts 16, including 3 surface lifts
Base elevation 7400′ (Arrowhead)
Summit elevation 11440′ (Beaver Creek)
Vertical drop 4040′ (main mountain – 3340′)
No. of trails 146
Acreage 1625
Beginner 34%
Intermediate 39%
Expert 27%
Average snowfall 310″
Snowmaking Yes (605 acres)
Night skiing No
Nursery facilities Yes, Small World Playschool, from 2 months to 6 years, on lower level of Park Plaza; rates vary by hours and peak/off peak, $78–95 full day, reservations required (☎970/845-5325); skiing 3–14, snowboarding 7–14 (rates vary, around $100 per day, rentals not included)

Intermediate

Warm up on the wide blue cruisers of the **Rose Bowl**, a quiet spot that gleams in the morning sun. For long thigh-burners and cascading terrain, take Redtail down to the Larkspur lift. From the summit of Larkspur, you can work on your speed, duck into a well-spaced aspen glade, or launch off rollers on the wide-open trails back down under the lift. The short blacks in **Larkspur Bowl** are among the few here that aren't knee-trembling double diamonds. To the left are the long, rolling, tree-studded runs under the Strawberry Park and Elkhorn lifts. These lead back to the village, skirting the cat track from the Redtail Lodge. Gentle in pitch, the **glades** between Bachelor Gulch and Arrowhead are perfect for first powder turns through the trees. The seldom-crowded runs of patchy Arrowhead are a good trek from Beaver Creek.

Expert

The Birds of Prey downhill takes place primarily on **Golden Eagle**, which is groomed regularly and super slick, while neighboring Peregrine and Goshawk are generally left to bump up. After it's dumped, the steep fall line, pines, and cliffs of **Royal Elk Glades** on Grouse Mountain are an in-bounds nirvana. If it's aspens you seek, head to golden **Thresher Glade** off the Larkspur or Strawberry Park lifts, home to plenty of tight tree lines. Backcountry gates, right off the Birds of Prey summit, access powder fields and gullies off Beaver Creek's so-called Bald Spot. Both here, and off either side of the Grouse

Mountain summit, riders taking their chances outside the boundary are conveniently funneled back into the ski area. Never ski alone, and check the backcountry box, on p.196 for more information.

Freestyle

There's a strong tradition of tree riding at Beaver Creek. As at Vail, the woods hide a plethora of carefully constructed slides, both in the numerous official jib lines stretching from summit to village on the front face and in more tucked-away spots. Even though local riders hit up Beaver Creek's steep glades and backcountry whenever the snow cooperates, the terrain parks and features here are well designed. Once the snow has built up enough, the Centennial park features a well-maintained superpipe and a good variety of hits and rails, as well as a cribbed-out yurt. There's also a baby park in the kids' learning area and a slightly bigger minipark off the Birds of Prey summit.

Lift tickets, lessons, and rentals

Beaver Creek operates on a shared **ticket** with Vail (see p.196). Packages and prices at Beaver Creek's **ski school** (℡970/845-5300 or 800/475-4543) are similar to Vail's, with stimulating programs for kids and the Burton Method Center snowboard option. Beginners benefit from their own indoor meeting place, where they can chat to instructors and watch instructional videos before heading onto the snow. Beaver Creek's adaptive school is at ℡970/845-5465; five-day lift passes within Vail resorts are available for $99. The resort runs a number of **telemark** programs (℡970/845-5313), including beginner lessons twice a week. Equipment is available to rent from the Nordic Demo Center at the bottom of Strawberry Park lift, with workshops in McCoy Park scheduled regularly for both adults and children; prices start at $66 for telemark classes (lift ticket not included).

To test the latest skis, stop in at the Alpine Demo Center on-mountain at the Spruce Saddle Lodge. The Other Side (℡970/845-8969) blasts hip-hop from its tucked-away location among the quiet, upscale boutiques of the Beaver Creek Lodge and has been a focal point for the local snowboard scene for years. Pricey but reasonable quality rental packages ($30–40) are available in the village plaza from Vail-owned Beaver Creek Sports (℡970/845-5400) and affiliated snowboard specialists One Track Mind (℡970/845-5420); book online (Ⓦwww.rentskis.com) for a discount. Ski rentals are about $5 cheaper at Christy Sport's Avon store (℡970/949-0241) than in their Beaver Creek Lodge branch.

Accommodation

Lodging options in Vail are limited to **luxury hotels** and relatively expensive, though not necessarily lavish, **condos**. There are a couple of B&Bs and a handful of cheaper condos, lodges, and motels down valley in West Vail, Minturn, and Avon. Usually the cheapest way to stay in town is to book an early/late season special or last-minute, all-inclusive condo package through Vail Central Reservations (℡877/204-7881, Ⓦwww.vail.com). The Vail Valley Tourism and Convention Bureau (℡1-800/525-3875; Ⓦwww.vailonsale.com) offers significant discounts on its website for last-minute bookings.

Vail

Lifthouse Condos 555 E Lionshead Circle, Lionshead ℡970/476-2340 or 1-800/654-0635, Ⓦwww.lifthousevail.com. Mid-range for Vail, these small studios sleep four in a pinch and come with a kitchenette, queen bed, and queen couch pull-out. The management here is great and discounts are regularly available on the website. ❻

Park Meadows Lodge 1472 Matterhorn Circle, Vail ☎970/476-5598 or 888/245-8086, ⊛www .parkmeadowslodge.com. Small studio suites and one- or two-bedroom condos, all with kitchens or kitchenettes, between Cascade Village and West Vail. Laundry, odd outdoor tub, and rec room; on the bus line. Ask for discounts. One-bed ❺, two ❼

Roost Lodge 1783 N Frontage Rd, West Vail ☎970/476-5451 or 800/873-3065, ⊛www .roostlodge.com. Vail's cheapest option, this wooden motel is on the northern, less attractive side of I-70. Rooms are drab, but triples (two doubles, one twin) include a fridge and microwave and sleep up to five, there's a greenhouse pool and funky outdoor tub, and rates include basic continental breakfast, après-ski wine and cheese, and shuttle service to Vail. From ❸–❹

Sandstone Creek Club 1020 Vail View Drive, Vail ☎970/476-4405 or 800/421-1098, ⊛www .sandstonecreekclub.com. Squat, brown buildings on the opposite side of the freeway to town. In the disguise of a dated country club, this condo hotel may not be beautiful, but by local standards it offers great rates; amenities include indoor/ outdoor pool and spa, games room, library, and shuttle services. Rooms ❺, condos ❻

Sonnenalp Resort 20 Vail Rd, Vail Village ☎970 /476-5656 or 800/654-8312, ⊛www.sonnenalp .com. Bavarian owned and run, this is *the* Vail classic, a luxury hotel straight out of a snowy European Christmas card. Accommodations are split between three distinct buildings: the central Bavaria house, intimate Austria Haus, and more affordable country-style Swiss Chalet. Use of the well-appointed spa is included in the exorbitant rates. ❾

Tivoli Lodge 386 Hanson Ranch Rd, Vail ☎970/ 476-5615 or 800/451-4756, ⊛www.tivolilodge .com. One of Vail's more inexpensive options with traditional alpine architecture in a handy location, at the foot of Golden Peak. Spacious rooms are bland but comfortable and amenities include an outdoor pool, hot tub, and a sauna. A large continental breakfast is served in the dark and cozy lounge bar. ❻–❽

Vail Mountain Lodge 352 E Meadow Drive ☎970/476-0700 or 866/476-0700, ⊛www .vailmountainlodge-spa.com. Boutique-style hotel not to be confused with the resort's original luxury guesthouse, the more staid *Lodge at Vail*. Rooms

are comfortably stylish. Home to the exclusive Vail Athletic Club, boasting the town's only indoor climbing wall. ❾

Down valley

Beaver Creek West 0360 Benchmark Rd, Avon ☎970/949-4840 or 1-800/222-4840, ⊛www .beavercreekwest.com. Bland but clean, comfy, and affordable one- to four-bedroom condos in Avon next to Nottingham Park. There are three public hot tubs and a sauna by the outdoor heated pool. On the bus route. Hotel-style rooms ❹, condos ❺–❾

Comfort Inn 1061 W Beaver Creek Blvd, Avon ☎970/949-5511, ⊛www.comfortinn.com. Close to the freeway and a bit of a walk from downtown Avon, but this chain motel is bright, clean, and inexpensive; always ask for discounts. Rates include continental breakfast, and there's an outdoor pool and tub. ❸

Minturn Inn 442 Main St, Minturn ☎970/827-9647 or 800/646-8876, ⊛www.minturninn.com. Friendly B&B in a handsome 1915 hewn log home and chic new timber-frame lodge on the banks of the Eagle River, both tastefully decorated with handcrafted furniture and simple linens. Rooms in the airy lodge are the more spacious; some have their own fireplaces and jacuzzi tubs. Surprisingly reasonable rates include a full breakfast and après snacks and a sauna. Massage available. ❹

The Ritz-Carlton 1030 Daybreak Ridge, Bachelor Gulch ☎970/748-6200, ⊛www.ritzcarlton.com. New and exclusive "lodge" – actually a giant hotel, architecturally influenced by the great lodges of America's National Parks but blown all out of proportion. Right on the slopes, with an incredible spa and elegant Arts and Crafts-inspired rooms. ❾

Savory Inn and Cooking School 2405 Elliott Ranch Rd, West Vail ☎970/476-1304 or 866/728-6794, ⊛www.savoryinn.com. Large, attractive log B&B on the banks of Gore Creek, now home to a resident chef. Morning classes (open to the public) range in topic from basic sauces to Asian delicacies; classes in conjunction with dinner are held at the weekend. Rooms are spacious and country-mountain style, huge breakfasts and evening hors d'oeuvres are included in the rates, and there's a lovely outdoor tub. ❻

Eating

Vail dining options run the entire spectrum both in variety and price. Costs in Beaver Creek are prohibitive, but the few restaurants in cute Minturn, though geared primarily to visitors, are less expensive. For laid-back spots patronized by the locals, head to Avon and Edwards. Pick up **groceries** at City Market (☎970/476-1017); there's one in Avon, and one just north of the freeway exit in West Vail. In Beaver Creek, visit the deli in the *Hyatt* (opens 6.30am) for pastries, cereals, and snacks, and enjoy a picnic in the oversized Antler Hall.

On-mountain dining at both resorts is expensive. If you're on the front face at Vail it doesn't take long to nip down for a cheap slice or burrito in the village, but if you're going to fork out for lunch, skip busy *Eagle's Nest* and *Mid-Vail*. Choose *Wildwood* instead, which serves filling and tasty barbecue sandwiches and soups for around $10. The glorified cafeteria of timber-framed *Two Elk* boasts the best location, overlooking Vail's back bowls and the Gore Range. For a cheaper option try the *Blue Moon* at the top of the gondola, a standard grill, but a fine place for a Backbowls Brew and an appetizer.

The Blue Moose Beaver Creek Plaza, Beaver Creek ☎970/845-8666. Decent pizza, calzones, and subs at reasonable prices. 11am–midnight.

Campo Di Fiori 100 E Meadow Drive, Vail Village ☎970/476-8994. Airy, upscale Italian, serving moderately priced, tasty pastas without the stuffiness found in many of Vail's upper-end restaurants. Dinner from 5.30pm.

Cleaver's Deli 297 Hanson Ranch Rd, Vail Village ☎970/ 476-1755. Quick pit stop in the village for cheap stuffed bagels, breakfast pastries, and good deals on half-sandwiches and subs (under $5).

The Dancing Bear 2211 North Frontage Rd, West Vail ☎970/476-2290. Cheap, overstuffed bagels and coffee served by Deadheads. Sit-down service and evening entertainment, too, but it's all about the early-morning takeout counter, deep in valley locals on their way to work. 7am–10pm.

DJ MacAdams West Lionshead Plaza, Lionshead ☎970/476-2336. The chefs whip up a mean hangover cure in this tiny 24-hour diner, a greasy gem in Vail's shiny crown. Fruit crepes and waffles compliment the heavier egg scrambles and omelets, all fresh and affordable.

The Flying Burrito 675 W Lionshead Circle, Lionshead ☎970/479-6356. Lunch in a tortilla for under $6. The usual beans, rice and meat combinations are on the bland side, but this small café is right by the gondola.

Jafas West Lionshead Plaza, Lionshead ☎970/479-5288. Inexpensive Aussie café and bar serving Fosters, Vegemite on toast, and meat pies to the homesick. The name is an abbreviation, and under constant debate – Just Another Friendly Aussie is the official version.

La Cantina Vail Transportation Center, Vail Village ☎970/476-7661. The best deal around is found in the insalubrious setting of the town parking garage. With huge burritos under $5 and $2 tacos, great margaritas, free, unlimited chips and fresh salsa, and the bus home just a stumble up the stairs, it seems inconsequential that the "dining room" is little more than a few tables crammed into a corner of the garage lobby. 11.30am–10pm.

Pazzo's 122 East Meadows Drive, Vail Village ☎970/476-9026 (also Avon: 82 E Beaver Creek Blvd ☎970/949-9000). Pizza, calzones, and subs are satisfying, the pasta so-so; but this place is warm and busy on the coldest, quietest night, inexpensive for Vail, with laid-back, friendly staff. Daily for lunch and dinner; breakfast at Vail location only.

The Saloon 146 N Main St, Minturn ☎970/827-5954. Atmospheric turn-of-the-century restaurant in the pretty wood-fronted Victorian railroad town of Minturn. Classic Mexican entrees ($10) are complemented by steak, quail, and fish, but it's the potent margaritas that are the real treat. Bar from 3.30pm, meals from 5pm.

Vendetta's 291 Bridge St, Vail Village ☎970/476-5070. Though a successful Italian dining room operates downstairs, fine dining isn't really the point here; as the village's late-night hangout, it attracts kids passing on Bridge Street who stop by for pizza by the slice ($3) in the front room or head upstairs for beer by the pitcher. Makes a good grab 'n' go lunch spot, too. Pizza served until 2am, deliveries until midnight.

Bars and entertainment

By the modest standards of American ski resorts, Vail's **nightlife** is among the best in the country, with the action centered on Bridge street in Vail Village. Local DJs play nightly, but bigger shows are scheduled over the weekend. A few major bands are brought to town each season to entertain the holiday crowds, with shows held in the Dobson Ice Arena.

Pick up a copy of the free *Vail Daily* (ⓦwww.vaildaily.com) or weekly *Vail Trail* for listings. Vail has two small movie theaters, each with two screens: the Cascade Village, next to Vail Cascade Hotel, and the Crossroads Cinema, in the Vail Village Crossroads Mall (movieline ☎970/476-5661). In Beaver Creek, the plush Vilar Center for the Arts, 68 Avondale Lane (☎970/845-8497 or 1-888/920-2787, ⓦwww.vilarcenter.org), runs an eclectic program of performances and films. Local winter **events** range from the sedate – ex-President Ford has lit the Christmas tree in Vail Village for the past thirty years – to both the official and unofficial on-mountain spring madness at the end of every season (ask a local for the lowdown).

8150 143 East Meadow Drive, Vail Village ☎970/479-0607. Serious club space with a sprung dance floor and an open-minded attitude to bookings. Music at least five nights a week, with a schedule that includes visiting DJs, big-name old school hip-hop crews, ridiculous tribute bands, and local fundraisers.

Bully Ranch 20 Vail Rd, Vail Village ☎970/476-5656. Annually voted the best hotel bar in town, this large, busy spot in the Sonnenalp is known for its après-ski mudslides. Tasty, if expensive, appetizers prevent the alcohol from hitting too hard.

The Club 304 Bridge St, Vail Village ☎970/479-0556. Après-ski acoustic singalongs and hardcore heckling are the norm during stage shows held in this dingy basement bar.

Club Chelsea *Vail Village Inn*, S Frontage Rd ☎970/477-2280. Lounge bands, martinis, bottled oxygen, and cigars, in a long-running Vail club that thinks it's in 1980s Manhattan.

Garfinkel's 536 E Lionshead Circle, Lionshead ☎970/476-3789. Large sports bar right next to the gondola, staffed primarily by antipodeans. Crowded at après, but patronized by young seasonals in the quiet midweek evenings, who come for the pool tables and good beer.

The George 292 E Meadow Drive, Vail Village ☎970/476-2556. This comfy basement bar only vaguely resembles the English pub it aspires to be, though dark leather booths provide some good corners for nursing a pint. Low-key atmosphere with busy pool tables, and a reasonably priced pub grub menu including fish & chips, bangers & mash – and that famous British dish, the Philly cheese steak. 3pm–2am.

Half Moon Saloon 2161 North Frontage Rd, West Vail ☎970/476-4314. Large weekend breakfasts and evening beer and tunes are the norm at this diner-cum-music venue. On the schedule are acoustic nights, comedy showcases, a weekly free taco bar, and hefty doses of mountain funk and blues.

Kaltenberg Castle Lionshead Plaza, Lionshead ☎970/479-1050. This conversion of the old Lionshead gondola building into a massive mock-palace comes complete with lederhosen-wearing entertainers and giant vats for the brewing of Bavarian beer. Subsidary of a brewery that's owned by the Bavarian Royal Family.

The Red Lion 304 Bridge St, Vail Village ☎970/476-7676. Classic Vail joint, crammed during après with an older crowd, here for the singalongs and requests played by guitarist and entertainer Phil Long.

The Tap Room/Sanctuary 333 Bridge St, Vail Village ☎970/479-0500. The *Tap Room* bar and restaurant draws a young, stylish crowd for après drinks and snacks. Upstairs, the urbane *Sanctuary* club and lounge is knowingly chic, complete with velvet rope and the occasional "Private Party Tonight" signs.

Other activities and attractions

Snowshoe tours, dog sledding, winter fly fishing, ice-skating, and more can be organized through the Vail Activities Desk (☎970/476-9090 or ☎800/475-4543), located in the Lionshead Gondola building, or through the Beaver Creek resort concierge, in the town plaza (☎970/845-9090). Multi-activity tour operators include Nova Guides (☎970/827-4232 or 888/949-NOVA), known for their nonskiing snowcat and snowmobile tours (from $60 per hour), and Vail Valley Activities (☎970/547-1594).

At the top of the gondola is the Adventure Ridge activity center (daily from 2.30pm); the place really comes into its own when the other lifts have closed and the alpenglow bathes the quiet mountain in rosy light. More typical activities like tubing ($18), ice-skating ($8 rentals, free with own skates), snow-

Colorado Ski Museum

Learn about Colorado's skiing pioneers at the **Colorado Ski Museum and Hall of Fame**, 231 S Frontage Rd (Tues–Sun 10am–5pm; $1; ☏970/476-1876, ⊛www .skimuseum.net). Exhibits include photographs, competition memorabilia, and equipment charting the evolution of skiing in the state, with a special emphasis on the lasting influence of World War II's 10th Mountain Division (see p.135). New inductees are added to the Hall of Fame annually, and the museum schedules public events in their honor.

mobiling ($62 for one, $78 for doubles, $18 for kids), and snowshoeing are offered alongside high-adrenaline ski-biking and thrill-sledding, high-speed snowtoys that are most exciting once it's dark, as you get to navigate down the empty slopes with only a headlamp to light the way. There's even an indoor laser tag course ($13), and parents with cash to spare can sign kids up for a night of chaperoned mayhem ($60).

Vail and Beaver Creek operate a couple of **cross-country ski centers**, the largest and most magical of which is Beaver Creek's McCoy Park (☏970/845-5313), with 32km of trails located at the top of the Strawberry Park lift. Call ahead to reserve nature treks or gourmet picnic tours, book lesson packages (from $55), or to register for the monthly Snowshoe Adventure Series fun runs ($20) or annual Snowshoe Shuffle, the largest such race in the US. The Vail Nordic Center is located by the golf course in East Vail (daily 9am–5pm; ☏970/476-8366), offering fifteen kilometers of track, a restaurant, ice rink and skate rentals, and evening sleigh rides. There's no fee to use the track and rentals are reasonably priced (from $15 for skis, $12 for snowshoes). Backcountry ski and snowshoe tours are regularly scheduled in conjunction with the Vail Nature Center – including monthly moonlight trips ($25). To book lessons, call the Nordic Ski School, based in Golden Peak Lodge (☏970/476-8366).

Other local activity centers include the Black Family ice rink (☏970/845-9090) in Beaver Creek and the indoor Dobson Ice Arena (☏970/479-2271). Facilities at the Avon Recreation Center, 325 Benchmark Rd (Mon–Thurs 6am–10pm, Fri 6am–9pm, Sat–Sun 8am–9pm; ☏970/748-4060), include a pool complex with waterslide, sauna, jacuzzi, and gym.

Listings

Avalanche hotline ☏970/668-0600 or ☏303 /275-5360 (statewide).
Backcountry weather conditions ☏970/827-5687.

Bookshops Verbatim Booksellers, 450 Lionshead Circle ☏970/476-3032, Mon–Sat 9am–8pm, Sun 10am–6pm. Lovely bookstore, with informed staff and a coffee shop.

Snowboard Outreach Society

Involved, compassionate, and dedicated, the **Snowboard Outreach Society** (☏970 /845-7040, ⊛www.sosoutreach.org) belies the stereotype of Vail as a shallow, commercial place. SOS volunteers have taught snowboarding to over 8000 underprivileged kids since the charity was formed in 1993. Based in Avon, the society works with Vail Resorts and other sponsors to stage the SOS Outreach Series, now the largest competitive snowboarding series in Colorado. All proceeds go toward the teaching program, and enthusiastic volunteers are recruited from the ranks of competitors. New volunteers are always needed – from regular instructors to helping hands at special events.

Forest Service Holy Cross Ranger District ☎/970-827-5715, Eagle Ranger District ☎/970-328-6388.
Internet Vail Library, 292 W Meadow Drive ☎970/479-2184 (Mon–Thurs 10am–8pm, Fri 10am–6pm, Sat–Sun 11am–6pm).
Library See "Internet" above.
Medical Vail Valley Medical Center (hospital), 181 W Meadow Drive ☎970/476-2451, ◉www.vvmc.com. Affiliated clinics in Beaver Creek (☎970/949-0800) and Edwards (☎970/926-6340). GPs through Colorado Mountain Medical, Vail number

☎970/476-7600, offices throughout Eagle and Summit counties.
Pharmacy Vail Valley Medical Center (see above) or City Market, 2109 N Frontage Rd, West Vail ☎970/476-1621.
Post office ☎970/476-5217 (also post offices in Minturn, Avon and Edwards).
Police ☎970/479-2200.
Road and weather conditions ☎970/479-2226.
Taxi Locals Limo ☎970/904-5466, Vail Valley Transportation ☎970/476-8294, High Mountain Taxi ☎970/524-5555.

Sun Valley

The ski resort of **SUN VALLEY**, taking in the towns of the Wood River Valley – **Ketchum**, **Warm Springs**, and to an extent **Hailey**, twelve miles south – has been attracting moguls and movie stars since its inception in the 1930s. At that time, Union Pacific Railroad chairman Averell Harriman discovered his railroad was obliged to maintain a passenger service. Having nowhere for passengers to travel, he decided an alpine ski center would be an ideal draw and soon after sent Austrian ski champion Count Felix Schaffgotsch on a mission to find snowy, treeless slopes sheltered by higher mountains. Having turned down Aspen for being too high, the Count decided **Dollar Mountain**, here in the relatively gentle foothills of the Sawtooths near the old sheep-ranching village of Ketchum, fit the bill.

Sun Valley was an instant success. The hill itself boasted the world's first chairlift, based on a hoist used for hauling bananas into ships' holds, and Hollywood stars like Marilyn Monroe and Gary Cooper were soon hitching rides up to the top and Ernest Hemingway was calling the area home. Today, Sun Valley Resort and Ketchum remain the most cosmopolitan and highly priced pieces of real estate in the state, though the downhill action now centers not around Dollar Mountain but the larger and steeper **Bald Mountain** (9150ft), known locally as "Baldy."

The fact that Ketchum is in the business of making money out of tourism is obvious – scores of restaurants, shops, and galleries line the town's streets, and the hard-worked mountain staff is not always as cheerful as at other Idaho ski hills. Just north of Ketchum is the village of Warm Springs – a suburb of sorts

Mountain info

Phone ☎1-800/786-8259
Snow phone ☎1-800/635-4150
Website ◉www.sunvalley.com
Hours Thanksgiving Day to end of April 9am–4pm (access to Seattle Ridge and bowls closes at 2.45pm)
Price $65
No. of lifts 19 including 7 quads and 3 surface lifts
Base elevation 5750´
Summit elevation 9150´
Vertical drop 3400´
No. of trails 75
Acreage 2054
Beginner 36%
Intermediate 42%
Expert 22%
Average snowfall 175˝
Snowmaking Yes, 30 percent
Night skiing No
Nursery facilities Yes, 6 months to 6 years (☎208/622-2288).

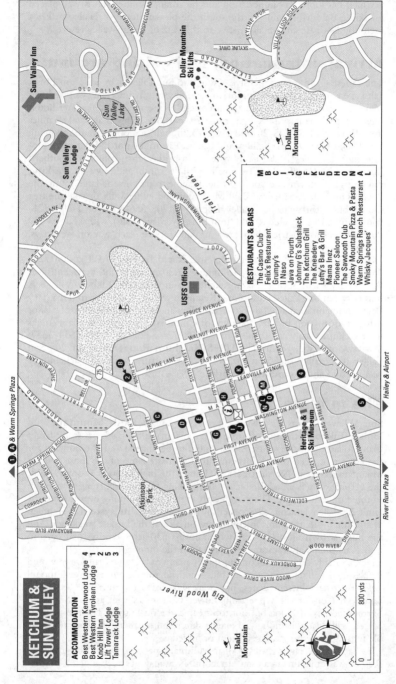

KETCHUM & SUN VALLEY

ACCOMMODATION
Best Western Kentwood Lodge	4
Best Western Tyrolean Lodge	1
Knob Hill Inn	2
Lift Tower Lodge	5
Tamarack Lodge	3

RESTAURANTS & BARS
The Casino Club	M
Felix's Restaurant	B
Grumpy's	C
Il Naso	I
Java on Fourth	J
Johnny G's Subshack	G
The Ketchum Grill	F
The Kneadery	K
Lefty's Bar & Grill	E
Mama Inez	D
Pioneer Saloon	H
The Sawtooth Club	O
Smoky Mountain Pizza & Pasta	N
Warm Springs Ranch Restaurant	A
Whisky Jacques'	L

– which has more accommodation and restaurant facilities and is well placed for skiing Bald Mountain. To the south the pleasant town of Hailey makes a useful budget base and an alternative to the glitz of the up-valley resorts.

Arrival, information, and getting around

The easiest – and most expensive – way into Sun Valley is by **air** from Boise, Salt Lake City, or Seattle; both Horizon and Skywest fly into Hailey's Friedman Memorial Airport. A bus into town costs $16 one way, though many hotels offer a complimentary pick-up service. By **car**, Sun Valley is about 150 miles from Boise via I-84, US-20, and Hwy-75, though the longer route following US-21 and Hwy-75 (via Stanley and Galena Pass to the north) is far more picturesque. Sun Valley is also easily reached from the urban centers of southern Idaho via US-93 (off I-84 at Twin Falls, 83 miles south) and Hwy-75. **Parking** can be tight in town, and your best bet may be to park in the large lot on the River Run Base Area below Bald Mountain, and either walk or take the free shuttle bus into town. Sun Valley Express (☎208/336-4038 or 1-800/821-9064) runs a **bus service** to and from Boise (via Twin Falls), with a fare of $59 one-way, $89 round-trip. There are four daily services each way on weekdays, six on weekends.

Getting around is easy: Ketchum Area Rapid Transit (KART, ☎208/726-7576) runs a free service (every 15 minutes; 7.30am–midnight) between River Run Plaza, Warm Springs Plaza, Ketchum, Sun Valley, and Elkhorn Village. A **taxi** between Sun Valley Resort and Ketchum will set you back around $7; try Bald Mountain Taxi (☎208/726-2650). For an excellent selection of visitor **information**, stop by the Chamber of Commerce, Fourth and Main streets in Ketchum (daily 8.30am–5pm; ☎208/726-3423 or 1-800/634-3347, ⓦ www.visitsunvalley.com). The **USFS Ketchum Ranger Station**, 206 Sun Valley Rd (daily 8am–5pm, ☎208/622-5371), runs a useful backcountry weather and **snow conditions hotline** (Dec–April) on ☎208/622-8027.

The mountain

Sun Valley consists of two separate ski areas, **Bald Mountain** and **Dollar/Elkhorn**, the site of some of the original lifts. "Baldy" is vastly larger than Dollar/Elkhorn (which is best suited to beginners) and is renowned for the consistent steep pitch of its runs. It also boasts some of the most opulent mountain lodges in North America. Though the highest point is only 9150ft, the vertical drop is an admirable 3400ft, making for thigh-burning runs of up to three miles in length. There are nearly eighty trails running over the mountain's 2000 skiable acres, all accessed by an impressive **lift system** – eighteen lifts in total – that ensures lines are rare on all but the busiest weekends. And the huge **snowmaking** system, which covers 630 acres, ensures that even in lean years there's always some fresh snow on the mountain.

Due to Baldy's steep and constant pitch, many of the green runs here would be classified as blue at most other hills – indeed, some even have small mogul fields on them. Intermediates, however, will thrive on runs like the green Southern Comfort or Upper and Lower College, as well as on the Warm Springs face, exhilarating but not too steep to be off-putting. The mountain is dotted with black diamonds, so expert skiers and boarders will have no trouble finding something to keep them occupied.

It's hard to believe that tiny Dollar Mountain, peeping up above Sun Valley Resort, was once the area's star attraction. Nowadays it's very much a **begin-**

ner's hill, with seventy percent of the runs reserved for them and the remaining thirty percent designated as intermediate. There's only 718ft of vertical drop, but the wide, easy-angled runs provide a great introduction to those not quite ready to tackle the more challenging slopes a couple of miles west. Freestyle snowboarders, though, may want to head here for the solid **halfpipe**.

Beginner

Dollar Mountain provides easily negotiated lifts, and all the runs on the Dollar face are gently angled. Once you're feeling confident head across to the mountain's Elkhorn face for the small selection of slightly steeper and longer runs. When ready to take on Baldy start off on Upper and Lower College from the top of the fast-moving Lookout Express quad. Be wary of the greens beneath Seattle Ridge Lodge – anywhere else these would be blues.

Intermediate

If you like to cruise long, rolling blues and work on your technique, Baldy is your mountain. The **Warm Springs Face** is a real leg burner, and if you want to push yourself try taking on the more challenging blacks (Upper Greyhawk, Upper Hemingway, and Upper Cozy) that can be accessed along a cat track to skier's left halfway down the Warm Springs Face. Don't worry too much if you find them more than you can handle, as they revert to blue runs further down the mountain. At the top of Lookout Chair in the open Mayday Bowl are Lefty, Farout, and Sigi's, three relatively easy blues that run out into the easy green cruiser of Broadway. Weaker intermediates should try the challenging green runs beneath Seattle Ridge Lodge such as Christin's Silver, Muffy's Medals, and Gretchen's Gold.

Expert

Although only 22 percent of Baldy is rated advanced, this still gives plenty to go at on a mountain this big. Baldy is steeped in open bowls with Lookout and Easter among the best and long, challenging bump runs like Limelight, on the Warm Springs face. More secluded slopes can be accessed across the steep and narrow Firetrail beneath Seattle Ridge into the relatively open glades of Christmas Bowl.

Freestyle

Given its size and status, it's surprising that Sun Valley **lacks a terrain park or halfpipe**, although there are plans to develop one on Baldy in the near future. Nevertheless, boarders will love the constant pitch of Baldy, where the only flats are on the top of the mountain. There are plenty of freeriding options in the bowls of Easter and Mayday, or head across to Warm Springs Face, where wooded terrain is available beside runs such as Limelight, Picabo's Street, and Fire Trail. For decent hits try the cat tracks off Warm Springs Face and I-80, where there are small kickers beside every snow cannon.

Lift tickets, lessons, and rentals

Sun Valley is one of the most expensive resorts in North America. It pays to shop around for seasonal and accommodation package discounts. Early and late-season **rates** can be as much as $20 a day less than peak season (roughly mid-Dec–end March), which are around $65 per day for adults, $36 per day for children 12 and under, $45 per day for seniors (over 65). These rates allow you to ski both Baldy and Dollar Mountain; beginners who want to stick to

Winter sports outfitters

Below we've listed a few of the best area outfitters, where you can expect to pay around $30 a day to rent skis or boards, $15 per day for boots.

Backwoods Mountain Sports cnr of N Main St and Warm Springs Rd ☎208 /726-8818. One of the valley's best outdoor stores includes a particularly impressive array of cross-country skis and snowshoes.

Board Bin & Girl Street cnr of Fourth and Washington sts ☎208/726-1222, ⓦwww.boardbin.com. Ketchum's best boarding shop, loaded with all the latest gear. If it's one of your first days boarding, stop in to rent a "buttpad," a wise

investment that should dull the pain of some of your bigger spills.

Ski Tek 191 Sun Valley Rd W ☎208 /726-7503. The best place for high-end demo skis and affordable tune-ups.

Sturtevants 314 N Main St ☎208/726-4501; also Warm Springs Village ☎208 /726-SKIS. "Sturtos" stocks a wide range of ski and boarding equipment and the Warm Springs store is handy for dropping off gear after a day on Baldy.

Dollar Mountain can get tickets for $25 per day adults, $20 kids. A season discount pass for $150 gets you $20 off the daily rate. An adult season pass is a whopping $1750.

Sun Valley's **ski school** (☎208/622-2248 or 2231, ⓦwww.sunvalley.com) has a solid reputation and long tradition, for all levels. Beginners should head for Dollar Mountain, while more experienced skiers will find ski school desks at River Run Plaza (☎208/622-6148) and *Warm Springs Lodge* (☎208/622-6357). Two-hour ski-and-board lessons cost $44, children's lessons (skiers 4–12, boarders 7–12) are $85 per day including lunch, and younger skiers and boarders pay $45 for a one-hour lesson. Private lessons cost $93 per hour with each additional person (up to five) paying $20, but note that lift tickets are not included in any of the above prices. Additional services include adult race clinics ($65 for three hours), three-day women's clinics ($330), and masters and disabled lessons (call for specific details). If you need to **rent gear**, good quality equipment is available either in the town (see box above) or at the rental shops at the base of Warm Springs Lodge and River Run Plaza.

Accommodation

Regardless of your budget, the first key to securing suitable **accommodation** in the Sun Valley area is to book as far ahead as possible. During the winter high season, it's not uncommon for hotels and inns to be booked solid months in advance, and inexpensive beds are relatively hard to come by. If you're having trouble finding a room, check with the **Sun Valley Central Reservations** (☎1-800/634-3347, ⓦwww.visitsunvalley.com). Visit the Chamber of Commerce for **condominiums** and **homes** – often the best deal if you're coming with a group, these vary enormously in the range of facilities and prices, from as little as $60 to several hundred dollars per night.

Sun Valley Resort

Sun Valley Resort Sun Valley and Dollar rds ☎208/622-2151 or 1-800/786-8529. Built in 1936 as a luxurious mountain resort, Sun Valley proper has expanded considerably over the years to include a wide mix of high-end accommodation that now includes the original 600-room lodge

(**❼**), the more modern *Sun Valley Inn* (**❻**), *Sun Valley Condominiums* (**❺**), and a small number of luxurious guest cottages starting at $600 per night. Prices can drop considerably in spring and autumn, and special ski packages can also be a good deal – four nights' accommodation with three days' skiing can be as low $245 per person for double occupancy. The entire resort has a vast selection of facilities including two pools, an ice rink, golf course, tennis courts, restaurants, and a movie theater. **❻**

Ketchum

Best Western Kentwood Lodge 180 S Main St ⊤208/726-9963 or 1-800/805-1001. Comfortably furnished rooms with kitchens, some with balconies and fireplaces, and a good location in downtown Ketchum. There's also an indoor pool, hot tubs, workout room, guest laundry, and restaurant on the premises. **❺**

Best Western Tyrolean Lodge 260 Cottonwood St ⊤208/726-5336 or 1-800/333-7912. Designed along the lines of an Austrian ski lodge, the *Tyrolean* is within easy walking distance of both the River Run lifts and downtown. The rooms are big and airy and many have lovely mountain views, and there's a complimentary continental breakfast served daily. An outdoor pool, hot tubs, sauna, and exercise room round out the package. **❺**

Knob Hill Inn 960 N Main St ⊤208/726-8010 or 1-800/526-8010, ⓦwww.knobhillinn.com. Located about a mile from the base of Baldy, this 24-room, Austrian Alps theme inn is one of Ketchum's finest accommodations. The beautifully appointed rooms include queen beds, marble bathrooms, and balconies with fine mountain views. There's a cozy guest library and bar in which to relax, and an indoor pool and hot tub. **❽**

Lift Tower Lodge 703 S Main St ⊤208/726/5163 or 1-800/462-8646. Perhaps the best value in town, with basic but comfortable rooms with two beds, refrigerator, TV, and phone. Amenities include a free continental breakfast and hot tub, and both River Run ski lifts and downtown are within walking distance. **❸**

Tamarack Lodge 291 Walnut Ave N ⊤208/726-3344 or 1-800/521-5379. The *Tamarack* has well-appointed rooms made all the more cozy by their fireplaces, with features including balconies and open-beam ceilings and microwaves, fridges, and coffee makers. The lodge has an indoor pool and outdoor hot tub, and is right in the middle of town. **❻**

Hailey

Airport Inn 409 Cedar St ⊤208/788-2477. Down by the Friedman Memorial Airport, the *Airport Inn* has fairly plain rooms with queen beds, some with kitchenettes, but is better value than most of the accommodation in Ketchum, which means it's well worth making reservations. Facilities include a hot tub and free coffee in the lobby. **❹**

Hailey Hotel 201 Main St ⊤208/788-3140. Originally a Basque boarding house, the rooms here are quite plain and the bathroom is down the corridor, but it's popular as a budget option so again reservations are recommended. **❹**

Povey Pensione 128 W Bullion ⊤208/788-4682 or 1-800/ 370-4682. This 110-year-old home is one of the oldest buildings in town and has a welcoming Old West feel to it, as do the homey rooms with antique furnishings, pastel wall coverings, and shared baths. Breakfast included. **❺**

Wood River Inn 601 Main St ⊤208/578-0600 or 1-877/542-0600. A modern inn with good-sized rooms with queen beds and complimentary continental breakfast, plus an indoor pool and hot tub. **❺**

Baldy's lodges

Baldy has some of the most opulent and impressive dining lodges in the Rockies. Their timber and river rock construction and luxurious interiors of pile carpets and marble bathrooms are more reminiscent of a classy hotel than ski lodges, and it takes a while to get used to clomping around them in ski boots without expecting to be asked to leave.

River Run Lodge ⊤208/622-2101. A spacious but busy dining area with deli cafeteria-style facilities where you can enjoy excellent pizza slices or soup and sandwiches for $7, or relax in upholstered armchairs over a beer or coffee. On Thursday evenings you can catch live jazz here.

Seattle Ridge ⊤208/622-2101. Set on a ridge at 8680ft, this oversized log-and-glass edifice is an architectural gem. The views, especially from the deck, are spectacular. Enjoy fine dining here; dishes such as mesquite-grilled chicken, salmon, swordfish, and prime rib feature on the menu, at around $20 an entree.

Warm Springs Lodge ⊤208/622-2101. This huge log, rock, and glass lodge is perfect for relaxing after making your way down the long slopes of Warm Springs Face. There's usually a live band playing slopeside outside, and it gets lively when the skiing is over for the day.

Eating

There's an excellent range **restaurants** in Ketchum, the majority either lining Main Street or located off it on either side between Second and Sixth streets; reservations may be necessary during peak seasons, though the nightlife is generally low-key. Down the valley, Hailey can be noticeably cheaper than Ketchum or the resorts for dining, if not necessarily better.

Sun Valley Resort

Bald Mountain Pizza & Pasta Sun Valley Mall ☎208/726-3838. Tasty pizzas and pastas at good prices in a family-friendly, relaxed setting. Pizza by the slice and take-out also available.

Gretchen's Sun Valley Lodge ☎208/622-2144. Overlooking the ice rink, the lively restaurant features filling breakfasts and a good range of traditional fare (steaks, pastas, and the like) the rest of the day – a full dinner will set you back $15–20.

The Konditorei Sun Valley Village ☎208/622-2235. The best breakfast spot in the village, though also good later in the day for its full range of Austrian cakes and pastries. Beer and wine are also served.

Ketchum

Felix's Restaurant 960 N Main St ☎208/726-1166. Located in the *Knob Hill Inn* (see overleaf), this restaurant has gained a strong following for its Spanish/Mediterranean-influenced dishes, including a fantastic paella. Entrees can run up to $20.

Il Naso corner of Fifth St and Washington Ave ☎208/726-7776. A popular spot with locals for fine Italian dining in urbane surroundings, with entrees from $15 upwards. If you're looking for something romantic, this is the place to head for.

Java on Fourth 191 Fourth St ☎208/726-2882. A cool, relaxed atmosphere – perhaps a little too relaxed on the part of the staff – pervades this coffee house that also serves pastries and cake. The deck overlooking the sidewalk is a great place to hang out.

Johnny G's Subshack 371 Washington Ave ☎208/725-7827. No-nonsense, filling submarine sandwiches ideal for those on the go.

The Ketchum Grill Fifth St and East Ave ☎208/726-4660. Housed in an 1884 postmaster's cabin, this highly recommended restaurant features a wide selection of dishes ranging from burgers and fries to entrees like linguine with quail and sundried tomatoes or grilled duck breast with mountain huckleberries, but don't expect much change from $20. Save room for the killer desserts as well. Open for dinner only.

The Kneadery 260 Leadville Ave ☎208/726-3856. A Ketchum institution and one of the most popular breakfast spots in town, with good omelettes and

a laid-back, woodsy atmosphere. No smoking.

Lefty's Bar & Grill 213 Sixth St ☎208/726-2744. *Lefty's* does basic, good-value bar food that goes perfectly with the typically bustling atmosphere. There's also an assortment of pinball and pool tables to play on after eating.

Mama Inez Seventh St and Warm Springs Ave ☎208/726-4213. Great southwestern-style Mexican food served in what feels like someone's home. The salsa is spectacular, and specials include chicken jalapeño, fresh fish, and killer veggie burritos topped with vegan red and green mole. Expect to pay around $10–15 for entrees.

Pioneer Saloon 308 N Main St ☎208/726-3139. This atmospheric, old-style pioneer bar is a Ketchum favorite. The prime rib is fantastically done, and the assorted shrimp, scallop, and steak entrees are also quite good ($12–20). It's a popular aprés-ski spot, so it's worth calling in for a beer even if you don't want to eat. Be prepared to queue, though.

Smoky Mountain Pizza & Pasta 200 Sun Valley Rd ☎208/622-5625. Excellent, affordable pizza and pasta and a friendly atmosphere make this a hit with families and the budget conscious.

Warm Springs Ranch Restaurant 1801 Warm Springs Rd ☎208/726-2609. A comfortable, relaxing place, with creek-side deck dining in summer. There's a wide choice of dishes, including great BBQ chicken and ribs, fresh mountain trout, and filet mignon, none of which should set you back much more than $20. The children's dishes are also very good.

Hailey

Java on Main 310 N Main St ☎208/788-2444. Good for a quick coffee and fresh-baked goods before heading off for a day in the mountains.

Sun Valley Brewing Co 202 N Main St ☎208/788-5777. A highly rated brewpub producing a dozen mouthwatering beers to go along with an eclectic menu than crosses all borders; standouts include Thai curry pasta, homemade bratwurst, and chicken pot pie, all for around $10.

Viva Taqueria 305 N Main St ☎208/788-4247. A local favorite for well-priced Mexican meals, including very filling burritos, best enjoyed with one of several beers made south of the border.

△ Main Street in Telluride, with mountains in background, CO

Bars and entertainment

Most bars are bustling after the lifts close but it can be relatively sedate later in the evening for a resort the size of Sun Valley. There are no major venues for **live music**, but many bars and restaurants still feature bands. Heading out for an après-ski cocktail isn't your only option after a day on the hill. **Cinemas** in town include the Opera House (☎208/622-2244) in Sun Valley Village, which screens movies nightly (including ski movies), and Ketchum's Magic Lantern, 100 Second St E (☎208/726-4274), which has four screens and features mainstream releases. If nothing good is on, you could always go **bowling** at the six-lane Sun Valley Bowling Alley (☎208/622-2191; $3.75 per game) in the Sun Valley Village.

Sun Valley Resort

Duchin Bar & Lounge *Sun Valley Lodge*
☎208/622-2145. A genteel atmosphere that's reminiscent of Sun Valley's old days, with an orchestra and ballroom dancing for entertainment as you sip your cocktails.

Ketchum

The Casino Club 220 Main St ☎208/726-9901. This former casino is a bit quieter than most of Ketchum's other bars, though the earthy atmosphere is still friendly. Pool tables rather than a dance floor provide the main entertainment, though the exuberant bartenders can also be a show.

Grumpy's 860 Warm Springs Rd. The name belies the atmosphere – friendly staff and clientele, great burgers, and large quantities of beer make this an excellent place to meet fellow travelers and locals alike. Especially popular for a quick drink after a day on the hill, which can easily turn into an all-night session.

The Sawtooth Club 231 Main St ☎208/726-5233. A big hit with the après-ski crowd. The attractive pine-paneled bar is a chatty place to have a beer, and upstairs there's a restaurant serving good mesquite-grilled duck, steak, trout, and salmon.

Whisky Jacques' 251 Main St ☎208/726-5297. Live bands ($3–5) play some nights in the pleasant log interior, filling the large dance floor with a slightly older crowd. Invariably busy and buzzing with both locals and visitors, it also serves pizza, sandwiches, and burgers, and there are pool tables if dancing isn't your thing.

Hailey

Red Elephant Saloon 107 Main St ☎208/788-6047. While not always as lively as those up in Ketchum, this bar still moves and grooves until midnight. The pub grub is decent as well.

Other activities and attractions

Though nowhere near as impressive as the **cross-country skiing** areas around Galena Lodge in the Sawtooth NRA an hour's drive north, there are a couple of decent spots to work up a sweat in the Sun Valley. The closest option is the **Sun Valley Nordic Center** (☎208/622-2250; $12; rentals available), just past the *Sun Valley Lodge*, where thirty miles of meticulously groomed trails are open to skiers and snowshoers. It's not much of a backcountry experience, though, as most of the trails are within view of houses. A better choice is the free **Wood River Trails System** that runs twenty miles south from Ketchum to Bellevue along gently inclined slopes. While it doesn't have a real "mountain" feel to it, the trails are well maintained and it's a great place to enjoy a good workout.

Powder-hounds may want to look into a **backcountry** skiing/boarding tour in the nearby Boulder and Sawtooth mountains. There's a vast amount of skiable terrain here, and with a guide – or without if you're experienced – huge swathes of untracked snow can be found. Backcountry huts and yurts are also available, supplying great overnight stops for multiday tours. Contact Sun Valley Trekking (☎208/788-9585) or Venture Outdoors (☎208/788-5049) for details; prices start from around $100. To experience the ultimate, most expensive ski

experience, check in with Sun Valley Heli Ski (☎1-800/872-3108, ⊛www
.svheli-ski.com); prices for a day's worth of **heliskiing** start at around $500.

The small **Ketchum–Sun Valley Heritage and Ski Museum**, corner of
First Street and Washington Avenue (Dec–March daily 11am–4pm; free), holds
a fairly rote collection of exhibits on local geology, Native Americans, and pio-
neers along with some interesting notebooks and diaries that belonged to
Ernest Hemingway. The skiing section, focusing on local Olympic successes and
Sun Valley's Hollywood connection, is sparse considering the area's ski heritage.

The main action in Ketchum is **shopping**, from stores devoted to skiing and
climbing gear to high-end galleries and jewelry shops. Of the many **galleries**,
the most worth stopping by are the Sun Valley Center for the Arts and
Humanities, 191 Fifth St E at Washington (☎208/726-9491), a nonprofit
organization that displays a wide range of local work.

Listings

Avalanche hotline ☎208/788-1200 ext. 8027.
Bookstore Chapter One Books, 160 N Main St,
Ketchum ☎208/726-5426.
Internet Access by the hour available at Wood
River Technologies, 2nd Floor, Jones Building, cor-
ner of Main and Fourth streets ☎208/726-5553,
and Newslink, corner of Sun Valley Rd and
Leadville. Rates vary from $3 to $5 per half-hour.

Medical St. Luke's Hospital, 3.5 miles south of
Ketchum on Hwy-75 ☎208/727-8800.
Pharmacy Chateau Drug Store, Giacobbi Square,
Fourth St, Ketchum ☎208/726-5696.
Post office 154 Fourth St W ☎208/726-5161.
Road conditions hotline ☎888/432-7623.

Schweitzer Mountain

Sixty miles south of the Canadian border, **SCHWEITZER MOUNTAIN** is
a relatively undiscovered little gem of a ski hill that sits above the delightful
town of **Sandpoint** on the northwest shore of **Lake Pend Oreille** (pronounced "Pon-du-ray"). Skiers and boarders will find that Schweitzer
Mountain, set in the rugged Selkirk Mountains, is northern Idaho's best ski
hill, with a wide variety of uncrowded slopes to cater for all levels of ability
and enough to keep you occupied for a good few days. Once a small and
quaint hideaway, this ever-expanding resort is now one of the state's largest ski
resorts, dominated by two impressive bowls that feature sensational views and
a variety of fantastic runs manageable by all but novices. If you base yourself in
Sandpoint, rather than on-mountain where facilities are more limited, you'll
get a taste of the eclectic lifestyle of the Idaho Panhandle's most appealing
town. Although it's still a working timber town, a heavy sprinkling of outdoors
and artsy types have given this buzzing little settlement a more bohemian,
eclectic feel than anywhere else in the Panhandle.

Arrival, information, and getting around

Although driving into Sandpoint is impressive from every direction, entering
from the south via Hwy-95 over the graceful span of **Long Bridge** is the
most stunning approach. From the town you'll see Schweitzer Mountain rising up to the north, and it's several miles of twisting, turning mountain road –
off Hwy-95 a couple of miles north of town – before you arrive at the slopes.

The local **bus service**, the North Idaho Community Express (NICE, ☏208/263 7287), runs four times a day to and from Coeur d'Alene ($9 round-trip), stopping within walking distance of downtown at the Riverside Building on Hwy-95. The town also has the only **train** stop in Idaho. Amtrak's *Empire Builder* route that runs between Chicago and Seattle pulls in at the station on the north end of Railroad Street (11.30pm westbound, 2.30am eastbound).

Information is available from the helpful Chamber of Commerce, 900 Fifth Ave (daily 8.30am–5pm; ☏1-800-800-2106, 208/263-2161, ⓦwww.sandpointchamber.com); the biannual *Sandpoint Magazine* ($2) available here has comprehensive listings of current events.

The mountain

The small, European-style base village sits 2400ft below the highest point on **Schweitzer Bowl** (6389ft). Adjacent to Schweitzer is **Outback Bowl**, accessed by a huge sixpack. The skiing tends to be a little quieter on this side of the mountain, although it's rare to find liftlines on either side. Both bowls have a mix of open slopes and glade skiing, served by six lifts in total. There are nearly sixty trails and a terrain park among the mountain's 2500 total acres. Beginners should head for Happy Trails and the Enchanted Forest, which drop off below the village, and for intermediates The Great Divide and Loophole offer superb views over the lake. Advanced skiers have several options, including Schweitzer Bowl's challenging bumps beneath Great Escape, while in the Outback Bowl exciting double blacks like Misfortune and Whiplash can be accessed from The Great Divide.

Beginner

Happy Trails and Enchanted Forest are gentle greens given over exclusively to beginners, children especially. From these progress on to South Bowl and Gypsy, accessed from Chair 1, or the wide open blue of Midway.

Intermediate

Schweitzer is excellent for intermediates, with almost half the mountain's runs graded blue. Especially popular is **The Great Divide** along the ridge between South Bowl and Outback Bowl, which connects with Loophole to offer a fast, carving run down to the village. Catch superb views over the lake on the way down. Outback Bowl contains several cruisers through the trees, while below the Great Escape Quad, blacks such as White Lightning and Stiles provide more of a challenge.

Mountain info	
Phone ☏1-800/831-8810 or 208/263-9555	
Snow phone ☏208/263-9562	
Website ⓦwww.schweitzer.com	
Operating times Late Nov to early April daily 9am–4pm	
No. of lifts 9 including one six-person chair, 2 surface lifts and 2 handle tows	
Base elevation 4000′	
Summit elevation 6400′	
Vertical drop 2400′	
No. of Trails 59	
Acreage 2500	
Beginner 20%	
Intermediate 40%	
Expert 40%	
Average snowfall 300″	
Snowmaking Yes (47 acres)	
Night skiing Yes, Fri–Sat 3pm–8pm from late Dec	
Nursery facilities Kinder Kamp, 4 months to 6 years, $50 full day, $40 if out of diapers	

Expert

Start your exploration of Schweitzer with a warm-up along The Great Divide before dropping off either side into blacks such as Sundance and JR in South Bowl or steeper double blacks Misfortune and Whiplash in Outback Bowl. Head up Chair 1 and onto South Ridge to access the steep black A–D chutes or, at the far end, double black South Bowl chutes, all of which provide a mixture of open glades and more close-packed trees. On Outback there are some challenging double black diamond steeps off North Ridge where the open upper slopes and lower glades are great fun after a fresh dump, but get here quick as it soon gets tracked out.

Freestyle

If you're looking for powder stashes, steeps, and trees head to Outback Bowl where it's easy to dart into the trees from virtually any run, and the north facing slopes here can be expected to hold good snow when the more open, sunny South Bowl is icing over. Decent kickers and hits to be found off the various open blues beneath Chair 1 and the Great Escape quad, and the terrain park is located here too, featuring eight hits, seven rail slides, one fun box, and a 250ft halfpipe with 15ft walls.

Lift tickets, lessons, and rentals

Adult day **tickets** cost $42 ($35 half-day), kids (7–17) are $32, and seniors (65-plus) pay $37. Children 6 and under ski free with a paying adult. Night skiing (3–8pm) costs $12 for adults. Beginner **lessons** are reasonable at $49 including lift ticket and rentals, and private lessons are $150 per half-day. Children's lessons (7–12) are $65 for a full day, or for ages 4–6 it's $75 for a full day including lunch and childcare. **Rentals** are available from The Source in the mountain village (☎208/255-3063), from $25 a day for skis and $30 for snowboards.

Accommodation

There's a selection of accommodation both on the mountain and down in cheaper Sandpoint. Make reservations if possible, as the better places in both locations tend to fill up quickly. Some motels and hotels in town offer money-saving **ski-and-stay packages** – enquire for special offers.

Schweitzer Mountain

Selkirk Lodge ☎1-800/831-8810, ⊛www
.schweitzer.com. The ski-in/ski-out lodge has a European feel with comfortable, cozy en-suite rooms featuring pine furniture. Many have great views over Lake Pend Oreille, others look over the slopes. Many rooms also feature a wet bar, microwave, and refrigerator. There's also an outdoor pool and three outdoor hot tubs. ❺

White Pine Lodge ☎1-800/831-8810, ⊛www
.schweitzer.com. Fully furnished condos feature an attractive northwest architectural style, full kitchens, and fireplaces. Guests also have use of an outdoor pool and two large outdoor hot tubs. ❼

Sandpoint and around

Best Western Edgewater Resort Motor Inn 56 Bridge St ☎1-800/635-2534, 208/263-3194,

⊛ edgewater@netw.com. Upmarket lodging with large, well-appointed rooms with cable TV – the more expensive rooms also have hot tubs. The hotel has an indoor pool and offers ski-and-stay packages. ❻

Coit House 502 N Fourth St ☎208/265-4035, ⊛wehsetk@juno.com. A Victorian house within walking distance of downtown. The four guest-rooms have been tastefully restored and are decorated with Victorian antiques, and all have their own bath, air con, and cable TV. ❺

Country Inn 470700 Hwy-95 S ☎208/263-3333. Basic but good-value rooms with microwaves and fridges two miles south of town. There's also a hot tub. ❷

K-2 Inn at Sandpoint 501 N Fourth Ave ☎208 /263-3441. A popular downtown hotel with small but cozy rooms. The beds are large, and the bathrooms have possibly the world's most powerful showers. Advance reservations recommended. ⑤

Lakeside Inn 106 Bridge St ☎ 1-800/543-8126, ⓦ www.sandpointlodging.com. In a pleasant park setting at the mouth of Lake Pend Oreille and Sand Creek, this is one of the best-located hotels in town. Still within walking distance of downtown, the spacious rooms include kitchens, and there's complimentary breakfast and indoor and outdoor hot tubs. ④

Page House B&B 506 N Second Ave ☎ 1-800 /500-6584, 208/263-6584, ⓦ www.keokee.com /pagehouse. The homey, beautifully furnished rooms in this 1918 house each have a separate

theme – Victorian, Depression-era, and country-style – and have cable TV and private phones. The house overlooks Sand Creek and is within walking distance of downtown. ⑤

S&W Motel 3480 Hwy-200 E ☎ 208/263-5969. A couple of miles out of town on the road to Hope, but very fairly priced and rooms have queen beds, stove, and refrigerator. There's also a hot tub for guests. ②

Super 8 Motel 476841 Hwy-95 N ☎ 1-800/800-8000, 208/263-2210. Plain but perfectly adequate rooms with queen beds and complimentary coffee, and a guest hot tub. Close to the Schweitzer Mountain turn-off. ②

Eating, drinking, and entertainment

There's a surprisingly good selection of **bars** and **restaurants** clustered within a few blocks of each other in Sandpoint's downtown area. The focal point of the local entertainment scene is the Panida Theater, 300 N First Ave (☎ 208/263-9191), which hosts stage shows, art house cinema shows, and concerts.

Schweitzer Mountain

Chimney Rock Grill ☎ 208/255-3071. The best restaurant on the mountain, featuring a cozy timbered interior with good bar food as well as a restaurant specializing in fresh regional cuisine such as local trout and salmon. Open for breakfast (from 7am), lunch, and dinner.

Lakeview Cafe ☎ 208/255-3071 ext. 2223. The most popular spot for a beer or coffee, located on the deck outside *Tap's Bar*.

Mojo Coyote Cafe ☎ 208/255-3037. Ideal for a mid-morning or afternoon break, the *Coyote* is located on the first floor of *Selkirk Lodge* and also does breakfast.

Outback Cafe ☎ 208/255-3067. Famed for its stuffed Idaho potatoes and relaxed, laid-back atmosphere, the deck here at the bottom of Outback Bowl is a real sun trap and makes a good spot to meet up for lunch.

Sandpoint

Bangkok Cuisine 202 N Second Ave ☎ 208/265-4149. Good-value Thai food in an easy-going environment; lunchtime specials start at $5.

Eichardts 212 Cedar St ☎ 208/263-4005. A lively, friendly bar with a dozen microbrews to choose from. They also serve decent bar food which won't set you back more than $10, and there's an upstairs games room with pool table, board games, and darts. Local rock bands perform on weekends.

Floating Restaurant Hwy-200, East Hope ☎ 208/264-5311. Based beside the marina at East Hope,

the bobbing boats and lakeside views make this one of the most atmospheric restaurants in the area. The food is very good and seafood is unsurprisingly the specialty – try the mouthwatering local salmon. An entree will set you back $15–20, and there's a fine range of microbrews to enjoy while watching the sun set over the lake.

The Hydra 115 Lake St ☎ 208/263-7123. A friendly, reasonably priced restaurant with very good prime rib. Vegetarians will appreciate the huge salad bar, and there's a good selection of wines and microbrews. The subdued lighting and woodland-inspired décor make for a relaxing atmosphere.

Ivano's 124 S Second Ave ☎ 208/263-0211. A fine Italian restaurant with a good selection of traditional dishes from $10 to $20. Closed Sundays.

Kamloop's Bar and Grill 302 N First Ave ☎ 208/263-6715. A busy bar popular with Sandpoint's younger residents. The décor is pretty uninspired and the welcome can vary from curious to indifferent, but it can be worth checking out for the regular live music sessions.

Monarch Mountain Coffee Shop 208 N Fourth Ave ☎ 1-800/599-6702. As a favored haunt of local outdoor types, this is a good place to get information on trails and such, along with a great variety of beverages, from fresh-roasted coffee to tea, chai, and even Argentinian *mate*. The breakfast burritos are a fine way to start the day, and they also serve tasty baked goods. Closed Sundays.

Panhandler Pies 120 S First Ave ☎ 208/263-2912. Famed for its fine home-baked pies, with a selection of over twenty just for dessert. Filling breakfasts cost around $5, and lunch and dinner twice that. Open Mon to Sat from 6am, Sun from 6.30am.

Pend Oreille Brewing Co 220 Cedar St ☎208/263-7837. The beer is brewed on the premises and you're encouraged to try something new each round by the friendly bar staff – the Scottish ale is tops. The atmosphere and décor are loosely that of an English pub, and there's a good bar menu.

Power House Bar and Grill 120 E Lake St ☎208/265-2449. Located in the town's original powerhouse just north of Long Bridge, with great

views across the lake and town and up to Schweitzer Mountain. The atmosphere is casual and prices are reasonable – the burgers in particular are good, as are the weekend breakfast specials.

Second Avenue Pizza 215 S Second Ave ☎208/263-9321. Popular with locals for well-priced pizzas – a large will set you back around $12 – and a comprehensive selection of micro-brews. If you're really hungry go for the "Juke Box Special'" which weighs a massive seven pounds and contains pretty much every ingredient you can think of. The calzones are also recommended.

Other activities and attractions

Cross-country skiers have over 30km of trails to go at beneath the base of the mountain ($10 a day) with something to suit all skill levels, and there's also a **snowshoe** trail too ($4). There's a **snowskate park** open Friday and Saturday evenings, or if you want to get away from the hurly-burly on the mountain and don't mind a bit of air and noise pollution, **snowmobile** tours are available in the surrounding backcountry and northwest toward idyllic Priest Lake (☎208/263-6959, ⓦwww.allaboutadventures.com).

Listings

Avalanche hotline ☎208/765-7323.
Bookshop Vanderford's, 201 Cedar St, Whitefish ☎208/263-2417.
Internet East Bonner Library, corner of Cedar and Division streets, Sandpoint.
Medical Bonner General Hospital, 520 N Third Ave, Sandpoint ☎208/263-1441.

Pharmacy Sandpoint Super Drug, 602 N Fifth Ave, Sandpoint ☎208/263-1408.
Post Office 210 N Fourth Ave, Sandpoint ☎208/263-2716.
Road conditions ☎1-888/432-7623.

Big Sky

Quite often, the massive, relatively uncrowded **Big Sky Resort** boasts the first skiable snow in the Rockies – the resort can open as early as October (week-ends only), though the official season lasts from mid-November to mid-April. The Montana resort was the brainchild of American newscaster Chet Huntley, who, with other major investors, bought a huge chunk of Lone Mountain in 1969 with the aim of developing a mountain resort in harmony with its surroundings. After current owner Boyne Developments took over, these developments have continued apace, but for now nature still holds the upper hand at the rugged and wild ski hill where moose and bear spotting are not unheard of.

The resort is divided into three mountains (Lone Mountain at 11,166ft, Andesite Mountain at 8800ft, and Flat Iron Mountain at 8092ft), which have plenty to keep most skiers occupied, though beginners may feel a little left out, with less than a fifth of the terrain open to them. Intermediates and experts are much better served.

Most amenities can be found at either the fine and expansive Mountain Village Base Area, the Meadow Village six miles from the resort, and the Canyon, three miles from the Meadow Village. For a more authentic Western experience there are some decent options strung out along the surrounding Gallatin Valley.

Arrival and information

Big Sky is 45 miles south of Bozeman, home to an airport served by airlines including Northwest, Delta/Skywest, United and Horizon. A shuttle service links the airport to Big Sky ($27 one way, $45 round-trip; ☎406/388-6404).

Alternatively, drive south down US-191 along the scenic Gallatin Valley, turning west on Hwy-64 for the eight-mile drive up to Mountain Village. For more information contact the **Chamber of Commerce** in West Fork Meadows (Mon–Fri 9am–5pm, Sat 10am–4pm; ☎406/995-3000 or 1-800/943-4111, ⓦwww.bigskychamber.com), or check out the free *Lone Peak Lookout* newspaper for listings and events.

The mountains

Big Sky is famed for empty slopes, reliable snow, and some of the most extreme in-bound skiing in North America. Of the three peaks that make up the resort, **Lone Mountain** stands high above the rest, but since every run off the top is a double black diamond relatively few skiers head up here. Take the thrilling return ride up in the fifteen-seat gondola just to view the magnificent summit panorama over three states – Montana, Idaho, and Wyoming. On the north side of Lone Mountain the slow Challenger double chair leads to yet more serious expert-only terrain. On the lower slopes, the sunny, easy-angled runs are best for beginner.

Lone Mountain is well linked to **Andesite Mountain**, where there are excellent wide, open, undulating blue runs which vary in quality and difficulty. It's not unusual to find bumps on many of these runs too – the result of relatively heavy usage. Similar to Lone Mountain, a few beginner runs congregate at the lower portions of the hill; it's also the spot for most freeriders to head – though note the natural halfpipe on Lone Mountain's Lower Morningstar too. East of Andesite is **Flat Iron Mountain**, the lowest of Big Sky's three peaks and another spot with wide open runs cutting through heavy tree cover.

Mountain info
Phone ☎1/800/548-4486 or ☎406/995-5000
Snow phone ☎406/995-5900
Website ⓦwww.bigskyresort.com
Opening hours Late Nov to late April daily 9am–4pm
Price $56, under 10 free
No. of lifts 15, including 15-passenger cabin to summit of Lone Mountain, 3 high-speed quads plus 4 surface lifts.
Base elevation 6800′
Summit elevation 11150′
Vertical drop 4350′
No. of Trails 202
Acreage 3600
Beginner 17%
Intermediate 25%
Expert 58%
Average snowfall 400″
Snowmaking Yes (10 percent of trails)
Night skiing Yes, Christmas to mid-March
Ski school Snowsports School ☎406/995-5743
Nursery facilities Yes – from 6 months at Handprints (☎406/995-3332, reservations required, from $70 per day).

On-mountain refreshment options are limited; other than the busy *Dugout Restaurant* at the top of Andesite you'll have to head down to Mountain Village or over to Moonlight Basin Lodge below Lone Mountain's Pony Express Lift for lunch.

Beginner

Beginners should head for the Swift Current Express that runs up the lower slopes of Lone Mountain and accesses Mr K, Lone Wolf, and White Wing (these are also accessible off the Explorer double chair). Mr. K has a slow skiing zone for the less confident, while first timers will feel comfortable on the new Mighty Magic carpet lift at the base of Lone Mountain. Andesite Mountain has open greens cut between the trees beneath the Southern Comfort chair. Try Deep South, a long loop which gives you time to get a feel for your skis or board.

Intermediate

It can be a little exasperating for intermediates to have to constantly stare up at Lone Mountain and realize its snow-laden upper slopes are expert only, but there's plenty of exciting skiing lower down. Crazy Horse and Calamity Jane, accessed off Swift Current Express and Gondola 1, provide a good warm-up, though they can be relatively busy. Avoid the crowds and head to the sunny, open glades of Blue Moon or the more challenging runs beneath the Shedhorn chair. Over on Andesite, Tippy's Tumble, Ambush, and Big Horn are speedy cruisers, perfect for carving.

Expert

Expert skiers and boarders are spoiled for choice at Big Sky. Take the tram to the top of Lone Mountain and start with the easier double blacks of Marx or Lenin before dropping into a range of runs through the trees beneath Shedhorn. For one of the mountain's largest challenges, sign in with ski patrol and hike off to the insanely steep Big Couloir or A-Z Chutes; full avalanche gear is required for these runs. Lone Mountain's South Face is less daunting, but you can still find slopes of up to 50 degrees. The terrain beneath the Challenger chair provides in-bound skiing as challenging as any in North America, varying from the vertical tree run of Little Tree to the open and bumped-out expanse of Big Rock Tongue.

Independent backcountry options

Big Sky's guides will not take clients on backcountry trips out of boundaries, but they will guide on more extreme terrain such as A-Z Chutes and Big Couloir. Most riders at Big Sky won't need to bother going out of bounds as there's enough quality snow and challenging runs on Lone Mountain. Big Sky has a cat ski operation run by Montana Backcountry Adventures (☎406/995-3880, ⊛www.skimba.com), located a mile north of the resort at the entrance to Moonlight Basin Ranch. They operate 1800 acres of backcountry terrain in the Lee Metcalf Wilderness Area and offer clients a daily average vertical of 12,500ft. There are plans to extend the ski-able area in the coming years. Powder skis and boards are required (rentals are available) and full avalanche safety gear is provided. As far as heliskiing goes, there are no permanent operations in the area. Montana Powder Guides (☎406/587-3096) in Bozeman can arrange trips in the Northern Bridgers.

Less confident riders should head across Turkey Traverse from the Lone Peak triple chair to the wide open bowl of South Wall, a relatively forgiving black with a long run out at the bottom. Five new gladed runs have been opened on Andesite – Blue Room (north facing so the snow stays in good condition), Congo, Bear Lair, Ambush, and Wounded Knee.

Freestyle

Freestylers have a fairly large and sparsely populated terrain park and a large halfpipe on Andesite Mountain, accessed from the Ramcharger High Speed quad, and a less challenging natural halfpipe on Lower Morning Star on Lone Mountain. The double black off the top of Lone Mountain, and the tree runs beneath the Shedhorn Lift, provide challenging hits in a natural environment.

Lift tickets, lessons, and rentals

Lift tickets vary from $58 for a single day to $364 for a seven-out-of-eight day ticket. Discounted passes are available for juniors (11–17), college students with ID ($46), and over-70s (half-price). Children under 10 ski for free (up to two per paying adult). Half-day tickets (12.30–4pm) are $46. There are also various discount offers aimed at frequent skiers, and season passes vary from $405 for a ten-day pass to $955 for a full-season pass. The **ski school** has a very good reputation and employs a number of European instructors. Group lessons cost $38 per half-day, lift ticket not included. Private lessons start from $170 for two hours for up to three people, and specialist mogul, powder, and telemark lessons are also available. Big Sky is a big resort and it's worth considering taking a guide if you can afford it, as there are invariably powder stashes waiting to be discovered by those in the know. Half a day costs from $240, full day $390 for up to three people. Big Sky's Mountain Hosts service also offers a free tour of the mountain for intermediate and better skiers daily from the bottom of Gondola 1.

Rentals are available from the ski school or from Grizzly Outfitters (☎406/ 995-2939) in Meadow Village or Lone Mountain Sports (☎406/995-4471; ⓦwww.lonemountainsports.com) in Mountain Village. High-performance ski packages (skis, poles, and boots) start at $40; snowboard packages, featuring step-in bindings and boots, are around $35.

Accommodation

Try to get **accommodation** in Mountain Village as it saves the drive (or shuttle bus) up the ski hill, often a hassle after heavy snow. Most of the accommodation here is run by the resort (☎1-800/548-4486, ⓦwww.bigskyresort.com), and many hotels in the area offer excellent-value ski packages.

Mountain Village

Huntley Lodge The resort's original hotel recently spruced up the still rather drab rooms a notch. The facilities, though, are excellent, and include a swimming pool, hot tubs, workout room, and the popular *Chet's Bar & Grill* (see "Bars and entertainment," p.223). Rates include a free buffet breakfast, and ski-and-stay packages help cut the cost. ❼
Moonlight Basin Lodge 1 Mountain Loop Rd ☎406/995-7700, ⓦwww.moonlightspa.com. Located at the base of Powder River Run a mile west of Meadow Village, this sumptuously

designed hotel is an attractive combination of timber and river rock. Rooms are just as beautifully decorated and will have you basking in the lap of luxury. Facilities include the excellent *Timbers* restaurant (see overleaf), a workout room, heated outdoor pool, and the Moonlight Spa, where you can get a great après-ski massage. ❽
Shoshone Condominium Hotel Ski-in, ski-out suites with private bedrooms, full kitchens, gas fireplaces, and balconies, plus access to *Huntley Lodge*'s health club, sauna, steam room, and lap pool. In summer a four-person condo can be had

for little more than $200 per night. **8**

Summit at Big Sky The *Summit* features large, elegant rooms, most with good mountain views along with wet bars, small kitchens, fireplaces, and large tubs. There is also a workout room and an on-site spa. **8**

Off the mountain

Best Western Bucks T-4 US-191, less than a mile south of the Big Sky turn-off ☎406/995-4111 or 1-800/822-4484, ⓦwww.buckst4.com. *Buck's*, a former hunting lodge, exudes far more personality than most Best Westerns. Though rooms are standard – comfortable queen beds, TV, coffeemaker – the common areas are anything but, including a pleasant lobby with fireplace, large country hall hosting the occasional concert, and a highly recommended restaurant (see below). Rates include a complimentary buffet breakfast. **6**

Big EZ Lodge 7000 Beaver Creek Rd ☎406/995-7000 or 1-800/244-3299, ⓦwww.bigezlodge.com. Located high above Meadow Village and a winding half-hour drive from Lone Mountain, the lodge, originally designed as the owner's personal residence, features thirteen art-filled suites, breathtaking views, a guest's-only gourmet dining room, and a huge outdoor hot tub. Expensive ($300 per night and up) but worthwhile package. **9**

Golden Eagle Lodge Meadow Village ☎406/539-4600. Well located for the shops in Meadow Village, the *Golden Eagle* has a range of relatively plain but perfectly adequate rooms varying in facilities from bunks to queen beds, and there's also a full restaurant and bar on site. They also provide excellent-value long-term accommodation (from $525/month), so if you're looking to spend a season skiing or working at Big Sky this is a good option. **6**

Rainbow Ranch Lodge US-191, five miles south of the Big Sky turn-off ☎406/995-4132. A dozen attractive, individually decorated rooms only a few steps from the Gallatin River. There's an outdoor hot tub, Western-style lounge featuring a roaring fireplace and overstuffed leather couches, and a very fine restaurant and wine cellar (see overleaf). **7**

River Rock Lodge Westfork Meadows ☎406/995-2295 or 1-800/995-9966. Fine lodging choice with attractive Western-style rooms featuring queen beds complete with down comforter and snug wool blankets, minibar, and coffeemaker. Rates are reduced in the off season. **6**

The 320 Ranch US-191, about a dozen miles south of the Big Sky turn-off ☎406/995-4283 or 1-800/243-0320. In business for a hundred years, accommodation is in cozy rustic log cabins; the larger ones have kitchenettes, although if you don't want to cook there's a good on-site restaurant. Cross-country skiing can be organized through the ranch. **6**

Eating

One thing you won't go short on around Big Sky is good food – there's a wide selection of fine dining spots both on the mountain, in the villages below, and strung out along the Gallatin Valley, from high-end, sophisticated **restaurants** to beer-swilling true-grit Western **bars**. If you're catering for yourself, check out the well-stocked Hungry Moose Market & Deli, 11 Skywood Rd, Meadow Village (☎406/995-3045).

Blue Moon Bakery Meadow Village ☎406/995-2305. Good coffee and fresh-baked bagels and pastries make this a great breakfast stop on the way up Lone Mountain. During the lunch and dinner hours, the menu expands to include pizzas, pastas, salads, and sandwiches.

Bucks T-4 US-191, less than a mile south of the Big Sky turn-off ☎406/995-4111. Probably the only Best Western restaurant featured in *Gourmet* and *Wine Spectator* magazines, *Bucks* specializes in imaginatively prepared exotic and local game. Stand-out entrees include the grilled New Zealand red deer in a port wine sauce and the pan-seared elk chop. Mains run from $20 to $35, and reservations are essential.

The Corral US-191, five miles south of the Big Sky turn-off ☎406/995-4249. Open for breakfast from 7am, but it's the prime rib ($10 or $20 portions), local rainbow trout, and Pacific halibut and salmon ($13–20) for lunch or dinner that make *The Corral* worth a visit. Also the place to come for a brew in a genuine Western roadhouse atmosphere.

Lone Mountain Ranch and Dining Lodge between Meadow and Mountain Villages ☎406/995-2782. Classic ranch-style cuisine, including Montana beef, local game, and poultry, plus seafood and vegetarian options in a stylish and intimate nonsmoking log lodge environment. Also does hearty buffet lunches and a chuckwagon dinner every Saturday night. Reservations required.

Mountain Top Pizza Mountain Mall ☎406/995-4646. Good pizzas served from lunchtime onwards. Expect to pay around $14 for a large with a few toppings; free delivery.

Rainbow Ranch Lodge US-191, five miles south of the Big Sky turn-off ☎406/995-4132. Expensive, but mains like cinnamon-cured pork chops on a bed of sweet potato hash ($23) and fine starters like lobster and rabbit ravioli ($10) make dinner here well worth the splurge. Ask to see the Bacchus Room, an extraordinary 10,000-bottle wine cellar complete with "weeping walls."

Sundog Café ☎406/996-2439. Located right beside the lift ticket booths, the *Sundog* is a con-venient place to stop off for a quick breakfast before you hit the mountain or for a midday break, with a tasty range of soups, chili, sandwiches, wraps, and baked goods, plus great coffee. Expect to pay around $7–10 for a decent lunch.

Timbers at Moonlight Basin Lodge 1 Mountain Loop Rd ☎406/995-7777. Though you can ski up to the bar and deli here for lunch, it's best for din-ner at the magnificent *Timbers Restaurant*, home to a massive stone fireplace. Highlights of the menu include the tenderloin of Montana beef topped with wild mushrooms, a sauteed Michigan venison loin, and Alaskan cod and chips. Entrees average around $25.

Bars and entertainment

Allgood's Bar & Grill Meadow Village ☎406/995-2750. Attracting a younger crowd, this bar and grill specializes in barbecued ribs and chicken ($12–14) and is also open for breakfasts (omelets $6–8). The lively bar has a pool table and darts.

Chet's Bar & Grill ☎406/995-5784. Located in *Huntley Lodge* and busy immediately after the lifts close thanks to a happy hour that includes nightly entertainment. You can also chance your hand at the poker table here. If you stay around after happy hour try the delicious smoked pheasant quesadilla appetizer, or the chargrilled buffalo strip steak main. Appetizers average $8–10, entrees $15 up.

Dante's Inferno ☎406/995-3999. One of the liveliest bars in Mountain Village, also serves lunch and dinner with a northern Italian theme, with entrees coming in at $12–22. It's one of the busiest places to hit after the lifts close and remains lively through to the early hours.

Lolo's ☎406/995-3455. *Lolo's* is invariably busy, especially during the après-ski happy hour when drinks specials compliment a selection of appetiz-ers, snacks and pizzas. Attractions include a dance floor, fooseball, and pool tables.

The Lone Wolf ☎406-995-7521. In Meadow Village center on Little Coyote Drive, the Lone Wolf is one of the newest and liveliest spots at Big Sky, with regular live music and such occasional delights as a mechanical bull. They also specialize in well-priced fresh wraps and huge burritos, plus après-ski appetizers.

M.R. Hummers Mountain Mall ☎406/995-4343. One of the most popular après-ski spots in the village, with a friendly vibe and great baby-back ribs to go with your beer, plus filling sandwiches for under $10.

Other activities and attractions

There's not a great deal to do either in Mountain Village or in the villages lower down the mountain. However, shoppers will find a reasonable selection of stores offering Montana-made souvenirs, and complimentary ski movies are shown nightly at the slopeside Roosevelt Amphitheater in Mountain Village's Yellowstone Conference Center.

Back out on the snow, **cross-country skiers** will find over thirty miles of some of the best trails in the US at Lone Mountain Ranch (☎406/995-4644 or 1-800/514-4644), a couple of miles down Hwy-63 from Mountain Village, with lift passes costing around $10 a day and ski rental available from around $15. **Snowshoes** can also be rented from Lone Mountain Ranch for use on some of their trails, or from Big Sky Sports (☎406/995-5840) or Grizzly Outfitters (☎406/995-2939) for use on Moose Tracks, a snowshoe trail that starts at the base of Andesite and Lone mountains in Mountain Village. Expect to pay around $15 per day. If you'd rather have someone else do the hard work, **dogsled rides** are available with Spirit of the North (☎406/995-3424), and

Lone Mountain Ranch (☎406/995-4644) and the 320 Ranch (☎406/995-4283 or 1-800/243-0320) organize evening **sleigh ride dinners**. You can also see mountain dogs in action every Saturday evening at 5pm when there's a free Ski Patrol Search and Rescue Dog Demo – meet outside the Plaza in Mountain Village. And in an area where *A River Runs Through It* was shot, keen **anglers** may want to cast a line even in winter – if so, Gallatin River Guides (☎406/995-2290) organizes local winter fishing trips.

Listings

Avalanche reports Gallatin National Forest Avalanche Center ☎406/587-6981, ⓦwww.mtavalanche.com.
Bookstore Moose Rack Books, *Huntley Lodge* 1 Lone Mountain Trail, Mountain Village ☎406/995-2551.
Internet Available for those who use Big Sky Central Reservations.

Medical Big Sky Medical Clinic, 100 Beaverhead Trail (behind *Huntley Lodge*) ☎406/995-2797.
Pharmacy Lone Mountain Pharmacy 3090 Pine St, Blue Mall, West Fork Meadows ☎406/995-3149.
Post office Big Sky Post Office, 55 Meadow Village, Suite 2 ☎406/995-4540.
Road conditions ☎406/586-1313.

Big Mountain

Big Mountain is by far northern Montana's biggest and best year-round mountain resort. Though locals have been skiing it since back in the 1930s, it's only recently that it's been elevated to any sort of premier status. In winter, the mountain averages 335 inches of snow, blanketing some 3000 acres of skiable terrain that are suitable for all comers. Most visitors take their skiing and boarding quite seriously, though this doesn't stop it from being a laid-back place, even backwoodsy. The mountain's remote location means that liftlines are rarely of any consequence, and crowds soon disperse among the bowls, trees, and eighty-odd trails.

The main downfall is the habitual cold, foggy weather – you may occasionally find yourself skiing in near-whiteout conditions, although the mountain's abundant trees act as a good visual aid in such conditions. The tree cover thins the further up the mountain you go, where you'll start to come across picturesque "snow ghosts" – trees coated thickly in rime, ice, and snow

Eight miles from the resort, **Whitefish** is easily one of the coolest towns in the Rockies. Set beside Whitefish Lake, and with Glacier National Park only 25 miles away, the attractive Western-style downtown area bustles with a young, outdoor-oriented population. There was no permanent white settlement in this area until 1883, prior to which fur trappers and loggers had passed through the region only on occasion. Things took off with the arrival in 1894 of the Great Northern Railway, and the town developed so quickly that the streets remained spiked with tree stumps where the original forest had been quickly cut down – hence its early nickname of "Stumptown."

Arrival and information

Whitefish sits astride US-93, which rolls into town from Kalispell thirteen miles south. Rimrock Bus Service (☎406/862-6700) operates a daily **bus** service to and from Kalispell and Missoula from Your C-Stop gas station, 403

2nd St. **Glacier Park International Airport** (☎406/257-9994) is mid-way between Kalispell and Whitefish on US-2 and is served by Big Sky, Delta, Horizon and United Express. Note that the "international" tag only comes from the fact that you can fly to Canada from here. The airport **shuttle** (☎406/752-2842) costs $15 to both Kalispell and Whitefish.

Information is available from the **Chamber of commerce** (June–Aug Day Mon–Fri 8am–6pm, rest of year 9am–5.30pm; ☎406/862-3501 or 1-877/862-3548), located in the Whitefish Mountain Mall to the south of town on US-93, and from a small counter in the railway depot ☎1-800/858-3930.

The mountain

The 360-degree exposure of the resort and copious annual snowfall ensure that you should always be able to find stashes of untracked snow. Expert skiers and boarders have some of the best **tree skiing** in North America to go at, especially on Connie's Couloir above Hellroaring Basin, while the double black East Rim on the south side of the mountain provides a more open challenge.

Intermediates will revel in the long, open blues, especially on the south side of the mountain, where there's over 2000ft of constant pitch. Beginners don't fare quite so well (although the Platter lift and Chair 6 are free all day – a good deal) and have little other than a selection of greens around the base area and a couple of more demanding runs from the summit. It's worth taking the **Glacier Chaser** chair up to the café at Summit House whatever your ability level to enjoy the wonderful panoramic views.

The nearly eighty marked runs are serviced by eight chairlifts and three surface tows, and there's also a halfpipe, boardercross run, and freestyle jumping area to go at. Boarders can head not only to a decent terrain park, but the mountain holds a fine selection of bowls, wind rolls, and tree runs, along with some great intermediate and advanced terrain in Hellroaring Basin (although steer clear of dropping onto Russ's Street, an interminably long cat track down to the base of the mountain).

Beginner

Most beginners' runs are off Chair 3, including the long and winding Home Again, and a number of runs drop down through the trees below the mountain's base. There are only a couple of beginner runs from the top of Big Mountain – Caribou, which wends its way down the North Side, or the more challenging traverse of Russ's Street, which includes a few blue pitches.

Intermediate

Big Mountain is a wonderful spot for intermediates who like to clock up the miles, with the likes of Inspiration, Toni Matt, and The Big Ravine off the Glacier Chaser chair providing long, fast, open, and continuous pitch runs ideal for getting up speed and practicing your carving turns. On the North Side of the mountain the runs are shorter but just as much fun, although you may find that short liftlines develop from time to time at the Big Creek Express chair which takes you back to the summit. Goat Haunt is a popular blue here, dropping off the ridge followed by Momentum and swooping down between the trees to open glades.

Expert

Expert riders are spoiled for choice in terms of tree skiing, with everything from the chance to veer off from groomers such as Toni Matt and into the trees on either side to the groves and more open glades of the double black East Rim on the south side of the mountain. Equally, there are plenty of lines of differing degrees of difficulty through the trees of the black Good Medicine area, which you can drop into from The Big Ravine.

Also worth checking out are Schmidt's Chute, which runs through well-spaced trees but is nice and steep – it's accessed by turning straight back on yourself after coming off Glacier Chaser – while the steep launch into Bighorn on the North Side is a highly charged way of getting into this side of the mountain.

Freestyle

Big Mountain is excellent for freestylers – not only is there a 350ft halfpipe and a terrain park with various hits, jumps, tabletops, quarterpipes, etc off Whitetail run on the North Side of the mountain, there's also Knox Landing, a freestyle jump hill to skier's right of Big Ravine run on the front side. In addition the natural features of the mountain also provide heaps of top-quality entertainment – head over to North Side for hidden powder stashes and a wide variety of lines through the trees beneath Inspiration, or for something a little less challenging the open glades and less severe gradients of the sunny North Bowl Face are well worth exploring.

Lift tickets, lessons, and rentals

Lift **tickets** cost $47 adults, $34 children (7–18) and $39 seniors (62-plus). Kids under 6 ski for free, and beginners happy to stick to chairs 2, 3, and 6 and Easy Riders can get a ticket for $26. Early and late-season skiers will find that rates drop as low as $20–25 per day in Nov/Dec and April. Night skiing ($14) is also available Fri and Sat from late Dec to early March. Note that with a full-day ticket if don't like the conditions and return your ticket within an hour you can get a ticket for use another day.

Big Mountain Ski and Snowboard School (☎406/862-2900, ⊛www.bigmtn .com) is located at the base of the mountain and offers ski and board lessons for $30 half-day ($42 including equipment rental), $48 full day, with similar rates for kids. A half-day of private lessons will set you back $155 (one or two people), with additional skiers charged $50.

Equipment **rental** is available from Big Mountain Sports (☎406/862-2900) at the base of Chair 2, where you can also get repairs and tune-ups. Rates vary from $22 per day for shaped skis, boots, and poles to $28 per day for boards and boots. There's also a ski and board demo center at the summit of Big Mountain. Other options include Snowfrog, 903 Wisconsin Ave (☎406/862-7547), en route to Big Mountain, with a good range of ski equipment for sale or rent here, and Stumptown Snowboards, 128 Central Ave (☎406/862-0955), your standard self-consciously cool board shop with a good range of gear for sale and rental.

Accommodation

With a convenient bus between town and the resort, you can quite freely choose your base. Slopeside lodging can be booked through central reservations (☎1-800/858-3930). There is relatively limited accommodation directly downtown in Whitefish, so be prepared to walk or drive into town unless you book far in advance.

Allen's Motel 6540 US-93 S ☎406/862-3995. Basic but clean rooms that are among the best deals in town, with rooms for up to four people for only $80. ❶

Alpinglow Inn Big Mountain Village ☎1-800 /754-6760, ☜www.alpinglow.com. Good-value slopeside choice, with two outdoor hot tubs, on-site restaurant, and decent amenities. ❺

Best Western Rocky Mountain Lodge 6510 US 93 S ☎1-800/862-2569, ☏406/862-1154. Large rooms with queen beds and some with fireplaces, plus free continental breakfast, pool, hot tub, exercise room, guest laundry, and shuttle service. ❸

Bunkhouse Travelers Inn & Hostel 217 Railway St ☎406/862-3377. There's the option of bunk accommodation ($13) or a clean and basic private room for $30. The hostel has a communal kitchen and dining room and a laundry, no curfew, and a good location within easy walking distance of downtown.

Duck Inn 1305 Columbia ☎406/862-3825 or 1-800/344-2377, ☜www.duckinn.com. A good-value, quiet, and friendly little inn overlooking Whitefish River with decks and fireplaces in each room, free breakfast, and a guest hot tub. Closed Nov–Jan. ❸

Edelweiss Big Mountain Village ☎406/862-5252 or 1-800/228-8260, ☜www.stayatedelweiss.com. One of a number of condos and inns on Big Mountain, the *Edelweiss* offers finely furnished condos with fireplaces and balconies with spectacular views of the Flathead Valley. ❻

The Garden Wall 504 Spokane Ave ☎1-888/530-1700, ☜www.wtp.net/go/gardenwall. A restored five-bedroom 1920s B&B with a stylish range of period décor and furniture throughout. The breakfasts are excellent, as is the owner's advice on the local outdoor scene. ❺

Grouse Mountain Lodge 1205 US-93 W ☎406 /862-3000 or 1-800/321-8822. One of the premier lodgings in town, *Grouse Mountain* has cozy but somewhat drab rooms with queen beds and plenty of guest facilities including indoor and outdoor hot tubs, indoor pool, sauna, tennis courts, mountain bike rentals, and a free shuttle service. ❼

Hibernation House 3812 Big Mountain Rd ☎406/862-1982 With their ski-and-stay packages, this is one of the better deals you'll find around the mountain; rooms come with queen beds and bunks and it's a very short walk to the nearest lift. ❸

Eating and drinking

The mountain has plenty of spots to grab a meal or a drink, but Whitefish is the best small town in Montana for **eating** and **drinking**, with a wide range of restaurants and bars packed into the downtown area. Be warned, though, that most places are busy, especially on weekends and holidays, so you may need to reserve a table.

Baker Ave Bistro 10 Baker Ave ☎406/862-6383. A popular in-town breakfast spot for bagels, omelets, and coffee before heading up to Big Mountain.

Bulldog Grill 144 Central Ave ☎406/862-5601. A friendly atmosphere, fine local beers, and large,

filling burgers make this a good place to hang out if you're not looking for anything sophisticated – both the male and female bathrooms contain a large collection of centerfolds.

Great Northern Bar & Grill 27 Central Ave ☎406 /862-2816. A great place to meet folks out to have a good time and drink plenty of beer. A boisterous setting, good-value bar food, Ping Pong tables, and bands on weekends ensure you can easily end up here a lot longer than planned. If you're on a budget stop in for the 4–6pm happy hour.

Hellroaring Saloon ☎ 406/862-6364. In this base area spot, you can get better than average bar food and stay until the late hours drinking.

Logan's Bar & Grill *Grouse Mountain Lodge*, 1205 US-93 W ☎ 406/862-3000. One of the finest restaurants in town offering contemporary regional fare such as peppercorn-crusted elk *carpaccio* and seared salmon fillet, served up in a cozy mountain lodge setting. An entree costs around $20.

Moguls Bar and Grill ☎ 406/862-1980. Smart mountain choice for the après set, but they serve meals throughout the day too.

Truby's 115 Central Ave ☎ 406/862-4979. The best wood-fired pizzas in town along with a warm and welcoming atmosphere ensure that it can be hard to get a table at *Truby's*. There's a shady deck alongside, and the bar staff are a great source of information on the local outdoor scene.

Whitefish Lake Restaurant ☎ 406/862-5285. Situated at Whitefish Lake Golf Club on US-93 west of town, this is one of the more upmarket restaurants in town with especially good seafood and prime rib. Expect to pay around $20–25 for an entree.

Whitefish Times 344 Central Ave ☎ 406/862-2444. Coffee and cakes in wonderfully relaxing surroundings, where you can lounge on a sofa and read from the wide range of complimentary magazines and newspapers.

Red Lodge

On the eastern edge of the Absaroka-Beartooth Wilderness, stunningly situated **Red Lodge Mountain Ski Area** is not unlike Aspen before the big money moved in, though a similar trend has started here, and how long it will continue to keep its friendly, down-home feel is open to conjecture. Reasons popularity is on the rise include the dry Montana powder, uncrowded and challenging runs, and superb panoramas across rugged mountains to the west and the slate-flat plains to the east. And when the lifts close head back down to the town of Red Lodge, where you'll find a **downtown** area which is small but full of character. It's anchored by the lovely red-brick *Pollard Hotel*, where guests back in 1897 watched the Sundance Kid and cronies rob the bank across the street when this was a genuine Wild West frontier town, attracting some of the West's most colorful characters including Buffalo Bill and Calamity Jane as well as the Sundance Kid.

Arrival and information

Red Lodge is some sixty miles southeast of Billings, whose Logan Field Airport is the biggest in Montana. To get here from Billings follow I-90 west then US-212 south into the fanged peaks of the Beartooth Mountains. US-212 (Broadway Avenue) runs north-south through the town, before becoming the Beartooth Highway on its way to Yellowstone National Park – unfortunately this spectacular high-level road is closed in winter. The **Chamber of Commerce** is at 601 N Broadway Ave (Mon–Sat 9am–5pm, reduced hours in winter; ☎ 406/446-1718, ⊛ www.redlodge.com), but for information on the Absaroka-Beartooth Wilderness Area and the Beartooth Highway, head instead for the **Beartooth Ranger Station**, three miles south of town on US-212 (Mon–Fri 8am–4.30pm; ☎ 406/446-2103).

The mountain

Six miles above town, **Red Lodge Mountain Resort** is spread over two mountains with seven **chairlifts** accessing 1600 acres of predominantly intermediate terrain. The highest of the two mountains is Grizzly Peak (9416ft), which has a maximum **vertical drop** of 2400ft and a network of 45 trails that vary from easy greens like Turnpike to lovely blue cruisers such as Barriers, which provides some fine views back down toward the town. There's also a series of more demanding blacks, including the vicious moguls on Upper Continental, as well as the double black tree skiing on East Parks. On Nichols Peak (9390ft), which tends to hold better snow (**average snowfall** for the resort is 250 inches a year), you'll find mainly blacks and double blacks – True Grit is one of the steepest runs in the region – although intermediates can enjoy the reasonably strenuous Latigo and Meeteetse Trail runs. Snowboarders are also well catered for with two well-designed **terrain parks**. A **snowmaking** system that covers forty percent of marked trails keeps things running smoothly when Mother Nature doesn't feel like helping out.

Beginner

Beginners have a limited amount of terrain available to them as there are no green runs from the top of either Grizzly or Nichols Peak. Complete beginners will want to start off on the **Mighty Mite** tow in front of the main lodge before heading over to the very mellow Miami Beach right of the lodge. After building up confidence head up the triple chair to Grizzly and Nichols from where runs such as Easy Street and Turnpike glide down to join Auto Bahn back to the base. From the triple chair you can also access the restaurant at Midway Chalet for lunch.

Intermediate

Intermediates should head to the top of Grizzly Peak where Barriers and Lazy M provide long, swooping runs back to base. **Nichols Peak** is a fun leg burner down to the base of the Cole Creek quad. Try the trees on the strenuous **Meeteetse Trail** all the way to the Palisades Lift. Though crowds are rarely a problem at Red Lodge, the further you venture from the base the more the numbers thin out, especially in the Cole Creek and Palisades areas.

Expert

Although there are no exceptionally long runs at Red Lodge, experts will still find plenty to challenge them, especially in the widely acclaimed **Cole Creek** drainage below Nichols Peak. Warm up on Hellroaring before heading into the trees to take on the double black of Coal Chute or True Grit, one of the steepest runs in the region. On Grizzly, less confident riders should try the reasonably steep but forgiving Thompson's for well-spaced trees. For more of a challenge try the bumps on Upper Continental and the double black tree skiing of East Parks.

Freestyle

Red Lodge's history of catering to boarders dates as far back as 1983 when it was the first resort in Montana to allow snowboarding. Today, this is reflected in an excellent **terrain park** located on Lower Continental and Hancock. It's accessed by the triple chair and the Willow Creek chair and has numerous bumps, jumps, rollers, a tabletop, and several rails. On the mountain itself the glades of the Cole Creek drainage provide plenty of scope and challenge for all levels.

Lift tickets, lessons, and rentals

A full-day **lift ticket** is $37, juniors (13–18) are $34, under-12s are $15, and seniors (over 65) are $30. Beginners content to stick to the lower mountain can purchase a $25 ticket (under-12s $12). There are special deals on "Mellow Mondays" and "Terrific Tuesdays" from the start of the season through mid-April, when adult all-day tickets are $28. Various excellent-value ski-and-stay packages are available through Central Reservations (☎1-800/444-8977, ✉res@redlodgemountain.com), which can effectively bring the cost of skiing and accommodation down to as little as $50 per day per person.

A full-day **ski lesson** is $42 for beginners, $65 experienced, including lift tickets and gear rental, while snowboarding costs $49 and $72 respectively. There's a lower age limit of 13 for skiing and none for boarding. Ninety-minute group clinics are also available for $30 for both skiing and boarding, and private lessons cost $75 for 90 minutes, with each additional person (up to four) paying $30 or $115 for three hours (additional person $40). Children age 7–12 are catered for with beginners' packages costing $39; more experienced skiers will pay $44. Ski and board **rentals** from the Winter Sports Center at the mountain's base are a reasonable $18 per day for skis, boots, and poles ($21 shaped skis, $35 high-performance package) and $35 per day for snowboards and bindings.

Accommodation

Most of the **accommodation** in Red Lodge is conveniently situated on the town's main street, Broadway, thus putting most bars and restaurants within easy walking distance.

Bear Bordeaux 302 S Broadway ☎406/446-4408. A lovingly decorated downtown B&B with bright, colorful rooms that have great mountain views. There's a hot tub, filling breakfasts, and an enormous video library (each room has a VCR). ❹
Chateau Rouge 1505 South Broadway ☎406/446-1601 or 1-800/926-1601, ✆www .chateaurouge.com. Spacious but cozy alpine-style one-room studios with kitchenettes and queen

beds, and two-floor, two-bedroom condo apartments with kitchens and fireplaces which can sleep four (or more at a squeeze). There's also an indoor pool, hot tub, and free continental breakfast. ❺
Comfort Inn 612 N Broadway ☎1-888/733-4661. Decent-sized rooms with cable TV and dataports. Extras include a free continental breakfast, indoor pool, hot tub, and guest laundry, although you still

get pretty much the standard chain motel atmosphere. Located at the south end of town within walking distance of downtown. ❺

The Pollard Hotel 2 N Broadway ☎406/446-0001 or 1-800/678-8946, ⓦpollardhotel.com. Built back in 1893, this is one of Montana's finest and most historic hotels and Red Lodge's first brick building. Local heroes like Buffalo Bill and Frederick Remington used to spend the night here before the hotel fell into disrepair. Renovated in the early 1990s to a high standard, it includes extras such as bathrobes, private balconies, and good mountain views from some of the rooms. The lounge and bar – roaring fire, oak paneling and worn leather chairs – are pure Montana class. *Greenlea's*, the hotel's restaurant, is also excellent (see p.000). ❺

Red Lodge Inn 811 S Broadway ☎406/446-2030. Plain but clean rooms within walking distance of downtown. There's also an indoor pool. ❹

Rock Creek Resort Five miles south of town on US-212 ☎406/446-1111 or 1-800/667-1119. At Red Lodge's fanciest resort, you can choose between staying in log-and-stone lodge, or in condos set among private grounds. Heaps of facilities including a restaurant, indoor pool, health club, tennis, horseback riding, and mountain biking. Decent ski packages are often offered. ❻

Willows Inn 224 S Platt Ave ☎406/446-3913. A Victorian B&B with five attractive rooms decorated with period furniture, located one block east of Broadway. There are also three six-person guest cottages with kitchens on the same lot for similar rates. ❺

Yodeler Motel 601 S Broadway ☎406/446-1435, ⓦwww.yodelermotel.com. Clean, comfortable rooms in an alpine-style building, within walking distance of downtown. A large outdoor hot tub, dataports, and cable TV add value. ❹

Eating

The majority of Red Lodge's **restaurants** and **bars** are strung along Broadway Avenue, which makes for a fairly lively scene in the evenings. Still, the only time the town really goes off is at holiday weekends or during a major event.

Bogart's 11 S Broadway ☎406/446-1784. A family restaurant serving a wide range of sandwiches, complimented by good pizzas and Mexican food, for around $10–12 per head. Nonsmoking.

Greenlea's *Pollard Hotel* ☎406/446-0001. The classiest dining downtown, *Greenlea's* features wood-grilled steaks, a fine wild mushroom risotto, delicious fresh-baked breads, and superb desserts, plus a lengthy wine list. Entrees will set you back around $25.

P.D. McKinney's 407 S Broadway ☎406/446-

1250. It doesn't look too stylish from outside, but you can get a good-value filling breakfast or diner-style lunch here – try the breakfast omelets which should keep you going for most of the day.

Red Lodge Pizza Company 123 S Broadway ☎406/446-3933. A great combination pizzeria and brewhouse with one of the largest ranges of beers in town. On Mondays and Tuesdays there's an "eat all you can" salad and pizza bar for $7.95; the rest of the week expect to pay $11.95 upwards for a large pizza. Nonsmoking.

Bars and entertainment

Red Lodge's bars provide a lively and friendly taste of traditional Montana, but don't expect anything in the way of dance clubs or big-name bands performing.

Bear Creek Saloon Seven miles east on Hwy-308 ☎406/446-3481. Any bar that has pig racing as well as Montana's first "velcro wall" has got to be worth a visit. Decent bar food (charbroiled steaks, burgers, seafood, and chicken breast sandwiches) and a good-natured, beer-swilling atmosphere make for a memorable experience.

The Bull 'n Bear 19 N Broadway. A no-frills establishment where you can see local bands and real cowboys crowding the bar.

Snow Creek Saloon 124 S Broadway. This always-busy bar is a popular après-ski joint with locals and visitors alike, making for a fine and unostentatious place to sink a beer.

Other activities and attractions

The **Red Lodge Winter Carnival** has a different theme each year (☎406/446-2610). Locals and visitors take part in such wacky races as the

Cardboard Classic, in which snow craft made only of cardboard, tape, and glue hurtle down the mountain. Every March the **National Ski-Joring Finals** take place in which more than 100 competitors on skis are pulled by galloping horses around an oval course. There's **cross-country skiing** and **snow-shoeing** at Red Lodge Nordic Center (☎406/446-9191), located two miles west of town on Hwy-78. Here you'll find 15km of groomed trails, full rental facilities, and a yurt in which to relax and refresh afterwards.

Listings

Avalanche report ☎406/446-2610.
Bookshop Broadway Bookstore, 13 S Broadway ☎406/446-2742.
Internet Red Mountain Library, 8th/Broadway (Tues–Sat 1–6pm) Free ☎406/446-1405.
Medical Beartooth Hospital & Health Center, 600

W 21st St ☎406/446-2345.
Pharmacy Red Lodge Drug, 101 S Broadway ☎406/446-1017.
Post office 119 S Hauser ☎406/446-2629.
Road conditions ☎406/252-2806.

Grand Targhee

Grand Targhee on the Wyoming/Idaho border is far less daunting than its rugged neighbor Jackson Hole, but that doesn't seem to dampen people's expectations. It's easy to understand why the myth of Targhee's severity spreads, as long-range snapshots of the resort undoubtedly focus on the bulky, jagged Grand Teton peak that overshadows the slopes, towering up 13,800ft in the background and blotting out much of the horizon. However, a quick peek at the trail map and the actual skiable terrain reveals an abundance of wide-open blues spilling down the mountain, along with a substantial green web of runs by the base. To be sure some terrain is suitable for advanced riders only, but this is not a mountain for show-offs or adrenaline-crazed kamikazes looking to break the sound barrier. Plain and simple, the thrills here are all about blasting through powder, an arcing spray of snow behind you and large swathes of untouched terrain ahead.

As the "Snow From Heaven, Not From Hoses" bumper stickers throughout the Teton Valley affirm, powder is this resort's strongest attribute. In an average year over forty feet of fresh powder falls, while in an amazing season sixty feet come down. Even with these impressive figures, the slopes remain blissfully secluded, though with a lift and terrain expansion program in the

Mountain info

Phone ☎307/353-2300 or 1-800/827-4433
Snow phone ☎1-800/827-4433 ext 1352
Website ⊛www.grandtarghee.com
Price $47
Operating times Dec to mid-April daily 9am–4pm
No. of lifts 4
Base elevation 8000′
Summit elevation 10,000′
Vertical drop 2000′
No. of trails 40
Acreage 2000
Beginner 10%
Intermediate 70%
Expert 20%
Average snowfall 500″
Snowmaking Minimal
Night skiing No
Nursery facilities Kid's Club, ages 2 months to 5 years, ☎307/353-2300 ext 1326

works thing may not stay so quiet for long. The only other group besides locals and the powder-hound contingency that seems to have already caught on are families, who take advantage of the affordable prices, quality ski school, and kids-ski-free programs.

Remarkably enjoyable for its unpretentious nature and plentiful powder days, its not all good news at Grand Targhee. For starters, when storms get hung up on the surrounding peaks, they also wreak havoc on visibility, and it's possible to vacation in "Grand Foghee," as locals sometimes call it, for several days and never see the towering Tetons above. Off-slope activities are minimal, as Jackson, weather permitting, is 45 minutes away. The nightlife scene is meager at best and nearby **Driggs**, Targhee's closest town base twelve miles away across the border in Idaho, has few options.

Arrival, information, and getting around

Located just inside the Wyoming border though accessible only via Idaho's Hwy-33, Grand Targhee's isolated location means there's no quick and fast way to get here. By **air**, the two closest options are the Jackson Hole airport forty miles away (see p.239), or the airport in Idaho Falls ninety miles away, which is serviced by SkyWest (℡1-800/221-1212) and Horizon (℡1-800/547-9308). Shuttles from Idaho Falls Regional Airport are run by Alltrans (℡307/733-3135; $30–85 depending on group size), while rental car offices here include Avis (℡208/522-4225 or 1-800/897-8448) and Hertz (℡208/529-3101 or 1-800/654-3131). A daily round-trip **shuttle bus service** from Jackson and Teton Village to the resort is run by Targhee Express, leaving Jackson Hole at 7–8am depending on your location and returning at 4.15pm; reservations are required by 9pm the night before (℡307/734-9754; $20, or pay $60 with lift ticket).

The Teton Valley Chamber of Commerce is located over in Driggs at 81C Main St (Mon–Fri 9.30am–3.30pm; ℡208/354-2500, ⓦwww.tetonvalley chamber.com). As there's **no public transportation**, a car is necessary if you're planning on exploring anywhere outside the resort. Driggs' R&S Auto Rentals, 180 N Main St (℡208/354-2297), has a limited selection of cars for rent.

The mountain

Except for the frequent times when low-lying clouds blot out nearly all visibility, getting a handle on Grand Targhee's layout is a breeze. Of the two peaks, **Fred's Mountain** has longer liftlines – perhaps a pair of skiers in front of you as opposed to none. The 1500 acres here are accessed via the Shosone (quad), Blackfoot (double), and Dreamcatcher (quad) lifts, the latter riding to Fred's peak at 10,000ft. Thanks to Teton Vista Traverse, a long green that curls its way down from the top, everyone save for absolute first-timers can ride up Dreamcatcher to enjoy some of the finest views of the Tetons.

Grand Targhee's second peak, **Peaked Mountain** (pronounced "Peak-ed"), has undergone recent changes. It was formerly reserved for guided snowcat skiing but the addition of the Sacajawea quad opened up 500 glade-filled acres for the common man. Around 1000 acres are still set aside for the snowcats, though the resort's master plan calls for the addition of more lifts and even a day lodge, meaning the days of exclusive snowcat terrain may be numbered. Until more lifts are added, boarders especially should take note that the traverse from Peaked back to the base area requires lots of speed to clear without stalling out.

As far as **off-piste terrain** goes, the mountain's backside, completely out-of-bounds and accessed via a short hike up to Mary's Nipple, is a thrilling expert-only zone lined with massive cliffbands; over the years, several top ski film companies have shot riders testing the limits of sanity here. If you'd like to get a look, hire one of the local guide companies listed in the box below.

Beginner

Though absolute beginners may find themselves heading down the same few trails and riding the same lift all day, Grand Targhee's secluded slopes and top-notch ski school make this a good resort to learn the sport. From the base area, the four-person Shoshone lift heads up some 400ft to access the **Beginner Area**, home to a half-dozen unnamed greens. Besides these, the only other green run is the winding top-to-bottom **Teton Vista Traverse**, accessed via Dreamcatcher – bring a camera for some majestic snaps or you'll be kicking yourself the whole way home. After comfortably riding these greens, check the daily grooming report and head for any of the groomed blues; all should be broad enough for even the widest of turns.

Intermediate

Save for a few especially steep and rocky areas, nearly all of Grand Targhee's in-bound terrain is suitable for intermediate riders. The best place to get your bearings is the wide, typically groomed blues like **Wild Willie** and **Sweetwater** on Fred's Mountain and Peaked's **Dreamweaver**. After that, step up to steeper runs such as **Floyd's Fantasy**, whose precipitous pitch straight down the fall line allows for maximum speeds. If looking to push through some powder, head for the Blackfoot double and run laps down **Blackfoot Bowl** and the barely defined **Lost Warrior** blue/black run, keeping an eye out for powder stashes in the wide, tree-studded face in-between. Thanks in part to the creaky double lift, this area on the resort's northern edge is the place to come when everything else is tracked out.

Expert

When it really dumps scoring fresh tracks all day should take your mind off the lack of super insane faces. The steepest in-bound blasts are the **Patrol** and **Instructor** chutes atop Fred's Mountain. A bit more dicey are the snow-safety control areas that contain **The Good**, **The Bad**, and **The Ugly**, as well as

Snowcat skiing and local backcountry options

Though slowly shrinking in size as the resort's in-bounds terrain grows, the upper reaches of Peaked Mountain are still home to around 1000 acres of mainly steep, wide-open terrain set aside exclusively for **snowcat skiing**. As the resort's program runs only when conditions merit firing up the snowcats, you're nearly guaranteed a spectacular, powder-filled experience. If booked for a full day, expect seven to ten runs on nearly 2500ft of vertical – obviously you'll want to be in good shape before signing on. Reservations are required at least a day before; a full day (lunch included) is $275 per person, a half-day $200 (☏1-800/827-4433 ext 1355).

If looking to head further afield into true **backcountry** terrain, including nearby Teton Pass (see p.242) and Grand Teton National Park, there are two good local **guide companies**. Besides guided tours, Yostmark Backcountry Tours, in Driggs (☏208/354-2828, ⊛www.yostmark.com), offers telemark and split board rentals and avalanche courses. Rendezvous Tours, in Alta on 1110 Alta North Rd (☏1-877/754-4887, ⊛www.skithetetons.com), does much the same along with overnight hut-to-hut tours, where guests camp out in one of several high-altitude yurts. Check both companies' websites for further details and prices.

the double blacks on Peaked's northern face. Grab a ski patroller atop the Sacajawea chair and ask to be pointed to the legendary **Das Boot** run hereabouts – but keep in mind that a good-sized cliff lies below and this is truly experts-only stuff. Another option, when the gates are open, is the fifteen-minute hike up to **Mary's Nipple** from the top of Dreamcatcher; backcountry rules are in effect, so don't go it alone and check in with the patrollers before heading up.

Those searching for tree runs need to look low on the mountain – the best place to dig around are the clumps of pines off Peaked's slashing **Shadow Woman**. Last, but certainly not least, expert skiers with a bit of cash to burn should seriously consider a day in Peaked's guided **snowcat skiing** area (see box on p.233).

Freestyle

With no purpose-built park or halfpipe, it takes a bit of searching to find Targhee's best freestyle spots. For guaranteed air scope out the down-right frightening cornice drop leading into **The Good**, **The Bad**, and **The Ugly** areas accessed off the Dreamcather lift. **Lady's Waist**, reached via the same lift, is a natural halfpipe that's likewise worth exploring.

Lift tickets, lessons, and rentals

Offering great bang for the buck, Grand Targhee's **lift tickets** run around $50 for an all-day pass, with decent savings of a few dollars daily on multiday rates. Kids' and seniors' tickets are closer to $30 per day, though keep in mind that with the resort's ski-and-stay packages one child (14 and under) per parent skies for free. True beginners and those unaccustomed to carving through powder should take advantage of the resort's well-respected **ski school**, home to some of the best powder skiing instructors in North America. Group rates begin at $35, while private lessons run $60 an hour ($30 each additional person). The ski school also offers lessons in the art of telemarking.

As for **rentals**, the resort's own ski and board rental shops – Edge Pro Shop and Phat Fred's – have a decent selection of gear. Down in Driggs, skiers can get better equipment at Peaked Sports, 70 E Little Ave (☎208/354-2354), while boarders should stop in at Big Hole Sports, 65 S Main St (☎208/354-2209), whose line includes Ride, Sims, and Lib Tech. Telemark skis and splitboard rentals are available at Yostmark Mountain Equipment, also in Driggs at 12 E Little Ave (☎208/354-2828).

Accommodation

If it's five-star **accommodation** you're after, think about visiting a different resort. Grand Targhee has around a hundred rooms spread across a trio of handy, if unspectacular, slopeside lodges, while the rest of the decidedly plain options are sprinkled along the access road and Driggs' main drag. Those staying at the resort get access to a gym, outdoor pool, and huge hot tub – plus the chance to be first in line on a powder day – while those closer to Driggs have slightly better eating and drinking options nearby. For a home or condominium, check with Grand Valley Lodging (☎1-800/746-5518, ⊛www.grandvalleylodging.com), who manage affordable properties sleeping from four to twenty a night. Note that the resort offers a range of **ski-and-stay packages** for as low as $225 per person for three days/three nights; see the resort website for details.

Grand Targhee Resort

Sioux Lodge ☎208/353-2300 or 1-800/827-4433. Featuring a large portrait on Shoshone Chief Targhee on one outside wall, this condo-style lodging is the best slopeside deal if in a group, with studios, lofts, and two-bedroom units, all with full kitchens, that sleep two to eight people. ❾

Targhee Lodge ☎208/353-2300 or 1-800/827-4433. The sixteen basic motel-style rooms, which all have two queen beds, are decent if rather overpriced. The draw is the convenient ski-in/ski-out access. ❻

Teewinot Lodge ☎208/353-2300 or 1-800/827-4433. Like Targhee's other two lodges, the best feature here is the location. It too is a bit pricey, though the 46 units here are more opulent, each furnished in a Western theme with lodgepole pine furniture and two queen beds. Facilities include a guest lounge with fireplace and a small indoor hot tub. ❻

Driggs and around

Best Western Teton West 476 N Main St ☎208/354-2363 or 1-800/528-1234. Though characterless, the forty standard motel chain rooms here are clean and comfortable and there's also an indoor pool and hot tub. Located about one mile north of Targhee turn-off. ❹

Intermountain Lodge 34 Ski Hill Rd ☎208/354-8153. Conveniently located on the road to Grand Targhee, the *Intermountain* has a collection of basic two-bed log cabins with kitchens that can squeeze up to four, along with six smaller rooms with single queen beds and a microwave. The hot tub here is great after a day on the slopes, as is the on-site coin laundry. All rooms have cable TV, and the office rents out VCRs and movies as well. ❹

Pines Motel Guest Haus 105 S Main ☎208/354-2774 or 1-800/354-2778. Attractive rooms in a c.1900 log cabin on Driggs's main drag. Some rooms share bathrooms, and there's a hot tub and an ice skating rink on site. For $10 extra you get breakfast too. ❹

Teton Teepee Lodge 470 West Alta Rd, Alta ☎307/353-8176 or 1-800/353-8176, ⊛www.tetonteepee.com. In the hamlet of Alta, between Driggs and the resort, this handsome, teepee-like structure divides between plain guestrooms circled around a large common area and two bare-bone male and female dorm rooms downstairs. A communal experience, rates include fine family-style breakfasts and dinners, as well as shuttle trips to the slopes. Other extras include a top-notch game room and TV lounge, on-site ski shop (demo rentals available), tuning bench, and a large outdoor hot tub. Three-night minimum. ❹

Eating and drinking

Eating out in and around Driggs is a simple affair. Choices are limited to the affordable **restaurants** strung along or just off Main Street, plus a couple of spots in Victor, a short drive south of town. The **nightlife** situation is a sadder tale; unless there's a happening band playing at the *Knotty Pine*, choices are limited to beers at the *Royal Wolf* and the après-ski scene at the resort. If stocking up on **supplies**, Barrels & Bins at 36 S Main St (Mon–Sat 9am–7pm) has a fine selection of health foods, while Broulim's next door is a run-of-the-mill supermarket (Mon–Sat 7am–11pm).

There's even less choice when it comes to eating and drinking in Grand Targhee. The moderate-to-expensive menu at the *Targhee Steakhouse* includes filet mignon ($24) and grilled salmon ($18) at night, and the breakfast buffet is a good choice ($10). The cheaper option is *Snorkel's Bistro*, with a simpler menu including pizzas ($14) and grilled sourdough panninis ($8). The most original dining option is the sleigh ride dinner ($32; reservations required on ☎307/353-2300 ext 1355), where grilled meats are served up in a forest-enclosed yurt. Back at the base, the *Trap Bar* is where everyone staying at the resort gathers at the end of the day to knock down $10 pitchers and blood-warming drinks like a "Chocolate Fog," a potent hot cocoa and brandy concoction, to the beat of frequent country and blues performances.

Bunk House Bistro 285 N Main St ☎208/354-3770. The best bet for a filling start to the day, the friendly *Bunk House* serves huge portions of "cowboy cuisine" 7am–2pm daily, with dinners on Fri and Sat only. A mean huevos rancheros is the star of the expansive breakfast menu, while lunch features wraps, quesadillas, and the like.

Knotty Pine 58 S Main St, Victor ☎208/787-2866.

Rustic establishment with separate bar and dining-room menus; top choice is the full rack of ribs, which will set you back around $15. After dinner, the *Pine* – which holds the valley's sole full-liquor licence – turns into the region's top live-music venue; call ahead to find out what bands are on tap. Daily 4pm–close.

Latino's Delight 190 N Main St. Though it's far from fancy this small café with spotted vinyl booths serves authentic Mexican food – and $5 goes a long way toward a filling meal. The *flautas* are especially good. Daily 6am–10pm.

Miso Hungry Café 165 N Main St ☎208/354-8015. Colorful café with a hippyish vibe that's the best place in town to whittle away an hour over a cappuccino or glass of fresh juice. As far as vittles go, breakfast options include oatmeal, waffles, and breakfast burritos, while lunch choices include homemade soups and tofu noodle bowls ($6). Open for dinner on Fridays only (6–9pm), when a filling vegetarian option is typically served. Mon–Fri 7.30am–5.30pm, Sat 8am–3pm, closed Sun.

Royal Wolf Depot St ☎208/354-836. One block west of Main Street, this excellent smoke-free bar, serving up a great array of pub grub, from burgers to seafood, with a few entrees topping out over $15. Nearly a dozen microbrews on tap help keep things lively, though no hard liquor is served. Daily 4pm–close.

Tony's Pizza 364 N Main St ☎208/354-8829. Hand-tossed pizzas are the specialty at this pizzeria, notable for the antique gondola hanging out front. A short menu of pastas and calzones, along with wine and local beers, rounds out the menu. Delivery available after 5pm. Daily 4–10pm.

Victor Emporium 45 N Main St, Victor ☎208/787-2221. This classic general store/soda fountain on Victor's main drag is a must stop for milkshakes, including locally grown huckleberry and raspberry varieties. Closed Tues.

Other activities and attractions

The resort has limited activities to occupy your time, save for skiing. Near the base area is a mainly-for-kids **tubing park**, which opens daily at 5pm, and a free **ice-skating rink** (open daily; rentals $5). The resort also has a 15km **Nordic skiing center** (☎307/353-2300 ext 1352; trails pass $10), a **dog sledding** program (☎307/353-2300 ext 1355; $115), and free guided **snow-shoe** tours of the surrounding Targhee National Forest – for which a minimum group of three is needed (☎307/353-2300 ext 1352; rentals $12). Those looking for less adventurous pursuits can happily spend quality time at the on-site **spa**, offering up a wide array of massages, wraps, salt scrubs, and the like (open daily; ☎307/353-2300 ext 1358).

If you're in search of more cosmopolitan pursuits you'll need to head to Jackson (see opposite).

Listings

Avalanche hotline ☎307/733-2664.
Bookstore Dark Horse Books, 76 N Main St, Driggs (Mon–Sat 9–6pm, Sun 9–2pm).
Library Alta Library, 469 W Alta Rd, Alta (Mon & Fri 1–5pm, Tues & Thurs 11am–8pm, Wed 11am–5pm).

Pharmacy Corner Drug, cnr of Main Street and access road (Mon–Sat 9.30am–6.30pm, closed Sun).
Road conditions ☎800/827-4433.

Jackson Hole

Our mountain is like nothing you have skied before! It is huge, with variable terrain from groomed runs to dangerous cliff areas and dangerously variable weather and snow conditions. You must always exercise extreme caution. You could become lost. You could make a mistake and suffer personal injury or death. Protect yourself – understand the trail map and ask questions before you proceed. Obey all trail signs and markers. Please think and be careful. Give this special mountain the respect it demands!

sign posted at top and bottom of the Tram, Jackson Hole

At most other resorts, a warning such as this would be sheer hyperbole or even fear mongering, but at **Jackson Hole**, it's fact. This *is* a special mountain, arguably the best in the country for confident intermediates and advanced skiers and boarders to challenge themselves on run after run. Fifty percent of the terrain is rated experts-only, and its huge vertical drop (4139ft) lags behind only Big Sky, Montana, and Whistler/Blackcomb, British Columbia, in North America – many a slider has stepped up to the slopes cocky and over-confident only to be left quickly humbled. Respect both the slopes and your abilities, though, and you'll have a field-day on the potent mixture of terrain, from silky groomers and deep powderfields to precipitous bowls and unpatrolled backcountry – just don't expect to wake up feeling pain-free the next morning.

The area around Jackson Hole is breathtaking. Wyoming's Grand Teton and Yellowstone national parks are just to the north, and some 97 percent of rugged Teton County is federally owned or state managed, a majority of it untrammeled wilderness; one highlight of a visit here is taking time away from the slopes for some close-up views of the soaring Tetons and the wildlife in the parks. Less inspiring is the hodgepodge cluster of Western lodges and alpine chalets that make up **Teton Village**, the resort's continually expanding base area. Only a fifteen-minute drive to the southeast, though, is the energetic town of **Jackson**, centered around a Western-style town square that's jammed full of park-visiting tourists during the summer months and blissfully calm during the far more relaxed winter season.

Opened in 1965, the resort has changed much in the past decade. On top of a much-needed lift system upgrade including the addition of an eight-person gondola in 1997, the base village has grown rapidly, with new day lodges, condos, and resorts popping up yearly, including the recent arrival of a *Four Seasons*. Not that this should worry purists too much: it's still good value, and the mountain itself – save for a bit more grooming here and there – remains as rough and brutally honest as ever.

Mountain info

Phone ☎ 307/733-2292
Snow phone ☎ 307/733-2291
Website ⊛ www.jacksonhole.com
Price $60
No. of lifts 10, including an aerial tram and eight-person gondola
Base elevation 6311′
Summit elevation 10450′
Vertical drop 4139′
No. of trails 76
Acreage 2500
Beginner 10%
Intermediate 40%
Expert 50%
Average snowfall 402″
Snowmaking Minimal (about 150 acres)
Night skiing No
Nursery facilities Cody House, Teton Village, ☎ 307/739-2691; 2 months to 3 years, plus ski programs for older kids

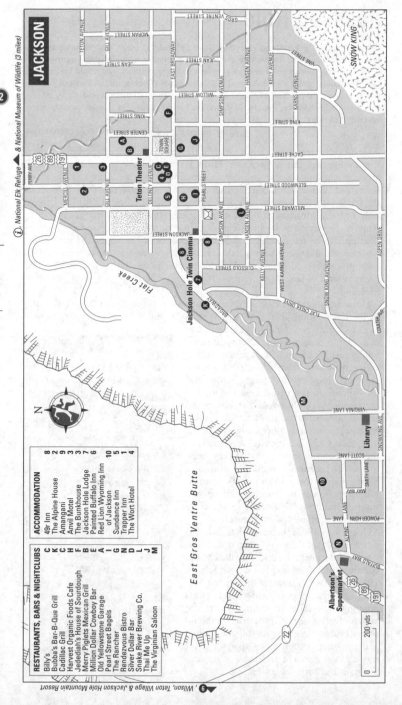

JACKSON

SNOW KING

Flat Creek

Teton Theater

Jackson Hole Twin Cinema

East Gros Ventre Butte

Library

Albertson's Supermarket

RESTAURANTS, BARS & NIGHTCLUBS	
Billy's	C
Bubba's Bar-B-Que Grill	K
Cadillac Grill	H
Harvest Organic Foods Cafe	F
Jedediah's House of Sourdough	B
Merry Piglets Mexican Grill	E
Million Dollar Cowboy Bar	A
Old Yellowstone Garage	I
Pearl Street Bagels	G
The Rancher	N
Rendezvous Bistro	D
Silver Dollar Bar	L
Snake River Brewing Co.	J
Thai Me Up	M
The Virginian Saloon	

ACCOMMODATION	
49r Inn	8
The Alpine House	2
Amangani	9
Anvil Motel	3
The Bunkhouse	3
Jackson Hole Lodge	7
Painted Buffalo Inn	6
Red Lion Wyoming Inn of Jackson	10
Sundance Inn	5
Trapper Inn	1
The Wort Hotel	4

Arrival, information, and local transport

Jackson Hole is slightly off the beaten path. The closest major city, Utah's Salt Lake City, is a five-hour drive away, which is why many out-of-state visitors **fly** into tiny Jackson Hole Airport, ten miles north of town. United, American, Continental, Northwest, and SkyWest all service the airport during the winter months, and landing on the runway within Teton National Park is a breathtaking experience. Check to see if your accommodation will pick you up; if not, taxis cost $20 into Jackson, $30 to Teton Village. While not as convenient, it's often cheaper to fly into Salt Lake City's international airport (see p.259); from there, Jackson Hole Express (⊕307/733-1719 or 1-800/652-9510, ⓦwww.jacksonholebus) runs two **shuttles** a day for around $50.

Useful only for those planning to spend time off the slopes, the helpful **Jackson Hole and Greater Yellowstone Visitor's Center** (daily 9am–5pm; ⊕307/733-3316, ⓦwww.jacksonholechamber.com) is at 532 N Cache St. Your best source for up-to-date information is the free *Jackson Hole Daily*.

Though not absolutely necessary, **renting a car** can make getting around a whole lot easier, especially if you're thinking about visiting the nearby national parks; agents in Jackson include major chains like Alamo, Avis, Budget, National, and Thrifty (see p.26 for contact info), plus Eagle (⊕307/739-999 or 1/800-582-2128). If sticking to public transport, the local START **bus** network (6am–11pm; $2, free within town; ⊕307/733-4521, ⓦwww.startbus .com) runs frequent services from several spots in town to Teton Village. **Taxi** services include AllTrans (⊕307/733-3135) and Teton Village Taxi (⊕307/732-2221). If heading to **Grand Targhee** (see p.231), a must-do if staying for a week or more, Targhee Express buses head off between 7–8am; reservations are required by 9pm the night before (⊕307/734-9754; $20, or $60 with lift ticket).

The mountain

Jackson Hole may be one of the few resorts around wild enough to attract the occasional moose foraging on its slopes, but you should save your wildlife spotting for the lifts; you'll have plenty of other natural obstacles – namely boulders, sudden drop-offs, glades, and the like – to worry about while skiing.

The mountain is divided into three areas; starting from right to left on the trail map there's **Apres Vous Mountain**, the **Casper Bowl** area, and the much-vaunted **Rendezvous Mountain**, each offering progressively more difficult terrain. Save for the two short quads that run from the cluster of condos on the resort's northern end, all of Jackson Hole's base lifts leave from the same general area in the Village, making moving about the slopes a simple affair. The most popular lift is the **Tram**, where it's common for first-track fanatics to begin lining up as early as three hours before opening on a powder day. It takes just over ten minutes to haul 63 passengers up 4139 vertical feet, dropping them off at the spectacular, wind-blown summit of Rendezvous Mountain (10,450ft), below which a free-riding nirvana awaits. The speedier eight-person **Bridger Gondola** drops off its passengers below Casper Bowl, and is well worth sticking to on the days when the line for the Tram is out-of-hand. It takes two quads to ride to the peak of the mountain's final chunk, Apres Vous Mountain (8481ft), one reason why this portion of Jackson Hole is relatively under-skied. That makes it a good bet on busy days – especially **Saratoga Bowl**, which hides powder stashes after the rest of the mountain is ridden out.

Beyond the resort's five boundary gates lies some of finest accessible **back-country** skiing and riding on earth; expert sliders should seriously think about giving it a look, but only after taking the necessary precautions; see the box on p.242 for more.

Beginner

Jackson Hole is not a good place for **beginners**. While there are a half-dozen bunny slopes near the base area suitable for never-evers and younger kids, there's very little terrain for the next step up. Only ten percent of the resort's runs are suitable for beginners, all of which can be accessed via the base area's Eagle's Nest double and Teewinot quad, leading to somewhat log-jammed learning slopes during busier periods. After graduating from these two lifts, Apres Vous Mountain is the place to go – though keep in mind that some of the blues here could easily be rated blacks at less demanding resorts.

Intermediate

Intermediates are best off working their way across the mountain from right to left, beginning with Apres Vous Mountain. Stretching down from the top of the mountain's eponymous quad, both **Werner** and **Moran** are good places to loosen up, undulating nicely and leading down some of the most beautifully groomed corduroy on the mountain. Both runs are also worth returning to later in the day, once calf- and thigh-burn have ruled out the tougher stuff. After a few laps, cut across Apres Vous on the **Togwotee Pass** transfer to Casper Bowl's triple, which enters into some of the finest intermediate terrain at the resort. It's a bit dicier than Apres Vous, studded with sudden dips and pockets of trees, but is also home to groomers like **Easy Does It** and **Casper Lift Line**, both wide enough to attract the Casper Carvers, Jackson's dedicated alpine-boarders. The **Moran Woods**, rated black and located far to the left looking down atop the triple, is a superb spot to test out your tree riding skills. Once you're ready for a change, cruise down to the base and catch your breath – you're going to need it – riding up the Bridger Gondola. While options from atop the gondola are myriad, no trip would be complete without a nonstop, 3000ft top-to-bottom race down either **Gros Ventre** (pronounced "Grow Von") or **Sundance**, both spilling nearly straight down the fall line.

Unless you're only planning on taking a few photos and hitching back down, don't bother heading up the **Tram** without being certain of your skills. For a good test, head down the **Amphitheater Bowl** from the Gondola Summit to the Thunder quad. From the top of Thunder, pick your way down **Grand** to the Sublette quad, from which you'll be able to check out **Laramie Bowl** and the steep, double black **Alta Chutes** while riding up; if the former seems within the realm of possibility, knock yourself out. If not, head to your right off the lift down **Hanging Rock** to **Rendezvous Trail** for the long, snaking trip back to the base.

Expert

Rendezvous Mountain is the reason Jackson Hole is arguably the pre-eminent advanced ski area in North America. Though waits for the tram ride up can dampen spirits, the unforgettable vistas and routes down more than make up for it. On the ride up, look to your left when nearing the top for anyone attempting **Corbet's Couloir**, a 10–20ft cornice drop into a narrow, steep, and tree-choked no-fall zone. Though tackling Corbet's – or at least claiming to – is the benchmark for Jackson Hole bragging rights, the unmarked **S&S Couloir** next to it is even more difficult, requiring a visit to the ski patrol for approval first.

Unless you're dead set on cruising the heralded **Hobacks** first, a good strategy once up top is to ride only the top half of the mountain, running laps on Sublette and Thunder. On a powder morning, though, head straight for this justifiably famous corner of Jackson Hole, where nothing is off limits and some 2000 vertical feet of powder fields await. In less than pristine conditions, the Hobacks can get sketchy, loaded with icy bumps that boarders especially will want to avoid. The rest of Rendezvous is nearly as memorable. A laundry list of the finest marked areas include: the tree- and rock-free **Rendezvous Bowl** at the top, a wide and windy choose-your-own-adventure style bowl littered with big bumps; the steep, rock-strewn **Alta Chutes** (1, 2, & 3) leading into Laramie Bowl; and the **Cirque**, which after a storm holds onto snow like a catcher's mitt. Runs not on the trail map but worth asking around about include the **Toilet Bowl**, a double black run with big-air possibilities below Paint Brush, and **Paradise Lost**, a tricky, formerly off-limits gully between North Hoback and Lower Sublette. Tree skiers on Rendezvous should look to the skier's right of **Bivouac** and around **Bird In The Hand**, both off Cheyenne Bowl, for the best glades.

Areas beyond Rendezvous worth exploring include Moran Woods (see "Intermediate" above), the tree-studded line under the gondola, and **Saratoga Bowl** on Apres Vous's far side, a fine place to lose the crowds should there be any. An even better place to leave the others behind is the resort's immense 3000-acre-plus **backcountry**; as long as you're not solo and have the experience, heading out off-piste is a can't-miss opportunity (see box overleaf).

Freestyle

With all the steep thrills, natural pipes, and cliff jumps found across the mountain, you can't blame the resort for its half-hearted attempts at improving its terrain parks. Located toward the bottom of Apres Vous between Werner and Hanna, the park has a collection of mainly smaller hits used for the most part by younger riders, while the pipe, though short, is well maintained with 17ft high walls. Half the mountain over, **Dick's Ditch** (named for a patrolman who survived an hour-long avalanche burial here in 1966) and the unmarked **Dude's Ditch**, running above Dick's along the left side of Amphitheater, are two natural pipes whose do-it-yourself spirit seem more in line with Jackson's vibe. It's no secret that the biggest kickers exist out in the backcountry, mainly in Rock Springs Canyon; if you're looking for big air, befriend a local and beg for the insider scoop.

Lift tickets, lessons, and rentals

At over $60 a pop, **lift tickets** at Jackson Hole are not cheap, and savings through multiday packages are minimal – the only way you can really save are the ski-and-stay packages offered by Jackson Hole Central Reservations (☎1-800/443-6931). In response to the difficult nature of the slopes, Jackson Hole's respected **ski school**, founded by Olympic gold-medal skier Pepi Stiegler, offers up a wider range of programs than the average resort. Though not a recommended mountain for beginners, the school does offer the typical first-timer courses ($70), including Burton's Learn-To-Ride system for newbie boarders (see p.534 for more on this program) and a comprehensive kids' program. Beyond the basics, the school runs plenty of **clinics** for stronger intermediate and advanced riders looking to ratchet their skills up a notch. Other options include private lessons, where you can design your own itinerary (around $500 a day; up to five per group), and guided backcountry tours (see box overleaf).

Jackson Hole's backcountry

Few places in North America reward **backcountry** skiers and snowboarders as much as Jackson Hole. The resort's backcountry **gates** access merely a portion of the explorable off-piste areas in the Brider-Teton National Forest and Grand Teton National Park, but it's a wonderland of natural bowls, chutes, and thigh-burning runs up to 4000ft in length, if also extremely dangerous. Not a single inch is patrolled and deadly avalanches are not unheard off; during the 2000–2001 season, slides killed five people in Teton County. If you do not have a partner and the appropriate safety equipment and experience, don't even think about heading out here.

The most popular entry gate, atop Rendezvous Bowl, leads into Cody Bowl and Rock Springs Bowl, from where it's possible to ride back into the lower Hobacks. Hooking up with one of the resort's ski school backcountry **guides** (T307/739-2663 or 1-800/450-0477) is highly recommended. A full-day tour for a group up to five runs around $450, while a half-day for a similarly sized group costs $250–350. For more backcountry experience, the ski school's three-day backcountry **camp** ($500), run twice a year and covering safety equipment and etiquette along with plenty of off-piste exploring, is likewise worth investigating.

The ski school also offers guided trips into nearby **Teton Pass** (8429ft), one of the favorite local backcountry entry points. Accessed via a parking lot on Hwy-22 just west of Wilson, bootpack trails lead into a mountain playground of powder-packed bowls than can often be skied as late as June. A pair of well-respected outfits near Grand Targhee offer tours here (see box on p.233 for details), as does Jackson Hole Mountain Guides (T307/733-4979 or 1-800/239-7642, Wwww.jhmg.com), which also runs a wide range of tours and camps listed in detail on its website.

A final option, mainly for those who'd rather not earn-their-turns hiking up, is **heli-skiing** with High Mountain Heli-Ski Village (T307/733-3274, F307/733-3529, Wwww.heliskijackson.com), into the Snake River, Hoback, Teton and Gros Ventre mountain ranges. A day consists of six runs (10,000–15,000 vertical); stop into the office at the *Snake River Lodge* in Teton Village for full details.

However you choose to head out-of-bounds, check **current conditions** on T307/733-2664 or Wwww.untracked.com/forecast. A good local **shop** to pick up tips, safety gear, and maps in town is Gear Revival, 410 Pearl St (T307/739-8699).

To **rent** equipment in Teton Village, head for the Bridger Center; skiers can choose from K2, Rossignol, Salomon, and Atomic packages ($25–30) at JH Sports (T307/739-2690), while the Hole in the Wall Snowboard Shop (T307/739-2689) offers demo packages with, amongst other brands, the latest Burton, Salomon, and Lib Tech boards ($35). In Jackson, Hoback Sports, 40 S Milward (T307/733-5335, Wwww.hobacksports), carries a full range of quality skis and boards.

Accommodation

Jackson doesn't function like a ski town. During winter, in-town **accommodation** rates actually drop by up to thirty percent compared to the far busier summer season, when millions funnel through town en-route to Teton and Yellowstone national parks. The slopeside rates in Teton Village, though, remain much the same for both peak seasons. With good public transportation available, staying in town is a wise choice for those looking for a wider range of eating and drinking options, as well as those who want to save some cash – although Teton Village's *Hostel X* is an amazing deal by any standard. Whatever your plans, check first with Jackson Hole Central Reservations (T1-800/443-6931) as they can help arrange great **ski-and-stay packages** throughout the region. Both Jackson Hole Resort Lodging (☎307/733-3990 or 1-800/443-8613, ⓦwww.jhresortlodging.com) and Rendezvous Mountain Rental (☎307/739-9050 or 1-888/739-2565, ⓦwww.rmrentals.com) manage a full range of condos, townhouses, and such.

Jackson and around

49r Inn 330 W Pearl St ☎307/733-7550, ⓦwww.townsquareinns.com. This downtown motel is nothing fancy, but the rooms, decorated in a curious combination of rustic Western décor and standard motel fittings, are much larger than average. Extras include two very large hot tubs and a skimpy continental breakfast. A few two-room suites are available for larger groups. ❸

The Alpine House 285 N Glenwood St ☎307/739-1570 or 1-800/753-1421, ⓦwww.alpinehouse.com. Billed as a "Country Inn," the *Alpine House* offers B&B accommodation in a bright, cheerful 21-room house. Decked out in light-colored timber, the place has a Scandinavian feel, and rooms are well-appointed, right down to guest robes and slippers. Packages including ski passes or cross-country expeditions are good value. ❻

Amangani 1535 North East Butte Rd ☎307/734-7333, ⓦwww.amangani.com. The only US property of the renowned Indonesian Aman resort group, the *Amangani* vies with Teton Village's *Four Seasons* for most luxurious accommodation in the region. Housed in a gorgeous redwood and sandstone temple-like structure on a butte between town and the slopes, highlights include a heated cliffside pool, spa treatments, and windowside tubs in every suite. With rates *starting* at $700 a night, though, only those with money to burn need apply. ❾

Anvil Motel 215 N Cache St ☎307/733-3668, ⓦwww.anvilmotel.com. Situated at one of the busier intersections in town, it's not the quietest spot but is very central. Rooms are small, the interiors are in good shape (the motel was built in 1991), and the fridge and microwave in each room are a useful bonus. A bunker below the motel contains *The Bunkhouse*, one big joyless dorm space that's only worth considering if you're traveling solo. ❸

Jackson Hole Lodge 420 W Broadway ☎307/733-2992 or 1-800/604-9404, ⓦwww.jacksonholelodge.com. A range of units is available at this motel-lodge, located near the town center. The standard rooms are small with either one or two queen-size beds, while the studio and condo units all have full kitchen facilities and can sleep up to six people ($250). Guest amenities include heated indoor pool, two hot tubs and a sauna. ❺

Painted Buffalo Inn 400 W Broadway ☎307/733-4340 or 1-800/288-3866, ⓦwww.paintedbuffalo.com. Good value inn a few blocks from the town center, with facilities that are a cut above some of its neighbors. The 140 rooms have one or two queen beds, there's a large heated indoor pool and an on-site coffeeshop serving sandwiches and baked goods. ❹

Red Lion Wyoming Inn of Jackson 930 W Broadway ☎307/734-0035 or 1-800/844-0035, ⓦwww.wyoming-inn.com. One of the best in the upper mid-range market, the *Red Lion* is completely nonsmoking and includes free continental breakfast, laundry, and Internet access. There are coffeemakers in each of the 73 guest rooms, and suites all have a gas fireplace and hot tub; a huge log fireplace gives the lobby a cozy lodge feel, too. ❼

Sundance Inn 135 W Broadway ☎307/733-3444 or 1-888/478-6326, ⓦwww.sundanceinnjackson.com. Small, basic motel with a great central location. The owners are friendly and helpful, and there's a free continental breakfast included as well as a "social hour" (5–6pm) with hot drinks and homemade cookies. ❹

Trapper Inn 235 N Cache St ☎307/733-2648 or 1-800/341-8000. Central motel whose rooms have queen- or king-size beds (some with fridge) and amenities including small indoor and outdoor hot tubs and a guest laundry. ❹

The Wort Hotel 50 N Glenwood St ☎307/733-2190 or 1-800/322-2727, ⓦwww.worthotel.com. Built in 1941, this is Jackson's most venerable high-end property, combining old-world style with modern facilities that include two large hot tubs, a grill-bistro, and an attractive bar (see p.245). Rooms are furnished with enormous lodgepole pine beds and big TVs, and bathrooms have full-size tubs. ❼

Teton Village

The Alpenhof Lodge ☎307/733-3242 or 1-800/732-3244, ⓦwww.alpenhoflodge.com. Classic Tyrolean lodge which offers 42 handsomely appointed guest rooms, some with fireplaces and balconies. Extras include a heated outdoor pool and hot tub, sauna, ski shop, and laundry. There's a casual bistro as well as the *Alpenhof Dining Room* (see p.245). ❼

Best Western The Inn at Jackson Hole 3345 McCollister Dr ☎307/733-2311 or 1-800/842-7666, ⓦwww.innatjh.com. Standard three-star chain motel accommodation, offering 83 mid-size rooms with either one queen bed or two doubles, along with a few lofts. Amenities include heated outdoor pool and hot tubs, laundry, and on-site tuning shop and the village's only sushi restaurant. ❽

Four Seasons ☎1-888/402-7888, ⓦwww .fourseasons.com. The largest and newest slope-side structure is worth a peek even if not staying here, if just to check out the rough-hewn stones and native artifacts in the main lounge. Elegant suites come with marble bathroom counters and leather couches, while the heated outdoor pool, massive fitness center and spa, and full ski concierge services are all to be expected for nightly rates starting in the $500 range. ❾

Hostel X ☎307/733-3415, ⓦwww.hostelx.com. Excellent slopeside hostel accommodation, with a lounge with fireplace, TV and game room, ski lockers and tuning room, microwave oven (no kitchen),

coin-operated laundry, and a ping-pong and pool table. Each four-bunk room is rented as a unit, and usually requires a five-night minimum stay ($50 for one or two, $63 for three or four). There's also a few rooms with king-sized beds, and all rooms have private bathrooms.

Snake River Lodge and Spa 7710 Granite Loop Rd ☎307/732-6000, ⓦwww.snakeriverlodge.com. The attractive lobby, decorated with antler chandeliers, deep leather couches, and river rock fireplace, sets the tone for this ski-in/ski-out lodge, only a short step down the luxury ladder from the *Four Seasons* next door. Accommodations include deluxe queen- or king-bed rooms and even more luxurious one- to three-bedroom suites, all loaded with extras like goose-down comforters, cotton robes, and granite countertops. Guests get access to the onsite spa and the indoor/outdoor pool and hot tubs within. Rates include breakfast. ❾

Eating

Jackson's **restaurants** more or less divide between good-value family favorites and high-end eateries, with not too much in between. Most establishments are located within easy walking distance of Town Square and, regardless of price, have a generally laid-back vibe. As winter is the off-season in town, a good percentage of restaurants close early and are open for breakfast and lunch only.

Teton Village's **slopeside dining** breaks down in a similar manner. Along with the pricier options reviewed below, there's a decent range of smaller cafés – like *Bridger Bagels* in the Bridger Center and the *Village Café and Bar* in the Village Center – that offer affordable breakfasts and lunches.

Though future plans call for more restaurants on the slopes themselves, the current situation is a bit dire; the best options – cafés atop the tram and gondola – are notable mainly for the views.

Jackson

Billy's 55 N Cache St ☎307/733-3279. Connected to the much fancier *Cadillac Grill* (see below), this is a cheery place to sit on a barstool and tuck in to an enormous cheeseburger ($6 including fries) in a 1950s diner ambience. Daily for lunch and dinner.

Bubba's Bar-B-Que Grill 515 W Broadway ☎307/733-2288. Located a long walk (or short drive) west of town square, this is the best place in town to fill up on barbecued babyback ribs, sandwiches, burgers, and steaks, all at great value. It's also the premier locals' breakfast venue, so expect at least half an hour wait for a table on weekend mornings. A huge omelette with grits, biscuits, and coffee is around $5. Open 7am–9pm daily.

Cadillac Grill 55 N Cache St ☎307/733-3279. Fancy Art Deco restaurant on the main square, offering the same huge burgers as *Billy's* but also buffalo, wild boar, caribou, antelope, and seafood

entrees for $12–20. A two-for-one happy hour special (5–7pm) in the jazz bar helps pass the wait. Reservations recommended. Daily 11.30am–2pm & 5.30–10pm.

Harvest Organic Foods Cafe 130 W Broadway ☎307/733-5418. Health food store with a veggie counter in back. Menu items include garden burgers, tofu dishes, baked goods, gourmet sandwiches, and thick fruit smoothies. Eat in the small dining area or order to go. Daily 8am–6pm.

Jedediah's House of Sourdough 135 E Broadway ☎307/733-5671. The casual and inexpensive *Jedediah's*, famed for their fluffy sourdough pancakes, also serves massive egg platters as well as filling sandwiches at lunch. Daily 7am–2pm.

Merry Piglets Mexican Grill 160 N Cache ☎307/733-2966. Reliable and inexpensive Tex-Mex entrees ($9–12) go nicely with the restaurant's famed margaritas, which you can get by the "half-yard." Daily for lunch and dinner; takeaway also available.

Old Yellowstone Garage 175 Center St ☎307 /734-6161. One of Jackson's finest restaurants, offering flawless service and a (brief) northern Italian-themed menu which changes daily. Items often include rare elk tenderloin and roasted sweet pepper risotto (entrees $22–28), accompanied by a choice wine list. On Sunday night the menu is ditched altogether in favor of an all-you-can-eat pizza extravaganza ($15). Daily dinner only.

Pearl Street Bagels 145 W Pearl Ave. Fresh and tasty bagels, from tomato-herb to cinnamon-raisin, plus the finest cappuccinos in town. Daily 6.30am–6pm.

Rendezvous Bistro 380 S Broadway (next to Albertson's) ☎307/739-1100. Well-priced bistro which locals try to keep secret. Starters include a perfectly salted French Onion soup and fresh oysters. Mains range from simple fish and chips to lamb chops and ahi tuna, all of which are recommended. A good selection of bottled wine under $30 adds to the attraction. Mon–Sat 5.30–10pm.

Thai Me Up 75 E Pearl St ☎307/733-0005. Standards like Pad Thai alongside lots of interesting seafood variations as well as vegetarian/vegan selections (entrees $12–16) keep Jackson's best Thai restaurant busy. The food is fresh and well-presented and the service pretty quick too. Takeaway and delivery also available. Daily from 6pm.

Teton Village and around

Alpenhof Dining Room and Bistro *Alpenhof Lodge* ☎307/733-3462. Fine dining restaurant with an extensive wine list and a menu including Western exotica such as venison, buffalo, and elk along with continental standards like foie gras and duck confit (entrees $25–35). Meals at the lodge's bistro are more moderately priced ($10–15), and a large log fire lends a warm and cheerful ambience. Reservations advised.

Game Fish *Snake River Lodge* ☎307/732-6040. Pricey, but the eclectic Southwestern combinations – elk quesadillas, grilled trout with roast corn cakes, crispy rabbit with a cranberry compote – ensure a memorable dinner. Expect to pay around $70 for two, including drinks.

Masa Sushi *Best Western The Lodge at Jackson Hole* ☎307/733-2311. Standard sushi and sashimi menu in this cozy upstairs nook, a nice change from buffalo burgers. Prices are reasonable (two-piece sushi orders $3–4), and reservations advised. Closed Mon.

Nora's Fish Creek Inn 5600 W Hwy-22, in the nearby hamlet of Wilson ☎307/733-8288. Popular locals' spot for a huge, leisurely breakfast of pancakes or omelettes. Lunch and dinner menu features tasty prime rib, salmon, and trout along with homemade desserts, at moderate prices. Reservations advised especially on weekends.

Nightlife and entertainment

Up in Teton Village, the raucous *Mangy Moose* fills quickly once the lifts shut down, and the classier **bars** in the *Snake River* and *Alpenhof* lodges pull in those looking to sip wine rather than guzzle beer. In Jackson, the year-round tourist trade has made the town Wyoming's liveliest, but you need to know what's happening on which night as people tend to pack in to one or two places and abandon the rest. Check the free *Jackson Hole Daily* for details on bands and special happy hour sessions. Beyond pints and pool cues, Jackson has several central **cinemas**, including the single screen Teton Theater (☎307/733-4939) off Town Square and the Jackson Hole Twin Cinema, across the post office on Pearl Street.

Jackson

Million Dollar Cowboy Bar 25 N Cache Drive ☎307/733-2207. Cheesy it may be, but everyone who visits Jackson at least ducks in to this hugely touristy Western-themed watering hole, to sit on one of the saddles at the bar, get out on the dancefloor with the other self-conscious tourists, or even indulge in a little drunken karaoke. There are also four pool tables. Cover most nights $5. Daily noon until late.

The Rancher 20 E Broadway. There's nothing remotely stylish about this upstairs pool hall on Town Square, but it's the drinking venue of choice for a mostly younger crowd who lounge around the eight full-size tables downing $6 pitchers of Bud. Happy hour 4–7pm. Daily until late.

SilverDollar Bar *Wort Hotel*, 50 N Glenwood St. This is the closest thing to an upscale bar in town, but it's still pretty relaxed and casual; hosts mellow country bands, singers, and piano players of variable quality. The silver dollars embedded in the bar-top number 2032. No cover charge.

Snake River Brewing Co 265 South Millward ☎307/739-2337. Highly recommended brewpub

located several blocks southeast of Town Square and thus frequented mainly by locals. The pastas and wood-fired pizzas ($9–12) are well worth trying, but it's the award-winning and constantly rotating beer ($3.50 a pint) selection that packs 'em in. The afternoon happy hour – $2.50 pints and delicious jumbo pretzels for a buck – is an especially joyous occasion. No smoking. Daily noon–midnight
The Virginian Saloon *Virginia Lodge*, 750 W Broadway. Just your basic watering hole, but a good place to retire to for happy hour (4–7pm) and watch a game on the big-screen TV. Daily from noon until 11pm or midnight.

Teton Village and around
The Mangy Moose ☎307/733-9779. The *Moose*, liberally strewn with Western bric-a-brac, is

Jackson Hole's legendary ski-bum hangout, famed for its aprés-ski sessions that segue into rowdy evenings of live rock or reggae. The bustling upstairs dining room does decent burgers, chicken, and pasta, best chased down with a locally brewed Moose Juice Stout; the *Moose's Belly* downstairs dishes up a pretty ordinary $7 skiers' breakfast buffet. Cover charge for live bands $5–10. Daily from 11am until late.
Stagecoach Bar 5755 W Hwy-22, in the nearby hamlet of Wilson ☎307/733-4407. Worth the drive for its renowned Thursday "disco night" – for which you're encouraged to dress up – as well as Sunday's crowded "Church" sessions, an extremely popular open-mike affair. Pool tables, darts, and a jukebox provide the entertainment on other nights.

Other activities and attractions

The Old West wooden boardwalks surrounding Jackson's Town Square are lined with galleries, souvenir emporiums, and other tourist attractions that may divert you for a bit. Afterwards, drive the short distance north to the **Grand Teton National Park** (ⓦwww.nps.gov/grte; $20 per car) for some breathtaking views; if you stick to Hwy-191 you won't have to pay an entry fee. For information on exploring some of its hundreds of miles of trails on snowshoes or cross-country skis, stop in at the Moose Visitor Center (daily 8pm–5pm; ☎307/739-3399) a few miles north of the airport.

En-route to the park, you'll pass the elegant **National Museum of Wildlife Art** (daily 9am–5pm; $6; ⓦwww.wildlifeart.org) and, across the highway, the 25,000-acre **National Elk Refuge**, established in 1912 to protect the elk's winter range. With as many as 10,000 elk foraging here in winter, the photo opportunities are stupendous – the Teton Range towers in the background – especially on the sleigh rides through the refuge organized by the museum (daily 10am–4pm; $15; ☎307/733-5771).

Cross-country skiing and snowmobiling

The Jackson Hole Nordic Center (daily 8.30am–4.30pm; ☎307/739-2629) in Teton Village has several looping **cross-country skiing** trails of variable ability adding up to 17km in total. Trail fees are $8, rental packages range $18–22, and lessons are available. Far more impressive are the half- and full-day tours that the Nordic Center runs into Grand Teton National Park. Full-day tours run $160 for the first person, $40 for additional person, including lunch.

Skirmishes over recent leigslation and environmental impact studies mean **snowmobiling** opportunities may be up in the air, but if you're interested in the sport, you're not likely to find a more exhilarating locale. Currently, tours run by local outfitters include rides past buffalo and elk to Old Faithful in Yellowstone National Park (around $200 per driver, $80 for passenger); trips over Togwotee Pass (around $150 per driver, $75 for passenger), featuring great views and large meadows; and a Granite Hot Springs excursion that travels through Granite Canyon to 110-degree springs, where you can take a dip in a snow-rimmed pool before tucking into lunch (around $150 per driver, $75 for passenger). Companies to check with include Jackson Hole Mountain Tours

(☎307/733-6850 or 1-800/633-1733, ☜www.jacksonholesnowmobile.com) and High Country Tours (☎307/733-5017 or 1-800/524-0130).

Listings

Avalanche hotline ☎ 307/733-2664.
Banks Foreign exchange and 24-hour ATM access are available at Jackson State Bank, corner of Center St and Deloney Ave. Other ATMs include Bank of Jackson Hole, corner of Cache St and Broadway, and Community First, corner of Glenwood St and Pearl Ave.
Hospital St John's, 625 E Broadway ☎ 307/733-3636, has 24-hour emergency care.
Internet Teton County Library (see below) has a row of 15min access terminals which are free of charge and in high demand; expect a short wait.
Library Teton County Library, 125 Virginian Lane

(Mon–Thurs 10am–9pm, Fri 10am–5.30pm, Sat 10am–5pm, Sun 1–5pm; ☎307/733-2164).
Laundry Soap Opera, 835 W Broadway (daily 7am–10pm; ☎307/733-5584).
Pharmacy Inside Albertson's supermarket (see below).
Post office Jackson: 220 W Pearl Ave ☎307/733-3650 (Mon–Fri 7.30am–5.30pm); Teton Village: ☎307/733-3575 (Mon–Fri 9.30am–4pm).
Supermarket Albertson's, at the junction of Broadway and Hwy-22 (daily 6am–midnight; pharmacy hours Mon–Fri 9am–9pm, Sat 9am–7pm, Sun 10am–4pm).

The Best of the Rest

Bogus Basin, Idaho

A short drive north of Boise, the Bogus Basin Ski Area (9am–10pm; $37; ☎208/332-5100, ☜www.bogusbasin.com) is a welcome alternative to more glamorous Sun Valley; you can ride its 2600 acres of terrain all day and still have some change left over for a night out. The sixteen-mile drive in on Bogus Basin Road is an adventure in itself, with a seemingly endless array of switchbacks affording sensational views of Boise. With season passes for locals only $399 (and for kids an unbelievable $29), it can get quite busy on weekends, but it's a friendly atmosphere, and liftlines can be a chatty affair. The sixty-odd runs are rated twenty percent beginner, forty-five percent intermediate, and thirty-five percent advanced, served by seven lifts. Beginners should check out Nugget Cat Track and Easy Way Down, which give a good overall feel for the mountain. Intermediates will find a great selection of wide open runs such as Ridge and Playboy, and there are plenty of black diamonds, like Lower Nugget or Second Chance, if you want to push yourself a bit. There's also a terrain park with a nice selection of quarterpipes, rails, and jumps. A ski bus ($8 round-trip; ☎208/459-6612) operates weekends and holidays from various locations in Boise. The Bogus Creek Lodge, at the base of the mountain, is where you'll find the busy *Deerpoint Café*, ticket sales, and ski and board rental. Halfway up the mountain is the Pioneer Lodge, home to *Bogus Bob's Grill* and the *Firewater Bar*, where there's good pub grub and a deck with mountain views. The only on-mountain accommodation is at the well-appointed *Pioneer Inn Condominiums* (☎208/332-5200, ☜www.pioneercondos.com; ❻).

Bridger Bowl, Montana

Bridger Bowl Ski Area (☎406/587-2111 or 1-800/223-9609, snow report ☎406/586-2389, ☜www.bridgerbowl.com), twenty minutes north of Bozeman on Hwy-86, has a reputation for being an extreme skier's haven. This becomes immediately apparent at The Ridge, towering above the main slopes and accessed via a steep 500ft hike. You'll need to sign in with ski patrol and have an avalanche transceiver, shovel, and partner to ski or board it. Those who don't quite have the experience for this should head for the black diamonds in the North Bowl or the double blacks beneath The Nose, while intermediates will have a blast on steep Emil's Mile and on several beautiful cruisers through the open glades. Pretty much everything on the lower mountain is suitable for newbies. Typically open by early December, the 1240 skiable acres are serviced by seven lifts that access some 2000ft of vertical drop from a top elevation of 8700ft. The most notable number here is the average snowfall – some 350 inches a year. Refreshingly, in the increasingly corporate world of ski resorts, Bridger Bowl is run as a private, nonprofit ski area; consequently, a lift ticket costs only $34 and rental packages start at under $20. On weekends and holidays the Bridger Bowl Ski Bus ($5; ☏406/586-8567) leaves from various locations in Bozeman from 8am. There are no places to stay on the hill, but there are several options for a meal, including the basic *Jim Bridger Lodge* in the base area and the elegant mid-mountain *Deer Park Chalet* – a filling lunch here will set you back around $10–12.

Brundage, Idaho

Eight miles north of McCall, Brundage Mountain Resort (☏208/634-7462 or 1-800/888-7544, snow report 208/634-SNOW, ⓦwww.brundage.com) has the enviable combination of receiving some of the lightest powder in Idaho and virtually no liftlines. The 1300 acres of terrain here are served by three chairlifts and a couple of tows. The top elevation of 7640ft allows for a vertical drop of 1800ft, and from the summit there are great views of the remote Seven Devils Range, the Wallowa Mountains in eastern Oregon, Payette Lake, and the Frank Church-River of No Return Wilderness. Good beginner runs include Temptation for its fine views and variety of slope angles, and Main Street, an easy, open blue above the day lodge. Intermediate skiers will enjoy 45th Parallel and Engen, which are wide and great for practicing your carves. For advanced skiers there are the bumps of ungroomed Stair Steps or the tree runs of Black Forest, while experts should head toward the steep tree skiing of Hidden Valley. Lift tickets are around $32 full day ($26 half), with decent discounts for seniors and those 18 and younger. There's also a backcountry snowcat operation here – the highest peak used is nearby Granite Mountain (8478ft). Half-day trips start at around $125 per person, full day $200, and overnight trips staying in a yurt with two full days skiing and all meals are around $495. For more information, call ☏208/634-7462 ext 120.

Discovery Basin, Montana

One of Montana's lesser-known ski areas, Discovery Basin (daily 9.30am–4pm, late Nov to Easter; ☏406/563-2184, ⓦwww.skidiscovery.com) is also one of the state's most challenging. Though it is easily accessible from Missoula, Butte, and Helena, liftlines are a rare sight and there's a good mix of terrain, making it popular with families. There are forty trails in total, with the steepest of the bunch located on the challenging backside of the hill; indeed, this is some of the trickiest in-bound skiing in the state. Beginners and most intermediates will need to stay on the front side of the mountain, where there are some easy-angled runs through very open glades such as the green Red Lion and Tenderfoot, or the more challenging and considerably steeper blues of Southern Cross and Berkeley. In total, the mountain offers 360 acres of terrain and a vertical drop of 1300ft, accessed by four chairlifts. Lift tickets are $25 and there's a good, no-frills lodge at the base of the mountain where you can also rent gear.

Eldora, Colorado

Boulder's unofficial ski hill is Eldora (☎303/440-8700, ⓦwww.Eldora.com; adult $33, child/senior $20), just forty minutes away on public transit ($3.50), a route popular with locals and students from the University of Colorado. Perched on the Front Range of the Rockies, Eldora's annual snowfall (311 inches), size (680 acres), and summit elevation (10,600ft) are rather modest by Colorado standards, but tickets are cheap and the terrain varied enough to keep beginners and intermediates entertained. Wide open greens and blues lie adjacent to mellow glades, icy moguls, a small rail-oriented terrain park, hand-groomed superpipe, and 45 km of cross-country trails. Weekends are not ideal if you're not used to crowds, as even the hectic pace of the lodge can be unsettling. From Denver or anywhere to the south, Loveland (see p.164) is just as close, and much better to boot. If you're coming overnight, which visitors rarely do, stay in Boulder, a considerably less expensive and more entertaining option than the resort's neighbor, Nederland.

Monarch, Colorado

Overlooked by many on their way to Crested Butte, Monarch (☎719/539-3573 or 888/996-7669, ⓦwww.skimonarch.com; adult $39, junior $17) at least has its position atop the Continental Divide going for it. The light, dry powder that falls regularly here (350 inches, with no snowmaking) somewhat compensates for the five slow lifts, smallish 670 acres, and the most basic of base lodges. It's also uncrowded and inexpensive, with a small bunny slope for beginners, gently meandering trails for intermediates, and deep stashes, perfectly pitched and spaced, with hidden drops and log slides found in the glades days after a storm. Snowcats offer advanced riders another 900 acres of bowl and tree skiing ($180 for the day, advance booking highly recommended). Avoid the fusty *Monarch Mountain Inn* down the road from the ski area in favor of lodging eighteen miles down valley in Salida. Ski-and-stay packages start at $42. North of the strip of motels on Hwy-50 is a historic redbrick district with restaurants, B&Bs, hot springs, and a sweet skatepark.

Silver Mountain, Idaho

The approach to Silver Mountain (daily 9am–4pm; adults $31, juniors $22; ☎1-800/204-6428, 208/783-1111, snow report 1-800/204-6428, ⓦwww .silvermt.com) is quite peculiar. Instead of driving to the base, resort goers head up via the world's longest single-stage gondola from Kellogg, which transports you over three miles and 3400ft up to the Mountain Hause (5700ft), floating directly over the remnants of the area's past mining operations en route. It's not the most scenic way to start the day, but the ragged landscape is soon left behind as you ascend the steep, forested slopes and enjoy a panorama that features three states (Washington, Idaho, and Montana). From the gondola, a series of five chairlifts gives riders access to over fifty runs, spread over 1500 acres of rarely crowded terrain. Beginners don't own much of that terrain, but should enjoy Claim Jumper, which has good views of the Silver Valley, while intermediate skiers and boarders will have a field day on runs like the open Silver Belt and Sunrise and the more challenging black-to-blue Steep and Deep. Experts can tackle the easy open glades and powder of South of the Border, the fun steeps of The Meadows, a nice open area that can be traversed for some good tree skiing, and climb to the top of Wardner Peak (6200ft) for back-country action. There's a comfortable *Super 8 Motel*, 601 Bunker Ave (☎208/783-1234 or 1-800/785-5443), right beside the gondola, and eating options around the top of the gondola include *Moguls Lounge*, for soups, steaks, and a range of microbrews and wine, and the *Mountain Hause Grille*, good for burgers, chili, and pizza.

Silverton, Colorado

Just one creaky old double chair ascends Silverton Mountain (☎970/387-5706, ⓦwww.silvertonmountain.com; $99), the latest and most innovative ski area to open in the state. An hour north of Durango and a couple of hours east of Telluride, this double-diamond wonderland has no lodge, no liftlines, and, extraordinarily, no groomed runs – just excellent backcountry skiing with the tangible advantages of avalanche control and uphill transportation.

The old chairlift provides access to 1600 acres of Bureau of Land Management steeps, glades, and chutes. Short hikes and a shuttle bus pick-up extend the choice of runs off the 12,300ft summit. All skiers, in groups of six to ten, are accompanied by guides, and tickets are limited to forty per day. Snowfall averages 425 inches annually and fresh tracks are the norm. One route down involves a couloir so tight and rocky that even the hardcore are advised to use a strategically placed rope to abseil to safer slopes; avalanche beacon, probe, shovel, and suitable backpack are required (available to rent for $15). A scant choice of B&B and motel accommodation is available six miles down the road in the former mining town of Silverton (see ⓦwww.silverton.com for details).

Ski Cooper, Colorado

Training ground for the World War II soldiers of the 10th Mountain Division (see p.000), Ski Cooper (☎719/486-2277, ⓦwww.skicooper.com; adults $33, juniors $17) is an inexpensive family alternative to the ski resort behemoths of Vail and Summit County, both over thirty miles away. There's not much to the 400-acre area, just a few lifts and a basic lodge that never gets too busy. A hand-ful of intermediate, tree-lined trails spill off the 11,700ft summit ridge in both directions; the wide, bunny slope meadow rises gently above the lodge; and 25km of cross-country trails wind through the woods below. For $234 snowcats trans-port riders up the spectacular open bowls and glades of Chicago Ridge, high on the Continental Divide above the ski area. Hot lunch is provided and a gourmet dinner in the heated yurt of the Tennessee Pass Cookhouse is available for $55. Alternatively, investigate neighboring Leadville, a Victorian redbrick mining town that offers an inexpensive and eclectic range of lodging and dining alter-natives.

Snowbowl, Montana

Of Missoula's two ski hills, the 905-acre Montana Snowbowl (☎406/549-9777, snow report ☎406/549-9696, ⓦwww.montanasnowbowl.com; $30) is the larger, home to some challenging skiing and boarding. Located twelve miles northwest of town off I-90 at the Reserve Street exit (look carefully for

Colorado's Gems Card

Seven of Colorado's more basic ski areas are collectively known as the **Gems**. Register for a free Colorado Gems Card online at the state's umbrella ski area organization, Colorado Ski Country (☎303/837-0793, ⓦ www.coloradoski.com), to get $10 off an adult lift ticket at Arapahoe Basin (p.117), Loveland (p.164), Monarch (p.249), Ski Cooper (opposite), and Sol Vista (below).

the signs as it's remarkably poorly advertised), it can get pretty busy on weekends, when a free shuttle bus (☎406/549-9777) leaves from various locations in Missoula. From a highest point of 7600ft, there's a very respectable vertical of 2600ft. Despite a general lack of beginner runs, Second Thought, which wends its way gently between trees, is a good place to start. Intermediates can head to Longhorn and Grandstand for sustained steepish pitches, and advanced skiers and boarders will enjoy the challenges of East Bowls below Big Sky Mountain, the bumps on Grizzly Chute and Angel Face, and the 500 acres of tree skiing. There are cafés on the mountain, while the lively *Last Run Inn* at the base is a lively après-ski spot. Accommodation on the mountain includes the ski-in/ski-out *Gelandesprung Lodge* (☎800/728-2695, $30–60) where double rooms go for as little as $42 per person per night including a one-day lift ticket.

Sol Vista, Colorado

Formerly known as Silver Creek, Sol Vista Golf and Ski Ranch (☎800/757-7669, ⓦ www.solvista.com; adult $39, junior $17) was reborn as a year-round family condominium community, with golf in the summer and skiing in the winter. Fifteen miles down valley from Winter Park (a much better option), the ski area is an anomaly among other Rockies resorts. Its 406 acres spill off a summit elevation of only 9202ft, and it averages a paltry 220 inches of snow each year. With a slightly optimistic definition of black runs, Sol Vista won't suit the accomplished skier, but families and beginners may appreciate the lack of crowds, gentle slopes, and clearly demarcated terrain. Sol Vista does have some novelty value: for $500, private groups can rent the entire East Mountain section of the resort for three hours of night skiing.

Wolf Creek, Colorado

Wolf Creek (☎970/264-5639 or 800/754-9653, ⓦ www.wolfcreekski.com; adult $43, junior/senior $25) averages 465 inches of powder a year, among the largest falls in all Colorado. The snow that falls on this south-central resort is dry and light, drawing riders from around the state; an abundance of rocky open bowls, cornices, and glades help to attract an expert freeriding crowd. Wolf Creek is, however, hard to reach, an hour either way from Durango or Alamosa and 200 miles from Albuquerque or Colorado Springs, and the layout of the ski area is wide but squat (the quoted 1604ft of vertical seems generous). Even with the recent addition of a new lift – bringing the total to six – long traverses and short descents are the norm. This is less of an issue for novice and lower intermediate skiers, who will likely spend most of their time on the lift-served slopes immediately above the base area. Lodging is available on both sides of Wolf Creek Pass, sleepy South Fork, or in Pagosa Springs, a somewhat faded spa.

Utah and the Southwest

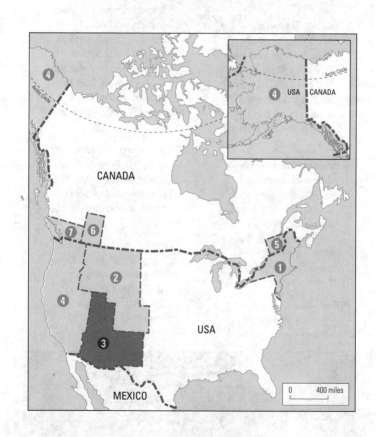

chapter 3

Highlights

* **Lone Star Taqueria** Enjoy mouth-watering fish tacos only minutes from the entrances to both Big and Little Cottonwood canyons in suburban Salt Lake City. See p.261

* **The Alta experience** Alta's skier's-only policy along with powder days aplenty, antiquated lifts and old world lodges all add up to one of the most original and memorable ski-trip experiences in the country. See p.262

* **Brighton backcountry** Scene of countless snowboard video and photo shoots, the extensive backcountry off Brighton's lifts is some of the finest untrammeled terrain in Utah. See p.267

* **Park City** One of North America's finest ski towns: by day ski the trails at one of three world-class resorts, by night sample the gourmet cuisine on Main Street. See p.270

* **Snowbird's tram** The finest way to take in Snowbird's breathtaking scenery and equally stunning terrain is on its speedy aerial tram – grab a window perch for the best views (and to avoid the stench of 125 sardine-packed passengers). See p.286

* **Taos** Varied slopes and spicy, southwestern cuisine attract skiers to the precipitous New Mexican peaks above dusty pueblos. See p.300

* **Grizzly** Ski the steep, two-mile run at Snowbasin where the Men's 2002 Olympic Downhill Skiing events were held. See p.310

3

Utah and the Southwest

n the Southwest, the only states with substantial ski activity are **Utah** and **New Mexico**; the resorts dotted around Salt Lake City in northern Utah – an area in many ways more closely connected to the Rockies than the Southwest – dominate the landscape. About a dozen ski spots are located under an hour's drive of the city, an asset shown off to great effect during the **2002 Winter Olympics**, which had events taking place throughout the vicinity. Yet the finest characteristic of Utah's resorts is not their accessibility, it's the hefty amount of light, dry **snow** that falls yearly. The arid desert air to the west and moisture released by nearby Great Salt Lake create powder perfect for off-piste expeditions or gentle cruising.

On the outskirts of Salt Lake City the **Cottonwood Canyons** are strafed with the biggest storms, when early-morning coffee is often accompanied by the boom of World War II-era howitzers blasting away at their avalanche prone slopes. Little Cottonwood Canyon, 25 miles away from Utah's capital, averages 500 inches of snow per year and is home to steep **Snowbird** and the throwback resort of **Alta**. Both are large enough for an extended stay on their own, but with interconnected lifts their nearly 5000 combined acres add up to arguably the finest downhill experience in North America – at least for skiers (Alta does not allow snowboarding). Next door, Big Cottonwood Canyon includes **Brighton**, which takes on a lot of those snowboarders turned away at Alta, and quieter **Solitude**.

Another cluster of resorts is in **Park City**, a former mining-boomtown thirty miles east of Salt Lake City. The vibrant community, home to the Sundance film festival, boasts three large ski areas that may be less adventurous and snowy than those in the Cottonwood Canyons but provide more of interest for your time off the slopes. The most central, **Park City Mountain Resort**, can be accessed via a chairlift from downtown. Due west is **Deer Valley**, an impeccably groomed resort that, like Alta, bans snowboarders. Unlike Alta, its patrons often seem more interested in a gourmet lunch than squeezing in a few more runs. A five-minute drive out of town sits **The Canyons**, Park City's largest resort and probably best overall option, with an wide selection of intermediate and advanced trails laced across eight peaks.

Of Utah's remaining resorts, the two most notable are **Snowbasin**, forty miles north of Salt Lake City and still somewhat of a locals' mountain, and **Brian Head Resort**, between the capital and Las Vegas, nothing to go out of your way for.

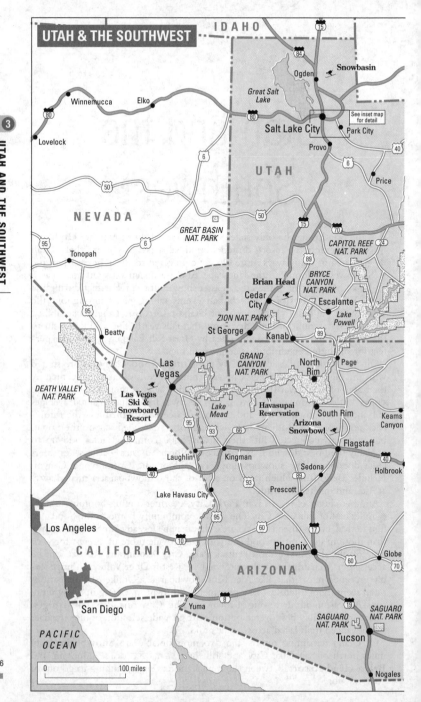

UTAH & THE SOUTHWEST

IDAHO

Winnemucca   Elko

Lovelock

NEVADA

Tonopah

Beatty

DEATH VALLEY
NAT. PARK

Los Angeles

CALIFORNIA

San Diego

PACIFIC
OCEAN

Ogden   Snowbasin

Great Salt
Lake

Salt Lake City   Park City

Provo

UTAH

Price

GREAT BASIN
NAT. PARK

CAPITOL REEF
NAT. PARK

Brian Head

Cedar
City   BRYCE
CANYON
NAT. PARK

Escalante

Lake
Powell

ZION NAT. PARK

St George   Kanab

GRAND
CANYON
NAT. PARK   North
Rim   Page

Las
Vegas

Las Vegas
Ski &
Snowboard
Resort

Lake
Mead   Havasupai
Reservation   South Rim   Keams
Canyon

Arizona
Snowbowl

Laughlin   Kingman   Flagstaff

Sedona   Holbrook

Lake Havasu City   Prescott

Phoenix   Globe

ARIZONA

Yuma

SAGUARO
NAT. PARK   SAGUARO
NAT. PARK

Tucson

Nogales

0   100 miles

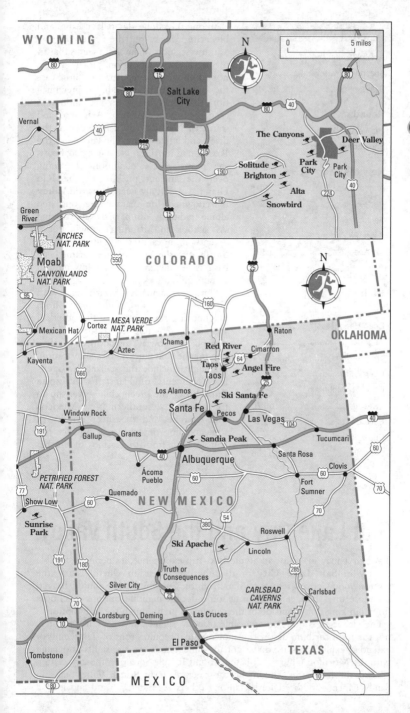

WYOMING

N

0   5 miles

Salt Lake
City

The Canyons   Deer Valley

Solitude   Park
Brighton   City   Park
                              City
         Alta
      Snowbird

Vernal

Green
River

ARCHES
NAT. PARK

Moab

CANYONLANDS
NAT. PARK

COLORADO

N

Mexican Hat   Cortez

MESA VERDE
NAT. PARK

Raton

OKLAHOMA

Kayenta

Aztec   Chama   Red River   Cimarron

Taos   Angel Fire
Taos

Los Alamos   Ski Santa Fe

Window Rock   Santa Fe   Pecos

Gallup   Grants   Sandia Peak   Las Vegas

Albuquerque   Santa Rosa   Tucumcari

Ácoma
Pueblo

PETRIFIED FOREST
NAT. PARK   Quemado

Show Low   NEW MEXICO   Fort
                                                          Sumner

Sunrise
Park   Ski Apache   Roswell

                                               Lincoln

Truth or
Consequences

Silver City   CARLSBAD
                                                        CAVERNS   Carlsbad
Lordsburg   Deming   Las Cruces   NAT. PARK

Tombstone

El Paso   TEXAS

MEXICO

Among the adobe, desert landscapes and blistering heat of the rest of the Southwest, snow of any kind seems like an incongruous juxtaposition. Storms might not dump with the regularity of those further north, but like in Utah, any precipitation that does break on the mountain ranges of New Mexico, **Arizona**, and southern **Nevada** falls as powder of the driest and lightest type. The tail end of the Rockies, in northern New Mexico, boasts the most reliable conditions. Looming over the ancient pueblos of the Rio Grand, wonderfully steep **Taos Ski Valley** is renowned for maintaining outdated alpine traditions – in part, by emphasizing ski school and banning snowboarders. Twenty minutes in the hills above arty **Santa Fe**, the eponymously named ski basin is considerably more mellow, both in terrain and attitude.

Though regularly swarming with Southwesterners (including many from neighboring Texas), none of the other ski areas in the region really has the terrain or dependable snowfall (or both) to justify a trip for the sole purpose of a ski vacation. Highlights include the spectacular open-bowl descents of Flagstaff's **Arizona Snowbowl**, the green chili served up in the cafeteria at southern New Mexico's **Ski Apache**, and the sheer novelty of snowboarding on fresh, real powder just half an hour from the casinos of the Las Vegas Strip.

Salt Lake City and the South Valley

Though it may make for an atypical ski-trip experience, it's perfectly feasible to stay in **Salt Lake City** or its suburban extension when visiting the Cottonwood Canyon resorts of Alta, Brighton, Snowbird, and Solitude. In fact, for those on a budget or wanting some decent nightlife options to choose from, bunking down outside of the canyons is pretty much the only option.

The city itself is quite an agreeable place to spend a few days, if ultimately not the most thrilling destination nor one that requires tons of sightseeing or extended exploration. If you've got the time, check out the sights associated with the Mormon Church, all based around Temple Square in the city center.

Its southern suburbs, known by the catch-all term **South Valley**, take in Sandy, Murray, and West Jordan among others. Admittedly bland and loaded with strip malls, auto-dealerships, and other trappings of suburban life, the Valley nonetheless is conveniently located and affordably priced.

Arrival and local transport

Four miles from downtown, **Salt Lake City International Airport** (℡801/575-2400) is serviced by nine major airlines – a large percentage of flights are run by Delta/SkyWest – so finding an affordable ticket even during the heart of the ski season is not out of the question. Amtrak **trains** arrive a few blocks southwest of the city center at 340 South 600 W Temple (℡1-800 /872-7245, ⓦwww.amtrak.com), while the Greyhound **bus terminal** is located downtown at 160 W South Temple (℡801/355-9579 or 1-800/231-2222, ⓦwww.greyhound.com).

Local transport boils down to two choices: utilizing the efficient public transport/shuttle bus system or renting a car. Unless you plan on doing plenty of hopping around, opt for the former, as the snaking roads through Big and Little Cottonwood Canyons can be a perilous affair best left to experienced mountain drivers. Also, throughout the entire ski season a **4WD vehicle or snowchains are mandatory**, which can raise the price of renting substantially. The airport has all the major agencies (see p.26 for contact details) if you're interested.

For those willing to deal with the minor hassles of public transport, the Utah Transit Authority (UTA; ℡801/743-3882, ⓦwww.rideuta.com) **bus system** is the way to go. From 6am to 6pm daily, buses starting from the Midvale Trax Station 7200 head up the both Big and Cottonwood Canyons every fifteen minutes. Check their website for detailed route, park & ride, and pricing information.

For a **shuttle bus** straight from the airport to the Cottonwood resorts (or from the resorts to Park City), book ahead with All Resort Express (℡435 /649-3999 or 1-800/457-9457, ⓦwww.allresort.com), Canyon Transportation (℡801/255-1841 or 1-800/255-1841, ⓦwww.canyontransport.com), or Lewis Bros. Stages (℡801/359-8677 or 1-800/826-5844, ⓦwww.lewisbros.com). Rates average $25 per person one-way, though cheaper group rates are available.

Accommodation

Salt Lake City has a fine range of **accommodation**, and happily most establishments don't hike up their prices during the ski season and also offer good deals on lift ticket packages. **Downtown** is a 45-minute drive away from the Cottonwood Canyons' resorts; to trade in the convenience of city living for a shorter drive, consider **South Valley**, home to a large collection of chain

hotels. Wasatch Front Ski Accommodations (☎1-800/762-7606, ⊛www.wfsa
.com) rents an array of one- to five-bedroom **condos** and homes in the
foothills of the South Valley.

Downtown Salt Lake City

Brigham Street Inn 1135 E South Temple
☎801/364-4461 or 1-800/417-4461. This historic
mansion is the city's most luxurious and peaceful
B&B, thanks in large part to its location several
blocks east of downtown toward the mountains.
Each of the nine guestrooms has its own private
bath – some have fireplaces too – and the breakfasts are beautifully presented. ❺
Deseret Inn 50 W 500 South ☎801/532-2900 or
1-800/359-2170. This downtown motor lodge is a
real throwback to a bygone era; though far from
smart, its rooms are clean and comfortable, and
the location is unbeatable for the price. ❷
Hotel Monaco 15 W 200 South ☎801/595-0000
or 1-877/294-9710, ℗801/532-8500, ⊛www
.monaco-saltlakecity.com. The interior of this
upscale boutique hotel, housed in a former bank,
could fairly be described as "funky"; lime green
ceilings, loud, striped wallpaper, and contemporary
furniture that betrays a North African-influenced
Art Deco theme. The hotel's *Bambara* restaurant is
also one of the city's best (see opposite). ❺
Peery Hotel 110 W Broadway (300 South)
☎801/521-4300 or 1-800/331-0073,
⊛www.peeryhotel.com. This refurbished 1910
downtown landmark – the oldest hotel in Salt Lake
City – has elegant rooms kitted out with plush furnishings and extras like Internet terminals and ter-
rycloth bathrobes. While a handful of the eighty-odd
rooms are on the small side, the rest are above-
average size. As a business hotel, rates drop considerably on weekends. Midweek ❹, weekend ❸
Ute Hostel 21 E Kelsey Ave ☎801/595-1645. This
small and worn private hostel, located a mile or so

south of downtown, has dorm beds and a couple
of double rooms. You can't reserve a bed, but it's
worth calling a day or two ahead to check whether
they'll have room; just phone on arrival and someone will pick you up from the airport, Amtrak, or
Greyhound. Dorms $20, private room $25.

South Valley

Best Western Cottonwood Inn 10695 South
Auto Mall Drive ☎801/523-8484, ⊛www.cotton-
tree.net. Chain hotel located among auto dealer-
ships off of 10600 South, which intersects with I-
15. The 110 rooms – ranging from standard king-
bed options to family suites with two queens and a
pull-out couch – are perfectly serviceable, and
useful extras include a 24hr indoor pool and hot
tub, guest laundry, and complimentary hot breakfasts. Several ski packages offered as well. ❹
Crystal Inn Midvalley 818 East Winchester St
☎801/685-9300 or 1-888/685-9300, ⊛www
.crystalinns.com. Boasting slightly larger rooms
than the typical chain-hotel accommodation, the
Crystal Inn is located just off the I-215 belting and
close to the canyon resorts' entrance. Extras
include a complimentary hotel shuttle, indoor hot
tub and pool, and free hot breakfasts and movie
rentals. Some rooms face the highway, so ask for a
quieter one if possible. ❺
Majestic Rockies Motel 8901 South State St
☎801/255-2313, ⊛www.majesticrockies.com.
Small, slightly grubby-looking small motel offering
up perhaps the cheapest beds within a short drive
of the canyon access roads. Best for those on a
budget; its rooms are decently clean and some
have small kitchenettes. ❷

Eating, drinking, and entertainment

Though Salt Lake City has a perfectly good selection of **restaurants**, it lacks
an atmospheric dining district. If you like to compare menus, the only downtown area with much potential is the block or two on either side of West
Temple, south and east of the Salt Palace. In the South Valley, a good place to
start is the entrance to Big Cottonwood Canyon, around which several
worthwhile restaurants and taverns are located.

While nobody would claim that Salt Lake City is a swinging town, they don't
roll up the sidewalks here when the sun goes down either. Most drinking venues are technically **private clubs** (see box on p.259), but a handful of brewpubs and taverns exist in which membership is not required. For current movie
and club **listings**, pick up a copy of the free *City Weekly*, distributed seemingly everywhere.

Downtown Salt Lake City

Restaurants

Baba Afghan Restaurant 55 E 400 South
☎801/596-0786. Vegetarians and those with a hankering for something far removed from American chow will enjoy *Baba*'s Middle Eastern menu. Entrees $8–13. Closed Sun.

Bambara *Hotel Monaco*, 15 W 200 South ☎801/363-5454. With a different menu daily, this expensive restaurant features some of the city's most eclectic choices. A sample meal might include buffalo carpaccio as an appetizer, followed by either New Zealand elk or Portuguese fisherman's stew ($25), a steamy concoction of lobster, cockles, shrimp, mussels, and scallops. Like the hotel itself, the restaurant interior is a chic, post-Deco affair. Daily for breakfast and dinner; lunch Mon–Fri only.

Lamb's Restaurant 169 S Main St ☎801/364-7166. This atmospheric eatery, a city stalwart since 1939, dishes up great breakfasts best eaten at the long shiny counter. Excellent-value set meals are served throughout the day, while entrees such as steaks or chops run from $13 to $20. Closed Sun.

Market Street Grill 48 W Market St ☎801/322-4668. This New York-style bar and grill is a firm locals' downtown favorite. Fresh seafood, especially oysters, is the main draw, though steaks in all shapes and sizes are served along with filling breakfasts too; entrees $15–30. Open from 6.30am Mon–Sat, 9am Sun.

Mikado 67 W 100 South ☎801/328-0929. Among several sushi places in town, this one is better value than most (two-piece sushi plates $4–5) and very central. The combination plates for two or more are a good value.

Red Iguana 736 W North Temple. Inexpensive Mexican tacqueria, with flavorful burritos and enchiladas, as well as excellent moles, a specialty of the Oaxaca region. Located a mile west of Temple Square. Most entrees under $10.

Bars and clubs

Dead Goat Saloon 165 S West Temple ☎801/328-4628. Raucous, semi-subterranean saloon, with live loud music most nights; emphasis is on blues and rock. Cover $2–10.

Port O'Call 400 S West Temple ☎801/521-0589. A big, beery place spread over three floors and heaving on weekends, *Port O'Call* is a decent good place to get among the locals to drink, dance, or shoot a game of pool. A sports bar vibe permeates, so don't bother stopping by if that's not your style.

Squatters Pub 147 W Broadway ☎801/363-2739. Casual, friendly brewpub that offers a range of beers and several TV sets for sports enthusiasts.

The menu includes all the bar basics like nachos, burgers, pasta, and salads. 11am until late.

South Valley

Asian Star Chinese Cuisine 7350 S Wasatch Blvd ☎801/733-4888. Tucked inside the Canyon Racquet Club, this bright establishment is the place to head for Chinese food. The service is superb, and it's hard to go wrong when choosing from the extensive and fairly priced menu. One item that should not be passed up is the honey shrimp.

Cotton Bottom Inn 2820 E 6200 South ☎901/273-9830. Small and unpretentious tavern specializing in what many locals consider to be the finest burger in town, including a pungent garlic version. Open Mon–Sat until 1am, 8pm on Sun.

Hog Wallow Pub 3200 Big Cottonwood Canyon Rd ☎801/733-5567. A bit tricky to find – look for the turn-off opposite the *Canyon Inn* at the mouth of Big Cottonwood Canyon – this friendly bar fills up with a friendly, youthful crowd once the slopes close. A local favorite, the *Hog* hosts live bands ranging from reggae to local rock Thurs–Sat, and both pub grub and plenty of local microbrews are on offer.

Lone Star Taqueria 2265 E Fort Union Blvd ☎801/944-2300. Two miles west of the Big Cottonwood Canyon access road sits this highly recommended Mexican fast-food eatery. Simple and authentic, *Lone Star* offers over a dozen varieties of tacos and burritos loaded with fresh ingredients. The fish tacos ($2.75), the house specialty, are worth writing home about, served with fresh grilled fish, cilantro, lime, and a mouthwatering jalapeño mayonnaise. Easily the best of the cheap eats options in the South Valley, if not the entire city.

Market Street Grill – Cottonwood 2985 E 6580 South ☎801/942-8860. A spin-off of the *Market Street* in downtown Salt Lake City (see above), this casually upscale eatery is a great choice for a splurge in the South Valley area. It specializes in seafood, and you can expect to pay $20–25 per entrée. There's a fine wine list and even finer brunch menu, the latter offered on Sundays only.

Porcupine Pub and Grill 3698 E Fort Union Blvd ☎801/942-5555. Located by the mouth of Big Cottonwood Canyon, this bar is a favorite post-slope stop for locals and visitors alike. The loft-like blonde wood interior attracts a slightly upscale crowd, here to choose from an extensive menu that ranges from pizzas ($10) to more expensive mains like filet mignon ($24) and halibut ($20). There are also over twenty beers on draft, heavy on local microbrews. If you're looking for a more raucous environment, head for the roadhouse-styled *Canyon Inn* (☎801/942-9801; $5 temporary membership) next door instead.

Equipment rental and lift tickets

Renting gear in Salt Lake City could not be any easier. Indeed, it's even possible to rent equipment at the airport while waiting for your bags to arrive. Each of the Cottonwood resorts has a variety of rental options, and we've listed those options along with each resort. But if you're the type who likes to show up with board or skis in hand, check with the following spots first; all of these establishments also sell **discounted lift tickets** to most if not all of Utah's resorts.

Lift House 3698 E 7000 South ☏801/943-1104 or 1-800/330-4754. Located by the mouth of Big Cottonwood Canyon, the highly regarded Lift House boasts quality skis and a knowledgeable staff. Overnight tune-ups available too. Daily 8am–7pm.

Milo Sport 3119 E 3300 South ☏801/487-8600 or 1-877/504-1500. The top retail snowboard shop in the city, with a great selection of everything from boards to goggles. No rentals available, but the spot to hit up for new gear and information on the local scene.

Ski'nSee ☏1-800/722-3685, ⊛www.skinseee.com. A good one-stop shop for groups with both skiers and boarders, with six locations throughout the region. Most convenient are the downtown location at 135 W 500 South (☏801/295-1428) and the store leading to the Alta/Snowbird access road at 2125 E 9400 South (☏801/942-1780). Ski packages include K2, Salomon, and Rossi

($15–32), while boards range from basic K2 step-ins ($23) to Burton and Salomon demos ($33). Snowblades, helmets, and even snow pants also rented. Book online and save around $5 per rental. All locations open from 8am.

Utah Ski & Golf ☏1-800/858-5221, ⊛www.utahskigolf.com. Chain with several locations throughout the region most notable for its two convenient airport shops (8am–10pm), located by the luggage carousels in each terminal. Competitive prices, but the selection of skis and boards aren't the best. Everything from gloves to helmets rented as well in case you've forgotten them at home, and definitely worth popping into for discounted lift tickets.

Wasatch Touring 702 E 100 South ☏801/359-9361, ⊛www.wasatchtouring.com. Located downtown, this is a top stop for local backcountry information. Rentals include telemark packages ($30).

Alta

The town of **Alta**, a silver mining camp in the 1860s with a permanent population numbering in the thousands, was home to fewer than a dozen hardy souls when Alf Engen visited in 1935 to scout out possible ski areas for the Forest Service. Even though the area surrounding the town tucked into the top end of Little Cottonwood Canyon was stripped of all trees and pockmarked with mines, it didn't take Engen long to realize its potential. By 1939, the country's second chairlift – Idaho's Sun Valley (see p.205) had the first – opened here and within a decade four of Alta's five lodges were built. Over the next fifty years little changed, and therein lies Alta's charm. While other resorts loudly embrace all things modern, Alta has tenaciously held onto its roots, embracing tradition over convenience at nearly every turn – including **skiing over snowboarding**.

Indeed, Alta is such an anachronism that it's almost easier to define the resort by what it isn't than what it is. Alta is not like Deer Valley in its pampering, nor is it an intricate resort village like Park City. Look elsewhere for ski porters, souvenir shacks, or buzzing nightclubs. And Alta is definitely not for snowboarders; riders have never been allowed, and in all likelihood won't be invited to ride the lifts anytime soon.

Add to this that lifts tend to creep along at a glacial pace, lift tickets are priced at bargain rates, and no new overnight lodge has been built since 1962 and it's easy to imagine Alta as a resort on the brink of disaster. Yet the resort has never

Mountain info

Phone ☎ 801/359-1078

Snow phone ☎ 801/359-1078

Website ✆ www.alta.com

Price $40, $64 Alta/Snowbird combined

Operating times Mid-Nov to mid-April daily 9.15am–4.30pm

No. of lifts 8 lifts, along with several surface tows

Base elevation 8530′

Summit elevation 10550′

Vertical drop 2020′

No. of trails 54

Acreage 2200

Beginner 25%

Intermediate 40%

Expert 35%

Average snowfall 500″

Snowmaking Yes (50 acres)

Night skiing No

Nursery facilities Yes, ☎ 801/742-3042; reservations requested

been in better shape, due in large part to miraculously light, near perfect **snow**, averaging over 500 inches per season. Storms rolling overhead are commonly measured in feet not inches, and when they blanket the ski area's impressive mix of beginner to daringly expert terrain, Alta's faults are instantly forgiven. Recent links with neighboring **Snowbird** haven't hurt Alta's standing either – their 4700 combined acres of terrain can now be skied on one ticket – and nowadays the little resort that could (or wouldn't) is regularly ranked along with Vail and Whistler as one of the continent's top ski destinations.

Arrival, orientation, and getting around

Stretched out for less than a mile along the end of **Hwy-210** near the eastern end of Little Cottonwood Canyon, Alta is under an hour's drive from both Salt Lake City's airport and downtown, weather and traffic permitting. For details on shuttles, buses, and the like from the airport and Salt Lake City, along with information on the canyon road's stringent winter regulations, see p.259.

Traffic on weekend and holiday mornings can be fierce, though, and during these times plan on hitting the canyon road no later than 8am. During snowstorms, Hwy-210 is frequently shut down for avalanche control, and even when it's open the twists and turns make for slow going. Park at the canyon entrance and use the UTA bus network unless you have both experience driving on snow and a 4WD (or tire chains). Tune your radio to 530 AM when nearing the canyon for current road conditions.

Alta doesn't have a village to speak of, just two **base areas** – Albion and Wildcat – consisting of basic day lodges and parking lots. Strung slopeside in between the two are the resort's lodges, while the opposite side of the road holds a church, tiny post office, and the *Shallow Shaft* restaurant. Free **shuttles** head down the canyon to condos and Snowbird, a half mile and one mile away respectively.

The mountain

Alta's 54 total runs are vastly underestimated. There are at least twice as many spread across the mountain than revealed on the trail map and in many areas the only thing holding you back from finding more is your imagination and ability. Whether it's grilling a local for their favorite chutes on a creaky lift ride up or looking for fresh lines to tackle off one of the many long traverses cutting across the mountain, it pays to be inquisitive.

Known as Alta's "frontside," much of the area above the Wildcat Base spills off of **Mount Baldy** and the **Peruvian Ridge**, which together form the boundary with Snowbird. The north face of Peruvian Ridge is where Alta's steepest tree skiing can be found, while the western face of Baldy higher up is highlighted by powder-filled bowls. More challenging bowls are located a lift over off **High Traverse**, a ridge-riding bumpy transfer accessing many of Alta's top runs.

The resort's "backside," pretty much everything west of High Traverse, is where most of the beginner's and intermediate terrain is located. Directly above the Albion Base Area, a trio of lifts accesses the **Albion Basin**, a web of greens and blues that bolster Alta's reputation as a fine destination even for first timers. From the top of the Albion Basin, the Sugarloaf quad cuts back toward the frontside – and the gates to Snowbird's Mineral Basin – while the Supreme triple chair leads to the intermediate/advanced **Point Supreme** peak, home to superb tree runs and under-visited bowls both in and out of bounds. High up and in between these two lifts, **East Castle** and **Devil's Castle** are – when not closed due to Avalanche control – two of the finest in-bounds, powder-catching bowls in the state.

There's no denying the antiquated nature of Alta's **lift system**. With only one detachable quad (Sugarloaf) among the resort's eight lifts, the slow chairs and resultant frequent lines require a certain level of patience. If you're not the type who can spend twenty minutes cheerily discussing the previous run, hit up Snowbird and its high-speed quads and tram instead. One thing that might help pass the time is the beauty of the surrounding area, as the **panoramic alpine views** available across this narrow top end of Little Cottonwood Canyon are remarkable. (For information on skiing in this off-piste region, see the box on "Backcountry skiing in Little Cottonwood and beyond", p.288.)

Beginner

Somewhat unusually for a mountain beloved by experts, Alta has plenty to offer first-time skiers. Above the Albion Base Area, the Albion and Cecret doubles and Sunnyside triple chairs lead to the heart of Alta's easygoing terrain, a good-sized patch that's home to a dozen or so green and relaxed blue trails. Best runs to practice linking turns include the long and winding **Crooked Mile** and the shorter **Sweet 'N Easy**, lined by trees on either side. No black runs cut through this area, keeping this ample portion of the Albion Basin the happy domain of beginners. For those having problems mastering the nuances of skiing powder, the resort also grooms, weather permitting, one run off every lift.

Intermediate

There's not a single lift at Alta that's off-limits to intermediate skiers. Warm up on **Rock 'N Roll** or **Big Dipper** spilling down off Point Supreme at the resort's eastern end. While much of the rest of the mountain is open for exploration, particularly the blues below the Sugarloaf lift, avoid the **Wildcat** woods toward Snowbird and the busy **High Traverse**, bumpy as a camel's back and a road to nothing but perilous steeps. When you're ready to dabble with some bowl skiing, don't miss **Ballroom**, suitable for confident intermediates during almost any conditions, but most exhilarating after a storm.

Expert

Not every advanced run worth skiing here requires a traverse or hike, but expert skiers will increase their options tenfold if willing to do so. A case in point is **High Traverse** cutting down the center of the ski area. Off the undulating traverse's frontside, skiers can bail out early down various chutes or tough it out to **Alf's High Rustler**, the resort's defining run, which plunges down a precipitous fall-line over 1000ft, ending at the deck of the *Goldminer's Daughter* lodge. For more of a challenge hit **Eagle's Nest** due west, a similarly steep fall but this time through cliff-laced trees. And off High Traverse's "backside," bowl after bowl – **Yellow Trail**, **East Greeley**, **Greeley** – access some of Alta's finest steep and deep terrain, the best stashes logically located the furthest out on the traverse. From the hike to powder-fields of **East Castle** and **Devil's Castle** to the steep chutes under the Wildcat chair off the Peruvian Ridge, the ski area to both sides of High Traverse is simply bursting with excellent expert terrain waiting to be explored. The out-of-bounds backside of **Catherine's Area** to the east, a north-east facing area known locally as Rocky Point, holds fields of fresh snow and cliffs in equal measure. **Wildcat** and **Westward Ho** in-bounds on the resort's opposite side hoard scores of tree-shots that dump you a short skate back to the lifts.

Freestyle

Alta has no dedicated terrain park but you'll have no problem scouting out wind lips, rollers, and variable sized cliffs to launch from. For some of the most insane freestyle terrain in the area, you'll need to hike up or book a cat ski tour into nearby **Grizzly Gulch** (see backcountry box on p.288), home to an array of backcountry jumps and some massive gaps.

Lift tickets, lessons, and rentals

Lift tickets are a bargain at only $40 per day. Passes for kids 12 and under go for $33, while an Alta/Snowbird day pass shoots up to $64 – only necessary, considering the extra costs, if you *must* ski both in a day.

With a staff used to skiing after heavy storms, Alta's **ski school** (☎801/359-1078) is the premier resort for learning how to ski powder properly. Named after local legend and US Olympic Ski Team coach Alf Engen, the school offers courses for beginners up to experts, ranging in costs from $35 for a two-hour class to $420 for an all-day, one-on-one lesson. If you always wanted to learn how to telemark, the school's two-hour workshop ($45) is recommended.

For high-quality **rentals**, pop into the Deep Powder House (daily 8.30am–6pm; ☎801/742-2400, ⓦwww.deeppowderhouse.com), located by the entrance to the *Alta Lodge*. Packages run $30–50 for Volkl, Atomic, Salomon, and Rossignol planks with high-end boots to match. If you'd rather show up skis in hand, see p.262 for a list of recommended outlets down in the valley.

Accommodation

Alta's old-world character is displayed in its odd collection of five independent **lodges**, spaced evenly over half a mile in front of the ski hill. They're all expensive but they at least include meals, and four of them offer **dorm beds** (usually not as cheap as a typical dorm bed elsewhere). Other nearby options include the accommodations at Snowbird a mile down the road (see p.289), or the **condos** offered by Canyon Services (☎801/943-1842 or 1-800/562-2888, ⓦwww.canyonservices.com) and Hellgate Condominiums (☎801/742-2020, ⓦwww.hellgate-alta.com) in between the two resorts. Keep in mind that while accommodation in the South Valley (see p.260) can be much cheaper, if you're staying slopeside when the canyon road closes for avalanche control – which happens quite frequently – you and your fellow guests will have the slopes to yourselves. During times of especially heavy snowfall, however, you won't even be allowed outside of your lodge, so bring extra reading materials just in case.

Alta Lodge ☎ 801/742-3500 or 1-800/707-2582, ⓦ www.altalodge.com. For many long-time visitors to Alta, this lodge is still the original and the best. Owned by the mayor of Alta, Bill Levitt, this 65-year-old lodge (the "new" wing was added in the 1960s) seems almost dowdy with its dark timber and lack of adornment, but it has an air of quiet comfort and genteel leisure. The fifty-plus rooms range in size and features, although none has a television. Communal amenities include a couple of saunas and hot tubs along with a cozy upstairs bar. Rates include breakfast and a delicious three-course dinner; double ❽, dorm ❺

Alta Peruvian Lodge ☎ 801/742-3000 or 1-800/453-8488, ⓕ 801/742-3007, ⓦ www.altaperuvian.citysearch.com. Rooms in this fifty-year-old rambling lodge run the gamut from dorms up to two-bedroom suites and chalets. There's a heated outdoor pool and hot tub, and live bands visit the *Peruvian's* bar on occasion. Per-person rates include breakfast, lunch, and dinner, plus an Alta lift pass; room with shared bath ❻ (per person), with private bath ❼ (per person), dorm ❻

Goldminer's Daughter ☎ 801/742-2300 or 1-800/453-4573, ⓦ www.alta.com/lodge/goldmine.html. Though the least aesthetically inspiring of Alta's lodges, *Goldminer's Daughter* is the most affordable and conveniently located by the ski lifts.

Rooms are similar to those of a slightly rundown motel, while dorms are standard rooms with four single beds crammed into them. There is a small sauna and hot tub and the property's most appealing feature, ideal for lunch, is its large sun-deck. All rates are per person and include breakfast and dinner; single ❺, double ❹ (per person), dorms ❹

Rustler Lodge ☎ 801/742-2200 or 1-888/532-2582, ⓕ 801/742-3832, ⓦ www.rustlerlodge.com. The best choice for those who want modern comforts and don't mind paying a bit extra for them. Rooms all have TV and phone, and a heated outdoor pool, hot tub, steam room, and full fitness center are all on site. Dorm beds are available too; choose between the cheaper six-bed room with TV and bath, or a three-bed with shower, toilet, and sink. All rates include breakfast and dinner; doubles ❽ (per person), dorms ❺

Snowpine Lodge ☎ 801/742-2000, ⓕ 801/742-2244, ⓦ www.thesnowpine.com. There's typically a sociable gathering by a fireplace or around the lodge's lone television set at Snowpine. The cheaper rooms have shared bathroom facilities, and there are no telephones in rooms; dorms are divided into small cubicles with two bunks and separate storage space in each, giving a communal ski-hostel experience with a modicum of privacy. Rates are per person and include breakfast and dinner; private bath ❻, shared ❺, dorms ❹

Eating and drinking

Meals are included at all of Alta's lodges, so there's not an overwhelming need for **restaurants** in town. For a change of pace after a few days of eating in the same spot, a visit either to the local *Shallow Shaft* or restaurants at Snowbird (see p.289) is a must; beyond these you'll have to head into the valley (see p.261 for recommendations).

Nightlife at Alta mostly revolves around the "private-club" (see box on p.259) lounges located in each lodge. *The Sitzmark Club Lounge* in the *Alta Lodge* is perhaps the most popular après-ski spot and the hangout of choice for the local ski patrol. The resort's ski instructors tend to drink at the *Rustler Lodge's* lounge, a classy spot with leather lounge chairs and a marble-top bar, while everyone tends to congregate at the *Peruvian Lodge's* bar whenever a live band is on tap.

Albion Grill Albion Base Area ☎ 801/742-2500. Cafeteria preferred by locals for affordable breakfasts of pancakes and French toast. Later in the day, a fine vegetarian chili is offered along with burgers, pizza, and a decent salad bar. Mon–Fri 8.30am–5pm, Sat–Sun 8am–5pm.

Alta Lodge ☎ 801/742-3500. Mainly the domain of guests, it's possible to drop in for lunch or reserve a dinner spot in this unpretentious dining room, where communal tables add to the convivial environment. The chef has been working here for

more than thirty years, and each evening he offers a dependable if not gourmet choice of three entrees (typically a beef, fish, and veggie option). On Sundays an elaborate, belly-busting buffet is served 6–9pm ($28).

Collins Grill On-mountain ☎ 801/799-2297. Sit-down restaurant located mid-mountain on the second level of Watson Shelter, where diners don slippers and warm up by a roaring fire while waiting to be served. While the cafeteria a floor below satisfies with beers and buckets of fries, *Collins* lists finer fare such as shrimp pasta ($15) and a bison burger with cilantro pesto spread ($13). Lunch only (11.30am–3pm).

Joanies Main road, by entrance to *Alta Lodge* ☎801/742-2221. A friendly café with superb views over the mountain's front face. Quick and cheap breakfasts (bagels, egg sandwiches, and omelettes) along with light lunches and dinners (wraps, deli sandwiches, salads) are offered along with espresso drinks and, best of all, fruit-filled smoothies. Three microbrews are on tap for a chilled après-ski. Daily 8am–8pm.

Shallow Shaft Main road, across from *Alta Lodge* ☎801/742-2177. Open for more than three decades, this intimate institution serves the finest food in Little Cottonwood Canyon. It's run by a husband-and-wife team, and meals here are sophisticated and delicious, with starters like crab-stuffed mushroom caps ($8) and entrees of house-smoked salmon ($22) and a delicious rack of lamb ($31). The atmosphere is perfectly cozy, with old mining gear on the walls and a few tables using old Alta single chairs as seats. Affordable take-out pizzas are also available. Reservations essential. Daily 6–10pm.

Other activities and attractions

Save for **backcountry skiing**, the only alternate outdoor option is the resort's basic 5km **cross-country ski track** (☎801/742-9722; pass $7, rentals $15). The *Rustler Lodge* offers a small menu of **spa services**, but the decadent Cliff Spa (see p.290) at Snowbird is far superior.

Listings

Avalanche hotline ☎801/742-0830.
Pharmacy The closest pharmacy is located a mile down the road at Snowbird; see p.290 for details.

Post office There's a small post office across from the *Rustler Lodge* on the main drag; Mon–Sat 9am–noon.

Brighton

Boarders regularly outnumber skiers at **Brighton**, Utah's oldest ski resort, situated at the head of Big Cottonwood Canyon. They're there for the plentiful freestyle terrain, extensive grooming (moguls are scarce indeed), and the resort's long-standing allegiance to the sport. Not that others don't take advantage of the slopes as well; with kids skiing free, Brighton attracts a large family contingent, and it's also the sole resort in the area with a substantial **night riding** operation, having some two dozen runs open until 9pm, six nights a week.

Though markedly smaller than its Cottonwood Canyons companions, runs here are no less thrilling, and families in particular should find the compact size more manageable to negotiate. Even more important, the ski area receives the same remarkable quantity of feather-light **snow** as its neighbors. Don't plan a full week around Brighton, even with Solitude next door. It does, however, deserve at least a day or two of your time, more if you plan on doing some **backcountry** exploring.

With Brighton's relatively small size comes a serious lack of slopeside amenities. Environmental restrictions prevent the building of new structures, so the only overnight options are a twenty-room lodge and a small selection of private cabins and homes for rent. Dining options are limited, with a cafeteria, general store, and a bar being the sole choices.

Mountain info

Phone ☎801/532-4731 or 1-800 /873-5512

Snow phone ☎801/532-4731

Website ⊛www.brightonresort.com

Price $40, $24 for night riding (4pm–9pm), children 10 and under free

Operating times Mid-Nov to mid-April Mon–Sat 9am–9pm, Sun 9am–4pm

No. of lifts 7

Base elevation 8755′

Summit elevation 10500′

Vertical drop 1745′

No. of trails 65

Acreage 850

Beginner 20%

Intermediate 40%

Expert 40%

Average snowfall 500″

Snowmaking Yes (200 acres)

Night skiing Yes, Mon–Sat

Nursery facilities No

Arrival and getting around

Via Hwy-190, Brighton is only thirty minutes from downtown Salt Lake City, less than an hour from its airport, weather permitting. For arrival and transportation details in Salt Lake City, see p.259. Though not as treacherous as the access road up Little Cottonwood Canyon, Hwy-190 still has plenty of twists and curves and shuts down regularly for avalanche control. Call ☎801/536-5778 for the latest road conditions. UTA buses riding back down Big Cottonwood can take you to Solitude should you want to ride there or visit any of the resort's restaurants.

The mountain

Brighton's 850-acres cup like a "C" around the base area, with the steepest and most varied terrain located toward either end. On one side the **Millicent** double chair rises 1100ft to access the resort's most exciting in-bounds terrain, a semi-bald slope loaded with rocky outcrops, swooping gullies, treacherous chutes, and wide-open spaces on which to carve. A handful of blues and greens mean all but true beginners can ride up "Milly" to scope out the terrain. On the opposite end of the "C," the **Great Western Express** quad zips up nearly 1750ft to a tightly spaced web of over a dozen runs ranging from perilous steeps to evenly pitched blues like Elk Park, the resort's longest run.

In between Great Western and Millicent, the mountain flattens out. The **Snake River Express** and **Crest Express** quads lead to its upper portion, home to short intermediate and advanced tree runs. Also accessible from here is Sunshine, a peak-to-base green that allows even rookies to gasp at the incredible view of massive peaks rolling into the horizon off the resort's backside. Below are mostly easy intermediate and beginner trails, along with the resort's halfpipe and terrain park.

Surrounding the entire perimeter of the ski area is acre upon acre of lift-accessible **backcountry**. The heavenly terrain surrounding the resort can quickly turn hellish – avalanches occur frequently – so do not cross the boundary without proper gear, a local guide, and information on the latest conditions from the ski patrol huts located by each of the four lifts that access the area.

Beginner

Though only twenty percent of the ski area is rated suitable for beginners, green runs are well spread across the mountain so there's little chance first-timers will get bored. Add to this an experienced ski school and it's easy to see why locals consistently vote it Utah's top family resort. Even on weekday afternoons the green runs can be crowded with three-foot tall kamikazes bombing downhill.

Intermediate

With blue runs spiraling down every lift, intermediates could spend nearly a full day exploring the slopes without riding the same run twice. Intermediates should make a point of exploring **Millicent**, running laps on both the area's eponymous double chair and the shorter Evergreen, another double that runs closer to the border with Solitude resort. **Easy Out**, **Backdoor**, and **Perris Bowl** all offer a taste of the undulating terrain found on this side of the ski area. Toward the ski area's center, the trees below **Hawkeye Access** will entertain confident riders with tight BMX-like paths laced with rollers, log-slides, and banked turns. Higher up the steeper runs just off the Crest Express quad – including **Snow Drift** and **Wren Hallow** – are good trails to test if you're ready to step up to Brighton's blacks.

Expert

Experts will spend most of their in-bounds time on the Great Western and Millicent chairs. Great Western leads to more straightforward blacks, along with **True Grit** and **Clark's Roost**, two of the mountain's steepest runs and good spots to search out powder. On the resort's opposite end, Millicent's terrain is a jumble of fall lines tossed across an invariably rolling surface. If you're looking for the most difficult run head to Mount Millicent's peak, from which **Elevator** rockets straight down through a rocky no-fall zone. While these runs are all notable, a good chunk of expert locals come to Brighton for one thing; backcountry access. Top areas include the tree-choked runs in **Hidden Canyon** that lead back to the Great Western lift and the steep blasts on **Wolverine Cirque** reached via a hike off of Millicent. The Crest Express is also popular for its access to the couloirs of **Pioneer Peak**.

Freestyle

Brighton spends a considerable amount of money on its freestyle terrain. The **halfpipe** above the Majestic lift is only of fair quality, but the **terrain park** located below it improves every year, and includes a few rails along with several large kickers. To better experience the freestyle potential at Brighton as a whole, follow the lead of local riders and search out the natural jumps located across the mountain, especially off Millicent. Out of bounds, there are even more options, as evidenced by the video and photo shoots that take place out here throughout the season.

Lift tickets, lessons, and rentals

A **day pass** (9am–4pm) at Brighton costs $40; $25 for night skiing (4–9pm). Kids 10 and under ride for free every day, no strings attached, and seniors pay $10. To save a few bucks off adult tickets, purchase passes at the outlets listed on p.262. Single-ride passes ($8) are useful for those headed straight to the backcountry, who won't be reusing the lifts time and again. The **ski school** (☎801/532-4731 ext 234)) here is both relaxed and recommended. Program rates range from $25 for a group lesson up to $275 for a full-day, one-on-one session, and first-time boarders can take advantage of the **Burton Method Center**, where $90 pays for learner's lift ticket, lessons, and a Learn-To-Ride board (see p.534 for more on this program). The resort rents out **equipment**, but it's best to skip lots of screaming children in the rental lines by arriving gear in hand. Boarders can rent at the Bottom Line Snowboard shop a few miles before the resort, where Salomon demos, Swallow Tails for powder days and even split boards are available (☏801/293-1642; daily 8am–6pm). For ski and board rental recommendations outside of the canyon, see p.262.

Accommodation, eating, and drinking

The resort's only slopeside **accommodation** option is the twenty-room *Brighton Lodge* (☏801/532-4731; $135), the alpine equivalent of a highway motel. Though nothing fancy, it's at least affordable and has an outdoor hot tub, free basic breakfasts and a communal TV room. Multinight package deals are available, as are a few slightly cheaper private hostel rooms with shared baths. Mount Majestic property management (☏1-888/236-0667, ⓦwww .mountmajestic.com) has a handful of private cabins for rent slopeside, and more accommodations can be found a mile down the road at and around Solitude (see p.293), or in Salt Lake City (see p.260).

Eating choices are limited too. The *Alpine Rose* is a basic cafeteria, and *Molly Green's* next door is Big Cottonwood Canyon's most rollicking evening establishment and a friendly place to down a few beers along with simple pub grub. It's a private club so you may have to pay a small fee to enter. In the morning, a general store at the resort's entrance dishes up egg sandwiches and stocks items like sunscreen in case you've forgotten anything.

Park City

Despite Brigham Young's strictures against prospecting for precious metals – he feared a Gentile "Gold Rush" – seeds for the town of **PARK CITY** were planted in the 1860s with the establishment of silver mining camps. The resultant rowdy days, which saw its Main Street lined with nearly thirty saloons established to satisfy the needs of hard-drinking miners, may never come back, but another recent growth spurt, thanks in large part to the 2002 **Winter Olympics**, has set Park City booming once again.

For the casual visitor the increase in accommodation, restaurants, and nightlife options makes a convenient destination even more convenient – though perhaps slightly less authentic and more expensive. Already one of the easiest ski towns to reach – Salt Lake City's international airport is less than a 45-minute drive away – the town, home to three world-class ski resorts and the winter **Sundance Film Festival**, is now one of the most well-rounded ski destinations in the Americas.

The closest ski area to Park City's six-block long historic Main Street and connected to it via a ski lift is **Park City Mountain Resort**, the oldest of the three resorts and still dotted with boarded-up mines. Due north of this is **Deer Valley**, the smallest of the three and easily the most luxurious. Though the resort's reactionary snowboarding ban does little to help its stuffy reputation, its flawlessly groomed slopes, attentive service, and gourmet restaurants earned it top overall resort honors in *Ski* magazine's 2001 reader survey. Furthest away, four miles south of Main Street, is **The Canyons** – not to be confused with "the Canyons," local-speak for the nearby Cottonwood Canyons – the largest ski area in the group and still growing. Though each have their own personal-

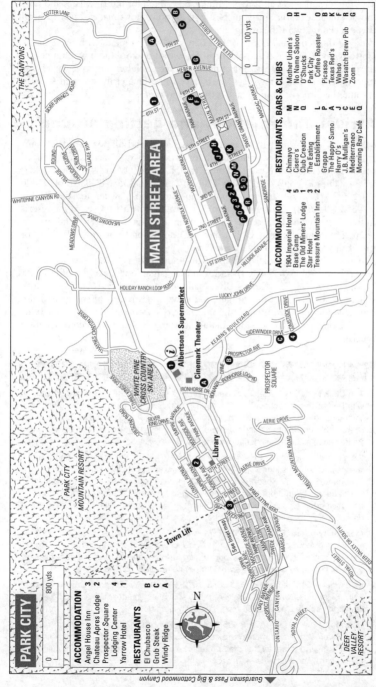

MAIN STREET AREA

0 — 100 yds

RESTAURANTS, BARS & CLUBS

Chimayo	4	Mother Urban's	D
Cisero's	5	No Name Saloon	H
Club Creation	1	O'Shucks	I
The Eating		Park City	
Establishment	L	Coffee Roaster	O
Grappa	P	Picasso	B
The Happy Sumo	A	Texas Red's	K
Harry O's	J	Wahso	F
J.B. Mulligan's	C	Wasatch Brew Pub	R
Mediterraneo	E	Zoom	G
Morning Ray Café	Q		

ACCOMMODATION

1904 Imperial Hotel	4
Base Camp	5
The Old Miners' Lodge	1
Star Hotel	3
Treasure Mountain Inn	2

PARK CITY

0 — 800 yds

ACCOMMODATION

Angel House Inn	3
Chateau Apres Lodge	2
Prospector Square	
Lodging Center	4
Yarrow Hotel	1

RESTAURANTS

El Chubasco	B
Grub Steak	C
Windy Ridge	A

N

Guardsman Pass & Big Cottonwood Canyon

ities, the terrain across all three is similar, best suited for intermediates and not-too-advanced experts, and your best bet, if you've got time, is to **sample all three** if skiing, two if boarding.

It's worth noting that none of Park City's resorts competes with those in the Cottonwood Canyons (Alta, Brighton, Snowbird, and Solitude) when it comes to snowfall, natural beauty, and difficulty of accessible terrain, so if you're visiting for more than a few days you'd have to be financially strapped – or an absolute beginner – to not make a trip out to them.

Arrival, information, and getting around

Salt Lake City's airport is 35 highway miles away, and **airport shuttle** companies ferry passengers back-and-forth for around $30 one-way. Recommended operators include All Resort Express (℡435/649-3999 or 1-800/457-9457, ⓦwww.allresort.com), Park City Transportation (℡435/649-8567 or 1-800 /364-8472, ⓦwww.parkcitytranportation.com), and Powder for the People (℡435/649-6648), all of whom also run shuttles from Park City to the resorts in the Cottonwood Canyons as well. If planning on renting a car at the airport, see p.259 for information. Unlike at the Cottonwood Canyons, a 4WD car or tire chains are not essential in Park City.

In town, there's a small **information center** at 528 Main St (Mon–Sat 10am–7pm; ℡435/649-6104) and a much larger one near the Prospector Square district on 750 Kearns Blvd (daily 9am–6pm; ℡435/658-4541). Both supply the usual array of pamphlets and news on current happenings, and also can help sort out overnight lodging. The city's **website** (ⓦwww.parkcityinfo.com) offers much the same, including some last-minute accommodation specials.

Rental and retail shops

The Click Park City Plaza, 1890 Bonanza Drive ℡435/940-9004. Snowboard shop with Burton demo packages ($25 a day with deals on longer rentals) along with a limited but quality selection of soft goods. Good also for information on local skate scene, which heads to the indoor spots in SLC or Provo in winter when Park City's Park Avenue skatepark is buried under snow. Daily 8am–8pm.

Jans 1600 Park Ave ℡435/649-4949 or 1-800/745-1020, ⓦwww.jans.com. The largest of eight Jans in the area – including rental shops at Deer Valley (℡435/649-2680) and Park City Resort (℡435/649-4950) – is also the pre-eminent overnight tuning spot in town, from simple waxes ($10) to full ski ($37) and board ($30) tune-ups. Also good for ski (Rossignol, K2, Salomon, Volkl, and more) rentals, with great deals on four- to seven- day packages; their snowboard rental pool is minimal.

Max Snowboard Rentals 1284 Lowell ℡435/647-9699 or ℡1-800/525-0314, ⓦwww.maxsnowboards.com. Country-wide chain with convenient PCMR and Canyon locations. Competitively priced Burton, Ride, and Nitro snowboard packages, with both step-in and strap-binding systems. Daily 8am–7pm.

Milosport 1351 Kearns Blvd ℡435/658-1616, ⓦwww.milosport.com. Only rents out basic Salomon boards, but if looking to buy snowboarding gear this should be your first stop as they stock a wide range of quality brands.

Surefoot 1284 Empire Ave ℡435/649-6016, ⓦwww.surefoot.com. Though retail only, Surefoot is worth mentioning in case you're looking to buy a new ski boot. Using high-tech gadgetry, the staff promises a perfect fit by building you a custom fit foot-bed. Well worth the extra cost.

Most of what there is to see and do is easily accessed via Park City's efficient and free **bus** network (☏435/615-5301; daily 7.30am–10.30pm), with routes as far out as Kimball Junction. Another option is the **trolley** (10am–10pm; free) that runs the length of Park City's busy drag every fifteen minutes. If **renting a car** in Park City, useful for day-trips, try Budget (☏435/645-7555 or 1-800/237-7251), Enterprise (☏435/655-7277 or 1-800/455-8661), or Park City Car Rental (☏435/658-0403 or 1-888/472-7524). Parking on Main Street can be problematic, though spots are typically available in the **parking garage** on Swede Alley east of the main drag.

Park City Mountain Resort

Park City Mountain Resort (PCMR) sits snug up against Park City's historic downtown. Its Town Lift heads down all the way to Main Street, and the base area is only a ten-minute walk away. Located in between Deer Valley and the Canyons, the resort's overall aesthetic sits squarely between the two as well. Not as groomed and pampered as Deer Valley, nor as isolated and natural as The Canyons, PCMR is the most average of the three. It's not that the resort does anything wrong. It's home to a social **base village**, with several plazas, an ice-skating rink, rental shops, and laid-back restaurants to choose from. It has an **excellent lift system**, including four high-speed sixpacks, which does a fantastic job of spreading visitors across the slopes. And it presents varied terrain, especially suited for intermediates. It's more that the resort does little that is spectacular, while its competitors improve at a faster clip.

On the slopes, the hundred named **trails** face in nearly every direction, allowing the sun to work its magic as riders negotiate their way around the hill. The majority are short trails, with the main exceptions the experts-only areas around the **McConkey** and **Jupiter** bowls, home to some of the best accessible terrain on the Wasatch's east side.

Beginner

Beginning skiers and riders are basically relegated to the northern quarter of the resort. Within walking distance of the base area, the **First Time** triple and **Three Kings** double chairs access small, dedicated beginner areas. Beyond the few runs here, the rest of the resort's greens cut across blues and blacks, so look for signs before leaping down a trail. At over three miles long, **Home Run**, accessed via the Payday and Bonanza sixpacks, is by far the top green here. A wonderfully wide groomer, it's tailor-made for boosting confidence – as long as it stays uncrowded. Toward the end of the day

Mountain info – Park City
Phone ☏435/649-8111
Snow phone ☏435/647-5449
Website ⌨www.parkcitymountain.com
Price $60
Operating times Dec to mid-April daily 9am–4pm
No. of lifts 14
Base elevation 6900′
Summit elevation 10,000′
Vertical drop 3100′
No. of trails 100
Acreage 3300
Beginner 18%
Intermediate 44%
Expert 38%
Average snowfall 325″
Snowmaking Yes (500 acres)
Night skiing Yes (First Time and PayDay lifts only)
Nursery facilities No, but Annie's Nannies (☏435/615-1935) in town is a licensed child care option

and on busy weekends, the long and snaking run gets jammed with traffic. When looking to step up, the first blue worth hitting is **Payday**, which starts off flat and only gradually gets steeper. After that, head over to King Con to pick your way down **Temptation**, **Climax**, and **Monitor**.

Intermediate

PCMR's slopes are best suited for intermediates. Except for the double chair to Jupiter Bowl, every lift accesses at least one blue run, meaning you can spend days here working your way back and forth across the resort's ridges before familiarity sets in. The most obvious lift to hit is the King Con high-speed quad, which accesses a dozen or so rather short blues spilling across the fall line down to **Broadway**, a gully that connects back to the lift. **Temptation**, a good warm-up and the widest run of the bunch here, offers up groomed thrills with a set of rollers at the top end and a wide turn toward the bottom. The steepest King Con blues, all side-by-side, are **Sitka**, **Shamus**, and **Liberty**, each offering a quick blast of speed before depositing you back in the Broadway gully. One lift over, the Silverlode sixpack accesses several more must-hit blues, including **Parley's Park,** which, snow permitting, boasts a few beginner's jumps, and **Hidden Splendor**, an often bumpy freeriding blast with patches of trees to dive into on either side.

Confident intermediates should head toward the high-speed McConkey's sixpack lift. There are three marked blues well worth riding plus an unnamed pinballesque trail that snakes under the lift, strewn with banked turns, branches to dodge, and stomach-churning rollers; it may be the most addictive run in the resort.

Expert

While it's possible to hit a black from nearly every lift at PCMR, expert riders should concentrate on riding up either McConkey Bowl's sixpack or Jupiter Bowl's slower double. McConkey's lift heads up some 1200ft in five minutes to access **McConkey Bowl**, steep and especially deep on powder days. While here, take time to explore the lines located in the massive double black glades entered via **Tycoon**.

Rather than hiking up to Jupiter Peak via the McConkey chair, save your energy by taking the lift to the top of **Jupiter Bowl**, which warms up nicely in the early afternoon sun. To reach the double chair, you'll want to keep your speed via Jupiter Access as it flattens out considerably. Once atop Jupiter Bowl, the options seem boundless. If feeling lazy, blasting directly down the liftline is tricky enough, though don't stray too far right as you may get mired in deep, flat basin. More challenging terrain is located both to the left and right. Heading left down the mountain leads to runs like **Portuguese Gap**, a hair-raising sheer shot through an alley of trees, and **Scott's Bowl**, a steep, wide open powderfield. Beyond here, the **Pinecone Ridge** area holds dozens of double black chutes to choose from. While well worth visiting, keep in mind that all of these chutes dump off into Thayne's Canyon, giving you a 30- to 45-minute trek up a pair of lifts back to Jupiter Bowl.

Bump skiers will want to run some laps on the creaky Thaynes double chair, which gives burning thighs plenty of time to rest after blasting through the moguls that regularly form on **The Hoist**, **Thaynes**, and **Double Jack**. **Silver King**, located underneath the Ski Team lift back toward the base area, is one of the steepest blazed trails on the mountain.

Freestyle

Riding high after successfully hosting all of the Olympic snowboard competitions in 2002, PCMR poured bucket-loads of money into improving and expanding its freestyle terrain. The stand-out feature here is the **Eagle Superpipe**, cut by the same pipedragon brought in for the Olympic competitions and one of the best halfpipes in the country. Should the nearly 20ft-high walls prove too daunting, the **Payday Halfpipe** one lift ride away is slightly smaller. Trailing only slightly behind The Canyons, PCMR's three terrain parks range from the basic **First Time** park up to double-lined **King's Crown**, located above the base area and home to a half-dozen progressively larger jumps along with twice as many rails and boxes.

Lift tickets, lessons, and rentals

As the only resort in Park City with night skiing, there's quite an array of **lift tickets** to choose from here, including All Day (9am–9pm) for $67, Twilight (12.30–9pm) for $58, and Night Skiing (4–9pm) for $28. You can typically save a few dollars at local ski shops or by looking into multiday passes. The **ski school** at PCMR has earned a solid reputation and offers an in-depth array of classes, though the base area can get crowded with competing classes. Group lessons start at around $60 to all-day, one-on-one lessons for over $500. Advanced workshops on topics ranging from skiing bumps to riding in the park are available, and beginning boarders should note that Burton's Learn-to-Ride program is utilized (see p.534 for more information). **Rentals** are available in the Legacy Lodge for around $30 per day, though you'll get a better price and selection at the stores listed on p.272.

Deer Valley

Confident in the notion that you can't please all the people all the time, **Deer Valley** has cultivated a particular niche for skiers – and skiers only – since opening nearly 25 years ago. If your dreams hinge on impeccably groomed slopes, ultrafine dining, and the absence of those pesky snowboarders, this may be the hill for you – as long as you've got the money. It's true that lift tickets are only a few dollars more than Park City's other resorts, but so is everything else – from rentals to lessons to lunch – which adds up to a tidy sum at day's end.

Even if you're more likely to spot fur trim than duct tape decorating the fancy one-piece ski-suits frequently worn here, the overall vibe is surprisingly relaxed, due in equal parts to typically superb conditions and an attentive staff. Run like a top-notch hotel, the resort boasts one employee for every four guests and from the moment of your arrival – when parking lot employees unload your skis for you – odds are you'll never be out of sight of a helpful employee's green jacket.

Mountain info – Deer Valley

Phone ☎435/649-1000 or 1-800/424-3337

Snow phone ☎435/649-2000

Website ⊛www.deervalley.com

Price $65

Operating times Dec to early April daily 9am–4pm

No. of lifts 19, including 1 four-person gondola

Base elevation 6570′

Summit elevation 9570′

Vertical drop 3000′

No. of trails 88

Acreage 1750

Beginner 15%

Intermediate 50%

Expert 35%

Average snowfall 325″

Snowmaking Yes (600 acres)

Night skiing No

Nursery facilities Infant to 12 years, reservations essential; ☎435/645-6648 or 1-888/754-8477

The **terrain** spreads across four rounded peaks, ranging in size from the 7950ft Little Baldy to the top of Empire Canyon at 9570ft. The best-groomed resort in North America, Deer Valley has an army of around twenty snowcats that head out nightly to groom three-quarters of the runs on these peaks – they even smooth out fresh snowfall, much to the consternation of powder hounds. Though rumours prevail that you'll find more corporate moguls on the slopes here than bumped-out ones, in reality the resort has several steep, bumped, and wooded areas for expert skiers to play around in. That said, Deer Valley's strongest suit is its intermediate and beginner terrain, the majority of it groomed so spectacularly that you'd almost need to want to crash in order to do so. One trail that shouldn't be missed regardless of your abilities is Deer Valley's most conspicuous display of wealth, **Last Chance**, an easy blue that meanders past sculpture-fronted multi-million dollar homes regularly featured in architectural magazines.

Beginner

Statistically only a small percentage of the mountain is devoted to beginning skiers. But the resort's smooth runs open up many of the blue runs to all but the most basic of beginners. If a newbie, you are best off learning turns on **Wild West**, by the Snowpark Lodge. All other beginners can spend the day traveling up over a dozen lifts, sampling runs on each of the resort's five summits. Greens and easy blues are spread all across the resort – even Empire Canyon, the most challenging peak, has a small "family area" with a pair of greens – meaning if you can link a turn with at least a semblance of confidence you won't spend your day stuck on the same run or same lift.

Intermediate

The majority of Deer Valley's blue runs are so neatly groomed that it's easy to feel as if you've raised your skills overnight after running the long straight trails that predominate. A top spot to do laps is Flagstaff Mountain's **Northside Express** quad, which zips over five equally fun intermediate runs that are far enough away from the base to remain crowd-free throughout the day. When you feel like stepping up some, head for the double blues on Bald Mountain, including **Wizard** and **Tycoon**, where slightly steeper pitches have you testing your own personal speed limits. Double blues **Orion**, **Solace**, and **Conviction** in Empire Canyon can determine whether you're ready to move up to blacks.

Expert

Step one: snag a handy expert-only trail map, outlining all of the resort's black diamond terrain. Step two: head for **Empire Canyon**, the ski area's premier expert zone snuggled up against Park City Mountain Resort's northern border and separated only by a rope. It's one of the few areas not groomed into a carpet nightly, and top runs include the short but sweetly steep **Daly Bowl** and **Daly Chutes**, along with the wide-open **Empire Bowl**. One peak over, **Flagstaff Mountain** boasts a tight patch of glades in the steep Ontario Bowl along with some good warm-up mogul runs under the Red Cloud triple chair. One more peak over, **Bald Mountain** is home to the final clutch of worthy expert runs, a string of mogul fields, and a pair of small black diamond bowls accessed via the Mayflower and Sultan triples. It's also worth noting that the resort offers a complimentary Black Diamond tour of the mountain daily, a good opportunity to pick the mind of a local skier for more information.

Freestyle

Despite the rising popularity of skiers riding the pipe and running laps in terrain parks, Deer Valley has yet to create any specific freestyle terrain. **Champion**, a mogul run on the resort's front face, has played host to the World Freestyle Skiing Championships, and there's a slight chance you may be able to huck off a few jumps there when visiting. In any case, if freestyle terrain is important to you head to PCMR or The Canyons instead.

Lift tickets, lessons, and rentals

Deer Valley limits **lift-ticket** sales to 5000 a day – purportedly to limit not lift-lines but crowds at the restaurants – so if it's a busy period purchase the $65 pass in advance (kids $35; seniors $45). To save a few bucks, buy multiday tickets, or stop by a local ski shop for discounted tickets. The **ski school** is a well-trained, enthusiastic lot (several-hundred dollar tips are not uncommon) making this a great place to learn the sport or brush up on technique. Semi-private morning or afternoon lessons (maximum of four students) cost $95 per session, while private lessons cost the same amount per hour. The children's program consists of a full-day lesson plus lunch, a good deal at $115. The resort's **rental shop** in the Snow Park Lodge rents out high-quality skis (and snowblades) in good condition. Prices are high – packages range from $40–50 a day – so you're better off renting from a local Park City outfitter if cost is a concern (see box on p.272).

The Canyons

Having changed its name and ownership several times since opening as Park City West in 1968, **The Canyons**, purchased by the American Ski Company (ASC) in 1997, has benefited significantly from the corporate makeover. Over a dozen new lifts have doubled the in-bounds terrain to a hefty 3500 acres, and slopeside additions have started to put a dent in Deer Valley's real-estate sales. But with the ASC in financial purgatory – in 2002 they had to sell off Heavenly (see p.358) – plans to expand the terrain by a much as another 2500 acres are probably on hold for now. Even so, it remains the largest resort in Park City and edges out its two competitors on diversity of in-bounds terrain, freestyle opportunities, and out-of-bounds options.

The mountain's 146 **trails** – an exaggeration, as several are merely cat tracks – are spread even and wide across eight peaks, the highest being the celebrat-

Mountain info – The Canyons

Phone ☎ 435/649-5400

Snow phone ☎ 435/615-3456

Website ⊚ www.thecanyons.com

Price $58

Operating times Dec to mid-April daily 9am–4pm

No. of lifts 16, including 1 eight-passenger gondola

Base elevation 6800′

Summit elevation 9900′

Vertical drop 3190′

No. of trails 146

Acreage 3500

Beginner 14%

Intermediate 44%

Expert 42%

Average snowfall 325″

Snowmaking Yes (200 acres)

Night skiing No

Nursery facilities: Yes, infant to 4 years; ☎ 435/615-8036 or 435/615-3402

ed **Ninety Nine 90** (9990ft). Though the size of the resort helps scatter the crowds, it also hinders reliable grooming and makes getting around quickly a hassle. To access most of the terrain you first have to reach mid-mountain either by the base's eight-person **Flight of the Canyons Gondola** or via the creaky Golden Eagle double chair. The gondola is clearly the better option, though on weekends lines can be long so arrive early. Once dropped off by the Red Pine Lodge, it's still another catwalk and one or two lift rides away from where you want to be. After you've finally reached your destination it's easy to speedily run lap after lap until your lungs give out.

As the farthest mountain from Main Street, The Canyons is typically the least crowded Park City resort. An open-air gondola shuttles passengers back and forth from the main parking lot to the base area, ending what used to be a laborious process. The **base village**, like the mountain, has received several additions over the last few years – most notably the towering *Grand Summit Hotel* (see p.281) – but a five-year, $500-million "master plan" is still in the works. For now, the main plaza – known as the Forum – plays host to the occasional concert and is encircled with a small collection of retail shops and food shacks; visitors in the know skip the latter and stock up at the cheaper 7-11 at the resort's entrance.

Beginner

True first-time skiers and boarders are better off at Deer Valley and Park City Mountain Resort respectively, as very few trails here are rated green. On a more positive note, the main beginner's chair – the **High Meadow quad** – is located mid-mountain, giving newbies the opportunity to ride up the gondola with everyone else (something kids seem to enjoy immensely). Once you're ready to try out something a bit more challenging, head up the Saddleback quad to the runs listed below.

Intermediate

Intermediate skiers looking for a warm-up should head straight toward the Saddleback quad from the gondola drop-off to either **Snow Dancer** or **Kokopelli.** The first is an archetypal blue run, while the flatter second trail connects to **Echo**, another fine blue and the easiest route down to **Snow Canyon**. This is the resort's widest run and perfect for giant carving turns, a good location for a group of mixed abilities; the Snow Canyon lift is speedy, there's a day lodge to take breaks in, and unlike many other areas here it's nearly impossible to get lost and split up. After a few rounds, continue down to the

Super Condor Express quad to check out **Boa**, a blue that indeed winds like a snake down from Murdock Peak. From the same lift, try the steeper **Aplande** and **Kestrel** runs that branch off of **Apex Ridge**. Confidently handle these and you're ready to stomp the resort's black diamond terrain.

The resort's opposite end is teeming with even more blues, and a trip to the secluded runs off **Peak 5** and the newer **Dreamscape** reveals a flatter, less congested part of the resort. While the extra-long and curvy blues below, particularly **Serenity** and **Harmony**, require plenty of speed to clear without stalling, they're worth hitting if just to check out the ritzy homes being built alongside and to dart under the overpasses on the way.

Expert

Black diamond runs are scattered across every peak, the best accessed via the Super Condor, Saddleback, and Ninety Nine 90 express quads. Upon exiting the gondola, most expert riders make straight for the latter lift and peak **Ninety Nine 90** – especially on powder mornings, when the trip turns into a leave-the-stragglers-behind mad dash. Top runs on this peak include the often bumped-out **94 Turns** and **Charlie Brown** a hair-raising double black shooting straight down a steep, tree-clogged slope. Once the snow gets tracked out up top, head down the mountain to ride **Diamond Ridge** under the Tombstone Express quad; running along a ridge spine, hidden stashes abound in the trees to your left.

One lift over, Saddleback Express leads to **The Pines** on one side and **The Aspens** on the other, both impressive glades that take quick turns to navigate successfully. Further north, the ridge-riding **Super Condor Express** is the place to come on crowded days as the steep and narrow chutes attract only the most confident, while the slightly less steep north-facing runs collect the most snow.

Another lure for experts is the **backcountry access** points off the tops of Peak 5 and Ninety Nine 90. Don't even consider heading out unless you're experienced and with someone who knows the routes, as you may well end up lost in Big Cottonwood Canyon somewhere below Solitude (see p.291). Though not technically backcountry, a safer bet is the terrain on **Murdock Peak**. Regularly patrolled and an easy twenty-minute hike from the Super Condor lift, the exhilarating steep chutes here should satisfy all but the most hard-core.

Freestyle

While Park City Mountain Resort has the better halfpipe, The Canyons is the better overall **freestyle** spot. The main **park**, CIA (Canyons International Airport), is conveniently located under the Red Hawk quad within view of the base area and is home to an impressive bank of rails and progressively bigger tabletop jumps. The resort's two **halfpipes** (one a kiddie pipe) are less impressive, although several of the natural pipes listed on the trail map are worth exploring. The best of these is **Canis Lupis**, a long natural gully with banked walls up to 15ft high along its length.

Lift tickets, lessons, and rentals

The Canyons **lift tickets** sell for $59 (kids and seniors $31), though cheaper tickets ($50–55) are sold in town at local ski shops and even cheaper $46–50 tickets can be purchased at the ski and snowboard shops in Salt Lake City (including those in the airport). The ski school offers a typical array of courses starting at around $100 for a morning/afternoon group lesson; call ☎435/615-

3449 for more information. As for **rentals**, the resort stocks a decent selection of Rossignol skis and snowboards (step-in only), but the outfitters listed on p.272 are a better bet.

Accommodation

All three ski areas are so close to town, so there's no pressing need to choose slopeside **accommodation**, though it's available in abundance. Regardless of where you bunk down, if you're with a group of four or more you'll almost certainly do better to **rent a condo**. Besides the PCMR and Deer Valley reservations services listed below, agents with a comprehensive list of properties include AAA Lodging and Ski Reservations (☎435/649-2526 or 1-800/522-7669, ⓦwww.ski-res.com) and Around Town Lodging (☎435/645-9335 or 1-800/347-3392, ⓦwww.aroundtownlodging.com). A final option, only worth looking into during the busiest times or if on a budget, are the chain hotels at **Kimball Junction**, off 1-80 about eight miles north of town; try the *Hampton Inn* (☎435/645-0900, ⓕ435/645-967, ⓦwww.hamptoninn.com; ④) or the *Best Western Landmark Inn* (☎1-800/548-8824, ⓦwww.bwlandmarkinn.com; ④).

Note that during the busiest periods – especially around Christmas and the Sundance Film Festival – rates rise exponentially for all types of accommodation, and you'll need to book well in advance.

Downtown Park City

1904 Imperial Hotel 221 Main St ☎435/649-1904 or 1-800/669-UTAH, ⓦwww.1904imperial .com. An original building from Park City's mining days, the *Imperial* is now the town's most central B&B. Its ten rooms are small but cozy and the parlor windows overlook Main Street. There's a hot tub as well. Rates vary between rooms depending on size. ⑤

Angel House Inn 713 Norfolk Ave ☎435/647-0338 or 1-800/264-3501, ⓦwww.angelhouseinn .com. Perched on a hill above Main Street, this friendly ten-room B&B features artistic touches in every room and healthy breakfasts. The rooms require booking well in advance, in part because you can ski under Park City Mountain Resort's "Town" lift straight to the inn. There are also three apartments across the road, which can sleep 4–6 people each and have full kitchen and dining facilities ($250–350). ⑥

Base Camp 268 Main St ☎435/655-7244 or 1-888/980-7244, ⓦwww.parkcitybasecamp.com. Formerly the *Park City Hostel*, this centrally located 68-bed establishment includes a small but well-equipped communal kitchen, Internet lounge, and laundry. The four-bed dorm rooms (which can be rented as private rooms during slow times) are small, but the management is friendly and upbeat. No lock-outs. Dorm bed $35, private room ⑤

Chateau Apres Lodge 1299 Norfolk Ave ☎435/649-9372 or 1-800/357-3556, ⓦwww.chateauapres.com. Worth considering for its convenient location and relatively low rates, but the drab double rooms are well past their prime

and have tiny bathrooms. There are also two sex-segregated dorms, each with twenty metal-frame bunks on a concrete floor that's reminiscent of an army barracks; only book here if you can't get into the *Base Camp* hostel (see above). Rates include continental breakfast. Dorm beds $28; rooms ④

The Old Miners' Lodge 615 Woodside Ave ☎435/645-8068 or 1-800/648-8068, ⓦwww.old-minerslodge.com. This restored 1893 lodge houses a simple but comfortable B&B. The communal areas are a bit dowdy, but the quiet and central location compensates. The twelve rooms vary quite a bit in size and décor, including one whose entrance mimics an old mine shaft. ⑤

Prospector Square Lodging Center 2200 Sidewinder Drive ☎435/649-7100 or 1-800/453-3812, ⓦwww.prospectorlodging.com. This corporate conference center, located a short bus ride from Main Street, offers regular hotel rooms that can sleep four in a pinch and a range of condo units for 4–8 people. Useful extras in every room include fridge, microwave, and coffeemaker, and there's a heated hot tub. ⑥

Star Hotel 227 Main St t☎435/649-8333 or 1-888/649-8333, ⓕ435/649-5746. It's hard to believe that a cheerful old boarding-house style hotel with creaky beds, saggy furniture, and cluttered common areas exists in the heart of posh Downtown. Great value for the unfussy guest as rates include breakfast and dinner. ③ per person, ⑥ double

Treasure Mountain Inn 255 Main St ☎435/649-7334 or 1-800/344-2460. This broad, ugly Sixties edifice, built in two sections separated by an outdoor pool, has spooky corridors straight out of *The Shining*. Its best feature is its location, smack in the center of town, and most rooms have useful extras like a fridge, kitchenette, and coffeemaker. Some two-bedroom units also available. ❹

Yarrow Hotel 1800 Park Ave ☎435/649-7000 or 1-800/927-7694, ⓦwww.yarrowhotel.com. Best for families, this full-service hotel and conference center outside of the downtown core by the Albertson's supermarket has large standard rooms with fridges and coffeemakers, as well as one-bedroom suites with kitchenettes. Other facilities include a heated outdoor pool and hot tub, and the local movie theater is a short walk away; rates include a buffet breakfast. ❻

Park City Mountain Resort

Park City Mountain Reservations ☎1-800/222-7275, ⓦwww.parkcitymountain.com. The resort's official lodging service can help sort you out with everything from a hotel room on Main Street to slope-side condos sleeping the largest of groups. Be sure to confirm the location of the property before booking; many of their condos are miles from the slopes. ❹–❾

Shadow Ridge Resort 50 Shadow Ridge St ☎435/649-4300 or 1-800/451-3031, ⓦwww.shadowridgepc.com. A five-minute walk from the lifts, this ski-vacation stalwart offers a range of plain one- and two-bedroom suites with full kitchen facilities, plus a small, heated outdoor pool, spa, sauna, and fitness center. Other extras include underground parking, laundry, and free après-ski snacks in the lounge. Hotel ❼, 1–2 bedroom ❽

Snow Flower Condominiums 400 Silver King Drive ☎435/649-6400 or 1-800/852-3101, ⓦwww.snowflowerparkcity.com. Ski-in ski-out complex by the PCMR's Three Kings Lift. Though the complex itself is far from stylish, the full-service condos for 2–12 people are comfortable enough and all feature kitchens, fireplaces, cable TV, and VCRs, and balconies, and guests have access to a pair of heated outdoor pools, laundry, underground parking, and movie rentals. ❽–❾

The Canyons

Grand Summit Resort Hotel ☎1-888/CANYONS, ⓕ435-649-7374, ⓦwww.thecanyons.com. Unlike most of the American Ski Company's other *Grand Summits*, this classy five-star slopeside resort complex feels both well designed and well constructed. Plush hotel rooms and suites are superbly equipped and amenities include a full range of fitness/spa facilities, indoor/outdoor heated pool and hot tubs, underground parking, as well as exquisite dining at *The Cabin* restaurant (see p.283). A basic room goes for $330 during winter. ❾

Sundial Lodge ☎1-888/CANYONS, ⓕ435-649-7374, ⓦwww.thecanyons.com. Ski in Ski out condominium lodge with both studio-style hotel rooms (winter $239/summer $129) and condos that sleep up to six people ($459/$349), plus two outdoor hot tubs with plunge pools. ❽–❾

Deer Valley

Deer Valley Lodging ☎435/649-4040 or 1-800/453-3833, ⓕ435/647-3318, ⓦwww.deervalleylodging.com. Manages almost thirty lodges, townhouses, and condo complexes clustered together in two distinct areas: Snow Park, near the chairlifts base, and Silver Lake Village, in the heart of the ski area almost halfway up the mountain. The high-end properties tend to be large and very comfortably appointed, with full-service kitchens, hot tubs, stone fireplaces, and mountain views, but there are not many one-bedroom places available – and even the smallest of these go for $340–400 per night in winter. For something approaching good value, a two-bedroom apartment or townhome is set up to accommodate four adults at $400–600 per night. ❾

Stein Eriksen Lodge ☎435/649-3700 or 1-800/453-1302, ⓦwww.steinlodge.com. The most salubrious address in Deer Valley's Silver Lake area, with award-winning restaurants and basic necessities like hand-painted tiles in guestroom kitchens. Probably worth the money to anyone who can contemplate spending upwards of $700 a night. ❾

Eating

For many, sampling Park City's fine **restaurants** is an integral part of the town's vacation experience. Few ski areas offer so many varieties of cuisine to choose from, and with the pick of the restaurants lined up on Main Street, you can cruise a bit and compare menus before deciding. That said, you'll likely need a reservation to get a table at any of the more upmarket places, and prices on the whole are fairly expensive. One name that inevitably crops up in discussions of the best-of-the-best is dynamic chef-restaurateur Bill White, who owns and oversees three of the most popular and expensive restaurants in town – *Grappa*, *Chimayo*, and *Wahso* – along with the newer *Windy Ridge*, an upmarket deli a short drive from Main Street. Those on a really tight **budget** may want to load up at the Albertson's supermarket (see "Listings") or head north to I-80 and Kimball Junction, home to a stand of fast-food restaurants.

As far as **resort dining** is concerned, both The Canyons and Park City Mountain Resort offer a perfectly adequate mix of crowded cafeterias, smaller specialty shacks (waffles, Krispy Kreme, etc), and beery après-ski venues. Sitting down to eat at Deer Valley, though, may very well be the highlight of your day; even the Snow Park Lodge's cafeteria features delicacies like roasted garlic cloves and sautéed veal – though the more pedestrian-sounding turkey chili takes top marks.

Park City

Chimayo 368 Main St ☎ 435/649-6222. Bill White's attempt at "cutting-edge contemporary Southwestern cuisine" lives up to its promise. Appetizers include a goat-cheese and mozzarella chile relleno with a poblano and pumpkin-seed pesto. Entrees, such as barbecued spare ribs with a chipotle and caramelized pineapple glaze ($30), are just as adventurous. Daily for dinner only.

The Eating Establishment 317 Main St ☎ 435/649-8284. A family-friendly menu starring babyback ribs, pasta primavera, breaded veal cutlets, and chicken-fried steak ($14–18). The breakfasts are classic American: greasy, big, and popular with locals. Daily 8am–10pm.

El Chubasco Park City Plaza, 1890 Bonanza Drive ☎ 435/645-9114. Whether you're after a big plate of burritos or just a sanity check on the menu prices in Park City, this strip-mall Mexican grill fits the bill. All the usuals – tacos, enchiladas, tamales, and moles – are in the $5–8 range. Lunch and dinner daily; take-out and delivery available.

Grappa 151 Main St ☎ 435/645-0636. The eldest of Bill White's Park City restaurants boasts the most satisfying and expensive Italian menu in town. Start with a grape and gorgonzola salad, and move to cedar-planked sea bass or scaloppini of turkey saltimbocca style (entrees $26–36). Dinner only, reservations essential.

Grub Steak Prospector Square, 2200 Sidewinder Drive ☎ 435/649-8060. Reliably good steaks (served with baked potato), ribs, and even buffalo keep this restaurant popular with families. Prices are a tad more than you might expect given its location well away from Main Street; entrees run $16–30. Dinner daily, lunch Mon–Sat.

The Happy Sumo 838 Park Ave ☎ 435/649-5522. Of the local sushi spots, this is the pick for its location – centrally tucked behind Main St where fewer tourists wander. Lunch and dinner Mon–Sat.

Mediterraneo 628 Park Ave ☎ 435/647-0369. Though the menu may not be as eclectic as *Grappa*, patrons of this convivial Italian restaurant

don't seem to mind one bit. The fairly priced standards ($12–18), such as spaghetti with meatballs or the spicy *penne all' arrabiata*, are both superb and filling. Complimentary foccacia comes straight from the wood-fired oven, as do an assortment of Neapolitan-style pizzas and fish specials. Recommended. Dinner daily from 5pm.

Morning Ray Café 268 Main St ☎ 435/649-5686. You may have to wait and it's not especially cheap, but the basic breakfast menu of omelets, bagels, and muffins is worth it. The lunch menu includes creative salads, sandwiches, and vegetarian items. Daily 7am–midnight, and until 2am Fri & Sat.

Park City Coffee Roaster 221 Main St. With the popularity of the larger breakfast places on Main Street, it's worth knowing about this tiny espresso bar with its own fresh-roasted coffees and slim selection of fresh muffins and pastries. Daily 7am–6pm.

Picasso 900 Main St ☎ 435/658-3030. Although this Spanish restaurant at the bottom of Main Street does have a full menu with lots of spiced and marinated meats and seafood, the mix of drink and tapas is the real draw. Tapas items $6–10, entrees $16–26. Live music Fri–Sat. Open daily 5pm–midnight.

Texas Red's 440 Main St. Get up to your elbows in ribs with spicy sauce ($15) at this amiable and affordable Main Street joint. Daily 11.30am–10pm.

Wahso 577 Main St ☎ 435/615-0300. The third of Bill White's restaurants is also where he's most likely to be found actually cooking. The menu is an adventurous marriage of French and Asian cuisine, and the wine list is mind-bendingly complete. The opulent interior features several intimate curtained booths, perfect for enjoying exquisite dishes like Chilean glazed sea bass and a spicy Szechuan filet mignon (entrees $22–30). Open daily for dinner only, reservations essential.

Windy Ridge 1250 Iron Horse Drive ☎ 435/647-0880. This yuppie-style deli is a local favorite for original sandwiches ($5–8), filling salads, freshly made soups, and daily specials like spinach and mushroom lasagne ($6). Its location, far from the bustle of Main Street, ensures an easygoing atmosphere.

Zoom 660 Main St ☎435/949-9108. Owned by Robert Redford, this hip bar/restaurant has an eye-catching interior of timber, copper, and glass wrapped around an open kitchen, where chefs toss about Thai BBQ shrimp, pastas, risotto, and flaming rib-eye steaks with steely precision (entrees $17–22). Watching them work while tucking into a $10 burger or smoked turkey sandwich at the bar is worth every penny. Daily for lunch and dinner.

Park City Mountain Resort

Legends *Legacy Lodge*. This slopeside bar is superbly situated with huge windows looking straight onto skiers as they head down at day's end. There is a relaxed mood with big chairs, a roaring fire, and usually a fairly unobtrusive acoustic duo; membership is required.

Moose's Upper Plaza ☎435/649-8600. One of several like-minded restaurants scattered about the resort's base area, dishing out greasy break-fasts ($3–8) and grilled burgers ($7) and BBQ pork sandwiches ($8) at lunchtime.

Pig Pen A rowdy après-ski venue one flight up in the resort plaza building behind the skating rink. They skirt Utah's membership issue surrounding bars by serving up burgers and nachos. There is a pool table, foosball, and even table-tennis, making for an ideal environment for a beery dissection of the day's events.

The Canyons

The Cabin *Grand Summit* ☎435/615-8060. Expensive dining featuring an American West and Southwest menu heavy on beef and lamb dishes (entrees $18–34) and boasting an extensive wine

list and full bar. Reservations recommended.

Doc's *Grand Summit*. Classy bar that makes for a good place to end a day of sliding around, either sitting at the leather-and-brass bar or, on warmer days, on the deck overlooking the gondola. Good cocktails ($7) and an average beer selection to go along with an assortment of soups and sandwiches in the $7–9 range. A more low-key spot for après-ski is the BBQ joint *Smokies*, also near the gondola base.

Deer Valley

The Mariposa *Silver Lake Lodge* ☎435/645-6715. The best of Deer Valley's restaurants, where appetizers like dill cured salmon are $11, rack of lamb costs $37, and a charbroiled yellowfin tuna steak $36. The desserts come draped in all manner of dining awards. Tues–Sun 6–10pm.

Royal Street Cafe *Silver Lake Lodge* ☎435/649-1000. Formerly *McHenry's*, the quintessential ski-bum experience continues at the café's schmoozy deckchair "beach." Inside, things have brightened up considerably with items like Asian cured duck confit ($9) and a roasted game hen and shiitake mushroom pot pie ($11) making decent choices if you want to forsake the large and tasty burgers. Daily 11.30am–9pm.

Snow Park Lodge Cafeteria *Snow Park Lodge* ☎435/645-6632. While both the breakfast buffet and tasty lunches served here are worth swooning over, it's the all-you-can-eat evening seafood buffet ($50) that's especially recommended. Every evening except Sunday, seemingly every seafood species is on display, from seared yellowfin tuna to Cajun crabcakes to fresh tiger shrimp and sushi rolls. There are always a few meats at the carvery as well, though you may want to skip those to save room for selections from the dessert table. Evening reservations are essential.

Nightlife and entertainment

Park City holds itself up as a **nightlife** capital, which it undoubtedly is by Utah standards. Except during the Sundance Film Festival, there's nothing really wild going on; just a handful of bars in which to get boisterous after a day in the mountains and a club or two that host bands and DJs. Utah's club membership requirements are enforced here as well (see box on p.259). For **listings** of upcoming events, check the weekly *Park Record* newspaper or the free *Park City's E.A.R.*, a monthly entertainment rag.

For a tamer evening out, Hollywood's biggest blockbusters are shown at the Cinemark Theater (☎435/649-6541), 1776 Park Ave, behind the Albertson's supermarket, while an art-house flick is featured every Fri and Sat at 8pm, Sun at 6pm, in the public library's auditorium, 1255 Park Ave (☎435/615-8291, ⓦ www.parkcityfilmseries.com).

Cisero's 306 Main St ☎435/649-5044. The base-ment bar of *Cisero's* Italian restaurant has a band or DJ playing at least a couple of nights a week. The house band is a basic blues-rock affair com-prising the owner and his friends, and there's a small dance-floor and a couple of pool tables.

Club Creation 268 Main St ☎435/615-7588. Though originally conceived as an all-ages dance-hall, *Club Creation* recently morphed into yet another Main Street bar – albeit one that boasts a stylish neon-and-steel interior as opposed to a bra-hatted moosehead. There are still DJs and some dancing on weekends, and the bar can whip up an extensive range of rum-based drinks.

Harry O's 427 Main St ☎435/647-9494. The only place big enough to put on name bands and large Latin or funk combos, *Harry O's* is pretty well unchallenged as the town's "major" nightclub. There's little rhyme or reason to their line-up, and on any evening you might encounter a fourteen-piece ensemble or just about any species of DJ. Cover $5–20.

J.B. Mulligan's 804 Main St ☎435/658-0717. Though typically only hopping when there's a blue-grass, reggae, or rock band playing, *J.B.*'s is ideal for a beer – they pour a nice Guinness – and game of pool. Bands usually play three nights a week, during which the cover is $5–10.

Mother Urban's 625 Main St ☎435/615-7200. As befits a bar that hosts mainly jazz and original acoustic acts, this is a dark, subterranean room reached via a steep staircase. The musical vibe is usually a mellow one, although performers vary from angst-ridden singer-songwriters to superb New Orleans jazz/funk combos. There are also free big-screen movies on Monday nights. Cover $5–10.

No Name Saloon 447 Main St. Formerly called the *Alamo*, and still often referred to by that name, *No Name* doesn't have bands or DJs, just a juke-box and lots of lively talking and drinking. There's a basic list of bar sandwiches, with occasional après-ski specials. Busy enough midweek, the place is packed to bursting on weekends with an even mix of locals and visitors.

O'Shucks 427 Main St. There's no actual enter-tainment at *O'Shucks* beyond a couple of televi-sions and an occasional acoustic strummer/war-bler, but if the crowd isn't at the *No Name Saloon*, odds are they'll be here. Additional attractions are free peanuts and a decent garlic burger.

Wasatch Brew Pub 250 Main St. Overrated brewpub located at the top of Main Street. Though the beer's marketing is clever – the slogan for the brewery's Polygamy Porter, "Why just have one," caused a mini-uproar a few years back – Utah's impotent liquor laws leave the suds lacking in both flavor and punch. The bar menu of fish and chips, burgers, salads, and the like is decent enough, but unless you're here to watch a game on one of sev-eral TVs, it's not a strong enough draw. Daily 11am–midnight.

Other activities and attractions

Time spent pursuing one of the many non-downhill winter sports – or visit-ing Utah Olympic Park – may be in order if you're here a few days. Those looking for less active pursuits can enjoy a day in a **spa** – try the Park City Racquet Club (☎435-615-5400), training center of the US Ski Team, or the Silver Mountain Spa (☎435/649-6670, ⓦwww.silvermountainspa.com) – or shopping at the sixty-odd **outlet shops** (ⓦwww.shopparkcity.com) out by Kimball Junction.

The Utah Olympic Park and other winter sports

Six miles north of Main Street, the **Utah Olympic Park** (☎435/658-4200, ⓦwww.utaholympicpark.com; $7) is Park City's most lasting reminder of the Olympic games. It's mainly a touring facility, and visitors can watch training sessions as athletes launch themselves off one of six ski jumps or slide down twisting bobsled/luge track. Throughout the winter, the center also runs a bob-sled public passenger ride program, allowing visitors to hit speeds of 80mph; reservations are required and the cost is $200 per person.

Park City's most accessible **cross-country skiing** area is the White Pine Cross-Country Ski Area (☎435-615-5858, ⓦwww.whitepinetouring.com; $10 trail pass), 18km of trails spread across the centrally located Park City Golf Course. More worthwhile are the guided cross-country and snowshoe trips

Sundance Film Festival

Held during the second half of January, Robert Redford's once maverick **Sundance Film Festival** (☎435/328-3456, ⓦwww.sundance.org) sees the downtown area overrun by what locals refer to as P.I.B.'s ("people in black"). Even though the festival has grown into the sort of establishment happening it once sought to undermine, every year still sees some unexpected gems emerge, and last-minute **tickets** can usually be had. An intriguing alternative is the **Slamdance Film Festival** (☎323/466-1786, ⓦwww.slamdance.com), showcasing only first-time directors working with restricted budgets and run over the same ten days in January.

run by both White Pine Tours (same details as above) and the nonprofit **Norwegian Outdoor Exploration Center** (☎435/649-5322 or 1-800 /649-5322, ⓦwww.outdoorcenter.org). Both offer personalized jaunts into the local backcountry for around $20 per hour, per person. Other day-off options include **snowmobile** tours through the Wasatch backcountry – check with High Country Snowmobile (☎435/645-7533 or 1-800/404-7669, ⓦwww .highcountrysnow.com) – or a **sleigh ride** over at the Homestead Resort (☎435/654-1102, ⓦwww.homesteadresort.com).

Finally, if you've got kids in tow, a trip to the **Gorgoza Park** (☎435/658-2648, ⓦwww.gorgozapark.com; daily noon–8pm) can provide some relief. A fifteen-minute drive away (call for directions), this overpriced playground offers lift-serviced tubing ($18 for two hours) and gocart-like snowmobiles for 5–12 year-olds ($6 for six laps). Rail addicts may also be interested in checking out their **jib park** ($15–20), littered with a handful of tabletop jumps and around a dozen rails.

Listings

Avalanche hotline ☎435/658-5512.
Banks Park City Bank, 820 Park Ave (Mon–Fri 9am–5pm, Sat 10am–4pm; ☎435/658-3730); Wells Fargo, 1776 Park Ave (Mon–Fri 9.30am–4.30pm, Sat 10am–4pm; ☎435/649-2384). The most centrally located 24hr ATM is the Bank One machine at 614 Main St.
Bookstore Dolly's, 510 Main St (daily 10am–10pm; ☎435/649-8062).
Internet access Park City Public Library (see below; free); Alpine Internet Coffeehouse, 758 Main St (daily 8am–10pm; ☎435/649-0051; $5 per 30min).
Library Park City Public Library, 1255 Park Ave (Mon–Thurs 10am–9pm, Fri–Sat 10am–6pm, Sun 1–5pm; ☎435/615-5600).

Medical center Snow Creek Emergency & Medical Center, 1600 Snow Creek Drive (Mon–Fri 9am–7pm, Sat–Sun 10am–6pm; ☎435/655-0055).
Pharmacy Albertson's, 1880 Park Ave (Mon–Fri 9am–9pm, Sat 9am–7pm, Sun 11am–5pm).
Police 445 Marsac St ☎435/645-5050; emergencies ☎911.
Post office 450 Main St (downtown) and 2100 Park Ave (hours and phone for both are Mon–Fri 9am–5.30pm, Sat 9am–1pm; ☎1-800/275-8777).
Supermarket Albertson's, 1880 Park Ave (open 24hrs).
Taxi Ace Cab Co ☎435/649-8294; Powder for the People ☎435/649-6648.

Snowbird

The phrase "steep and deep" is thrown around breezily in describing ski resorts, but at **Snowbird** it's a fact. Very few mountains in the US and Canada match Snowbird's hair-raising collection of chutes, cirques, cliffs, and knee-knocking straights, and even fewer can top the 500-plus inches of light, perfect powder that falls annually, allowing the resort to regularly stay open a whopping 200 days-plus per season. And, now that skiers can also visit neighboring Alta on a single shared lift ticket, it's easy to see why ski magazines consistently rate this picturesque end of Little Cottonwood Canyon one of North America's premier mountain destinations.

Some might argue over the aesthetics of the tiny village, a collection of avalanche-proof concrete bunkers including the *Cliff Lodge*'s imposing twelve-story tower, but it's impossible to deny the stark beauty of the canyon rising on either side. No wonder that Ted Johnson and Derek Bass, the resort's founders, were attracted to this slice of real estate. Bass remains in charge, and his free-spirited grit – he was the first person to scale the highest peak on each of the seven continents – helps define the resort and the ski-it-if-you-can attitude that prevails. The planners' inclusion of a 125-passenger aerial tram (known, appropriately enough, as The Tram) proved to be their best design choice, allowing riders to quickly ascend from the base area to Hidden Peak (11,000ft), then run 3000ft laps for as long as their legs and lungs hold out.

The resort spills down in three easily negotiable directions from Hidden Peak. Looking down from The Tram, to the right are the steeps of Peruvian Gulch, and to the left the larger Gad Valley, home to a diverse range of terrain with superb pockets of trees. Off the backside is the Mineral Basin, drawing intermediate and advanced sliders to its undulating, wide-open slopes. Whichever you choose, plan on arriving early and riding hard, as the fresh powder on the mountain gets tracked out impossibly fast. Snowbird's only true faults lie in a serious lack of off-slope activities and affordable slopeside accommodation. You can find both in Park City; here it's all about the slopes.

Mountain info	
Phone ☎801/742-2222	
Snow phone ☎801/933-2100	
Website ◎www.snowbird.com	
Price $56 Tram plus chairlifts, $47 chairlifts only, $64 Alta/Snowbird combined	
Operating times Mid-Nov to mid-May 9am–4pm	
No. of lifts 11, including a 125-person tram	
Base elevation 7760′	
Summit elevation 11,000′	
Vertical drop 3240′	
No. of trails 85	
Acreage 2500	
Beginner 27%	
Intermediate 38%	
Expert 35%	
Average snowfall 500″	
Snowmaking Limited	
Night skiing Very limited; Wed & Fri on Chickadee	
Nursery facilities The superb Camp Snowbird (☎801/933-2256); 6 weeks to 3 years; reservations two weeks in advance	

Arrival, information, and local transport

Tucked away toward the far end of Little Cottonwood Canyon's access road (**Hwy-210**), Snowbird is thirty miles from Salt Lake City's airport, 25 miles from its downtown. See p.259 for practical information on services from the airport and greater Salt Lake City area.

It usually takes 45 minutes to an hour to arrive from downtown or the airport, less than half that from the South Valley, but during snowstorms and busy weekend mornings the trip can be substantially longer. On weekends, arrive as early as possible and park either in the Gad Valley lot (ticket sales available) or on the bypass road north of the tubing hill. During storms you may have no choice but to wait as the narrow canyon road is frequently closed. Consider using the UTA bus network unless you have experience driving on snow and a 4WD or snowchains.

The resort's village is small and centered around the **Snowbird Center**, near the Tram's loading deck. If planning on heading up to Alta to ski or grab dinner, **free buses** run the mile-long route regularly.

The mountain

For a bird's-eye view of Snowbird's burly terrain, hitch a ride on the **Tram**. Actually two trams (one red, one blue), the 125-person flying buses travel nearly 3000 vertical feet, zipping to the 11,000ft Hidden Peak in seven breathtaking minutes. Nab an open window perch if possible.

Look out your left at broad-shouldered **Mount Baldy** (11,068ft), on whose rocky peak the US Freeskiing Nationals take place annually. Between Baldy and the tramline is the predominantly expert area **Peruvian Gulch** that contains many of the resort's steepest runs. On the opposite side of the tram line is the larger **Gad Valley**, a mixture of more steeps, impressive clusters of trees, a stream of meandering blues, and, toward the bottom, some rare true greens. Also here, tucked away on the resort's western edge, are Snowbird's steadily improving terrain parks.

The newest available terrain – and gateway to Alta – is the south-facing **Mineral Basin**. With 500 acres spilling off the backside of both the Tram and Little Cloud lift, looking over an impressive vista of peaks rolling off into the horizon, this least crowded portion of the mountain has become a haven for intermediates to kick back on less daunting 1500ft laps.

Beginner

Snowbird bruises both the bodies and egos of beginners. One of its longest green runs, **Emma**, would probably be rated a black diamond by many East Coast resorts, and other greens slice across blue and black runs. Besides the absolute beginner **Chickadee** slope sandwiched between the *Cliff Lodge* and Snowbird Center, the only lift for never-evers is Baby Thunder. After mastering these limited runs, head for the greens in the Mineral Basin, although most should really be graded blue.

Intermediate

Though clearly more an experts' mountain, Snowbird has plenty to offer intermediates willing to work their way across the slopes. Warm up with the resort's longest trail, **Chip's Run**, which snakes 2.5 miles down Hidden Peak back to the Snowbird Center, passing through the heart of the Peruvian Gulch area. Next head for the Mineral Basin, where running laps in the sun off the two high-speed quads could occupy an entire morning. **Powder Paradise** is wide open enough to allow for safe spills off its lively rollers, while all the blazed runs leading down from the Baldy Express chair should prove a blast. Back on the front side, the Gad Valley has more worthwhile blues, the best of which are accessed via the Gad 2 chair. Try **Bananas**, steep at the top though mellow further down, and **Bassackwards**, second only to Chip's in length and just as curvaceous.

Expert

Throw a dart blindfolded at a trail map of Snowbird and odds are you'll hit not only an expert trail but one that's a memorable ride. As with other rugged mountain resorts like Jackson Hole and Crested Butte, the black and double black diamond slopes here require vigilance and a healthy dose of looking before you leap. But if you explore smartly and manage to time your visit during a snowstorm, get ready for a perfect day of face shots and high-speed thrills. Classic runs include the fear-inspiring double-black chutes of **Great Scott** and **Upper Cirque**; **Silver Fox**, a nearly pencil-straight drop down the entire front face; and **Regulator Johnson**, a wide-open bowl beneath the Little Cloud chair. Once the most obvious powder lines seem spent, consider hiking the ridge up to **High Baldy** or head over into the **Thunder Bowl**, which tends to stockpile hidden stashes. For **trees**, head into the upper reaches of the Gad Valley, where hard-charging lines can be had off to the skier's right of **Bananas** and in the trees spilling off of **Tiger Tail**. Be sure to pick carefully, though, as the Gad Valley hides some nasty cliffs.

Freestyle

While hunting down natural terrain features is still the sport of choice for many, Snowbird has begun making concessions for the jibbing and hucking crowd. Still not on par with Park City's two snowboard-friendly resorts or

Backcountry skiing in Little Cottonwood and beyond

Although the 4700 combined acres offered by Alta and Snowbird are more than enough terrain for most, experts looking to explore further into the **backcountry** of Little Cottonwood Canyon and beyond are spoiled for choice. The most adventurous option is the **Ski Utah Interconnect Tour**, an excursion run by Utah's skiing board that visits fiver resorts in one day through a combination of in-bound, terrain, and backcountry routes (☎801/534-1097, ⊛www.skiutah.com; $150). From the resorts themselves, it's possible to book off-piste tours through the ski schools or to head into the backcountry independently if you're with someone who knows the routes. At Snowbird, for example, a hike off the Gad 2 chair and past the resort boundaries leads into the **White Pine Canyon**, a locals' favorite, from where it's possible to curve back into the resort to the Baby Thunder chair or to ride down to the access road.

If you'd like to spend the entire day in the backcountry and be carted back up to the top after each descent, the most thrilling (though expensive) option is **Wasatch Powderbird Guides**, a heliskiing/boarding outfit in the Snowbird base area ($700/day, meals not included; ☎801/742-2800 or 1-800/974-4354, ⊛www.heliskiwasatch .com). Recent battles with conservationists have threatened to limit flying days drastically or even shut the operation permanently – you can read their arguments at ⊛www.saveourcanyons.org – so call ahead for the latest details. Reservations are typically needed weeks in advance.

A cheaper option is to take a **cat skiing** tour in **Grizzly Gulch Bowl**. Located above Alta, Grizzly Gulch has long been a favorite filming spot for both pro boarders and skiers. Alta's tours – which snowboarders can join – run around $200 for five trips up to the 10,500ft peak; call the Alf Engen Ski School for details (☎801/359-1078).

For more **information on local backcountry options**, stop by Wasatch Touring in Salt Lake City (see p.262 for details) or pick up a copy of *Wasatch Tours*, by Alexis Kelner and Dave Hanscom, or for the most insane routes *The Chuting Gallery*, by Andrew McLean. Both are available in bookstores throughout Salt Lake and Park City. For current conditions in Little Cottonwood Canyon, call ☎801/742-0830.

Safety precautions are always in effect when exploring backcountry outside of resort boundaries. See p.31 for full details.

Brighton one canyon over, Snowbird's **terrain parks** have received major upgrades. The primary park, located off the **Baby Thunder** lift, boasts a line of quality rails along with some decent jumps, while the **Baby Emma** park holds bumps for beginners along with a mediocre halfpipe.

Lift tickets, lessons, and rentals

Unless you've received your **tickets** as part of a ski-and-stay package, get passes at the Smith's supermarket chain or ski rental outlets in Salt Lake City (see p.262) for savings of upwards of $15 on the $56 one-day **lift ticket**, good for the aerial tram plus lifts. A $47 day pass covers chairlifts only, a good deal if you're not obsessed with getting maximum vertical; the Alta/Snowbird combined ticket costs $64. Multiday passes can save up to $10 per day, and up to two children (12 and under) ski free on chairlifts with any adult.

Snowbird's slightly pricey but well-respected **snow school** (☎801/933-2170) offers the usual spread of beginner courses, though remember it's not a prototypical first-timer's mountain. The school does run several "workshops" and camps for intermediate to expert skiers and boarders, and you'd be hard pressed to find a better resort to get lessons on riding both powder and ultra-steep terrain expertly.

The best **equipment rental** option at the resort is Sportstalker II on the top level of the Snowbird center. Decent demo packages cost $25–35; see p.262 if you want to rent before arrival.

Accommodation

Accommodation at Snowbird is expensive. There are no dorm beds available and the four local lodgings are all owned by the resort. If you're on anything resembling a budget, you'll need to secure accommodation down in Salt Lake City (see p.260). Everything here is booked via Snowbird Central Reservations (☎1-800/640-2002), which offers an array of weekend, full-week, and early/late-season packages. The *Cliff Lodge* (❸–❾), the resort's only full-service hotel, dominates the village. The architectural showcase inside is a massive glass-walled atrium looking out on the Peruvian Gulch area, and the entire building – from the lobby to rooms to the spa – is adorned with Oriental rugs, many part of Dick Bass's personal collection. Choose from rather plain queen-bed suites (with in-room glass-walled showers) to deluxe two-bedroom suites. Guests have access to the spa (see p.290), a large game room, room service, and heated ski lockers. The other resort options – *Iron Blossom Lodge*, *Lodge at Snowbird*, and *The Inn* – are all similarly priced timeshare condo complexes (❼–❾), offering studio and one-bedroom condos complete with saunas, hot tubs, and lounges.

You could always stay a mile up the road at Alta (see p.265) or check with the *Blackjack Lodge*, between the two resorts, to see if any of their ten studio or one-bedroom condos are available (☎1-800/343-0347, ⊛www.blackjacklodge.com; ❼–❽).

Eating and drinking

Snowbird contains a respectable collection of **restaurants** spread throughout its small village. The majority of choices are located either in the Snowbird Center or the *Cliff Lodge*, and once you've lost your enthusiasm for these, it's a thirty-minute drive down to the South Valley or a bit further into downtown Salt Lake City (see pp.260–61 for recommendations). Also worth a visit is the superb and expensive *Shallow Shaft*, a mile up the road at Alta (see p.267).

When night falls, the majority of guests turn out the lights early, so consider bringing along your Scrabble board – or a designated driver for the drive back up from Salt Lake City. Save for the smoky *Tram Club* and the odd night when a restaurant's lounge gets hopping, slopeside **nightlife** is nearly nonexistent.

The Aerie *Cliff Lodge* ☎801/933-2160. Located on the *Cliff Lodge*'s tenth floor, this intimate Asian-themed eatery serves up Snowbird's finest food, with jaw-dropping views and prices to match. The menu, featuring ahi tuna, New York strip, and duck breast tossed in pasta, is bolstered by an extensive wine list. Live jazz is played in the lounge Wed, Fri, and Sat, and there's also an expensive sushi bar open nightly. Mornings are more relaxed, with a phenomenal all-you-can-eat breakfast buffet ($15) starting at 7am. Dinner reservations recommended.

The Forklift Level 3, Snowbird Center. Across from the Tram entrance, this casual café is the best place for a good-value sit-down breakfast or lunch. The filling, basic breakfasts – omelets, French toast, hash browns – run $5–8, while a lunch of soup or salad and a sandwich – the corned beef is tops – costs a few bucks more. Beer and wine served.

General Gritts Grocery Level 1, Snowbird Center. Small grocery convenient for stocking up on snacks and other slope necessities or for downing a quick coffee and egg sandwich before dashing upstairs to get on the tram.

Keyhole Junction *Cliff Lodge*. Snowbird's Tex-Mex restaurant, most impressive for its tequila selection of some two dozen varieties. Fine for a decent meal and a strong margarita, but if you're craving tacos a drive down to Salt Lake City's *Lone Star Taqueria* is a must (see p.261).

The Steak Pit Level 1, Snowbird Center. The resort's oldest restaurant sticks to the standard steakhouse formula; several cuts of beef are offered, most massive, along with butter-drenched hunks of seafood and bottomless bowls of salad. The décor is uninspiring, though quite honestly no one seems to mind.

Tram Club Level 1, Snowbird Center. The sole nightspot of note in the village. If it weren't for the Tram's engine room visible against one wall, this large and dark "private club" could easily be mistaken for a low-key hotel cocktail lounge. Unless there's a live band on, you'll have to make do with a couple of pool tables, jukebox, and row of TVs. If hungry, skip the pub grub and grab a pizza from *Pier 49 San Francisco Pizza* up one level.

Wildflower *Iron Blossom Lodge* ☎801/933-2230. An attractive and cozy dinner-only Italian restaurant located a short walk south of the Snowbird Center. Pastas, including vegetarian ravioli, run $15–20, entrees $20–30. The dessert menu includes a lip-smacking hazelnut torte ($8). Reservations recommended.

Other activities and attractions

With such a compact base area, there's not much to do on a day off. The most popular nearby attraction is the **Cliff Spa** (daily 6am–10pm; $20 for Snowbird guests, $30 all others; ☎801/933-2225, ⓦwww.cliffspa.com), a massive complex located on the top levels of the *Cliff Lodge*. The highlight is the gorgeous adults-only rooftop pool and hot tub, though the eucalyptus steam room and variety of scrubs, wraps, and massages ($75–200) earn high marks as well. If that's too relaxing an option, there's a tiny **ice-skating rink** ($7) off the *Cliff Lodge* and a small **tubing hill** ($5) as well. If money is no concern, check with the Snowbird Activity Center (☎801/933-2147 or ext 2147 if staying at the resort), which can arrange snowmobiling, sleigh rides, and even spring fly-fishing trips.

Listings

Avalanche hotline ☎801/742-0830.
Internet The business center in the *Cliff Lodge* has connections; check with concierge for availability.

Pharmacy The Snowbird Pharmacy (☎801/359-1720) on Level 2 in the Snowbird Center is open daily 9am–5pm.
Post office Located in Snowbird Pharmacy; informal hours (☎801/742-2376).

Solitude

Were it not for its more notable neighbors – Brighton next door, and Alta and Snowbird one canyon over – **Solitude** would be a major magnet for powder hounds both regionally and nationally. As it stands, the resort embodies its name, remaining the least crowded of the four Cottonwood Canyon resorts. Even on weekends and at the busiest of holiday periods, liftlines are often insignificant. Of course, die-hard fans of the mountain – mainly day-trippers along with a healthy dose of slopeside condo owners – wouldn't want it any other way.

The ski area itself may not be the steepest, deepest, or most freestyle friendly in Utah, but most resorts would kill for Solitude's bountiful snowfall and 1200 varied acres of skiable terrain. What those acres lack in beginner runs is compensated for in both intermediate and expert terrain; there's at least a full day or two without much repetition, and the relative paucity of skiers ensures that fresh powder stashes can be found even days after a storm.

Mountain info

Phone ☎ 801/534-1400
Snow phone ☎ 801/536-5777
Website ⊛ www.skisolitude.com
Price $44
Operating times mid-Nov to mid-April daily 9am–4pm
No. of lifts 8
Base elevation 7988′
Summit elevation 10,035′
Vertical drop 2047′
No. of trails 64
Acreage 1200
Beginner 20%
Intermediate 50%
Expert 30%
Average snowfall 500″
Snowmaking Minor
Night skiing No
Nursery facilities No

At the base, the resort's attractive pint-sized **village**, designed by Intrawest, the same folks behind the base villages at Whistler, Keystone, and Stratton, is cautiously expanding. Emulating the success of nearby Deer Valley, several new high-end condo complexes and a collection of rather pricey restaurants draw more overnight guests, though the overall buzz is still light years away from Park City. Even if you've got cash to burn, the village remains best suited for self-entertaining families and others willing to bed down early.

Arrival and resort transport

Located a dozen miles up Big Cottonwood Canyon's Hwy-190, Solitude is under an hour's drive from Salt Lake City's airport and only half that from its downtown. For information on the airport, shuttle services, and other transportation practicalities from Salt Lake City, see p.259. Not as treacherous as the access road up Little Cottonwood Canyon, Hwy-190 still has plenty of twists and curves and shuts down regularly for avalanche control. Call ☎ 801/536-5778 for the latest road conditions.

The resort has two entrances, one to the smaller Moonbeam Center area and another to the Village at Solitude. The latter holds all of the resort's accommodation options and most of the restaurants, though for day-trippers there's little difference between the two. The resort's Nordic Center is located beyond both, closer to the entrance to Brighton.

The mountain

Save for a rocky face directly below the resort's highest point (10,035ft), nearly all of Solitude's **ski area** is open for exploration. The eastern third of the ski area's frontside is nearly all intermediate terrain, while the small handful of runs suitable for beginners are stuck on the lower half of the mountain by the base areas. The rest of the front face is split between long curving blues, half-a-dozen groomed blacks, and several steep, tree-studded experts-only areas.

Except for the Eagle Express quad, the **lifts** across this front section are slow and antiquated doubles. On the backside, the Honeycomb Return, the resort's newest quad, zips riders out of 400 acres of patrolled in-bounds "backcountry" known as **Honeycomb Canyon.** Though always spectacular, in the past the only way out of this backside canyon was an insanely long traverse that left most boarders knuckle-rowing for hundreds of yards.

To dive into the area's unpatrolled **backcountry**, check with the resort's Back Tracks program (☏801/534-1400, ext 2225), where ski patrol guides lead group tours. Other options further afield include the heliskiing and snowcat tours out of Little Cottonwood Canyon, located on the opposite side of Honeycomb Canyon; see the box on p.288 for details.

Beginner

There aren't a whole lot of green runs at Solitude, so they tend to jam up first. All of the greens are located on the lower half of the mountain, and you'll have to improve your abilities rapidly in order to ride up top for the best views. The Moonbeam II triple leads to most of the greens, but the winding **North Star** off the Sunrise triple chair is the longest, most enjoyable beginner run on the hill.

Intermediate

Save for the Honeycomb Return lift that leads out of the experts-only Honeycomb Canyon, intermediate skiers can ride every other lift on the mountain. The speedy Eagle Express quad leads to a dozen blues, including the wide-open **Sunshine Bowl**. For more of a challenge, head to the Summit double for a thigh-burning swirl from peak to base down **Dynamite** to **Deer Trail**, or try the seclusion of **Sol/Bright,** a run that forms the border with Brighton. Keep your speed on the latter or you risk stalling out on several flat spots.

Expert

For fresh lines, experts will have a field day off the Powderhorn, Summit, and Honeycomb Return chairs. The Powderhorn double accesses most of the ski area's blazed blacks, including regularly groomed Diamond Lane, but it's also the route to **Here Be Dragons**, a severe double-black blasting through trees down the Honeycomb Canyon's ultra-steep southern wall. In the opposite direction off Powderhorn, more steep double-black tree runs await on **Middle Slope**, **Parachute**, and **Milk Run**. One chair over, the Summit double accesses perfectly spaced-out tree shots through the **Headwall Forest** as well as the mouth of **Honeycomb Canyon**, as close to backcountry conditions as possible while still in-bounds. The south side is more forested and difficult, while areas like **Prince of Wales** and **Black Bess** on the opposite face are straight powder shots down the canyon floor back to the Honeycomb Return quad.

Freestyle

Solitude has no terrain park. For freeriding, various-sized banks and humps typically form along **Eagle Ridge** across the resort's top ridge, and jumps are sometimes built above **Sol/Bright** as it curves out of sight from the rest of the resort. If you want park-built jumps head to Brighton.

Lift tickets, lessons, and rentals

Instead of paper **lift tickets**, Solitude has followed the lead of many European resorts, using recyclable Access Cards that are automatically scanned at the base of each lift. An adult all-day pass runs $45, while children 13 and under save $20. Minimal savings are available on multiday passes, and there is a pay-by-the-ride option ($45 for ten lift rides) if you're planning on skiing for short periods of time over several days. Another choice is the $60 Solbright pass, which allows you entrance to both Big Cottonwood resorts. Private **lessons** start at $65 per hour, while group classes begin at $40 (☎801/536-5730). The resort **rents** skis ($25–40) and boards ($28–36) from both base areas, but if you'd rather arrive with gear in hand see p.262 for outlets outside of Big Cottonwood Canyon or p.270 for the board-only Bottom Line Snowboard shop a mile away.

Accommodation

The facades of Solitude's half-dozen slopeside **accommodation** options are meant to evoke a European flavor, but inside the style and amenities are pure modern American. The 46-room *Inn at Solitude* features bland **hotel** rooms and suites in the four-star range, with amenities such as a heated outdoor pool and hot tub, fitness room, and ski lockers leading straight to the slopes (❼). Better choices are available at the five other condos. The single-bedroom *Alpine Creek* condos are the most affordable at $275 a night, though the one- to three-bedroom *Eagle Springs* complex (❾) may be the best choice, housing an indoor pool (use shared by all the properties). The *Creekside* units are the most luxurious (❿), with ski-in, ski-out access, wood-burning fireplaces, and the best views of the surroundings. All are managed by the resort (☎801/536-5700 or 1-800/748-4754).

Besides the limited choices up the road at Brighton (see p.270), one of the few other options is the *Silver Fork Lodge* (☎801/533-9977 or 1-888/649-9551, ⓦwww.silverforklodge.com; ❺), only a mile from the ski area. Home to eight antler-filled rooms and a restaurant (see below), facilities at this affordably priced and sociable B&B include a sauna, TV lounge, and small game room.

See p.260 for spots in downtown Salt Lake City and the South Valley.

Eating and drinking

Solitude offers some decent **restaurants**, though none in the base area exudes a great deal of atmosphere. Fine dining is available at *St Bernard's* in the *Inn at Solitude*, where the simply prepared entrees are priced in the $15–25 range and include braised lamb shank, veal schnitzel, and grilled salmon, complemented by an extensive wine list. More expensive and more adventurous are the five-course meals served at *The Yurt*, an authentic Mongolian tent located a short cross-country ski trip up the mountain's slopes. Reservations are essential (☎801/536-5709) and the $80 per person fee includes ski or snowshoe rentals. More affordable family dining is available at the *Creekside*, while sandwiches and an excellent chicken chili accompany cold microbrews in the *Thirsty Squirrel* pub. On-mountain, the *Sunshine Grill* catches the sun until early afternoon, providing a fine picnic-like setting for its burgers and cafeteria-style meals.

Outside the village, the *Silver Fork Lodge*, a mile away (see "Accommodation" above), does a large breakfast menu of tasty platters like salmon Benedict and gut-busting portions of sourdough pancakes ($8–12). The cozy lodge atmosphere is also worth a stop for dinner, when seared trout salad and an array of steaks go for $16–25.

Beyond renting movies from the Stone Haus snack shop in the village center or briefly hitting the *Thirsty Squirrel* (which shuts at 9pm), **nightlife** options are nonexistent. See pp.260–61 for recommended places in South Valley and downtown Salt Lake City.

Other activities and attractions

Solitude's off-slope attraction of note is its **Nordic center** (℡801/536-5774), sandwiched between the Sunrise chair and neighboring Brighton. The $10 trail pass accesses some 20km of mixed-ability trails winding around 500ft of vertical rise on the resort's tree-coated lower slopes. Rentals ($8–16) and lessons ($35–45) available, as are backcountry tours.

Santa Fe

Past canyons of red rocks and groves of quaking aspens, sixteen miles from the sunny plaza and dusty adobe homes of **Santa Fe**, the presence of a ski resort may come as a bit of a surprise. Even more surprising is the fact that Santa Fe ski basin, rising from the New Mexican desert, has one of the highest base elevations in the States. Because of the altitude and arid climate, when it snows, the powder that falls on the Sangre de Cristo range is light and dry. Unfortunately consistent snowfall is not reliable this far south.

In a dry spell the basin can feel small, though for its size Ski Santa Fe offers an impressive variety of terrain. In prime conditions, tight trees and widely spaced glades offer intermediates and above-challenging off-piste riding, while extensive beginner slopes and easy blues are complemented by a handful of both groomed and bumped-out blacks. There's no pipe and not much of a park, but tickets and lessons are good value and the weather reliably sunny. The ski basin is a day area, without any of the frills of a larger resort, but the choice of lodging, dining, and entertainment off the slopes is a world apart from the typical ski town offerings.

Mountain info
Phone ℡505/982-4429
Snow phone ℡505/983-9155
Website @www.skisantafe.com
Price $44
Operating times Last week in Nov to first week in April daily 9am–4pm
No. of lifts 6, including 2 surface; new Millennium lift scheduled imminently
Base elevation 10,350′
Summit elevation 12,053′
Vertical drop 1703′
No. of trails 44
Acreage 660 (expansion due)
Beginner 20%
Intermediate 40%
Expert 40%
Average snowfall 225″
Snowmaking Yes (275 acres)
Night skiing No
Nursery facilities Yes, ℡505/988-9636, from 3 months to 4 years

One of the oldest cities in the US, Santa Fe is startlingly beautiful, even if the suburbs have sprawled, and the city mandates that insist on adobe everything – from motels to supermarkets – give the place a rather surreal air. Founded by Spanish missionaries over a decade before the Pilgrims arrived on American soil, Santa Fe is now very much a tourist destination, with its numerous galleries, museums, restaurants, and theaters appealing to a largely upmarket contingent. Fortunately it's much thinned out in the winter and just as appealing. Temperatures are relatively balmy, though the thermometer can drop to freezing at night, and off-season prices, if not exactly cheap, are a welcome change from most North American resorts.

Arrival, information, and getting around

Albuquerque Sunport **Airport** is a 45-minute drive south on I-25; tiny Santa Fe municipal airport is primarily used by private planes. Renting a car from one of the major agencies at Albuquerque is a better alternative than taking a Sandia Shuttle bus to Santa Fe ($23; ☎505/474-5696 or 888/775-5696, ⓦwww.sandishuttle.com), especially considering there is no public transportation from the town to the ski area. Hwy-475, the winding access route, begins on Artist Road just off Washington Street on the northeastern corner of the plaza. The sixteen-mile route climbs through pinon and juniper trees on the outskirts of town, then morphs into Hyde Park Road, winding up through the Santa Fe National Forest. Parking at the basin is free, but difficult to find in the center of town. Greyhound buses stop out at 858 St Michael's Drive (☎505/471-0008), while trains on the *Southwest Chief* route pull in at Lamy, seventeen miles southeast. Lamy Shuttle vans ($16 one-way; ☎505/982-8829) make the trip into town once a day and reservations are required. Santa Fe Trails buses – (Mon–Fri 6am–10.30pm, Sat 8am–7.30pm, Sun 10am–6pm, 50¢; ☎505/438-1464) cover downtown, the Cerrillos Road strip, and outlying visitor attractions. Pick up a schedule from the **visitor center**, two blocks west of the plaza at 201 W Marcy St (Mon–Fri 8am–5pm; ☎505/955-6200 or 800/777-2489, ⓦwww.santafe.org).

The mountain

Curved under Tesuque Peak, little Santa Fe ski basin is roughly divided into two areas. Most of the lifts serve the slopes directly above the lodge with runs that spill off the long, barren ridgeline skier's left of the Tesuque Peak chair and culminate in a gently rolling meadow of greens. This is the busy side of the mountain with the easier green and blue trails running down between chairs 1 (the Santa Fe Super Quad) and 2 (Sierra) becoming particularly crowded. In contrast, the tree shots, rock drops, small bowls, and rollercoaster cruising runs in the valley rider's right off the Tesuque summit are often deserted, perhaps because of the long traverse currently needed to access the lower, less intimidating trails. This is bound to change with the installation of the Millennium lift, the first stage in an expansion to open up the Raven's Ridge area on the far side of the valley – an area currently only accessible to those prepared to hike. While upper ridgeline trails like North and South Burn are subject to the negative effects of the dry desert winds, most of the ski basin is better sheltered. The lower slopes are a veritable suntrap, and powder lurks in pockets among the steep trees under Tesuque long after a storm.

Beginner

The lower slopes of the mountain are all wide, mellow, gently rolling greens but, as the thoroughfares back to the base lodge, they tend to be traffic-prone. **Sunnyside**, under the Sierra chair, is a little less busy and stays bathed in the sun late in the day. Advanced beginners should be able to handle the mellow, quieter blues off the summit.

Intermediate

Though there isn't much blue marked on the trail map, Santa Fe is a great mountain for progressing intermediates, particularly those who want to get off the groomed trails. Stumpy, gently pitched and widely spaced glades, short blacks, sheltered powder fields, and patches of steeper trees are all within the realm of the intermediate ready to step it up. The slopes under Chairs 1 and 2 are traditional groomers, good for cruising and carving. For powder, South Burn is an easy off-piste playground. More difficult are the trees and glade runs skier's right off Tesuque, which get easier the further along you drop in off the Sunset cat track.

Expert

In dry spells, experts may tire of Santa Fe quickly. There are only a few fast, groomed blacks, though mogul skiers can lap the staircase under Chair 3, dropping into the short, steep, bumped-out chutes of Easter Bowl. But it's in terms of off-piste terrain that Santa Fe shines. The vertical drop may not be huge, but there are sweet tree shots under the summit that open up into rocky glades and small, sheltered powder bowls; the best stuff is under the Sunset cat track.

Hike out into the Alpine Bowl on the ridge opposite Tesuque Peak, which drops back down toward the lodge, or take the low-profile Tesuque Peak gate off the summit. The glades here funnel out at the Big Tesuque parking turnout, a few bends in the road below the ski area on Hwy-475.

Freestyle

The terrain park at Santa Fe, when it exists at all, is minimal and it's better to head to Angel Fire (see p.307) for rails and kickers. But the natural terrain contains a cascade of rollers and cat tracks, hidden logslides, and, in the bowls under Tesuque Peak, a catalog of rocks to launch off. None of the hits is really huge here, and the short vertical drop takes away the fear factor. To get to the Big Rock, a fearsome launching point for hucksters, drop in midway along the Sunset cat track. For small cliffs, head down into Easter Bowl directly below the summit.

Lift tickets, lessons, and rentals

Half-day **tickets** can be purchased (#33) for either the morning (9am–12.30pm) or afternoon sessions. Season passes are pricey (over $700), but the Skier Plus card, cheapest if bought before December ($30), provides $10 discounts on day tickets. Best value for those planning a multiday trip in January is the Millennium pass ($139), which offers unlimited skiing in that month, plus the $10-a-day discount at other times. All passes can be bought online and used at Santa Fe and its sibling resort, Albuquerque's little Sandia Peak (see p.309).

Lessons are good value, especially the novice package that includes two same-day lessons, beginner lift access, and gear for just $58. Group lessons start at $30. Specialist clinics are aimed squarely at Santa Fe residents, as they are offered primarily in multiweek formats. A dedicated team of volunteers and donors behind the Adaptive Ski Program of New Mexico (℡505/995-9858, ⓦwww.adaptiveski.org) keeps prices low. Book at least two weeks in advance for a two- ($40) or four- ($60) hour lesson, with equipment and lift tickets included.

It's best to rent your equipment from town. Beyond Waves, 1428 Cerrillos Rd (℡505/988-2240), offers quality snowboard packages from $21 and up; the skate shop doesn't open until midday, so you need to book the night before. The staff at Santa Fe Mountain Sports, 607 Cerrillos Rd (☎505/988-3337), are very active in local skiing programs. In addition to rentals, the shop offers boot fitting and tuning services. Sangre de Cristo Mountain Works, 328 S Guadalupe St (☎505/984-8221), is the place for info on avalanche classes (run by Search and Rescue and St John's College), telemark clinics, and backcountry guides.

Accommodation

Santa Fe has few budget **accommodations** – most are strung along Cerrillos Road (Hwy-85) – but the standard compares favorably to the average ski resort. Winter prices are a bargain compared to the busier summer season, and real luxury is available for just a few dollars more than what you'd pay at the cheaper properties. Prices are higher in the center of town, though there's always the option of a charming B&B – the city is flush with them.

Alexander's Inn 529 E Palace Ave ☎505/986-1431 or 888/321-5123. Arts and Crafts home dating from 1903, offering five immaculate bedrooms, secluded garden cottages, and three separate rental houses equipped with full kitchens. Breakfast and tea can be taken indoors or out on the porch. ❸–❻

El Paradero 220 W Manhattan Ave ☎505/988-1177, ⓦwww.elparadero.com. Spanish farmhouse, dating from 1800, that has been comfortably renovated and now boasts fourteen elegantly decorated rooms. It's close to the center of town, and great breakfasts and teas are served daily. ❹

El Rey Inn 1862 Cerrillos Rd ☎505/982-1931 or 800/521-1349, ⓦwww.elreyinnsantafe.com. Best of the motels out on Cerrillos, this whitewashed Spanish colonial complex offers cool gardens and a tiled outdoor jacuzzi. Of the 86 rooms, those in the North Courtyard are the most basic but the most affordable. All are clean, continental breakfast is included, and kitchenettes are available. ❸; check online for winter discounts and ski packages.

Fort Marcy Hotel Suites 320 Artist Rd ☎505/982-6636 or 800/745-9910, ⓦwww.fortmarcy.com. Converted condominiums on Ski Basin Road right outside town, with spacious and tastefully decorated one-, two- and three-bedroom suites. Amenities include an indoor pool, tub, laundry, continental breakfast, and discounted lift tickets. From ❸ per person

Hotel Plaza Real 125 Washington Ave ☎505/988-4900 or 877/901-7666, ⓦwww.buynewmexico.com. Centrally located mid-range hotel with a courtyard and pretty colonial facade. Public spaces are light and airy, and rooms are comfortable – though not quite as individual as you would expect from a "boutique" hotel, as it claims to be. ❹

Hotel St Francis 210 Don Gaspar Ave ☎505/983-5700 or 800/529-5700, ⓦwww.historicstfrancis.com. This distinguished, small hotel seems like a transplant from a European city, despite the adobe facade. Comfortably furnished with heavy antiques in lieu of the prevalent southwestern rugs and artifacts typical of Santa Fe lodging, it's a quiet oasis steps from the galleries and restaurants around the Plaza. Ski package prices are a bargain over summer rates. From ❸

Inn of the Anasazi 113 Washington Ave ☎505/988-3030 or 800/688-8100, ⓦwww.innoftheanasazi.com. Opulent, dark, and stylish, this downtown hotel was modeled on the ancient Anasazi pueblos. This theme is a little overplayed and the atmosphere unashamedly grand, but rooms are luxuriously appointed (with fine linens, organic toiletries, and so forth) and there's a highly reputed restaurant on site. ❼

Santa Fe Budget Inn 725 Cerrillos Rd ☎505/982-5952 or 800/288-7600, ⓦwww.santafebudgetinn.com. Clean, no-frills, two-story adobe motel six blocks from the plaza. ❷

Santa Fe International Hostel 1412 Cerrillos Rd ☎505/988-1153, santafehostel@quest.net. Located in an ancient motel on a shabby part of Cerrillos Rd surrounded by rundown cars, the hostel rates high on traveler atmosphere but less so on creature comforts. Beds are crammed into small rooms, and both the plumbing and heating have seen better days. $15, private rooms ❶

Santa Fe Motel & Inn 510 Cerrillos Rd ☎505/982-1039 or 800/930-5002, ⓦwww.santafemotel.com. Quiet, remodeled adobe motel a short walk from downtown. Some of the rooms have their own patios and kitchenettes, an extended continental breakfast is included in the reasonable rates, and discounted lift tickets are available. ❸

Ten Thousand Waves Hyde Park Rd (Hwy-475) ☎505/982-9304, ⓦwww.tenthousandwaves.com. Eight serene suites and cottages in the enchanting, peaceful grounds of a Japanese-style spa (see "Other activities and attractions", opposite). Four miles out of town, it's the closest lodging to the ski area. ❼

Eating

Even the most culinary-adept ski towns have nothing on Santa Fe. Stellar **restaurants** at both ends of the price scale serve creative chile-laced dishes (both red and green – there's an important distinction, as the locals will inevitably tell you), and it's easy to stumble upon somewhere good without even trying. There's nothing special about dining at the ski area, which relies on the traditional cafeteria format; pack a lunch from the deli counters at Whole Foods, 753 Cerrillos Rd (☎505/992-1700), or Wild Oats markets, 1090 St Francis Drive (☎505/983-5333).

Banana Café 329 W San Francisco St ☎505/982-3886. Stylish Thai restaurant with an inventive menu that goes well beyond green curry and pad thai, with dishes like pineapple fried rice and mango shrimp. Reasonably priced, too. Mon–Sat 11am–2pm & 4–9pm.

Café Oasis 546 Galisteo St ☎505/983-9599. Crunchy, quirky café that serves healthy breakfasts all day, along with salads and sandwiches at lunch and a eclectic selection of entrees like lamb curries and tempeh burritos ($11–15) in the evenings. Rather besotted with the body's "integrity" to the point that aluminum cooking pots are eschewed, vegan dishes are prevalent but meat – organic, of course – is firmly on the menu. Mon–Thurs 10am–midnight, Fri 10am–2am, Sat 9am–2am, Sun 9am–midnight.

Carlos' Gosp'l Café 125 Lincoln Ave ☎505/983-1841. Little deli where hearty chowders and substantial sandwiches are doled out to the constant musical accompaniment of gospel and soul.

Cleopatra Café Design Center, 418 Cerrillos Rd ☎505/820-7381. Since the dining area is essentially patio furniture set in the middle of the Design Center's cavernous warehouse, the ambience here is a little peculiar. Regardless, the falafel, gyros, and other Middle Eastern dishes are cheap and authentic, right down to the treacle-thick Turkish coffee. Mon–Sat 11am–8.30pm.

El Tesoro Café 500 Montezuma Ave ☎505/988-3886. Tucked away in the Sanbusco Mall, chefs at this breezy little diner rustle up fresh southwestern dishes for breakfast and lunch, along with crisp salads and stuffed sandwiches. Great value. Mon–Sat 8am–6pm, Sun 11am–5pm.

Horseman's Haven Café 6500 Cerrillos Rd ☎505/471-5420. This atmospheric greasy spoon is way out by the highway on Cerrillos Road, next to the Texaco Station. Inexpensive breakfasts, lunches, and dinners are meaty and laced with chile, and the warm little dining room is littered with horses: plastic horses, paintings of horses, and all manner of equine paraphernalia. Mon–Sat 8am–8pm, Sun 8.30am–2pm.

Mu Du Noodles 1494 Cerrillos Rd ☎505/983-1411. It doesn't look like much from the outside, but the pan-Asian noodle dishes here are both affordable and tasty, with specials like Vietnamese sweet and sour rockfish and Malaysian coconut-steeped laksa. The restaurant is within easy walking distance of the youth hostel and close to the Cerrillos Road motels. Mon–Sat 5.30pm–close.

The Plaza Bakery 56 E San Francisco St ☎505/988-3858. Easy to locate – though tricky for parking – this longtime Plaza café makes a good coffee and pastry pit stop en route to the ski area; it's not a bad place to pick up a sandwich for lunch either.

Zia Diner 326 S Guadalupe St ☎505/988-7008. A diner without the grease, the comfort food served in this large, airy restaurant is excellent; just the mashed potato and gravy have been luring back regulars for years. Daily 11am–10pm.

Bars and entertainment

Evenings in Santa Fe are geared more toward dining out than raucous **nightlife**, and many of the better bars are attached to restaurants. There's usually some performance or other going on at the restored Lensic Performing Arts Center, 211 W San Francisco St (☎505/988-1234); for listings, pick up a copy of the free alternative weekly, *The Reporter*. Santa Fe has several indie **movie houses**, including the Jean Cocteau, 418 Montezuma Ave (☎505/988-

2711), the arty Plan B Cinemateque, 1050 Old Pecos Trail (☎505/662-8763), and the *Cinema Café*, a restaurant-cum-bar-cum-movie house with comfy couches that claim to have the largest selection of beer and wine in the state.

The Cowgirl Grill 319 S Guadalupe St ☎505/982-2565. Named the best après-ski spot in the country by *Outside Magazine* – who just happen to have their offices across the street, so may be just a little biased – the frozen margaritas here are outstanding, happy hour is timed to coincide with the end of the ski day, and a barbecue-heavy grill menu is served until 1am.

The Paramount 331 Sandoval St ☎505/982-8999. Often schedules out-of-town DJs and bands; the large dance floor, which doesn't get busy until late, is complemented by the cozier *Bar B* next door, a more intimate spot for cocktails.

Pranzo 540 Montezuma Ave ☎505/984-2645. The stylish, dimly lit bar area of this highly rated Italian restaurant (they even make their own noodles!) is the perfect spot for an early evening cocktail.

Second Street Brewery 1814 Second St ☎505/982-3030. Family-friendly brewpub offering discounts to skiers on the production of their lift ticket; full menu served from lunch until 10pm Sun–Thurs, until 11pm Fri–Sat.

Warehouse 21 1614 Paseo de Peralta, ☎505/985-4423. Cavernous teen center down by the train station that holds all-ages shows, mostly punk or hip-hop, on the weekend.

Other activities and attractions

One obvious thing to do with some spare time is to check out a few of the **galleries** and **museums** dotted throughout town, from tiny commercial spaces to major collections like the Museums of Indian Culture and Folk Art, the Georgia O'Keefe Museum, and the Center for Contemporary Arts. More active off-slope pursuits are plentiful, in part thanks to the dry, sunny weather down in town. Central DeVargas Park **skatepark** in the center of town has been superseded by a gnarlier one way down off Cerrillos, on Camino Carlos Rey. There's an indoor pool, waterslide, spa, ice rink, and gym at the sparkling Genoveva Chavez Community Center, 3221 Rodeo Rd (Mon–Fri 6am–10pm, Sat 8am–8pm, Sun 10am–6pm; pool or rink admission $4, skate rental $2; ☎505/955-4001). Fishing, hiking, rock climbing, horseback riding, and mountain biking are available in winter in the dry desert hills around town. Contact the visitor center for more information, or stop in at one of the local outdoor stores (see above).

The road back into town from the ski area passes the spa of **Ten Thousand Waves**, Hyde Park Rd (☎505/992-5025; Sun–Mon and Wed–Thurs, 9.15am–10.30pm, Tues 4–10.30pm, Fri–Sat 9.15am–midnight, $13.50–27 per person). Scents of cedar and sage waft over private and communal hot tubs, dotted on a hillside above town in a landscaped open-air compound. The overt Japanese design is tastefully executed. Expensive massage and spa services are also available.

Listings

Avalanche hotline Santa Fe National Forest ☎505/753-7331.

Bookstore Collected Works, 208 San Francisco St ☎505/988-4226.

Internet Santa Fe Public Library, 145 Washington St ☎505/955-6780.

Medical St Vincent Hospital, 455 St Michael's Drive ☎505/983-3361.

Police 200 Lincoln Ave ☎505/955-6576.

Post office 120 S Federal Place ☎505/988-6351.

Road conditions ☎800/432-4269.

Search and rescue ☎505/827-9300.

Taxi Capital City Cab ☎505/438-0000.

Taos

Amid the native pueblos of the arid Sangre de Cristo mountains, **Taos Ski Valley** offers some of the most spectacular, challenging, in-bounds terrain in the States and the snow, when it comes, is light, dry, and deep. The resort itself, however, is minuscule, a tiny hamlet of alpine lodges in a narrow valley surrounded by precipitous peaks. The lack of build-up echoes much of the traditional bent of the resort; indeed, it seems that many principles have been preserved to honor skiers who yearn for the old days. Ski school is sacrosanct, lodging is all-inclusive, and, most conspicuously, snowboarders are absent.

This last fact endures despite the best tactics of the Free Taos movement – local riders known to hike up the mountain in protest at their exclusion. The closest options for snowboarders remain the smaller resorts of Angel Fire or Red River (see pp.307–309), each around an hour away on the edge of the Enchanted Circle, a highway loop through the Sangre de Cristo range which has Taos Ski Valley at its mountainous center.

Nineteen miles south down winding Hwy-150, the arty, adobe town of Taos sprawls on a dusty high-desert plateau, abutting the edge of the Rio Grande gorge. While the native village of Taos Pueblo had its origins over a thousand years ago, the settlement two miles to the south – now crammed with galleries, inns, and excellent restaurants – was founded by Spanish colonialists in the 1630s, becoming part of the US in 1848. Artists and writers have flocked to Taos since the turn of the last century, most notably D.H. Lawrence and Georgia O'Keeffe, followed by waves of subsequent New Age bohemians. The marked contrast between the town and the mountain adds a surreal quality to a ski vacation here. Look no further than the distinct architecture of the two places; also, the ski area receives 312 inches of snow annually to the town's 35.

Arrival, information, and transport

It's around a three-hour drive from Albuquerque Sunport **Airport** to the ski area. The 135-mile route passes through Santa Fe, then follows dusty Hwy-68 up to Taos. Rio Grande Air runs three flights daily from Albuquerque to Taos airport (from $79 each way, ☏877/435-9742, ☻www.riograndeair.com), and car rentals are available at both airports. Shuttle service to the ski area from Albuquerque is provided by Faust's Transportation (☏505/758-3410, $40 one-way), which also runs buses from Santa Fe ($25) and serves as the local taxi

Mountain info	
Phone ☏505/776-2291 or 800/776-1111	
Snow phone ☏505/776-2916	
Website ☻www.skitaos.org	
Price $49, with significant discounts early and late season	
Operating times Last week in Nov to first week in April, 9am–4pm	
No. of lifts 12, inc. 2 surface	
Base elevation 9207′	
Summit elevation 12481′ (lift served 11819′)	
Vertical drop 2612/3244′	
Number of trails 72	
Acreage 1096	
Beginner 24%	
Intermediate 25%	
Expert 51%	
Average snowfall 312″	
Snowmaking Yes, all beginner and intermediate slopes	
Night skiing No	
Nursery facilities Yes, Kinderkare (☏505/776-2291 ext 1331) for ages 6 weeks to 2 years.	

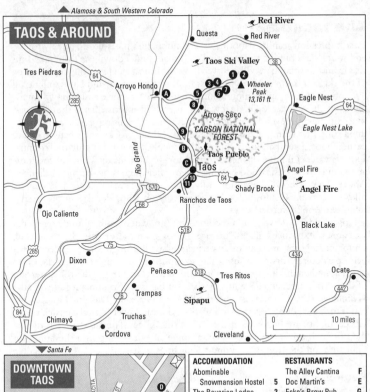

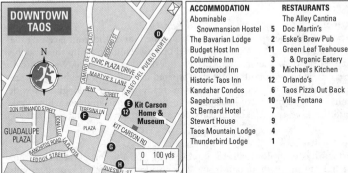

ACCOMMODATION		RESTAURANTS	
Abominable		The Alley Cantina	F
Snowmansion Hostel	5	Doc Martin's	E
The Bavarian Lodge	2	Eske's Brew Pub	G
Budget Host Inn	11	Green Leaf Teahouse	
Columbine Inn	3	& Organic Eatery	H
Cottonwood Inn	8	Michael's Kitchen	D
Historic Taos Inn	12	Orlando's	B
Kandahar Condos	6	Taos Pizza Out Back	C
Sagebrush Inn	10	Villa Fontana	A
St Bernard Hotel	7		
Stewart House	9		
Taos Mountain Lodge	4		
Thunderbird Lodge	1		

service. Greyhound TMN&O buses from Albuquerque (from $24) and Santa Fe (from $14) stop at the bus station in Taos on Hwy-168, 1386 Paseo del Pueblo Sur (℡505/758-1144), a few blocks south of the **visitor center** at the Paseo del Cañon junction (℡1-800/732-8267, ⓦwww.taoschamber.com).

Public **buses** depart Taos for the ski valley 6.45am-3.30pm daily as part of the Chile Line system. Reservations are suggested for both the ski bus and the residential Green Chile line, as both run on irregular schedules. Red Chile Line buses run on a regular half-hour schedule between Ranchos de Taos to the south and Taos Pueblo (Mon–Sat 7am–6pm, limited Sun service 8am–5pm; ℡505/751-4459).

The mountain

First impressions can be daunting as the mountain's precipitous, thickly forested lower slopes outline the moguled runs that plunge down the front face. Lifts rise from the small base village over these technical steeps to the central spine of the ski area, a sunny ridge with less intimidating greens and blues spilling off left and right. The upper mountain is divided into two extensive bowls invisible from the slender valley below. Beginners and intermediates should spend most of their time in the middle of these basins, cruising down gentle tree-lined runs. Encircling each bowl are the cliffs, chutes, rocks, and steeps that have earned Taos a reputation as one of the toughest mountains in the country. Experts can ski double diamond terrain top-to-bottom on Taos, but the foot-access only West Basin and Highline ridges offer the best in-bound challenges. Above the east bowl, the summit of Kachina Peak is reached via a 45-minute hike – a trip aficionados will make repeatedly on a powder day, since it results in an extra 662ft vertical drop.

Taos is seldom crowded and stashes of fresh powder can be found among the ski area's extensive glades of evergreens long after the last snowfall. Unfortunately, the area can often be plagued with drought; the past decade has been particularly dry with just a few exceptional years. Even when the powder is abundant, hiking or traversing is often necessary to get the thirty percent of the terrain not served by lifts. Each basin has a mid-mountain rest stop: the *Whistlestop Café* to the west and the *Phoenix Grill* and *Bavarian Lodge* to the east. From here, long traverses follow the ski area's lower boundary back to the village, nightmare highways at the end of the ski day. The alternative is to take the lifts back up to the resort's central spine and then drop into the bumps or tight trees on the front face, a direct shot back to base.

Beginner

The small **Strawberry Hill** learning area at the foot of the front face isn't the most reassuring spot for novices, squeezed in between steep bump runs and the village. Head onto the sunnier, mellow, tree-lined runs in the **West Basin**. These can be lapped on lift 8 and are bordered by well-groomed blues that are simple to dip in and out of when you're ready to progress. Beginners with stamina have the option of heading down the long trails under Kachina Peak toward the *Phoenix Grill* –be prepared for a potentially tiring traverse out.

Intermediate

Intermediates with no desire to improve may find the terrain at Taos rather limited. Both upper mountain basins contain just a handful of groomed trails – plenty for a day of exploration, but really not enough to amuse those who want to cruise endlessly for days. Try the mid-mountain **Walkyries** chute, bowl, and glades before venturing further.

Expert

Trails all over the mountain twist through glades, inconceivably tight trees, and gullies. On the front face, Al's is the classic bump run, a mogul staircase flanked by shorter shots cut through the trees. For chutes and steeps accessible without hiking, check out the High T lines under lifts 2 and 6 in the **West Basin** or traverse under **Kachina Peak** from the top of the Kachina lift. To hike to the summit, start at the top of the spine above ski patrol headquarters (check in first) then ski out along the Highline Ridge.

△ The slopes at Park City Mountain Resort, UT

Freestyle

Taos recently capitulated to the whims of younger skiers and set up a couple of big kickers, hip, quarterpipe, and rail over on Maxie's trail. The move was so successful that now they're even talking about building a halfpipe. Still, finding something natural to huck off at Taos is simple. Easiest to access are the rocks in Walkyries and above Longhorn.

Lift tickets, lessons, and rentals

Day **tickets** at Taos ($49) are relatively cheap – even cheaper late spring – and skiers save $10 on day tickets and receive discounts on lessons, demos, food, and lodging with the purchase of a Taos Card ($30 if bought by mid-December).

The **Ernie Blake Ski School** is synonymous with Taos, at least to the legions of annual returnees. Disciples of all abilities sign up for "Learn to Ski Better" weeks (prices include lift tickets and cost $200–450 depending on the season). Two-hour group lessons ($37) and good-value, all-inclusive beginner packages ($60) are also available. Childcare is available and Junior Elite all-day programs, again, are good value compared to programs at major resorts in other states.

Resort **rentals** are good quality and reasonably priced, with packages from $20 to $32. There are a couple of stores in the valley, including Boot Doctors (☎505/776-2489) and Cottam's (☎505/776-8719). For a bargain, stop in at the Adventure Ski Shop in Taos, 303 Paseo del Pueblo Norte (☎505/758-9744); packages cost $9–24.

Accommodation

Resembling an alpine hamlet, Taos Ski Valley encompasses a handful of small condo complexes, traditional lodges, and charming B&Bs, most within walking distance of the lifts. Only the bland modern facade of the *Inn at Snakedance* hotel seems out of place. Aside from the new version of the *Edelweiss Lodge*, currently under construction, the resort has no plans to join the trend for building new mountain villages; this is a sleepy place.

Most B&Bs in the Taos area are represented by the Taos Association of Bed and Breakfast Inns (☎505/776-5826, ⊛www.taos-bandb-inns.com). An alternative to the rather expensive ski valley accommodations are the adobe–clad motels that line Hwy-68 south of Taos. In town, luxury inns and stylish vacation rentals surround the central plaza. Taos Central Reservations (☎505/758-9767 or 800/821-2437, ⊛www.taosweb.com/plan/tcr) represents more than 200 properties around town; for lodging in the ski valley, contact the valley Chamber of Commerce (☎800/992-7669, ⊛www.taosskivalley.com).

Taos Ski Valley

Abominable Snowmansion Hostel 476 Taos Ski Valley Rd ☎505/776-8298, ⊛www.taosweb .com/hotel/snowmansion. Friendly HI hostel in an arty hamlet at the bottom of the road up to the ski valley. The Chile Line ski bus (50¢) drops off outside. In addition to the ramshackle dorms and private suites, there's a pool table, piano, lounge, and large kitchen. $19–22, private rooms from ❷

The Bavarian Lodge Mid-mountain ☎505/776-5301, ⊛www.thebavarian.net. Austrian-style chalet stuffed with old-world antiques, located in an isolated spot mid-mountain and notable for its excellent Bavarian restaurant (see p.306). Each room is individually decorated, some have kitchenettes, and there's a fitness room and hot tub. ❽, 6–8 person suite ❾

Columbine Inn 1288 Taos Ski Valley Rd ☎505/776-5723, ⊛www.columbineinntaos.com. A couple of miles from the ski area, the *Columbine* blends the wooden beams of a ski lodge with the space and frilly décor of a motel. Each room has a microwave and mini-fridge; some have small lofts. Rates include airport pickup from Taos and a generous continental breakfast. ❸

Kandahar Condos On-mountain ☎505/776-2226 or 800/756-2226, ⊛www.kandahar-taos.com. Small condos, rather dated but inexpensive for Taos, and right on the slopes. Each sleeps six, and there's a communal indoor tub, game room, and laundry. ⑥

St Bernard Hotel 12 Sutton Way ☎505/776-2251, ⊛www.stbernardtaos.com This exclusive lodge is a little piece of the Alps transplanted to New Mexico, complete with worn wood paneling, cozy carpeted bedrooms, and collages of family members on the walls. Specializes in all-inclusive ski weeks (including full board and tuition). Modern, comfortable condo accommodation is also available. $1350–1790 per week including lift, lessons, full board, and lodging; condo rates up to $400 less per person.

Taos Mountain Lodge Hwy-150 ☎505/776-2229, ⊛www.taosmountainlodge.com. A mile down valley from the resort, the owners of this quiet, pretty little place have eschewed the prevalent alpine style in favor of the modern southwest. Each of the ten suites is stylishly kitted out, some with traditional kiva fireplaces, and all have kitchenettes and satellite TVs. There's also an outdoor tub. For the best rates, book online; rooms sleep 4–6. ⑤

Taos

Budget Host Inn 1798 Paseo del Pueblo Sur ☎505/758-2524 or 800-323-6009, ⊛www .taosbudgethost.com. An attractive adobe exterior disguises a standard cheap motel. The rooms are adequate and fridges and microwaves are available. The rates are some of the cheapest in town. ❶

Cottonwood Inn Junction of Hwy-150 and 230, El Prado-Taos ☎505/776-5826 or 800/324-7120, ⊛www.taos-cottonwood.com. Beautiful, romantic adobe mansion located in the cottonwoods halfway between town and ski valley. The seven stylishly decorated rooms include traditional kiva fireplaces, hot tubs, or steam showers. Tasty breakfasts and afternoon appetizers included. ❹–❻

Historic Taos Inn 125 Paseo del Pueblo Norte ☎505/758-2233 or 888/519-8267, ⊛www.taos inn.com. Dating from the 1800s and in operation as a hotel since 1936, this popular hotel has 33 stylish rooms, many small in size but big in atmosphere. Centrally located, the *Inn* has long hosted visiting luminaries, with the atrium lounge serving as the town's social hub. ❸

Sagebrush Inn 1508 Paseo del Pueblo Sur ☎505/758-2254 or 888/449-8267, ⊛www.sage-brushinn.com. Rooms here are basic, but this courtyard adobe motel, built in 1929 and once patronized by Georgia O'Keefe, still manages some charm. Local musicians play in the whitewashed lounge on weekends. ❹

Stewart House 46 Hwy-150 ☎505/776-2557 or 888/505-2557. Out on the desolate plains just northwest of town en route to the ski valley, this wooden ranch is perfectly at home in the Southwestern desert, its bright colors and higgledy piggledy courtyard typical of the bohemian New Mexican style. The rooms are comfortable and stylish, and an old barn out back (with full kitchen) sleeps six. ❸, barn ❼

Eating, drinking, and entertainment

The absence of places to **eat** in the Ski Valley is counterbalanced by an abundance of restaurants in Taos proper, many of which are better value than typical ski town offerings. Neither spot has a buzzing **nightlife**, although in Taos there's a thriving coffeeshop scene with jazz, folk, and blues often on tap. Pick up a copy of *Tempo*, the arts and entertainment weekly of the *Taos News*, for listings. There's a multiplex, the Storyteller Cinema, 110 Old Talpa Rd (☎505/758-9715), in town, and independent films and documentaries are sporadically screened at the Taos Center for the Arts, 133 Paseo del Pueblo Norte (☎505/758-2052), which has a busy schedule of lectures, dance, and theatrical performances. At the ski area, popular events include January's annual wine-tasting festival.

On-mountain dining is limited. Most popular is the resort-run *Martini Tree* (☎505/776-2291) bar in the rafters upstairs, which serves pizza and sushi but stops serving alcohol at 7pm. Mid-mountain, the independently owned *Bavarian Lodge* (see p.306) makes the best lunch stop. The small general store in the resort is pricey; pick up groceries in Taos at Smith's supermarket, 221 Paseo del Pueblo Sur (☎505/758-3711). For gourmet deli food, stop at Cid's, 623 Paseo del Pueblo Norte.

Taos Ski Valley

The Bavarian Lodge Mid-mountain ☏505/776-5301/8020. Outside, a sunny terrace bustles with one-piece ski suits; inside, in a space heavy with antique European wood, the atmosphere is dark and cool. Enjoy goulash ($5) accompanied by a cold Spaten beer, and followed by apple strudel, itself reason enough to make the journey up the mountain. Fondue nights are held weekly; prices $14–25. Lunch and dinner.

Crossroads Pizza ☏505/776-8866. Opposite the *Thunderbird Lodge*, this quiet pizzeria turns out homemade pastas in addition to tasty thin-crust pizza. It's not cheap, with pies starting at $12, but beats driving down to Taos at the end of a long day. 11am–close.

The St Bernard Hotel ☏505/776-2251. Slopeside bar attached to the quintessential Taos hotel, with stadium seating on the roof for viewing those neatly schussing down the mountain. Café lunches and family-style dinners.

Tim's Stray Dog Cantina ☏505/776-2894. Southwestern diner and bar in the resort center with uninspiring but reasonably priced dishes, though the peppers that grace the green chile cheeseburgers are home-roasted and tasty. On weekends, it's as rowdy as things get in the valley. 8am–9pm.

Taos

The Alley Cantina 121 Teresina Lane ☏505/758-2121. The grill menu at this bar is nothing special, but it's the town's premier music venue and one of the few places to get a drink after 10pm.

Doc Martin's 125 Paseo del Pueblo Norte ☏505/758-2233. The southwestern cuisine served in the atmospheric *Taos Inn* may be somewhat overrated, but the *Adobe Bar,* in the atrium, is one of the busiest nightspots in town, swaying to the sounds of live jazz.

Eske's Brew Pub 106 Des Georges Lane ☏505/758-1517. Adobe walls, low ceilings, and small rooms set this brewpub aside from the more typical wooden bars of its ilk. Different ethnic cuisines are served daily (from sushi to fish and chips), bands are scheduled on the weekends, and their very own specialty, green chile flavored beer, is served in addition to a more palatable selection. Mon–Thurs 4–10.30pm, Fri–Sat 11.30am–10.30pm, Sun 11.30am–10pm.

Green Leaf Teahouse and Organic Eatery 105B Queznel St ☏505/751-4212. Healthy edibles in calm, New Age surroundings. There's usually an open mike video screening or musical soiree scheduled. Thurs–Sat 11.30am–4pm, Mon–Wed, 11.30am–9pm.

Michael's Kitchen 304 Paseo del Pueblo Norte ☏505/758-4178. Conveniently located opposite Adventure Ski Rental. Day skiers from Santa Fe line up here for cheap, giant Southwestern breakfasts, pancakes, and pastries. Diner fare served later in the day is equally inexpensive, but somehow not as satisfying. Daily 7am–8.30pm.

Orlando's 1114 Don Juan Valdez Lane (Hwy-64) ☏505/751-1450. Little more than a shack, this funky (and funkily decorated) restaurant en route to the ski area is marked by a giant outdoor fire pit. The food is hearty Southwestern and great value; you can eat for under $10.

Taos Pizza Out Back 712 Paseo del Pueblo Norte ☏505/758-3112. On the north side of town, this friendly shack serves inventive pizzas along with filling and reasonably priced calzones, pasta, and salads. Daily 11am–close.

Villa Fontana Hwy-522 ☏505/758-5800. Of the more upscale restaurants in Taos, this Italian place just north of the turn-off to Hwy-150 (Ski Valley Rd) is perhaps the most romantic, and the north Italian cooking is reliably creative and fresh. Entrees are $18–24, and reservations are a good idea. Daily 5.30pm–close.

Other activities and attractions

Though the avalanche danger can be high, experienced **cross-country** skiers and snowshoers can explore trails that wind through the Carson National Forest right from the ski area. Contact the ranger office on Cruz Alta Road in Taos (☏505/758-6200) for maps and advice. The nearest developed cross-country ski area is the Enchanted Forest in Red River (☏505/754-2374; trail passes from $7.50, rentals $11, beginner packages from $30), which boasts 24km of trails in 400 acres of wilderness. **Snowmobiling** trips in the ski valley are organized by Big Al of Wilderness Adventures (☏505/751-6051, from $55). A large indoor ice rink (admission $4, rentals $1) and concrete **skatepark** (free) are located in the Youth and Family Center at the top of Paseo del Cañon.

Taos Pueblo

Settled for over 1000 years by the Tiwa Indians, the two adobe complexes of the Taos Pueblo – Hlauuma, the north house, and Hlaukwima, the south house – together form the oldest continually inhabited community in the US. Though most of the tribal community now lives in modern homes elsewhere on the reservation, the 150 or so residents of the pueblo eschew electricity or running water and maintain their ceremonial traditions. Visitors are only permitted to enter the pueblo's public spaces (daily 8am–5pm; $10; ☎505/758-1028, ⓦwww.taospueblo.com), though the entire village is closed from February to April. Fees are charged per camera (still cameras $10, video cameras $20).

Of the seven excellent **museums** in town, the Kit Carson House and Millicent Rogers Museum are the most impressive, the former for its evocation of frontier life, the latter for its extensive collection of traditional and contemporary Native American and Hispanic arts and crafts.

Listings

Avalanche hotline Carson National Forest Ranger Office ☎505/758-6200.

Bookstore Taos Book Shop, 122D Kit Carson Rd, ☎505/758-3733.

Highway report hotline ☎1-800/432-4269.

Internet Taos Public Library, 402 Camino De La Placita ☎505/758-3063, call for hours.

Medical Mogul Medical, slopeside ☎505/776-8421; Holy Cross Hospital, 1397 Weimer Rd, Taos ☎505/758-8883.

Pharmacy Smith's Supermarket, 221 Paseo del Pueblo Sur, ☎505/758-3711.

Post office 318 Paseo Del Pueblo Norte, Taos, and in the ski resort center, ☎800/275-8777.

Police 107 Civic Plaza Drive ☎505/758-2216.

Search and rescue ☎505/758-8876.

The Best of the Rest

Angel Fire, New Mexico

Angel Fire (☎505/377-6401 or 800/633-7463, ⓦwww.angelfireresort.com, adult $45, teen $36, junior $28) tries to be the snowboarder's substitute for Taos, but topography stands in the way. Despite a well-groomed pipe and small terrain parks, the 445-acre mountain just isn't that challenging. Though a handful of steep, bumped-out blacks cover the backside, the entire front face spills sideways off gentle Heading Home ridge, with trails falling in an awkward diagonal and lift access painfully slow. The summit elevation is a respectable 10,677ft, but Angel Fire sits in a bleak, wide-open valley that receives a meager 210 inches of snow a year. Not that you'll have much reason to stay, but neither the resort itself nor the scrappy neighboring town of Eagle's Nest can be described as cozy. They do have plenty of places to stay and eat (for information, contact the Angel Fire Chamber of Commerce, ☎505/377-6401 or 800/633-7463, ⓦwww.angelfirechamber.org); the more attractive hotels and motels of Taos are only forty minutes away, linked to Angel Fire by a free daily ski shuttle.

Arizona Snowbowl, Arizona

Tiny Arizona Snowbowl (☎928/779-1951, ⓦwww.arizonasnowbowl.com, adult $40, junior $22) boasts splendid natural terrain just fifteen minutes above the college town of Flagstaff. Set in the Kachina Peaks Wilderness, the resort boundaries encompass acres of open bowl terrain off Humphreys Peak (12,643ft) – the highest point in Arizona – in addition to its cut trails. The Agassiz chair accesses rockdrops and long powder shots of the Upper Bowl and a handful of fast, steep-groomed blacks, acres of trees, windlips, and natural gullies. Experienced riders should leave the boundaries to take advantage of the numerous descents on the backside of the Upper Bowl; take normal backcountry precautions. Gentle intermediate runs like Southern Belle spill off the lower Sunset Triple, and the open Hart Prairie meadow is an impressively large learning area with 50 segregated acres served by three lifts. There's also a small terrain park here when conditions permit (monitor conditions by calling the Flagstaff snow report, ☎928/779-4577). If planning an overnight trip, Flagstaff's inexpensive motels and B&Bs (☎928/774-9541 or 800/842-7293, ⓦwww.flagstaffarizona.org for info and reservations) are better value than the basic ski lodge at the foot of Snowbowl Road.

Brian Head Resort, Utah

Tiny Brian Head Resort (☎435/677-2035, ⓦwww.brianhead.com; adult $38, junior $25) is quite family friendly, with some eighty percent of its trails rated green or blue. Just outside of Cedar Breaks National Monument – thus surrounded by stunning red-rock scenery – and covered by an annual average of 400 inches of light desert powder, the 540-acre ski area spreads across two peaks, the smaller of which (Navajo) is dedicated to beginners and children with a dozen soft blue and green trails. It's a short shuttle ride to the opposite peak (Giant Steps), layered with longer blue cruisers and several short black diamond blasts. All the runs are short by Utah's standards, but with a dearth of liftlines it's easy to run lap after uninterrupted lap on 1000 vertical feet. Still, experts will quickly tire of the options unless conditions are prime and steeper Brian Head Peak (11,307ft) opens, accessible by foot or via a $5 snowcat ride. There isn't an inordinate amount of freestyle terrain, but there are two small terrain parks and a halfpipe with 12ft walls. Located three hours north of Las Vegas and four hours south of Salt Lake City, Brian Head is best considered as a stopover on a longer road trip. The resort does have a hotel, *The Cedar Breaks Lodge* (ⓦwww.cedarbreakslodge.com), and several condo complexes, with more accommodation in outlying towns like Parowan and Cedar City, fifteen- to thirty-minute drives away.

Las Vegas Ski and Snowboard Resort, Nevada

A smudge of snow above the crags of the desert, Las Vegas Ski and Snowboard Resort (☎702/385-2754, ⓦwww.skilasvegas.com; adult $30, junior $23) looks like a white thumbprint from the Strip – and doesn't seem much bigger once you've made the twenty-minute drive up to the Spring Mountains. Snowmaking augments the 120 natural inches of super-light desert-dried powder that falls annually. Turn up here after a storm to take advantage of the trees and canyons that flank the 640 acres. In normal conditions, the rolling slopes served by the area's three lifts are plenty to keep beginners busy and entertaining enough to amuse even experts for an afternoon – though the alleged terrain park and halfpipe are not much more than bumps of snow. On the other hand, that's no matter, as the most compelling reason to head out this way is to take a break from the bustle of Vegas and to keep you out of the casinos during daylight hours.

Red River, New Mexico

Red River (☎505/754-2223, ⓦwww.redriverskiarea.com; adult $46, junior $32), a 290-acre ski area 45 minutes northeast of Taos, has traded in on its Gold Rush heritage to create a family-friendly theme park of a ski resort. It's not particularly exciting or challenging, and unlikely to grab your attention for too long unless you've got kids in tow, but the small mountain is a reliable place for snow in an area often devoid of it. This is due largely to decent snowmaking facilities that counteract occasional droughts and the effects of warm daytime temperatures. Only a few runs are pitched steep enough to satisfy experts, and novices may find the limited green terrain nerve-racking during busy periods. Intermediates are well served with several long cruising runs (try Boomtown first), and mini-rippers have plenty of natural bumps to launch off, in addition to a small terrain park. Practically all of the area's inns, condominiums, and lodges are within steps of the slopes, and facilities are dressed up Western style.

Sandia Peak, New Mexico

With Santa Fe ski basin just an hour to the north, few head out of their way to ski its smaller sister resort, Sandia Peak (☎505/242-9133, ⓦwww.sandiapeak.com; adult $38, junior $29). Those that do find a nice surprise; while there may be only 200 acres to ride, accessed by painfully slow lifts, this is a fun – and quite scenic – little mountain. It's reached via the world's longest aerial tramway, which rises 4000ft from Albuquerque's dusty eastern suburbs (note: novices should drive up to the base lodge off the Crest Scenic Byway/Hwy-536, where the rental shop, ski school, and bunny slope are located). Surrounded by endless plains, dotted with stumpy volcanic peaks, views from the 10,378ft summit are spectacular. The slopes can be reminiscent of those on the East Coast – relatively meager snow coverage, trails cut into gullies and sandwiched between the trees, the entire area only a few runs wide – but there are long greens and blues that twist and roll for two and a half miles down a 1700ft vertical drop, cruising territory where even experts can spend an afternoon zipping around. If for some reason you intend to stay the night, consider the comfy dorm beds in the clean, attractive *Sandia Mountain Hostel* (☎505/281-4117; $14), at the intersection of Hwy-14 and the Scenic Byway.

Ski Apache, New Mexico

Just two and a half hours northwest of El Paso, Ski Apache (☎505/336-4356, ⓦwww.skiapache.com; adults $45, juniors $29) comes as a surprise considering its proximity to the Mexican border. Eleven lifts access the mountain's 750 acres, which are topped off by a 11,500ft summit. That high elevation, along with good snowmaking facilities, keep conditions decent, in spite of relatively low annual snowfall. Below the summit, the ungroomed Apache Bowl provides intermediates with some widely spaced glades and the occasional powder stash, while beginners are well served by gentle paths that also snake through the ski area's many trees. Run by the Mescalero Apache, the ski area is less than twenty miles from Ruidoso, a fast-growing mountain resort (Ⓦwww.ruidoso.net) best known as a stop on the international horse race circuit. Good-value ski-and-stay packages are available via either resort's website.

Snowbasin, Utah

Were it not for the world-class ski areas in the neighborhood, Snowbasin (Ⓣ801/620-1000 or 1-888/437-5488, Ⓦwww.snowbasin.com; adult $52, junior $29) would undoubtedly be a premier downhill destination. Only a forty-minute drive north of Salt Lake City, the resort made headlines hosting the downhill skiing events of the 2002 Winter Olympics, which has at least put it firmly on the radar. But until slopeside lodging is more substantial, the resort's rugged 3200 acres are more than likely to be blissfully deserted, visited mainly by local day-trippers. If you're in the region for an extended stay consider hitting Snowbasin on a Saturday when Park City and the Cottonwood Canyons get ultra-busy. An efficient lift system, including two gondolas, accesses a wealth of terrain (blanketed in 400 inches of powder each year) ranging from groomed cruisers and powder-filled trees to some of Utah's most technical chutes and cliffs. Experts should try Grizzly, a two-mile long, seriously steep screamer on which the men's Olympic downhill events were held. Atop the mountain and slopeside sit fancy, new day-lodges, with some tasty cafeteria food on offer. The closest accommodations are the handful of options in tiny Eden a few miles away or the larger selection of choices in Ogden twenty minutes away, though many visitors choose to stay in livelier Park City (see p.270).

Sunrise Park, Arizona

Over 200 miles east of Phoenix, Sunrise Park (Ⓣ928/735-7669 or 800/772-7669; adult $38, junior $22) is the largest ski area in the state at 800 acres, and the White Mountains are reliably covered with snow (250 inches annually), but Arizona Snowbowl (see p.308) is a far more well-rounded destination. There's no going off the trails, which are mainly geared toward beginners and intermediates, and jumping is frowned upon everywhere except in the small terrain park. Surrounded by undeveloped tribal lands, dining and accommodation in the immediate area is restricted to the resort's *Sunrise Lodge* – which has reasonable lift- and lodging-packages (from $108 per person for two nights) but not much else. Consider basing yourself in Eagar or Springerville, two relatively charmless service towns thirty minutes down Hwy-260.

The West

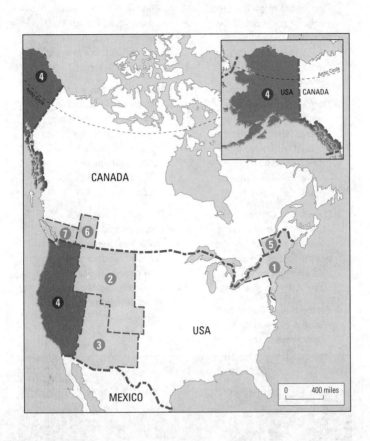

4

THE WEST

✳ **Mammoth and June mountains** Tops in North America for a varied selection of jibs, kickers and pipes, from mini to super-duper. See p.322

✳ **Nevada casinos** Après ski with a twist; from the shabby nostalgia of Crystal Bay gambling dens to the high rise giants of Stateline and Reno. See p.332

✳ **Donner Summit** Easily accessed backcountry above Lake Tahoe, blitzed by heavy storms and littered with red rocks, cliffs and railway gaps. See p.342

✳ **Dave's Deli** Cheaper than bringing your own lunch, this tiny take-out counter at the foot of Squaw Valley might be the best deal in Tahoe. See p.351

✳ **Timberline in Summer** Scores of freestyling campers, training

Olympians and relaxed day-trippers head to Oregon's Mt Hood for summer skiing. See p.379

✳ **Mount Baker** Ride through deep powder – the 1998–1999 season had a world record 1140 inches of accumulation – at Washington's premier ski area. See p.394

✳ **Heliskiing from Valdez** Home of big mountain riding in North America, a pristine, untouched bounty of treacherous steeps and giant bowls accessible only by heli-copter. See p.407

✳ **Diamond Peak and Homewood** Views of the lake from these small, Tahoe resorts rival any in the region, and tickets are considerably cheaper than at neighbors Heavenly and Squaw. See pp.411 and 412

The West

From tiny oases of pine and snow high above the deserts of southern California to barely penetrable glaciers that dominate the landscape in Alaska, winter resorts are found along the length of America's **West Coast**. The majority are situated just a few hours inland on mountains that catch the full force of precipitation off the Pacific. The dense, moisture-rich snow that results can truly be said to dump: six feet in a single day is not unheard of.

Alaska, home to the steepest, most challenging terrain on the continent (and only nominally a part of "the West"), gets hit the hardest. Breaching the Chugach Mountains just outside **Valdez**, Thompson Pass regularly receives the highest snowfall in the US (a whopping 81 feet in 1953) and is the hub of **heliskiing** in the state. Though vacations to this awe-inspiring state are generally taken with a helitrip planned, the quiet resort of **Alyeska**, forty minutes west of Anchorage, is of sufficient size to make the long-distance trip worthwhile.

The resorts of **Washington** are among the more accessible in the country. **Snoqualmie** is only a 45-minute drive from downtown Seattle, while **Crystal Mountain** and **Stevens Pass** are an hour or so further. Of these three small, laid-back ski areas, Stevens Pass has the most highly rated terrain – only super-seded in the state by modest **Mount Baker**, a no-frills freerider's dreamland close to the Canadian border.

Mount Bachelor is the **Oregon** equivalent, though its cascading slopes are not as steep. Just outside the friendly town of Bend, it's further inland than other ski areas in the Northwest, so the snow is much lighter. The state's other major resorts are all located on the arresting volcanic peak of Mount Hood, less than an hour's drive from Portland. **Hood Meadows**, **Ski Bowl**, and **Timberline** are relatively small and flat, and the area, with its glacial snow-fields, is more notable for its thriving summer camp scene.

A significant problem with planning a trip in Alaska or the Northwest is the weather: drizzling rain occurs even at higher altitudes and the mountains can be shrouded in thick, damp fog. In **California**, the ocean-borne snow that falls on the lofty Sierra Nevada range is not much drier – warm temperatures result in the occasional rainstorm creating "powder" that's so dense and sticky that it's referred to as Sierra Cement – and storms that dump the thick, wet stuff frequently result in the mandatory use of **snow chains** for your tires. However, with a warmer climate and the dry Nevada desert to the east, sunny days at California ski areas are the norm. Four hours northwest of San Francisco, stunningly blue **Lake Tahoe** straddles the borders of both states. No fewer than fifteen alpine resorts cluster around its shores, from tiny family-run areas like Boreal and Donner Ski Ranch to the giants of **Heavenly** and **Squaw Valley**. Skiing has a long history in this region: the first recorded ski lift in the

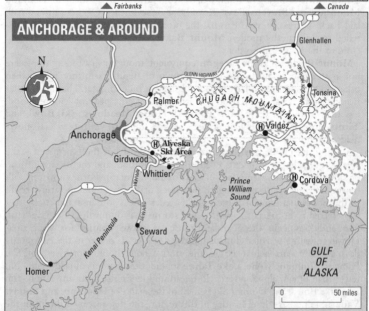

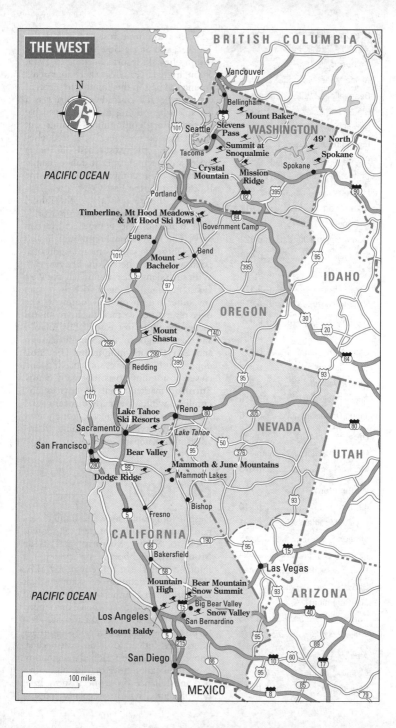

US was a tow rope installed in 1910 in Truckee, and Sugar Bowl was one of the nation's first ski resorts, opening in 1939. Though the larger resorts here are ranked among the best in the country in terms of the skiing, each operates primarily as a day area with lodging and dining available in the resort communities strung out along the lake's shores. As is true elsewhere along the west coast, lift ticket prices are much cheaper in Tahoe than at ski areas of a comparable size in the Rockies or on the East Coast.

Three hours south of Tahoe, **Mammoth** is quietly earning a worldwide reputation for its pipes and terrain parks. The huge, sprawling mountain also has plenty to satisfy more traditional skiers who flock here from Los Angeles. With such dense, heavy snowfall, the West Coast manages a longer ski season than any other region on the continent. The only resorts not to rack up huge annual inches are those just east of Los Angeles and San Diego, in the San Bernardino and San Gabriel mountains. The most popular use extensive snowmaking and clever positioning to compensate: **Snow Summit** markets itself to novices and families, while **Bear Mountain** and **Mountain High** have gone after younger freestylers, transforming themselves into skateparks on snow.

Big Bear

Despite unreliable snowfall, limited terrain, and an insufficient vertical, crowds flock to **Snow Summit** and **Bear Mountain**, neighboring ski areas just a hundred miles east of downtown LA. With a long tradition of skateboarding and surfing in Southern California, and not much to attract the experienced downhill rider to either ski area, it's little surprise that snowboarders outnumber skiers here. Indeed, over the past decade, Snow Summit has developed a reputation as a terrain park innovator – its diminutive size and reliance on artificial snow have not prevented it from regularly topping magazine polls as the **best terrain park** in North America. In 2002 both Big Bear resorts came under the same ownership, and the bulk of Summit's rails and boxes moved to Bear Mountain. Now billed as an "all-mountain terrain park," the entire ski area is dotted with hits and jibs, essentially a skatepark on snow. Summit, meanwhile, has been firmly repositioned to accommodate the novices and families who help fill the place to capacity on the weekends.

The two tiny ski areas are ten minutes apart, rising above Big Bear Lake City, a woodsy, sprawling resort that blends almost imperceptibly with the more workaday Big Bear City on the eastern edge of the lake. Cradled in the San Bernardino Mountains, the eight-mile long lake is within three hours of San Diego and the southern California hinterlands. Many winter visitors view the resorts as **day areas**; evenings are quiet and the towns are generally sleepy.

Arrival, information, and getting around

The crucial element in figuring out **journey time** to Bear is traffic. Midweek, with no rain, fog, or rockslides to snare up Hwys-330 and 18 – the two-lane route that winds steeply up into the San Bernardino Mountains from I-10 – the drive should take under three hours from either San Diego or Los Angeles, sites of the

BIG BEAR

SAN BERNARDINO MOUNTAINS

San Bernardino
National Forest

Barstow &
Las Vegas

Big Bear Discovery
Center-USFS

NORTH SHORE DRIVE

Big Bear City
Airport

GREENWAY DRIVE

Big Bear
City

Redlands

Big Bear Lake

BIG BEAR BOULEVARD

Library

FOX FARM ROAD

Bear Valley Community Hospital

BIG BEAR BOULEVARD

MOONRIDGE ROAD

Big Bear
Lake City

& San Bernardino

& Fawnskin

RESTAURANTS
El Jacalito	F
Fred & Mary's	H
Grizzly Manor Café	E
Ingrid's Deli	I
Madlon's	B
North Shore Café	A
Pine Knot Coffee House	G
Pong's	D
Sushi Ichiban	C

ACCOMMODATION
Adventure Hostel	2
Black Forest Lodge	3
Eagle's Nest	4
Escape Condos	9
Gold Mountain Manor	1
Grey Squirrel Resort	7
Honey Bear Lodge	6
Northwoods Resort & Conference Center	5
Wildwood Resort	8

SNOW SUMMIT
RESORT

Bear Valley

8182 ft

BEAR
MOUNTAIN
RESORT

8490 ft

8805 ft

SAN BERNARDINO MOUNTAINS

0   1 mile

N

Mountain info

Phone ☎909/866-5766
Snow phone ☎800/BEARMTN (Bear);
800/SUMMIT-1 (Summit)
Website ⊛www.bigbearmountainresorts.com
Price $43; night tickets $26; half-night session $18.

Bear Mountain

Operating times Mid-Nov to mid-April
Mon–Fri 8.30am–4pm, weekends and holidays 8am–4pm
No. of lifts 12, including 3 surface
Base elevation 7140′
Summit elevation 8805′
Vertical drop 1665′
No. of trails 34
Acreage 748 total acres, but only 198 acres of trails
Beginner 30%
Intermediate 40%
Expert 30%
Average snowfall 100″
Snowmaking Yes (198 acres, 100% of trails)
Night skiing No
Nursery facilities No, skiing from age 4, snowboarding from age 6

Snow Summit

Operating times Mid-Nov to mid-April
Mon–Fri 8.30am–4pm, weekends
8am–4.30pm, night session hours and days of operation vary according to the season and snow conditions
No. of lifts 11
Base elevation 7000′
Summit elevation 8200′
Vertical drop 1200′
No. of trails 31
Acreage 230 skiable (620 under permit)
Beginner 10%
Intermediate 65%
Expert 25%
Average snowfall 75″
Snowmaking Yes (198 acres, 100% of trails)
Night skiing Yes, hours vary
Nursery facilities No, skiing from age 4, snowboarding from age 6

closest airports. Hwy-38 is the alternate route to take on busy weekends, adding a few miles but with less traffic and fewer bends in the road. To really reduce mountain driving, take Hwy-18 in from the north, a route across the bleak high desert that is usually the last road into the mountains to be subject to chain control.

The City of Big Bear Lake stretches along almost the entire southern shore of its namesake, flanking Big Bear Boulevard (Hwy-18). Summit is right off the highway on Summit Boulevard, east of the small cluster of stores and restaurants known as The Village, while Bear Mountain is ten minutes up Moonridge Drive, the next major junction. **Parking** at both mountains is free, though the closest lots can fill to capacity on busy weekends. A shuttle transports skiers from the auxiliary lots.

MARTA (Mountain Area Regional Transit Authority; $5; ☎909/584-1111) buses run two to four times a day (Mon–Sat) between Bear and San Bernardino, connecting with Los Angeles area Metrolink trains (☎909/808-5465, ⊛www.metrolinktrains.com; $8.50 for the 1 1/2 hour journey to LA Union Station) and Greyhound bus services (Los Angeles $10, San Diego $20). MARTA also operates the **local bus service** around Big Bear Lake and Big Bear City (Mon–Sat 6.30am–6pm, Sun 8.30am–9pm, $1), running hourly in both directions along Big Bear Boulevard, stopping at the base of Snow Summit and detouring up Moonridge Drive to Bear Mountain; Dial-A-Ride service is available throughout the valley ($2; 6am–6pm). Pick up a route map and schedule from the Chamber of Commerce and Resort Association **visitor center** at 630 Bartlett Rd (Mon–Fri 8am–5pm, Sat–Sun 9am–5pm; ☎1-800/4-BIGBEAR, ⊛www.bigbearinfo.com).

The mountains

Even though Bear Mountain's and Summit's terrain parks are world class, the **mountains** they inhabit are minuscule in size; each has only around 200 acres of trails. When the Santana winds carry in a big storm (a rare occurrence) and the off-piste glades become skiable, 400 or so acres more are added to each. The waters of artificially created Big Bear Lake – the valley was dammed back in 1884 to water the citrus groves of the Inland Empire – allow for impressive snowmaking capacity, which significantly increases coverage. Still, bushes and dirt gullies between trails are the norm. On weekdays, either ski area makes a fine spot to introduce a novice to the slopes, with plenty of flat terrain. Those who ski only occasionally will also enjoy the novelty of skiing at this latitude, cruising on mellow sunlit trails with views out across the lake. Experts not interested in terrain parks should head elsewhere.

Snow Summit

Summit maintains a small selection of **parks** on the western slopes of the ski area – though these days the monster rails have been replaced for the most part by mini-jibs. In addition to a beginner's rail park, there are small jumps and rollers in the family park zone under Chair 9, and a beginner line running parallel to the bigger tables and rails on Westridge, the top-to-bottom park run that first made Summit famous. The **pipe** on ZZYZX is dug into the slope to make best use of the limited snow, though the walls still get patchy at times.

Outside of the terrain park, skiers have several options including a wide meadow, perfect for **beginners**, and the relatively secluded, slow skiing-only family park at the top of the All Mountain Express lift. Unfortunately, the latter is one of the first areas to close when snow coverage dwindles, along with the marginally steeper slopes under Chair 7. Avoid Summit Run, the gentle summit-to-base thoroughfare back to the lodge, as it's a minefield of shaking, snaking beginners and reckless speed demons. Confident **intermediates** should try the small bowl under Chair 6, as the short double diamond would barely classify as a black at another resort.

Bear Mountain

Bear Mountain offers jibs in a variety of sizes, constructions, and combinations: single barrel round rails, double and triple barrel rails, flat rails, ledge rails, boxes and mail boxes straight, curved, and angled. Terrain features can be found on almost every run. The resort's **pipes** are decent, both located on the lower slopes and accessed by the speedy Goldrush quad lift. The small but adequately furnished **snowskate park** is beside the base area sundeck. In addition to the pro park on Gold Rush, there are hits and rails for all abilities scattered liberally around the western slopes of the ski area, beneath the Silver, Goldmine, and Showdown peaks. Only Bear Peak, home to Geronimo, the most convincing **black run** in the valley, is jib-free. When it dumps, Geronimo offers access to the trees and gullies of Bow and Deer canyons. Though irrelevant much of the year, Bear Mountain's soft boundary policy means unlimited access to the surrounding canyons of the San Bernardino National Forest, should there be any snow in them. Occasionally conditions are good enough for explorations in the neighboring San Gorgonio Wilderness; make further inquiries at local boardshops or the ranger station.

Lift tickets, lessons, and rentals

Ticket sales are limited to avoid overcrowding – it's not unusual for weekends to sell out in advance, particularly over the holidays – so book in advance on the resort website. **Tickets** are valid at both resorts, and spending the morning at one and the afternoon at the other is perfectly viable, though a more likely combination is to ride Bear Mountain during the day and switch to Summit at night. Unusual deals include the "ride free on your birthday" offer and up to $17 credit if you turn your ticket in by 1pm. Midweek season passes to both mountains start at $199 if bought before June. Once the season has started, the full pass costs $799.

Lift-and-lesson (no gear) packages start at $56. Two-hour group classes cost $25–30; kids' packages are good value, from $46 for the day ($11 extra for rentals). Bear Mountain has two additional programs to those offered at Summit: the Burton Kid's Method Center, for budding snowboarders 12 and under, and USARC (United States Adaptive Recreation Center; ℡909/584-0269, ⓦwww.usarc.org) adaptive skiing programs. Resort **rentals** are decent brands but expensive, worn, and limited in selection. You're better off renting from stores in town. Pokey Goldsmiths, 42071 Big Bear Blvd (℡909/866-2728), between the two resorts, carries a decent inventory of skis (from $11.50) and boards (from $20), clothing, helmets, and cross-country ski rentals. Alpine Sports, 41530 Big Bear Blvd (℡909/866-7541), is a ski specialist, and Leroys, 598 Paine and 41925 Big Bear Blvd (℡909/866-4887), is the dedicated snowboard shop.

Accommodation

Complexes of tiny wooden cabins cluster in the pines along Big Bear Boulevard, past their prime but still quaint in a summer camp sort of way. Typical resort condominiums are limited; more luxurious are the valley's B&Bs, many located on the quieter north shore of Big Bear Lake. Their central online agency is A Big Bear Bed & Breakfast Experience (ⓦwww.bigbearbnb.com). To rent a deluxe mountain home in the area, try Blue Skies (℡909/442-2422, ⓦwww.bigbearproperties.com) or the visitors center (℡1-800/4-BIGBEAR, ⓦwww.bigbearinfo.com).

Adventure Hostel 527 Knickerbocker Rd ℡909 /866-8900 or 1-866/866-5255, ⓦwww.adventurehostel.com. Located in the center of Big Bear Village, complete with free Web access, linens, lockers, and cheap ski packages (from $50 midweek). Furnishings may be minimal, but there is a kitchen, game room, and no curfew. Reservations recommended, especially on weekends. ❷

Black Forest Lodge 41121 Big Bear Blvd ℡909/866-2166 or 1-800/255/4378, ⓦwww.blackforestlodge.com. Slightly dated, mock-Bavarian lodge in the heart of town, offering chintzy motel rooms, tiny cabins, and family chalets. The ski shop on the property has discounted rates on older gear. Kitchen suites are available, and room rates are reasonable; from ❷, ski packages from $58 per person.

Eagle's Nest 41675 Big Bear Blvd ℡909/866-6465 or 1-888/866-6465, ⓦwww.bigbear.com/enbb. Attractive wooden B&B and cabins in the center of

town. Room décor varies considerably, particularly in the cabins. ❹

Escape Condos 41935 Switzerland Dr ℡909/866-7504 or 1-800/722-4366, ⓦwww.bigbearescape .net. Large wooden complex at the foot of Snow Summit. All of the small two- and three-bedroom condos are individually decorated – most seem straight out of the 1970s. ❹–❽

Gold Mountain Manor 1117 Anita ℡909/585-6997 or 1-800/509-2604, ⓦwww.goldmountainmanor.com. Impressive 1920's log mansion located on the quieter north shore. Eleven elegant rooms range in character from floral Victoriana to rustic cabin, each with their own fireplace. The friendly owners whip up tasty breakfasts, while their labradors flop winsomely on comfy couches next to the pool table. ❺–❼

Grey Squirrel Resort 39372 Big Bear Blvd ℡909 /866-4335 or 1-800/381-5569, ⓦwww .greysquirrel.com. Near the lake, with small, comfy cabins sleeping 2–14 and a roster of private homes for rent close by. The indoor tub is a little musty and the furnishings past their prime, but cabins are clean and quiet. Cabins from ❹, homes from ❻

Honey Bear Lodge 40994 Pennsylvania Ave ☎909/866-7825 or 1-800/628-8714, ⓦwww .honeybearlodge.com. Cheap accommodation for those prepared to cram six into a loft. All are simply decorated, and include fridges, microwaves, and wood-burning stoves. The economy motel rooms are spare and lifeless. Loft sleeping six from ❸, economy rooms from ❶, discounts for multiday bookings.

Northwoods Resort and Conference Center 40650 Village Drive ☎505/866-3121 or 800/866-

3121, ⓦwww.northwoodsresort.com Overpriced and a bland atmosphere, though there's a heated outdoor pool and tub, and since the place has 147 rooms to fill, discounted rates are often available. ❻

Wildwood Resort 40210 Big Bear Blvd ☎909/878-2178 or 888/294-5396, ⓦwww .wildwoodresort.com. Large complex of white painted cabins on the outskirts of town, clean and good value, especially midweek. Most have kitchens and fireplaces, and there's an outdoor tub. Extravagantly themed suites in the lodge range from leopard-print and vines of the Jungle Room to the sea murals and plastic fish of the Castaway. Suites ❺, ski packages from $49 per person.

Eating

Restaurants are strung along the length of Big Bear Boulevard, with few outstanding choices. Vons supermarket is on the eastern side of town, at 42170 Big Bear Blvd (daily 7am–11pm; ☎909/866-8459). Outdoor barbecues, pasta bars, cafeterias, coffeeshops, and sports bars are located in the wooden complexes at the base of both resorts, with "beach" areas right on the slopes.

El Jacalito 40629 Lakeview Drive ☎909/878-2131. Simple, inexpensive, and authentic Mexican café famed for its 99¢ tacos and weekend breakfasts. Open daily.

Fred & Mary's 607 Pine Knot ☎909/866-2434. Californian gourmet dining in a garlanded cottage right in the center of the village. Try creative pasta dishes like the handmade carrot gnocchi ($14–20). Fri–Sat 5–10pm, weekdays 5–9pm, closed one or two days midweek (call for days, which vary).

Grizzly Manor Cafe 41268 Big Bear Blvd ☎909/866-6226. Loved for its good value (breakfasts around $5) and the intentionally ornery staff. The only thing larger than the hearty meat, egg, and hash brown breakfasts are the lines out the door on busy weekends. Breakfast daily, lunch when they feel like it.

Ingrid's Deli 42530 Moonridge Rd ☎909/866-8122. Inexpensive breakfast and sandwich pit stop on the road up to Bear Mountain.

Madlon's 829 Big Bear Blvd ☎909/585-3762. Hansel and Gretel cottage presided over by a theatrical owner; each night's gourmet offerings are top notch, from steak to veggie specials. Expensive; reservations suggested. Dinner from 5pm nightly;

brunch Sat–Sun 8am–2.30pm.

North Shore Café 39226 North Shore Drive ☎909/866-5879. Reasonably priced, quiet, elegant café in the little hamlet of Fawnskin, on the opposite side of the lake to the ski areas and close to most of the area's B&Bs. The menu is upscale on Friday and Saturday nights, when the chef produces French-American entrees like hazelnut trout and filet mignon in lieu of the usual burgers, pastas, and salads.

Pine Knot Coffee House 535 Pine Knot Ave ☎909/866-3537. Crunchy coffeehouse in the village, serving up pastries and espresso in comfortable surroundings.

Pong's 42104 Big Bear Blvd ☎909/866-4400. The atmosphere is a little bland, but the kitchen turns out fresh Chinese, Japanese, and Thai dishes a cut above the usual Chinese-American restaurants, and you can eat well for under $10.

Sushi Ichiban 42151 Big Bear Blvd ☎909/866-6413. Best day to visit is Thursday after the staff has made its fresh fish run on Wednesday. Really excellent sushi, along with good udon noodles. Sun–Tues & Thurs 11am–9pm, Fri–Sat 11am–10pm.

Bars and entertainment

Dead midweek, the town is not much better on the weekends. Big Bear's **après-ski** has a low-key beach vibe, with crowds hanging out on the wooden decks and in the slopeside bars of the resorts. Off the slopes, try *Chad's Place*,

40740 Village Drive (℡ 909/866-2161), a sprawling sports bar with pool tables, foosball, a dance floor, and tiny stage where bands up from the city rock out on Friday and Saturday nights; or *Murray's*, 672 Cottage Lane (℡ 909/866-1444), a karaoke country-rock dive. The Village is home to a handful of arcades and the two **theaters**, located on Village Drive and Pine Knot Ave (℡ 909/866-5115). Few big-name acts grace the stage at the Big Bear Lake Performing Arts Center, 39707 Big Bear Blvd (℡ 909/866-4970), though the local Community Arts group puts on regular shows. The Bowling Barn, 40625 Lakeview Drive (℡ 909/878-2695), is a perennial family favorite, with rock 'n' roll and country bands leading dances on weekends.

Other activities and attractions

With little in the way of a resort center and just a handful of kitschy stores, Big Bear offers few off-slope activities. **Cross-country** skiers and **snowshoers** of all abilities are free to explore the valley's hills and glades after the purchase of an Adventure Pass ($5 per day), valid in the surrounding San Bernardino National Forest and neighboring areas. Passes can be bought, snowshoes rented ($12), and trail maps collected at the Big Bear Discovery Center on North Shore Drive (Hwy-38), just west of Fawnskin (daily 9am–5pm; ℡ 909/866-3437).

Horseback rides are available through Baldwin Lake Stables (℡ 909/585-6482), and backcountry 4WD tours with Off-Road Adventures (℡ 909/585-1036). The concrete alpine slide at Magic Mountain is open year-round ($4), alongside a sledding hill ($18; $12 from 5 to 9pm). The Real Deal Ride Shop, 42124 Big Bear Blvd (℡ 909/878-5935), sponsors the neighboring Grandville **skatepark**, 42118 Big Bear Blvd (Sat–Sun 10am–6.30pm, weekday hours vary; $10, pads required), a decent collection of smallish wooden quarterpipes, fun boxes, and rails housed in a warehouse and adjacent lot.

Listings

Bookstore Big Bear Book and Bean, 596 Pine Knot Ave ℡ 909/878-4083.

Internet Big Bear Branch Library, 41930 Garstin Drive ℡ 909/866-5571; call for hours.

Medical Bear Valley Community Hospital, 41870 Garstin Drive ℡ 909/866-6501.

Pharmacy Rite Aid, 42146 Big Bear Blvd ℡ 909/866-2211.

Post office 472 Pineknot St/247 Centerwood St, both ℡ 800/275-8777.

Road conditions and weather ℡ 909/866-ROAD.

Taxi Big Bear Shuttle and Taxi, ℡ 909/585-5514 or 800/214-5273.

Mammoth and June

Though not the largest ski area in California – both Heavenly and Squaw Valley are bigger – **Mammoth** is, well, mammoth, a great white hump of a dormant volcano strewn between the Ansel Adams Wilderness and the squat resort town of Mammoth Lakes. On holiday weekends skiers from Los Angeles take the five-hour drive north to the Inyo National Forest, where the mountain majestically crests Adams' beloved "Range of Light," the jagged eastern

Sierras. Sitting at a higher altitude than Lake Tahoe and hit sporadically by heavy Sierra storms, Mammoth boasts one of the longest seasons in the US, rarely closing before July. This, in combination with an aggressive program of terrain park and pipe building, has brought freestyle pros en masse to the area to train in recent years. A mix of decent off-piste skiing, both in and out of bounds, and acres of twisting blues and easy greens makes the mountain one of the most technically diverse in California. If that weren't sufficient, Mammoth has an uncrowded little sibling, **June Mountain**, which provides more freestyle terrain and pistes just twenty minutes down the road.

The architecturally bland town of **Mammoth Lakes** sprung from a tiny settlement after the first chairlift opened in 1955. Today, it's an amalgamation of boxy strip malls along two wide, perpendicular roads (Main Street and Old Mammoth Road), crisscrossed with condominiums. Though the lower slopes of this expansive mountain snake to the western edge of Mammoth Lakes' condo sprawl, the Main Lodge and gondola are a twisting fifteen-minute drive up the mountain. In partnership with ski area construction giant Intrawest, the resort is developing a small modern village of condo suites, stores, and bars, designed as the hub for a **new gondola** which, when fully operational, will whisk skiers straight up the mountainside from Main Street and provide more of a pedestrian gathering place in the town itself.

Arrival, information, and getting around

Most visitors **drive** to Mammoth, 325 miles north of Los Angeles on Hwy-365, a straight shot up through the arid Owens Valley. A 4WD is not strictly necessary, though once on Hwy-203 into town the roads can become thick with soft Sierra snow. Though there are perennial expansion plans for the tiny Mammoth Lakes airstrip, currently the closest major **airport** is Reno (℡775/328-6400, see box p.333), 165 miles north on Hwy-365. Getting to Mammoth by bus is complicated: the Crest bus (℡1-800/922-1930) runs from Mammoth Lakes on alternate days to Carson City in the north and Ridgecrest to the south, where the Pride or Kern Regional Transit buses connect to Greyhound services in Reno and Mojave. Some bus services include lodging and lift tickets and run from major cities in California. Try Pacific Sports Tours (℡310/798-1234, ⊛www.mammothskitours.com) or Sierra Tours (℡714/667-1111 or 1-888/667-1110, ⊛www.sierratours.com); weekend packages start at $175.

The resort has an excellent free **bus** system so long as you don't want to go anywhere in a hurry after 5.30pm. Night service is limited to central locations, running on the half-hour until 11pm Sun–Thurs and midnight Fri–Sat. Pick up a route map from the combined Mammoth Lakes and US Forest Service **visitor center** at the eastern entrance of town on Hwy-203 (daily 8am–5pm, ℡760/924-5500 or 1-888/466-2666, ⊛www.visitmammoth.com), an excellent resource for local backcountry and hot springs information.

Driving up the mountain on Hwy-203 to the Canyon and Main Lodges is easy midweek and excruciating on the weekend. There are pay lots near the lodges, but it's less hassle to leave cars in town and take the bus or, when operational, the new gondola.

Mammoth Mountain

The first lodge to be built, imaginatively named the **Main Lodge**, is high on the ski area's northern boundary, from where the Panorama gondola provides the fastest route to the long summit ridge, while speedy lifts access the small

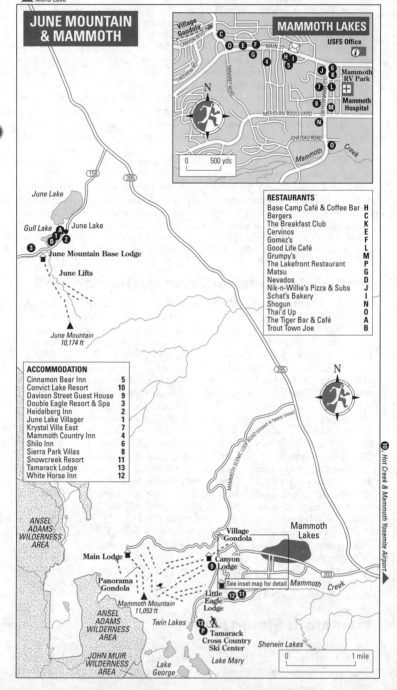

JUNE MOUNTAIN & MAMMOTH

MAMMOTH LAKES

USFS Office

Mammoth RV Park

Mammoth Hospital

MAIN ST

MERIDIAN BOULEVARD

CHATEAU ROAD

Mammoth Creek

0   500 yds

N

Mono Lake

Village Gondola

CANYON BLVD

LAKEVIEW BLVD

MINARET ROAD

OLD MAMMOTH RD

June Lake

158   395

Gull Lake   June Lake

June Mountain Base Lodge

June Lifts

June Mountain
10,174 ft

395

MAMMOTH SCENIC LOOP ROAD (closed in heavy snow)

N

RESTAURANTS

Base Camp Café & Coffee Bar	H
Bergers	C
The Breakfast Club	K
Cervinos	E
Gomez's	F
Good Life Café	L
Grumpy's	M
The Lakefront Restaurant	P
Matsu	G
Nevados	D
Nik-n-Willie's Pizza & Subs	J
Schat's Bakery	I
Shogun	N
Thai'd Up	O
The Tiger Bar & Café	A
Trout Town Joe	B

ACCOMMODATION

Cinnamon Bear Inn	5
Convict Lake Resort	10
Davison Street Guest House	9
Double Eagle Resort & Spa	3
Heidelberg Inn	2
June Lake Villager	1
Krystal Villa East	7
Mammoth Country Inn	4
Shilo Inn	6
Sierra Park Villas	8
Snowcreek Resort	11
Tamarack Lodge	13
White Horse Inn	12

ANSEL ADAMS WILDERNESS AREA

Main Lodge

Panorama Gondola

Mammoth Mountain
11,053 ft

ANSEL ADAMS WILDERNESS AREA

Twin Lakes

JOHN MUIR WILDERNESS AREA

Lake George

Village Gondola

Mammoth Lakes

Canyon Lodge

See inset map for detail   Mammoth Creek

Little Eagle Lodge

Tamarack Cross Country Ski Center

Lake Mary

Sherwin Lakes

0   1 mile

203

Hot Creek & Mammoth Yosemite Airport

backside bowls and serve the pro park and superpipes. High, bald, and exposed, the upper mountain terrain underneath Panorama suffers most from the gusty winds that often plague the resort.

The new gondola links the town up to **Canyon Lodge**, a sheltered base area good for beginners and nervous intermediates. On the mountain's southern boundary is **Little Eagle Lodge**, home to forested greens in the mountain's lower altitude, heavily gladed flanks. Great in fresh powder, this area can get too much sun and become soggy in spring, and is a little too flat for novice snowboarders.

Those with tickets already in hand have even more choices as to where to start their day. To avoid the crowds around the various lodges, park in turnouts on Hwy-203 before you reach the Main Lodge, which will give you direct access to the lifts next to the *Mill Café* and the South Park terrain park.

As if the location of all the various lodges weren't confusing enough, successful navigation of the ski area itself takes time. Dotted with rocky outcrops, ridges, and valleys, and crisscrossed with 27 lifts, the area requires a **trail map** as a necessary companion at first. At least most of the chairlifts are quick and efficient, though Mammoth gets extremely busy on holiday weekends.

Mountain info – Mammoth

Phone ☎760/934-0745 or 1-800/MAMMOTH

Snow phone ☎760/934-6166 or 1-888/SNOWRPT

Website ⊛www.mammothmountain.com

Price $60 full day, $48 half day

Operating times Nov–June daily 8.30am–4pm

No. of lifts 27, including 3 gondolas (though 2 are really the lower and upper parts of one route), 8 high-speed quads, and 2 surface

Base elevation 7953'

Summit elevation 11,053'

Vertical drop 3100'

No. of trails 150

Acreage 3500

Beginner 25%

Intermediate 40%

Expert 35%

Average snowfall 384"

Snowmaking Yes (477 acres, 48 trails, 33% of mountain)

Night skiing No

Nursery facilities Yes, Small World Childcare Center in Mammoth Mountain Inn for daycare from newborn to age 12, ☎760/934-0646, skiing and snowboarding ages 4–12

Beginner

Sheltered by trees and out of the paths of faster skiers, the beginner chair and slopes at the Canyon are generally quieter than their equivalents at the Main Lodge. Confident beginners can progress to longer greens and mellow blues off **Chair 17** in the same area. For something a bit more challenging, try the handful of long trails under the **Eagle Express**. Novice snowboarders should avoid this area until confident holding speed on the flat, especially since the lower altitude of this area of the mountain can result in slow slush on sunny days.

Intermediate

Avoid the exposed, crowded trails off the Main Lodge (Panorama) gondola and take Chair 12 to the quieter trails of the **Outpost**. On the opposite side of the mountain, take a cruise through the tall pines high above Little Eagle base, a gently rolling gladed area perfect for an introduction to power. Lifts serving the varied intermediate trails around the Canyon Lodge can be appallingly busy at times; try those above the *Mill Café* instead, particularly if you're ready for a longer challenge. Mid-mountain blacks are short and open, only truly difficult when the wind creates white-out conditions.

Expert

Double diamond descents spill off almost every upper mountain lift, accessible from any one of the base lodges. Easier **groomers** are found at upper mid-mountain, off chairs 9 and 5 or the Facelift express, and on the backside Outpost area behind the Main Lodge. For **open bowl** skiing, cornices, and chutes head up the gondola to the summit and be prepared to hike or traverse for the best lines. Along the summit is the **Dragon's Tail**, popular for its powder-filled trees. Keep your speed once the pitch starts to flatten or you'll be hiking out. More technical skiing, moguls, cliffs, and stubby glades spill off the precipitous mid-mountain knobs below Rogers Ridge and above Chair 22, though these areas are closed unless conditions are ideal.

Freestyle

Mammoth offers some of the best freestyle options in the country and the only downside is that everyone else knows it too. The so-called **super-duper pipe**, regular **super pipe**, and **pro park** are located above the Main Lodge. Running parallel to the pro park is a more modest line, with a handful of midsized table-tops and smaller rails. There's also an entire alternate set over in **South Park**, off Chair 20, with both huge and beginner kickers, and a separate trail of rails. South Park works best in the morning, as it gets too slushy here later on. A few smaller hits and an infrequently groomed **minipipe** are located just above the Canyon Lodge. If you're nervous around crowds, try June Mountain, emptier midweek (see opposite). Oustide the parks Mammoth is a rollercoaster of a mountain. On a powder day, take your pick of lines, from open bowl floaters to serious cliffs and tight landings off the mid-mountain ridges.

Lift tickets, lessons, and rentals

Day **tickets** to Mammoth are a few dollars cheaper during the week. Best deal is the early-purchase season pass, which costs only $399, $800 cheaper than the regular season pass. Sold only in April, the pass allows unlimited access to Mammoth and June from May until the end of the following season; ride for eight days and the pass will have been paid off.

Though the resort-owned **rental** shops carry good equipment and deal with the weekend crowds fairly well (book in advance on the website to ensure the gear is available), prices are steep – up to $55 for demos. Grab coupons from the visitor center and head to Footloose Sports, a huge ski shop and bootfitter on the corner of Main Street and Old Mammoth Road (☎760/934-2400) or

---

Independent backcountry options

Home to Mount Whitney, at 14,494ft the tallest mountain in the continental US, the jagged peaks of the Eastern Sierra offer some of the most challenging backcountry descents in the country. Just south of Mammoth are the Sherwins, a rust-colored range of bowls and steep chutes. Right off the backside of the resort is the infamous Hole in the Wall, a tricky, avalanche-prone route that drops down to Twin Lakes and the Mammoth Lodge. As always, proper equipment and a local guide are essential. Contact the Sierra Mountain Center, based in Bishop (☎760/873-8526, ⓦwww .sierramountaincenter.com), for day tours, overnight winter camping and hut trips, powder descents, and avalanche courses.

to Wave Rave, 3203 Main St (☏760/934-2471), one of the oldest snowboard stores in the States.

Lessons for adults and kids (☏1-800/MAMMOTH) are available at both the Canyon and Main lodges. Mammoth is one of the few ski areas in the States that starts kids on snowboards at the same age as skis – group lessons are offered from the age of 4. Adult novices interested in the "First Time" all-inclusive lift, lesson, and equipment package ($81) need to make reservations with the resort at least 72 hours in advance. Three-hour adult group lessons (from $55) are scheduled for the morning; shorter afternoon sessions (from $35) are offered to beginners only. Telemark, park, and pipe sessions are offered at the weekends, and limited **adaptive lessons** and gear are available; book at least seven days in advance on ☏760/934-2571.

June Mountain

Fifteen miles north of Mammoth Hwy-158 branches off Hwy-395 and climbs past the sleepy June Lake village to **June Mountain ski area**, which escapes the worst of the area's weekend crowds. For such a small area, June has a surprising diversity of **terrain**, though the more challenging gladed slopes are only really skiable when there's fresh, deep snow. There's a ticket window at the base of the lower slopes, but the day lodge is higher up, at the top of the J1 double chair – a lift so painfully slow that you need to figure in an extra twenty minutes to your morning commute. And an extra twenty minutes at the end of the day, too – because the lower slopes are so unreliable, skiers typically have to download on the J1 double to get back to the parking lot.

Past the day lodge, sheltered, treelined greens fill a flat valley below two small peaks: Rainbow (10,040ft), which has a handful of blues designated for **family skiing**, and slightly steeper June (10,174ft), which boasts the mountain's short but sweet black chutes the area's larger terrain park features. Great for

Mountain info – June	
Phone ☏760/648-7733 or 1-888/JUNEMTN	
Snow phone ☏760/934-2224	
Website ⊛www.junemountain.com	
Price $47 full day, $37 half day	
Operating times Dec–April J1 lift 7.30am–5pm, others 9am–4pm (J2 opens at 8.30am)	
No. of lifts 7, including one rope tow	
Base elevation 7545'	
Summit elevation 10,174'	
Vertical drop 2590'	
No. of trails 35	
Acreage 500+	
Beginner 35%	
Intermediate 45%	
Expert 20%	
Average snowfall 250"	
Snowmaking Yes (20 %)	
Night skiing No	
Nursery facilities No nursery, but kids' sports school from age 4	

beginners and intermediates who don't mind skiing the same runs all day and for groups who want to minimize their chances of losing each other, June is also renowned for its **parks** and **superpipe**. Back when snowboarders were a novelty, Mammoth made its smaller sibling something of a holding pen for these new creatures, and terrain features blossomed on June's secluded slopes; in fact Mammoth locals still drive to June to hit the rails and ride the expertly groomed pipe. The resort also offers a good range of smaller hits and a mini jib park.

The rickety June Meadows Chalet day lodge, with its cafeteria, bar, and small store, opens at 8am and by lunchtime the outdoor deck is busy with barbecues and groups of kids. Further up the mountain, the *Stew Pot Slim* shack serves barbecue and chili on sunny days. There are only a couple of places to eat in June Lakes (see "Eating" below) and no bus service between June and Mammoth.

Lift tickets, lessons, and rentals

Tickets bought independently here are some $10 cheaper than at Mammoth, while season passes are practically given away (just $99 for students, in recent years). The chalet (see above) holds a slim selection of **rentals** and the June Ski School, which offers **lessons** for a few dollars less than Mammoth. Propaganda, 2587 Hwy-158 (☎760/648-7399), is the area's core snowboard store.

Accommodation

The older **condo** complexes offer great deals, particularly midweek, but everything quickly fills on peak weekends. For rental agencies try Mammoth Reservations (☎760/934-8372 or 1-800/223-3032, ⓦwww.mammothreservations.com), which has a hut opposite the post office on Main Street, or Mammoth Sierra Reservations (☎760/934-8372 or 1-800/325-8415, ⓦwww.mammothsierraonline.com). There are a few modern chain **motels**, a handful of rather shabby all-inclusive ski lodges, and a hostel. The resort manages a few slopeside properties with the older *Mammoth Mountain Inn*, at the Main Lodge, best situated for first tracks but severely limited for dining options; closer to town is *Juniper Springs*, a plush condo–hotel next to the Little Eagle base. Sleepy June Lakes is better known for fishing than skiing, so rates here are generally cheaper in the winter. June condo rentals (☎1-800/462-5589, ⓦwww.rainbowridgereservations.com) and June Lake Properties (☎760/648-7705 or 1-800/648-JUNE) are where to start.

Mammoth

Cinnamon Bear Inn 113 Center St ☎760/934-2873 or 1-800/845-2873, ⓦwww.cinnamonbearinn.com. More like an upscale motel than a B&B, benefits include a full breakfast, jacuzzi, central town location, and good midweek ski packages. A few kitchens and kitchenettes are available. ❸–❻

Convict Lake Resort Rte 1 off Hwy-395 ☎760/934-3800 or 1-800/992-2260. Perched beside a deep mountain lake in a remote spot about fifteen minutes from Mammoth Lakes, the cabins here are clean but basic. Most sleep 2–8, with a couple of large houses sleeping up to 34. There's a fisherman's general store, and an expensive, highly rated, seemingly out of place French restaurant in the resort. ❹–❾

Davison Street Guest House 19 Davison Rd 619/544-9093 (out-of-town number). Hostel close to Canyon Lodge. Dorm beds from $20, all in small rooms that can also be rented individually. Large A-frame lounge on top floor with great views and couches that double as extra beds.

Krystal Villa East 137 Laurel Mountain Rd ☎760/934-2669 or 1-800/237-6181. Budget condos in the Mammoth "ghetto," the name given to the older part of town. Not particularly pretty outside or in, but it is comfy. All the suites have wood stoves and TVs and there's a laundry room, video library, spa, sauna, and pool. Especially good midweek and long-stay deals. ❸ per night, sleeps 4–6.

Mammoth Country Inn 75 Joaquin Rd ☎760/934-2710, ⓦwww.mammothcountryinn.com. Centrally located, family-run B&B that feels like a small lodge. All rooms have private baths, cable TV, and VCRs and are decorated with Western themes. A hearty breakfast and evening snacks are served in the small lounge. ❸–❺

Shilo Inn 2963 Main St ☎760/934-4500 or 1-800/222-2244. A cut above the usual brand motels with spacious rooms containing microwaves and fridges. Amenities include laundry facilities, a generous continental breakfast, and an indoor pool, tub, sauna, and steam room. ❹

Sierra Park Villas 286 Old Mammoth Rd ☎760/934-4521 or 1-800/422-2624, ⓔspv@qnet.com. Inexpensive and fairly spacious condos in an apartment-style complex in the center of town near Vons supermarket, the movie theaters, and on the Mammoth shuttle route. There's a sauna, outdoor tubs, laundry room, and cable. ❺

4

Snowcreek Resort Old Mammoth Rd ☎760/934-3333 or 1-800/544-6007, ⊛www.snowcreek.com. Large, quality condo complex on the outskirts of town, seemingly under continuous expansion – including, most recently, deluxe suburban townhouses. Rates include complimentary access to the impressive Snowcreek Athletic Club. ❺–❾
Tamarack Lodge Lake Mary Rd ☎760/934-2442 or 1-800/237-6879, ⊛www.tamaracklodge.com. Located on the shores of Twin Lakes just outside town, both the lodge and the surrounding 29 cabins provide an elegant rustic retreat. Built in 1924, the renovated cabins retain their old-fashioned ambience; all have full kitchens and no televisions, and most are surrounded by deep snow in the winter. Breakfast is available in the lodge's fancy *Lakefront Restaurant* (but not included in the price) and mulled wine is served in the afternoons. Ski packages available. Cabins from ❺, lodge rooms ❸ with shared bath, ❺ with private bath.
White Horse Inn 2180 Old Mammoth Rd ☎760/924-3656, ⊛www.whitehorse-inn.net. Intimate B&B in a quiet part of town, decorated with care by brothers Doug and John, who have used the house as a repository for antiques and artifacts from around the world. Facilities include an outdoor tub, billiard room, rec room, and lounge. ❹

June Lake

Double Eagle Resort and Spa 5587 Hwy-158, ☎877/648-7004. Spa and fitness center in beautiful surroundings with a highly rated restaurant, *Eagle's Landing*, on the premises. Cabins are new and attractively furnished, but rather expensive for the size. ❼
Heidelberg Inn 85 Boulder Lake View Drive (Hwy-158) ☎760/648-7718. In the 1930s the inn was a hunting lodge for the Hollywood glamour set, and still seems stuck in the days of board games and daily socials. The lounge is dominated by stuffed animals (not the cuddly type) and a giant fireplace. Suites are old-fashioned but clean, and all have kitchens. ❻
June Lake Villager 2640 Hwy-158 ☎760/648-7712, ⊛www.junelakevillager.com. Fifties-style motel that's cheap, clean, and right in the center of town. Some units have kitchenettes and fireplaces, and there's a rather dingy indoor jacuzzi. ❶

Eating

Mammoth lacks the array of **restaurants** typical of most ski towns, and though there are a few good spots, looking for a meal can be like trawling through an LA suburb. People often drive to eat, prices are steep, and fast food is a staple. For self-catering visit the always busy Vons **supermarket**, at 481 Old Mammoth Rd (☎760/934-4536). The Village Market, 6805 Minaret Rd (☎760/934-3232), is pricier but has a good deli selection. On-mountain, the new McCoy Station food court is a sparkling canteen serving a wide selection of dishes. Of the base lodges, the cozy *Mill Café*, with its high wood rafters, practically compels the ordering of expensive chili or hot chocolate. The Main and Canyon lodges house huge, hectic **cafeterias**.

Base Camp Café and Coffee Bar 3325 Main St ☎760/934-3900. Inexpensive pasta dinners, burgers, and overstuffed sandwiches are served in this low-key café.
Bergers 6118 Minaret Rd ☎760/934-6622. Good value, with huge portions, the best burgers in town (from $4.25) and generous salads. Gets hectic on the weekends.
The Breakfast Club 2987 Main St ☎760/934-6944. Breakfast is served through lunchtime in this relaxed café, which runs its own in-house bakery.
Cervinos 3752 Viewpoint Rd ☎760/934-4734. Frequently booked well in advance, this is Italian fine dining at its best. Whole roast garlic with fresh breads, seafood pasta, tender meat, and stuffed local trout are served in elegant, simple surroundings. Expensive.

Gomez's Main St and Mountain Blvd ☎760/924-2693. A sit-down family restaurant that's good value considering the size of the portions. Huge burritos under $10 and the nachos are big enough to share.
Good Life Café 126 Old Mammoth Rd ☎760/934-1734. *Good Life* serves healthy, tasty breakfast and lunches, catering to veggies and the budget-conscious, though the decor's a bit tacky. Their salads are top quality: huge and fresh, with plenty of interesting sprouts and nuts.
Grumpy's 361 Old Mammoth Rd ☎760/934-8587. Billed as a "Sports Restaurant," the grill menu on offer is decent and the bar gets packed out on weekends with sports fans.
The Lakefront Restaurant Tamarack Lodge ☎760/934-3534. French-California cuisine – think

seared scallops and wild blueberry tart – in an old-fashioned, intimate setting. Entrees $20–30; reservations essential on weekends.

Matsu 3711 Main St ☎760/934-8277. Cozy and inexpensive, tucked away at the top of town, *Matsu*'s simple Pan-Asian dishes include teriyakis, stir-fried wok dinners served with egg flower soup and rice, and the popular tofu (or beef, or chicken) rice bowl.

Nevados Main St and Minaret Rd ☎760/934-4466. Packed on weekends, this large, muraled dining room is a laid-back, upscale California grill. Influences are eccentric, resulting in dishes like lobster wonton taquitos, and everything comes with a different sauce, aioli, or vinaigrette. The desserts are fantastic. Best value are the prix-fixe dinners ($30). Daily from 5.30pm.

Nik-n-Willie's Pizza and Subs 76 Old Mammoth Rd ☎760/934-2012. Inventive menu, on the higher side price wise for pizzas, though salads and sandwiches are reasonable. Daily 11.30am–9pm.

Schat's Bakery 3305 Main St ☎760/934-6055. Pseudo-European bakery turns out tasty breads and sweet pastries. Skip the restaurant out back, which is overpriced and of a much lower standard. Breakfast and lunch.

Shogun Sierra Centre Mall, Old Mammoth Rd ☎760/934-3970. Though the sushi here is nothing exceptional, the fish is fresh and the menu offers teriyaki, tempura, and other Japanese standards. There are karaoke showdowns on Tuesdays and Saturdays. Expensive. Daily from 5pm.

Thai'd Up 625 Old Mammoth Rd ☎760/934-7355. Hidden away behind Von's market, this little Thai café offers some of the spiciest food in town, though the quality of their pad thai and curries can be hit or miss. There are a few tables, but most people get their food to go. Entrees $8–10, dinner only.

June Lake

The Tiger Bar and Café 2620 Hwy-158, June Lake ☎760/648-7551. Western diner and bar established in 1932, serving an extensive grill menu, decent Mexican food, and huge breakfasts, all at affordable, diner prices. Breakfast until 11.30am, dinner from 5pm.

Trout Town Joe 2750 Hwy-158, June Lake ☎760/648-1155/7170. An anomaly among June Lake's small selection of dated stores and motels, this bright, arty café dishes up espresso drinks, freshly baked pastries, and healthy sandwiches ($5–6).

Bars and entertainment

For a ski town that is full of young freestylers, the choice of **bars** and **clubs** here is surprisingly poor. The resort itself occasionally stages a club night in one of its lodges, usually in conjunction with one of the freestyle competitions held regularly on the mountain. Check the *Good Times Weekly* paper for listings. The Minaret and Plaza **theaters**, both at 439 Old Mammoth Rd (☎760/934-3131), are frequently packed.

Clock Tower Cellar 6080 Minaret Rd ☎760/934-2725. Comfortable basement pub in the *Alpenhof Lodge*, with a good pool table, darts, and foosball.

La Sierra's 3789 Main St ☎760/934-8083. Few leave here sober on a Saturday night. Attractions for the younger crowd include an array of pool tables and a small stage, occasionally graced by hip-hop crews or bands from LA.

Looney Bean 3280 Main St ☎760/934-1345. Ramshackle café with mismatched chairs and creaky tables, where Mammoth's youth congregate to read magazines, play board games, check the Web, and get their shot of caffeine. Open until 10pm on the weekends.

Whisky Creek Main St and Minaret Rd ☎760/934-3498. Good microbrewery and restaurant, packed on weekends with an older, out-of-town crowd in for live rock, blues, and comedy. On Wednesday nights, in the upstairs bar the younger, local crew is out in force, with a DJ holding court.

The Yodler Slopeside at the Main Lodge ☎970/934-0636. Owned by the resort, this two-story chalet offers classic après in a remarkable impression of an alpine hostelry.

Other activities and attractions

The most inviting off-slope activity is visiting one of the many natural **hot springs**. Closest to Mammoth is the free Hot Creek (open from dawn to dusk), at the end of unpaved Hot Creek Hatchery Road, three miles south of the Mammoth Lakes exit off Hwy-395. A 4WD vehicle is recommended for access

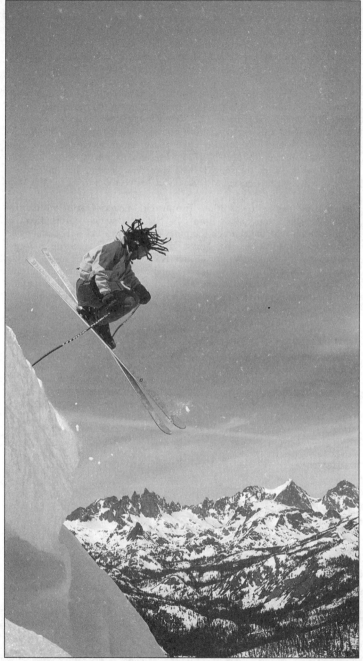

△ Skier jumping off cliff, Mammoth Mountain, CA

throughout the winter, with the last section of the road sometimes only passable on foot. Despite Forest Service warnings about the potential dangers of scalding water and heavy chemicals churned up by episodic volcanic activity, lounging in the creek is the sublime Mammoth experience. Don't bathe at the foot of the wooden steps leading into the gorge, where the topography is changeable and the hot springs most active, but head upstream to the large, shallow pool.

At the southern end of town on Old Mammoth Road, the stylish **Snowcreek Athletic Club** has a pool, tubs, racquetball courts, and a fitness center (☎760/934-8511, day pass $17, five days $55). A number of companies run snowmobile trips; try Mammoth Snowmobile Adventures (☎760/934-9645) by the Main Lodge. Opposite the visitor center on Hwy-203, the outdoor ice skating rink (☎760/924-7733, $7 session, $3 rentals) is open daily for public **skating**. When the snow is deep enough, a sledding hill (☎760/934-7533) operates in the trees off Minaret Road, between the town and the Main Lodge.

Mammoth resort owns the **Tamarack Cross-Country Center** (☎760/934-2442, trail passes from $14 half-day), which covers 45km of groomed trails winding through the pines out by Twin Lakes. For route suggestions in the Inyo National Forest (☎760/924-5500), pick up a Winter Recreation map from the Visitor Center/Ranger Office. Some of the marked snowshoe trails start right in town. The center also keeps information on backcountry routes further afield, around luminous Mono Lake and into the dramatic Hoover, John Muir, and Ansel Adams wilderness areas, where motorized vehicles are prohibited.

Listings

Avalanche hotline ⊛ www.csac.org/Bulletins/Calif/current.html.

Bookstore Booky Joint, Minaret Village Mall (next to Vons) ☎760/934-3240 (daily 8am–8pm).

Car rental Mammoth Car Rental ☎760/934-8111, U-Save Auto Rental ☎760/934-4999.

Internet Mammoth Lakes Library, 960 Forest Trail ☎760/934-4777 (hours vary).

Medical Mammoth Hospital, 85 Sierra Park Rd ☎760/934-3311.

Pharmacy Rite Aid, 26 Old Mammoth Rd ☎760/934-8561.

Post office 3330 Main St ☎760/934-2205.

Police 568 Old Mammoth Rd ☎760/934-2011.

Road conditions ☎1-800/427-7623, chain control info on ☎760/924-5285.

Taxi Mammoth Shuttle ☎760/934-3030.

Weather ☎760/934-7669.

Lake Tahoe

The striking blue waters of **Lake Tahoe**, the largest alpine lake in North America, serve as a focal point for an area of fifteen distinct alpine ski areas in the central Sierra Nevadas. Though the eastern third of this breathtakingly beautiful body of water laps into Nevada, the region is more distinctly split by the poles: the sprawling, suburban **south shore**, a stretch of flashy casinos, tacky strip malls, wedding chapels, and motels surrounded by sublime wilderness, and the more understated **north shore**, a string of compact towns, with architecture reminiscent of a Yogi Bear cartoon, nestled among white fir and Jeffrey pines.

The variety of accommodations and amenities are as varied as you'll find in any North American resort, with lodging strung around the lake in the form of condo villages, dated forest cabin motels, towering casino hotels, and private houses perched precariously above the water. But it's the diversity of affordable skiing **terrain** that's unbeatable, from small day areas to large mountain resorts. In the south, huge **Heavenly** looms directly over the casinos. Close by is **Sierra at Tahoe**, a mid-sized, family-oriented day area with killer terrain parks and excellent tree skiing, while **Kirkwood**, at 35 miles southwest of the lake the most remote of the Tahoe resorts, offers wonderful open bowl skiing, challenging, cliff-strewn freeriding terrain, and an excellent learning environment.

The giant of the north shore is **Squaw Valley**, famed for its six peaks, open bowls, and rocky cliffs. **Alpine Meadows** has little in the way of a resort base but attracts a loyal local following to its steep terrain. **Northstar** is a condo resort, popular with families and intermediates, but also with mogul bashers and tree fanatics.

A number of smaller Tahoe resorts are covered in "The Best of the Rest" section at the end of this chapter. These include **Sugar Bowl**, the first modern ski resort in Lake Tahoe; **Boreal**, now almost entirely a terrain park; the little family-oriented areas of **Donner Ski Ranch** and **Soda Springs**; and value-for-money **Mount Rose**, perched atop the eastern ridge of the lake.

In this nook of the Sierras where up to four feet of powder in 24 hours is not unusual, where over 300 sunny days are logged annually and daytime tem-

Getting to Tahoe

From northern California there are two primary routes into the Tahoe Basin. I-80, the only interstate to cross the Sierra range, is a straight shot 200 miles up to Truckee and the north shore from San Francisco, often taking less than four hours, weather and traffic permitting. When storms hit Donner Summit (7239ft), the gateway to the Tahoe basin, snowplows and chain-up checkpoints can potentially stretch the last hour of the trip into another three or four. Chains are mandatory for all vehicles except 4WDs fitted with snowtires; if you don't have any in your trunk, chain crews will happily sell them to you at significantly inflated prices. From Truckee, the north shore towns of Tahoe City and Kings Beach are reached in 20–30 minutes along winding two-lane roads. It takes at least 45 minutes to drive from Tahoe City to South Lake Tahoe.

From Sacramento, the journey to the south shore follows Hwy-50, taking about the same amount of time as the northern route in good conditions. Hwy-50 narrows to two lanes over Echo Summit and, though plowed regularly, can still be treacherous in poor conditions; traffic can be as much of a problem as inclement weather. Factor in at least an extra couple of hours on weekends and holidays, and expect to crawl around the lake during the morning and afternoon ski commute.

Amtrak **trains** stop in Truckee on the California Zephyr route from Chicago to the Bay, while Greyhound buses serve both Truckee and South Lake from Reno and points west. The **Bay Area Ski Bus** (℗925/680-4386, @www.recreation4fun.com) runs day-trips to all the major Tahoe resorts. Trips leave pick-up locations throughout the Bay Area between 4 and 5am, returning around 9pm.

Busy Reno/Tahoe International is around 45 minutes east of the lake via I-80 (north shore) or Hwy-395 to Hwy-50 (south shore), and most major car rental agencies have a presence at the airport. Booking in advance is recommended, particularly for 4WD vehicles. For direct transfer to South Lake, the Tahoe-Casino Express (℗775/705-2424 or 800/446-6128) costs $34 round-trip. The only direct passenger transport from the airport to the north shore involves more costly private shuttles, like The No Stress Express (from $41 one way, ℗888/4SHUTTLE, @www.nostressexpress.com).

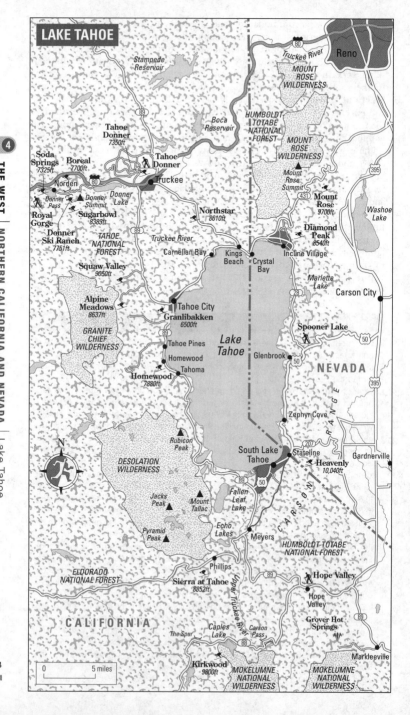

LAKE TAHOE

Reno

Truckee River

MOUNT ROSE WILDERNESS

Stampede Reservoir

Boca Reservoir

HUMBOLDT-TOTABE NATIONAL FOREST

MOUNT ROSE WILDERNESS

Mount Rose Summit

Tahoe Donner 7350ft

Soda Springs 7325ft

Boreal 7700ft

Norden

Donner Summit

Donner Lake

Tahoe Donner

Truckee

Mount Rose 9700ft

431

395

Washoe Lake

Donner Pass

Royal Gorge

Donner Ski Ranch 7751ft

Sugarbowl 8383ft

Northstar 8610ft

Diamond Peak 8540ft

TAHOE NATIONAL FOREST

Truckee River

Carnelian Bay

Kings Beach

Crystal Bay

Incline Village

Squaw Valley 9050ft

Marlette Lake

Carson City

28

Alpine Meadows 8637ft

Tahoe City

Granlibakken 6500ft

Spooner Lake

50

GRANITE CHIEF WILDERNESS

Tahoe Pines

Homewood

Tahoma

Lake Tahoe

Glenbrook

NEVADA

395

Homewood 7880ft

Rubicon Peak

DESOLATION WILDERNESS

Zephyr Cove

CARSON RANGE

South Lake Tahoe

Stateline

Gardnerville

N

Jacks Peak

Mount Tallac

Heavenly 10,040ft

207

Pyramid Peak

Fallen Leaf Lake

Echo Lakes

89

50

ELDORADO NATIONAL FOREST

Meyers

HUMBOLDT-TOTABE NATIONAL FOREST

Phillips

CALIFORNIA

Sierra at Tahoe 8852ft

89

Hope Valley

Hope Valley

89

Grover Hot Springs

The Spur

Caples Lake

Carson Pass

88

Markleeville

0   5 miles

Kirkwood 9800ft

MOKELUMNE NATIONAL WILDERNESS

MOKELUMNE NATIONAL WILDERNESS

peratures are often mild, "poor conditions" generally means slush, not unforgiving ice, and the ski season regularly lasts well into May.

North shore

Twelve of the region's ski resorts are located on Tahoe's **north shore**, from a handful right on the water to those high on the peaks surrounding the Tahoe basin. This varied choice of terrain coupled with a serene atmosphere lures hordes of Californians every weekend, as opposed to the gamblers and out-of-state tourists who tend to flock to the busier, brighter south shore.

Landlocked **Truckee** and lakeside **Tahoe City** are the most convenient winter bases in terms of dining, nightlife, access to the area's minimal public transportation, and proximity to the widest selection of ski areas, including **Squaw Valley** and **Alpine Meadows**. Less expensive accommodation is found further east, in the casinos and condo villages of lakefront settlements or down among the rustic cabin resorts of the sheltered west shore.

Arrival, information, and getting around

For driving directions to Tahoe from the Bay Area and Reno, see box p.333. **Public transportation** on the north shore is made up of an incredibly confusing system of town trolleys, ski shuttles, and infrequent TART (Tahoe Area Regional Transit) buses. Getting to and from a ski area is manageable with a bit of advance planning, but there are no services in the evening. Shuttles to all the resorts run from Tahoe City, Truckee, and the north and west shores daily, in most cases only once a day. The TART ($1.25 single; 7am–6pm; exact change required; ☎530-550-1212) service runs once hourly along the north shore from Incline Village to Tahoma and every other hour between Tahoe City and Truckee (8am–4pm). The Truckee Trolley ($1, free to skiers; 7am–5pm; ☎530/587-7451) heads east from downtown along Donner Pass Road to Sugar Bowl and Donner Ski Ranch and west to Northstar. Dial-a-ride ($3; 8am–5pm; ☎530/587-7451) shuttles on demand are available within Truckee and to outlying areas; 24-hour reservations required. Schedules are available at local visitor centers (and ⊛www.laketahoetransit.com); the official North Lake

Reno

Sprawling **Reno** has swelled in recent years with suburbanites searching for an affordable home in the sun, close to the slopes and scenery of Tahoe but without the heavy snows or stringent housing regulations. Basing yourself here is a cheap and decidedly different alternative to the average ski vacation. Midweek ski-and-stay packages at the casinos start at just a few dollars more than a regular lift ticket (from $59 per person), though prices can rise over $100 at the weekends. Just be prepared for a daily commute of at least 45 minutes each way, and check that a ski shuttle service is part of the deal.

The Peppermill ☎866/926-4653 or 775/826-2121, ⊛www.peppermillreno.com Not in the center, but inexpensive and consistently well-rated. Waterfall pool and health club. From ❷

Reno Hilton ☎800/501-2651 or 775/789-2000, ⊛www.renohilton.com. Huge, with ski and snowboard store, bowling

center, driving range, and health club. From ❶

Sands Regency ☎800/648-3553 or 775/348-2200, ⊛www.sandsregency.com. Another reliable giant with ski and snowboard shop on the premises; good-value packages. From ❶

Despite the urban moniker, **Tahoe City** is little more than a sprawling village. The main drag, Hwy-28 (also known as North Lake Boulevard), is lined with dated motels, stores, restaurants, and bars. Traveling east along Hwy-28, you pass the almost indistinguishable homes, vacation houses, and condo complexes of Lake Forest, Dollar Point, **Carnelian Bay**, and **Tahoe Vista**. There are few restaurants here and infrequent bus services make it hard to manage without a car. Nearby **Kings Beach** is the most convenient lakefront settlement for Northstar, Diamond Peak, and Mount Rose. Further east California and Nevada meet at **Crystal Bay**, the north shore's smaller, shabbier version of the glitzy Stateline in south shore. Built in the Sixties, the resort community of **Incline Village** has a sizeable permanent population more evident in summer. The town contains a few, mostly family-style restaurants, dive bars, and strip malls. On the western edge of Tahoe City, at the terminus of Hwy-28, Hwy-89 (or West Lake Boulevard) dives down around the sheltered west shore of the lake, passing a handful of popular restaurants, residential communities, and low-key marinas en route to Homewood ski area. South of Homewood are the modest, log cabin resorts of tiny **Tahoma**, among the lake's best bargains. Hwy-89 follows the mostly unpopulated Truckee River Valley for fifteen miles, passing the ski resorts of Alpine and Squaw before meeting I-80 in **Truckee**. Gateway to the north shore from both Northern California and Reno, Truckee was once a boisterous settlement fueled by the lumber industry and construction of the Southern Pacific railroad; remnants of its past echo around the wooden walkways and buildings of preserved **Commercial Row**. Today it's a bustling collection of stores, restaurants, bars, and the still-functioning historic railway depot, which houses the Chamber of Commerce **visitor center** (daily 8.30am–5.30pm; ☎530/587-2757).

Tahoe Resort Association's **visitor center** is in the center of Truckee, at 245 North Lake Blvd (Mon–Fri 9am–5pm, Sat–Sun 9am–4pm; ☎530/581-6900). A novel option for moving around the lake is the expensive *Tahoe Queen* paddlewheeler (from $90, with lift tickets) that ferries skiers once a day from south shore to north shore resorts.

It's hardly surprising considering the lack of public transit options that most visitors bring cars, resulting in horrendous **traffic**, particularly on weekends, when what looks like a short distance on the map can turn into a tedious, gridlocked slog along icy, winding roads.

Accommodation

It's best to pick a **place to stay** close to your resort of choice. Most properties get booked up at the weekends and holidays months in advance, but prices of hotels and motels are practically halved midweek. Condominiums are generally the cheapest option; with a bewildering multitude of properties, your best bet for one-stop condo and vacation home rentals is to call the advisors at Lake Tahoe Central Reservations, ☎888/434-1262, ⊛www.mytahoevacation .com. Managed by the North Lake Tahoe Resort Association, they maintain an immense listing of who's renting what. For the brave, **winter camping** is permitted at Sugar Pine Point State Park (☎530/525-7982), south of Tahoma on the west shore; the Sierra Club also maintains a few backcountry huts in the area (☎530/426-3632, ⊛www.sierraclub.org)

For Squaw Valley, Alpine, and Northstar lodging, see resort entries.

Tahoe City

Granlibakken 625 Granlibakken Rd ☎530/583-4242 or 1-888/543-3221, ⊛www.granlibakken .com. Large but serene conference resort in the middle of the forest just south of Tahoe City, with townhomes, condo suites, and good midweek ski packages. Tiny ski hill on the property, plus a sauna, hot tub, and outdoor heated pool. Hot breakfast buffet included. Ski packages from $84; regular room rates from ❹ .

Lake of the Sky 955 N Lake Blvd ☎530/583-3305. Basic motel opposite the Safeway on the eastern edge of Tahoe City. Clean and inexpensive. Continental breakfast included. ❸

Mayfield House 236 Grove St ☎530/583-1001 or 1-888/518-8898, ⓦwww.mayfieldhouse.com. Friendly and comfy B&B in the heart of TC, built in 1928 but modernized with cable TV and videos, whirlpool tubs or steam showers. Connecting rooms and separate garden cottage available; discount lift tickets, homemade trail mix, and freshly baked muffins are provided for days on the mountain or the snowshoe trail out the back door. ❺–❽ , ski packages from $95 per person.

The Peppertree 645 North Lake Blvd ☎530/583-3711 or 1-800/624-8590, ⓦwww.peppertreetahoe.com. While this block motel looks rather incongruous among the wooden homes of Tahoe City, rooms are a decent size and have great views of the lake. Coffeemakers, cable TV, hot tub, and within walking distance of everything Tahoe City has to offer. Midweek, rooms booked in person are usually far cheaper than the rack rate; $75 per person ski packages. ❹

Sunnyside Restaurant and Lodge 1850 West Lake Blvd ☎530/583-7200 or 800/822-2754, ⓦwww.sunnysideresort.com. Elegant, relaxed wooden lodge right on the lake, just south of Tahoe City on the quiet west shore; it's worth paying extra for a room with a view. Wholesome continental breakfast and homebaked cookies included. The parking lot spills over on Wednesday nights, when locals swarm around the large river rock fireplace and bar area for half-price fish tacos. ❹–❼ ; midweek lift-and-lodging packages less than $100 per person.

Tamarack Lodge 2311 North Lake Blvd ☎530/583-3350. Though rather dated and shabby, this historic lodge offers the cheapest lodging in the area, and most rooms and cabins come with useful kitchenettes. One mile east of Tahoe City. ❷

Truckee

Best Western Truckee/Tahoe Inn 11331 Hwy-267 ☎530/587-4525 or 800/824-6385, ⓦwww.bestwesterntahoe.com. Friendly, independently owned motel franchise offering ski packages and shuttles to downtown Truckee and selected resorts. Amenities include a filling breakfast buffet, beer and wine in the lounge, on-site café, laundry, fitness center, and outdoor tub. ❹

The Inn at Truckee 11506 Deerfield Drive ☎530/587-8888 or 888/773-6888, ⓦwww.innattruckee

.com. Modern motel rather than the cozy hostelry suggested by the name, but clean, convenient, and inexpensive. Sauna, tub, and continental breakfast are added bonuses; book online and save by naming your own price. Regular rate ❹ (midweek), ❺ (weekend) for four sharing.

Richardson House 10154 High St ☎530/587-5388 or 888/229-0365, ⓦwww.richardsonhouse .com. Classic Victorian B&B, diligently restored, with six antique-filled ensuite rooms and a two-room suite; all have feather beds. Of the many good-value ski packages and midweek specials offered by the amenable owners, the most unique is Dotcom Bomb, a half-price deal strictly for unemployed techies. ❹–❻

River Street Inn 10009 East River St ☎530/550-9290, ⓦwww.riverstreetinntruckee.com. Turreted building on the river, stylishly remodeled with warm colors. Comfy lounge and breakfast area; each of the nine snug rooms features a private bath and TV/VCR. ❹

Tahoe-Truckee Hostel 10117 East River St ☎530/582-9823, ⓦwww.highlandia.com. Right on the river in downtown Truckee, hostelers get the choice of a double room or two bunkrooms downstairs. Full kitchen, laundry facilities, and lounge area with cable TV; book exchange and free local calls. ❶ , linens extra.

Truckee Hotel 10007 Bridge St ☎800/659-6921, ⓦwww.truckeehotel.com. Full marks for historical atmosphere, but scoring slightly less on creature comforts. In the business for over 125 years, the floors of this charming hotel are crooked, the tubs claw-footed, the furnishings Victorian. Only eight of the 37 rooms have private baths, and you'll want to ask for a room on the opposite side of the building to the railway tracks if you're a light sleeper. ❸

The rest of the north shore

Clair Tappaan Lodge 19940 Donner Pass Rd, Norden ☎530/426-3632. Large Sierra Club hostel (no membership necessary) on Donner Summit, with 140 bunks arranged in two-person cubicles, small group rooms, and single-sex dorms (bring a sleeping bag or linens). Read a book from the library in front of the roaring fire or take a cheap ($14) cross-country ski lesson. Three daily hearty meals included in the price, and small chores assigned. ❷

Ferrari's Crown Resort 8200 North Lake Blvd, Kings Beach ☎530/546-3388 or 1-800/645-2260. Rather bleak but very clean, cheap, and friendly motel on the shore in Kings Beach. Indoor tub with window on the lake, cable TV, spacious rooms, kitchenettes available. ❷

Rockwood 5295 West Lake Blvd, Homewood ⓦwww.rockwoodlodge.com. Established in 1939, this mansion has five bedrooms, each with a private bath and seating area; the owners maintain a tranquil atmosphere (no shoes in the house), offering continental or delicious full breakfasts and tempting evening sweets in the communal parlor. ⑤–⑦

Rustic Cottages 7449 North Lake Blvd, Tahoe Vista ⓣ530/546-3523 or 1-888/7RUSTIC, ⓦwww.rusticcottages.com. Built in 1925 and recently remodeled by a couple who make metal furniture for Pottery Barn. Not surprisingly, the eighteen tiny but pretty cabins feature wrought iron beds, TV/videos (the office has a free library of over 300 movies), fridges, microwaves, and coffeemakers; some have full kitchens and fireplaces. Most have queen beds; a few squeeze in up to six. Homemade muffins, coffee, and juice available every morning; excellent value. ②–⑥

The Shore House 7170 North Lake Blvd, Tahoe Vista ⓣ530/546-7270 or 1-800/207-5160, ⓦwww.tahoeinn.com. Romantic, wooden B&B right on the lake; the outdoor tub is practically on the beach. Nine small rooms, each with its own outdoor entrance and gas fireplace. ⑥

Sun n' Sand Lodge 8308 North Lake Blvd, Kings Beach ⓣ530/546-2515, ⓦwww.sunandsandlodge .com. Remodeled motel on the shore, next to *Steamers* restaurant (see opposite). Simple, clean, with fridge, microwave, and cable in every room; communal tub. Good-value ski packages, from $58 per person with tickets to Alpine. ②

Tahoe Biltmore 5 Hwy-28, Crystal Bay ⓣ775/831-0660, ⓦwww.tahoebiltmore.com. Basic, motel-style rooms above the very pink and dated casino, and in a separate "motor lodge" out back. The latter are quieter and less expensive – though on busy weekends it can be hard to escape crowds of people out to spend money. Hot tub and ski packages available. Regular rates ③ for four, as low as ①

Tahoe Lake Cottages 7030 West Lake Blvd, Tahoma ⓣ530/525-4411 or 1-800/852-8246. The modest cottages arranged on a concrete motor court are rather cramped but inexpensive and pleasantly decorated, with tiny kitchens and communal outdoor tub. One-bedroom cottages sleep up to four; two bedrooms also available. Call for ski packages. ⑤–⑦ Mention Rough Guides to the owner for a discount.

Eating

There's no shortage of **restaurants** to suit all tastes and budgets on the north shore, with a good concentration of quality, inexpensive spots around Tahoe City and Truckee. You can also stock up at one of the 24-hour or late-night supermarkets around the lake or visit either branch of New Moon Natural Foods, 11357 Donner Pass Rd, DMV Plaza, Truckee, (ⓣ530/587-7426), or 505 West Lake Blvd at Granlibakken Road, Tahoe City (ⓣ530/583-7426), all-organic health food stores.

Tahoe City

Fiamma 521 North Lake Blvd ⓣ530/581-1416. Polished but laid-back Italian restaurant, with great salads and pasta specialties. Not quite budget, but still affordable; reservations suggested. From 5.30pm.

Fire Sign Cafe 1785 West Lake Blvd, Sunnyside ⓣ530/583-0871. The best breakfast in Tahoe City with an extensive menu of home-baked muffins, pancakes, and waffles with fresh blueberry-raspberry sauce, and eggs every which way. They also serve excellent salads and overstuffed sandwiches for lunch, though breakfast is served all day. Daily 7am–3pm.

Lakehouse Pizza, 120 Grove St ⓣ530/583-2222. Après-ski pizza hangout and breakfast spot right on the lake. The food is decent and reasonably priced, but it's the view that draws the crowds. 7am–10pm.

Mandarin Villa 120 Grove St ⓣ530/583-1188. Quiet Chinese joint above *Lakehouse Pizza* with

great views of the lake; good for vegetarians. 11.30am–9.30pm, closed Mon.

Tahoe House 625 West Lake Blvd ⓣ530/583-1377. Almost two dozen varieties of freshly baked breads; breakfast pastries, sandwiches, gourmet meals, and wine to go. 6am–6pm.

Yama Sushi 950 North Lake Blvd, Lighthouse Shopping Center ⓣ530/583-9262. The long sushi counter, dining room, and sake bar are usually packed. In addition to sushi, light meat and veggie dishes are available. All-you-can-eat special Tues–Thurs, half-price sake and beer on Wed. Open from 5pm.

Truckee

Casa Baeza 10010 Bridge St ⓣ530/587-2161. Next to the *Truckee Hotel*, this whitewashed cellar with its formica tables and cavernous bar serves authentic alternatives to the bright, faux-Mex barns on the lakefront. 11.30am–2pm & 4–10pm.

Dragonfly 10118 Donner Pass Rd, Old Town

☎530/587-0557. Asian fusion dishes, from affordable noodle bowls to more expensive entrees including an Asian noodle bowl filled with filet mignon, caramelized onions, and Chinese long beans, complemented by a huge selection of wine. Décor is Far Eastern colonial; the upstairs location affords views over Old Town Truckee, particularly in warm weather when the balcony is open. Try appetizers at the bar for alternative après. 11am–2.30pm & 5.30–9.30pm.

Java Sushi 11357 Donner Pass Rd, Truckee ☎530/582-1144. Good tunes, good sushi, and great all-you-can-eat lunch specials. Daily 11am–2pm & 4.30–10pm.

Squeeze In 10060 Donner Pass Rd, Old Town ☎530/587-9814. Satisfied customers have been squeezing into this narrow brick room since 1974, lured by an astounding 57 varieties of fluffy omelets, each around $8–9. Lunch is served but breakfast is better. 7am–2pm, no credit cards.

Tacos Jalisco 11400 Donner Pass Rd ☎530/587-1131. No-frills taqueria, with whopping veggie burritos for only $3. 10.30am–9pm.

Truckee Bagel 11448 Deerfield Drive ☎530/582-1852. Tucked away behind McDonalds off Hwy-89 is the best bagel shop on the north shore, though neither the coffee nor the dining room is anything special. Best bets are the apple bagels and cinnamon twists. Weekdays 6am–4pm, weekends 7am–3pm.

Wild Cherries Coffee House 11249 Donner Pass Rd ☎530/582-5602. Cheap granola, hot breakfast bagels, and fresh, if pricey, smoothies. Homemade soups at lunch. 6am–6pm.

The rest of the north shore

Angela's Pizzaria 7000 West Lake Blvd, Tahoma ☎530/525-4771. Small pizza parlor with giant

calzones, sandwiches, and beer by the pitcher, all reasonably priced. Tues–Thurs 11.30am–9pm, Fri–Sat 11.30am–9.30pm, Sun 5–9pm.

Café 333 333 Village Blvd, Incline Village ☎775/832-7333. Creative California cuisine, so tasty it's hard to tell that healthy, low-fat cooking is their goal. Try the roasted rack of lamb rubbed with dijon and rosemary served with a red wine demi glaze. 7.30am–3pm & 5.30–9pm.

Hiro Sushi 8159 North Lake Blvd, Kings Beach ☎530/583-4476. Locals drive round the lake for owner Hiroshi's early evening all-you-can-eat hour and generous sushi rolls. 5–10pm, closed Mon.

Log Cabin 8692 North Lake Blvd, Kings Beach ☎530/546-7109. The tiny cabin rivals the Firesign for best breakfast on the north shore, using fresh ingredients to concoct extraordinary waffles and ingenious egg dishes. Mon–Fri 7am–1.30pm, until 2pm Sat–Sun.

Old Post Office 5245 North Lake Blvd, Carnelian Bay ☎530/546-3205. Early morning deliveries of omelets and home-fried potatoes, with hot sandwiches for lunch. 6.30am–2pm.

Soule Domaine 9983 Cove St, Kings Beach /Crystal Bay ☎530/546-7529. Romantic log cabin serves upscale, American dishes; expensive, but memorable. Reservations highly recommended. From 6pm.

Steamers 8290 North Lake Blvd, Kings Beach ☎530/546-2218. Beachfront grill a notch above average. The extensive menu includes excellent pizza and a roster of local brews. 11am–11pm.

Stoney Ridge Café 6821 West Lake Blvd (Hwy-89), Tahoma ☎530/525-0925. A novel take on breakfast with biscuits and gravy, sourdough French toast, and Asian scrambles. Healthy lunches and wholesome, more elegant, and expensive dinners. Daily except Tues 7am–2pm for breakfast and lunch; Thurs–Sat dinner 6–9pm. No credit cards.

Nightlife and entertainment

The north shore might not have the big-name casino shows of South Lake, and there's hardly a raging club scene anywhere outside of Stateline, but there are a handful of popular **bars** (some with decent local live music). Movie theaters are located in Incline Village, Kings Beach (Brockway), Tahoe City (The Cobblestone), and Truckee (Martis Village). Call ☎530/546-5951 for films and times. The free *North Tahoe Truckee This Week* (ⓦwww.tahoethisweek) runs listings of upcoming events. Annual festivals include the Snowfest carnival in March and May's Ski and Sail/Gates and Wake contests held both on local slopes and on the water.

Bar of America 10042 Donner Pass Rd, Truckee ☎530/587-3110. Corner hangout with a Western motif; live music with regular open-mike nights.

Jimmy Bongo Velvet Lounge 881 Tahoe Blvd, Incline Village ☎775/833-2623. This club and

martini bar is garishly kitted out, has decent tunes, and is open late on busy weekends.

Lake Tahoe Brewing Co 24 Stateline Rd, Crystal Bay ☎775/831-5822. Excellent beers, eclectic menu including wood-fired pizzas, and live music Fridays.

Sierra Vista 700 North Lake Blvd, Marina Mall, Tahoe City ☎530/583-0233. Sports bar on the lake with a fairly consistent stream of well-known bands. Tourist Club 10010 Donner Pass Rd ☎530/587-8688. Dive bar on the historic Truckee boardwalk. The long bar is propped up by older locals, while a younger crowd hangs around the pool table in the back.

Other activities and attractions

Individual ski areas offer some or all of the usual off-slope activities found in the more typical self-contained resorts – dog sledding, tubing, ice-skating, and snowmobiling – but the north shore has numerous independent operators offering the same. If **snowmobiling** in Tahoe choose an operator that takes tours up to Mount Watson, the highest point on the north shore. Try TC Sno Mo's (☎530/581-3906) in Tahoe City; Snowmobiling Unlimited (☎530/583-5858) at Brockway Summit, south of Truckee; or the monthly moonlit trips from Northstar (☎530/562-2267). For a mellower experience, try one of the track operators, such as Tahoe Snowmobile Adventures (North Tahoe Regional Park, Tahoe Vista, ☎530/546-6115): instruction is included.

For **cross-country and snowshoeing** pick up a USFS (United States Forest Service) Sno-Park permit, available from The Backcountry (see rental box opposite) and other sports stores ($5 a day, $25 a season) and head out to Blackwood Canyon, Paige Meadows, Sugar Pine Point, or one of Tahoe's many other USFS spots and regional parks open for winter use. Some have backcountry huts; others a few kilometers of groomed trails to complement the acres of backcountry terrain. Royal Gorge, 9411 Hillside Drive, Soda Springs (☎800/500-3871, ⓦwww.royalgorge.com), is the largest cross-country resort in North America with a whopping 330km of trails, ten warming huts, four trailside cafes, a pee-wee center for kids 4 and older, a shuttle bus, and four surface lifts. Tahoe XC, 925 Country Club Drive, Tahoe City (☎530/583-5475, ⓦwww.tahoexc.org), offers two warming huts and 65km of forested trails close to Tahoe City.

The small but well-designed transition-heavy **skatepark** in Truckee is right off Hwy-267, just south of town; it dries fairly quickly following a storm. Go winter **fishing** on the lake on the *Kingfish* (☎530/525-5360, boats depart the Homewood marina). The most luxurious **spa** is at Squaw Creek (☎530/583-6300); an alternative is the body treatments at the Yogic Arts Center in TC (☎530/583-3391), which also runs daily drop-in **yoga** classes.

Listings

Avalanche hotline ☎530/587-2158.

Bookstore The Bookshelf, Gateway Mall, Truckee ☎530/582-0515, and Boatworks Mall, Tahoe City ☎530/581-1900.

Internet Free in local libraries: Truckee, 10031 Levone Ave ☎530/582-7846, Mon & Thurs 10am–8pm, Tues, Wed, Fri & Sat, 10am–6pm. Tahoe City, 740 N Lake Blvd ☎530/583-3382, Tues, Thurs, Fri 10am–5pm, Wed noon–7pm, Sat noon–4pm. There are also libraries in Kings Beach (301 Secline Drive, ☎530/546-2021) and Incline Village (846 Tahoe Blvd, ☎775/832-4130).

Medical Tahoe Forest Hospital, 10121 Pine Ave, Truckee ☎530/587-6011, ⓦwww.tfhd. Tahoe Truckee Medical Group (☎530/581-8864, ⓦwww.ttmg.net) has offices in Tahoe City, Truckee, and Squaw Valley, providing urgent care and treating sports injuries.

Pharmacy Longs Drugs, 11411 Deerfield Drive, Crossroads Shopping Center, Truckee ☎530/587-5770; Tahoe City Pharmacy, 599 North Lake Blvd, TC ☎530/583-3888.

Post office 950 North Lake Blvd, TC (Mon–Fri 8.30am–5pm, Sat noon–2pm); 10050 Bridge St, old town Truckee (Mon–Fri 8.30am–5pm, Sat 11am–2pm); both ☎1-800/275-8777. Local branches all around the lake.

Road conditions Caltrans on ☎916/445-7623 or 800/427-7623, ⓦwww.dot.ca.gov (though Caltrans covers Lake Tahoe and the Reno area, there is also a separate road conditions line for Nevada: ☎775/793-1313).

Taxi Tahoe Truckee Taxi ☎530/583/8292 or 530/582-8294.

Weather Tahoe hotline ☎530/546-5253.

North shore rentals

The Backcountry 11400 Donner Pass Rd, Truckee ☎530/582-0909; 255 North Lake Blvd Tahoe City ☎530/581-5861, ⓦwww.thebackcountry.net. Scruffy locals' spot renting all manner of backcountry gear; the best source of backcountry info in Tahoe.

Dave's Ski and Board Rentals 620 North Lake Blvd, Tahoe City ☎530/583-6415; 10200 Donner Pass Rd, Old Town Truckee ☎530/582-0900; Hwy-89 at Squaw Valley Rd ☎530/583-5665; 8299 North Lake Blvd, Kings Beach ☎530/546-5800. The Tahoe City branch is the hub of this local chain. Dave's has online rentals and offers the fifth day free, in addition to clothing rentals and deals on last season's demo gear.

Granite Chief 11368 Donner Pass Rd Truckee ☎530/583-2832; Squaw Valley ☎530/583-2832, ⓦwww.granitechief .com. Huge barn in Truckee complemented by a smaller store on the road into Squaw Valley, with decent rates. Backcountry rentals include avalanche beacons and helmets.

Totally Board 10062 Bridge St ☎530/582-1584. Skate and board shop a good source of local knowledge. Reasonably priced rentals for the area, and doesn't get the weekend crush common to Dave's.

South shore

Straddling the border of California and Nevada, the sprawling settlement along Lake Tahoe's **south shore** personifies civic schizophrenia. Officially two adjacent municipalities, shiny high-rise casinos, and expeditious wedding chapels flank Hwy-50 right up to the Nevada border in **Stateline**, abruptly giving way to the shabby motels and strip malls of California's South Lake.

Skirting the lake, the highway is the commercial vein of the sprawl. On the western edge of town, it splits at the so-called Y; route 50 heads inland toward Sierra, Kirkwood, and the road back to the Bay Area, while Hwy-89 continues to the north shore.

Looming above the south shore are the peaks of **Heavenly**, the region's largest ski area. Thirty-seven acres of old motels were cleared to make way for the resort's new gondola and pedestrian center, the only resort in the States where the creation of a new village has reduced, rather than increased, the number of lodging units in the area.

Most of the south shore's appeal revolves around 24-hour entertainment, inexpensive restaurants, and a huge variety of lodging, from dirt-cheap motels to quiet vacation homes that rent for less than their equivalent on the north shore.

Arrival, information, and getting around

For general info on getting to the Tahoe region see box on p.333. The Lake Tahoe Visitor's Authority (☎530/583-3494 or 1-800/288-2463, ⓦwww .bluelaketahoe.com) is your best source for pre-trip planning and reservations. Once in town, pick up coupons, free maps, and guides from the Tahoe-Douglas Visitors Center at the Round Hill shopping center, just north of Stateline in Zephyr Cove (☎775/588-4951, ⓦwww.tahoechamber.org; Mon–Sat 9am–5pm).

The sprawling nature of South Lake means that nearly everyone drives, and the journey up and down Lake Tahoe Boulevard (Hwy-50) soon becomes familiar. Fortunately, it's much easier to get around here on **public transit** than on the north shore. Public STAGE buses (daily 6am–1am; ☎530/542-6077) run from Stateline to the junction of Hwy-50 and Hwy-89 north. Bus Plus

Backcountry: Donner Summit and around

If you've ever picked up a ski magazine or drooled over a snowboard video, you'll recognize the red rocks, stubby pines, Southern Pacific train tracks, and snow pillows off Donner Summit. For $199 ($225 weekends), **Pacific Crest Snowcats** will guide you through the snowy peaks between Sugar Bowl and Squaw; reservations highly recommended (☎530/581-1761 or 1-888/SWAYBACK, ⓦwww.swayback.com). Highly respected and in the business since 1979, **Alpine Skills International** training school, Hwy-40 at Donner Pass, Norden (☎530/426-9108, ⓦwww.alpineskills .com), teaches specialized backcountry skills to skiers and snowboarders in the area; leads local hut tours; holds regular winter mountaineering, camping, and avalanche classes; and organizes trips to Tioga Pass and Mount Shasta. Guiding services available include **NASTC** and **AMP** (see box opposite), who offer backcountry classes in addition to in-bounds off-piste training courses. Visit The Backcountry store in Tahoe City or Truckee (see box p.341) for more information on local backcountry routes.

($3; ☎530/542-6077) provides door-to-door service, 24 hours a day. Free casino **shuttles** collect gamblers and clubbers from most of the hotels and motels on the south shore, and Heavenly, Kirwood, and Sierra all provide free shuttle service to their resorts from multiple pick-up points (see resort listings for details). North shore resorts are served by a once-daily ski shuttle; buses depart from the larger hotels and casinos, and the journey is free with the purchase of a lift ticket (call ☎775/883-2100 for reservations and the most up-to-date info on pick-up locations).

Traffic can be a nightmare on weekends, particularly along Emerald Bay Road (Hwy-50) out toward Sierra, Kirkwood, and the Bay Area. Better to take Pioneer Trail from downtown Stateline or continue straight along Lake Tahoe Boulevard from the Y, backroutes to the little hamlet of **Meyers**.

Accommodation

Lodging on the south shore can be refreshingly inexpensive compared to more traditional ski areas, but most accommodation is depressingly unattractive, at least from the outside. Two giant timber and stone condo hotels, the *Marriott Timber Lodge* and *Grand Residence* (from ❻; ☎530/542-6600/8400, ⓦwww .marriot.com), dominate Heavenly's new pedestrian village. Centrally located on Hwy-50 (Lake Tahoe Boulevard) close to the casinos, the village makes a pleasant gateway to the gondola. The cheap motels that line Hwy-50 on the California side are densely clustered, though the further out toward the Y, the less expensive. Try to see your room before paying as quality varies dramatically. Midweek, the casinos of **Stateline** are the best value for money, with room specials from $39 and standard ski packages for around $80 per person. *Caesars* (☎1-888/829-7630, ⓦwww.caesars.com) and *Horizon* (☎775/588-6211, ⓦwww.horizoncasino.com) are probably the choice of the lot, with the *Lakeside Inn* (☎775/588-7777, ⓦwww.lakesideinn.com) a low-key alternative to the glitz. If you're budgeting for a large group or want some semblance of a traditional mountain atmosphere, your best bet is to rent a **home** or **condo** away from the motel strip; there are more homes to rent in the Tahoe area than in any other ski resort region in the States. Try Lake Tahoe Accommodations (☎530/544-3234 or 1-800/544-3234, ⓦwww.tahoeres.com); Tahoe Management (☎775/588-4504 or 1-800/624-3887, ⓦwww.tahoevacations .com), a good source for slopeside condos; or Tahoe Rental Connection (☎530/542-2777 or 1-800/542-2100, ⓦwww.tahoerentalconnection.com), for cabins and family homes at low rates.

North American Ski Training Center

For those not quite ready to step it up to the backcountry, the **North American Ski Training Center** (NASTC), based in Truckee, offers multiday, off-piste freeskiing camps held within resort boundaries (Alpine, Squaw, Kirkwood, and Sugarbowl are local resorts used). Course fees include evening tech talks, meals, and video training sessions; lodging packages are available through each resort. Training is primarily aimed at improving the technique of advanced intermediate to expert alpine skiers, though snowboarders and freebooters are welcome. All Mountain Professionals (AMP; ⊛ www.allmountainskipros.com, ☎ 888/754-2201) is a similar operation, aimed at recreational skiers keen to sample the off-piste experience. With more emphasis on backcountry skiing than NASTC, most AMP courses begin within the ropes at Sugar Bowl, before progressing out the resort gates to take on Donner Summit.

Black Bear Inn 1202 Ski Run Blvd, South Lake ☎ 530/544-4451 or 877/232-7466, ⊛ www .tahoeblackbear.com. Stylish five-room logwood mansion with a spacious lounge and zen-like garden. Three private cabins sit at the rear of the property, behind the hot tub pagoda; homecooked breakfasts and pre-dinner drinks served. ❼–❾

Blue Jay Lodge 4133 Cedar Ave, South Lake ☎ 800/258-3529, ⊛ www.bluejaylodge.com. Clean, friendly, and affordable motel, close to casinos and the Heavenly gondola, with coffeemakers and laundry facilities. From ❷, ski packages available.

Camp Richardson 1900 Jameson Beach Rd, Hwy-89 (west of the Y), South Lake ☎ 530/541-1801 or 800/544-1801, ⊛ www.camprichardson .com. A short drive but a world away from the strip malls of South Lake, this comfy Depression-era lodge and cabin complex is set in forested grounds beside the lake. Some of the small cabins are slicker than others; all have kitchens and are pleasantly decorated, as are the simple lodge rooms. Neither have televisions or phones and breakfast is not included. Cross country center and outdoor hot tub on the premises. Cabins sleeping 2–8 from $20 per person; lodge rooms from ❸, ski packages available.

Doug's Mellow Mountain Retreat 3787 Forest Ave, South Lake ☎ 530/544-8065, ℮ hostelguy @hotmail.com. You have to be pretty mellow to deal with the lax housekeeping and the cramped sleeping arrangements at Doug's house, but it's a cheap place to cook and crash and is the south shore's most enduring hostel. $15 for a dorm bed.

Fantasy Inn 3696 Lake Tahoe Blvd, South Lake ☎ 800/367-7736, ⊛ www.fantasy-inn.com. Circular beds, faux-satin drapes, jacuzzi in the bedroom, and twin heads in the showers. With ostentatious theming and a chapel on the premises, this gussied-up motel isn't everyone's idea of romantic, but it's an experience at the very least. ❽

Fireside Lodge 515 Emerald Bay Rd, South Lake ☎ 530/544-5515 or 800/692-2246, ⊛ www .tahoefiresidelodge.com. On the west side of town, this old motel has been completely overhauled with log pine furniture, wood paneling, quilts on the beds, and fieldstone (gas) fireplaces. Each room has a TV/VCR and kitchenette; there's a pool table in the rec room and afternoon snacks and continental breakfast served in the "gathering room." From ❸, ski packages available.

Inn at Heavenly 1261 Ski Run Blvd, South Lake ☎ 800/692-2246, ⊛ www.innatheavenly.com. Older sibling of the *Fireside Lodge*, another revamped motel masquerading as an inn. Very similar, except that the small rooms are more gratuitously themed. Close to Heavenly, the cabins (really houses) are spacious, with pool tables and private outdoor tubs. From ❺, midweek specials and ski packages available.

Lakeshore Lodge and Spa 930 Bal Bijou Rd, South Lake ☎ 800/448-4577, ⊛ www .tahoelakeshorelodge.com. Despite the Eastern Bloc exterior, this lakefront hotel has been pleasantly furnished and all rooms have fantastic lake views. Perks include on-site spa services and a hot tub right on the beach; neighboring townhouse-style condos share the facilities. From ❺, ski and spa packages available.

Sorensen's 14255 Hwy-88, Hope Valley ☎ 530/694-2203 or 1-800/423-9949, ⊛ www .sorensenresort.com. Christmas-card village tucked among the aspens midway between South Lake and Kirkwood. Draped in Christmas tree lights, the quaint cabins sleep two to six. The Chapel and Saint Nick's are favorites, transplants from a bygone Santa's Village. No phones or TV, but a tiny café, store, and cross-country center on the premises. Weekends usually booked months in advance. ❹–❾

Zephyr Cove Resort 760 Hwy-50, Zephyr Cove ☎ 775/588-6644, ⊛ www.tahoedixie2.com. On the opposite side of town to *Camp Richardson*, most cabins are slightly shabbier but have cable TV (no phones). RV and tent camping available, with full hook-ups; simple lodge rooms are located above the restaurant; and fishing, snowmobiling, and riverboat tours leave from the premises. Cabins sleeping 2–10 from $30 per person, lodge rooms from ❷, RVs $25, tents $15.

Eating

The south shore has no discernible **restaurant** epicenter and most of the locally favored spots are actually tucked away in nondescript strip malls. Nevertheless, there's no shortage of moderately priced bar and diner food, plus a few highly rated healthy options. Casino **buffets** tend to be more about quantity than quality and are no longer such a bargain; the most popular is the Forest Buffet on the top floor of *Harrah's* (℡775/588-6611; dinner from $16.95). Multiple branches of practically every fast-food outlet jostle for space along Hwy-50, alongside a number of 24-hour supermarkets (see listings). Grass Roots, 2040 Dunlap Drive at the Y (℡530/541-7788, open until 7pm), is the natural food alternative. All the listings below are in South Lake unless otherwise noted.

Alpen Sierra 3940 Lake Tahoe Blvd (Hwy-50 at Pioneer Trail) ℡530/541-7449. Bright and airy coffeeshop run by the local Tahoe roaster. Open from 6am daily.

Alpina Café 822 Emerald Bay Rd ℡530/541-7449. A large selection of Alpen Sierra coffees, tempting pastry counter, and inexpensive soups and sandwiches.

Bountiful 717 Emerald Bay Rd ℡530/542-4060. Perhaps the best breakfast on the south shore, with organic vanilla french toast, pumpkin pancakes, and fluffy egg and tofu scrambles served in a pastel roadside hut. Huge and healthy salads, sandwiches, and rice bowls for lunch. Expect to wait and bring cash; no cards or checks. Tues–Sat 8am–3pm, Sun 8am–2pm.

Cafe Fiore 1169 Ski Run Blvd ℡530/541-2908. With over 100 wines (Californian and Italian) but only seven tables, in this cute, candlelit cottage assures diners of thoughtful attention to detail, reflected in both the service and delectable Italian menu. Creative pasta entrees (each around $20) like the cognac-sauteed seafood linguine can be split, but you wouldn't want to. Daily 5.30–9.30pm, reservations required.

Frank's Restaurant 1207 Emerald Bay Rd ℡530/544-3434. Classic coffeeshop diner with extensive menus and highly rated breakfasts. Mon–Sat 6am–2pm, Sun 7am–2pm.

Freshies 3330 Lake Tahoe Blvd ℡530/542-3630. Hidden away in the Lakeview Plaza, this colorful lunch spot is tropically themed, packed with locals, and offers discounts on their Hawaiian-influenced menu in relation to how much fresh powder has fallen on the mountains. Daily 11am–10pm.

Mott Canyon 259 Kingsbury Grade (Hwy-207) ℡775/588-8989. Valued for its late-night pizza, burgers, and stir-fries. When all else is closed, this bar is rammed with hungry drinkers partaking of the past-midnight happy hour. 11am–4am, food until 3am.

The Naked Fish 3940 Lake Tahoe Blvd ℡530/541-3474. Sushi of an extremely high standard. Good music, stylish décor, chilled sake, and innovative Asian fusion dishes make this one of the most interesting, tasty restaurants on the south shore. From 5pm nightly.

Red Hut 2723 Lake Tahoe Blvd ℡530/541-9024/229; Kingsbury Grade ℡775/588-7488. Two branches of this quintessential waffle house (locals favor the quieter spot on Kingsbury Grade) offer carb-loaded breakfasts and greasy lunches. Daily 6am–2pm.

Sorensen's Cafe 14255 Hwy-88, Hope Valley ℡530/694-2203. Tiny dining room serving hearty food like beef burgundy stew and barbecue chicken alongside an excellent wine list, all in a magical country setting. A top breakfast stop en route to Kirkwood or Grover Hot Springs; reservations suggested for dinner. Daily 7.30am–9pm.

Sprouts 3123 Harrison Ave (at Hwy-50 and Alameda St) ℡530/541-6969. Informal, inexpensive, mostly organic café. From overstuffed burritos and bagels to wholesome veggie rice bowls, fresh muffins to fruit smoothies, the food is fast filling. Daily 8am–10pm.

Bars and entertainment

South Lake might not have quite the raging **nightlife** claimed by the brochures, but there's certainly a much wider variety than in most ski areas; each casino offers a few big-name shows a season in addition to regular comedy and musical revues and, of course, gambling. Most drinking spots in South Lake are of the sports-bar variety, and also serve food. Live music is generally scheduled on weekends, with regular blues-rock for the tourist-oriented après, leaning toward baggy-shorts punk and a smattering of funk and hip-hop in local hangouts. Grab a copy of the free weekly, *Lake Tahoe Action*, for listings. Movie lovers can choose from bargain matinees at the Horizon Stadium, 50 W Hwy-50 (℡775/589-6000), and the new multiplex in the Heavenly Village.

Club Nero *Caesars Casino* ℡775/586-2000. This casino club with go-go cages is the spot to get hammered, even if you'd avoid this sort of scene at home. Lifties favor dollar drink Mondays and two-for-one Wednesdays. Cover – and music – varies.

The Beacon Bar and Grill *Camp Richardson* ℡530/541-0630. Overpriced restaurant on the lake which hosts happy hours and events, and whose claim to fame is the tasty rum-runner cocktail.

The Christiana Inn 3819 Saddle Rd ℡530/544-7337. Warm up with fireside après at the bar of this old-fashioned, alpine-style inn. Located at Heavenly's California base. Live jazz and blues Fri–Sat 9pm–1am.

Hoss Hoggs 2543 Lake Tahoe Blvd ℡530/541-8328. Barbecue spot that runs a happy hour from 4 to 7pm daily, with local bands taking to the small stage a few nights per week.

Mulligan's 3600 Lake Tahoe Blvd ℡530/542-1095. American sports bar take on an Irish pub, with darts, a pool room, and giant TV screen; a reliable, if not always inspiring, place to dance on the south shore, with hip-hop, Latin, and occasional live bands. Drink specials during football games and free jukebox on Monday nights.

The Pub Tahoe 4093 Lake Tahoe Blvd ℡530/542-4435. Après spot with happy hour appetizers and low-key, live music nightly, located opposite the Heavenly gondola.

Strange Brew Coffee & Cyber Lounge 2660 Lake Tahoe Blvd ℡530/542-4169. Young staff serve up inventive latte variations, chai, and snacks in this rather dilapidated arts space. Evening diversions include open-mikes and ambient DJs. Mon–Thurs 7am–11.30pm, Fri 7am–midnight, Sat 8am–10pm, Sun 7am–9pm.

The Tudor Pub 1041 Fremont Ave ℡530/541-6603. Run by an English expat, this attic bar might not quite replicate a British country pub, despite the horsey British brasses and Olde Worlde prints, but they pull a fine pint of ale behind the bar. Fish and chips or bangers and mash are served up with Boddingtons and Guinness, accompanied by whichever local musicians are playing that night.

Turn 3 2227 Lake Tahoe Blvd ℡530/542-3199. Small, divey sports bar decked out in racing paraphernalia. They host a weekly karaoke night and the occasional local punk band. Pool, darts, and video games.

Other activities and attractions

You could spend an entire week outdoors on the south shore and never step foot in a ski resort. Pick up cross-country information sheets from any Lake Tahoe visitor center or stop in at the Forest Service, 870 Emerald Bay Rd

Backcountry: Mont Tallac and around

Visible from the lake, the giant snowy cross etched into the side of Mount Tallac is a signpost to the south shore's most popular backcountry downhill descent. Part of the snowmobile-free Desolation Wilderness, home to a number of other peak descents, other well-travelled winter areas include the Carson Range around Heavenly and the Carson Pass area out toward Kirkwood. Though it's not as well-known as the Donner Summit region to the north, don't expect total solitude in the southern backcountry. As always, the company of a local guide is highly recommended. **Sierra Ski Touring** (℡775/782-3047) guides lead trips throughout the region, offering avalanche courses, ski mountaineering treks, snowboard-specific expeditions, spring corn camps and navigation, first aid and wilderness first responder classes. Great resources include ⊛www.tahoebackcountry.net, complete with route suggestions and links to local backcountry ski groups, and the comprehensive website of the north shore's outstanding Backcountry store, a fountain of advice and information for the entire region (see box on p.341).

South shore rental shops

Cutting Edge Sports 3930 Lake Tahoe Blvd ☎877/700-3343, ⊛www.cuttingedgesportstahoe.com. Expert tuners offer good-quality board rentals, even at the cheaper strap-in level ($18–30).

Shoreline 259 Kingsbury Grade ☎775/588-8777 and **Trinity** 1060 Ski Run Blvd

☎530/544-1621. In addition to boards they have a small but excellent selection of freestyle and regular skis. Rates $20–32, boots $10.

Tahoe Boot & Ski Works 2277 Lake Tahoe Blvd ☎530/544-8060. Specialty boot fitting and ski tuning for skiers who can tell the difference.

(☎530/573-2600). Cross-country centers include the charming **Hope Valley**, 14655 Hwy-88 (lessons $30, rentals from $12; ☎530/694-2266), located on the road toward Kirkwood, which offers Full Moon tours and snowshoe treks along 100km of sheltered groomed and marked backcountry trails. Inexpensive Camp Richardson, 1900 Jameson Beach Rd (half-day trail pass $5, rentals $15; ☎530/542-6584), maintains flat trails on and around the beach and has markers to National Forest trails up into Desolation Wilderness. Spooner Lake, Hwy-28 just north of Hwy-50 (half-day trail pass $12, rentals $16, lessons $38; ☎775/749-5349 or 888/858-8844), is the most developed of the three, with over 80km of groomed trails, including a scenic flat loop through aspen groves and more technical climbs with wonderful views of the lake. In addition to a couple of warming huts, the area maintains two tiny backcountry cabins, sleeping up to four; linens are provided and the main lodge is just a few kilometers away. For more information on the Kirkwood Cross-Country center, see p.367.

Along with cross-country trails, the entire Tahoe basin is laced with National Forest and park trails open for private **snowmobile** use; both the USFS and visitor centers keep information sheets and maps on where to go. Of the South Lake commercial tour operators, the best Tahoe vistas come courtesy of Zephyr Cove Snowmobile Center (☎775/588-3833), the largest operator in the region. Husky Express dogsled rides in the Hope Valley meadow require reservations (☎775/782-3047). **Sleigh rides** are offered by Borges Sleigh Rides (☎530/541-2953), who leave for a trip into the woods from the meadow next to Caesar's Casino; and the Camp Richardson corral (☎530/541-3113), on the lakeshore west of town. Neither trip is particularly remote or adventurous, but both hold a certain family appeal. More giggles are likely at Hansen's Saucer Hill (1360 Ski Run Blvd, ☎530/544-3361), with **tubing and sledding** at $6 an hour (9am–5pm, some holiday weekends until 9pm).

Grover Hot Springs State Park (pool: Mon–Fri 2–9pm, Sat–Sun noon–9pm; ☎530/694-2249) is 35 minutes south of the lake on Hwy-89, four miles west of Markleeville. The alpine valley setting beyond is desolately beautiful and makes a great **winter camping** spot. For indoor swimming, head to the large **recreation center** at 1180 Rufus Allen Blvd (☎530/542-6056); geared to local residents, fitness classes and use of the lap pool, gym, and ice rink are refreshingly affordable. The small **skatepark** in Bijou Community Park (1201 Al Tahoe Blvd) is usually cleared out by spring, but the best skatepark in the area is just across Hwy-207 (Kingsbury Grade) in Gardnerville, Nevada. For more information head to Skatin' Worshippers, 3444 Lake Tahoe Blvd (☎530/542-3444).

Listings

Avalanche hotline ☎530/587-2158.
Internet El Dorado County Library, 1000 Rufus
Allen Blvd ☎530/573-3185, Tues–Wed
10am–8pm, Thurs–Sat 10am–5pm; Strange Brew
Coffee & Cyber Lounge, 2660 Lake Tahoe Blvd,
☎530/542-4169, Mon–Thurs 7am–11.30pm, Fri
7am–midnight, Sat 8am–10pm, Sun 7am–9pm.
Medical Barton Memorial Hospital, 2170 South
Ave ☎530/541-3420.
Pharmacy Longs Drugs, 2358 Lake Tahoe Blvd
☎530/544-1500.
Post office Six stations, including 1046 Al Tahoe
Blvd, CA and 233 Kingsbury Grade, NV (both ☎1-
800/275-8777).

Road conditions Caltrans on ☎916/445-7623 or
1-800/427-7623, ☜www.dot.ca.gov (though
Caltrans covers Lake Tahoe and the Reno area,
there is also a separate road conditions line for
Nevada: ☎775/793-1313).
Supermarkets Albertsons, 1030 Al Tahoe Blvd
☎530/541-5113; Raley's, 4010 Lake Tahoe Blvd
☎530/544-3418, and 1040 Emerald Bay Rd
☎530/541-5160; Safeway, 1020 Johnson Lane
☎530/542-7740, and Round Hill Mall ☎775/588-
2130.
Tahoe hotline ☎530/546-5253.
Taxi Yellow Cab Co, Stateline ☎775/588-1234.

Squaw Valley

Few people dispute that **Squaw Valley USA** is a great ski mountain. Prices,
management, new development, environmental issues, weekend crowds – these
may all be topics for criticism, but the vast, varied terrain full of bowls, cliffs,
rocks, couloirs, cornices, and trees spread across six challenging peaks have
made Squaw one of the most beloved, busy resorts in the West.

Of course, popularity is nothing new here. The resort played host to the
Winter Olympics in 1960, a mere eleven years after it was opened and has
retained a loyal clientele ever since. It was built on privately owned land, and
thus is not subject to the usual planning restrictions imposed by National
Forest tenancy, and the owners have consistently upgraded the slopes with the
latest advances in ski lift technology, allowing quicker, greater access to the
mountain's terrain. The owners have also resisted any attempts to make Squaw
part of a mega ski-corporation, permitting a distinctly buttoned-down atmosphere to thrive. Though expensive, the ski area doesn't feel like an exclusive
millionaire's club, as Aspen and Vail do at times.

Most visitors swarm to the slopes on the weekend, leaving at the end of the
ski day for Truckee or the north shore, rather than staying in the boxy, concrete
hotels or small condo complexes in the sleepy Olympic Valley. Squaw is hoping this will change as a large chunk of land near the mountain base was
recently sold to developers Intrawest and the first phases of the new Village at
Squaw have now been completed. New restaurants and public spaces are
encouraging day-trippers to linger after 4pm, where once it was primarily
locals and lifties who remained.

Arrival, orientation, and getting around

Squaw is located in Olympic Valley, six miles north of Tahoe City and twelve
miles south of Truckee and I-80 on Hwy-89. The journey from Truckee can
actually be quicker during busy periods, avoiding the heavy traffic coming
north from around the lake.

The new village is slowly eating into the giant free parking lot at the foot
of the mountain, with pay parking structures currently under construction

right by the slopes. Avoid long walks by making an immediate left once in the lot and taking the Far East Express lift to the rest of the mountain, or opt for the satellite lot across the creek behind the *PlumpJack Inn* (see p.350).

Public transportation is available but infrequent, as most visitors come by car. The Squaw Ski shuttle (free; ☎530/581-7181) leaves Incline Village at 7.50am daily, stopping in Tahoe City at 8.30am and arriving at Squaw at 8.55am. The return shuttle departs at 4.30pm. Call for collection from the west shore and for details of additional scheduling during peak periods. Reserve at least twelve hours in advance for buses from the south shore or Reno ($5 round-trip; ☎866/769-4653). Olympic Valley is on the limited Tahoe City-Truckee TART route (see p.335), while complimentary shuttles from the *Resort at Squaw Creek* (see p.350) run hourly from noon to 11pm between the hotel and Tahoe City, and from the Boatworks Mall in Tahoe City 12.30–11.30pm. The hotel is accessible from the base area during ski hours by local shuttle or the Squaw Creek lift, and nonguests are permitted to use the service.

The mountain

There are only a few named runs at Squaw so riders usually refer to the

names of the lifts; graded green, blue, or black to describe the type of terrain they access. From the base, the aerial tram swings over the steep face and red rocks of **Broken Arrow** across to **High Camp**, a facility housing restaurants, swimming pool (open from March onwards), and ice rink. The tubing hill and vast beginner slopes are located here – one of Squaw's attractions is that novices aren't stuck at the bottom of the mountain, but have access to the same views and restaurants as everyone else. The funitel gondola carries skiers up to the **Gold Coast** cafeteria, nestled between the imposing butte, steeps, and moguls of **Squaw Peak** and the intermediate runs on the front face of **Emigrant.** On a busy day, the overlooked Squaw One chairlift can be the fastest way up the mountain. To the left of funitel's base are Snow King and KT-22. Notorious KT-22 is the downhiller's choice – steep and littered with challenging chutes, cornices, and cliffs. Offering excellent views of Lake Tahoe at its summit, forested **Snow King** has both tight tree lines and gentle cruising runs that lead back down valley to the *Resort at Squaw Creek.* When the upper mountain lifts are shut down due to high winds – fairly common at Squaw during storms – Snow King is the sheltered alternative, but its lower altitude means that the snow is often heavy and wet.

The most remote of all Squaw's peaks is **Granite Chief**. On a powder day, locals hike the summit to drop into the open bowl and trees beneath. The exit from these trees below is one of the few spots where riders need to keep their speed. Other traps include the traverse between Gold Coast and Central Park (Squaw's smaller terrain park); the gully that leads to the base of Silverado; the exposed ridge that stretches from Emigrant to High Camp; and Mountain Run, the cat track from High Camp to the village. Everyone ends up on this gentle, winding 3.2 mile route at some point. The trail's long, flat stretches are not problematic for skiers, but can be tricky for novice snowboarders. Stay skier's left and take Olympic High or Sunnyside instead.

Beginner

Total beginners should take the cable car to the top of the mountain for the superb views and gentle bunny slopes at **High Camp**. Next step is **East Broadway** above the Gold Coast restaurant. From here it's an easy progression to the gently rolling **glades** off Gold Coast and Emigrant lifts.

Intermediate

Shirley Lake and tougher **Solitude** access long cruisers, spiced with easy lips and rollers. The tree runs here are mellow and the snow usually better than down mountain. After a recent storm, try the forested runs on **Snow King**. Siberia lift accesses more challenging blues, while the Sunnyside route to the base area is a confidence builder. Intermediates who like to cruise have the fewest options of any group at Squaw, as there just aren't that many long, blue trails.

Expert

KT-22 is known for its cornices, cliffs, and steeps. Try Cornice II and Solitude for less difficult terrain and fields of moguls. For trees head to **Snow King** or **Granite Chief** – both have powder stashes long after the rest of the mountain is tracked. The steep red cliffs at the top of **Broken Arrow** are definitely extreme, but it's possible to drop in below for an easy flowing powder cruiser. Headwall and the backside of Emigrant should keep bump-bashers busy.

Freestyle

Squaw has challenging freeriding for all levels and a top-class superpipe. The mountain's crammed with drops and natural hits. Central Park is the small but permanent **snowboard area**, with its own chairlift, a few giant tabletops, hips and rails, and an pipe that's floodlit at night. There's a well-cut **superpipe** on Squaw Peak packed with pros and most easily accessed from Siberia chair. This is usually the site of the boardercross course and assorted large tabletops and rails, but their existence is highly dependent on snow conditions, scheduled contests, and the whims of Squaw Valley management.

Lift tickets, lessons, and rentals

Perhaps because of its reputation as the best mountain on the north shore, Squaw hasn't yet bought into the notion of competitive **rates**. Even midweek season passes bought at the cheapest preseason rate are prohibitive, with half-day tickets barely a break either. Night skiing is included, but it's limited unless you're using the terrain park. The best deal is the Frequent Skier pass, which, for $5, gives holders every fifth day free in addition to discounts on midweek tickets. Families fare better as tickets for kids 12 and under are just $5.

Lessons are available for all levels and include telemark packages, advanced ski clinics, and group freestyle sessions in the terrain park. It's a decent school with a great learning area, but it's not cheap. Packages including rentals and tickets can top $100, though half-day lessons start at around $42. Private adaptive ski lessons are available at a twenty percent discount (☎530/581-7263).

Regular and demo boards and skis are good quality in the resort **rental shops**, but up to $10 more expensive per day than the local branch of Dave's (on Hwy-89 at the Squaw Valley turn-off, next to the 7-11; see p.341 for more details. Snowshoes and telemark skis are available.

Accommodation

Accommodation at Squaw is pricey. The *Olympic Village Inn* (☎530/581-6000 or 1-800/845-5243, ⓦwww.vioa.com) and *Squaw Valley Lodge* (☎530/583-5500 or 1-800/922-9970, ⓦwww.squawvalleylodge.com) are both bland but comfortable condo hotels; suites sleeping four start at around $190 a night. Squaw Valley Central Reservations (☎1-800/403-0206, ⓦwww.squaw.com) can find you area rooms for around $100 per person (midweek or low season), much more for Village condos. Squaw Valley Realty (☎530/583-3451, ⓦwww.squawvalleyrealty.net) has a much larger selection of condos for rent in Olympic Valley, all on quiet mountain streets, and most within twenty minutes walk from the lifts. If you stay anywhere nearby, it will be a good fifteen-minute journey to Tahoe City's bars and restaurants, and it's easy to feel stranded here if you don't have a car. Check the north shore listings on p.336–38 for accommodation closer to the action.

PlumpJack Squaw Valley Inn 1920 Squaw Valley Rd ☎530/583-1576 or 1-800/323-7666, ⓦwww.plumpjack.com. The eccentrically stylish interior and zen-like courtyard – with pool, hot tubs, and mountain views – dramatically contrast with the drab exterior. A luxury hotel with a relaxed atmosphere, it's the preferred choice of Tahoe regulars and locals in need of spoiling. Their tasty breakfast buffet is included (see restaurant listing below). Discounted midweek packages often available. ❼–❾

Resort at Squaw Creek 400 Squaw Creek Rd ☎530/583-6300 or 1-800/403-4434, ⓦwww.squawcreek.com. Boxy, luxury hotel that offers a retro take on opulence. Amenities include an outdoor spa, ice rink, cross country trails, and its own lift to access the rest of the mountain. Expensive ski packages start at $150 per person.

Eating, drinking, and entertainment

Though the new Village is gradually attracting more **restaurants**, Squaw's dining options are still limited. Tahoe City and Truckee offer a much wider variety for taste and budget when it comes to après-ski dining and **drinking** (see p.338–40). On-mountain, *High Camp* lures big spenders with tablecloths and pool-side dining, while the Gold Coast cafeterias are also pricey; the complex at the foot of the mountain is best for cheap snacks. Meanwhile, The Squaw Valley General Store, Far East Center (☎530/581-7129), makes killer sandwiches.

There always seems to be some kind of **festival**, competition, or promotional event going on here, from mogul series to the annual Spring Schwing snow-golf tournament. Look for screenings of films shot at the resort and evening clinics or lectures from local pros and industry stalwarts.

Balboa Cafe Village at Squaw Valley ☎530/583-5850. New from the PlumpJack partnership, a version of their well-known *Balboa Cafe* in San Francisco. Upscale brasserie, featuring the likes of steak *frites* and seared salmon (in the $20–25 range) with an unfortunate theme park-style facade. 11.30am–late, dinner menu 6–10pm.

Dave's Deli Olympic Plaza ☎530/581-1085. The pile of boards propped against the wall outside this tiny food counter indicate its undying popularity. Practically as cheap as bringing your own food, Dave's is one-stop shopping for early-morning Odwalla juice, breakfast muffins, picnic snacks, and cheap beer.

Mother Barclay's Cafe Squaw Valley Mall ☎530/581-3251. Breakfast and lunch dishes in giant portions at reasonable prices. Don't expect to move, let alone ski immediately after a full serving of blueberry pancakes. 7am–3pm.

PlumpJack Squaw Valley Inn 1920 Squaw Valley Rd ☎530/583-1576. One of the best restaurants in the Lake Tahoe area, frequently booked out and with a wine list you'd expect from a partnership that also owns one of San Francisco's top wine retailers. Tasty, high-end California cuisine, with all sorts of influences, and a short bar menu if you just want to snack and take in the scene. Open for breakfast, lunch, and dinner, daily 7.30am–10pm (dinner after 5.30pm weekdays, 5pm weekends).

Red Dog Bar and Grill Far East Center ☎530/581-7261. Out in the parking lot, this spot has long been the favorite drinking haunt of lift ops. Occasionally schedules evening entertainment, but gets raucous regardless. 3–10pm.

Wildflour Baking Company Olympic House ☎530/583-1963. Be the first to answer the daily general knowledge quiz correctly and win a fresh chocolate chip cookie. Their gigantic cinnamon rolls are also available in High Camp at *Wildflour Too*. Open from 7am.

Other activities and attractions

The **tubing hill** and **ice rink** at High Camp are open until the last cable car heads down at 10pm. High Camp's **swimming** lagoon opens in March, daylight hours only. Discover great **snowshoeing** trails along Squaw Creek, behind the *Olympic Village Inn* at the far end of Squaw Valley Road; 18km of **cross-country** trails around the *Resort at Squaw Creek* (trail passes $13, $6 after 3pm; ☎530/581-6637); and a very small climbing wall in the cable car building (☎530/583-ROPE).

Listings

For other listings, see Lake Tahoe's north shore, p.340.

Medical Truckee Tahoe Medical Group, Squaw Valley office ☎530/583-3439 or ☎530/581-8864.

Post office 1600 Squaw Valley Rd ☎530/583-5126 (Mon–Fri 7.30am–4pm).

Alpine Meadows

Attracting a dedicated following on Tahoe's north shore, **Alpine Meadows,** is something of a ski resort paradox; popular with families, it's also a haven for hardcore freeriders. Not that a simple glance at the slopes would reveal this diversity: the undulating terrain spreads out further than the view from the lodge suggests, yet the number of groomed trails is fairly small. The in-bound terrain is more akin to a backcountry experience, while an atypical open-boundary policy makes the actual surrounding backcountry accessible from the mountain's lifts. But if Sierra Cement – heavy, wet, dense snow – sets in and advanced riders are reduced to skiing groomed trails, Alpine can be a bit, well, boring.

The facilities and mountain can seem pretty limited for a day area that's priced at the same level as giants like Squaw and Heavenly. Still, the lodge seems perennially filled with families and large groups, attracted by the small and gently rolling beginner area, sprawling intermediate terrain, teen programs, and Alpine's lift and off-site lodging deals.

Arrival and getting around

Alpine is located on Hwy-89, just north of Tahoe City and thirteen miles south of Truckee and I-80. Staying west of Tahoe City or in Truckee is the best way to avoid heavy north shore traffic on busy mornings.

Free **parking** is available close to the base of the mountain, but prime spots get filled fast and late arrivals have to choose between a long walk and pay parking right by the lodge. Free Alpine ski **shuttles** (☏540/581-8225) pick up between 8 and 8.45am from points on the north shore and from Squaw Valley, departing at 4.30pm. The west shore route runs at 8.15 and 9.15am, stopping in Tahoe City en route, returning at 2 and 4pm. There is also a west shore shuttle serving the back bowl's Sherwood Chair on weekends and holidays. Pickups are at 8.45 and 9.45am, departing from the Sherwood Chair hourly 2–4pm. TART buses stop at the Alpine turn-off on Hwy-89, connecting to the ski area parking lot buses; see p.335 for TART info.

Mountain info
Phone ☏530/583-4232 or 800/441-4423
Snow phone ☏530/581-0963
Website ✆www.skialpine.com
Price $56
Operating times Mid-Nov to late May daily 9am–4pm
No. of lifts 14, including 1 high-speed six pac and 3 surface
Base elevation 6835'
Summit elevation 8637'
Vertical drop 1802'
No. of trails 100 + (but many are short and really all part of the same run)
Acreage 2000
Beginner 25%
Intermediate 40%
Expert 35%
Average snowfall 495"
Snowmaking Yes, served by 12 out of 14 lifts
Night skiing No
Nursery facilities No

The mountain

Alpine's front slopes funnel down in a semicircle to the **base lodge**, making it relatively easy to navigate; the trail map is rather misleading. The high-speed Summit Six is the fastest route to both front and back bowls. Within minutes of opening time on a powder day, lift-accessed blacks are cut with trails and skiers are hiking out along the ridges. Intermediate and advanced riders with their own gear can skip the crowds by getting the weekend ski shuttle from Tahoe's west shore to the Sherwood **lift** on the back side, which gets the sun first thing. Like most of the lifts here, the Sherwood triple can be achingly slow.

Alpine is notorious for **high winds**, particularly on exposed Ward Peak where whiteouts are not unusual; the mountain is best avoided during storms. Sunny conditions can make the back bowls boggy by lunchtime, so groups start congregating at the cabana-like *Ice Bar*. This sheltered Mid Mountain Chalet restaurant has more of a family atmosphere, while the large deck of the base lodge is always crammed on sunny days, close as it is to the bunny slopes, park, and pipe.

Beginner

The segregated beginner terrain, located at the foot of a steep rise and next to a parking lot, is rather limited and uninteresting. Kids are better off with a small whoopdedoo terrain park, along with the reassurance of being close to everyone else. This is precisely what makes navigating the next level of greens a bit intimidating for most adult learners, as the trails are crammed into a busy valley route back to base. But Alpine works well for adventurous advanced beginners and progressing intermediates, with short, challenging blues mixed in with fun, gentle, treelined gullies (try Skateboard Alley first, then the tighter Hot Wheels) and a wide, gently undulating "Family Ski Zone."

Intermediate

The blues directly **above the lodge** – in the Alpine bowl and off the Roundhouse lift – are classic downhill runs, some narrow and winding, others long, wide, and thigh burning. Escape the crowds and head to the all-blue area off the **Scott** and **Lakeview** chairs – a protected, treelined assortment of moguls and groomed cruisers mixed with a few gentle rollers, mellow lips, and mini glades. These slopes are blessed with both the afternoon sun and a nice view of Tahoe from the top of Scott peak. Keep speed on the traverse out toward **Sherwood Chair**, as it's flatter back here than it looks on the trail map.

Expert

Alpine has few groomed blacks. The back bowl of **Ward Peak** gets the sun in the mornings and has relatively mild gradients, spiced up with a few cliff bands. The further you hike the fresher the powder – but watch your exit in this area, because it flattens out abruptly. Hike to your left on the front face of Ward for steep couloirs into pillows of powder through awesome glades. On the opposite side of the valley, even snowboarders find it fairly easy to traverse, rather than hike, to the steep ledges skier's right off **Scott Chair** – a woodsy area with super technical cliffs.

Freestyle

Slow to accept snowboarders, management is catering more and more to young riders and twin tip skiers. Freestylers can take advantage of a **superpipe dragon** and a **park** that, though small, is consistently improving – and well suited to progressing young huckers and wannabe rail monsters, with its own lift and convenient location right by the lodge. The natural draw, meanwhile, has always been the rock-littered powder fields; when the snow's good, there's no shortage of objects to drop off and lips to launch.

Lift tickets, lessons, and rentals

Alpine's regular day rates, season **tickets**, and prepay 10-Paks are among the most expensive in Tahoe. However, in a bid to attract a younger crowd, the resort has recently initiated a $19 ticket for the single lift that serves the terrain park, an incredible bargain for Tahoe; call before heading over to make sure the deal is still in place. Free POWDR cards, available at over 300 NorCal and Nevada ski shops – but not in Tahoe – give a $20 discount on preselected mid-week days (usually two or three per week, outside the holidays). Interchangeable tickets for parents are available, allowing couples to trade-off babysitting duties.

Beginner **lessons** including lift tickets start at $60; intermediate/advanced lessons from $36 (lessons only). Alpine offers a full roster of multiday clinics for skiers and snowboarders, including women's camps and instructor training. The Tahoe Adaptive Ski School (TASS) is headquarted here (☎530/581-4161, ⓦwww.skinastc.com/tahoe.htm); a half-day lesson including ticket and equipment is $50.

For local alternatives to Alpine's small and rather pricey **rental shops**, see the box on p.341. Telemark skis, blades, and snowshoes are also available at the mountain.

Practicalities

The resort consists of little more than a base lodge, a couple of on-mountain food stops, and a small but generally luxurious selection of **condos** and **vacation homes** clustered in the trees between Hwy-89 and the mountain. Lodging packages throughout Tahoe can be booked through Alpine Central Reservations (☎1-800/949-3296, ⓦwww.skialpine.com). The only hotel in the immediate area is the wood-shingled *River Ranch* lodge (☎530/583-4264 or 1-800/535-9900, ⓦwww.riverranchlodge.com, ❹–❺), comfortable if slightly old-fashioned, situated by the tumbling Truckee River.

Opposite River Ranch is *Thunder Ridge Café*, 150 Alpine Meadows Rd #2 (☎530/583-6896, ⓦwww.thunderridgecafe.com), serving inexpensive, healthy **breakfasts** (try the veggie-egg scrambles or $3 pancake and French toast half-orders), huge deli sandwiches, and thin-crust pizzas. Breakfasts to go are available at the resort from *Treats* (in the base lodge) and *Coffee Connexion*.

For all manner of north shore listings, see pp.336–40.

Northstar

Known as Tahoe's best resort for families, with all the pros and cons that entails, **Northstar** is not nearly as intimidating as nearby Squaw nor does it contain the untamed bowls, steeps, and drops of its neighbors to the south. What this quiet, compact resort does have is forested, manicured slopes ideal for intermediates and all within an easily navigable layout. A recent expansion (on Lookout Mountain) has increased expert terrain, and Northstar's terrain parks are improving as well, making it a more well-rounded choice.

Unobtrusive condo complexes and timber-clad homes are scattered throughout the extensive grounds, and development has focused more on understated modernization than hurried expansion. The lifts are speedy and on-mountain lodges sparkling, but there is precious little going on after the runs close, with only a handful of restaurants and shops in the tiny pedestrian village. Now in partnership with Colorado resort developers East West, a more aggressive program of growth promises more village lodging, restaurants, stores, an ice rink, brewpub, and spa.

Arrival, information, and getting around

Northstar is located on Hwy-267, six easy, flat miles south of Truckee and six steep, winding miles north of Kings Beach and the lake. During a storm the road from Northstar back to Truckee is usually clear, while traffic to Kings

Mountain info

Phone ☎530/562-1010 or 800/466-6784 (800/GONORTH)

Snow phone ☎530/562-1330

Website ⊛www.skinorthstar.com

Price $57

Operating times late Nov to mid April, 8am–10pm

No. of lifts 15, including 1 gondola, 3 tows, and 2 magic carpets

Base elevation 6330′

Summit elevation 8610′

Vertical drop 2280′

No. of trails 70

Acreage 2420

Beginner 25%

Intermediate 50%

Expert 25%

Average snowfall 350″

Snowmaking Yes (50%)

Night skiing Limited night riding, tubing, and snowbikes in small Polaris Park on holiday weekends

Nursery facilities Yes, ☎530/562-2278, ages 2–6, skiing ages 3–12, snowboarding 4–12; Mommy, Daddy & Me is a free Saturday program sharing teaching tips with parents of children aged 3–5.

Beach gets gridlocked as cars chain up to take on Brockway Summit. Those traveling from Reno and the east can get directly to Hwy-267 off I-80 on the new Truckee bypass, exit 188B. (See p.333 for travel to the north shore).

Free **parking** is available in tiered outdoor lots, the terraced system making for a longish walk despite the proximity to the base of the mountain. Be sure to note the color and number of your terrace, as it's easy to get confused. A people-mover carries weary skiers back through the lots at the end of the day, departing from the roadside edge of the village.

With no public transportation to or from Northstar after 5.30pm, those staying in the resort will almost certainly need a **car**. For day visitors, Area Transit **shuttles** ($1.50; free to skiers) run to Northstar hourly approximately 7am–5.30pm from Tahoe Vista, Kings Beach, and Truckee, connecting with north shore TART services (see p.335). An additional once-daily free ski shuttle serves Incline Village, Crystal Bay, and Kings Beach; pick up a TART schedule or call ☎530/587-7451 to plan your journey – otherwise risk an hour-long wait at the bus stop. Shuttle service from Reno and South Lake is also free, but you need to be an early riser who doesn't mind spending the entire day at the resort, since there's only one service daily. Buses depart from the larger hotels and casinos, some of which also sell discounted lift tickets to nonguests. Reservations are suggested; call ☎775/883-2100 or 1-888/883-2106 for the most up-to-date info on pick-up locations.

The mountain

Northstar's **layout** could hardly be simpler. The mid-sized ski area incorporates three navigable faces, traversing is minimal, and riders are never more than a lift ride away from trails leading back to base.

The gateway to most of the ski area is at the top of the gondola (nonskiing gondola tickets are $10), home to the multistory Lodge at Big Springs, mid-mountain rentals and demo centers and a kids' learning area. All trails on the front face funnel to this base, spilling down the valley between Mount Pluto's east and west ridges. It's difficult for families and groups to lose each other, but the wide, central runs often resemble a human pinball game. Overcrowding in beginner areas is accentuated due to the large numbers of less experienced skiers. The blues here are groomed, flanked by gladed trees and dotted with mini-terrain features. With advanced skiers in the minority, it's less crowded on the backside, where the rather overrated black diamond trial markings put off intermediates who could most likely handle the terrain. The challenging Lookout Mountain is even more deserted, particularly outside holiday periods.

Of the north shore resorts, sheltered Northstar is the place to visit for powder in the trees. The lower slopes can suffer from sogginess, however, and the mountain's lower altitude also means that the resort has to close earlier than its neighboring resorts.

Beginner

The problem for never-evers is that – aside from a small teaching zone – Northstar has only a few true greens, all of which are busy thoroughfares to the mid-mountain lodge. **Village Run**, the green below the gondola which links mid-mountain to the base, is quieter earlier in the day – everyone else tends to stay higher up – but gets packed in the afternoon rush home. It also has a tendency to be patchy and slow during warm spells. More confident beginners should try the front face blues; most are gentle enough to learn on. These runs have a pitch particularly suited for novice snowboarders who often find bunny slopes a bit too flat. Riders note that Village Run is best avoided completely until you feel confident pointing straight on the flat; take the gondola down instead.

Intermediate

Blues on the front face are easygoing, ideal for the beginning intermediate. Virgin tree skiers can weave in and out of the widely spaced woods right of the **Vista Express**. The front face blacks are slightly overrated and most competent intermediates could handle any of the short, sheltered runs off the East or West ridges. Ignore the black diamond marking on the backside and try **Sierra Grande** and **Challenger**, endless cruisers well within the grasp of confident intermediates.

Expert

With the Lookout Mountain expansion, Northstar has added a handful of long and genuinely steep groomed blacks, bump, and tree runs to its resume. Most of the tree runs are evenly pitched, but can get bumped out in the absence of fresh snow. Head left off the top of the Lookout lift for a short but sweet pinball shot on the edge of the boundary. On the backside ski the acres of gladed trees and bumped trails. These are popular with traditional alpine skiers who run speed laps down **Iron Horse** or through the moguls of **Burn Out**. Rarely open, **Sawtooth Ridge** is less manicured than the rest of the mountain. If it's powder you crave, this is the spot.

Freestyle

There's not much in the way of natural jibs and drops, but for intermediates who don't want to get too airborne, the mountain is littered with smaller, groomed terrain features. Check out the mini-rollers and berms off the Vista Express lift. Although Squaw and Sugarbowl have traditionally attracted more of the north shore's high-caliber riders, Northstar has been improving its park terrain with new boxes and more rails. The superpipe is now closer to the mid-mountain lodge in a shadier spot and the regular pipe is occasionally open at night (at lower rates, since you have to hike). The parks are rarely crowded midweek and certainly less intimidating than elsewhere.

Lift tickets, lessons, and rentals

Northstar's Double Whammy season pass can be used at sister south shore resort Sierra at Tahoe, and starts at just $249 when bought preseason. Six packs for $159 cut day prices in half, and significantly discounted tickets can be purchased through NorCal and Reno area partner stores (check online for store details). For a rather hefty registration fee ($79), Vertical Plus entitles members to one free midweek ticket at Sierra or Northstar, daily ticket discounts, electronic ticketing, members-only lines, and a wristband that logs your vertical ascents (via the lift gates); the more vertical you log, the more discounts on food and equipment..

Lesson packages for beginners start at $69 for gear, half-day lesson, and all-day ticket; regular group lessons are $39. Free lessons are offered to advanced intermediates twice daily (except Saturdays and holidays) on a first-come, first-served basis. Mini-shredders can join classes at the age of 4 – most ski areas restrict snowboard lessons to 7 and above – and mini-terrain parks groom the next generation of freestylers.

Northstar's large **rental** facility uses precision Snowell tuning machines, but equipment is geared toward beginners and rates are high. Very few non-step-in boards are available, though skiers can take better advantage of the mid-mountain demo facility. For local alternatives, see p.341.

Practicalities

The village at the base of the resort is on the brink of major development, but for now facilities are relatively limited. The bulk of Northstar's **accommodation** is found in small condo complexes and mountain homes scattered around the surrounding estate. Lift-and-lodging packages booked through the resort start at around $91 per person, and guests have access to the outdoor lap pool, hot tubs, saunas, and fitness center of the Swim and Racquet Club.

On-mountain **eating** choices are confined to one of two cafeterias. Atop Mount Pluto, the light and airy *Summit Deck & Grille* is a cut above the usual ski area canteen, with a menu that includes stir fries and fish tacos. At the top of the gondola the *Lodge at Big Springs* has a sunny deck with views of the new superpipe, and includes a Mexican themed bar and café, coffee stand, and grill. *Cippolini's* (☎530/562-2245), located next to the *Alpine Sports Bar* at the base of the mountain, serves excellent pizzas and calzones. The *Timbercreek*, in the village (☎530/562-2250), serves gourmet California cuisine in a formal dining room, complemented by a café menu of creative salads, burgers, and other variations on grill staples. A huge breakfast buffet is available from 7.30 to 10.30am. Alternatively, pick up coffee and a quick snack at the Village Food Company (☎530/562-2253), which sells expensive breakfast specials, sandwiches, and sushi in addition to a wide selection of gourmet groceries.

If you're after regular **evening entertainment**, this is not the place to stay. See north shore listings on p.339–40 for suggestions in nearby Truckee or Kings Beach.

Heavenly

Heavenly, the largest ski area on the West Coast, straddles two states from its perch above South Lake, its long, white tendrils clearly visible from the north shore. On the California side, Tahoe's most extensive vertical seemingly runs right into the lake, while the Nevada trails overlook the dusty expanse of Carson Valley.

With endless cruisers, terrifying glades, deep gullies, and steep chutes to negotiate, skiers are more often focusing on their next turn rather than the shimmering lake or the valley below. That's not to say it's all high-level intermediate or expert terrain – there are a few beginner runs and Heavenly does cater to families (offering the youngest daycare anywhere in the region) – but novices will find better opportunities in the smaller resorts on the north shore.

Now part of the Vail Resorts portfolio, Heavenly is currently in the midst of a long-term redevelopment plan; recent additions include a high-speed gondola that accesses the mountain from Stateline, the bustling, casino town just east of the California border. The resort is close to the majority of the region's lodging, located directly off Hwy-50, and the resort's pedestrian village is here as well. Those entering Heavenly from its Nevada base can stay in dated condos, a quiet residential alternative to the south shore sprawl.

Mountain info	
Phone ☏775/586-7000, vacations 800/2-HEAVEN	
Snow phone ☏775/586-7000, press 1	
Website ⊛www.skiheavenly.com	
Price $59, peak season	
Operating times Late Nov into May Mon–Fri 9am–4pm, Sat–Sun & holidays 8.30am–4pm	
No. of lifts 29, including 1 gondola, 1 aerial tram, 8 surface	
Base elevation 6540′	
Summit elevation 10040′	
Vertical drop 3500′	
No. of trails 85	
Acreage 4800	
Beginner 25%	
Intermediate 45%	
Expert 35%	
Average snowfall 360″	
Snowmaking Yes (almost 70%)	
Night skiing No	
Nursery facilities Yes, from 6 weeks to 6 years, reservations required, ☏775/586-7000, ext 6911; skiing from 4, snowboarding from 7	

Arrival and getting around

For information on Reno airport, car rental, and directions to South Lake Tahoe, see the box on p.333. Once in South Lake, there's no need to drive to the slopes. Aside from the comprehensive STAGE public transport (see p.341), Heavenly runs an efficient **free shuttle system** to all base lodges (daily 8am–5.30pm; ☏775/586-7000). Buses on four routes pick up from all but the most residential areas, stopping every 20–30 minutes at hotels and the blue shuttle bus signs dotted throughout town.

For drivers, free parking lots serve Heavenly's four base areas. Beginners should head for the **California Lodge**, located in a residential neighborhood at the top of Ski Run Boulevard. Right on South Lake's main drag, the **gondola** is the most convenient mountain access point for intermediate and above skiers, who ascend over two miles on a stunning twelve-minute flight to the heart of the ski area – with an optional stop at the Observation Deck for a picnic lunch with one almighty view. Heading up the mountain from neighboring **Boulder** and **Stagecoach** lodges in Nevada takes some trail-navigating skills but makes a handy traffic-dodging option on busy weekends, especially if coming from Reno or the north shore.

The mountain

Before the gondola was built, Heavenly was tricky to navigate, with miles of winding, flat cat tracks linking a confusing network of 29 lifts. Finding your way around still requires a trail map and tedious traversing, but the gondola has improved the situation with an easily accessible center point. Complimentary **mountain tours** leave the top of the tram daily at 10am, but don't expect to get oriented immediately. The more informative "Ski with a Ranger" programs are just as good an introduction to the terrain, and provide an insight into local fauna and geological history at the same time.

There's a certain charm about exiting a chairlift and confronting large opposing arrows directing skiers into one state or the other. As a general rule, the **California side** is more crowded, with a wider array of terrain, including Heavenly's halfpipe, all but one of the area's green runs, and the majority of groomed blacks. Over the hill on the **Nevada side** are miles of thigh-burning blues and glades; the sheer couloirs of the mountain's double diamond canyons are tucked against Nevada's eastern boundary, but are just as much of a trek to reach from either state. Restaurants are located on-mountain and at the base lodges in both states. When it's time to leave, there's no shame in downloading to either base in California. There is no skiable route to the base of the gondola, and the low-altitude black runs above the California Lodge are tough even when the snow is at its best.

At the top of the gondola (a $20 ride for nonskiers) is the **Adventure Park** (10am–3pm, sleds and tubing $10/hour), aimed at families looking to break up their ski day with tubing runs and short snowshoe and cross-country trails; should you be interested in more extensive trail networks, there are several far better operations on the lake detailed on p.345.

Beginner

Heavenly's claim that 25 percent of its slopes is rated for beginners is frankly preposterous. There are barely ten green runs across its broad expanse, with only one green-rated trail on the Nevada side. Never-evers should consider the flat meadows of Sierra or Kirkwood instead. Advanced beginners should be fine, however, as many of Heavenly's blues are wide and gentle. Take the gondola to the **Tamarack** sixpack, which accesses a cluster of blues around the top of the gondola and the East Peak lodge, including wide, sweeping Orion. Novice snowboarders are advised to avoid flat Skyline Trail, a tedious traverse even for accomplished riders.

Intermediate

Miles of blue trails suit all levels of intermediate riders, from nervous skiers inching their way down gentle, wide roads and stopping every few turns to look at the view, to those beginning to take mellow bumps in their stride. If you tire easily, stay on the Nevada side, which offers a large concentration of runs in a relatively compact area. Blue trails on the California side are found in smaller pockets that are separated from each other by acres of glades; if you don't want to loop the same few runs, you'll need to make at least a couple of long traverses. For bumps and gullies, try Bettys, a split-groomed run (half smooth, half with moguls) off the Ridge chair above the California tram.

Bettys is next to Ridge Run, one of Heavenly's best cruisers with expansive views across the lake. To get the heart racing, tackle **Olympic Downhill**, the carver's choice, running top-to-bottom on the Nevada face. Smooth glades are off the Olympic chair, under the Sky Express, or anywhere off the Skyline trail.

Expert

After a storm, traverse across Milky Way Bowl to the death-defying chutes and cliffs of **Mott** and **Kilbrew Canyons**, only open when there's sufficient snow. If you choose Kilbrew, be prepared for a painful traverse to the Mott Canyon lift. For steep trees, head to the **North Bowl** along Nevada's western boundary or to **Dipper Knob** above the canyons. For rolling gladed terrain, try **Maggie's**. If the back canyons are closed and the trees are pitted and hard, Heavenly has little to offer the advanced skier. Classic downhill blacks are few; **The Face** and bumpy **Gunbarrel**, dropping precipitously down to the California lodge, might be notorious for scaring the pants off beginners, but at low altitude the snow here is the worst on the mountain, plagued by rocky patches and slushy bumps. Stick to the upper-mountain **Ellie's** or **Little Dipper** blacks instead.

Freestyle

Trying to fight its reputation of having the weakest terrain parks on the south shore, Heavenly has developed super long boxes and rails in the parks on Yahoo (California) and Olympic (Nevada), including beginner jibs on California's groove. For natural hits, explore Skiways and Maggie's Canyon for gullies, natural pipe hits, and berms of powder. A waterfall is tucked away in the North Bowl, and Killbrew is cliffdrop central. Away from the busy wide cruisers, Heavenly's shorter, more winding blues offer plenty of rollers, dips, and bumps to occupy the intermediate.

Lift tickets, lessons, and rentals

The least expensive season pass, bought by November, costs a reasonable $299 and even the full-priced version costs much less than a comparable pass at Squaw. Save on daily **tickets** prepurchased under the ski corporation's free-to-join PEAKS or Perfect 10 programs (especially useful if you also plan on riding Vail's Colorado resorts the same season), or check regional newspapers for current local deals. Sporting goods store REI sells day passes for a $10 discount.

No matter how good the teaching staff is, lack of suitable terrain makes the adult beginner **lessons** (priced at $89) a bad deal. For intermediates and above there are several worthwhile all-day clinics (from $75), and adaptive lessons are also available, though expensive; advance booking required (☎775/586-7000 ext 9-6218).

The **rental fleet** available at all base lodges is basic with few options to choose from. This particularly applies to snowboarders, who are required to visit the Heavenly-owned Boardinghouse (☎530/542-5228) in town for anything more advanced than the most forgiving, high-flex beginner board. For less expensive alternatives, see the south shore box on p.346. The many branches of Heavenly Sports (☎530/544-1921) cater better to skiers, with a couple of stores dedicated specifically to demo-level ski gear.

Practicalities

Although the mountain proudly touts the new "village" at the base of the gondola, it's not part of the resort and is really nothing more than a couple of

Marriott hotels in the midst of the malls and motels along Hwy-50. You can stay closer to the ski area in one of the mountain homes surrounding the California lodge, or condos off Kingsbury Grade, close to the Nevada base. Lodging packages offered through Heavenly are typically arranged at other properties along the south shore (see p.342–43); ski-and-stay-free packages are good value for infrequent skiers, especially outside peak season.

Though each of Heavenly's three base lodges houses a decent, if rather sterile **place to eat** – beer, burgers, and a salad bar in the creaky California Lodge; Tex-Mex and tequilas in Boulder Lodge's Cantina; pricey pizza at Stagecoach Lodge – money is better spent at one of the on-mountain restaurants, particularly in good weather. Both the Sky Deck barbecue (on the California side) and the East Peak lodge (on the Nevada side) also offer the typical burgers and cafeteria fare, but with better views. The sundeck, cafeteria, and full-service pseudo-gourmet restaurant at the top of the California Lodge tram has views out over the lake. For a faster, hand-warming hot chocolate pit stop, stop at *Patsy's Hut*, right by the beginner trails. A pricey but alluring alternative is to order an upmarket picnic lunch from Mountain Catering, who will dig a table and chairs out of the snow, adorning it with fresh cut flowers, silverware, and china; midweek only, reservations required (☎775/586-7000, ext 9-6228). Regular brown-baggers can leave their lunches in lockers at the top of the gondola and, on a warm, clear day, return to the Observation Deck for a picnic complete with stunning view.

There's little point in showing up early for breakfast or hanging around for **après** (though the California Lodge sometimes has live music), with better options in South Lake – see p.344–45 for recommendations.

Sierra at Tahoe

It's not uncommon for **Sierra at Tahoe** to sell out on weekends, when both day-trippers from the Bay Area and local families are drawn to its chilled-out community atmosphere. Unlike some of its mega-resort neighbors, there's not much in the way of a base area at Sierra – just a couple of warren-like wooden buildings – and little variety in natural terrain save for steep, well-spaced trees. What the resort lacks in amenities, though, it makes up for in character and service, from meandering trails hemmed in by towering California pines and constantly evolving terrain parks to great beginner and kids programs and substantial value passes.

A word of warning: though Sierra gets dumped on during storms, the northwest facing slopes suffer from aptly named Sierra Cement worse than Heavenly or Kirkwood. Get a few warm days and the snow in the trees melts and drips onto the powder below, transforming it into a sticky oatmeal.

Arrival, information, and getting around

Twelve miles southwest of South Lake, Sierra is the first resort reached on Hwy-50 coming in to South Lake from the west. Between South Lake and Sierra, Hwy-50 winds perilously up Echo Summit. Free **shuttles** depart from multiple locations on the south shore five times over the course of the morning, returning from Sierra hourly throughout the afternoon; call ☎530/541-7548 for pick-up times and reservations. The handy West Slope shuttle ($17

Mountain info

Phone ☏530/659-7453

Snow phone ☏530/659-7475

Website ⊛www.sierratahoe.com

Price $53

Operating times Mid-Nov to (usually soggy) mid-April 9am–4pm weekdays, 8.30am–4pm weekends and holidays

No. of lifts 10, including 3 high-speed quads and 2 surface lifts

Base elevation 6640′

Summit elevation 8852′

Vertical drop 2212′

No. of trails 46

Acreage 2000

Beginner 25%

Intermediate 50%

Expert 25%

Average snowfall 480″

Snowmaking Yes

Night skiing No

Nursery facilities Yes, Wild Mountain, ☏530/659-7453, ext 270, excellent program from 18 months to 5 years; skiing from age 3, snowboarding from 4

round-trip, but includes a $10 discount on lift tickets; ☏530/541-7548) picks up from Sacramento, Folsom, and Placerville on weekends and holidays.

If driving in from the east, use the route described on p.342 to avoid South Lake traffic. For general directions to South Lake, see box on p.333

The mountain

The misconception that Sierra is a small resort – it encircles a hefty 2000 acres – has been propagated by the rather odd decision to place two of the **high-speed quads** right next to slower chairs. This parallel ascent speeds up liftlines when busy, but hardly opens up accessibility. Moving around Sierra's three faces involves considerable traversing.

The best trees, bump runs, and occasional rocky outcrop loom above the base area on the steep front face of **Huckleberry Mountain**, accessed by the Grandview Express. From the summit, it's a short traverse to the mellow blues, glades, and terrain parks of the backside. The slow **Nob Hill** double chair also departs from the base area, depositing skiers on the ridge above the cruising territory of the West Bowl; it's also the most direct lift for the upper mountain halfpipe and pro-hucker terrain park. The superpipe sits alongside the never-ever meadow in the valley floor and can be lapped on the short Easy Rider Express.

When the powder is fresh and deep, the tree skiing ranks among the best in the country, much less Tahoe. Be careful, though; aside from the normal hazards of riding in the trees – hidden obstacles, hitting solid wood at speed – the thick trunks of Sierra's evergreens combined with the region's heavy, wet snowfall create prime conditions for deep **tree wells** (see p.536).

On top of tree runs, experts can explore out of bounds via five backcountry gates. Advanced riders pay an extra $25 on top of their lift tickets for a three-and-a-half hour **ski-patrol led tour**, which includes instruction in backcountry skills, the use of avalanche transceivers, and an escape from the mountain crowds into uncut, untracked powder. This is an excellent introduction to off-piste skiing, one of the best deals for advanced riders in the country.

Beginner

Though there are many beginners at Sierra, there's not a ton of green terrain. There is a wide, rather busy meadow close to the lodge, which has its own lift but is shared by the superpipe and tubing tow. There are also a few very long, winding runs down the front face, easily mistaken for cat tracks, which get cluttered with bodies on busy days. Fortunately, most of the blues here are tame enough for progressing beginners; head for the **backside** trails first, but steer clear of the busy terrain parks.

Intermediate

After warming up on the backside runs and exhausting the long, sheltered, occasionally moguled West Bowl cruisers, confident intermediates can take some of the blacks on the front face. Directly above the lodge, the wide, steep **Lower Main** blue serves as a good transition between the two. For an introduction to powder and tree skiing, try the backside's gentle glades under the El Dorado lift.

Expert

The long, narrow, steep blacks on the front face get bumped out fast. The terrain here pitches and rolls, dropping steeply in places. For tight trees stay right off the front face chairlifts. To the left, drop off the **Sugar N Spice** cat track into more gladed forests but keep an eye out for rock drops, stumps, and fallen logs. The **Avalanche Bowl** is a tucked-away powder patch under the Nob Hill lift.

Freestyle

Catering to the loyal, local freestyle contingent, the parks here are well built and busy, even though their location on the mountain's flattest runs can be frustrating in slow conditions. Warm up on the artificial rollers and small kickers littering the mellow backside runs before taking on the **Alley Park** under its own access lift. Though the Alley Park may be short and flat, the jumps and rails are anything but. The **halfpipe** under Nob Hill doesn't suffer just because there's a **superpipe** down by the lodge; both are groomed. Sierra also maintains a decent snowskate park and permits their use mountain-wide.

Lift tickets, lessons, and rentals

Only a few dollars cheaper than Heavenly or Squaw, Sierra is costly for its size if you don't take advantage of the many promotions and lodging packages offered locally. Purchase your **ticket** at South Lake sporting goods stores for a $6 discount or pick up Value Season Vouchers from NorCal and Reno ski shops (including REI) for significant low-season discounts. Young adult tickets (ages 13–22) are around $10 cheaper than full adult price; kids' and seniors' tickets are more deeply discounted; and those under 5 ski free. Sierra runs the Double Whammy **season pass** in conjunction with sister resort Northstar (see p.357). The cheapest version (midweek only, bought preseason) costs just over $200 and can be purchased online.

Group **lessons** begin at just over $30 per two-hour session. As at sister resort Northstar, advanced instruction is offered free. Sierra is also home to a Burton Learn-To-Ride center (see p.534). Two-day packages don't come cheap but do include specially designed beginner boards, one small group lesson, and one private lesson ($170). The resort maintains a well-equipped, heavily used **rental** department at typical California resort prices. Cheaper rentals are available in town (see p.346).

Practicalities

With **no accommodation** at the ski area, Sierra runs lift-and-lodging packages in conjunction with South Lake hotels and motels (see p.342–43). The tone for resort **dining** is set by the PUVs (Pizza Utility Vehicles) that circumnavigate the parking lots at day's end; food at the resort is fuel plain and simple, so don't expect any gourmet chili or ethnic interpretations. At the base lodge, an outdoor expresso cart and bakery offer quick breakfasts. Later in the day, in good weather everyone hangs out on the barbecue deck with bag lunches; when it's colder, the action moves upstairs to a simple sports-bar pub. At the top of the front face, the *Grandview Grill* serves up the expected array of items; the best value are the wraps, big enough for two, and a roof deck affords great lake views. Lastly there's a warming tent and snack stop in the West Bowl, where mean barbecues are held on sunny weekends.

Kirkwood

Volcanic sentinels high on the crest of the Sierras surround **Kirkwood**, the most remote Lake Tahoe ski area, some 35 miles southwest of the lake along scenic Hwy-88. The powder that falls into this snowtrap is considered the lightest and deepest in the region – find yourself here on a mid-week powder morning and lines are yours for the taking, a marked contrast to the furiously tracked-out slopes elsewhere in Tahoe. Often described as a smaller version of Squaw, it does share the same box canyon layout, wide open bowls, above-treeline rocky terrain, and formidable chutes, cornices, and forested gullies, but the differences are mostly to its advantage: smaller crowds, a retro feel, and greater affordability.

Indeed the trappings of a modern resort have been sluggish to develop here, dating back to when the Sierra Club sued the Forest Service upon the opening of the ski area in 1972, not taking kindly to the intrusion upon this pristine valley. Most lifts are slow and the resort remains little more than a cluster of condo complexes at the base of the mountain, despite the construction of a few additional luxury residences and a so-called "village" – really just a condo-hotel, a small pedestrian plaza, ice rink, and a couple of outlying buildings.

Mountain info

Phone ☎209/258-6000, central reservations ☎1-800/967-7500

Snow phone ☎1-877/KIRKWOOD

Website ☷www.kirkwood.com

Price $54

Operating times Late Nov to early May daily lifts 9am–4pm, lodge 7.30am–7pm

No. of lifts 12, including 1 express quad and 2 surface

Base elevation 7800′

Summit elevation 9800′

Vertical drop 2000′

No. of trails 65 plus many unnamed bowl runs

Acreage 2300

Beginner 15%

Intermediate 50%

Expert 35%

Average snowfall 500″

Snowmaking Yes (but only 4 runs)

Night skiing No

Nursery facilities Yes, ages 2–6, at the Mini Mountain Center next to the Red Cliffs Day Lodge (☎209/258-7274); skiing ages 4–12 and snowboarding ages 7–12 at the Mighty Mountain Center in Timber Creek, ☎209/258-7754

Arrival and getting around

The resort's own hype on being the closest Tahoe resort to Sacramento and the Bay Area is not strictly true. On a clear day with no traffic, Hwy-88 could be considered a shortcut, but it's also a winding, two-lane mountain road, cursed by frequent avalanche closures. While Carson Pass on Hwy-88 south from the lake is usually cleared quickly, skiers coming from the west are not so lucky. Call the snow report before setting out.

From the south shore, take Emerald Bay Road south and look for the Hwy-89 junction just after the California agricultural checkpoint in Meyers. Turn right onto Hwy-88 eleven miles down the road in Hope Valley. For information on Reno's airport, car rental, and general directions to South Lake Tahoe, see the box on p.333. A free shuttle makes a daily run from motels and hotels on the south shore; call the resort for pick-up schedule. If driving, try to get into the parking lot next to the day lodge. A free shuttle runs between outer parking lots, Timber Creek beginner area, and the lifts.

The mountain

Kirkwood is a seriously challenging mountain when conditions are right, loaded with black groomers and acres of rolling powder fields, steep chutes, cliffs, and gullies. There are a few dedicated beginner slopes and a fair cross-section of terrain for intermediates, but those looking for miles of cruising terrain should go to Heavenly instead (see p.358).

The front face of the mountain is a small horseshoe-shaped valley curved around Kirkwood Meadows. Timber Creek, the treelined never-ever area, marks the western boundary. In the center is the "village" and a cluster of lifts that access the front-face steeps, a handful of intermediate runs, beginner cruisers, and traverses over to the backside. The Red Cliffs day lodge sits at the base of the eastern boundary, five minutes walk from the central lifts.

Chairlifts here are both numbered and named, but numbers are more commonly used. Chair 2, swinging above the pro terrain park, is the gateway to the cornices, rocks, intermediate cruisers, and glades of Kirkwood's large backside area. Keep your speed when returning past the base of this lift, as the trail funnels into a run that goes slightly uphill. Off the summit of Chair 2, rolling blues spill through the trees to a flat meadow in the center of the backside bowl, home to the *Sunrise Grill*, Kirkwood's barbecue deck and suntrap. Slow Chair 4 climbs to Kirkwood's farthest boundary, accessing a wide-open bowl of intermediate and advanced cruisers, the long Wave cornice, powder fields, and small cliff drops. You can also traverse back toward the front face from the top of Chair 4, dropping off Thunder Saddle through the technical, cliff-strewn descents of the eastern slope of Eagle Bowl. The lone high-speed quad on the mountain – Chair 6 – accesses only black terrain.

Beginner

The **Timber Creek Day Lodge**, reached via a free shuttle from the main village, has the most secluded beginner runs, its own lift, mini-terrain park, and access to next-step blues. On the main mountain try the slopes under Chair 1 that run down the center of the base area, wide cruisers popular with beginner skiers though too flat for beginning boarders.

Intermediate

The lower slopes of the front face are ideal for intermediates. Accessible from both Timber Creek and the main village, they are fairly short but offer a good variety of terrain. Keep to the runs off Chairs 5 and 7 unless you're really confident on steeps. For long, rolling cruisers, head to the blues on the backside, following the traverse from Chair 1 to Chair 2. Once at the far boundary, traverse under **The Wave** cornice (watching out for leaping skiers from above) for a taste of powder in Devil's Draw and mellow glades off Fawn Ridge.

Expert

Only the best (or craziest) attempt the towering **Sisters**, one of Kirkwood's signature bands of rock that crest the horseshoe ridge. But there are many less treacherous challenges from the double-diamond downhiller's **Wall** to multiple chutes descending from the horseshoe rim of the front face. Not known for moguls, Kirkwood's bumps are usually found directly under Chair 6. Hike to rider's left off, past the larval fingers of Glove Rock, for some of the best powder stashes and tree runs. If you head to the less crowded back bowl and traverse across to **Thunder Saddle** you'll get to choose either open powder fields or the short, steep chutes below the **Cirque**.

Freestyle

After a recent storm, the mountain *is* the terrain park. Check the natural half-pipe gullies in and under Palisades Bowl and the cornices, rocks, and rollers under Chair 4. There's a rather tattered **superpipe** under Chair 5 taking up the entire width of a run. Try the hits and jibs above the pipe or head to the **park** under Chair 2 – larger, occasionally windblown, but better maintained. Baby kickers are found over by the Timber Creek beginner area.

Lift tickets, lessons, and rentals

Kirkwood was the first Tahoe resort to introduce an affordable **season pass** and its midweek version is still one of the best deals in the country, with few blackout days. Passes can be purchased online, include discount guest tickets, and are least expensive if bought before the end of November (from $199). Members of discount mega-market Costco can pick up Kirkwood four-packs for day discounts of over $10 a ticket.

Beginner **lessons** are held both on the wide, flat meadow in front of the main village and at the secluded Timber Creek area, home to the Mighty Mountain kids' center. Advanced packages are offered, including women's camps and NASTC (North American Ski Training Center) multiday residential programs for advanced skiers. Lessons begin at $40 for group sessions and can be prebooked on ☎209/258-7245.

The resort currently has a monopoly on **rentals** in the valley, making ski packages extremely expensive; expect to pay $30 for a basic package and $50 for demos. See the box on South Lake rentals (see p.346) for more sensible places to rent beforehand.

Accommodation

One advantage of Kirkwood's size and layout is that almost all of its **accommodations** are ski-in, ski-out, located either right on the slopes or across the access road. Managed by the resort (reservations ☎1-800/967-7500), lodging is limited to a small selection of condos. Anchoring the tiny pedestrian village are the *Mountain Club* and *Lodge at Kirkwood*, both large, luxury condo-hotels decked out in the usual timber and stone, but without the oppressive scale common to recent mountain developments elsewhere. Units range in size from hotel studios to three bedrooms, and use of the Mountain Club spa is included. Other recently built condos include the luxury *Snowcrest*, *Meadow Stone*, and *Timber Ridge* lodges. Of the older buildings, *Sun Meadows* is a little shabby but closest to the village while *Thimblewood* and *Edelweiss* are apartment-style complexes across from Timber Creek day lodge. **Rates** start at $139 for a hotel-style room, $199 for a one-bedroom condo, with various ski-and-stay deals.

Most riders seeking nightlife and budget accommodation choose to base themselves on the south shore (see p.342–43). If you want to be on the Kirkwood side of Carson Pass, an alternative is *Caples Lake* (☎209/258-8888, ⓦwww .capleslakeresort.com; rooms ❹, cabins ❺), ten minutes down the road at 1111 Hwy-88. The creaky lodge has a warm dining area and clean but spartan rooms, while its collection of rustic fishing cabins sleep 4–6 and are a better deal; wood-burning stoves and a sauna are among the amenities. A more upmarket cabin resort is *Sorensen's* in Hope Valley, halfway between Kirkwood and South Lake – see p.343 for details.

Eating, drinking, and entertainment

There are only a couple of **restaurants** here. Like everything at Kirkwood, they're steps from the slopes and function as both on- and off-mountain dining. Tahoe's predominance as a weekend destination is aptly demonstrated by the fact that *Off the Wall* (☎209/258-7365), the resort's showpiece restaurant in the timber-and-stone *Lodge at Kirkwood*, is only open for dinner Fridays, Saturdays, and holidays. Bistro standards like burgers and chili are served daily at lunch. *Monte Wolfe's*, in the base of the *Mountain Club* (☎209/258-7246), is an odd combo of mountain canteen and coffee shop, not much in the way of food but the couches and books are nice touches. Red Cliffs day lodge has a better selection of **cafeteria** standards (taco bar, burgers, sandwiches) and a fine choice of beers. Timber Creek lodge is a cafeteria by day and pizza place on Friday, Saturday, and holiday evenings.

Down on Hwy-88 is the *Kirkwood Inn* (☎209/258-7304), an atmospheric, rough-hewn log cabin founded by pioneer settler Zachary Kirkwood in 1864. The skillet breakfasts dished out here are large enough to slow down the hungriest skier and lunches – hearty burgers, potatoes, and plenty of cheese – and are best followed with a nap. Happy hour drinks and tacos are served 3–5pm.

Nightlife is pretty much nonexistent; Kirkwood holds its regular resort-sponsored parties in South Lake. The slightly sterile *Bub's Sports Bar and Grill* (☎209/258-7225), across the road from *Off the Wall*, has video games, pool, and big-screen TVs to occupy the quiet evenings.

Other activities and attractions

Kirkwood's **cross-country** center (☎209/258–7248) is highly rated with 80km of upper elevation trials, three warming huts, and even a "kiddie kilometer" spiced up with animal cutouts. From the cozy, modern rental cabin on Hwy-88, beginners start out in the meadow and progress to gently climbing trails in the Eldorado National Forest; picnic, evening, and full-moon trips are regular offerings. Trail passes $20, lesson packages from $42, dogs permitted ($3).

Other off-slope activities include a small, inexpensive **tubing park** and an **ice rink** ($8 with rentals; Mon–Fri 2–6pm, Sat–Sun noon–6pm). More creative options include **dog sled** rides around Kirkwood meadow with Running Creek Sled Dogs (☎775/266-4720) or **ice fishing** on neighboring Caples and Silver lakes (contact the *Caples Lake* resort, see "Accommodation" above).

Mount Bachelor

Mount Bachelor lays claim to some of the finest cruising runs in North America, premium freestyle terrain, and hundreds of acres of perfectly spaced trees lining the volcanic slopes. Rising from central Oregon's high desert, the ski area essentially spreads 360-degrees around a single molten peak, the flanks of which are relatively flat. Curving trails dip and roll affably across the volcano's natural contours, with pockets of perfectly spaced trees that'll plaster idiot grins on the faces of adventurous riders.

Inconsistent **weather** is Mount Bachelor's sole drawback. During the first half of the season especially, it's possible that visibility will be low, winds excessive, and the top-third and backside of the mountain closed. You could just as likely show up for fresh powder every day – the resort averages a very respectable 350 inches of desert-air snow that's far drier than the maritime cement which falls on Mount Hood to the north. Consider visiting during the calmer spring season, which runs through the end of May. Regardless of when you visit, liftlines are virtually nonexistent.

As it's surrounded for miles on all sides by the protected timberlands of the Deschutes

Mountain info	
Phone ☎1-800/829-2442	
Snow phone ☎541/382-7888	
Website ✪www.mtbachelor.com	
Price $44, $47 holidays	
Operating times Mid-Nov to May Mon–Fri 9am–4pm, Sat–Sun 8am–4pm	
No. of lifts 12, including 2 surface tows	
Base elevation 6300′	
Summit elevation 9065′	
Vertical drop 3365′	
No. of trails 71	
Acreage 3683	
Beginner 15%	
Intermediate 50%	
Expert 35%	
Average snowfall 350″	
Snowmaking Minimal	
Night skiing No	
Nursery facilities Yes, 6 weeks to 10 years old; reservations required on ☎541/382-1709	

National Forest, Mount Bachelor's infrastructure is minimal. The main West Village Base Area along with the smaller Sunrise Lodge stopover and an attractive mid-mountain lodge contain restaurants along with rental and retail outfits, but the closest overnight options are located twenty- to thirty-minute drives away in either **Sunriver** or **Bend**. The former is a planned resort community, while the latter (and better) base is a vibrant mountain town of 55,000, with excellent accommodation, restaurant, and nightlife options. The locals are a friendly, healthy bunch, and considering that for several months of the year it's possible to get in a morning of riding on the slopes followed by an afternoon of golfing, hiking, or biking, it's not hard to see why.

Arrival and getting around

The closest **airport** is a regional strip in Redmond, twenty miles north of Bend; Horizon, United Express, and Skywest run direct flights from San Francisco, Seattle, and Portland. Portland international airport is a three- to four-hour drive away. Both airports have major car rental firms, including Avis, Hertz, and National.

Mount Bachelor is a relatively flat 25-mile drive from **Bend** to the northeast on the scenic Hwy-46 (Cascades Lakes Highway). **Sunriver** is a twenty-mile drive to the southeast on Hwy-45. Showchains or a 4WD vehicle are required for either route. Unlike the resorts around Mount Hood, Sno-Park parking passes are not needed. The town of Bend has no public transport. There are, though, resort-run **shuttle buses** running routes to Mount Bachelor from Bend's Park

PHOTO: JEFF CURTES

TAKE A TRIP TO **BURTON.COM** TO
FIND EVERYTHING YOU NEED TO
GET STARTED, GET PACKED
AND GET RIDING.

NEW TO SNOWBOARDING? HEAD
TO **LEARNTOSNOWBOARD.COM** TO
FIND A METHOD CENTER NEAR YOU.

LEARN TO RIDE IS MORE THAN A CALL TO ACTION;
IT IS A PROGRAM THAT BURTON SNOWBOARDS HAS
BUILT IN CONJUNCTION WITH THE BEST SNOWBOARD
INSTRUCTORS ALL OVER THE GLOBE. LTR™ BOARDS,
BOOTS AND BINDINGS ARE ENGINEERED TO MAKE
LEARNING TO RIDE EASY, PAINLESS AND FUN. OUR
GOAL IS TO HAVE YOU LINKING TURNS THE FIRST DAY
BECAUSE ONCE YOU DO YOU'LL BE HOOKED FOR LIFE.

MC
METHOD CENTER

WE WORK CLOSELY WITH RESORTS TO MAKE
SURE THAT METHOD CENTERS PROVIDE THE BEST
LEARNING ENVIRONMENT POSSIBLE. THE KEY TO
GOOD INSTRUCTION AND INDIVIDUAL ATTENTION IS
MAINTAINING A LOW STUDENT-TO-INSTRUCTOR RATIO.
OUR KIDS' METHOD CENTERS SPECIALIZE IN GETTING
GROMS 12 AND UNDER UP AND RIDING WITH THE BEST
OF 'EM. GO TO WWW.METHODCENTER.COM TO FIND THE
METHOD CENTER™ NEAREST YOU. WE PROMISE YOUR
LIFE WILL NEVER BE THE SAME.

REDEEM THIS CERTIFICATE AT THE BURTON METHOD
CENTER OF YOUR CHOICE FOR A 10% DISCOUNTED
LESSON. CHECK METHODCENTER.COM FOR DETAILS.

& Ride lot, inconveniently located a very long walk from downtown on the corner of Colorado and Simpson streets. Shuttles depart daily at 7am (weekends), 8.15am, 9.30am, and 11.15am and cost $3 one-way. Should you need a **taxi** in Bend, try Bend Cab (☎541/548-0919) or High Desert Taxi (☎541/475-5892).

The mountain

With its conical shape and speedy lifts, navigating Mount Bachelor is simple. Approximately three-fifths of the area is immediately accessible via the lifts, while the wilder southern face and peak are opened to experts when conditions allow.

The east-facing front face, the oldest skied section of the mountain, has all but two of the resort's dozen lifts. The highest and often closed **Summit Express** is the sole chair leading up the steeper top third of the mountain, a treeless expanse whipped by the wind into a powder and ice meringue. Below here a row of high-speed chairs access a fair chunk of the resort's intermediate terrain, beginner runs, and the superpipe and terrain parks that rightfully rank high on *Transworld Snowboarding*'s best-of lists. Nearby, right of the West Village base, is a large and treeless cinder cone that holds fresh lines for days after the latest storm. To climb this geological oddity, speed up its backside via Leeway, hiking whatever portion remains.

The remaining pair of lifts head up the newer **Northwest Territory**, which has quickly become a favorite of both locals and visitors even though northern winds mean temperatures can be markedly colder. The approximately thousand acres of terrain are worth the extra layer, as intermediates can run laps on Outback Express while experts stick to the Northwest Express chair, both high-speed quads accessing narrow trails that drunkenly weave up to 2400 vertical feet.

To the delight of the substantial snowboarding contingency, moguls are scarce from consistent **grooming** and wall-to-wall corduroy is a standard feature of most trails. All lifts are efficient with the sole exception being the Rainbow triple on the resort's eastern boundary. While you'll want to avoid this lift on a powder day, head here if it hasn't snowed recently to search out hidden stashes and some nice drops in the trees.

Beginner

Mount Bachelor is best suited for daring beginners willing to move around the slopes. Newbies and those looking to warm up rusty joints should head first to the **Sunshine Accelerator** chair and its pair of short, flat green runs. Outside of this small beginner zone, green runs are dappled across the lower half of the mountain's front face. This means beginners will need to hop from lift to lift, occasionally crossing more advanced runs. If looking to stick to one lift, stay on the Sunrise Express and run laps on **Marshmallow** and **Rooster Tail**, two tree-lined greens that curve pleasingly for around 800 vertical feet.

Intermediate

Half of the trails on Mount Bachelor are rated blue and virtually every one blows away the average cruiser. Cutting the front face in half, the Skyline Express quad leads to the first group of long, snaking blues with near-perfect pitches. Chugging down the widest trail, **Cliff Hanger**, feels like riding down the spine of a massive dragon, with immense ripples falling down its entire length. From here, head to the Summit Express quad to scope the views from Bachelor's peak. Both wide and impeccably groomed, **Beverly Hills** and **Healy Heights** are a carver's delight and the easiest way down, but if feeling confident cut further right to explore **Cow's Face** (see "Experts" below). In the opposite direction from Skyline Express, the Pine Marten Express quad cuts over several worthy blues en route to the resort's ultimate intermediate nirvana, **The Outback**. Taking up half of the heavily wooded northwest face and accessed via the Outback Express quad, The Outback consists of 1800 vertical feet of some of the finest intermediate terrain in North America. The six long, narrow runs here are full of dips and curves and the trees – especially those between **Down Under** and **Ed's Garden** – are spaced perfectly for exploration.

Expert

Experts who crave extended steep runs could easily become bored in a day or two, especially if the Summit Express chair is shut down. But those who don't mind trading plunges for curvaceous single black runs along with substantial glades could happily spend the season here. Off the Summit Express quad to the skier's right, **Cow's Face** is a wide region laced with gullies and intersecting fall lines. To the left, a traverse leads into the lower half of **The Cirque**, where the resort's steepest (though short) lines await. When winds are calm, two more difficult options open atop the summit. The first is a short hike to the mountain's peak, from where it's possible to bomb the entirety of The Cirque, launching off some major cornices. The second is the **South Ridge** gate, leading into the "controlled backcountry" of Bachelor's isolated southern face. Not shown on the trail map, this adrenaline-filled zone has hundreds of powderfield-to-glade lines that eventually bottom out at a traverse leading back around the mountain to the **Northwest Express** chair. A ride up here leads to the resort's second expert playground, a web of six single black runs that are just as enticing as The Outback (see "Intermediate" above) but steeper. Top runs include the narrow, plunging **Devil's Backbone** and **Spark's Lake Run**, which can be used to access more woods on the southern face before hitting the traverse back to Northwest Express.

Freestyle

Slightly ahead of Mount Hood Meadows for best freestyle terrain in the Northwest, Mount Bachelor has both amazing purpose-built playgrounds and natural features off which to jib and jump. The largest park is the **Air Chamber**, running nearly a mile in length beneath the Skyliner Express quad. Several rails dot the top and bottom of the park, while the middle holds a dozen or so jumps ranging from medium-sized to pro-only level. Should this park be too intense, smaller (though still challenging) jumps and rails are collected in a park beneath the Pine Marten Express quad. The resort also maintains an Olympic-caliber **superpipe** along with a baby halfpipe for first-timers. As for natural terrain, the mountain is loaded with hips, dips, and drops. Try befriending a local for a guided tour or start by exploring the trees around **Bushwacker** in The Outback for some BMX-style trails loaded with drops.

Lift tickets, lessons, and rentals

Lift tickets, self-scanned electronically at every lift, are affordably priced at $44 per day. Teens (13–18) pay $37, while tickets for kids 12 and under go for $26. Multiday tickets give savings of a couple of dollars per day. Mount Bachelor's **ski school** offers courses for ages 4 and up, ranging in cost from $50 for a two-hour class to $300 for an all day private lesson.

    Rentals, available at both base areas, start with basic $26 ski and board packages. High-performance packages are $35, while demos from the West Village ski shop are $40 for skis (Salomon, Volkl, Dyanastar) and $45 for boards (Burton, Salomon). If staying in Bend, stop by Skjersaa's Sport Shop, 130 SW Century Drive (daily 8am–6pm; ☎541/382-2154), for better priced packages starting at $22 and rising to $33 for demos.

Accommodation

With no slopeside **accommodation** on offer, your two base choices are Bend or Sunriver. Bend is a far better alternative with a decent range of budget lodging and access to the town's amenities. The only drawback is a scarcity of options within walking distance of downtown, but you're likely to arrive via car so it's only a minor inconvenience. For inexpensive options try one of the dilapidated motels a mile south of downtown on SE 3rd Street, like the *Sonoma Lodge* (☎541/382-4891; ❶) or *Cascade Lodge* (☎541/382-2612; ❶).

Bend Riverside Motel 1565 NW Hill St ☎541 /389-2363 or 1-800/284-2363, ⓦwww .bendriversidemotel.com. A ten-minute walk north of downtown, this two-story motel complex contains an array of suites and cottages, all with kitchenettes and fireplaces. The décor is somewhat dated, but worth overlooking for the competitive prices. The mini-suites and cottages each sleep up to four, while the full-suites can accommodate up to six. Amenities include a heated pool and hot tub. ❸

Mount Bachelor Village Resort 19717 Mount Bachelor Drive ☎541/389-5900 or 1-800/452-9846, ⓦwww.mtbachelorvillage.com The loft and 1–3 condo units at this pseudo-village perched on a canyon high above the Deschutes River are top of the line with easy access to Bend's downtown. All units have full kitchens, fireplaces and decks, and many have private hot tubs with views of Bend's city lights. Guests receive passes to the adjacent Athletic Club of Bend. ❻

Phoenix Inn Suites 300 NW Franklin Ave ☎541 /317-9292 or 1-888/291-4764, ⓦwww.phoenixinn .com. While lacking in character, this chain hotel has the distinct advantage of being on the edge of Bend's small downtown. All 117 rooms are suites with microwave, fridge, and a leather couch, and offer access to an indoor pool and hot tub. ❺

Riverhouse 3075 N Business 97 ☎541/389-3111 or 1-800/547-3928. Large, Seventies-era lodging spread across both sides of the Deschutes River a short drive north of downtown. Rates are very reasonable and there are a variety of rooms and suites to choose from. Amenities include an on-site laundry, continental breakfast, and an indoor pool. Good ski-package deals as well. ❸

Sunriver Resort ☎1-800/547-3922, ⓦwww .sunriver-resort.com. Known as one of the finest golfing retreats in the Northwest, *Sunriver* is a 3500-acre resort community south of Mount Bachelor that has a large collection of condominiums and hotel rooms in the centralized *Lodge Village*. It's an excellent destination resort if you're looking for personalized service along with access to private pools, spas, and restaurants but it's only minimally closer to the slopes than downtown Bend. Hotel ❺, condos ❼

Eating and drinking

Bend offers a diverse array of **restaurants** ranging from brewpubs to Thai cuisine, most within the small downtown core or on Galveston Avenue en route to the ski area. Mount Bachelor runs a few restaurants of its own, but as you're going to be sleeping in Bend (or Sunriver) it makes more sense to head back and eat in town so you can change prior to dinner. If you haven't brought along a packed lunch, stop in at the cafeteria at the mid-mountain *Pine Marten Lodge* for the typical resort spread along with some more original choices like soba noodles ($5).

Later in the evenings, Bend's **nightlife** scene is geared toward beers and conversation, with either of the two downtown brewpubs good bets. For live music check the listings section in the free weekly *The Source*, stacked in most downtown cafés and on street corners, as bands play at nearly a dozen locations throughout town. There are also two **cinemas**: the ten-screen Old Mill (☎541/312-2866) and the six-screen Pilot Butte (☎541/317-8312).

Bend Brewing Company 1019 NW Brooks St ☎541/383-1599. Slightly cramped, homey brewhouse with an excellent downtown location by the river. The regular menu, mainly salads and sandwiches in the $6–8 range, is bolstered by daily entrée specials like grilled strip steak ($16) and teriyaki tuna ($14). The beers aren't as tasty as the Deschutes Brewing Co's (see below), but the potent Outback Old Ale is a worthy entry.

Big O' Bagels 1032 NW Galveston ☎541/383-2446. Good stop for bagels or deli sandwiches on the way to Mount Bachelor from downtown. Daily 7am–3pm.

Cup of Magic 1304 NW Galveston ☎541/383-2446. Up the road from *Big O' Bagels*, this relaxed bungalow coffeehouse makes for a tasty breakfast detour. Choices include an array of fresh pastries along with a chalkboard full of espresso and chai concoctions.

Deschutes Brewery & Public House 1044 NW Bond St ☎541/382-9242. The Deschutes Brewery's airy downtown brewpub is the local's choice. The beer is fantastic and with a dozen or so on tap it'll take a few visits to sample them all (start with the Mirror Pond Pale Ale). Much of the food, from daily sausage specials to fresh bread, is also made at the brewery. Sandwiches and burgers run $8, while more substantial entrees like fish and chips and BBQ ribs go for $10–18.

Merenda's 900 NW Wall St ☎541/330-2304. This bistro on Bend's main drag has one of the most adventurous menus in town and should be your first choice for a splurge night out. Featuring French and Italian country cuisine, standout options include any of the wood-grilled fish and meats and the Monkfish stew ($18). The wine list is extensive, with up to 75 options available by the glass.

Pine Tavern 976 NW Brooks St ☎541/382-5581. Open since 1936, this riverside restaurant is Bend's most established eatery and firmly anchored in place with 200-year-old Ponderosa pines shooting up through the dining room and out the ceiling. Specializing in hearty meals, entrees include a filet mignon ($25), sirloin and shrimp ($23), and fresh catch of the day and lighter options like smoked salmon salad ($11). Reservations recommended.

Pizza Mondo 811 NW Wall St ☎541/330-9093. This casual "New York Style Pizza" joint serves up authentic pies for dining in, take-out, and delivery. Arrive before 5.30pm to take advantage of the post-slope special: two slices and a pint of beer (or soda) for $5.

Toomie's 119 NW Minnesota Ave ☎541/388-5590. The décor is rather plain but the food is anything but. Choose from spicy and delicious Thai entrées like *gaeng pehd* (a red coconut curry) and crispy catfish in the $12–18 price range.

Other activities and attractions

With acres of untrammeled wilderness nearby, there are plenty of worthwhile activities around Mount Bachelor. Below the ski slopes themselves is the resort's 50km tangle of **cross-country ski** trails. Trail fees are $12 per adult, with rentals available for $20. **Snowmobiling** trails are abundant hereabouts, and Safari Adventures offers a range of tours (☎541/385-5065, ⊛www.andrewmallory.com). If looking to **golf, fish, bike, or hike** during the spring season, there are quality options in every direction; see ⊛www.visitbend.com for more information.

More relaxed pursuits including **shopping** in Bend, both downtown and in the outlet shops in the Old Mill district as well as a tour of the town's **High Desert Museum**, 59800 S Hwy-97 ($5), where exhibits and nature trails illuminate the region's culture and wildlife.

Listings

Avalanche hotline ☎503/808-2400.

Internet access Several stations are available at the main library on NW Wall Street (see below).

Laundry Coin-Op Laundry, 120 NW Greenwood Ave (daily 7am–10.30pm).

Library 507 NW Wall St (Mon–Thurs 10am–8pm, Fri–Sat 10am–5pm, Sun 1–5pm; ☎541/388-6679).

Pharmacy In Ray's Food Place, 210 S Century Drive (Mon–Fri 9am–8pm, Sat 9am–7pm; ☎541/389-9117).

Post office 53 NW Oregon (Mon–Fri 9am–5.15pm).

Supermarket Ray's Food Place, 210 S Century Drive (daily 6am–11pm).

Mount Hood

An imposing, solitary peak, **Mount Hood** (11,245ft) dominates the skyline east of Portland. Viewed from the city, Oregon's tallest mountain appears to be a near perfect, smooth-sided volcano. Closer inspection reveals the sharp cone's true nature: pockmarked with multiple folds and grooves carved out by glaciers, winds and eruptions throughout millennia. Mount Hood's solitary position is both a curse and a blessing, as there's little between it and the ocean to catch incoming storms. This leads to whiteout conditions and dangerously high winds; 500 inch snowfall years are not uncommon. The snow is heavier and wetter than average, but provided you pack waterproof gear there's little to complain about.

Of Mount Hood's three major resorts – there are a couple of minor ski areas as well – **Mount Hood Meadows** is both the biggest and the best. Containing an excellent spread of intermediate, expert, and freestyle terrain, the resort competes with all but the biggest Western resorts. **Timberline** can boast the longest vertical drop in the US Pacific Northwest and substantial freestyle terrain, but only truly comes into its own during summer when both ski/snowboard camps and day-trippers take full advantage of the nearly **year-long season**. **Mount Hood Skibowl**, markedly smaller than both Meadows and Timberline, has an impressive night-skiing operation along with some technical in-bounds terrain.

The lack of a main base, and scant practicalities nearby, keep Mount Hood a commuter mountain; weekend crowds can be an issue. The closest town of size is **Hood River**, forty twisting highway miles north of Mount Meadows. Centered on a few small town blocks, it's better known for windsurfing in the Columbia River Gorge but is still worth considering for its extensive eating and drinking options. Closer to the resorts is tiny **Government Camp**, abutting Mount Hood's Skibowl and just ten- and fifteen-minute drives from Timberline and Meadows respectively. A one-street town lined with massive snowbanks, Govey (as it's known locally) basically hibernates during the winter months before getting overrun with campers come summer. Ten to fifteen miles east en route to Portland are a string of insignificant towns that serve as alternative bases.

Arrival and getting around

Portland's international **airport** is roughly sixty highway miles away from Mount Hood, so it's possible to arrive early in the morning and still get in runs before lunch. Renting a car, one with tire-chains or 4WD, before heading up is essential; all the major car rental firms run offices out of the airport. State-issued Sno-Park **parking permits**, which help pay for the area's extensive plowing operations, are likewise necessary, even for the resort lots, and can be purchased at the resorts themselves or area gas stations and the *Huckleberry Inn*. A daily pass costs $3, three-day $7, and annual $15.

There are two **highway routes** from Portland to Mount Hood. The straightest shot is due east on Hwy-26, approximately sixty miles away from downtown Portland. If stopping in Hood River or heading straight to Mount Hood Meadows, you can also go east via I-84 (past the photogenic Multnomah Falls) to Hwy-35 to ride up Mount Hood's northern flanks, seventy miles in total. This route is often quicker come weekends for Timberline as well, as day-trippers can clog slower Hwy-26.

For those staying in Portland, both Timberline and Mount Hood Meadows run **shuttle bus** services from downtown during busy periods. As times and prices change frequently, you're best off calling the resorts for details.

Mount Hood Meadows

Heavy snowfalls and a large, diverse selection of terrain ensures **Mount Hood Meadows'** standing as one of the finest resorts in the Pacific Northwest. Located on the sunnier and more sheltered east face of Mount Hood, Meadow still has many of the same weather issues, including white-out conditions and lift closures, as Timberline a short drive away. They're not quite as dramatic though, and even when the highest lifts are closed everyone save for those craving extended steeps has plenty to play on. When the entire mountain opens, experts will have little to complain about with the double black terrain of expansive Heather Canyon offering line upon exhilarating line of powder shots.

Save for the steep-sided slopes of Heather Canyon, most of the trails at Meadows twist and turn like narrow mountain highways down the slopes. There are few sustained straights, but visitors don't seem to mind, taking full advantage of the undulating terrain, dipping and weaving in and out of the trees and constantly exploring areas in-between blazed trails. The substantial snowboarding contingency here does just this, treating the entire mountain as one big terrain park. For purpose-built freestyle terrain, the resort has long been a favorite of park-rats and has more than

Mountain info – Mount Hood Meadows

Phone ☎503/337-2222
Snow phone ☎503/386-7547
Website ⊛www.skihood.com
Price $44 (8am–4pm, 11am–7pm, or 1pm–10pm), night $20 (4pm–10pm)
Operating times Mid-Nov to late April Mon–Thurs 8am–4pm, Fri–Sun 8am–10pm
No. of lifts 10, including 2 surface tows
Base elevation 4523´
Summit elevation 7300´
Vertical drop 2777´
No. of trails 87
Acreage 2150
Beginner 15%
Intermediate 50%
Expert 35%
Average snowfall 400˝
Snowmaking No
Night skiing Yes, 22 runs Fri–Sun until 10pm; during Jan and Feb, night skiing is often extended to Wed and Thurs as well
Nursery facilities Yes, 6 weeks to 6 years; reservations on ☎503/337-2222, ext 374

enough jumps, rails, and pipes to fill up a season, let alone a vacation.

Slopeside there's not a whole lot going on at Meadows. The Main Lodge is the larger of two base areas and where you'll find the ski school, rentals shops, and most food options. The Hood River Meadows base is useful only if you've got gear in tow and plan on sessioning the Hood River Express lift.

Beginner

Only a small percentage of Meadows' terrain is rated beginner. Most novice runs, perfectly pitched for learning, are located under the short **Daisy**, **Buttercup**, and **Easy Rider** chairlifts by the main lodge. A terrain park is also typically here, and some might find the freestylers whizzing by nerve-wracking. Beginners with confidence should head to the **Hood River Express** chair to run laps on the long, slow-zone blues running beneath it.

Intermediate

Heather Canyon aside, blue cruisers stretch across the entire mountain and even less confident intermediates will be able to work their way down from every chair. From the Cascade Express lift, a trio of wide blues – **Texas Trail**, **Catacombs**, and **Boulevard** – are perfect for warming up on. Nearby, **Ridge**

Run is another excellent blue, lined with trees on either side, loaded with drops and banked turns. On the opposite side of the mountain, the Shoot Star Express and Hood River Express chair both lead to the longer **Vanguard** and **Apollo** runs. Both are challenging with relatively steep pitches but wide enough for smooth carving. The entire area accessed via the Hood River Express lift is below the main lodge and designated as a slow-skiing zone. The weaving **Tamarack** and **Kinniknick** cruisers here are best except on warmer spring days when their lower portions become soupy and sluggish.

Expert

When open, **Heather Canyon**, a "controlled backcountry" zone, is the place to head. Accessed via the Cascade and Shooting Star chairs, the entire area is rated double black and hundreds of steep lines shoot down two powder-rich canyons (Newton Canyon is a smaller cleft on the resort boundary), both leading to a bumpy gully that leads to a double chair at the base. Below Heather Canyon is an even more extreme area, entered through two control gates off Park Place. This forested zone – including **Elk**, **Yoda**, and **God's Wall** – is for advanced experts only; be aware that there's a very large cliffband here, so don't dive in without a knowledgeable partner. In-bounds, try the line of mini-bowls to the skier's right of Mount Hood Express and the short steep shots off Tillicum toward the Shooting Star Express chair.

Another option is to take the **snowcat rides** from the top of Cascade up to within shouting distance of the peak. Well worth the $10 charge (per trip) to access a thousand extra vertical feet (including some nasty chutes) leading into Heather Canyon, it's usually only on offer for ten days in springtime.

Freestyle

Meadows has natural freestyle terrain in spades and some of the finest purpose-built parks and pipes on the West Coast. The bowls and trees off either side of Ridge Run are pockmarked with natural features, but there are hidden hits and cliff-drops from boundary to boundary. Pinning down the exact location of **terrain parks** before arriving is more problematic, as the resort often changes their location based on snowfall. In all but the worst conditions you can expect to find three top-notch terrain parks (best classified as medium, hard, and insane) and a pair of fresh-cut halfpipes. In March, look out for the Vegetate competition where both pros and amateurs launch off the biggest jumps.

Lift tickets, lessons, and rentals

Adult **lift tickets** are $44 and can be bought for three different "shifts": 8am–4pm, 11am–7pm, or 1–10pm. Kids (7–12) and seniors pay $25 for the same, and night-only tickets (4–10pm) cost $20 for everyone. The resort's ski school offers an array of courses, with a special emphasis on programs for youngsters. Classes start as low as $35 for a ninety-minute session. For rentals, there's no need to stop en route as the resort has a fine selection to choose from. The main rental station offers Rossignol skis ($25) and boards ($28), while the demo shop next door rents out high-end skis (Salomon, Volkl) and boards (Burton, Salomon) for $45.

Mount Hood Skibowl

Directly next door to Government Camp, **Mount Hood Skibowl** is best known for its substantial night-skiing operation. With some 350 acres of varied terrain lit every night, it's one of the largest in the country and draws visitors from Portland for midweek evenings. The resort is at a substantially lower altitude than its larger neighbors, so if conditions are wet or sticky head higher up to Timberline's or Meadows' smaller networks of night-skiing trails.

With short runs twisting through narrow tree-lined alleys, the entire lit area – open in the morning Friday through Sunday only, save holidays – feels cut from the same cloth as East Coast resorts. Taking up slightly more than half of the ski area, this tight warren of runs makes for a refreshing change from typical wide-open Western style skiing. Unfortunately, the steady mix of green, blue, and black runs (along with decent freestyle features) are hard to fully enjoy due to an antique lift system. Lines are rarely a problem, but the four lifts here are all painfully slow double chairs. Open only during the day and when conditions warrant, the remaining – and most decidedly different – area within the resort's boundaries is known as **The Outback**, which takes up several hundred acres of black and double black diamond terrain laced with chutes, glades, and copious cliff drops. It's worth exploring after a storm, and partnering up is recommended.

Slopeside, Skibowl has two **base areas**, East and West, both home to cafés and

Mountain info – Mount Hood Skibowl

Phone ☎503/272-3206
Snow phone ☎503/222-2695
Website ⊛www.Skibowl.com
Price $38 all day, $20 night only
Operating times Late Nov to mid-April Mon–Thurs 3.30–10pm, Fri 9am–11pm, Sat 8.30am–11pm, Sun 8.30am–10pm
No. of lifts 8, including 4 surface tows
Base elevation 3500′
Summit elevation 5027′
Vertical drop 1527′
No. of trails 65
Acreage 960
Beginner 20%
Intermediate 40%
Expert 40%
Average snowfall 300″
Snowmaking Minimal
Night skiing Yes, 34 runs nightly (until 10pm Sun–Thurs, 11pm Fri–Sat)
Nursery facilities Yes, 6 months to 6 years Fri–Sun only; reservations on ☎503/810-8391

rental shops. For The Outback, park at the West base. While there are some ambitious expansion plans afoot (including a condo complex and gondola linking up to Timberline), for now the biggest buzz slopeside occurs at the East base's **adventure park**, which includes several tubing lanes, kiddie snowmobiles, and a 500ft zipline. Call the main information line for individual prices.

Lift tickets, lessons, and rentals

At only $20, night **passes** are a great value; day passes running $38 are expensive for the amount of terrain, though kids ride for $10 less and those 6 and under ride for free. The resort does have a **ski school**, but both those at Timberline and Meadows draw better instructors with more choices. Ski **rentals** are affordably priced at $15–20 depending on night-only/full-day options, while boards jump up to $25–30.

Timberline

Timberline is known to skiers around the world because its slopes stay open year-round; see the box on p.379 for full details on the resort's unrivaled summer/fall period. During the winter/spring season, however, the tall and narrow ski area is less heralded, and deciding whether or not to visit depends on one main point: whether or not it's a "Palmer Day." The **Palmer Snowfields** cover the ski area's upper third, a powder-rich expanse loaded with bumps and folds to play in, and this is where the summer camps set up shop. It's an exhilarating zone that gives Timberline the longest vertical drop in the region, but unfortunately more often than not Palmer's lift shuts down in winter as high winds and heavy cloud cover batter the unsheltered peak.

If the Palmer quad isn't running, odds are high the next lift down, the Magic Mile express quad, will also be closed. The only other chair rising high above the resort's eponymous lodge, it leads to a satisfying clutch of wide blues and a few patches of glades. Call ahead to check on the status of these two lifts or better yet drive up – the snowphone is notoriously over-optimistic – to ask an employee before purchasing lift tickets.

The remaining chairs beneath Palmer and Magic Mile cover the lower half of Timberline, where dozens of trails criss-cross forested terrain. The runs here are fun enough, but only freestylers have adequate terrain for a full day of exploration. Jibbers and jumpers will have a blast on **Paint Brush**, a long terrain park loaded with rails and giant wedges. In the glades one run over, known locally as the **Bone Zone**, are scores of dips, lips, and hips. Across the remaining lower portion of the ski area there are a handful of worthwhile green, blue, and black runs, but fewer options than at Mount Hood Meadows a short drive away.

Regardless of the weather conditions, all visitors to the region should visit the resort for a tour, meal, or overnight stay at the *Timberline Lodge*; see the accommodation and restaurant reviews on p.378 and p.380 for details.

see the accommodation and restaurant reviews on p.378 and p.380 for details.

Mountain info – Timberline
Phone ☎1-807/754-6734
Snow phone ☎503/222-2211
Website ⊛www.timberlinlodge.com
Price $39, night $20
Operating times All year except two weeks post Labor Day; Winter/Spring season Sun–Thurs 9am–4pm, Fri–Sat 9am–10pm; Summer/Fall season 7am–1pm
No. of lifts 6
Base elevation 4950′
Summit elevation 8540′
Vertical drop 3590′
No. of trails 32
Acreage 1430
Beginner 30%
Intermediate 50%
Expert 20%
Average snowfall 350″
Snowmaking No
Night skiing Yes, two chairs open Fri, Sat, and holidays 4pm–close
Nursery facilities No

Lift tickets, lessons, and rentals

All-day adult lift **tickets** include the night-skiing session and are $38; juniors (7–12) pay $22, while kids 6 and under ski free. Night passes (4pm until close) are $18 for all ages, and summer tickets are $38 across the board. The **ski school** here is a good one, though there's not a huge array of beginner runs to learn on. Classes start as low as $45 for a two-hour lesson with lift pass and rentals. The resort **rents** K2 and Rossignol snowboards at $33 a day, while Rossignol and Salomon skis are rented out at $22; evening rates are $5–10 cheaper.

Accommodation

As the *Timberline Lodge* offers the only slopeside **accommodation** in the state, you'll probably be staying off-mountain. Government Camp is the most central accommodation base, and the small towns of Brightwood and Welches to the east are the next closest with limited but worthwhile choices. To the north of the mountain larger Hood River has dozens of hotels and motels to choose from (most with $25 lift ticket packages to Mount Hood Meadows) in a slightly more happening setting. If willing to tack on the extra drive time from Hood River, the large *Best Western Hood River Inn* on the banks of the Columbia River is one of the best options (ⓣ1-800/828-7873, ⓦwww.hoodriverinn.com; ③). Many visitors rent one of the cabins or fully stocked chalets in and around Government Camp; check with Cascade Property Management (ⓣ503/622-3212, ⓦwww.mthoodrentals.com) for details.

Government Camp and Timberline

Falcon's Crest 87287 Government Camp Loop ⓣ503/272-3403 or 1-800/624-7384, ⓦwww.falconscrest.com. Quaint, traditional B&B with a Christmas theme mixed in among a wealth of collectibles. Five individually decorated en-suite rooms are available (Safari Room, Mexicalli Suite, etc) and amenities include a TV lounge, a selection of wines and beers, and full breakfasts. Six-course gourmet dinners for $40 per person also offered with advanced notice. ⑤

Huckleberry Inn Government Camp Loop ⓣ503/272-3352, ⓦwww.huckleberry-inn.com. The top budget choice and most centrally located Government Camp accommodation, the *Huckleberry* has sixteen rooms above its restaurant. A few two-bedroom units with kitchens are available for $140 per night, while the rest of the plain though clean options are motel-style units cramming up to six visitors. A bunkroom sleeping groups of up to fourteen is also available for $160 per night. ③

Mount Hood Inn 87450 Government Camp Loop ⓣ503/272-3205 or 1-800/443-7777, ⓦwww.mthoodinn.com. A clean and simple inn at the bottom end of Government Camp's main drag, within walking distance of Skibowl. The majority of the sixty rooms available are generic motel-style, but eight suites with hot tubs and king beds are also available. All rooms have cable TV and fridge, and useful extras include underground parking, a laundry room, an indoor hot tub, VCRs for rent, and a basic continental breakfast. ⑤

Timberline Lodge Timberline ski area ⓣ503/622-7979 or 1-800/547-1406, ⓦwww.timberlinelodge.com. A tourist attraction in its own right, the *Timberline Lodge* was constructed in the 1930s as a WPA project. Sitting at 6000ft, the views are nearly as impressive as the structure itself, built with massive hand-hewn timbers and native stone. Grand enough to be used as the setting for *The Shining*, there are a total of seventy surprisingly affordable guestrooms, most with private bathrooms and cable TV. A handful of dorm rooms are available as well. Amenities include a sporadically open heated outdoor pool and hot tub. Dorms ③, guestrooms ④

The outlying eastern towns

The Brightwood Guest House 64725 E Barlow Trail, Brightwood ⓣ503/622-5783 or 1-888/503-5783. A cedar-paneled guesthouse off the Sandy River that can squeeze up to six. A koi pond by the front door hints at the interior of the one-bedroom home, laden with all manner of Oriental bric-a-brac. Amenities include a selection of movies to go with the TV and VCR, fully stocked kitchen, and a large breakfast delivered by the innkeeper who lives next door. ⑤

Hidden Woods B&B 19380 East Summertime Drive, Sandy ⓣ503/622-5754, ⓦwww.thehiddenwoods.com. Perfect for a couple or small family looking for some pampering, this friendly B&B's sole accommodation is a log cabin built in 1929. Located steps from both the Sandy River and an outdoor hot tub, the two-bedroom cabin is outfitted with a marshmallow-soft king bed, clawfoot bathtub, and a roaring fireplace. A six-course breakfast cooked to order included. ⑤

The Resort at the Mountain 68010 Fairway Ave, Welches ⓣ503/622-3101 or 1-800/669-7666, ⓦwww.theresort.com. Visited more come the warmer months for its golf course (which stays open most of the winter nonetheless), accommodations at this sprawling resort are a good deal during the winter season. A total of 160 rooms are available, spilt between standard double queen hotel rooms, studios with king beds and a pullout sofa, and one- and two-bedroom condo units. None would win any interior design awards, but with $20 lift ticket package deals and allowances for four guests in even the smallest rooms, bargain-hunters won't having anything to complain about. ④

Salmon River Retreat Brightwood ⓣ503/622-5706, ⓦwww.salmonriverretreat.com. This guesthouse on the banks of the Salmon River is a unique, memorable accommodation option. The attractive main house, surrounded by towering trees and a riverside deck with a firepit and hottub, is where meals are served. The three small bedrooms are in an annex next door, each loaded with comfortable accessories like feather beds and their own bathrooms as well. The genial innkeeper serves huge gourmet breakfasts daily, and she also offers creative package deals including massage treatments, bird-watching tours, and yoga classes. Next door, a cabin sleeping up to ten can also be rented. ④

Eating and drinking

The **restaurant** situation around Mount Hood is uninspired. Government Camp has only a couple of choices and the best eating out–options are found either in the *Timberline Lodge* or in the towns to the east. If you're visiting for more than a few days you may find the drive out worth it for a change of pace. **Nightlife** is equally low-key, with the *Rathskeller* and *Charlies* in Government Camp the main two bar choices. While the *Rathskeller* roars to life with DJs and bands during the summer camp season, both remain ghostly quiet during the winter season, suitable for a beer and basic pub grub but not much else.

Summer at Timberline

Significant snowfall, a permafrost base (not a glacier, as many inaccurately claim), and expert grooming allow Timberline to stay open **year-round**, the only ski area in the US to do so. Summer operations run from the beginning of May until the end of August, when the resort shuts down for two weeks for maintenance. Over the summer period, two lifts serve the extensive Palmer Snowfield (daily 7am–1.30pm). Mornings are frigid but by midday, when the sun beats down, conditions morph from packed ice to slush. Gate racers arrive early and are off the hill by noon, while jibbers hike late into the afternoon.

Summer tickets ($39) allow access to limited freeskiing terrain and a small terrain park and pipe, squashed on Palmer between the private fiefdoms of the **summer camps**. While the ski racing camps are content to simply lay out gates, diggers for the three longstanding freestyle camps – High Cascade (HCSC), Windells, and smaller Mount Hood – construct playgrounds of pipes, hits, and jibs, from mini hits and rails to superpipes and monster kickers. Pro riders descend here either on a mission to get the last bit of footage for next season's movies or to teach tricks to 10 year-olds. Though adolescents and recent high school grads make up the majority of campers, coaches, and counselors, older adults are welcome too. Adults are typically housed in separate accommodation, usually in semi-private rooms. Rates quoted are per week, and are at their most expensive mid-summer; in addition to the ones below, numerous university teams, ski clubs, and private organizations hold summer ski-training camps on Palmer (details on ⓦwww.timberlinelodge .com.in).

High Cascade Snowboard Camp ☏1-800/334-4272, ⓦwww.highcascade .com. With the largest area on the mountain, a Vans-sponsored skatepark, and a lodge right in Govey, HCSC can get hectic. Adults-only camps are offered at Hood over the summer and at Bachelor during the spring and fall. Mid-June to mid-August, $1395–1700; adult "No Frills" on-mountain only rate, $760.

Mount Hood Snowboard Camp ☏800 /247-5552, ⓦwww.campsnowboard.com. Offering camps at Timberline year-round and accepting only 36 campers per session, the more intimate environ-ment of MHSC is good for riders who want to avoid frenzied snake sessions on the hill; the focus here is strictly snowboarding. $875–1975; day campers are charged half-price.

Windells ☏800/765-7669, ⓦwww .windells.com. Palmer snowfield pioneers, Windells is based out of the old *Shamrock Motel* in Welches, removed from the Govey bustle. The camp's skatepark is legendary and four BMX tracks are hidden in the woods, from beginner to pro. Windells welcomes freestyle skiers in addition to snowboarders. Early June to late August, $1099–1599 per week.

Government Camp's Village Store (Sun–Thurs 8am–7pm, Fri–Sat 8am–8pm) sells basic snacks and beer, but for **groceries** you'll need to stock up en route.

Government Camp and Timberline

The Cascade Dining Room *Timberline Lodge* ☎503/622-7979. Beautifully situated with views of the slopes and mountains further afield, the *Timberline Lodge*'s elegant dining room offers decadent breakfast items like apple-strudel French toast ($10). Lunches are a simpler affair with various soups on offer along with fish and chips ($15) and a creamy linguini dish ($14). For dinner creative entrees include grilled salmon tandoori ($25) and rabbit stuffed with wild mushrooms ($25). Easily the finest restaurant in the area; dinner reservations are recommended.

Huckleberry Inn ☎503/272-3352. On Government Camp's main drag, this forty-year-old establishment dishes out the region's top breakfasts, including huckleberry pancakes ($6), cinnamon rolls and donuts (both $2) in a simple diner setting. Open 24 hours, lunch and dinner might be burgers ($6–8), chicken fried steak ($10), or fish and chips ($8), followed by a slice of fresh-baked pie or a thick milkshake.

Mount Hood Brewing Co 87304 E Government Camp Loop Hwy ☎503/622-0724. Owned by Timberline resort, this brewpub at the bottom of Government Camp's main drag has the most extensive menu in town. It's family friendly, and menu items here include bar snacks, sandwiches, and salads ($8–10), and entrees like grilled salmon ($18). The pizzas are best avoided, though the six draft microbrews on tap are quite good; try the Ice Axe IPA.

The Ram's Head *Timberline Lodge* ☎503/622-7979. As with everywhere else in the *Timberline Lodge*, this circular bar overlooking the entrance to the *Cascade Dining Room* is attractively decorated with historic photos and Depression-era paintings and woodwork. Along with spirits and homebrews from the *Mount Hood Brewing Co*, you might try Brazilian pulled-pork on a baguette ($11) or organic chicken pot pie ($11). Daily 11am–11pm, but note that it closes for lunch during slower periods.

The Taco Shoppe ☎503/272-3599. Delicious meat or veggie tacos wrapped in thick tortillas and topped with cilantro and diced onions are the specialty of this roadside shack across from the Village Store. No indoor seating, just take-out.

The outlying eastern towns

Panda Panda 24371 E Welches Rd ☎503/622-5165. Only worth a visit if you're craving ethnic cuisine, *Panda Panda* dishes out average Chinese food at reasonable prices. Beer and cocktails served, and take-out is also available.

The Rendezvous Grill 67149 E Hwy 26, Welches ☎503/622-6837. *The Rendezvous* is a popular stopover for both locals and day-trippers heading back to Portland. Favorites include a calamari appetizer with a lemon ginger dipping sauce and entrees such as cider-poached salmon ($20), crab and shrimp cakes ($17), and a superb rigatoni topped with house-smoked chicken ($18). The nightly dessert tray is correctly described as "devastating," featuring a rotating selection of six sugar-laden options. Reservations recommended. Closed Mon and Tues.

Other activities and attractions

Mount Hood Meadow's **Nordic center** (☎503/337-2222, ext 262) is a small 15km system. Passes run $10, with rentals costing $18. Several of the paths connect to ungroomed but scenic US **Forest Service trails**, of which there are miles in the area. Stop in at Government Camp's Val Inn Ski Shop (☎503/272-3525) for cross-country/snowshoe rentals and advice. Families should check out Skibowl's **adventure park**, mentioned on p.376. With **Portland** just over an hour's drive away, many vacationers spend off-mountain days visiting the city's museums, restaurants, and stores.

Listings

Avalanche hotline ☎503/808-2400.
Internet access Mount Hood Cultural Center and Museum, Government Camp ☎503/272-3301; hours vary.

Post office US Post Office, Government Camp (Mon–Fri 7.30am–4.30pm).
Road conditions ☎1-800/977-6368.

Crystal Mountain

Ringed by awesome volcanic peaks, which include the hulking 14,410ft Mount Rainier, **Crystal Mountain**, 76 miles southeast of Seattle, is primarily a day-use area and is suitable for all abilities. Its big selling point, and what makes it particularly enticing to experts, is its accessible, avalanche-controlled, and lightly patrolled **backcountry areas**. The ski area sits in a pocket of sorts, so although storms from the north and west are funneled into the valley, surrounding peaks catch a lot of the local snow. Though this generally leaves Crystal with less snow, what does fall here is of superior quality, relatively light and fluffy by regional standards.

The **resort area** itself is a modest operation with half a dozen small hotels, a day lodge, two bars, and a pokey general store. It only gets crowded on weekends when Seattleites descend on the mountain; otherwise the resort is sparsely visited. The nearest town is nondescript **Enumclaw**, 39 miles west, which doesn't add much excitement to a stay here; however, ambitious **development plans** for the resort – which envisage six more lifts and a passenger tram from base to summit, along with more base facilities – could change the picture dramatically.

Arrival and getting around

The closest international airport to Crystal Mountain is Seattle and Tacoma's **Sea-Tac airport**, 67 miles away. There's no shuttle service from the airport to the resort, so your best option is to **rent a car** (see box below). You could make a day-trip with the Ski and Snowboard Express Bus, which leaves from the Seattle area (Sat, Sun & holidays; ☏ 1-800/665-2122; $58 including lift ticket), or a similar trip with Beeline Tours (see box below). Highways 410, 164, and

---

Washington practicalities

Washington State's main international airport, **Sea-Tac**, fourteen miles south of downtown Seattle (🖰 www.airportsintl.com/sea.html), is the best launching point for trips to the main ski areas – although Vancouver, just over two hours' drive north of Seattle, is also worth considering as a hub, particularly if you can find cheaper flights or if you are primarily interested in visiting Mount Baker (see p.394).

In the absence of organized shuttle services to ski areas from the airport, your best bet is to pick up a **rental car** for the duration of your visit. Nine car companies have information counters in the baggage claim area, including major players like Alamo (☏ 206/431-7588 or 1-800/462-5266), Avis (☏ 1-800/331-1212), and Hertz (☏ 1-800/654-3131), along with the often slightly cheaper Dollar (☏ 206/433-5825) and Thrifty (☏ 206/246-7565). Useful information on **road conditions** for the state can be had via three telephone numbers, of which the Mountain Pass Report (☏ 1-800/695-7623) is most useful for skiers and riders. The State Highway Info Line (☏ 206/368-4499) gives out general information on all major highways, while avalanche conditions are outlined on ☏ 206/526-6677.

Two **bus companies** organize trips into the mountains from the Seattle area. Beeline Tours (☏ 1-800/959-8387, 🖰 www.beelinetours.com) offers day-trips to both Summit at Snoqualmie ($59 including lift ticket, or $35 without) and Stevens Pass ($35, transport only) on weekends. Another company offering similar service, but often also including accommodation on multiday trips, is Fun Shuttle (☏ 1-877/772-2746, 🖰 www.funshuttle.com); check their website for the schedule, which includes trips to Crystal Mountain, The Summit at Snoqualmie, and Mount Baker.

169 all head southwest to Enumclaw, from where Crystal Mountain is another 33 miles away along Hwy-410 and then six miles down a mountain road to the resort. While you can **get around** the tiny resort area easily on foot, shopping, dining, and entertainment options are so limited that it's well worth having **your own vehicle** if you intend to stay for more than a couple of days.

The mountain

Stretched across **four adjoining peaks**, which rise to around 7000ft, the bulk of the terrain on Crystal Mountain is quite varied. Most of the beginner terrain rises from the base area to give way to more taxing intermediate runs scattered throughout the ski area and expert runs at the fringes of the patrolled area. Beyond this perimeter, avalanche-controlled **backcountry areas** – the North and South Country zones – lie on either side of the ski area. These are accessed through gates which are opened after avalanche control, marked with signs warning you of the necessity of having a location device, a shovel and a companion, as well as advising that use is at your own risk.

Mountain info

Phone ☎360/663-2265
Snow phone ☎1-800/754-6199
Website ✪www.skicrystal.com
Price Adult day pass $43
Operating times Mid-Nov to mid-April Mon–Fri 9am–4pm, Sat, Sun, & holidays 8.30am–4pm
No. of lifts 10, including 1 surface tow
Base elevation 4400′
Summit elevation 7012′
Vertical drop 3100′ (including backcountry return)
No. of trails 50
Acreage 2300 acres (including 1000 acres backcountry)
Beginner 13%
Intermediate 57%
Expert 30%
Average snowfall 380″
Snowmaking Yes (35 acres)
Night skiing Yes, mid-Dec to mid-March, Fri–Sun 4pm–8pm; 65 acres; $20
Nursery facilities No; 4 years and up can be enrolled in daylong skiing for $65 per day

Beginner

The majority of Crystal Mountain's **green runs** are accessed from the base area's four lifts. The longest is the slow **Quicksilver Lift** that heads out to a gentle, long, uncongested run of the same name. This is an appropriate first stop after you've gained confidence on the easy first-timer Meadow area; it's also the place to sharpen skills before heading up on the **Forest Queen Express** to the winding, 3.5-mile-long Queens Run.

Intermediate

Although more than half the mountain's in-bounds terrain is designated intermediate, most of the blue runs are a little on the short side, with no particularly dedicated intermediate area. That said, intermediate skiers and riders have the run of the resort, finding decent, if short, runs from virtually every lift. The best selection of these is off **Rainier Express**, which heads up to the summit house. From here you can hook around the backside of the mountain to access the carefully groomed Lucky Shot, with its hugely enjoyable rollers and occasional steeper pitches, perfect for carved turns, or the adjoining Little Shot with its scattered trees. Alternatively, leave the summit and head over to **Green Valley**, served by the eponymous lift and containing the mountain's most adventurous blue terrain. This area is a good option for mixed-ability groups, since the groomed areas are generally straightforward and forgiving, while adjoining ungroomed and tree sections are much more technical.

Expert

The presence of steep chutes, huge drops, powder bowls, and tight trees give Crystal Mountain some of **most challenging terrain** in Washington. The best of the in-bounds expert terrain is found at the southern- and northern-most reaches of the resort, while the adjacent **South** and **North Country areas** are a great place to hunt out fresh tracks in steep basins or in the woods and chutes, respectively. Considered slightly less dangerous, the North Country generally opens first; after heavy snowfall you may have to wait until well into the afternoon for the South Country to open. Signs at the base of the main lifts advise which areas are open.

In the **south**, the High Campbell Chair leads to the double black **Powder Bowl**, which not only has generally forgiving snow, but also the option of hitting the lightly wooded Bear Pits area beyond. Those willing to take the fifteen-minute hike from the top of the chair out to **The Throne** (6600ft) will be rewarded with a magnificent powder descent. The Throne also marks the boundary of the in-bounds ski area, where two gates, one at the summit and one further down the ridge, allow access to both the **backcountry** and the Avalanche Basin. For the best snow in this basin, hike another fifteen minutes along the ridge to Silver King (7012ft), the highest peak in the ski area. From the top you can access Silver Basin, in the next valley over, where pockets of cold air keep snow dry and light, and its distance from the lifts ensures that it stays largely untracked.

At the **northern end** of the resort, the best expert runs are again at the perimeter, and can be accessed from either the **Rainier Express** or the **Green Valley** lift. Right Angle, as much for its dizzying views over the base area as for its steep, narrow profile, is the best run here. It follows on from Northway Ridge, an easy black run, along which are several **backcountry access gates** to the **North Country** area; the first of these gates leads into Paradise Bowl, the most straightforward run and a good introduction to the area. Though it's possible to follow a long, tortuous track back down to the base area from the North Country, it's far better to head down the unmarked Lower Northway, which follows an obvious course down the valley to the resort shuttle.

Freestyle

Freestylers should explore the **Boarder Zone Snowboard Park**, under the plodding Quicksilver Chair, for a mix of mainly intermediate-level tabletops and kickers. For **natural hits**, explore the gully below the Bear Pits run above the Rainier Express lift, or the ones along the sides of Kelly's Gap Road on the area's Northern Perimeter.

Lift tickets, lessons, and rentals

In addition to full-day **lift tickets** ($43 for adults; under-10s with paying adult free), the resort also offers slightly cheaper half-day passes, valid between noon and 4pm. Tickets for the Discovery Chair, which accesses only a large beginner run, cost $20 per day. **Private lessons** are pricey at $65 an hour, though you can save $10 by taking a lesson earlier or later in the day; additional students are charged just $10 per hour. **Group lessons** are another option, skiers paying $75 for a two-hour session and $85 for four hours; snowboarders pay a small amount more. The mountain's **first-timer's package** ($44 per day) includes a lesson, a lift ticket (for the Discovery Chair only), and full rental equipment. More unusual programs include the steep-skiing camp for advanced skiers and women-only ski clinics.

The quality of the **rental equipment** at the resort's own slopeside stores is reasonable enough: ski packages cost $27–33 per day, while snowboards and boots cost $33 per day. Alternatively, get your rental gear in Enumclaw, where Ski and Mountain Sports, off Hwy-410 (℡ 360/825-6910), rents performance ski packages for $30 and snowboards and boots for $25. If you are looking to demo truly **high-performance gear**, head to the enthusiast-run Rainier Rides, below the *Alpine Inn* (℡ 360/663-0182); they've got boards from Gnu, Supernatural, Burton, Nidecker, and Rossignol ($31 per day), as well as skis from Salomon, Rossignol, Völkl, Atomic, and K2 ($36 per day). Avalanche beacons are also available. Another good source of top-notch demo skis, as well as cross-country and snowshoe equipment, is Greenwater Skis on Hwy-410 (℡ 360/663-2235, ⓦ www.greenwaterskis.com); it's also the best place for repairs and tuning.

Accommodation

Though modest in quantity, the **slopeside accommodation options** at Crystal are reasonably varied, particularly midweek, when the resort-owned Crystal Hotels (℡ 360/663-2262 or 1-888/754-6400, ⓦ www.crystalhotels.com) offer **inexpensive packages**: two nights' lodging, tickets, breakfast, and an evening meal start at $160 per person. That said, there's nothing very fancy about the resort; accommodations mostly overlook the parking lots, and there aren't any great budget options. A few more choices are available in and around Enumclaw.

Alpine Inn Crystal Mountain ℡ 360/663-2262 or 1-888/754-6400, ⓦ www.crystalhotels.com. This slopeside Austrian-style chalet, bedecked with gingerbread woodwork and alpine hearts, contains small, spartan (no phones or TVs), immaculately clean rooms that can sleep up to four. ❹

Alta Crystal Resort Hwy-410, Crystal Mountain ℡ 360/663-2500 or 1-800/277-6475, ⓦ www .altacrystalresort.com. Upscale lodging in a gathering of quintessential Pacific Northwest log buildings, a ten-minute drive from Crystal Mountain. Units are decorated with dried flowers and log furniture, and come with kitchens, phones, TV, and VCR. Communal facilities include a heated pool and hot tub. Packages from $160 per night midweek include lift tickets for two. ❻

Crystal Mountain Lodging Suites ℡ 360/663-2558 or 1-888/668-4368, ⓦ www.crystalmtlodging-wa.com. Just a five-minute walk from the lifts,

these individually owned, outfitted, and decorated condo units are available for rent when not in use by the owners. Various sizes of chalets and suites can be had, sleeping up to four, all with full kitchens and fireplaces and with access to a heated outdoor pool. ❼

King's Motel 1334 Roosevelt Ave, Enumclaw ℡ 306/825-1626. Clean, efficiently run motel beside Hwy-410, 39 miles from Crystal Mountain. Larger units have kitchenettes and there's a laundry facility. Skier packages are offered which make the fifth night of lodging here in any one season free. ❷

Quicksilver Lodge Crystal Mountain ℡ 360/663-2262 or 1-888/754-6400, ⓦ www.crystalhotels.com. Bland but spacious motel-style rooms, with TVs and fridges, a five-minute walk from the slopes. The big bonus is the lofty communal sitting area with its crackling log fire. ❹

Eating and drinking

Since it's primarily a day-use area, the selection of **places to eat** at Crystal Mountain is tiny, while the larger range of possibilities in Enumclaw is unexciting. The cafeteria breakfasts in the main lodge are large and good value, and the *Summit House* serves on-mountain food like pizzas, pastas, soups, and salads, accompanied by stunning views of Mount Rainier. If you'll be here for a few days, stock up on **groceries** at the Safeway in Enumclaw beside Hwy-410, as the tiny market at Crystal Mountain stocks only the most essential items.

Pard's Place 1324 Hwy-410, Enumclaw. Family restaurant on the edge of Enumclaw, with filling lunches and dinners daily, plus breakfast on weekends.

Snorting Elk Cellar *Alpine Inn*, Crystal Mountain ☎ 360/663-7798. The cornerstone of Crystal Mountain's nightlife is this convivial basement bar, serving excellent pizza (from $15) and deli sandwiches ($5), along with the usual huge piles of post-ski nachos. Regular live music.

Alpine Inn Restaurant *Alpine Inn*, Crystal Mountain ☎ 360/663-7727. Sparsely decorated with antlers and antique skis, this is Crystal's best restaurant. The food reflects the simple but classy décor: steaks, salmon, pork tenderloin, wiener-schnitzel, and, for vegetarians, a roasted vegetable tower or eggplant and zucchini on crisped noodles and blue cheese. Most entrees run from $16; steaks are from $22.

Sourdough Sal's Day Lodge, Crystal Mountain. Overlooking the slopes, *Sal's* is best for slopeside drinks, including nine different microbrews. The fairly inexpensive menu includes soups, sandwiches, chili-cheese fries, good burgers, and veggie choices like wraps and grilled portobello mushroom. Live music on Friday and Saturday nights, which are usually busy.

Other activities

Local ski shops like Rainier Rides and Greenwater Skis (see "Lift tickets, lessons, and rentals" opposite) rent out **snowshoes** for around $19 per day; they also will provide sketch maps for local routes and can advise you where to head if you've brought your own cross-country skis. For an evening **massage** or soak in a **hot tub**, head to the East Peak Center (open weekends only; ☎360/663-2505), located above the main parking lot at the entrance to the ski area.

Listings

Avalanche line ☎206/569-2211.
Internet Enumclaw City Library, 1700 First St ☎360/825-2938.
Medical Enumclaw Community Hospital, 1450 Battersby ☎360/825-2505.

Pharmacy Safeway, 152 Roosevelt Ave E, Enumclaw ☎360/825-5023.
Post office 1742 Cole St, Enumclaw ☎1-800/275-8777.

The Summit at Snoqualmie

With the largest night-skiing operation in the US, **The Summit at Snoqualmie** courts the after-work ski crowd from Seattle, fifty miles away along I-90; in light traffic, it's only an hour's drive from downtown. As modest as it is convenient, facilities are virtually absent from the ski area, and the resort mainly serves as a great learning and cruising mountain for beginners and intermediates – though pockets of world-class expert terrain (much of it fearsome backcountry) are also tucked away here.

The **nearest town** to the ski area is the rather nondescript North Bend, twenty miles west along I-90; it's well served by a large adjacent factory outlet mall and a tiny, vaguely alpine-style, town center. The more picturesque town of **Snoqualmie**, named after the thundering Snoqualmie Falls, is only a couple of miles northeast of North Bend.

Mountain info

Phone ☎ 425/434-7669

Snow phone ☎ 206/236-1600

Website ⊛ www.summit-at
-snoqualmie.com

Price $42

Operating times Dec–April daily
9am–10pm

No. of lifts 26, including 4 surface tows and 2 magic carpets

Base elevation 2620′

Summit elevation 5450′

Vertical drop 2310′

No. of trails 65

Acreage 1916, plus 750 in the
backcountry

Beginner 34%

Intermediate 36%

Expert 30%

Average snowfall 444″

Snowmaking No

Night skiing Yes, Mon–Sat &
holidays 4pm–10pm; $24; 600
acres

Nursery facilities Yes

Arrival and getting around

Seattle's Sea-Tac airport, 56 miles away by I-90, is the closest **international airport** to The Summit at Snoqualmie. As the airport is not linked by direct shuttle service to the resort, the best option for **getting to the ski area** is to rent a **car** (see box p.381). Getting around the different parts of the ski area is made easy by **free shuttles** (Tues–Sun; every 15 minutes), though an equally easy solution is to commit to one area for at least half the day, and then use your car to swap areas.

The mountain

Originally four separate ski areas, The Summit at Snoqualmie is split up into three interconnected slopes on Mount Catherine – **Summit West**, **Summit Central**, and **Summit East** – and the stand-alone **Alpental**, a five-minute drive or shuttle bus ride away on the other side of the valley. In a quiet valley with varied terrain, Alpental is by far the most attractive of these areas; the others have a far duller profile, with most runs made even less appealing by their views over the I-90 corridor. Note that the four different ski areas have **different opening times**; though the entire area is generally open on weekends, it's still best to call or check the website for the current operating schedule.

The three adjoining Mount Catherine areas are best known for their **beginner-** and **intermediate-level** runs, as well as extensive **night-skiing** opportunities (illuminated by curiously dim lights). Summit West is the best learning area, with several gentle wide-open runs, while Summit Central is the centerpiece of the resort, balanced better across all ability levels. Summit East is the smallest area, and is often neglected, making it usually the least crowded; it features some of the ski area's longest **expert trails** and is also the starting point for the **cross-country trails**. Avalanche-prone Alpental is the **expert's playground**, particularly celebrated for its lift-accessible, avalanche-controlled (but unpatrolled) **backcountry terrain**; it's also where you'll generally find the ski area's best snow.

Beginner

The Summit at Snoqualmie is a great beginner mountain, with gently rolling hills and broad, groomed runs on many of the four slopes. **Summit West** is the classic place to learn, where even the wide blues are soon within reach for confident beginners. **Alpental** has a dedicated beginners area that's lightly used, giving you lots of peace to concentrate on your turns, with the bonus of slightly better snow than elsewhere in the resort.

Intermediate

Intermediate skiers and riders will have no problem finding lots of cruising and carving on wide runs in the three summit areas. **Summit Central** in particular has fine fall-line skiing both day and night, its gentle slopes and short runs making it easy to stay in control while enjoying making wide, arching turns. **Summit East** has narrow, cruising runs, while **Alpental** offers little intermediate terrain, since groomers can only get halfway up the mountain.

Expert

With the exception of bump runs under the Triple 60 chair at Summit Central and a few tree runs at Summit East, the vast majority of the **expert terrain** is at **Alpental,** where three-quarters of the trails are designated with a single or double black diamond. Generally, the terrain here gets harder as you move further up the mountain, so that the bulk of the most challenging, satisfying runs are off the dated two-seater **Edelweiss Chair,** which makes the last leg of the journey to the summit. After heavy snowfall it's worth exploring the terrain below the lift in the Edelweiss Bowl, where chutes, bowls, trees, and cliffs abound on the handful of short runs to the base. Alternatively, leave the top of the lift and zip down the beautifully consistent vertical of powder fields like Upper and Lower International on the front side of the mountain, which link with runs back to the base area. Alongside Upper International, **Adrenaline** is steeper but less-used, often having some of mountain's best snow. If you enjoy **freeriding through trees**, head out of Upper International to Snake Dance, where technical sections through trees and over boulders along the boundary of the patrolled area await.

Freestyle

The better of The Summit's two **halfpipes** is the 600ft-long pipe at Summit West, adjacent to the **terrain park**. Meanwhile, the pipe and park at Summit Central is unexciting, the slope being too flat and the features far too modest, though beginners might find it a good place to gain some confidence. In the search for **natural hits**, explore the stumps on Rip Cord under the Triple 60 lift; over on Alpental, investigate Snake Dance.

Lift tickets, lessons, and rentals

Day-only tickets ($42; 9am–5pm) are only a minor savings on full-day **lift tickets** (9am–10pm); you can also get a similar ticket that lasts from 1pm until 10pm. Tickets from 1pm to 5pm are available for $32. Savings of around 25 percent can be had on weekdays for all types of ticket. **Night-skiing passes** cost $24 all the time.

Private **lessons** are $50 per hour, though packages are available with discounts on tickets and rental gear. The resort also offers group lessons, though these are restricted to beginner packages: $55 buys a two-hour lesson, a limit-

Backcountry options

A further option from the top of the Edelweiss Chair (see above) is some terrific steep and rugged **backcountry**, full of thrilling (but hazardous) cliffs and creek beds; signs at the top of the chair update the area's status. To enter, the resort insists you take a tour with a patroller and obtain a pass before heading out. For information on the next tour, contact the ski patrol at the top of the lift. If you choose to enter the backcountry you should take avalanche beacons and a snow shovel with you.

ed lift ticket, and rental equipment. You can extend this program over three days for $99. The ski area also has a large kids' program of two- to four-hour group lessons, with lunch, for ages 3 and up.

Standard **rental gear** is available at the resort, with skis going for $27 per day and snowboards for $30. Also offered is the excellent-value rental "season pass," which will take care of your rental needs for the entire season; the pass costs $99 for skiers and $140 for snowboarders. For demo gear, the ski area's rental shops carry a good selection from several leading manufacturers.

Accommodation

As it's pretty much entirely a day-use area, **accommodation** at The Summit is limited to just one hotel, the *Best Western Summit Inn*, and one hostel-type place, the *Hyak Lodge* (see below for both). That said, there are several moderately priced self-contained apartments, chalets, and cabins available for short stays in the area; these can be viewed at ⓦ www.snoq.com. Otherwise, the closest accommodations are the motels of **North Bend** and more upscale lodges and bed-and-breakfasts near its neighbor **Snoqualmie**.

Best Western Summit Inn Snoqualmie Pass ⓣ425/434-6300 or 1-800/557-7829, ⓦwww.bwsummitinn.com. Predictably comfortable rooms managed by the nationwide chain. Facilities include pool, sauna, hot tub, and laundry. Ski packages offered, starting from $110 per night with tickets for two. ⓺

Edgewick Inn 14600 468th Ave SE, North Bend ⓣ425/888-9000. Decent motel at the easternmost edge of town. Some rooms have jacuzzis and water beds, and the motel has a laundry facility. ⓷

Hyak Lodge 370 Keechelus Boat Launch Rd, Snoqualmie Pass ⓣ425/434-5955, ⓦwww.parks.wa.gov/hyaklodge.asp. Originally constructed to house highway snowplowing crews, the *Hyak Lodge* has been converted into a pleas-

ant inn with dormitory-style guest rooms. Only works well for groups, though, as the minimum booking is four rooms (at $50 a night each), with a maximum of two people in each room.

North Bend Motel 322 E North Bend Way, North Bend ⓣ425/888-1121. Clean family-run motel within easy walking distance of North Bend's center. With TVs, phones, and the most reasonable rates in town. ⓶

Salish Lodge 6501 Railroad Ave SE, Snoqualmie Falls ⓣ425/888-2556 or 1-800/826-6124, ⓦwww.salishlodge.com. Rustic high-end hotel beside the bellowing Snoqualmie Falls. Its 91 rooms sport wicker furniture, down comforters, fireplaces, and hot tubs. Use of an exercise room is included; spa treatments are extra. ⓼

Eating and drinking

While there are a good number of places to pick up predictable cafeteria food at the mountain, off the slopes the options are thinner on the ground – and mostly in North Bend.

North Bend Bar & Grill 145 E North Bend Way, North Bend ⓣ425/888-1243. A large and efficiently run friendly bar, the best of several along the main street. Pub food includes salads, soups, and sandwiches (around $9) and, in the evenings, steaks (from $12) and decent quesadillas ($8), one of several good veggie options.

Robertiello's 101 W North Bend Way, North Bend ⓣ425/888-1803. Unpretentious little Italian restaurant with excellent homemade food, including simple antipasto dishes like fresh mussels, or mozzarella salad (each around $8). Entrees include pastas (around $14) with first-class sauces, as well as good meat and seafood dishes.

Salish Lodge 6501 Railroad Ave SE, Snoqualmie Falls ⓣ425/888-2556. Upscale lodge serves top-notch regional fare, based around fresh seafood and local vegetables; also offers one of the largest selections of wine in the region.

Twede's Café 137 W North Bend Way, North Bend ⓣ425/831-5511. Sparkling neon-lit diner with glossy plastic-clad booths, serving an array of breakfasts, but specializing in burgers: over 25 kinds are available for around $7 each, and are served with bottomless fries. Choose from options like the pizza burger with mozzarella or the teriyaki burger with pineapple.

Other activities

The main alternative activities offered by the ski area are **tubing** (Fri–Sat 9am–10pm, Sun 9am–6pm; $7), a kids' **snowmobile race track**, and **cross-country skiing** from the Nordic Center (Wed 9am–10pm, Thurs–Sun 9am–4.30pm; ⓦwww.summitnordic.com; $12). Located in Summit East, the center maintains 34 miles of tracked trails accessible via the Keechelus Chair, use of which – as well as a warming hut yurt – is included in the price of a pass. The center offers a variety of lessons to beginners and intermediates, along with cross-country ski rentals, which run around $20–30 a day or $80 for a season. **Snowshoers** can rent equipment for $15 per day from the center, and can also access the Keechelus Chair. Lastly, spring brings the **Bored Stiff Festival** to The Summit, which includes various events and trade-show style stands, competitions, and live bands.

Listings

Avalanche line ⓣ206/442-SNOW.
Medical Snoqualmie Valley Hospital, 9575 Ethan Wade Way SE ⓣ425/831-2300.
Pharmacy QFC Pharmacy, 460 E North Bend Way,

North Bend ⓣ425/888-2357.
Post office 208 Main Ave S, North Bend ⓣ1-800/275-8777.

Stevens Pass

Surrounded by National Forest Wilderness areas, **Stevens Pass** lies at the top of the eponymous pass, 78 miles west of Seattle on Hwy-2 to Wenatchee. Like all Washington state ski areas, Stevens is a fairly modest day-use area; the only real facility here is the swank new day lodge, which contrasts with the generally dated lift system. However, there's rarely a shortage of snow, and thanks to occasional storms surging in from the east with cool, dry air, Stevens often has much lighter snow than elsewhere in the Cascade Mountains.

For those visiting Stevens Pass for more than a day, the mock-Bavarian town of **Leavenworth**, 38 miles to the east, beckons with numerous hotels and restaurants. Bavariana is taken seriously here, and even the gas stations and supermarkets have altered their signs to conform to the old-German script that prevails throughout town. Kitsch though it may be, it's all done with good humor and leant some authenticity by the presence of a vibrant German-speaking community. Another attraction for those staying in the area for a couple of nights is **Mission Ridge**, a sizeable ski resort owned by the same people that own Stevens Pass, with varied terrain and great-quality snow; see p.413.

Arrival and information

Stevens Pass is 98 miles from Sea-Tac Airport or 78 miles from Seattle; the easiest way to get from either to the resort is **by car** along Hwy-5 and then Hwy-2. Alternatively, Beeline Tours runs **buses** on the weekend from Seattle to Stevens Pass (ⓣ1-800/959-8387, ⓦwww.beelinetours.com; $35). If you plan to stay overnight, be aware that all accommodation and services are a significant drive from the ski area, many in Leavenworth, where the Chamber of

Mountain info

Phone ☎206/812-4510

Snow phone ☎206/634-1645

Website ⓦwww.stevenspass.com

Price $43

Operating times Late Nov to mid-April daily 9am–10pm (until 4pm in the spring)

No. of lifts 10

Base elevation 3821′

Summit elevation 5845′

Vertical drop 1800′

No. of trails 37

Acreage 1125

Beginner 11%

Intermediate 54%

Expert 35%

Average snowfall 450″

Snowmaking No

Night skiing Yes, daily 4pm–10pm; $27; 394 acres

Nursery facilities Yes, from 3 months, ☎206/812-4510

Commerce on Hwy-2 and Ninth Street (☎509/548-5807, ⓦwww.leavenworth.org) can provide advance information.

The mountain

Stevens Pass spreads over a large basin in between two peaks, **Cowboy Mountain** and **Big Chief Mountain**. The upper reaches of conical Cowboy Mountain are carpeted with fierce, steep runs that, further down, give way to more intermediate terrain. By contrast, Big Chief Mountain is a less dramatic peak, with runs that drop off the high ridge that leads to the summit on both sides, bringing you back to the base lodge or down the opposite Mill Valley side, which is not visible from the base area. The slopes of Big Chief Mountain have a more consistent angle, with black runs barreling unremittingly down both sides of the mountain. Intermediates only get a look in around the fringes, while beginner terrain is concentrated at the base of the valley between the two peaks. Virtually all the beginner terrain, and almost all of the intermediate, is lit for night skiing every night until the spring.

Beginner

For beginners at Stevens, head for the **Daisy Chair**, within easy walking distance of the base area; it accesses the quiet green runs Tye Creek and Easy Street. More challenging are the blue runs off the **Hogsback Express**, particularly Rock 'N Blue. If it seems too crowded here, try the slightly steep but forgivingly wide Showcase, off the Big Chief lift.

Intermediate

Though it's tempting to just settle into doing the smooth blue cruisers off the **Hogsback** and the **Skyline expresses**, it's worth heading to the **Tye Mill** chair for a little variety. Also, don't ignore the much quieter blues on the **Mill Valley** side, perfect for cruising and laying down wide carves.

Expert

Stevens Pass offers three areas of **highly concentrated expert terrain**. The smallest is Cowboy Mountain, while both the front and back of Big Chief Mountain have long single and double black diamond runs with plenty of chances to dip into the trees. The upper reaches of Cowboy Mountain are accessed by the imposingly steep 7th Heaven chairlift, which leads to a variety of single and double black diamonds. The best snow is usually tucked away in the **Meadows**, though watch out for the many cliffs dotted around here. Two of the steepest, most intimidating runs on the mountain, **Bobby** and **Nancy Chute**, involve a couple of minutes hike; they're only open in good snow conditions.

On Big Chief Mountain, explore the **Big Chief Bowl** by the Double Diamond lift, where steep entrances between cliffs and trees put many off, leaving an expanse of attractive powder below. Further down, jump onto the immaculately groomed I-5, usually a near-empty run that allows for fast carving. Also off the Double Diamond chair is some excellent **freeriding**, particularly in the trees between the vicious Double Diamond bump run and the super-narrow Wild Katz. Along the same ridge is Tye Bowl, often with untracked powder, but protected by trees, short jumps, and rocks on the way in. The easiest way to access the bowl is a cut to skier's right a short way down the Tye Mill liftline; careful negotiation of obstacles then leads into this little-skied area. For sustained exploring, the best area to settle into is often the **Mill Valley** side. Look for tight trees around the Corona Bowl and further down around Shooting Star. For powder, explore the Polaris Bowl and Andromeda Face, both below the Southern Cross chair.

Freestyle

The Bent Monkey **freestyle park**, under the Brooks lift, offers fast approaches and dozens of features. The modest halfpipe at the base of the park is perfect for beginners. For a varied range of **natural hits** try Pegasus Gulch on the Mill Valley side, and some of the smaller cliffs in the Meadows area. In the latter, explore below the 7th Heaven chair and at the entrance to Tye Bowl beneath the Tye Mill lift – but take care to scope out jumps carefully, as many incorporate severe drops and awkward landings.

Lift tickets, lessons, and rentals

All-day **lift tickets** at Stevens cost $43, while from noon onwards they're $35, and at 4pm they drop to $27. All are valid until closing, which is 10pm in peak season. If you know you're going to ski at Stevens for several days in a season, consider buying the Harbor Advantage card ($59), which gives you your first lift ticket free and a discount of $5 on weekends and $10 on weekdays on further tickets. The card is also valid at Mission Ridge (see p.413), and if it's your birthday, you get a free lift ticket.

The Snow Sports Center at Stevens Pass (☎206/812-4510 ext 242) offers decent-value private **lessons** for $42 per hour, as well as starter packages for $50 per day or $99 for three days that include a lesson, lift ticket, and equipment. Lessons are also available for kids aged 3 and over. You'll find a good range of **rentals** from the Rossignol tech center in the Day Lodge; basic ski or snowboard packages start at $32 per day, while performance gear costs $39. An alternative source for ski and snowboard equipment is Der Sportsman, in Leavenworth at 837 Front St (☎509/548-5623 or 1-800/548-4145, ⓦwww.dersportsman.com).

Accommodation

The only way to stay at Stevens Pass itself is to bring your own **RV** – hookups are offered for $15. Otherwise, the nearest town with good **accommodation** is Leavenworth, which, as it's primarily a summer tourist destination, generally has plenty of beds free in winter. A few scattered options also lie east and west of Stevens Pass alongside Hwy-2, a little handier for skiing, though services are a bit dreary. The ski area's website (ⓦwww.stevenspass.com) lists a variety of stay-and-ski **packages** that include lift tickets also valid at Mission Ridge (see p.413).

Leavenworth

All Seasons River Inn 8751 Icicle Rd ☏509/548-1425 or 1-800/254-0555, ⓦwww.allseasonsriverinn.com. Upscale bed-and-breakfast a couple of minutes' drive from the town center, with half a dozen individually decorated rooms, most with private jacuzzi and all with gorgeous river views. ❹

Evergreen Inn 1117 Front St ☏509/548-5515 or 1-800/327-7212, ⓦwww.evergreeninn.com. Despite the alpine accents in the forecourt, this is just a simple, clean little motel. It's within easy walking distance of the town center and is a good value, with rates that include use of an outdoor hot tub and a light continental breakfast. Some of the cheapest available ski packages are offered here as well. ❸

Hotel Pension Anna 926 Commercial St ☏509/548-6273 or 1-800/509-2662, ⓦwww.pensionanna.com. Austrian-style lodge filled with heavy wooden furniture, feather beds, and other decor imported from the Alps. A good continental breakfast is included in the price, and ski packages are available. ❸

Run of the River 9308 East Leavenworth Rd ☏509/548-7171 or 1-800/288-6491, ⓦwww.runoftheriver.com. Laid-back, superbly comfortable inn in a log building one mile east of the Icicle River from Hwy-2. Rooms have high ceilings, handmade furniture, fireplaces, and jacuzzi. Weekday rates include ski passes for stays over two nights. ❼

West of Stevens Pass

Sky River Inn 333 River Drive East, Skykomish ☏360/677-2261 or 1-800/367-8194, ⓦwww.skyriverinn.com. The bland riverside motel is 15 miles west of Stevens Pass in Skykomish. Units are standard motel issue, although all rooms are equipped with fridges and phones, and some with kitchenettes. Ski packages, midweek, and multiday deals are available. ❸

SkyCabins Skykomish ☏360/793-7616, ⓦwww.skycabins.com. Two pleasant, very well-equipped riverfront cabins in Skykomish, one of which can accommodate groups of up to seven. Facilities include hot tub, fireplace, telephone, Internet connection, satellite TV, and washer/dryers. Both weekly and nightly rates are available; these are based on two people staying, with small additional charges for extra adults in a group. ❺

East of Stevens Pass

Nanson Creek Cabin Hwy-2, near milepost 82 ☏509/763-3394 or 1-866/459-8630, ⓦwww.nccabin.net. Well looked-after, lone-standing cabin around twelve miles from the resort; a good self-catering option for up to eight people. ❹

Rock Springs Custom Knives 19475 Hwy-2, near milepost 78 ☏509/763-3117. Run by a small knife-making business, these small, neat cabins – which all share an outside bathroom – are just four miles away from the slopes. ❷

Star Spangled Manor 15251 Hwy-2 ☏509/763-3157. Two simple rooms (no phone or TV) offered in a large roadside log building 18 miles from the ski area and 20 miles from Leavenworth, making it a convenient base for both. There's a choice of two restaurants in easy walking distance. ❷

Eating and drinking

After a day on the slopes, the *Bull's Tooth Pub & Eatery*, in the main Stevens Pass day lodge, offers the smooth Stevens Pass Amber Ale and good bar food. The bulk of the area's **dining** is in Leavenworth, where there's no shortage of mediocre, pseudo-Germanic eateries designed to draw in passing tourists. Some are more authentic, and a couple of spots offer cuisine other than German, adding much-needed variety to the scene. **Nightlife** in Leavenworth is minimal, though it's not hard to find a few cozy bars in which to have a drink – though you're unlikely to have much company unless it's a weekend night.

Leavenworth

Andreas Keller 829 Front St ☏509/548-6000. Basement restaurant with some of the most authentic traditional German food and surroundings in town. Staples include rotisserie chicken or sausages like knockwurst and leberkäse for $8, while daily specials start at $9. There's a selection of Bavarian beers on tap, including spicy wheat beers.

Bavarian Bakery 1330 Hwy-2 ☏509/548-2244. Simple bakery with fantastic fresh-baked goods and a couple of tables where you can enjoy a cup of strong German coffee.

Lorraine's Edel House 320 Ninth St ☏509/548-4412. A good alternative to the heavy Central European fare found elsewhere in town, *Lorraine's* serves great Asian food, including roast duck, grilled salmon, and fresh pasta dishes. One of the town's most upscale restaurants; main courses run from $11 to 17.

Los Camperos 200 Eighth St ☏509/548-3314. A curiosity in the land of wurst, this venue for excellent Mexican dishes is made all the more curious given its tucked-away-in-an-alley entrance. Succulent burritos for $8, or an extensive selection of combination platters, all around $10.

Mozart 829 Front St ☎509/548-0600. Located above the *Andreas Keller*, Mozart offers a gourmet spin on the German staples served below. Entrees include wienerschnitzel ($19), sauerbraten ($17), and – unusually – a rotating vegetarian choice (around $13).

Uncle Uli's Pub 902 Front St, Leavenworth ☎509/548-7262. Leavenworth's best pub, a favorite with ski area employees, serves a good range of microbrews and has a grill fired up for bratwurst and burgers. None of the other food selections – salads, potato soup, chili, and sandwiches – are anything special, but, largely under $6, most are good value.

West of Stevens Pass

Bush House Country Inn 300 Fifth St, Index ☎360/677-2223. Small local restaurant in an old hotel dining room, serving decent, moderately priced meals prepared from fresh ingredients – the only handy choice for those staying in Skykomish.

Dutch Cup Restaurant 927 Main St, Sultan ☎360/793-1864. Popular inexpensive diner that makes a good stop-off for breakfast (served from 6am) or a filling end to a day of skiing and riding – the menu's a predictable assortment of burgers, soups, steaks, and prime rib.

East of Stevens Pass

'59er Diner 15361 Hwy-2 ☎509/763-2267. 1950s-themed diner, located beside the *Star Spangled Manor*, roughly midway between the ski area and Leavenworth. Serves burgers ($6) and sandwiches ($5) as well as $11 blowout breakfasts, free if finished within 30 minutes.

Star Spangled Manor 15251 Hwy-2 Leavenworth ☎509/763-3157. Locals' bar with adjoining restaurant serving moderately expensive hearty American fare, including cooked breakfasts, burgers, sandwiches, and steaks.

Other activities and attractions

Unlike other Washington resorts, there are a lot of alternative activities around Stevens Pass and Leavenworth. There's a **tubing area** at the center of Stevens, near the beginner slopes, while **cross-country skiing** is offered between late November and mid-February on 25km of groomed trails. The trails begin from the Nordic Center, five miles east of the Stevens summit, where daily trail passes are $12 and ski rentals $19. Cross-country ski **lessons** are available – a first-timer's package with rental equipment and pass costs $30. Marked **snowshoe trails** also start at the Nordic Center, with snowshoe rentals costing $15. Once you've exhausted the cross-country skiing opportunities provided by Stevens, it's worth exploring the 24km of trails in and around Leavenworth groomed by its Winter Sports Club (☎509/548-5115, ⓦwww.skileavenworth.com).

In Leavenworth, after you've had your fill of poking around the various **art galleries** and craftsy **shops**, don't miss one of the town's most unique attractions, the lovingly assembled **Nutcracker Museum**, 735 Front St (Nov–April Sat & Sun 2–5pm; ☎509/548-4708, ⓦwww.nussknackerhaus.com; $2.50), where four thousand nutcrackers – some are up to five-hundred years old – are on display. Leavenworth is also a hub for **dogsledding**: Enchanted Mountain Tours (☎360/856-9168 or 1-800/521-1694) run half-day and overnight tours from around $250 for two people. A cheaper alternative is Alaska Dreamin' Sled Dog Company (☎509/763-8017), located nineteen miles north of Leavenworth in Plain, which offers half-hour rides for $30 per person.

Listings

Avalanche line ☎206/677-2414.
Bookstore A Book for All Seasons, 705 Hwy-2 ☎509/548-1451.
Medical Cascade Medical Center, 817 Commercial St, Leavenworth ☎509/548-5815.

Pharmacy Village Pharmacy, 815 Front St ☎509/548-7731.
Post office 960 Hwy-2, Leavenworth ☎1-800/275-8777.

Mount Baker

Tucked away just south of the Canadian border, in one of the highest parts of the Cascade Mountains, the modest **Mount Baker** ski area is known as one of the **best places to snowboard** in North America, with superb riding both in and out of bounds. It's really something of an icon for the sport: twenty years ago, boarding's pioneers started their activities here, and the resort remains an outstanding mountain to ride, with the banked slalom its mainstay.

Today, the plain, low-tech ski area has become something of a counter-cultural stronghold for snowboarders, who revel in the huge amount of **freeriding terrain**, as the whole area is riddled with cliffs, chutes, and steep, open bowls. But it's the vast quantities of deep wet snow – the 1998–99 season saw a world record 1140 inches accumulate – that particularly attracts riders (though this can make skiing difficult). In all, two-thirds of those on the hill are snowboarders, often dressed in heavy technical clothing, prepared for wet snow, frequent rain, and low visibility, thanks to the wildly fluctuating temperatures that come with Mount Baker's low elevation. In keeping with the small scale of the ski area, there's **no local resort infrastructure**, and for all but the most basic day lodge services you'll have to head seventeen miles back down the narrow alpine Hwy-542 (which snakes up to the ski area) to the town of **Glacier**. Even then, Glacier has no more than a few hotels, restaurants, a general store, and a snowboard shop; there's only a handful of extra services in **Maple Falls**, a further 6.5 miles west down the highway.

Mountain info	
Phone	☎360/734-6771
Snow phone	☎360/671-6771 or 604/857-1515
Website	⊕www.mtbakerskiarea.com
Price	$34
Operating times	Mid-Nov to May daily 9am–4pm
No. of lifts	10, including 2 rope tows
Base elevation	3500′
Summit elevation	5250′
Vertical drop	1500′
No. of trails	38
Acreage	1000
Beginner	24%
Intermediate	45%
Expert	31%
Average snowfall	645″
Snowmaking	No
Night skiing	No
Nursery facilities	No

Arrival

Bellingham International Airport, 56 miles east of Mount Baker, is the **nearest airport** – though Seattle's Sea-Tac Airport, 160 miles south (see box p.381), and Vancouver's international airport, about 100 miles northwest, are the nearest major hubs. With the exception of the Bellair Baker Shuttle (☎360/380-8800, ⊕www.enjoytheride.com), which provides transport up to the mountain from Bellingham (Sat only; $14 round-trip) or Glacier ($10 round-trip), the only practical method of getting to Mount Baker is a **car**. If you're driving to the ski area, you'd do well to get a 4WD vehicle, as there's often poor traction on the upper half of Hwy-542.

The mountain

Mount Baker divides neatly into two areas, both located off two peaks that are themselves part of a ridge that leads off the 9720ft Mount Shuksan. The **Panorama Dome** rises from the upper base area, around Heather Meadows Day Lodge, while **Shuksan** is located above the lower base area, which contains the White Salmon Day Lodge. The latter area is marginally more popular, as its base area services operate daily and it has a greater amount of terrain that spans all skill levels. Access to the bulk of the out-of-bounds backcountry riding is also from Shuksan. The Panorama Dome encompasses mostly black diamond terrain – though most of the ski area's easiest green runs are here as well – and its base area is open on weekends and holidays only.

Beginner

Though Mount Baker is not really known as a beginner resort, its inexpensive lift tickets and handful of easy runs at the base of the mountain make it a good place to learn. The gentle slopes in front of **Heather Meadows Lodge** and the single, longer green run off the **C7 quad** by the White Salmon Day Lodge are the best starting points. Once you've mastered basic turns you'll find **easy blues** to do off every lift – strike out first to the quiet Austin and Blueberry off the **C1 lift**.

Intermediate

The spaghetti-like collection of blue runs that descend into wide-open bowl-style terrain off the **C8** and **C5 chairs** are the best place for intermediates in search of easy cruising and carving. Beyond the five runs around these two chairs, though, there's not much choice elsewhere. Austin is the only major intermediate run off the Panorama Dome at the other end of the resort, and the short blue runs at its base are nothing special. If you feel like progressing onto **blacks** try North Face off the summit, which is generously wide, fairly quiet, and allows you to retreat to blue runs halfway down the mountain.

Expert

The bulk of the most incredible in-bounds terrain is on the **Panorama Dome** off the **C6 lift**. Ringed by cornices at its entrance close to the top of the chair, Razorhone Canyon is one of the most spectacular and varied options, with wide powder fields that dive into a steep narrow canyon harboring a plethora of **natural hits**. The best vertical here is right beneath the C6 lift: an open piste you can leave for fine **tree skiing** between old, evenly spaced cedars and firs down Cannuk's Delux – but be particularly alert for hidden obstacles. Also off Panorama Dome, following the line of the **C1 lift**, Chute is a wonderfully open powder field prior to its mad plunge through a narrow cut in the rocks, just wide enough for the half-dozen or so turns it takes to negotiate.

With all the great terrain on the Panorama Dome, it's easy to forget about the runs flanking the parallel-running **C4** and **C5 lifts** on the **Mount Shuksan** side of the ski area. Choose careful lines around the virtually unrideable cliffs and chunky drop-offs, or head down Gabl's below the lift for steep lines and fresh powder.

> ### Backcountry options
>
> Despite the fearsome in-bounds challenges, for many, the attraction of Mount Baker is the **backcountry terrain**, accessed off the top of the **C8 chair**. Avalanches are not uncommon, so seek out careful advice from the ski patrol and be sure to bring a companion, shovel, and location device. Well-defined tracks head out to powder bowls cradled above the cliffs of Razorhone Canyon, as well as in the opposite direction toward Mount Shuksan. Here, gates give access to slopes with a mix of near-vertical chutes and little powder bowls full of hits, gullies, and rideable cliff drops.

The Banked Slalom

As old as almost any tradition in the sport of snowboarding, the annual **Banked Slalom race** has attracted the cream of international competition to the slopes of Mount Baker since 1984. Held in late January, the race invites riders to compete on a course that begins with eight high-speed, gigantic slalom turns before dropping into a natural halfpipe where marker flags direct participants up – in places, at least – forty-foot high walls. With no TV coverage, sponsorship presence, prize money, or World-Cup points, the event is true to the sport's free-spirited, counter-cultural origins. Many old-school riders ignored the 1998 Olympics – dismissing them as too organized, commercialized, and nationalistic – so as not to miss this race and the opportunity to win first prize: a roll of golden duct tape on a chain. But as much as it's about celebrating the beauty of snowboarding, the Banked Slalom is also about heavy partying in Glacier.

Freestyle

Best known for its signature **natural halfpipe**, along a creek bed off the top of Chair 5, and home to the Banked Slalom race (see box above), Mount Baker also has a small groomed **terrain park** and halfpipe near the base of Chair 7. This is just as well, since, particularly in big snow years, the whole cauldron of natural pipe tends to fill with snow, leaving a disappointingly unimpressive indent. Off the Panorama Dome, Razorhone Canyon can be sessioned again and again for its many hits.

Lift tickets, lessons, and rentals

Lift tickets at Mount Baker vary in price according to the day of the week. Adult day passes, $34 on weekends, are $28 from Monday to Wednesday and drop to $26 on Thursdays and Fridays. **Group lessons** are also inexpensive at $22 per hour, while first-timer packages – which include a lesson, ticket, and equipment – will set you back $45. The ski school also offers more **specialized programs**, including lessons on using shaped skis, women's classes, disabled lessons, and a top-notch telemark ski program, widely considered the best in the region.

Though the choice of outlets at Mount Baker is minimal, the **rental equipment** offered is decent enough. Basic skis can be picked up for $26 per day, and snowboards for $32; performance packages for either will run you around $10 more per day. Also available for rent are telemark skis ($24), cross-country skis ($18), and snowshoes ($16). A good option is The Glacier Ski Shop, off Mount Baker Highway in Glacier (closed noon–3pm daily; ☎360/599-1943).

Accommodation

In the absence of onsite lodging at the ski area, the few roadside motels, cabins, and B&Bs in and around Glacier provide almost all the local **accommodation**. For those with an RV, there's free camping at the parking lot, though not any hookups. A good option for big groups is Mount Baker Lodging (☎360/599-2453 or 1-800/709-7669, ⓦwww.mtbakerlodging.com), a management company that sets up rentals in private cabins, sleeping up to ten. Refer to the website for details of the many properties, and watch for midweek specials; there's a two-night minimum stay at any of their properties.

Glacier Creek Lodge 10036 Mt Baker Hwy,
Glacier ☎360/599-2991 or 1-800/719-1414,
ⓦwww.glaciercreeklodge.com. In the heart of
Glacier, a convenient and inexpensive, though
well-worn, option. Choose from tiny motel units or
the dozen one- or two-bedroom cabins with
kitchen. Motel rooms ❷, cabins ❹
The Inn at Mt Baker 8174 Mt Baker Hwy, Glacier
☎360/599-1359 or 1-877/567-5526, ⓦwww
.theinnatmtbaker.com. Classy B&B in an airy, modern property six miles west of Glacier. Sleep on feather mattresses and down duvets, wake to magnificent mountain views and a filling gourmet breakfast. The communal guest lounge has a refrigerator stocked with snacks as well as a TV, VCR, and
video collection; there's also an outdoor hot tub. ❺
The Logs at Canyon Creek 9002 Mt Baker Hwy,
Deming ☎360/599-2711, ⓦwww.telcomplus.net

/thelogs. Two miles west of Glacier, pleasant cabins secluded from the road by woodland. Cabins
sleep up to eight in two bedrooms and come with
fireplaces and full kitchens. Three nights are regularly offered for the price of two. ❸
Mount Baker Bed and Breakfast 9434 Cornell
Creek Rd, Glacier ☎360/599-2299, ⓦwww
.mtbakerbedandbreakfast.com. Friendly B&B a
short drive west of Glacier, run by outdoorsy types
who pride themselves on making huge breakfasts.
Of the three available rooms, one has a private
bath. Everyone shares the outdoor hot tub. ❸–❹
Snowline Inn 10433 Mt Baker Hwy, Glacier
☎360/599-2788 or 1-800/228-0119,
ⓦwww.snowlineinn.com. Fairly nondescript, multi-
story motel with simple condos and studios, all
with kitchenettes and sleeping up to six.
Economical weekly rates are available. ❷

Eating and drinking

On weekdays, the White Salmon Day Lodge is the only dining option, serving
standard cafeteria food at the base of the mountain. On weekends, it's worth
seeking out the *Raven Hot Café* at the base of C4 and C5 for its spicy Mexican-
style grub. In **Glacier**, there's a small selection of decent restaurants, most doubling as bars for the town's minimal nightlife. The drive-thru *Mount Baker
Express*, a mile west of town, serves good snacks, particularly pizza and nachos,
to those looking for a bite on the fly. If you're planning on doing your own
cooking in Glacier, be sure to stock up before you get here, as the general store
has only basics.

Frosty Inn 7461 Mt Baker Hwy, Maple Falls
☎360/599-2594. Cheerful family-style restaurant
serving diner staples in a lounge overlooked by
multiple TV screens.
Milano's Pasta Fresco 9990 Mt Baker Hwy,
Glacier ☎206/599-2863. Simple bistro serving
homemade pasta that easily corners the local culinary scene. Ravioli's the specialty, with cheese,
meat, smoked salmon, or porcini mushroom varieties offered, each around $9. The ricotta cheese-

cake is also excellent, and there's a deli counter,
too, good for stocking up on picnic items.
Seven Loaves Restaurant and Bakery 9393 Mt
Baker Hwy, Glacier ☎360/599-2290. Bakery on the
western fringe of town with a simple restaurant serving fairly unimaginative pizzas, burgers, and tacos
– though local organic ingredients are used, and
there's something for everyone, from vegan to carnivore. The espresso and home-baked goods make
a good start to the day. Open for dinner Thurs–Sun.

Other activities

Entirely surrounded by National Forest land, the area around Mount Baker has
plenty of options for wintertime activities besides downhill skiing and snowboarding. Local rental shops (see "Lift tickets, lessons, and rentals" opposite) can
help out with **snowshoe**, **cross-country**, and **telemark ski rentals**, as well
as advice about where to head. The ski area itself manages a 4km stretch of
cross-country trails – though it's the self-reliant who explore more widely
in the National Forest lands that are rewarded with the more spectacular
scenery and peaceful trails.

Listings

Avalanche line ☎206/599-2714.

Banks ATM at Maple Fuels, Maple Falls ☎360 /599-2222.

Laundry Maple Fuels, Maple Falls ☎360/599-2222.

Medical St Joseph Hospital, 2901 Squalicum

Pkwy, Bellingham ☎360/734-5400.

Pharmacy Sumas Drug, 315 Cherry St, Sumas ☎360/988-2681.

Post office 7802 Silver Lake Rd, Maple Falls ☎1-800/275-8777.

④ Anchorage

If you're heading to the resort at Alyeska or the port of Valdez, base camp for most of Alaska's heliskiing outfits, you'll almost undoubtedly use **Anchorage** as a gateway. Erected rapidly on the spoils of oil, it's not an immediately attractive town, but it's not without charm either, and the location, ringed by miniature ice floes bobbing into the Cook Inlet from the Pacific, with the mighty Chugach Mountains as a backdrop, is nothing short of spectacular.

As the only major urban hub in the region, Anchorage is driven by an energetic young populace and the downtown bars and restaurants are affordable and laid-back. Stock up on provisions, rent a car or RV, or spend a night on the town; it's possible to ski in Alyeska and stay in Anchorage, usually a more economical alternative.

Arrival, information, and getting around

Use the Anchorage CVB, 524 West 4th Ave (☎907/276-4118 or 1-800/478-1255, ⊛www.anchorage.net), for advance planning. In town, head for the log cabin **visitor center** on the corner of W 4th Avenue and F Street (9am–4pm; Apri–May 8am–6pm). The **public transit** system here has limited hours and doesn't serve the airport or any ski area, though the occasional ski shuttles make it out to Alyeska. The five-mile journey from the **airport** to downtown costs $12 on the Borealis Shuttle (☎888/436-3600 or 907/276-3600), with taxis charging only a few dollars more; all major car rental agencies are represented at the airport. Anchorage's center is the easiest place to stay without a car, as all the bars, restaurants, and hotels are within walking distance of each

---

Alaska Marine Highway

The ferries of the **Alaska Marine Highway** system soldier on throughout the winter, serving southeast and south-central coastal towns. Though it's almost as cheap to fly, the ferries are a leisurely travel option for skiers with a few extra hours to spare and the desire to experience the beauty and solitude of the coastal fjords. Meals are available on board and lounges are furnished with reclining seats. Routes useful to heliboarders are those across Prince William Sound, running from Whittier (60 miles south of Anchorage) to Valdez and Cordova (Whittier–Valdez, $65; Valdez–Cordova, $34) and those sailing from Bellingham, in north Washington, up to Juneau and Haines (Juneau–Haines, $26). The Bellingham route is occasionally used by riders bringing motorhomes for the heliseason, who would rather pay the expensive fare (almost $1000 each way) than expose their rig to the winter hazards of the Alaska Highway. Service on all routes is limited to four or five trips per week and the schedule varies dramatically. Reservations, information, and timetables are available at ☎1-800/526-6731, ⊛www.akferry.com, or from PO Box 25535, Juneau, AK 99802-5535.

Motorhome rentals

A popular mode of transport for summertime visitors, **motorhomes** are inexpensive to rent during the winter, typically going for around half of the rates advertised on the company websites. Roadside parking during this period is generally available and many of the heli operators provide hookups for a nominal fee. Be sure to establish whether miles, cleaning, and linens are included in your quote before booking.

ABC Motorhome & Car Rentals 3875 W International Airport Rd ☎907/279-2000 or 800/421-7456, ⓦwww .abcmotorhome.com. Campers from $70 per day (sleeps two comfortably), 21ft motorhomes from $80 (sleeps three), with a three-night minimum.

Alaska Economy RVs 8825 Runamuck Place, #4 ☎907/561-7723 or 800/764-

4625, ⓦwww.goalaska.com. Cheap, with unlimited mileage: campers from $89 per day, motorhomes from $125.

Clippership Motorhome Rentals 5401 Old Seward Highway, Anchorage ☎907 /562-7051 or 800/421-3456, ⓦwww .clippershiprv.com. Rates start at $90 per day, with one hundred free miles per day.

other. Midtown's suburban grid of malls has a couple of great places to eat and hang out, but the area is tough to get to at night without a vehicle.

Accommodation

HI-Anchorage 700 H St ☎907/276-3635, ⓦwww .alaska.net/~hianch. Standard HI hostel (afternoon lockout, 1am curfew) in a building rather reminiscent of a prison, located downtown. $16 members, $19 nonmembers, private rooms ❶

Captain Cook 4th Ave at K St ☎907/276-6000, ⓦwww.captaincook.com. Feel like an oil baron between the wood-paneled walls of this luxury high-rise hotel. Downtown, with awesome views. ❻

The Copper Whale 440 L St ☎907/258-7999. Anchorage is full of B&Bs and this one is large, comfy, and downtown. For others see the Anchorage Alaska B&B Association site, ⓦwww.anchorage-bnb.com. ❸

Puffin Inn 4400 Spenard Rd, ☎907/243-4044 or 800/4PUFFIN, ⓦwww.puffininn.net. Inexpensive, clean, modern motel, close to the airport. Free airport shuttle, cable TV, continental breakfast, and newspapers. ❸

Spenard Hostel International 2845 West 42nd Place ☎907/248-5036, ⓦwww.AlaskaHostel.org. Closer to the airport than downtown, but laid-back and friendly, with three kitchens, three lounges (TV, quiet, and social) and no curfew. The "Winter Community" program offers cheap weekly and monthly rates. $16 for both members and non-members

Eating

Bear Tooth Theatre Pub 1230 W 27th Ave ☎907/276-4200. Order an inexpensive halibut burrito or pick up a pitcher of microbrew and settle down in front of the full-size movie screen.

Glacier Brewhouse 737 W 5th Ave ☎907/274-2739. Large and loud, serving consistently good microbrews and Alaskan variations on continental standards; alongside the pizza, pasta, and steaks are halibut and fresh king crab. Sister restaurant *Orso* (same address, ☎907/222-3232) specializes in Italian fine dining in a stylish setting.

Kumagoro 533 W 4th Ave ☎907/272-9905. The

place for a sushi fix or an inexpensive bowl of noodles.

Moose's Tooth 3300 Old Seward Hwy at 33rd Ave ☎907/258-2537. Classic pizza and brew stop for weary skiers, just off the highway back from Alyeska.

Snow City Café 1034 W 4th Ave ☎907/272-6338. Start the day with an omelet or fruit pancakes at this comfy café.

Thai Kitchen 3405 E Tudor Rd ☎907/561-0082. The local favorite for authentic Thai food at affordable prices.

Nightlife and entertainment

Pick up a copy of the *Anchorage Press*, **a free weekly,** for details of what's on in local entertainment. Begin a night of downtown bar-crawling debauchery with an early-evening martini at the elegant *Bernie's Bungalow*, 626 D St, then move on to *Humpy's Alehouse*, 610 W 6th Ave (☎907/276-2337), for music and microbrews with the college crowd or to the *Pioneer*, 739 W 4th Ave (☎907/276-7996), for a good dive bar. *Chilkoot Charlie's*, 2435 Spenard Rd (☎907/272-1010, weekend cover charge), is a rough-and-ready Alaskan hangout, its sawdust-strewn barn offering a surprisingly wide variety of enter-tainment.

Listings

Equipment rental Scott Liska's Boarderline, branches at 5020 Fairbanks St ☎907/245-9800 (home to a small indoor skate park) and Diamond Center, 800 E Diamond ☎907/349-9931; Northern Boarder, 320 W 5th Ave ☎907/258-7972 (owned by Scott's brother Jay); Peter Glenn Ski and Sports,

1520 O'Malley Rd ☎907/349-2929 (also a pick-up location for the Alyeska ski shuttle).
Groceries New Sagaya City Markets, 900 W 13th Ave ☎907/274-6173; another branc at 3700 Old Seward Hwy ☎907/561-5173.

Alyeska

The largest ski area in Alaska, **Alyeska** is the only real destination resort in the state, offering terrain for all levels and a wide array of facilities as well. The steeps are here if you want them; an entire face is classified double diamond, and heliskiing and snowcat trips depart right from the base of the resort. The upper mountain is above treeline, in a giant glacial bowl with ridges and chutes more typical of resorts in Europe than the States, yet, as Alyeska hugs the coast, the base elevation is practically at sea level and temperatures are significantly milder than in Alaska's subzero interior. Topping a thousand inches twice in the late 1990s, the average snowfall is more than double the figure for Colorado resorts, so patchy coverage is rarely a problem.

The resort's impressive sixty-passenger tram, on-mountain restaurants, and the luxurious *Alyeska Prince* hotel were built in the early 1990s by a Japanese resort chain eager to push Alyeska out of relative obscurity and capitalize on a then-bustling Japanese market, which has since dwindled. Today, locals from Anchorage (45 minutes southeast) constitute a large part of the clientele. Alyeska is located in the small town of **Girdwood**, a collection of timbered homes tucked away in the spruce forest, with a handful of bed and breakfasts, a couple of cozy restaurant-cum-bars, and a few small shops mostly accessed by unpaved roads. Originally a mining settlement, Girdwood was practically a ghost town when the ski area opened in 1959. In recent years several new developments have sprung up in the surrounding area, but the permanent community still retains the laid-back spirit of the hippies who settled here in the 1970s.

Off-peak, the resort is practically deserted midweek, populated only by British skiers on surprisingly inexpensive package vacations.

Mountain info

Phone ☎907/754-1111

Snow phone ☎907/754-7669 (SKI-SNOW)

Website ⊛www.alyeskaresort.com

Price $36 for hotel guests, $46 non-Alaskans

Operating times Nov to May daily, weekly operations are limited to Dec to early April 10.30am–5.30pm

No. of lifts 9, including 60-person aerial tram and 2 surface lifts

Base elevation 250′

Summit elevation 3939′ (hikable in-bounds); 2750′ (top of highest chair)

Vertical drop 2500′

No. of trails 68

Acreage 1000

Beginner 11%

Intermediate 52%

Expert 37%

Average snowfall 628″

Snowmaking Yes (42% or 28 trails)

Night skiing Yes, Christmas vacation and Fri–Sat only, mid-Dec to mid-March, lifts close at 9.30pm, one of the largest lit areas in North America at more than 2000ft of lighted terrain, 27 trails

Nursery facilities Yes, skiing from 3, snowboarding from 5; private child-care at Little Bear's Playhouse in Girdwood, ☎907/783-2116

Arrival, information, and getting around

Flights land at Anchorage International, forty miles north of Girdwood along the Seward Highway (Hwy-1). The scenic route snakes along the Pacific inlet of Turnagain Arm, flanked by the snow-covered mountains of the southern Chugach range. Whales and seals can occasionally be seen cruising the shore while moose are known to stop traffic on the road. A ski shuttle makes a daily trip from Anchorage to Alyeska weekends and holidays, arriving at the Daylodge at 10am and departing at 5.30pm. Round-trip tickets are $12 and can be bought in advance at the Peter Glenn Ski Shop (see "Listings" opposite) or purchased on the bus. Private shuttles can be arranged with The Magic Bus (☎907/268-6311), but a car is highly recommended for exploring Girdwood, Anchorage, and the surrounding area. Even within Girdwood, bar-hopping involves a twenty-minute walk from one establishment to the next, and the closest market – the gas station on the Seward Highway at the Girdwood turn-off – is two miles from the *Alyeska Prince*. Free parking is available for skiers in lots beside the Daylodge and the *Alyeska Prince*. The Girdwood Chamber of Commerce **website** (⊛www.girdwoodalaska.com) has extensive local information.

The mountain

Due to limited midwinter daylight and chilly morning temperatures, lifts don't open until 10.30am. By mid-March snow conditions are best later in the day, and the sun is still high when the lifts close at 5.30pm. Departing from the *Alyeska Prince* and swinging over the North Face, the sixty-person **tram** is the fastest way to get up the mountain. The upper terminal houses the on-mountain restaurant and cafeteria, both with inspiring views across the Kenai Peninsula. From here expert riders can drop into the double black diamond North Face or head to the chutes and ridges off the summit of Mount Alyeska. Intermediates should make their way down the open bowl of the main face. Beginners start from the **Daylodge**, a twenty-minute walk from the hotel, at the foot of Alyeska's main face and home to a cafeteria and rental shops. To reach the summit, upper tram terminal, and on-mountain restaurants from the Daylodge, take Chairs 4 and 6. Chair 7 runs from the hotel to the Daylodge bunny slopes, but is only open during peak periods. The lodge itself may be closed midweek out of peak season and the entire ski area switches to week-end-only operations around the middle of April.

Alyeska can suffer from **erratic weather conditions**. If it's raining at the base, it's most likely snowing at the summit. This doesn't necessarily mean the lifts will be running: avalanche danger at these times (and right after) can be high, shutting the mountain down. Flat light and white-out conditions are a fairly regular occurrence, especially during the earlier months of the season. On weekends, one chilly alternative is to ski at night on Alyeska's extensive floodlit area.

Beginner

The mountain's limited green trails, close to the Daylodge, are accessed by a couple of surface lifts and the short, slow **Chair 3**. Never-ever slopes are isolated from faster skiers, but more advanced beginners must cope with traffic crossing from the front face toward the Alyeska Prince base. Long, wide cat tracks on the upper mountain are easy enough for those progressing to blues.

Intermediate

Almost all the terrain on the front face is suitable for intermediates. Riders can cruise from top to bottom on wide, gently winding paths or tackle shorter, steeper faces. From the top of the tram follow **Main Street** around to the bottom of Chair 6, the highest lift on the mountain. From the Chair 6 summit, follow Silvertip to **Ptarmigan Gully** for treeless, rolling expanses of cruising terrain and a handful of trails that descend to the Daylodge. If you prefer the shelter of forested slopes, drop into the trails directly below the tram building from South Edge to Sourdough. Though the mountain is regularly groomed, there are plenty of patches left bumped, and the moguled blacks on the front face are within the grasp of advanced intermediates. Served by its own lift from the Daylodge, **Tanaka Hill** is a classic blue, evenly pitched with a perfect fall line.

Expert

Hike to the couloirs and powder fields of Glacier Bowl and Headwall and test your endurance on the long **High Traverse** across the front face toward the steeps and glades of Max's Mountain or drop into the ungroomed North Face. From the tram station hike to skier's right up ridge for the North Face's steepest chutes or head left and down for stubby glades. In poor conditions, prepare to ski the lift-served front face only; it's better for freeriders, but less appealing to downhill carvers and off-piste veterans. The most challenging terrain is found directly below the upper tram terminal on Lolo's and Gear Jammer under Chair 1.

Freestyle

Even when conditions are poor on North Face and the upper mountain, Alyeska's naturally rolling terrain is perfect for freestylers. On the front face,

Independent backcountry options

Chugach Powder Guides run snowcat trips close to the ski area and heliski trips further into the Chugach range (see p.409). Valdez, Alaska's heliskiing central, is a six-hour drive. Locals hike around the ridge up on nearby Turnagain Pass. Hatcher Pass, just north of Anchorage near the town of Willow, is popular with the snowmobile crew. More information is available from the Glacier Forest Service office, Alyeska Highway at Brudine Road (℡907/783-3242).

launch off the network of cat tracks and natural hips. The biggest drops here are below the tram building. Lap Chair 6 for natural hits and bumps. Neither the pipe nor small terrain park is particularly impressive, but both are good for a laugh.

Lift tickets, lessons, and rentals

Alyeska is inexpensive compared to most North American resorts, particularly for visitors on multiday package deals; the cheapest day **tickets** are sold to *Alyeska Prince* guests ($30), and cheap night passes are on offer too. Beginners can ride Chairs 3 and 7 for around half the price of a regular ticket ($19). Sightseeing tickets for the tram are $12–16, but there is no charge after 5pm, when the surrounding peaks are bathed in late afternoon light.

The Mountain Learning center caters to beginners; prices for visitors are best if booked as part of an all-inclusive package. Two-hour **lessons** start at $30, with lift-and-lesson packages from $50. Women's midweek ski clinics are offered occasionally throughout the season. For two weeks in June, the upper reaches of Mount Alyeska host the Boarderline summer camp, where Anchorage and Girdwood locals build large kickers and erect jibs up in Glacier Bowl (☎970/245-5070 for information). Challenge Alaska (☎970/344-7339, ⊛www.challenge.ak.org) organizes adaptive programs at Alyeska for skiers with disabilities.

Rentals run from $23 for basic skis to $30 for boards. Beginner packages are only available from the Daylodge. More expensive performance and demo packages are offered at the Alyeska Prince shop, which also rents Nordic skis and snowshoes. Girdwood Ski and Cyclery (☎907/783-2453), on the way into town on the Alyeska Highway, is an alternative for backcountry rentals, used gear, and clothing.

Accommodation

The grand, frequently vacant *Alyeska Prince* makes a fine place to stay and is used for most all-inclusive packages. Stay in Anchorage (see listings p.399) if you want more restaurant choices, or rent a condo or chalet through Alyeska Accommodations (☎907/783-2000 or 888/783-2001, ⊛www .alyeskaaccommodations.com) to get access to kitchen facilities. Properties are reasonably priced ($100–300 per night) and range from modern studios to large luxury homes. It's best to stock up on **groceries** in Anchorage.

Alyeska Hostel Alta Drive ☎907/783-2222, ⊛www.alyeskahostel.com. Attractive cabin with one private room and two small dorms. Full kitchen; linens are available. Cash only. $12.50.

Alyeska Prince Hotel 1000 Arlberg Ave ☎907/754-1111, ⊛www.alyeskaresort.com. The only hotel in Girdwood reflects the resort owners' Japanese origins: cherrywood fittings, lots of gadgets, and sleek, high-tech styling. Half empty during winter (bargain rates are in effect midweek), the *Prince* has a fitness center with an elegant indoor pool, rental shop, Japanese steakhouse, slopeside bar, and a rather uninspired café. Ski packages from $100 per person. ⑥

The Glass House Lot 2, Brenner St ☎907/754-1470, ⊛www.girdwood.net/glass. The stained glass windows of this B&B make an arresting sight as you drive along the Alyeska Highway to the resort. The three suites are decorated in a Scandinavian style, and the house is bright and airy. ④

Winner Creek Bed and Breakfast Mile 2.9 Alyeska Highway ☎907/783-5501. Modern, elegant log home surrounded by trees. Spacious and comfortable, with a river-rock fireplace and welcoming kitchen. One of the three rooms sleeps four to five. Facilities include a hot tub. ④

Eating, drinking, and entertainment

Choosing **where to eat** in Girdwood doesn't take long. The cheery *Bake Shop*, on Olympic Circle close to the Daylodge (T 907/783-2831, 7am–7pm), is the spot for filling, inexpensive sourdough pancake breakfasts or soup and sandwich lunches. Next door, the tiny *Java Haus* (T 907/754-2827) provides a caffeine fix along with Internet access. Fans drive from Anchorage to visit the rustic *Double Musky*, Crow Creek Rd (T 907/783-2822; Tues–Thurs 5-10pm, Sat-Sun 4-10pm), a strange mix of New Orleans meets Alaska serving spicy seafood and steaks. Try the Creole crab-stuffed halibut ($25). *Chair 5*, Linblad Ave (T 907/783-2500), is more affordable, serving up inventive pizzas like Thai chicken and four-cheese pesto, along with burgers, microbrews, and pool.

On-mountain are a few pricey spots, including the *Glacier Express*, a burger joint perched above the North Face in the upper tram terminal, and the *Seven Glaciers* (Fri & Sat night only) on the floor above, a standard gourmet-style entry with steaks and seafood. Basic cafeteria snacks and hot drinks are available at the Daylodge, while around the corner, the *Sitzmark Bar and Grill* has a little more atmosphere with a busy **après** and the occasional band or DJ on Friday or Saturday nights.

Other activities and attractions

Dog sledding, snowmobiling, snowshoeing, and ski touring can all be arranged in Girdwood. Next to the *Alyeska Prince*, flat Moose Meadows is best for cross-country novices – rent skis or snowshoes from the hotel. Views of the famous Portage Glacier, a fifteen-minute drive south from the resort, are best seen from the air. Try Alpine Air (T 907/783-2360, from $69 per person), based at the tiny Girdwood Airport, to tour the Chugach Range and the fjords of Prince William Sound. Landings are allowed high on the glaciers if conditions permit. Whale-watching and iceberg cruises depart daily from Seward, two hours south of Girdwood.

Listings

Avalanche hotline T 907/754-2369.
Banks ATM in the *Alyeska Prince* and at the Tesoro gas station on the Seward Hwy.
Internet Gerrish Library, Hightower Rd T 907/783-2565 or *Java Haus* (see above).

Medical Girdwood Clinic, Hightower Rd T 907/783-1355.
Post office Hightower Rd and Linblade Ave T 907/783-2922.

Eaglecrest

Whether you're looking for a gentle introduction to Alaskan skiing, a warm-up for heliboarding in Haines (see p.409), or a stop-off en route to Anchorage, **Eaglecrest Ski Area** (T 907/790-2000, snow report T 907/586-5330, W www.skijuneau.com; adult $26, junior $18) is highly recommended. Among the fjords and spruce of Southeast Alaska, the open bowls and snow-encrusted glades of this 640-acre resort sit at the end of a rutted road on little Douglas Island, twelve miles from downtown Juneau. Owned by the city, Eagle Crest is only open Thursdays though Mondays (9am–4pm) and is alternately blighted and blessed by the heavy precipitation that drizzles down over the city. Snowmaking is no match for the warm temperatures that bring damaging rain and the ski area occasionally shuts down, even in the middle of winter, due to lack of snow. However, when the temperature drops, the gladed slopes and exposed ridgeline are blasted with coastal powder.

The mountain

After a storm Eaglecrest offers advanced intermediates and experts a day of epic powder riding. With only two tediously slow chairs and just a handful of traditional runs, **hiking** is an integral part of the experience. From the 2600ft summit of the upper lift, skiers stomp up toward **Pittman's Ridge**, worth the trek for the startling views across the water toward snowcapped Admiralty Island and the Pacific Ocean further west. To skier's left along the ridge, cornice hits lead into the short, open powder shots of the **West Bowl**, which funnels down into rocky trees. To the right are the steeper chutes and stubby glades of the **East Bowl**. Both end in a lengthy, flat traverse. The vertical drop, though 1400ft, seems short, but the rolling terrain and untracked powder fields are awesome.

Intermediates have only a handful of trails to choose from, and the small terrain park is usually icy. **Beginners** are slightly better off, learning on a small meadow with one surface lift (lit on Friday nights 4–9pm), separate from the rest of the mountain, then progressing to the greens and easy blues below the lower chair. Reasonably inexpensive (from $17) **lessons** and basic rentals are available from the day lodge, home to an excellent tuning shop. There's also a small cross-country area, suitable for beginners and intermediates ($5), and a lift-served tubing hill, open on Friday nights, weekends, and holidays. The Eaglecrest Ski Bus runs from points throughout Juneau on weekends and holidays only ($3 each way, call mountain for schedule).

Practicalities: Juneau

You'll be staying, eating, and generally hanging out in **Juneau**, an attractive Victorian port accessible only by sea or air. In addition to cruise ship tourism, the city benefits economically from its tenuous position as the seat of state government, a distinction continually under threat by those who would move the capitol to Anchorage.

Juneau has a wide range of **accommodation** including the small and pleasantly furnished *Silverbow Inn and Bakery*, 120 Second St (☎907/586-4146, ⓦwww.silverbowinn.com, from $88 B&B), run by an energetic couple from New York and a hub of the local arts scene. Seasonal events and movie screenings are held weekly in their backroom restaurant, and their bakery produces the best bagels in the state. Budget beds are available in the dorms at the rather austere *HI-Juneau*, 614 Harris St (☎907/586-9559, ⓦwww.juneauhostel.org; $10, chores, lock-out, and curfew), and cheap motel rooms, some with kitchenettes, at the *Driftwood Lodge*, 435 Willoughby Ave (☎907/586-2280 or 1-800/544-2239, ⓦwww.driftwoodalaska.com; from $49).

Shop for **groceries** at *Rainbow Foods*, Second and Stewart (☎907/586-6476), or grab inexpensive sandwiches from *Paradise Café*, 245 Marine Way (☎586-2253). A step up is *Hangar on the Wharf* (☎907/586-5018), a bustling bar and grill on Merchants Wharf with views across the Gastineau Channel, reservations suggested. For something a little quieter, try elegant *Di Sopra* for fresh halibut, creative pastas, and generous salads (entrees $12–20). Nearby is the cozy

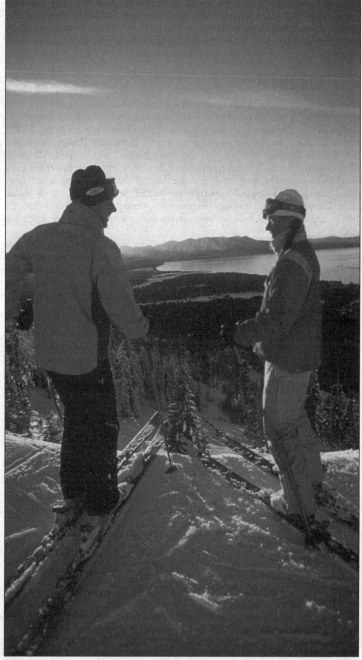

△ Couple standing over slopes, South Lake Tahoe, CA

and inexpensive *Fiddlehead* restaurant and bakery, 429 W Willoughby Ave (☎907/586-3150). **Bars** downtown are all within a stumble of each other and in winter draw a young crowd of snowboarders, outdoor guides, and off-duty fishermen. Don't miss the busy wooden saloon in the creaky *Alaskan*, 167 S Franklin St (☎907/586-9000), Juneau's oldest hotel and a venue for live music and open-mike nights. And visit the *Bubble Room*, hotel lounge of the dated but grand *Baranof Hotel*, 127 N Franklin (☎907/586-2660). The *Imperial* sports bar (241 Front St, ☎907/586-1960) is a fine spot for pool, air hockey, and arcade games.

Should you break a piece of gear or forget to pack vital **equipment**, stop in at Poseidon Snowboards, 226 Seward St (☎907/463-5655), or the Foggy Mountain outdoor store, 134 N Franklin St (☎907/586-6780). **Car rentals** are available at the airport (☎907/789-7821), nine miles north of downtown; try Rent-a-Wreck (☎907/789-4111) or Payless (☎907/780-6004).

Other activities and attractions

A small but efficient town bus service (☎907/789-6901, $1.25 each way) runs north to the residential suburbs, dropping passengers within walking distance of the covered wooden **skatepark**, 2400 Mendenhall Rd, or the highly regarded Alaskan Brewing Co 5429 Shaune Drive (☎907/780-5866; free tours and samples Thurs–Sat 11am–4.30pm). Dog sledding, ski touring, and short **heli-ski** descents can be arranged with one of Juneau's many guide services (enquire at the CVB), usually up on the vast Juneau icefield, 1500 square miles of glacial snow.

Heliskiing in Alaska

Heliskiing in Alaska is not all gnarly vertical descents, avalanche running, and near-death experiences. While it's true that most riders who make it up here are experts, you don't have to be a budding pro to tackle the terrain. Week-long helipackages are expensive and guides often find themselves catering to wealthy clients, most of whom are advanced intermediates, who prefer mellow terrain in the huge, open, untracked powder bowls of Alaska; satisfaction comes from laying down perfect turns, and avalanche danger is practically nil. No guide will push their group to ride harder than the weakest member can manage, so it's important to be honest about your abilities when booking and to choose skiing companions wisely. Guides will seek out the best terrain for the group, generally starting the day at the easier end of the scale. Runs of 4000 vertical feet are normal; expect to average four to eight runs a session.

Costs, location, and other factors

All guide services meet self-imposed safety guidelines. Choosing one over the other boils down to what type of package you're looking for and when you want to go. "Helitime," the time that you end up paying for the helicopter, is either priced by the number of runs, the guaranteed vertical feet you can be expected to log on your trip, or according to the Hobbs airtime meter in the helicopter, similar to a taxi's meter. Some guides still allow riders to jostle for

Heliskiing operators

Valdez

Alaska Backcountry Adventures, Valdez ☏907/835-5608, ⊛www.alaskaback country.com. ABA, the oldest operator in Valdez, maintains basic facilities and an RV camp by the Worthington Airstrip at Mile 29 on the Richardson Highway. Using a ski plane in addition to a chopper, ABA is more like a taxi than an all-inclusive operator, though guide service is now mandatory. Pay-by-the-run chips are available at $85 each with a minimum purchase of ten. A full day of helitime costs $595 including lunch; five-day packages start at $2975. That's without accommodation. ABA will arrange a reasonably priced hotel lodging in town or can set up RV rentals. The group's base area, known as Worthington Strip, has RV hook-ups (a $15 fee is charged if you bring an RV not rented through ABA). The Strip is also home to Phatz Ski Rental. Safety equipment is not included in the price, as many ABA regulars have their own, but all gear is available to rent. Ice climbing and kayaking are also offered.

Alaska Rendevous Heli-ski Guides ☏907/822-3300 (mid March to early May) or ☏307/734-0721 (off-season), ⊛www.arlinc.com. The recently constructed *Alaska Rendevous Lodge* sits at Mile 45, at the northern end of Thompson Pass, and has its own airstrip and tavern. Rooms are $50 per person for a shared room, $75 single. Previously operating out of the *Tiekel River Lodge* at Mile 56, this outfit was founded by Theo Meiner, a member of the avalanche advisory board for the National Ski Patrol and previously a guide with Valdez Heli-Ski. Two runs close to the lodge start at $230; a day package of six runs $720. Semi-private and private charters available. They also offer ice-climbing and backcountry touring.

H₂O Heli Guides, Valdez ☏907/835-8418 or 800/578-4354, ⊛www.h2oguides.com. Founded in 1995 by Dean Cummings, World Extreme Skiing champ, H₂O arranges for skiers to stay in downtown Valdez at the *Totem Inn*. It offers a multitude of three-, five-, and seven-day inclusive packages, including an annual women's week. A couple of down days are figured into each package and ice climbing, kayaking, and fishing are offered as alternative activities. Five-day/seven-night packages start at $3518 per person with daily rates from $690, including ground transportation, Salomon fat skis and boards, and all safety gear. Mid-Feb to late April.

Valdez Heli-Camps ☏970/835-3898, ⊛www.valdezhelicamps.com. All-inclusive packages based out of the operator's fifteen-room lodge in downtown Valdez. Meals are catered, with huge buffet breakfasts and dinners eaten in the lodge. A shuttle carries skiers to Thompson Pass each day, and lunch is served in their warming hut. A snowcat operates on down days, and alternative activities include fishing, kayaking, snowshoeing, cross-country skiing, dog-mushing, and ice climbing. Guests have the option of spending a night in an insulated ski touring hut on top of Stone Mountain ($435 per night for groups up to six; snowcat transportation, fuel, firewood, and waste disposal provided). $4367 for six days/seven nights, shorter packages include a two-day/one-night cat package from $495. One-day heliskiing from $621, one-day cat skiing $182. Lodge and meals only, $182 Transceivers included, but probes, packs, and shovels cost extra. Fat ski rental $35 daily. Early Feb to mid-May.

Valdez Heli Ski Guides ☏907/835-4528, ⊛www.valdezheliskiguides.com. The largest guide service in Valdez, operating out of the *Tsaina Lodge* on the Richardson Highway close to the Worthington Glacier and Thompson Pass. Founded in 1993 by Doug Coombes, an expert skier who has been guiding in Valdez since it all began. The Tsaina has luxury cabins, a bunkhouse, restaurant, and a bar. Three-, four- and seven-day packages are scheduled from early March to mid-May. A week-long steep skiing camp is also offered. Week-long packages cost from $4635 for lodging, meals, and helitime and include use of all safety gear and heli-pack. Powder ski rental from $23. One day, averaging six runs, costs $635. Lodging only is $200.

Cordova

Points North Heli-Adventures, Inc, Cordova ☎877/787-6784, ⊛www.alaskaheliski .com. South along the coast from Valdez, the small cannery town of Cordova is accessible only by plane or boat. Surrounded by mountains on the shores of the Orca Inlet, the town is home to Points North, the lone operator to fly into the southeastern Chugach. Lodging and base of operations are located at the converted Orca Cannery, run by Points North and now known as the Orca Adventure Lodge. On down days riders can take to the local ski hill, Mount Eyak, which operates one creaky single chair to the summit. Rates are $135 per night for lodging (all meals included) and $475 per heli-flight hour. Expect to pay around $600 a day for about 20,000–25,000 vertical feet. Visitor information is available from the Cordova Chamber of Commerce (☎907/424-7260, ⊛www.cordovachamber.com).

Girdwood

Chugach Powder Guides, Alyeska ☎907/783-4354, ⊛www.chugachpowderguides .com. CPG fly into the ski resort of Alyeska in the eastern Chugach an hour south of Anchorage in Girdwood (see p.400). A popular choice for skiers on a week-long Alyeska vacation looking to try their first runs from a helicopter. The average CPH client tends to be a little older and wealthier than at Valdez, though extra slots may be snapped up last minute by younger Anchorage locals. CPH runs a snowcat when the weather prohibits flying. Seven-day packages including lodging at the swanky *Alyeska Prince Hotel* and lift passes at the resort start at $3150 per person with daily rates from $575. (See Alyeska listings, p.403.)

Haines

Out of Bounds ☎800/HELL-YEA, ⊛www.alaskaheliskiing.com. The only heliskiing outfit in southeastern Alaska, Out of Bounds offers riders the vast expanses of the Chilkat, Takshunuk, and Takhinsha Mountains to themselves, with even the chance to name runs as they go as first descents are pretty normal here. The crew is a relaxed bunch and specializes in big mountain riding without the handholding, though they'll help you with car rentals and lodging if you need some suggestions. A large percentage of clients are returning filmmakers, photographers, and pro riders. Ten-day packages start at $3950, daily rates average $500. A guide school is also offered each spring. The closest international airport is in Juneau (see p.405), and three to four airlines fly daily up to Haines, so advance booking is not usually necessary; expect to pay $100–150 round-trip. Accommodation in Haines is available in pricey but clean motels (try the *Captain's Choice Motel*, on 2nd St downtown), cabins (*Bear Creek Cabins and Hostel*, ☎907/766-2259, a mile from town, also runs two dorm rooms), and a cluster of small B&Bs, many located in the historic clapboard buildings of Fort Seward, Alaska's only Army post pre-World War II; the Haines CVB, 122 2nd Ave (☎907/766-3155 or 800/458-3579, ⊛www.haines.ak .us), can help you choose, as can Out of Bounds. Most restaurants are closed for the season, but halibut fish and chips or milkshakes at the *Bamboo Room* diner on 2nd Avenue and Main (daily 6am–late; ☎907/766-2800) will hit the spot. Lunch is available next to the heli staging area in the form of burgers, pies, and fry-ups at the *33 Mile Roadhouse* (☎767-5510) out on the Haines Highway. *The Fogcutter*, 122 Main St (☎907/766-2555), is the drinking den of choice, though most riders eat dinner and collapse.

a single run, but these will usually be very close to the staging area and not necessarily the pristine experience you're looking for. More typical is the opportunity to take a spare place in a prebooked group for the day. The six-seat A-Star is the helicopter most often used; the common group size is four clients and one guide. All-inclusive packages are the **easiest** option as clients are guaranteed a seat. However, the guide service must reserve helicopters for the ski season, pay pilots' wages, and cover hefty insurance costs whether the helicopter flies or not. Even if the weather is bad, as it often is in Alaska**, pre-paid helitime is rarely refunded**. If you've booked a week and experience a long stretch of down days, substitutes of fishing and ice climbing may not be enough to make up for the expense, and you'll suddenly realize why jockeying for flights on a daily basis can make sense. If possible, aim to spend at least twice as many days in Alaska as you'd like to fly and consider an outfit close to a regular ski mountain or running a snowcat in addition to helicopters. Also establish exactly what's included in your rate as less-expensive guides may charge rental fees for use of a transceiver, probe, shovel, harness, and streamlined backpack that must be carried for safety by every rider.

Location is another factor. All Alaskan heli ops are based in mountain ranges close to the Pacific coast, where heavy snow results as warmer ocean storms meet the colder temperatures blowing south from the interior. **Valdez**, in the heart of the Chugach Mountain range, is the best known of the Alaskan heli towns. As the birthplace of the Alaskan heliskiing phenomenon it may no longer have the same pioneering buzz of ten years ago, but the area's many advantages include a range of operators to choose from and as much of a party atmosphere as you'll find in the Alaskan interior.

The disadvantage of Valdez is that (if not prebooked) you'll be fighting for flight time with all the other motorhome occupants parked up on Thompson Pass, 29 miles out of town. When the weather sets in and flight windows are brief, competition to get in the air can get a bit nasty. Points North, based in Cordova, and Chugach Powder Guides, based at Alyeska resort, also fly into the Chugach and are well out of the Valdez crush. Out of Bounds is the only operator with a permit in the southeast of the state, flying out of Haines, close to the Canadian Yukon border.

The **heliseason** runs from February to May. February is cold and dark, but most certain to have fresh snow – a mixed blessing as fresh snow increases the likelihood of instability and avalanche. The undisturbed, glacial peaks keep powder fresh for days. March is the most popular month, though still chilly. By late April, when summer's endless days approach, skiers can ride until nine or ten at night.

The Best of the Rest

49° North, Washington

A sixty-mile drive away from Spokane, 49° North (℡509/935-6649; Ⓦwww.ski49n.com; $34 adults, $27 juniors) is named for its location on the 49th parallel, nestled among acres of pristine forest in the lower Selkirk Mountains. Five slow, usually empty lifts access the 42 runs spread across 1100 acres. The terrain, covered by approximately 300 inches of snow annually, includes bumped-out runs, long cruisers, an Olympic-size halfpipe, and excellent backcountry freeriding in the East Basin. Free childcare and beginners' lessons are available.

Bear Valley, California

If Bear Valley (☏209/753-2301, ⊛www.bearvalley.com; adults $43, under-23s $36, juniors $15) were not so inconveniently located, it wouldn't be such a well-kept secret. Stranded between Lake Tahoe and Yosemite, the mountain is just east of Kirkwood (see p.364), yet only accessible in winter from the west, via a complicated network of backroads. Those who make the journey have a sizable 1280 acres of excellent bowls, cliffs, and cruisers to play on, all hit by the same heavy snows as its Tahoe neighbors (360 inches annually). Though beginners and intermediates will appreciate the lack of crowds here, it's freeriders who are best served. The extensive rocky terrain is exhilarating when conditions are right, and there are two small, well-designed parks and a pipe; it's all easily navigated by virtue of the mountain's thirteen lifts. Two-for-one midweek deals are offered on both lift tickets and lessons. Angel Camp is the nearest sizeable town, a winding 45 minutes away, but the resort's Home Run and a network of cross-country trails lead off the summit (8495ft) to tiny Bear Valley Village, where bunks in the comfortable *Base Camp Lodge* (☏209/753-6556, ⊛www.basecamplodge.com; ❶ and up) make an inexpensive alternative to the grander *Bear Valley Lodge*.

Boreal, California

The short vertical drop and limited terrain of Boreal (☏530/426-3666; ⊛www.skiboreal.com; adults $35, juniors $10) will not suit downhill speed demons, mogul fanatics, backcountry purists, or intermediates searching for long cruisers and a lake view. Yet the 380-acre resort on the western side of Donner Pass, eight miles west of Truckee, draws day crowds from as far away as the Bay Area, thanks to low ticket prices, extensive beginner terrain, decent parks, and various family-friendly offerings. Boreal is a day area, though its Nightline park is groomed specifically for evening sessions ($22; until 8pm weekdays, 9pm Fri & Sat), quite popular with Tahoe locals. There are wide open beginner meadows close to the lodge and under the Last Dutchman lift, and intermediates should be able to handle the backside's supposed black diamond runs, which are often deserted. Natural conditions aren't always tops, due to the strong Sierra sun and the lack of tree cover, but extensive snowmaking ensures that Boreal is usually one of the earliest California resorts to open. Just as good a reason to come this way is the Western SkiSport Museum (Wed–Sun 10am-4pm; free; ☏530/426-3313), adjacent to Boreal ski area and founded by the venerable Auburn Ski Club in 1969. The museum is crammed with memorabilia and photos from times when snow that had been carted down to San Francisco for a ski-jumping exhibition was pillaged by overexcited city dwellers for a massive snowball fight.

Diamond Peak, California

While the snow is of dubious quality, the facilities rather basic, and ticket prices relatively expensive for what you get ski-wise, Diamond Peak (☏775/832-1177, ⊛www.diamondpeak.com; adults $41, juniors $15) does offer some of the most spectacular north shore views of Lake Tahoe. Created as part of the Incline Village development back in the 1960s, the original ski area (once

known as Ski Incline) is now the lower part of the mountain. Short, intermediate runs spill off the ridge into a wide, sheltered canyon that slopes gently
down past the base lodge and parking lot. With only six lifts and a compact layout, getting separated for long is almost impossible. Novices may use the two
canyon beginner lifts for just $15 – no views, but a great price for Tahoe. The
ski area expanded upwards to 8450ft Diamond Peak in 1987, adding more
intermediate cruisers, a handful of seriously steep groomed blacks, stubby
glades, and the undulating, backcountry-style Solitude Canyon – awesome and
untracked in powder, but icy, sketchy, or closed when low-altitude conditions
prevail. Although dated condos flank the lower slopes, Diamond Peak is a day
area, witnessing family crowds only on weekends when the local residents and
Incline Village second-home owners come out to play. Snacks are available in
the base lodge cafeteria and mid-mountain *Snowflake* restaurant. To get to the
resort from the North Shore, take Hwy-28 to Incline Village, turn left on
Country Club Drive and follow Ski Way to the resort; from the south shore,
follow Hwy-50 to Hwy-28; turn right on Country Club Drive.

Dodge Ridge, California

Northwest of Yosemite, Dodge Ridge (℡209/965-4444, ⓦwww.dodgeridge
.com; adults $43, teens $35, juniors $15) is the closest resort to the Bay Area.
Though it's strictly a day area, the twelve lifts and facilities, including a mid-
mountain restaurant, allow riders to take full advantage of the resort's 815 acres.
Dodge Ridge markets itself toward families and is primarily suited to beginners and intermediates. There are some gentle cruising runs, sheltered bunny
slopes and above-average terrain parks packed with jibs. Recent expansion into
Boulder Creek Canyon has added 265 acres of more challenging trails, including the ski area's steepest, but most of the blacks are within the grasp of competent intermediates. The snow quality in this sheltered valley is decent, averaging over 300 inches annually. Rustic cabin and lodge accommodation is
available in the nearby hamlets of Pinecrest and Strawberry; if planning an
overnight trip, however, it's worth the extra hour or two to drive up to Lake
Tahoe (see p.332), with its smorgasbord of ski areas and more attractive locale.

Donner Ski Ranch, California

Ten miles west of Truckee, Donner Ski Ranch (℡530/426-3635, ⓦwww.don-
nerskiranch.com; adults $20, juniors $10) makes its hay by offering the least
expensive skiing in all of Tahoe, perhaps anywhere, especially on monthly value
days when tickets can be as low as $5. The six lifts are creaky and slow, there
are only 435 acres of mostly short, intermediate runs – though the snow is
some of the deepest in the region – and the lodge is small and neglected.
Group lessons are $20 with lift, lesson, and equipment packages $45 for skiers,
$49 for snowboarders ($30/40 for kids 5–12). The slopeside *Summit House* has
basic but inexpensive condo units ($130–250 per night, sleeping from two to
ten) and there are a couple of local bars where you can buy a beer and a burger, but Donner Ski Ranch is essentially a day area.

Homewood, California

The only Tahoe resort on the woodsy west shore, Homewood (℡530/525-
2900; ⓦwww.skihomewood.com; $44 adults, $27 juniors, kids under 10 free)
is fairly small at 1260 acres but there's a decent variety of terrain, including

glades and winding tree-cut runs primarily geared toward intermediates. The resort sits at lower altitude than most Tahoe ski areas, but has a traditionally high snowfall, averaging 450 inches a season, with the best snow found on the north-facing slopes and glades under the Quad chair. On a powder day, when the glades are dense with snow and the steep walls of Quail Face are open, even the hardcore will love Homewood. The terrain park and pipe are generally well maintained, with mostly smaller hits and jibs. Both the rustic North and reno-vated South lodges house ticket booths, reasonably priced cafeterias with var-ied menus, and rentals. Lift and lodging packages on the nearby west shore can be booked through the resort, starting at around $50; call ☎877/525-7669. Homewood is an easy six-mile drive from Tahoe City on Hwy-89. Free on-call shuttle service is available between Incline Village and all north shore stops to Homewood; call the resort in advance for details.

Mission Ridge, Washington

Seattleites find it hard to push an extra sixty miles east past Stevens Pass (see p.389) to the smaller ski area of Mission Ridge (☎509/663-6543, snow con-ditions ☎509/663-3200 or 1-800/374-1693, ⑩www.missionridge.com; $37 day lift ticket). But though its 2200 acres of terrain see only around 200 inch-es of snow a year, the flakes that fall here are among the lightest in the state, producing powdery conditions unfamiliar to the state's other major resorts. Though there are only four interminably slow lifts at Mission Ridge, lines are minimal even on busy days. Of its 35 marked trails only ten percent are begin-ner; the two dedicated beginner runs are accessed from Lift 1. Lift 2 takes you to the top of the mountain and probably accesses the most diverse terrain – not just plenty of gentle blues for those who want to develop their skills in peace, but the bulk of the advanced runs; choose between fast carving around the Bomber Bowl, where there are several great, manageable chutes, or the double black moguls on the other side of Lift 2. The ski area on the whole is pitched more toward intermediates, with sixty percent of the runs graded blue; the best cruisers are available off lifts 3 and 4. When conditions are good, it's worth ven-turing into the backcountry areas; most of which are accessed from Lift 2 by hiking or skating along Windy Ridge and the adjoining Microwave and Bowl Four. The latter of these has the mountain's best snow, typically loaded with feather-light powder perfect for laying down fat, even carves – but the hike to get here is the longest. Note that though the ski area welcomes backcountry skiers and will advise of conditions, they will not help in the event of an acci-dent, which becomes the responsibility of the county sheriff.

Mountain High, California

Of the small resorts found in the San Gabriel Mountains, the peaks that form the northwestern border of Los Angeles' suburban sprawl, Mountain High (☎760/249-5808; ⑩www.mthigh.com; for ticket prices see below) are the easiest to reach and have the only significant snowmaking program. Most vis-itors are beginners or younger freestyle skiers and boarders, who aren't both-ered by the lack of vertical or acreage, treating the resort more like a skatepark on snow. There are, however, enough cruisers to keep the casual intermediate content for a day. Mountain High is a much more realistic day-trip – or even, as the lifts don't close until 10pm, an evening out – from LA than Big Bear. Avoiding traffic, the trip is only a little over an hour from the city, and it's almost all on the freeway. Though neither the ski hill nor the local town of

Wrightwood has the resort infrastructure found at Big Bear, Mountain High has better snowfall records: some winters see more than 300 inches of snow. The resort has two separate peaks, East and West. The former has a couple of beginner areas, long intermediate cruisers, some short glades, and a tenuously rated "double-black" bump run when the snow's good enough, but the terrain features here aren't as well maintained as those at the West resort. The recently rebuilt East lodge, crowded on the weekends, houses a pleasant restaurant and bar, rental shop, and ski school, but midweek the slopes are practically deserted. Day tickets are sold on both the hour and point system. Four- or eight-hour tickets replace the usual day and half-day offerings, allowing riders to start their days whenever they please. Alternatively, a card loaded with 200 points costs around the same amount as an eight-hour ticket (but can be spread out throughout the season), with one lap on the Blue Ridge high-speed quad costing twenty points; taking the Mountain High express uses up fifteen; all others are ten apiece. To get here from east LA, San Bernadino, Orange County, and Riverside, take I-15, exit Hwy-138 West, and shortly after make a left onto Hwy-2.

Mount Baldy, California

Only 45 miles from downtown Los Angeles, Mount Baldy (☎909/981-3344, ⓦwww.mtbaldy.com, adults $40, juniors $25) is nevertheless underutilized by local urbanites. The 800-acre mountain has the steepest, most challenging slopes in southern California, making it a good place for day-tripping experts, but a lack of snowmaking (20 percent) and any meaningful improvements or full-bore marketing campaign prevent the resort from reaching its full potential. Beginners and intermediates are better off heading up to the more reliable conditions at Snow Summit (see p.316), while freestylers will probably want to skip the steeps of Baldy in favor of Mountain High's jibs and jumps (see p.413). Those with skateboarding roots might be the most satisfied – buried in the depths of the mountain among the steeps and glades is the Baldy fullpipe, a bit of a holy grail for boarding enthusiasts.

Mount Rose, California

Cresting the ridgeline between the Tahoe Basin and Nevada's dusty Washoe Valley, Mount Rose (☎775/849-0704 or 800/SKI-ROSE; ⓦwww.mtrose.com; adults $48, juniors $12) offers views of both lake and desert, with the highest base elevation in Tahoe. A large proportion of the resort's intimidating trails plunge down the fall line on both north and east flanks of the peak, a popular training ground for downhill racers. With few blue trails, the mountain's steep rise can be intimidating for intermediates; however, the wide, sheltered canyon at the base of the north face is perfect for novice skiers, segregated from the steeper runs and served by two slow-moving chairs. The spacious East Bowl accesses acres of glades and a small collection of man-made hits and jibs. Beginner lift, lesson, and gear packages are relatively inexpensive ($48), private lessons are cheap ($39), and advanced clinics are free.

The comfy Main Lodge cafeteria caters to a local Reno crowd with inexpensive food: fries are less than a buck, with almost all other items – sandwiches, pasta, breakfast – under $5. The Main Lodge also houses a coffeeshop and spacious bar. Mount Rose is the closest ski resort to Reno, 22 miles up steep, winding Hwy-431. Nearest lakeshore towns are Crystal Bay and Incline Village; Tahoe City is a good 45 minutes away without traffic. Ski shuttles depart Reno twice daily; reservations are recommended (☎775/325-8813 or check the website), and the charge is minimal with a full-price lift ticket, but $15 round-trip otherwise.

Mount Shasta, California

At 14,162ft, the volcanic peak of dormant Mount Shasta stands prominently in north-central California, much more of a draw than the Mount Shasta Board & Ski Park (☎530/926-8610 or 1-800/SKI-SHASTA, ⊛www.skipark.com; adults $33, juniors $17, night skiing $20) sitting on Shasta's southern flanks. Just three chairlifts serve its 425 acres, though admittedly there is a good mix of trails, decent glades, an improving selection of hits and jibs, a pipe, and night skiing (Wed–Sat 4–10pm). Still, many riders will be going to hit the back-country and ascend the peak in spring and early summer. This is not an under-taking for the inexperienced; you need to be in good shape, equipped with crampons and an ice-axe, and well-versed in backcountry practices. The weath-er can change with alarming speed, and several deaths occur every year. It's imperative to first contact the Mount Shasta Ranger District Office, 204 W Alma St (☎916/926-4511, ⊛www.shastaavalanche.org), for route suggestions, avalanche advisories, and the required hiking permits ($15); House of Ski, 316 Chestnut St (☎530/926-2359, ⊛www.shastaski.com), can also offer advice. Accommodation is plentiful at the foot of the mountain in Mount Shasta City, a charming, one-street town just off I-5 that has become a center for the American spiritualism movement, with all the alternative practitioners, spiritu-al bookstores, and organic restaurants that entails.

Mount Spokane, Washington

Only thirty miles from Spokane, Mount Spokane (☎509/238-2220; ⊛www .mtspokane.com; adults $31, juniors $27) is a nonprofit ski area spread over 2500 acres. Five double chairs access the 38 predominantly groomed, open blues. There are a couple of challenging bump and tree runs here, along with an adequate terrain park – though a halfpipe is noticeably absent. The avail-ability of night skiing on almost two-thirds of the mountain is one of the largest draws for local skiers. From Spokane take Hwy-395 north to Hwy-206 until you reach Mount Spokane Park Drive en route to the resort.

Snow Valley, California

Thirty minutes from LA's suburbs, Hwy-18 passes the little resort of Snow Valley (☎909/867-2751, ⊛www.snow-valley.com; adults $39, juniors $13) en route to Big Bear Lake and the crowded slopes of Snow Summit and Bear Mountain (p.316) – and so do most vacationers. In lean snow years, the upper reaches of this 240-acre resort are covered more in dirt than powder, and the snowmaking here is minimal; meanwhile, the Schighridj (pronounced Sky Ridge) terrain park is nothing compared with what Bear Mountain has to offer, and there's no busy resort town to offer diversions at the mountain's base. Yet all of this is precisely what makes Snow Valley attractive to young families, who can play on the gentle lower slopes without fear of being mown down by speed demons. Both the rental stores and ski school are well equipped for never-evers, though they occasionally run out of gear on busy weekends; book in advance. The lodge is very basic, but the cafeteria-style food is reasonably priced and picnics are permitted on the sunny, sheltered deck. All-inclusive (beginner lift, lesson, and rentals) packages are available for never-evers at just $39, a fantastic value.

Soda Springs, California

Tiny Soda Springs (☎530/426-1010 or 530/426-3666, ⓦwww.skisodasprings .com; adults $23, juniors $10) is the first ski area to catch the eye when heading up I-80 from the west. With two chairlifts and 200 acres of mellow green and blue terrain, it's a decent spot only for families and beginners – but not as good value as Donner Ski Ranch (see p.412), though use of two snowtubing tows and the sledding hill is included in the ticket price. Runs are short, but liftlines are rare. The base lodge houses a cafeteria, basic rentals (snowboards are pricey), and inexpensive snowshoes, a popular alternative to skiing the mountain.

Sugar Bowl, California

Often overlooked, Sugar Bowl (☎530/426-9000 or 866/THE-BOWL, snow phone ☎530/426-1111, ⓦwww.Sugar Bowl.com; adults $54, juniors $13) was Tahoe's first major ski resort; it opened back in 1939. It was even the first in the US to have a gondola (in 1953; today's updated version is still housed in the original wooden building), and Walt Disney was a founding investor – he filmed Goofy's *Art of Skiing* here in 1941, and one of the area's four snow-blasted peaks bears Disney's name. Hit full force by the storms that fall light and deep high on Donner Summit, powder days at Sugar Bowl reach epic dimensions, perfect for tackling the gnarly big mountain freeriding or the naturally segregated and refreshingly balanced terrain elsewhere. In the past decade an additional peak, Mount Judah, has been opened up to skiers, complete with a stylish day lodge. Other development plans have included faster lifts that access more terrain, like the Mount Lincoln quad which has made getting to the rocky fingers, chutes, and drops of The Palisades and '58 a slightly less formidable task. The favored accommodation is the original 1939 lodge, *The Inn at Sugar Bowl* (☎530/426-9000, rooms $130–340), which houses a cafeteria, coffeeshop, and upscale restaurant. Both the Main Lodge at the base of Mount Judah and the original Village Lodge have cafeterias and coffeeshops and the Mid Mountain lodge at the base of Mount Lincoln serves pizza, chili, sandwiches, and soup, in addition to refreshment of the alcoholic variety. To reach the resort, take exit I-80 on Donner Summit at Soda Springs/Norden, then turn right onto Hwy-40 east. Keep going past the gondola parking lot to the main lot at Mount Judah for fastest access to the slopes.

Tahoe Donner, California

Tahoe Donner (☎530/587-9444, ⓦwww.tahoedonner.com; adults $29, juniors $12) is often confused with Donner Ski Ranch, but with 14 runs on 120 acres it's only a quarter of the size. Right above the residential area of Truckee that shares its name, Tahoe Donner has gentle slopes used mostly by novices and local families. There are two chairlifts, a towrope, and a magic carpet. For its size, all-day tickets are reasonable, but half-day tickets are a bargain (adults $15; children 7–12/seniors 60–69 $7). Group lessons and beginner packages are slightly more expensive than at Donner Ski Ranch, but Tahoe Donner provides lessons for 3–6 year olds. Basic ski and step-in board rentals are available. Across the street is the excellent Tahoe Donner Cross-Country area, and there's a sledging hill just down the road ($4 per person). Take Northwoods Boulevard off Donner Pass Road, opposite Truckee High School. Follow the right branch where the road splits, passing the sledging hill and signs to the cross-country center; turn right on Slalom Way.

White Pass, Washington

Just north of Oregon, White Pass (☎509/672-4300; ⊛www.skiwhitepass.com; $37 adults, $24 juniors) is around thirty miles due south of Crystal Mountain – though direct routes between the two are closed in the winter, necessitating a substantially longer journey from Seattle. Crowds across the resort's 635 acres are minimal and, with a vertical drop of 1500ft and 350 inches of annual snow, skiing White Pass is a worthwhile alternative to other comparable Cascade resorts. Of the 32 runs, sixty percent are intermediate, and the rest are evenly split between beginner and expert. There is no terrain park or halfpipe, but there are plenty of good natural hits.

Guide: Canada

Canada

5

Québec

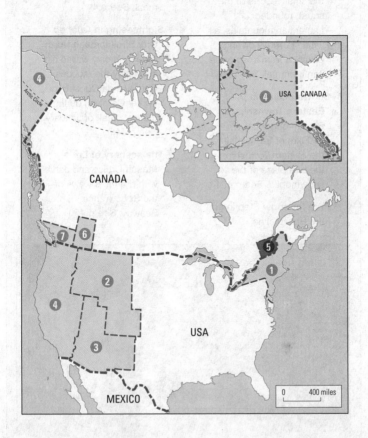

Highlights

✳ **Ski Tremblant** Quebec's premier ski area offers the region's most challenging terrain. See p.426

✳ **The Laurentians** Sample the small resorts of the squat, rounded Laurentian mountains, all within leisurely driving distance from cosmopolitan Montreal. See p.433

✳ **Snowmobiling in the Eastern Townships** Ride through the 2000km of trails within the Eastern Townships, the birthplace of the snowmobile. See p.444

✳ **Pray for snow** Stop in at the Benedictine monastery Abbaye Saint-Benoît-du-Lac, between the resorts of Magog and Owl's Head; the abbey is open to anyone who wants a restful night or a simple meal. See p.444

✳ **Sightseeing in Quebec City** Stroll through North America's only walled city and enjoy the raucous Carnaval de Québec (or Winter Carnival) during the last week of January. See p.445

✳ **The scenery of Le Massif** Cruise and carve with dramatic views of the St Lawrence Seaway. See p.450

5

Québec

Severe and protracted, **Québec**'s winters have caused locals to take their winter sports seriously. Even in the absence of Western Canada's lofty peaks, a multitude of **ski areas** have sprung up to service these passions, along with massive networks of cross-country trails and a sprawling web of snowmobile tracks. Downhill ski areas in the province are generally small, and nearly all are clustered around either dynamic **Montreal** or quaint, stylish **Québec City**, allowing you to mix a few urban diversions into a ski vacation and readily explore some of Québec's vibrant Francophone culture.

The bitterly cold, damp, and variable winter climate brings with it unpredictable **snow conditions**, and from one day to the next, heavy slush may be replaced by rock-hard ice. Typically, there is fairly heavy snow, often granular and crusty, along with icy areas that necessitate the use of sharp edges. Thanks to careful management by the resorts and their snowmaking facilities, however, skiing and snowboarding conditions are generally good, with the province's resorts offering plenty of **intermediate**-level terrain. Additionally, many ski areas have geared themselves toward **beginners**, offering excellent-value novice packages. **Experts** will find the terrain a little more limited, at least in comparison to elsewhere in North America, though the quality of gladed skiing in the province is some of the best anywhere. **Freestylers** are also particularly well-served by many of the province's ski areas, which often feature varied terrain parks, generally typified by smooth landings and transitions.

Because Québec only has one large-scale ski area, the all-inclusive resort **Tremblant**, many other areas have joined together to offer multi-area passes and accommodation packages; we've thus organized them first by area, then by resort. One grouping of these is set in Québec's most accessible mountain range, the **Laurentians**, its highlights mostly found in the five associated ski areas in the Saint-Sauveur Valley. Also worthwhile are the resorts of the **Eastern Townships** (Cantons-de-l'Est), a collective term for several towns with nineteenth-century origins that straddle the province's border with Vermont; these include the loosely bound Mont-Orford, Owl's Head, Mont-Sutton, and the independent Bromont. The province's remaining major ski areas are clustered around **Québec City**, where three resorts – Mont-Sainte-Anne, Stoneham, and Le Massif, which have joined forces to create formidable ski packages – are under an hour's commute from the center of town.

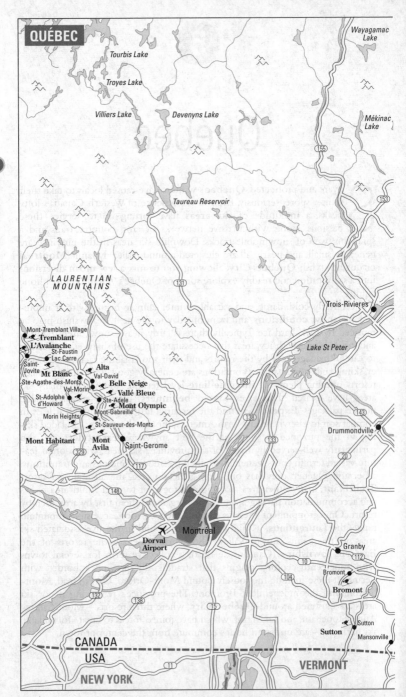

QUÉBEC

Tourbis Lake

Troyes Lake

Villiers Lake

Devenyns Lake

Wayagamac
Lake

Mékinac
Lake

Taureau Reservoir

155

153

131

Trois-Rivieres

LAURENTIAN
MOUNTAINS

Lake St Peter

158

Mont-Tremblant Village
Tremblant
L'Avalanche
St-Faustin
Lac Carre
Saint-
Jovite
Mt Blanc
Ste-Agathe-des-Monts
Val-Morin
St-Adolphe
d'Howard
Morin Heights
Mont Habitant

Alta
Val-David
Belle Neige
Vallé Bleue
Ste-Adele
Mont Olympic
Mont-Gabreille
St-Sauveur-des-Monts
Mont
Avila
Saint-Gerome

Drummondville

143

138

133

20

329

117

148

Dorval
Airport

Montréal

Granby

112

10

Bromont

Bromont

104

132

138

15

Sutton

Sutton

Mansonville

CANADA

USA

VERMONT

NEW YORK

11

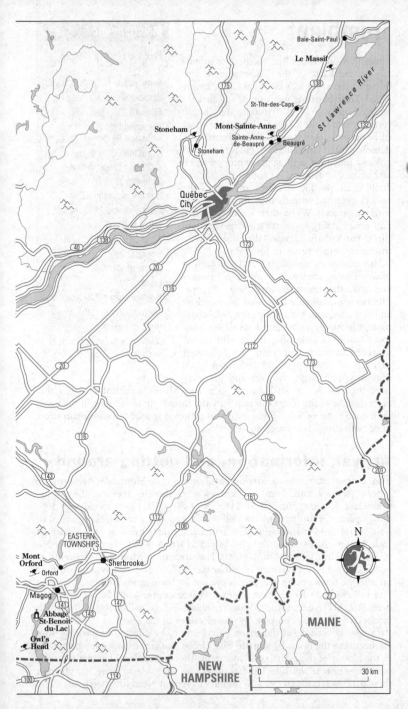

Tremblant

Fittingly, Mont-Tremblant, the highest mountain in the heart of the Laurentians, is also home to the province's largest ski area, simply called **Tremblant**. It was one of the first ski areas to open in North America; lifts began running here in the 1930s, making it a pioneer of resort-style ski tourism. Today, Tremblant's densely packed base village of cutesy, brightly-colored imitation eighteenth-century French architecture surrounds a couple of narrow cobbled streets. The ski area rises from the resort's core and spreads over four faces of a single mountain. While there's plenty of terrain for all ability levels, it's the expert terrain that's particularly noteworthy, outstripping that of any other resort in Québec.

The quality of the skiing at Tremblant, as well as its size, attracts so many to the mountain that the resort is struggling to cope. Liftlines are unusually long, and intermediate and beginner trails are usually crowded. What's more, the highly commercial resort environment can be a little off-putting, plus unreasonably expensive, particularly for beginners in need of equipment and lessons. A good option to help with the cost and get away from the crowded resort is to stay in nearby Mont-Tremblant Village, a tiny place 4km from the resort offering only the most basic services, or in the nearby service town of Saint-Jovite, which is gathered around a quaint main street lined with shops, boutiques, and cafés.

Mountain info	
Phone ☎819/861-2000 or 1-800/461-8711	
Snow phone ☎514/333-8936	
Website ⊛www.tremblant.ca	
Price Adult day pass $58	
Operating times Mid-Nov to mid-May daily 8.30am–3.30pm	
No. of lifts 13, including 1 gondola and 3 magic carpets	
Base elevation 230m	
Summit elevation 875m	
Vertical drop 645m	
No. of trails 92	
Acreage 610	
Beginner 20%	
Intermediate 30%	
Expert 50%	
Average snowfall 370cm	
Snowmaking Yes (464 acres)	
Night skiing No	
Nursery facilities Yes, from 12 months ☎1-888/736-2526	

Arrival, information, and getting around

The nearest international **airport** to Tremblant is Montreal's Aéroport de Dorval (⊛www.admtl.com), 120km away. A **shuttle service**, the Mont-Tremblant Express (☎514/631-1155 or 1-800/471-1155; round-trip $98; 2hrs) operates from here, but it's well worth it to rent a car, unless you plan to only spend time at the resort. Car rental companies based at Dorval airport include Avis (☎514/636-1920), Budget (☎514/636-0052), Hertz (☎514/636-9530), and Thrifty (☎514/631-8000). The drive from Montreal is straightforward – follow Rte 15 (which becomes Rte 117) to St-Jovite, where you turn off into the town center, keeping an eye out for the sign for Tremblant. Stay on Rte 117 until you arrive at the regional **visitor center** (daily 9am-5pm); from here, Rte 117 continues to Mont-Tremblant Village, while Rte 327 (which intersects 117) carries on past the visitor center to the resort.

If you're not staying at the resort, you're sure to be directed to **parking lots** connected to the resort by **shuttle bus**. Unless you arrive early enough to park in the closest of these lots, or if you arrive later in the day when early morning congestion at the base lifts has ebbed, it's advisable to drive straight past these parking lots for an extra 25 minutes to Versant Nord (the north side). The extra time invested in driving will easily be recouped, since all the Versant Nord parking lots are at the base of the lifts, saving not only the time required for a shuttle ride, but also time spent at the resort's busiest lifts.

Getting around the resort is easiest on foot, as the village is clustered around a single main street that links the Place Saint-Bernard, near the lifts, and the Place des Voyageurs, the public transport hub, from which the shuttle service to Mont-Tremblant Village leaves (daily 6am–11.20pm; every 30 mins; $1), as well as the shuttle buses to the parking lots and scattered resort-owned properties. Exploration further afield necessitates your own vehicle or a taxi; good choices are St-Jovite Taxi, ☎819/425-3212, and Taxi Tremblay, ☎819/686-2255.

The mountain

Mont-Tremblant divides into four distinct zones: two are on the northeast side of the mountain, and two are on the southeast side. The best way to explore the peak is to follow the sun, staying north in the mornings and moving to the south side in the afternoons, by which time you'll miss the worst of the early-morning crowds. Those who've purchased the **First Tracks** package (☎891/681-3000 ext 70601; $13) travel up the lifts at 7am to a leisurely continental breakfast at the *Grand Manitou Lodge* before heading down on virgin slopes. Apart from being a decent value, the First Tracks package is worthwhile as a way to beat the lines that form at the main base area for the lifts that open at 8.30am. Arriving early is key to missing the longest lines at the base, while delaying lunch until mid-afternoon (lifts close at 3.30pm) is another way to avoid the crowds – locals are generally unwavering about taking time out for lunch, leaving the slopes relatively quiet at midday.

Beginner

Beginners will find plenty of long green runs on both sides of the mountain, though some are best avoided on account of the crowds and their use by faster skiers. The trails on the **south side** can get particularly busy, especially the fairly narrow and flat Nansen Bas trail, which loops around to the base area. Generally, it's best for novices to stick to the upper mountain and the green runs served by the TGV lift. Better still is to head over to the **north side**, following the main green run P'tit Bonheur (which becomes Beauchemin Bas) all the way to the base area, hooking up with the relatively quiet Sissy Schuss of the Expo express lift. Absolute beginners will be pleased with the two oft-crowded **magic carpet lifts**, which can be used free of charge, near the base area on the south side of the mountain.

Intermediate

Unlike most of Québec's other larger ski areas, Tremblant is not ideal for intermediates. Although almost a third of the terrain at Tremblant is nominally graded at this level, this figure is deceiving, as many of the (often crowded) blue runs are either very short or lead in or out of green or black diamond terrain. Moreover, where black runs at other resorts are typically suitable for confident intermediates, the black diamonds at Tremblant generally deserve their grading.

The intermediate runs on the **south side** of the mountain are the busiest, with most skiers funneled down just two runs, **Beauvallon Haut** and **Alpine**, to as far as the base of the TGV lift at mid-mountain. From here, you can either cut to the **Curé Deslauriers** – an unusual, undulating trail – or head to the wide-open cruising runs of Beavallon Bas and Desserres, beneath the gondola. Take note, though, that the upper part of Desserres and the entire length of

Charron are only for strong intermediates willing to brave a black run. Of the black diamonds, groomed **Kandahar** is one of the most straightforward, with only one steep section. Separate from the rest of the south side is Versant Soleil, where three blue runs should be avoided unless there's been fresh snow: they're well used and can quickly get icy, thanks to the slope's frequent sun exposure.

The least busy run on the north side is usually **Duncan Bas**, off the Expo express lift. One black diamond trail on this face that's a little easier than its grading suggests is Géant, off the Duncan express lift. This broad, carving run is almost always quiet, a wonderful intermediate-level possibility few skiers and riders are aware of. But the true intermediate gems on this side of the mountain are the two unusually mellow flowing **gladed areas**, Réaction and Sensation. Access to these is again only for those willing to brave black diamond terrain, though: the narrow, bumpy, busy and often icy upper portion of Action is tricky, but still fairly easily conquered by a half-dozen wide traverses.

Expert

Most black diamond runs at Tremblant will prove challenging even to advanced skiers, and the few runs labeled as double black diamonds are just that. The best and quietest expert runs are on the **north side** of the mountain, where you can choose from the steep vertical of Banzaï and Duncan Haut or the narrow bump run CBC, on the fringe of the resort. The resort's steepest trail is Dynamite, with a gradient approaching 45 degrees, found further down the same face. Head over to the Edge lift, also on the north side, for some excellent glade running on Emotion, a testing freeriders' trail. Don't ignore the adjacent Réaction, where you'll find plenty of natural hits and an upper portion that's steep and lightly used.

On the **south side**, the slopes around the Le Soleil lift also contain some quirky and challenging gladed areas, particularly the Bon Viex Temps, which covers a large area. Meanwhile, the Les Bouleaux glades, though ultimately worth the effort, will require you to hike or herring-bone for a short distance. Of the runs serviced by the Le Soleil, the glades usually have the best snow conditions by far, as this sun-facing slope often has terrifying, icy conditions on the more exposed portions. On the main southern face, the black runs that drop alongside the TGV lift can be interesting to explore when the conditions are right and lift lines short. For a long, narrow, and uncrowded run try Ryan Haut (which becomes Ryan Bas); halfway down there's an option to turn onto the blue Charron, where you can enjoy linking broad carved turns beneath the gondola all the way back to the base.

Freestyle

Thoughtful planning and hard work went into building **Parc Gravite**, Tremblant's fine terrain park on the north side of the mountain. The park stretches virtually the length of the Lowell Thomas lift, one of the resort's least-used lifts, and includes a tremendous variety of hits, jumps, tabletops, high banks, and rails sections. The dramatically oversized halfpipe is world-class, and sits below speakers pumping out loud rock music that jars more often than the landings.

Lift tickets, lessons, and rentals

Tremblant has the most expensive **lift tickets** in Québec, and multiday tickets only cut the cost marginally. The Snow School (☎819/681-5666) offers a number of programs for both kids and adults, but is pricey: a ninety-minute group **lesson** costs $50 (four-person maximum) and private lessons start at $72/hour. You can save around $5 a time by taking the lessons in the afternoon rather than the morning, though it's the multiday snow school packages that are better value.

In and around the resort there are many places to **rent gear**. Half a dozen of these are slopeside outlets, the biggest of which is the Chalet des Voyageurs (☎819/681-3000 ext 45564), which offers a range of both skis and boards. The best places for the very latest in demo equipment are the Centre Burton (☎819/681-5802) and Centre Salomon (☎819/681-5502), both at the upper end of the resort village. Adult rental rates for skis, snowboards, or telemark skis average around $30/day, with half- and multiple-day savings available. Add around $10/day for high-performance gear. In Mont-Tremblant Village, you can pick up rentals for up to a third less than this from Yves Sports, 1908 ch Principal (☎819/425-1377), which stocks standard as well as performance skis (Dynastar) and Original Sin snowboards. Also in the village is Max Ski Service, 2047 ch Principal (☎819/425-3695), a specialist in demo ski gear offering rentals for $30/day and $75/three days.

Accommodation

Far and away the handiest place to **stay** is Tremblant, where you can do entirely without a car, heading directly to the runs from slopeside lodgings, below which are plenty of shops, cafés, and restaurants. With around 3500 beds, getting a place here is usually no problem. Contact Tremblant Reservations (☎418 /425-8681 or 1-800/567-6760, ⓦwww.tremblandt.ca) to book a room or inquire about ski packages, which include accommodation and passes. These start at around $125 per person for two nights in a dorm at the youth hostel, to around $200 for private rooms in modest environs and $300 for lodgings in the resort itself.

For **group accommodation**, check out Tremblant Sunstar (☎1-800/754-8736, ⓦwww.tremblantsunstar.com), which rents out condos and chalets with options ranging from studios to five-bedroom suites; most of these properties are served by a free shuttle bus service. If you don't mind foresaking convenience for intimacy you might opt for one of several **bed-and-breakfasts** scattered around **Mont-Tremblant Village**, also home to the youth hostel. Most of the other budget accommodation choices are motels in **St-Jovite**, while another option is the **Grayrocks** ski resort 3km from Tremblant – see p.455 for details.

Tremblant

Country Inn & Suites ☎1-866/763-6666. Comfortable, rather nondescript rooms at the lower end of the resort village. Facilities include a small gym and hot tub; a continental buffet is included in the price. ⑤

Fairmont Tremblant ☎418/681-7000 or 1-800 /441-1414, ⓦwww.fairmont.com. Luxurious slopeside hotel keen on pampering, with an extensive health club and fitness center. Bedrooms can be a little cramped, but all are comfortable enough, with subtle rustic touches in the decor. Suites include a simple kitchen. Ski packages can be surprisingly good value. ⑥

La Place St Bernard ☎819/861-2000 or 1-800 /461-8711. Actually three properties – St-Bernard, Johannsen, and Deslaureiers – in premier location surrounding the resort village's slopeside plaza. Lodging options, some of the best value in the resort, range from simple hotel rooms to spacious two-bedroom suites. All have faintly rustic furnishings and fireplaces. ⑥

Mont-Tremblant Village

Auberge la Porte Rouge 1874 ch du Village ☎819/425-3505 or 1-800/665-3505, ⓦwww.aubergelaporterouge.com. Modest motel-style lodge beside the white expanse of Lac Mercier in the center of Mont-Tremblant Village. Basic rooms are pine-furnished and meticulously clean, and have balconies with lake views; some have fireplaces and hot tubs. Breakfast and dinner are included in ski packages. ④

Auberge le Lupin 127 Pinoteau ☎819/425-5474 or 1-877/425-5474, ⊛www.lelupin.com. One of several B&Bs scattered around the village. All of *Le Lupin*'s nine country-style rooms, with brass beds and hardwood flooring, have private bathrooms; some have fireplaces, too. Ski packages available. ❸

Club Tremblant 121 rue Cuttle ☎819/425-2731 or 1-800/567-8341, ⊛www.clubtremblant.com. Spacious, good-value apartments in several scattered lodges, located midway between Mont-Tremblant Resort (free ski shuttle provided) and Village. Units range from one to three bedrooms; most have views of the ski hill and all feature fireplaces and full kitchens. Communal facilities include a fitness center with spa, pool, and hot tub. Only all-inclusive packages are offered. ❻

Hotel Mont-Tremblant 1900 ch Principal ☎819/425-3232 or 1-888/887-1111 ⊛www .hotelmonttremblant.com. A gray-and-white clapboard building originally built to house factory workers, this hotel beside Lac Mercier has 25 plain but comfortable motel-standard rooms. Rates include breakfast and evening meal, and ski packages are available. ❹

Mont-Tremblant Youth Hostel 2213 ch du Village ☎819/425-6008, ⊛www.hostellingtremblant.com. Friendly, well-equipped and looked-after hostel offering beds in simple dorms ($22.50; members

$18.50) sleeping up to ten people, as well as private rooms designed for two ($62; $50 for members). Facilities include laundry, TV room, and a kitchen. There's also a small pub on the premises and a shuttle bus service offered to the resort.

Résidences Mont-Tremblant 213 rue du Couvert ☎819/425-8974 or 1-800/567-6764. Cheerful, well-priced one- to three-bedrooms condos. Units have fully equipped kitchens and there's free access to the clubhouse's games room, hot tub, and sauna. Ski packages available. ❹

St-Jovite

Auberge Mountain View 1177 rue Labelle ☎819/425-3429 or 1-800/561-5122, ⊛www.aubergemountainviewinn.com. Straightforward, family-owned motel offering bed-and-breakfast accommodation; located a mile out of St-Jovite on the way to the Tremblant ski area, beside a cross-country ski network. Rooms are set back from the road, and most have fridges and fireplaces. Ski packages available. ❷

Motel Saint-Jovite 614 rue Ouimet ☎819/425-2761. Closest motel to the center of town has clean, standard units and modest prices. ❷

Normandie Motel 195 Rte 117 ☎819/425-3597. Highway-side motel with friendly owners, just south of St-Jovite; dated 1970s furnishings and rock-bottom prices. ❶

Eating

Together, the resort, Mont-Tremblant Village, and St-Jovite offer a wide selection of **dining options**, from expensive restaurants with excellent service to cheap pub grub (for the latter, see "Drinking and entertainment," opposite). The obvious place to head for **on-mountain food** is the busy *Grand Manitou Lodge* at the summit of the mountain, which offers a cafeteria, restaurant, brown bag area, and a spectacular setting. The cafeteria food here is reasonable, while the lodge's restaurant, *La Légende*, has fairly pricey French cuisine and fine mountain views. Alternatively, you can pick up lunch in the resort village itself, from any of the cafés or restaurants strung out between Place St Bernard and Place des Voyageurs. In the spring, head to the stalls grilling hamburgers and chicken at the base of the gondola.

Stocking up on **groceries** in both the resort and Mont-Tremblant Village is a decidedly pricey affair: the resort only offers a small deli, Les Delices du St-Bernard (☎418/681-4555), off Place St-Bernard beside the liquor store. There is a supermarket in Mont-Tremblant Village, but if you're going to make the journey from the resort, you might as well head to the cheaper and far larger supermarkets of St-Jovite.

Mont-Tremblant Resort

Au Grain De Café ☎418/681-4567. French-style café serving the best coffee in the resort, along with fresh pastries, is your best bet for a quick, inexpensive breakfast.

Coco Pazzo ☎819/681-4774. Upscale Italian restaurant with selections like roasted rack of lamb, grilled veal, and freshly made pastas; food also available "to go" from the adjacent shop where grilled sandwiches are reasonably priced at $6.

Crepêrie Caterine ☎418/681-4888. Small, popular, family-owned restaurant serving delicious if
expensive crepes in a variety of combinations. Try
the tasty crepe Benedict ($11) or indulge in the
chocolate crepes ($7).

La Grappe a Vin ☎819/681-4727. Friendly little
wine bar with plain bistro on the floor above. The
bar has a huge wine selection, with 40 by the
glass and another 130 by the bottle. The largely
regional menu ranges from simple upmarket
snacks – oysters, wild game patês, local cheeses,
fresh soups and salads – to full meals like the del-
icate Kyoto salmon with maple and sesame ($23),
a specialty. Vegetarians can choose from items
like the avocado gratin with tomato puree ($18).

Soto ☎418/681-4141. Fantastic sushi at astro-
nomical prices in a starkly stylish Japanese
restaurant. For the ultimate indulgence go for the
sasuke, an array of temaki and maki for $40.
Reservations required.

Mont-Tremblant Village

Auberge Sauvignon 2723 ch Principal ☎819
/425-7575. Popular regional restaurant close to
Lac Tremblant with several dependably tasty
choices from a well-priced, generally meat-based,

table d'hôte menu priced at $13–30. A trip to the
varied large salad bar is included or can be bought
on its own for $12.

Restaurant Lorraine 2000 rue Principale
☎819/425-5566. Family-style restaurant with a
lengthy diner-style menu based around sandwiches, pizza, barbecued chicken, and various pastas –
most choices are under $10.

St-Jovite

Antipasto 855 rue Ouimet ☎819/425-7580. Cute
brick-and-wood restaurant housed in an old train
station with memorabilia to match, serving delicious Caesar salads and a huge variety of brick-
oven pizzas and fresh pastas.

L'Escalope 597 rue Ouimet ☎819/425-3354.
Stylish restaurant with a gamey menu that'll send
vegetarians scampering. Choose from items like
ostrich medallions in brandy ($27), steaks (from
$24), salmon ($26) or the great Maritime seafood
platter ($39), which includes shrimp, scampi, and
rock lobster tail in garlic butter.

La Verre Bouteille 888 rue Ouimet ☎819/425-
8776. Simple bistro serving ample portions of
French staples like onion soup and mussels, as
well as steaks, at modest prices.

Drinking and entertainment

Place St-Bernard, adjacent to the base of the lifts, is most people's first stop
for a **drink** after their last run; there's live music here in the spring, too. As the
night goes on, the partying moves a short way downhill to the center of the
resort village, **Vieux-Tremblant**, where bars are a mercifully close stagger
away from one another. In contrast, the nightlife in Mont-Tremblant Village is
restricted to a quiet drink in a hotel bar, and the nightlife in St-Jovite is barely more than that.

For entertainment of a non-alcoholic variety, the two-screen Cinema Pine
movie theater in the Johannsen complex at the center of the Tremblant
Resort generally screens both a French film and a recent Hollywood release.

Café de l'Epoque Vieux-Tremblant ☎819/681-
4500. Somewhat scrappy place at the center of
the resort village with big TV screens, live music,
billiards and, sometimes, a heaving dance floor,
thanks to DJs and occasional live rock music.

Casey's Vieux-Tremblant ☎819/681-2855. Jovial
neighborhood-style bar with all the usual offerings
of potato skins, fries, burgers, and sandwiches.
Located on the southern edge of the Vieux-
Tremblant area.

El Diablo Vieux-Tremblant ☎418/681-4546. A
microbrewery with good pub food, sausages,
smoked meats, and big portions of tasty poutiné
(fries with melted cheese curd and gravy). Live
music, usually blues, on Friday and Saturday.

Le Shack Place St-Bernard ☎819/681-4700.
Slopeside sports bar serving the best burgers in
town to a hungry après-ski crowd.

Micro-Brasserie St Arnould 435 rue Paquette,
St-Jovite ☎819/425-1262. Popular brewpub a
block away from Hwy-117, decorated with hundreds of empty bottles and cans. You can choose
from a half-dozen distinctively local brews, including the tangy Riviére Rouge. Pizzas ($9) and pas-
tas ($10) are also served, though the pies made
with beer, like the onion beer pie ($10), are more
memorable.

P'tit Caribou Vieux-Tremblant ☎819/681-4500.
Usually the wildest bar in the resort, P'tit Caribou
regularly stays open until 3am.

Other activities and attractions

The Mont-Tremblant region brims with off-slope alternatives, particularly a large network of **cross-country** ski tracks (see below). There's also a selection of guided options offered by Tremblant's activity center (☎819/681-4848, ⓦwww.tremblantactivities.com), located just off the Place St-Bernard at the upper end of the resort village, including dogsledding, snowmobiling, horse-back riding, snowshoeing, ice climbing, and sleigh riding. The resort has its own **tubing** hill ($15/4hrs) and free **ice-skating** at Lac Miroir (skate rentals available). You'll also find several larger **pools** with **spa programs**. The largest is the recreation center Aquaclub La Source ($20 per session; big reductions available with multiday tickets; ☎819/681-5668), near the center of Mont-Tremblant resort; it's got an indoor beach, lagoon-style pools, and both in- and outdoor hot tubs. There's also a steam bath and fitness center where you can hire sports trainers. For more upscale pleasures visit Le Scandinave, 555 Montée Ryan (daily 10am–9pm; $30; ☎819/425-5524, ⓦwww.scandinave.com) in Mont-Tremblant Village. The Scandinavian-style spa includes a sauna, steam room, jacuzzi and waterfall; Swedish massages start at $50. The best place for a wider range of massages, as well as various other therapies and beauty treatments, is the Spa sur le Lac, 121 rue Cuttle (☎819/425-2731), part of the Club Tremblant complex; see p.430.

In Mont-Tremblant Village, you can go tubing at Aventures Neige, 850 rue Lalonde (☎819/429-5500 or ☎1/877-671-5500, ⓦwww.aventuresneige.com), a center which also offers kids the chance to race around in mini-snowmobiles and ice skate for free on Lac Moore. **Snowmobiles** can be rented from several places in the area, including the *Auberge Mountain View* (see review p.430); expect to pay around $90 for a three-hour rental of a basic machine, plus suit rental (around $15) and fuel. There are plenty of less-organized activities, particularly **tobogganing** and **snowshoeing**, for which it's best to seek local advice; the regional **visitors center** (see "Arrival, information, and getting around," p.426) can be particularly helpful.

Cross-country skiing

Cross-country skiing around Tremblant takes place in three areas, the largest of which, the **Domaine Saint-Bernard**, can be accessed from the Mont-Tremblant resort ($10 day pass available). Another area, the **Diable**, 12km from the north side of the ski area, offers 49km of groomed trails and 107km of ungroomed trails. Park entrance fees and the trail pass (together $11) are paid on arrival. Both ski areas incorporate warming huts into the network. The third main option is a section of the **P'tit Train du Nord**, part of a longer trail which starts near Montreal.

Listings

Bookstore Page à Page, Premenade Deslauries ☎819/681-4800. Good selection of English and French titles.

Car rental Budget, 583 rue Ouimet, St-Jovite ☎1-888/357-3157; National, 1595-A route 117, St-Jovite ☎819/425-3221.

Hospital Centre Médical St-Jovite ☎819/425-2728; nearest 24hr emergency service 40km away at the Hospital Laurentian St-Agathe ☎819/324-4000.

Internet *Au Grain de Café*, Le St-Bernard, Tremblant ☎819/681-4567; *Bistro Inter-Café*, 230 rue Principal, Saint-Jovite.

Laundry Lavoir Saint-Jovite Inc, 1121 rue Ouimet ☎819/425-8996.

Medical Ski Patrol ☎819/681-2000, or 819/681-5509 in emergencies.

Pharmacy Jean Coutu, 1065 rue Ouimet, St-Jovite ☎819/425-3757.

Post office 1098 rue Ouimet ☎819/425-2376.

Smaller Laurentian resorts

Amid the squat, rounded Laurentian mountains, in the almost continuous belt of scattered vacation homes spreading west from Montreal, numerous smaller ski areas have sprouted up as evening and weekend destinations for residents of Québec's largest city. They collectively cover enough terrain to sustain longer ski vacations, each area possessing all the usual amenities – cafeterias, rental gear, ski school, and day care – plus some luxurious accommodation and eating options scattered about. Staying here also allows for side-trips to energetic, cosmopolitan Montreal or for more relaxed poking around the immediate countryside.

The ski areas themselves, which are mostly grouped around the laid-back little towns of **Saint-Sauveur-des-Monts** and **Val-David**, are small scale, and few have more than a dozen short runs or greater than 200 meters of vertical rise. Together, though, the thirteen most significant of these smaller ski areas offer around 250 runs on 1000 acres of terrain – 35 percent beginner, 40 percent intermediate, and 25 percent expert – where conditions are bolstered by extensive snowmaking. If you're prepared to shuttle between the many different areas, you'll find yourself with a satisfying array of options.

Arrival, information, and getting around

While it's possible to get from Montreal to the ski areas without your own transport – Limocar Laurentides (☎514/842-2281 or 450/435-6767, ⊛www .limocar.ca) provides a daily **shuttle bus** service from Montreal's Terminus Voyageur, 505 boul de Maisonneuve Est, that stops at all the major Laurentian towns – you're far better off having your own vehicle. This will enable you to move freely between the five resorts and scattered local towns without needing to rely on the intermittent, weekend-only **shuttle service** (13 daily, details posted at base area drop-offs) provided by the resorts. **Car rental outlets** at Dorval include: Avis (☎514/636-1920), Budget (☎514/636-0052), Hertz (☎514/636-9530), and Thrifty (☎514/631-8000). Once you've got a car, getting there's not complicated: from Montreal, follow Rte 15 northwest into the mountains, where the exits to the many small settlements are clearly marked.

Local **information** for the whole valley can be obtained at La Vallée de Saint-Sauveur Chamber of Commerce, 228 rue Principal, St-Sauveur-des-Monts (☎450/227-2564 or 1-877/528-2553) and the La Maison du Tourisme des Laurentides, off Rte 15 at exit 39 (daily 9am–5pm; ☎450/436-8532, 514/990-5625 in Montreal, or 1-800/561-6673, ⊛www.laurentides.com). At either of these locations you can pick up the free, handy Laurentides tourist guide booklet, which contains all sorts of listings, as well as a couple of useful maps.

The mountains

The most accessible Laurentian ski areas are the **five associated areas** in the Saint-Sauveur Valley (☎450/227-4671 or 514/871-0101, ⊛www.montsaint sauveur.com), which are gathered around the laid-back little town of Saint-Sauveur-des-Monts, 60km northwest of Montreal along Rte 15. The largest of these areas is the flagship **Mont-Saint-Sauveur**, which, together with the interconnected, adjacent **Mont-Avila**, offers 46 trails, well-balanced between ability levels and many with night skiing. On the west side of Rte 15 from

Mont-Saint-Sauveur, **Mont-Olympia** is almost as large, but is geared more to beginners and has only limited night skiing. In contrast, **Mont-Gabriel**, 4km north along Rte 15, has only a couple of beginner trails, with the rest of the terrain split evenly between intermediate and expert. Along Rte 364, 6km to the west of Mont-Saint-Sauveur, **Morin Heights** is a largely intermediate mountain that's two-thirds lit for night skiing, with a few more advanced trails, including one good gladed area.

Of the independent resorts in the Saint-Sauveur Valley, the most accessible is **Mont-Habitant** (☎450/227-2637, ⊛www.monthabitant.com), located on Mont-Saint-Sauveur and Morin Heights. The eleven runs – with a vertical drop of 183m – are divided evenly between beginner, intermediate, and expert; there's snowmaking here, as well as night skiing daily until 10pm. **L'Avalanche** (☎819/327/3232), located near St-Adolphe-d'Howard, 18km northwest of Saint-Sauveur-des-Monts, operates ten runs with a vertical drop of 165m; its terrain is also split evenly between ability levels, although experts will find more challenging runs here than at Habitant. The upscale resort **Le Chantecler**, close to Saint-Adéle (☎450/229-3555 or 1-800/363-2420, ⊛www.lechantecler.com) is mainly intermediate- and beginner-oriented, offering 23 runs, sixteen of which are lit for night skiing on Friday and Saturday; the vertical drop is 201m.

The other big grouping of ski areas in the Laurentians is around **Val-David**, 20km past Saint-Sauveur-des-Monts on Rte 15; the average vertical drop here is around 150m. **Alta** (☎819/322-3206) is the biggest, with 22 largely beginner and intermediate runs, but does not have snowmaking, so it's only worth heading to after a recent snow. Also in the area are **Belle-Neige** (☎819/322-3311), with fourteen runs – again, mostly beginner and intermediate – and **Vallée-Bleue** (☎819/322-3427 ⊛www.vallee-bleue.com), which has seventeen runs, including some relatively easy expert terrain.

Beginner

Most of the smaller Laurentian ski areas have summit-to-base beginner runs, nicely separate from more difficult parts of the mountain, that are well equipped for absolute beginners. If everyone in your party is a beginner, then **Mont-Olympia**, with its twelve novice trails, is one of the best options.

Intermediate

All of the Laurentian resorts offer great blue terrain, making it hard to recommend one place over another. That said, **Mont-Gabriel**, where about half the terrain is rated blue, is a good option, as is **Mont-Saint-Sauveur**, which has plenty of blues, along with some relatively easy blacks. **Vallée-Blue** has decent cruisers for its size.

Expert

Experts searching for steeps and glades will find decent terrain at **Mont-Saint-Sauveur**, which is also the region's best resort for night skiing. Of the other four associated resorts, only Morin Heights has a dearth of expert terrain, with only one (albeit very good) gladed area really qualifying, despite the many blacks marked on the map. At **Mont-Habitant**, the situation is similar – the Sous-Bois is a fun tree run, but there's little else around. **L'Avalanche** is good for experts and crowd-free **Alta** with its rock-bottom prices is also tempting, but wait for a snowstorm, as snowmaking is absent here.

Freestyle

Many of the smaller Laurentian ski areas have made half-hearted concessions to freestylers; most have modest parks and a few offer halfpipes, but these are often poorly maintained. Notable exceptions are the **terrain parks** at Mont-Saint-Sauveur and Morin Heights, where the glades harbor good natural hits. Mont-Gabriel also has a decent **park**, with huge tabletops.

Lift tickets, lessons, and rentals

At the five associated Laurentian resorts, **lift ticket prices** on the weekdays run from $12 to $24 for a day pass; weekend passes cost about $10 more (this more or less holds true for the other, independent ski areas, as well). Tickets bought at Mont-Saint-Sauveur are the **most expensive** ($35, valid until 6pm; $30 from 3pm to closing, usually around 10.30pm or 9pm on Sundays), but these are valid at the other four associated resorts, though not so vice versa. Multiday packages (two days for $72; five days for $164) include skiing both day and night. If you'll be in the area for a while and plan to ski several places, it's worth calling or exploring ski area websites to look for deals. Some, like Mont-Gabriel's $15 passes, are offered all season, while others, like Le Chantecler's two-for-one deals, come and go.

    Ski schools are one of the great strengths of the smaller Laurentian ski areas; all the resorts can be relied upon for good instruction in remarkably inexpensive packages. Mont-Saint-Sauveur organizes two-hour group lessons for $22 (four-person minimum) or $49 if you also want a lift pass and rental equipment as well. Private lessons are reasonably priced at $40 per hour, and if a second person joins it's only $16 more.

    Rental options for skis and snowboards run from around $30 per day; don't expect a massive selection, particularly if you're looking for higher-end equipment. A better (and slightly cheaper) selection of equipment is available at ski retailers in Saint-Sauveur-des-Monts – try Sports Denis Parent, 217 ch Lac Millette (☎450/227-2700), half a kilometer northeast of Mont-Saint-Sauveur.

Accommodation

The Laurentians have an abundance of **accommodation**. The best place for an extended stay is Saint-Sauveur-des-Monts, as it's central, small-scale, close to a cluster of ski areas and generally well-equipped to deal with travelers; the tourist office (see p.433) has a comprehensive collection of leaflets and photos from local **B&Bs**. Also good choices are the service town of Saint-Adéle, bohemian Val David, or touristy Saint-Agathe. Although only a small part of the overall accommodation picture, you can find **slopeside lodging** at several ski areas, including upmarket Le Chantecler and Mont-Gabriel. Mont-Saint-Sauveur offers well-priced **condos** with two or three bedrooms starting at $288 per night, including lift passes for four people. It's worth calling any of the resorts (see "The mountains," pp.433–34 for contact info) to enquire about ski packages they may offer in association with local accommodation providers, as these usually work out to be very reasonable.

Auberge Swiss Inn 796 rue St-Adolphe, Morin Heights ☎450/226-2009 or 1-877/616-2009. Large alpine chalet B&B surrounded by woodland, a five-minute drive from Morin Heights. The plainly decorated rooms are a bit snug, but are an excellent value. Packages with breakfast and dinner at the attached Swiss-French restaurant are also available. ❷

Hostelling International le Chalet Beaumont 1451 rue Beaumont, Val-David ☎819/322-1972 or 1-800/461-8585. Excellent youth hostel in a huge chalet with crackling fires, great views, and cross-country ski trails from the door. Dorm beds cost $17.50 for members, $19.50 for nonmembers. There's a pick-up service from the nearest bus station.

Le Bonnet d'Or 405 rue Principale, St-Sauveur-des-Monts ☎450/227-9669 or 1-877-277-9669, ⊛www.bbcanada.com/bonnetdor. Elegant old Victorian property with individually decorated rooms and substantial continental breakfasts. ❸

Le Chantecler 1474 ch Chantecler, Ste-Adéle ☎450/229-3555 or 1-800/363-2420, ⊛www .lechantecler.com. Hugely popular family resort set beside eponymous ski area, in hulking stone buildings bedecked by steeps and gables. Rooms have pine furniture, most feature whirlpool baths, and many have fireplaces. Communal amenities include laundry, video rental, and sports center with pool, sauna, hot tub, squash, racquetball, and badminton. A generous and varied buffet breakfast is included in the price of rooms and evening meals can also be added into packages. Prices very reasonable, though the presence of noisy kids and signs of wear and tear in the building can be off-putting. ❸

Manoir Saint-Sauveur 246 ch du Lac-Mille, St-Sauveur-des-Monts ☎450/227-1811 or 1-800

/361-0505, ⊛www.manoir-saint-sauveur.com. Large hotel with 300 spacious but nondescript rooms and a comprehensive fitness center. Reasonable ski packages are available, and there's a complimentary shuttle to ski areas. ❻

Mont-Gabriel Resort 1699 ch du Mont-Gabriel, Ste-Adéle ☎450/229-3547 or 1-800/668-5253, ⊛www.montgabriel.com. Sprawling, modern resort at the base of the ski hill; its 135 units are a mix of standard hotel rooms and far prettier log cabins. Facilities include a fitness center with pool, sauna, and hot tub. ❻

Motel Le Joliburg 60 rue Principale, St-Sauveur-des-Monts ☎450/227-4651. Plain-looking motel located off Rte 364 at the northeast edge of town, with individually decorated rooms that bring it a cut above the rest. Room amenities include cable TV, fireplace, and fridge. ❷

Motel Saint-Sauveur 90 av Guidon, St-Sauveur-des-Monts ☎450/227-4628, ⊛www.st-sauveur .qc.ca. Brightly painted motel located opposite factory outlet shopping in a not very attractive part of town. Units are clean but unexceptional, and budget ski packages are available. ❸

Eating and drinking

There are plenty of places to **eat and drink** in the Laurentians; all of the resorts have decent slopeside cafeterias, and choices in most towns range from a quick crepe to fine dining. At Saint-Sauveur-des-Monts you'll also find fast-food and big chain supermarkets.

The **nightlife** options in the valley are pretty dull; if you're here for any amount of time, and don't mind the 120km round-trip, you really should head out to Montreal at least once. In the area, the most sociable places to drink are usually the ski-hill bars that draw crowds as night skiing tails off.

Local **cinemas** include Théâtre Saint-Sauveur, 22 rue Claude, St-Sauveur-des-Monts (☎450/227-8466), and Cinéma Pine, 24 rue Morin, Ste-Adéle (☎450/229-7655); keep in mind, though, that shows are usually in French.

Brûlerie des Monts 197 rue Principale, St-Sauveur-des-Monts ☎450/227-6157. Coffeehouse with wide range of inexpensive snacks and light meals.

L'Armorique 231 rue Principale, St-Sauveur-des-Monts ☎450/227-0080. Victorian house adjacent to the large church square at the center of the village, where many different types of excellent, moderately expensive crepes are served, along with salads, raclette, and fondue.

L'Eau á la Bouche 3003 boul Ste-Adéle, Ste-Adéle ☎514/229-2991 or 1-800/363-2582. Overlooking Le Chantecler's ski slopes, with would-be Provencal interiors – heavy beams and white plaster walls – is one of the finest dining establishments in the Laurentians. The frequently changing menu relies on local ingredients to pres-

ent renditions of generally French food. Foie gras often makes an appearance, as do game dishes such as the red-wine marinated venison (entrees around $35). A great way to end a feast is with the cheese platter, an excellent French and Québecois assortment. Prix-fixe dinners start at $55.

La Cage aux Sports 75 rue de la Gare, St-Sauveur-des-Monts ☎450/227-8787. Neighborhood sports bar with the best reasonably priced American bar menu in town; particularly good burgers.

Le Grand Pa 2481 rue de L'Eglise, Val-David ☎819/322-3104. Well-patronized local favorite in the middle of town; serves excellent Italian food in a simple environment. A perfect après-ski destination, the brick-oven pizzas here (from $18) can be washed down with pitchers of sangria or beer.

Mexicali Rosas 61 rue de La Gare, St-Sauveur-des-Monts ☎450/227-9021. Dependable dining experience from an Ontario-based chain. The fajitas ($14) are tasty, as is the selection of more varied combination plates like the burrito and beef tamale ($14).

Mont-Gabriel Resort 1699 ch du Mont-Gabriel, Ste-Adèle ☎450/229-3547 or 1-800/668-5253, ⓦwww.montgabriel.com. Top-notch French cuisine, with offerings like salmon with braised leeks and pork with ginger and orange. More reasonable prices than many of the upscale regional restaurants.

Other activities

The Laurentian mountains are well equipped to handle the steady stream of visitors looking for winter fun of all sorts. Aside from skiing or boarding, locals often **snowmobile**, **cross-country ski**, or **snowshoe** on a massive network of trails, including the Le P'tit du Nord. The Le P'tit Train du Nord linear park is on an old converted railroad bed and runs between St-Jérôme, 45km west of Montreal along Rte-15, and Mont-Laurier, 200km northwest. Use of the system, which is open for winter sports from December to mid-April, costs $7 per day. There's another 500km of **cross-country ski tracks** in and around the Saint-Sauveur Valley, many of which are free to use. Contact the tourist information office (see p.433) for their excellent pamphlets to all these areas; they also provide details of the many snowmobile rental companies, one of which is Récréation Centrale, Rte 15 exit 83 or 86, St-Adolphe-d'Howard (☎819/327-1234, ⓦwww.recreationcentrale.com). Récréation Centrale is on the doorstep of one of the largest networks of snowmobile trails in the region, and charges around $100 per day. Mont-Avila offers **snow-tubing** ($15 for two hours) and free **ice-skating**, while Mont-Gabriel has only snow-tubing ($9 for two hours).

Listings

Internet *Pause Café Internet*, 21 rue De L'Eglise, St-Sauveur-des-Monts ☎450/240-0056.
Laundry Buanderie de la Vallee, 9 rue Lanning, St-Sauveur-des-Monts ☎450/227-4710.
Medical Hospital Laurentien–Ste-Agathe, 234 rue St-Vincent, St-Agathe ☎819/324-4000.

Pharmacy Jean Coutu, 75 rue de la Gare, St-Sauveur-des-Monts ☎450/227-8488.
Post office 1727 ch Pierre Peladeau, Ste-Adele ☎450/228-3275.

The Eastern Townships

Wedged between Montreal and the Vermont border, the **Eastern Townships** (Cantons-de-l'Est) contain a handful of ski resorts that compete with those in the Laurentians. Though these resorts are further from Montreal and more spread out than the Laurentian resorts, they are generally larger and feature more interesting terrain, particularly expert runs and gladed areas. Together, the Eastern Townships offer more skiing acreage than Tremblant, the province's largest resort, and, as long as conditions at these lower elevations cooperate, the quality of the skiing is better. The closest of these ski areas to Montreal is the rapidly expanding **Bromont**, which courts night skiers, while **Mont-Orford**, **Mont-Sutton**, and **Owl's Head** rely on day traffic, luring visitors from farther afield with offers of interchangeable multiday tickets.

Arrival, information, and getting around

Montreal's Aéroport de Dorval (⊛www.admtl.com) is the closest major international airport, though Burlington airport in Vermont is also an option. While **buses** from Montreal (☎514/842-2281) do connect to the larger of the region's towns, such as Granby, near Bromont, and Magog, near Mont-Orford, the absence of public transport once you get there means that a car is necessary.

From Montreal, take route des Canton-de-l'Est (Hwy 10) and stop at the useful **information center** at exit 68 (Mon–Fri & Sun 8.30am–5pm, Sat 8.30am–6pm; ☎1-800/263-1068). The **Bromont ski area** is beside the main highway 10km past the information center (around 80km from Montreal), while **Mont-Orford** is 25km on from there. Both **Sutton** and **Owl's Head** are south of Hwy-10; the most straightforward way to get to Sutton is to follow Rte 139 south from Hwy 10 exit 68; for Owl's Head, leave Hwy 10 at exit 90, taking Rte 243 south. Of the four resorts, the drive to Sutton is the longest; allow an hour and a quarter to get there from Montreal, 105 km away.

Bromont

Despite the many diamonds on the trail map, **Bromont** is mostly an intermediate-level resort with meticulously groomed cruisers, night skiing until 10pm, and its own peak for **beginners**, Mont-Soleil. After mastering the beginners' peak, head to Brome on the main mountain, which winds down from the summit with great views; St Bruno and St Hubert, wide trails with pockets of trees, are also good for confident beginners.

Intermediates visiting Bromont will find nearly all the black diamond terrain in their grasp, thanks to the resort's careful grooming. Moguls are left on some sections of a few trails, but these are easy to dip in and out of. Some of the fastest carving can be found on Coupe de Monde and Knowlton, while changes in the steepness of Cowansville make for a more varied run. True **expert** terrain is limited, though Montreal does have a short steep section; there are also a few taxing turns to be found in the unnamed woods to the skier's right of the trail.

Lift tickets, lessons, and rentals

Lift tickets ($41 for eight hours) can be returned within thirty minutes of purchase for a voucher if snow conditions are poor. Tickets are also available for three ($31) or four ($33) hours, as are half-price tickets valid on the beginner lift only. **Lessons** for two cost $24 per person per hour, private lessons are $39 per hour, and bundled packages with equipment and lift ticket thrown in cost $35 for skiers or $40 for riders. Skiboard lessons are offered at $35 per hour. Basic **rentals** are available from $20 for skis and $25 for snowboards, with the best gear on offer for almost twice the price.

Mountain info – Bromont	
Phone ☎450/534-2200 or 1-866/BROMONT	
Website ⊛www.skibromont.com	
Price Adult day pass $41	
Operating times Mid-Nov to mid-April Mon–Thurs 9am–10pm, Fri 9am–10.30pm, Sat and Sun 8am–10.30pm	
No. of lifts 5, including 1 surface lift	
Base elevation 180m	
Summit elevation 565m	
Vertical drop 385m	
No. of trails 49	
Acreage 160	
Beginner 31%	
Intermediate 22%	
Expert 47%	
Average snowfall 483cm	
Snowmaking Yes (128 acres)	
Night skiing Yes (96 acres; $23)	
Nursery facilities Call to check	

Mont-Orford

At the northern end of the Appalachian Mountains, close to the small town of Magog, three peaks – Mont-Orford, Mont-Giroux, and Mont-Alfred-Desrochers – comprise the **Mont-Orford** ski area. There's plenty of terrain here for all skill levels, but those with a taste for tree skiing will particularly enjoy the resort's sustained steeps and narrow cuts. The tight trees are also useful to preserve the snow, which, along with Orford's relatively high elevation, usually ensures it has the best conditions of the eastern resorts.

Orford has several simple **beginner** runs; start with the gentle cat track 4km on Mont-Orford, which has views over Lac-Memphremagog and the Owl's Head ski area. Once you've conquered this, head to several easy greens on Mont-Giroux and then Mont-Alfred-Desrochers, where the easiest intermediate terrain is located. Narrow **intermediate** trails roll and wind on all three mountains, with wide trails and fast carvers dipping off every peak, particularly Mont-Alfred-Desrochers. For a first taste of the **gladed skiing**, head to Archade on Mont-Orford.

With its **expert** terrain, Mont-Orford goes one extra, assigning the dubious triple black diamond category to a couple of its steepest runs; while you will find 45-degree pitches on runs like Slalom off the La Quatuor lift, it's mostly just hype. Mont-Orford is, however, home to some of Québec's trickiest sections, in particular the various blacks that drop down the steep headwall on skier's right of the La Quad du Village chair on Mont-Orford. A single entrance here leads into more signed runs through the woods, where you'll find numerous ledges and boulders and no shortage of new lines to explore. If you're looking for fast groomers, try the winding Trois Ruisseaux or the steep Maxi on Mont-Orford; both are groomed twice daily. Boarders beware that the blacks on Mont-Giroux empty onto a tedious, long, and flat beginner trail.

The snowboard park off the La Mi-Orford chair provides plenty of challenges for **freestylers**, but to stay here would be to miss out on all the good natural hits scattered throughout the resort on runs like Mont-Orford's Contour.

Lift tickets, lessons, and rentals

In addition to day-long **lift tickets** ($36), Orford also sells morning and afternoon tickets for use before or after 12.30pm; however, the savings are so minimal that it's not really worth timing your visit to match. Multiday tickets also offer only minimal reductions – though if you buy a ticket for four days or more ($130) it becomes a "Ski East Pass" and can be used at both Sutton and Owl's Head as well. The standard **lesson** package offered is a two-hour session ($25) for a group of up to six people; private lessons will run you $36 per hour. Starter lessons include lift ticket and rentals for $55. The resort's **rental**

Mountain info – Orford

Phone ☎819/843-6548 or 1-800/567-2772

Website ⊛www.mt-orford.com

Price Adult day pass $36

Operating times Mid-Nov to mid-April, daily 9am–4pm

No. of lifts 8, including 2 surface lifts

Base elevation 310m

Summit elevation 850m

Vertical drop 540m

No. of trails 52

Acreage 244

Beginner 38%

Intermediate 32%

Expert 30%

Average snowfall 600cm

Snowmaking Yes (207 acres)

Night skiing No

Nursery facilities Yes, from 2 years

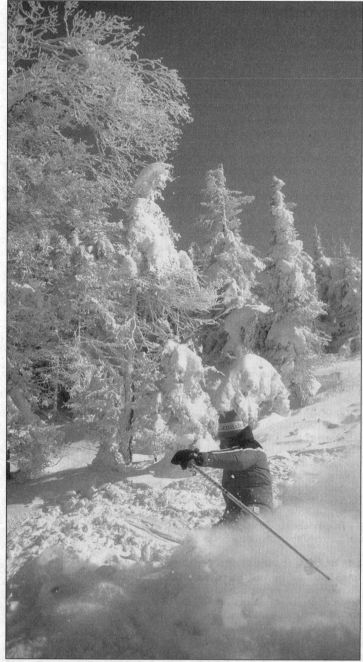

△ Skier carving through powder on Mont Tremblant, Québec

equipment is nothing special, but at least it's fairly cheap – skis and snowboards both go for $29 per day.

Mont-Sutton

Family-owned and friendly, **Mont-Sutton**, 11km north of the Vermont border, is known for its glade skiing – almost all the runs are gladed. Some have been widened enough to allow for grooming equipment, but most are too narrow for much carving. The presence of so many trees and the north-facing aspect of the entire ski area makes snow conditions in Sutton reliable all winter.

Sutton's lift system is well-designed, with almost every lift heading from base to summit. The mountain is also blessed with a layout that divides naturally into different **ability levels**. Much of the beginner terrain is at the western end of the resort and much of the expert is at the eastern, with intermediate terrain separating the two. A plus for snowboarders is the virtual absence of flat sections around the resort.

Given its gladed nature and the density of the narrow runs here, it's standard practice to jump between several runs on your way down the mountain, largely ignoring the map. Finding a different line each time is no problem, with the result that the ski area seems much bigger than it is. As a result, though, it's hard to recommend anything concrete, though that's no matter: the joy of exploration is a large part of the fun.

For a long time, Sutton resisted creating a terrain park, arguing that it had enough natural terrain for **freestylers**. Though they are right – creek beds, boulders, and drop-offs are abundant – they have capitulated, adding the Skill Zone; keep in mind, though, that if all you do is stay in the terrain park, you'll be missing out.

Mountain info – Sutton
Phone ☎450/534-2545
Snow phone ☎541/866-7639
Website ⊛www.mountsutton.com
Price Adult day pass $41
Operating times Late Nov to mid-April Mon–Fri 9am–4pm, Sat & Sun 8.30pm–4pm
No. of lifts 9; many are slow doubles from the 1960s
Base elevation 508m
Summit elevation 968m
Vertical drop 460m
No. of trails 53
Acreage 174
Beginner 32%
Intermediate 28%
Expert 40%
Average snowfall 480cm
Snowmaking Yes (104 acres)
Night skiing No
Nursery facilities Yes, from 2 years ☎450/538-1310

Lift tickets, lessons, and rentals

A full-day **lift ticket** at Mont-Sutton is $41. Those who can only ski beginner terrain should purchase the $21 ticket, which allows access only to two of the resort's lifts. A half-day ticket, valid before or after noon, will save you twenty percent. Those who purchase a ticket for four days or more will find themselves in receipt of a "Ski East Pass," a ticket that can also be used at Sutton and Owl's Head.

Four-hour group **lessons** cost $45, though a better-value package for $60 (skis) or $70 (snowboard) includes a lesson, gear rental, and a lift ticket; it's even cheaper if you're in a group of two, four, or more and purchase a package together. Private lessons cost $39 per hour. Sutton has a decent range of **rentals**, starting from basic skis at $16 per day to demo gear at $38 per day. Snowboards are $38 and snowblades are $23 per day.

Owl's Head

Within sight of the US border, **Owl's Head** rises up over the sprawling Lac-Memphremagog, offering not only fine vistas of the lake and surrounding rolling hills, but also a reasonably sized ski area with varied, well-groomed terrain. It's a good **beginner** mountain, though less for its layout and more for the fact that experts simply ski elsewhere, leaving the place quiet for new learners. Beginners who've begun to turn comfortably should try the easy blue Lily's Leap, which offers some great views as it winds down from the top of the mountain.

Intermediate skiers and riders have the run of the mountain: a grid of wonderful blue runs, ideal for fast, wide-open carving on even rolling terrain, covers the entire ski area, and many of the black diamond trails are well within reach for confident intermediates. In contrast, the amount of available **expert** terrain is limited to a few short steep sections around the liftline of the quad on the main mountain, where the narrow Grand Allée has spots that are 47 degrees. **Freestylers** should take note that the terrain park is the longest among the Eastern Townships, and is certainly worth a look.

Mountain info – Owl's Head	
Phone ☎450/292-3342 or 1-800/ 363-3342	
Website ✆www.owlshead.com	
Price Adult day pass $32	
Operating times Early Dec to late April daily 9am–4pm	
No. of lifts 7	
Base elevation 155m	
Summit elevation 747m	
Vertical drop 554m	
No. of trails 41	
Acreage 86	
Beginner 33%	
Intermediate 34%	
Expert 33%	
Average snowfall 457cm	
Snowmaking Yes (73 acres)	
Night skiing No	
Nursery facilities Yes, from 2 years	

Lift tickets, lessons, and rentals

Half-day **lift tickets** at Owl's Head will only save you $5–9 (depending on whether it's morning or afternoon) off the price of a full-day ticket ($32). Private **lessons** cost $35 per person, with extra students charged $18 each. An economical choice is the $90 ski-week package (offered midweek only), which includes ten hours of lessons, video sessions, and a fun race between participants. Group lessons are very reasonable at $17 per person per hour. Absolute beginner packages are $40 for skiers and $50 for boarders; these include an hour lesson, rentals, and a lift ticket. Outside of a package, **rental** rates start at around $20 for skis and $23 for snowboards.

Accommodation

Thanks to a busy summer season there's a surplus of **accommodation** in the Eastern Townships. Slopeside condos and hotels at the resorts are supplemented by inns, hotels, B&Bs, and motels in nearby towns, such as Granby (near Bromont), Magog (near Mont-Orford), and Sutton (near Mont-Sutton). Check with the information center (see p.438) for more listings, or call the resorts directly (or check their websites) for special deals. If you're after a ski package or a bed in one of Magog's many B&Bs, call a centralized reservation number (☎1-877/943-2744).

Bromont

Auberge au Vieux Manoir 871 rue Shefford
☎ 450/534-2502. Basic hotel in the center of
Bromont village with the cheapest available ski
packages. Sauna and bar. ❷

Auberge le Madrigal 46 boul Bromont ☎ 450/
534-3588 or 1-877/534-3588, ⊛ www.lemadrigal
.ca. Plush bed-and-breakfast in a modern wooden
house surrounded by trees. Eleven sleek but small
rooms available, some with private whirlpools. Ski
packages offered. ❸

Le Château Bromont 90 rue Stanstead
☎ 819/534-3433 or 1-800/304-3433, ⊛ www
.chateaubromont.com. Swank slopeside lodging;
some rooms have hot tubs and fireplaces. The fitness center includes indoor and outdoor pools. ❻

Orford

La Belle Victorienne 142 Merry Nord, Magog
☎ 819/847-0476 or 1-888/440-0476. Charming
B&B in a late-nineteenth-century house in downtown Magog, with a fireplace and indoor spa;
healthy gourmet breakfasts included. ❷

Motel de l'Outlet 480 ch Hatley Ouest, Magog
☎ 819/847-2609 or 1-877/847-2606, ⊛ www
.toile-magog.com/outlet. In a quiet neighborhood
of downtown Magog, just ten-minute drive from
the ski area, small, spotless rooms, with fridge and
microwave. Excellent ski packages are as low as
$50 per person for two to stay and ski. ❶

Village Mont-Orford 4969 ch du Parc ☎ 819/
847-2662 or 1-800/567-7315, ⊛ www.village-mont
-orford.com. The only lodging at the base of the
mountain has dull but comfortable one-, three-, or
four-bedroom condo units, with fireplaces. ❸

Sutton

Auberge Altitude 484 ch Boulanger ☎ 450/538-
1011, ⊛ www.aubergealtitude.com. The only
slopeside bed-and-breakfast has five rooms, with
or without private bathroom and fireplaces. ❸

Auberge des Appalaches 234 ch Maple
☎ 450/538-5799 or 1-877/533-5799,
⊛ www.auberge-appalaches.com. Cozy, fourteen-
room bed-and-breakfast with private bathrooms
and great valley views, 1.5km from the slopes.
Owners are enthusiastic outdoor types who regularly run snowshoe tours from the lodge – and
occasionally play snow volleyball. ❷

Auberge la Paimpolaise 615 rue Maple
☎ 450/538-3213 or 1-800/263-3213. One of the
few slopeside options is this Swiss chalet-style inn
with 28 rooms, a large outdoor whirlpool and a
bustling après-ski bar. ❷

Terrasse des Neiges ☎ 450/538-2202. A five-
minute walk from the slopes, this is the best budget option; the rooms are pretty standard motel-
style, though some have fireplaces. ❶

Owl's Head

Auberge Owl's Head ☎ 450/292-3342 or 1-
800/363-3342. Basic hotel rooms in the top floor
of the ski-area base lodge, with deals including
meals in the cafeteria and dinner in the lodge. ❷

Owl's Head Condo Apartments ☎ 450/292-
3318 or 1-800/363-3342. Plain condos ranging
from one to three bedrooms at the base of the ski
hill. Units are equipped with kitchens and fireplaces. Communal hot tub and sauna provided. ❷

Eating, drinking, and entertainment

A fair range of **restaurants** can be found around each of the three larger ski
areas, though the better establishments are in the nearby towns of Granby,
Magog, and Sutton. In contrast, the number of busy **drinking** spots is rather
small, though Bromont has a lively **nightlife**, thanks to skiers stopping off for
a drink after night skiing. The slopeside *Bromontais Resto-Bar* has a hopping bar
and dance floor, while the *Le Chateau Bromont* bistro bar (see "Accommodation" above) is a quieter, more elegant alternative. At Orford, the *Slalom Pub*
has a busy happy hour (4–6pm).

Later in the evening, head to the **bars** in nearby Magog and try the popular
La Grosse Pomme, 276 rue Principal. The more boisterous side of the après
scene at Sutton is in evidence at the *Auberge la Paimpolaise*, while for a more
laid-back atmosphere – and board games – try the *Auberge des Appalaches* (see
"Accommodation" above). Visitors to Owl's Head will find little except the
slopeside cafeteria.

Bromont

Auberge le Madrigal 46 boul Bromont
☎ 450/534-3588 or 1-877/534-3588. Relatively

expensive regional cuisine from a small menu at a
local B&B. Appetizers include snails, onion soup,
mussels, and shrimp in garlic butter (all $6–10);

entrees to try include the juicy Brome Lake duck and the ostrich, though less adventurous but excellent filet mignon and seafood can also be had (most $17–25).

Baffetto de Roma 80 boul Bromont ☎450/534-4050. Huge selection of inexpensive pizzas and pastas at a friendly restaurant that also will deliver locally.

Orford

La Merise 2329 ch du Parc ☎819/843-6288. Fairly expensive regional cuisine served amid local watercolors in a florally decorated dining room near the ski hill. The table d'hote menu is the specialty, and runs between $26 and $34 for five courses. The menu changes often, but try the linguine with cheese and whitewine sauce when available.

Tonnerre de Brest 2197 ch du Parc ☎819/847-1234, ☻www.tonnerredebrest.net. Popular restaurant near the Mont-Orford ski hill with mainly Belgian cuisine including crepes, mussels, and frites.

Sutton

Auberge la Paimpolaise 615 rue Maple ☎450/538-3213. Busy restaurant serving inexpensive regional and European dishes to an après-ski crowd.

Beetle Resto-Pub 19 Principale N ☎450/538-1717. Sutton's local drinking hole, with good-natured, though excessively smoky, atmosphere and reasonable pub grub.

Tartin Pizza 19 Principale N ☎450/538-5067. Small, no-fuss restaurant good for an inexpensive pizza or a slice of great cheesecake.

Other activities and attractions

Aside from downhill skiing and snowboarding there are plenty of other activities in the Eastern Townships. At the top of the list is snowmobiling, in the actual birthplace of the sport. There's also cross-country skiing and snowshoeing in the area, as well as **ice-skating** rinks at several locations, including Club Multi-Forme, 101 rue du Moulin, in Magog (☎819/847-4419), and at the base of Owl's Head, where you can also go **tubing**.

Snowmobiling

Supposedly invented by local entrepreneur J Armand Bombardier, **snowmobiling** is an integral part of life in the Eastern Townships. Local trails, of which there are around 2000km, are detailed on maps available from the regional information center (see "Arrival, information, and getting around," p.438). To use most of the network you'll need an **access pass**, available from centers that rent out snowmobiles like the Centre de Mécanique Magog, 9 boul Bourque, Omerville (☎819/868-2919). For a look at how the sport evolved from Monsieur Bombardier's early tinkerings, visit the Musée J Armand Bombardier (☎450/532-5300) in Valcourt, 40km north of Mont-Orford.

Cross-country skiing and snowshoeing

Along with snowmobiling, **cross-country skiing** is a major outdoor activity in the Eastern Townships, and two cross-country centers are particularly worthwhile. The bigger of the two is Parc du Mont-Orford, 3321 ch du Parc

---

Saint-Benoît-du-Lac Abbey

Between Magog and Owl's Head, off Rte 243 in South Bolton, lies the white-turreted **Abbaye Saint-Benoît-du-Lac** (☎819/843-4080, ☻www.st-benoit-du-lac.com), a functioning Benedictine monastery that overlooks Lac-Memphremagog. Around sixty monks live here, several under a vow of silence, along with a few nuns. The abbey is open to anyone who wants to stay, though donations are expected for food and lodging. You can also attend Eucharist (daily 11am) or Gregorian chants (Nov–May Mon–Fri 9–10.45am & 1.30–4.30pm, Sat 9–10.45am & 11.45am–4.30pm) as well as buy handmade cheeses and apple cider from the abbey shop.

(☎819/843-9855, ⊛www.sepaq.com; $9 for a day's skiing), a provincial park with 87km of trails ranging from gentle lakeside forays to major challenges on climbs up Mont-Chauve. The park also has a network of trails for snowshoers. The smaller Parc Sutton, midway between the village and the ski area, (☎450/538-4085; $3 for a day's skiing), offers 58km of marked trails, of which 40km are mechanically groomed; there's also 20km of snowshoeing trails. Rentals are available for both activities.

Listings

Internet *Tartin Pizza*, 19 Principale N, Sutton ☎450/538-5067; Centre d'Acces Communautaire, 858 Rte Missisquoi, Bolton ☎450/292-0396.
Laundry Lavoir Magog-Orford, 69 rue Laurier, Magog ☎819/868-1340.
Medical Centre de Santé de Sutton, 33 Principale S, Sutton ☎450/538-3983; CLSC Alfred-

Desrochers, 50 rue St-Patrice E, Magog ☎819/843-2572.
Pharmacy Parmacie Essim, 34–4 Principale N, Sutton ☎450/538-0055; Jean Coutu 448 rue St-Patrice, Magog ☎819/843-3366.
Post office 1288 ch Nicolas Austin, Austin ☎819/868-7777.

Québec City resorts

Clinging to the top of a 350ft cliff that towers over the broad St-Lawrence River, **Québec City** is the only walled city in North America, and exudes a charm usually associated with medieval Europe. Within an easy drive of the city are three modern ski resorts, all superbly geared toward intermediates but with enough terrain for both beginners and experts as well. The largest of these is **Mont-Sainte-Anne**, 40km away, where there's good terrain for every skill level of skier or rider. Nearest to town, only 6km beyond the city limits, is the low-key **Stoneham**, a locals' mountain with limited expert terrain, but loved for its proximity to the city and its wind-protected horseshoe valley – a good place to shelter from cold temperatures and harsh winds typical on many of the area's brutally cold winter days. The third main mountain in the area is the more remote **Le Massif**, an hour's drive away, 73km from Québec City; it's best known as much for its excellent views as its remarkable intermediate-level carving slopes that plunge down to the St-Lawrence Seaway. All three mountains receive plenty of snow, with Le Massif and Mont-Sainte-Anne on the front line in particular for storms traveling up the Saint-Lawrence Seaway – just watch out for an icy glaze that can form on all three from the combination of wind and weekend traffic.

Arrival, information, and getting around

Most international air traffic arrives in Montreal, leaving Québec City's own **airport**, 20km west of the city center, to cater almost exclusively to domestic flights. Airport **shuttles** provide service to several Downtown hotels (8.45am–10.20pm; 7–8 daily; $9), while **taxis** make the twenty-minute trip for $25. **Trains** from Montreal arrive on the northeast fringe of Québec City's old town at the Gare du Palais (Via Rail ☎418/692-3940 or 1-800/361-5390), which adjoins the long-distance **bus terminal** (☎418/525-3000) at 320 Abraham-Martin. From here you can get to Mont-Sainte-Anne on one of the local Orléans buses to Beaupré ($20), then take a taxi to the resort ($6).

The easiest transportation method between resorts is a **rental car** (see "Listings," p.455), particularly if you plan on visiting Le Massif, which has no direct shuttle service from Québec City. Stoneham is a 25-minute drive north of town off Rte 73, while both Mont-Sainte-Anne and Le Massif can be reached by following Rte 440 (which becomes Rte 138) northeast out of town. The turn-off for Mont-Sainte-Anne is 40km from Québec City, while Le Massif is a further 33km along Rte 138.

Hiver Express (☎418/525-5191, ⊛www.taxicoop-quebec.com; round-trip $23) runs a **ski shuttle** service from sixteen Downtown hotels and the tourist information office to both Stoneham and Mont-Sainte-Anne; pick-ups are at 8am and 10am, with services returning at 2.30pm and 4.30pm. Le Massif runs a complimentary shuttle linked with the Hiver Express service that leaves from Mont-Sainte-Anne's shuttle parking area. Hiver Express can also arrange private bookings for taxi services to the resorts, priced at $60 each way.

Mont-Sainte-Anne

Based around a single peak, **Mont-Sainte-Anne** is an easily navigable ski area; though it only spreads over a mere 400 acres, it offers a high-density trail system with plenty of variety. Steeps, bumps, glades, and high-speed cruisers are all well represented. The bulk of the trails are on the south side of the mountain, rising out of the base area and overlooking the mighty St-Lawrence River. The terrain here divides into two broad zones on either side of the L'Étoile Filante base-to-summit high-speed gondola. To the east is the mainstay of the resort's trails, and the vast majority of these are kept open until 10pm by a slick night-skiing operation. Most runs here are **intermediate**, with high-speed carving from summit to base. To the west of the gondola is a dedicated **expert** area, where you'll find the bulk of the resort's ten World Cup-standard race trails, featuring highly challenging terrain.

About a third of the ski area spills over the north and west sides of the mountain, where the vast majority of trails are **intermediate**, though **beginners** have decent alternatives to the more crowded front-side runs. The main attraction is the quality of the snow rather than the terrain; while the southern face of the mountain is prone to thaw in the sun – creating wetter, heavier powder and freezing overnight into icy patches – the northern side provides much better protection. The contrasting conditions of the two sides can easily be used to your advantage: you can ski the north side until the south has had a chance to properly soften in the sun, then head back to the north side once the south has become too slow and heavy. Get a quick overview of the more subtle features of the resort with the free **guide service** offered daily at 10am and 1.30pm from outside the summit lodge.

Mountain info – Mont-Sainte-Anne

Phone ☎418/827-4561

Snow phone ☎418/827-4579 or 1-888/827-4579

Website ⊛www.mont-sainte-anne.com

Price Adult day pass $47

Operating times Mid–Nov to early May Mon–Fri 9am–4pm, Sat & Sun 8.30am–4pm

No. of lifts 13, including 1 gondola and 6 surface lifts

Base elevation 200m

Summit elevation 900m

Vertical drop 700m

No. of trails 56

Acreage 428

Beginner 23%

Intermediate 46%

Expert 31%

Average snowfall 410cm

Snowmaking Yes (340 acres)

Night skiing Yes (15 trails; $22 adult night pass)

Nursery facilities Yes, from 6 months ☎418/827-4561

Beginner

Green beginner runs extend from summit to base on both sides of the mountain, most snaking down its entire length. The longest (and easiest) trail, **Le Chemin du Roy**, follows the gentle course of a road from top to bottom on the mountain's southern face – though it's largely a waste of time for those wanting to practice even shallow turns. **La Familiale** has a more consistent vertical, but it can get quite busy. Perhaps better than either are the green trails on the north side, where the snow is often better and the crowds thinner.

Intermediate

With almost half the ski area given over to intermediate-level terrain, blues are Mont-Sainte-Anne's great strength. All of the blue trails on the south side of the mountain start east of the gondola, most following smooth, steep grades down down to the gondola's base. When the main runs like Le Gros Vallon and La Beaupré get too crowded or tracked up, hook onto **La Traverse**, which heads west to the base of black diamond terrain before connecting with La Crête, leading back to the gondola. For those tired of unhooking their gear at the bottom of every run, try carving the furiously fast **La Tourmente** or **L'Express**; both are accessed off the L'Express du Sud lift. These two, along with the narrower, gentler **La Pichard**, offer some of the best night skiing runs for those not wanting to use the gondola. The north side of the mountain has cruising runs in frequently changing snow conditions; for an introduction to glade skiing, head for the fast, technical **glades** of La Vital Roy and La Sidney-Dawes.

Expert

Easily identified by a cluster of black diamonds on the south side of the trail map, the bulk of the expert area spreads west of the gondola, where the terrain is steep and the fall line beautifully even. There's nothing but blacks here, so don't worry about slower skiers or even the presence of many others. A couple of the least challenging expert runs, La Crête and La Beauregard, hug the perimeter of the resort, plunging from incredible views to the base of the Le Trip chairlift. Le Trip also services **La Brunelle**, a dense glade run that offers the most fearsome technical terrain on the mountain. From the base of this run, cut west to the La Sainte Paix chairlift, which services some of the **steepest trails** on the mountain, including La "S" and La Super "S". Both run side by side, differentiated only by the bumps on the former.

Freestyle

The mountain's main **terrain park** lies beneath the La Tortue lift, just below the summit lodge on the south side of the mountain. Few others use the lift, so it's easy to hit the same obstacles again and again, with the bonus that the lift runs directly over the park, allowing you to watch others tackling the same terrain. The park is spacious, nicely laid out, and has well-designed jumps that allow for smooth transitions and kind landings. The **mini-halfpipe** is an excellent place to learn to pump up the walls, while avoiding the intimidating speeds needed to pop out of the top of a regular halfpipe. The lower part of the park is devoted to intermediate and expert tabletops before hitting the **expert halfpipe** below the base of the La Tortue lift. From here, you'll have to head back down to the base area to return to the main park; don't miss the smaller terrain park on Le Court Vallon along the way. **Freeriders** should explore the natural hits and wind-blown lips on the sides of Le Gros Vallon and

La Montmorency, off the L'Express du Sud lift, or those beside L'Espoir in the expert area on the south face.

Lift tickets, lessons, and rentals

Mont-Sainte-Anne multiday **lift tickets** include night skiing; those running for three days or more must run consecutively, though they allow for one day off in the middle of the span. You can ski six days in a week for $225.

Private **lessons** are expensive at $65, while group programs are bargains: including equipment for either skiing or snowboarding and a day pass, they're priced from $44 for complete beginners (restricted lift pass) to $58 for beginners and $65 for intermediates. Note that the resort allows use of the two T-bars beside the base area free of charge, making it tempting to teach a friend to ski or ride since neither of you will waste valuable lift ticket time tottering around on the snow. Better intermediates and experts can join the HEAD Tyrolia Snowsports Academy, where a morning lesson is $44 and an afternoon lesson is $37. A five-day "X-5" pass for $200 includes access to all sessions (two per day), plus use of demo equipment and the clubhouse. Sessions focus on dealing with different terrain and grand-slalom technique, and free-skiing with video analysis is also included.

Most of the gear for **rent** by the resort is stock equipment, but at least the prices are reasonable, with skis costing $22 per day and snowboards $31 per day. For a better selection of higher-end gear and lower prices, check with the stores scattered along the highway in Beaupré.

Stoneham

Given the minimal vertical drop, it's the terrain between its three intercon-nected peaks that brings skiers and riders to **Stoneham**. Despite a grading system that claims over forty percent of the mountain for experts, the ski area is more appropriate for intermediates, since most black runs have generally been overgraded. Advanced skiers will find the resort pretty limited after a day or two.

The overcomplex **numbering system** for the peaks and trails can be confusing. Skiing and riding takes place on peaks 1, 2, and 4, on trails num-bered 1 to 61, although there are only thirty trails. What's more, many trails are further distinguished from one another by letters, and some – even though they have the same number – change from blue to black midway through. Still, orientation is relatively easy, as the peaks are all visible from one another, and most surround the small base area. The bulk of the intermediate and beginner terrain is on peak 2 at the center of the ski area, while peaks 1 and particular-ly 4 are graded as expert terrain. Two-thirds of the resort is open at night, mak-ing it the largest **night skiing** acreage in Canada.

Beginner

Stoneham is blessed with some superb beginner terrain, with long, broad trails that keep learners away from intimidating faster skiers. Absolute beginners should start in front of the base lodge on Trail 3; after mastering that, move on to Trail 2. Trail 6, which begins at the summit, snakes its way down a mellow road to the base of Peak 2; however, it crosses several intermediate trails, and can be too flat and crowded in many places. Better to try the slightly harder Trail 19 on for size – it's wide and steep enough to practice turns with plenty of space and momentum.

Mountain info – Stoneham

Phone ☎418/848-2415 or 1-800/463-6888

Snow phone ☎418/848-2415

Website ⊛www.ski-stoneham.com

Operating times Late Nov to early April Mon–Fri 9am–10pm, Sat 8.30am–10pm, Sun 8.30am–9pm

Price Adult day pass $36

No. of lifts 9, including 4 surface lifts

Base elevation 250m

Summit elevation 700m

Vertical drop 500m

No. of trails 30

Acreage 322

Beginner 20%

Intermediate 37%

Expert 43%

Average snowfall 360cm

Snowmaking Yes (277 acres)

Night skiing Yes (16 trails; $20 adult night pass)

Nursery facilities Yes, from age 2¹/₂; ☎418/848-2415 or 1-800/463-6888

Intermediate

Intermediate-level skiers have the run of the mountain. Moguls, glades, and even some double black diamond trails are manageable for stronger intermediates. Warm-up on the blue runs of Peaks 1 and 2, then try Trails 7 and 8 for long summit-to-base GS-style carving. After that, head across to Peak 4, and don't be intimidated by all the black diamonds on that part of the map: here you'll find wide rolling trails like 41 and 42, which have steep sections interspersed with mellower sections that allow you to catch your breath. Double black diamond Trails 45 and 46 over on Peak 4 may be within the grasp of confident skiers, but beware of becoming overconfident and skipping into the Peak 4 glades, which are truly expert terrain. Instead, try the black diamond segment of Trail 19 on Peak 2, a fast gladed section that you should be able to tackle fairly easily.

Expert

Peak 4 is the expert's mountain, with all but one trail designated black diamond. Though these aren't world-class in terms of difficulty, the absence of grooming leaves some runs, like narrow 49, bumpy and difficult. Some of the most challenging skiing and riding on the mountain (here snowbladers come into their own) is in the Peak 4 glades. Trail 47 is particularly steep, bumpy, narrow, and exposed, and a slow first run to scout the obstacles here is well advised. Another notable glade run, though with a shallower grade, is 41 on Peak 4, which partly follows the course of a frozen streambed, with jumps off summertime waterfalls and rapids. There are plenty of easier lines too, most on skier's right.

Freestyle

Stoneham's **terrain parks** are accessed via chairlifts that travel above the man-made features, allowing a preview of the fun to come. The tabletops have smooth takeoffs and landings, and there are plenty of rails and boxes. The park on Trail 4B is the longest, spanning summit-to-base on Peak 1 and incorporating around fifteen hits en route. A smaller terrain park is accessed off Lift A, also on Peak 1, and includes an excellent little halfpipe ideal for those new to freestyle. Part of this park can be reached through the double black diamond glade of Trail 10, though this way is best avoided, since many sideslip down this short trail, exposing a glut of gear-tearing roots and rocks. Some of the mountain's most incredible **natural drops** are found in the difficult glades over on Peak 4.

Lift tickets, lessons, and rentals

Day **lift tickets** cost $36 and are valid until 6pm. The day/night tickets ($32) are available after 12.30pm and are valid until closing. Multiday tickets – available for up to seven days – are good for both day and night skiing. **Lessons** are fairly low-key at Stoneham, but at only $30 per hour for private lessons, plus various discounts on equipment rental, they're a real bargain. The **rental** equipment available at the resort is respectable, ranging from basic ($18 per day) to high-performance skis ($38) and reasonably good snowboards ($32).

Le Massif

Towering above the vast expanse of the ice-laden St-Lawrence, **Le Massif** has some of the most spectacular views of any resort in the world. The area is within a UNESCO World Biosphere Reserve, and on many runs you'll turn a corner to be confronted and perhaps distracted by the spectacular scenery. Skiing- and snowboarding-wise, the focus of the mountain is largely on providing intermediate and expert terrain, though some beginner runs have been squeezed in at the edges.

Built along one side of a ridge, Le Massif is easy to navigate, with the vast majority of runs coming together at a single base area. Since the recent building of the summit lodge, the base area is no longer the focal point of the resort, which has more or less been inverted. If you're traveling in from Québec City, it's best to park at the summit station, which has all the same amenities as the base area. You'll start the day with a run and finish it with a lift back up to your car.

Beginner

Despite the presence of a surface tow at the summit lodge for absolute beginners, plus the possibility of riding all the way from summit to base on a green run, Le Massif is best avoided by those just starting out. The only green run on the lower half of the mountain – **La Combe**, which becomes L'Ancienne – is used to flush skiers from a large part of the mountain back to the base area, making it too busy for all but the most confident beginners. Those who do come here should concentrate on riding lift B and following a series of relatively quiet green trails back to the base of this lift. If you're confident, try the blue run **La Petite Rivére**, which is generally quiet and, though steep in places, very wide, allowing for wide turns.

Intermediate

As with other Québec City-area resorts, intermediates are well-served at Le Massif. A painstaking grooming regime means most of the groomed black diamond runs are well within the capacity of intermediates, and rarely much

Mountain info – Le Massif	
Phone ☏418/632-5876 or 1-877 /536-2774	
Snow phone ☏418/632-5876 or 1-877/536-2774	
Website ⊛www.lemassif.com	
Price Adult day pass $42	
Operating times Late Nov to late April Mon–Fri 9am–4pm, Sat & Sun 8.30am–4pm; Dec and Jan lifts close at 3pm daily	
No. of lifts 5, including 2 surface lifts	
Base elevation 45m	
Summit elevation 900m	
Vertical drop 875m	
No. of trails 30	
Acreage 220	
Beginner 20%	
Intermediate 31%	
Expert 49%	
Average snowfall 645cm	
Snowmaking Yes (154 acres)	
Night skiing No	
Nursery facilities Yes, from 3 years old	

harder than any of the blues. A fast, wide-open carving run is **La Petite Rivére**, which follows the backbone of a ridge straight down from the summit lodge; it's easy to vary this run by entering one of four different blues that branch off along the way. Although this center ridge has some of the most consistent vertical on the mountain, it's also well worth heading over to Chairlift C and exploring **La Fénoméne**, a fast but fairly easy black diamond run. The blues looping around Chairlift B are best avoided, as they're relatively short and usually some of the busiest around.

Expert

Le Massif's pride is its generally terrifying racecourse **La Charlevoix**. Diving down the southern perimeter of the resort, it's a fast, incredibly steep trail used for training world-class skiers. Unfortunately, this often closes it to the public, as do its frequently poor snow conditions. Instead, try La "42," which runs parallel to La Charlevoix almost the entire way. These are the only true expert-level runs in Le Massif, although the tight moguls of **La Pionche** (off Chairlift A) and the tricky but fairly gentle tree run of **Le Souis Bois** (off Chairlift B) are also worth exploring.

Freestyle

The two **terrain parks** at Le Massif are tiny compared to those at Mont-Sainte-Anne and Stoneham. A few small launches and rails have been built just above the summit lodge at La Grande Pointe, and a couple more between green runs La Combe and L'Ancienne near the base of the mountain. Since the parks are so limited, some of the best freestyle opportunities are in the woods: a good start is to explore the drops and jumps in Le Souis Bois off Chairlift B.

Lift tickets, lessons, and rentals

At Le Massif, those under 23 or over 55 can get $10 off the regular **day pass** price of $42. Another way of reducing costs by about ten percent is a multi-day ticket, sold in three- and five-day increments. The **ski school** at Le Massif offers reasonably priced private lessons at $39 per hour, and two-hour ski ($35) or snowboard ($44) group lessons. Despite the presence of a Rossignol Demo Center, ski **rentals** in Le Massif are nothing special (though prices are reasonable); you're better renting in Beaupré.

Accommodation

A bewildering range of **accommodation** options are on offer. The most developed resort, **Mont-Sainte-Anne** is the main center for slopeside accommodation, though **Stoneham** also has a smattering of options; only Le Massif is without lodging. If you don't mind a short commute in the morning and evening (ski shuttles are available – see p.446), it's worth staying in the much more stimulating surroundings of **Québec City**. Outside the winter Carnival (late-January and early February), you can also take advantage of reduced rates in the city. If you have your own vehicle and aren't bothered about being separated from the nightlife of Québec City, a handy place to stay is the service town and pilgrimage center **Sainte-Anne-de-Beaupré**. Sprawling along Rte 138 close to Mont-Sainte-Anne, it has a glut of inexpensive motels, plus plenty of skier and boarder-related services.

You should investigate the **ski packages** (☎418/827-5281 or 1-888/386-2754, ⊛www.fun2ski.com) offered by accommodations located in all four areas listed below. A good selection of properties have joined together with the resorts to offer economical packages which incorporate both lodging and the "Carte Blanche" lift ticket, available from two to seven days and valid at any of the three resorts. Deals start from around $250 for three days of skiing and three nights accommodation.

Mont-Sainte-Anne

Auberge le Refuge du Faubourg 1910 boul Les-Neiges ☎418/826-2869 or 1-800/463-5752, ⓦwww.refugedufaubourg.com. Roomy, simple condos in a bland building a short drive or shuttle ride from the slopes. Units come with one or two double beds, a full kitchen, and a wood-burning fireplace. Ski packages are offered at $176 for two including tickets. ❷

Chalets Mont-Sainte-Anne 1 rue Beau-Soleil ☎418/827-5776 or 1-800/463-4395, ⓦwww.chaletsmontste-anne.com. One- to five-bedroom condos beside *Chateau Mont-Sainte-Anne*; units have washer & dryer, kitchens, and fireplace. ❻

Chateau Mont-Sainte-Anne 500 boul Beau-Pré ☎418/827-5211 or 1-800/463-4467, ⓦwww .chateaumontsainteanne.com. Smart, rustic rooms and suites with balconies and kitchenettes; there's also a health club, pool, restaurant, and lounge. ❹

L'Auberge du Fondeur Rang St-Julien ☎418/827-5281 or 1-800/463-1568. Ugly concrete B&B in the midst of a cross-country skiing network. Facilities include sauna, waxing room, and a living room with fireplace. Ski-and-stay packages start at $69 per night. ❸

Beaupré

Auberge Baker 8790 ch Royal-Château-Richer ☎418/824-4478 or 1-866/824-4478, ⓦwww .auberge-baker.qc.ca. Wonderfully atmospheric bed and breakfast in a 150-year old farmhouse set well back from the busy Rte 138, just a ten-minute drive from the slopes. Rooms have rough-hewn beams, many curious nooks, and gloriously mismatched antique furnishings. Guests can use the communal kitchen, or can visit the superb in-house restaurant (see "Eating," opposite). Continental breakfast included and ski packages offered. ❸

Auberge la Camarine 10947 boul Ste-Anne ☎418/827-5703 or 1-800/567-3939, ⓦwww.camarine.com. Straightforward hotel rooms stylishly decorated with surreal art in a large wooden lodge beside Rte 138, a five-minute drive from the slopes. Many units are equipped with wood-burning fireplaces, and the inn's restaurant is the best in the area (see "Eating," opposite). Ski packages are available and prices are fixed throughout the ski season, making it a great deal at peak times. $292 with tickets for two. ❸

Motel St-Louis 9657 boul Ste-Anne ☎418/827-4298 or 1-800/736-4298, ⓦmotelstlouis.com. Basic, scrupulously clean motel – one of a dozen along Rte 138 in Beaupré, a ten-minute drive from the ski area – with fearfully ugly 1970s furnishings. Offers some of the best-value ski packages around. ❷

Stoneham

Condos Stoneham Stoneham Resort ☎418/848-2411 or 1-800/463-6888, ⓦwww.stonehamresort .com. Functional, well-equipped, and comfortable ski-in/ski out apartments, sleeping from two to eight. Units have balconies and fireplaces. ❸

Hotel Stoneham Stoneham Resort ☎418/848-2411 or 1-800/463-6888, ⓦwww.stonehamresort .com. Warm, comfortable, and spacious – though dull – hotel in a slopeside setting within the resort's tiny village. Avoid rooms above the ground-floor bars if you're a light sleeper. ❸

Québec City

Auberge St-Louis 69 rue St-Louis ☎418/692-2424 or 1-888/692-4105. You'll be hard-pressed to find a better low-budget deal located in the center of the old town. Rooms are basic and some share bathrooms. ❶

Hotel Nabiur Victoria 44 côte de Palais ☎418/692-1030 or 1-800/463-6283. ⓦwww.manoir -victoria.com. Dignified four-star hotel on the northern side of the old town, offering ski packages at around $160 per night for two. ❹

Le Chateau Frontenac 1 rue des Carrières ☎418/692-3861 or 1-800/441-1414, ⓦwww.fairmont.com. Formal, elegant Victorian hotel that's perched high in the old town, making it the city's most striking landmark. There are a huge variety of rooms from the pokey to the grand suite, along with some surprisingly economical ski packages. Sumptuous buffet breakfasts included. ❹

Québec Youth Hostel 19 rue St-Ursule ☎418/694-0755 or 1-800/461-8585, ⓦwww.cisq.org. Large, centrally located, impersonal hostel with dorm beds ($22, or $18 for HI members) and all the usual facilities – kitchen, laundry, lockers, internet access. No curfew.

Eating

All three resorts have a range of slopeside **dining** options, and there are plenty of supermarkets on the way from Québec City to Stoneham, or in Beaupré. The only resort where choices are limited is Le Massif, but the cafeteria food is exceptional, usually featuring fresh pasta, a seafood salad with smoked fish and mussels, and a selection of local cheeses. Save for a couple of worthwhile **restaurants** in Mont-Sainte-Anne and Beaupré, the area's best dining is in Québec City, where it's usually hard to find a bad meal. Look for *table d'hote* (set meal) menus created from fresh ingredients and offered at great prices. What follows is just a tiny selection of what's available; see also "Nightlife and entertainment" below for pub food options.

Mont-Sainte-Anne

Au Café Suisse 1805 boul Les-Neiges ☏418/826-2184. Twee Swiss-style restaurant with reliable fondues (from $20), raclettes ($24), and some more unusual items like Japanese-style steak with noodles and a curry broth. The *table d'hote* is worthy of the $30 price tag.

Beaupré

Auberge Baker 8790 av Royale, ☏418/824-4478 or 1-866/824-4478. Classy but relaxed restaurant in an eighteenth-century inn; the best in the area for Québecois cuisine. Try the hearty traditional items for an excellent introduction. Appetizers include Migneron de Bai St Paul ($6.50), a local cheese in phyllo pastry with maple syrup sauce, or an earthy yellow pea soup ($4). Entrees (around $16) include meat pies, pork meatball stew, duck, or salmon. The $27 *table d'hote* is a great way to keep tabs on spending.

Auberge la Camarine 10947 boul Ste-Anne ☏418/827-1958. The top restaurant in the area, with an eclectic variety of French, Italian, and Asian dishes (often fused) and a frequently changing menu. The food is of the highest standard, so expect a meal to cost up to $70 per person, excluding drinks. There's a wide selection of wine, with many half-bottles offered. Open only for dinner 6–8.30pm; reservations essential.

Stoneham

Feu Follet Stoneham Resort. Best restaurant in the base area, offering moderately expensive (mostly $10–20 per entree) but high-quality

Francophone cuisine – *moules et frites*, trout or fondue – as well as a surprisingly good selection of fajitas and even brochette of alligator.

La Capriccio Stoneham Resort. Unexciting Italian restaurant in Stoneham's base village. The food is well-priced, with a $7 lunch and a $13 dinner buffet on offer, but it's all a bit too stodgy. Better to choose pizzas from the menu, where you'll find the memorable "Veniccia" topped with snails and oysters.

Québec City

Aux Anciens Canadians 34 rue St-Louis ☏418/692-1627. Pricey (the table d'hote is $30) but worthwhile antique-furnished restaurant, serving huge helpings of some of the best Québecois cuisine, in one of the oldest homes in the city center. The menu includes caribou, duck, and meat pie and a superb maple syrup pie for dessert. After dinner, order up a "caribou" – a local sherry and vodka drink.

Le Buffet de L'Antiquarie 95 rue St-Paul ☏418/692-2661. Humble, stone-walled, diner-style restaurant amid the antique shops of the lower town, serving dependable, budget-priced versions of everyday Québecois cookery like *poutiné* (fries covered in gravy and curd), pea soup, or onion soup with melted cheese. Also has good cakes for dessert.

Les Fréres de la Côte 1190 rue St-Jean ☏418/692-5445. Friendly bistro at the east end of the old town's main nightlife strip, dishing out a range of delicioius pizzas, pastas, or fish and meat platters from an open kitchen, all set to thumping music. A good place to start a night out. Moderate prices.

Nightlife and entertainment

Of the three resorts, Stoneham generally has the wildest **nightlife**, thanks to the boisterous activities of night skiers from nearby Québec City. Mont-Sainte-Anne has its moments too, largely on weekends, while Le Massif is good for little more than a couple of après-ski beers. If you're serious about exploring local nightlife, **Québec City** is the best place to be, particularly during the

Winter Carnival (see box opposite given the range of bars and clubs in town, it's difficult to zero in on just a few. There are two main areas: rue St-Jean, within the city walls, or three blocks out of the walled city alongside the Grand Allée, which is where the bulk of the action is.

For information on the **latest events** in the area, check the listings section in the French daily newspapers *Le Soleil* and *Journal de Québec*, or in the free weekly *Voir* or the weekly English-language *Québec Chronicle Telegraph*. Another source of detailed information and programs for the city's theaters, symphony orchestra, and cinemas – the latter of which are mostly in the suburbs – is the Tourism and Convention Bureau (see box opposite). Tickets to most larger-scale events are sold by Admission (⊕1-800/361-4595, ⓦwww.admission.com).

Mont-Sainte-Anne

Chouette Bar Mont-Ste-Anne resort. Located in the main lodge, the *Chouette* is better set up for the longer night out than *ZigZag* (see below), thanks to a regular DJ and live music on weekend nights.
Saint Bernard 252 boul Beaupré ⊕418/827-6668. Enjoyable, large pub midway between the ski-hill and Beaupré, with a range of beers including some local brews and decent pub food, particularly the outstanding onion rings ($4) and delicious veggie fajitas ($13).
ZigZag Bar Mont-Ste-Anne resort. Near the gondola base, the *ZigZag's* sociable deck area is the place to head immediately after a day on the slopes.

Stoneham

Le Bar le 4 Foyers Main lodge, Stoneham resort. Casual place with, as the name suggests, four fireplaces, as well as several overstuffed sofas in many cozy nooks. The moderately priced bar food includes grilled baguettes, panninis, and pizzas ($8).
Le Pub St-Edmond Hotel Stoneham, Stoneham resort. Crowded Irish-style pub serving moderately priced pitchers of beer along with tasty, meat-centric bar food.

Other activities and attractions

Just about every **winter sport** imaginable can be found in the Québec City area. At the resorts, you'll find tubing, ice-skating, and an indoor climbing wall at Stoneham, and ice-skating, snowshoeing, dog-sledding, paragliding, sleigh rides, and snowmobiling at Mont-Sainte-Anne. Contact the resort helpdesks for details, or the Québec City tourism bureau (see box opposite) for more information on local opportunities, such as the outdoor skating rink at *Château Frontenac* (daily 11am–11pm; $2, skate rental $3). Other local stand-out activities are **cross-country skiing** and **ice-climbing** lessons, while **sightseeing** around Québec City is also very worthwhile.

Cross-country skiing

From mid-December to mid-April, the **Mont-Sainte-Anne Nordic Center**, 7km east of the ski area base, is open for cross-country skiing. The largest of its kind in Canada, the center boasts over 223km of trails, of which over half are set up for skating. There are plenty of trails through hardwoods and evergreens, plus expert possibilities to ascend and ski down some double black diamonds. The trails break down as 25 percent easy, 41 percent intermediate, and 34 percent expert. Day **tickets** to the network cost $15, with rentals running another $15; lessons are also available. Seven shelters are located around the area, three of which are equipped with wood-burning stoves and kitchen facilities. Overnight lodging in these are free (⊕418/827-4561 ext 408), though the more popular overnight option is the *L'Auberge du Fondeur* inn (see "Accommodation," p.452). An alternative cross-country option is to explore the more intermediate- and beginner-oriented rolling hills north of Québec City around **Camp Mercier**, where there are 192km of trails.

Québec City and the Winter Carnival

As North America's only walled city, filled with narrow, winding seventeenth- and eighteenth-century streets, **Québec City** has been designated a World Heritage Site by UNESCO. It's easy to spend at least a day wandering around the town, as well as exploring some of its collection of grand museums. The Greater Québec Area Tourism and Convention Bureau, 835 av Wilfrid-Laurier (☏418/649-2608 or 1-800/665-1528, ⊛www.quebecregion.com), can provide decent city maps and helpful pointers to get you started.

The city is at its most attractive during the Carnaval de Québec (or **Winter Carnival**), which begins on the last weekend in January and lasts a little over two weeks. It is presided over by the ridiculous, rotund mascot-snowman "Bonhomme," and the idea behind the carnival is to tempt people out of their homes in the frigid weather to celebrate the beauty of winter. It seems to work: the Québecois turn out in large numbers to view the incredible ice sculptures while drinking the local sherry and vodka concoction called a "caribou." Many activities are organized during the festival, as well, including sleigh rides, ice-skating, ice-climbing, dogsledding, and canoe races across the St-Lawrence River.

Ice-climbing

Diving down 105 meters where the Montmorency River meets the St-Lawrence, **Montmorency Falls** is higher than Niagara, though certainly far narrower. The falls are located beside the road 11km northeast of Québec City, and, when frozen, you can climb this mass of ice. L'Ascensation Ecole d'Escalade runs the world's largest **ice-climbing school** here, accepting adults and children (from nine years) alike; rates start at $60 per day (☏1-800/762-4967, ⊛www.rocgyms.com).

Listings

Bookstore Librairie Smith (Place Laurier, 2700 boul Laurier) is good for English-language books.
Car rental Thrifty, Château Frontenac (☏418/877-2870), or near the airport at 6210 boul Wilfred-Hamel (same phone).
Internet *Bar le Repit*, 2485 boul Ste-Anne ☏418/667-6584.

Medical Hospital de Ste-Anne-de-Beaupré, 11000 des Montagnards, Beaupré ☏418/827-3726.
Pharmacy Lavoie, 10989 boul Ste-Anne, Beaupré ☏418/827-3757.
Post office 105 rue Principale, St-Raphael ☏418/661-8423.

The Best of the Rest

Gray Rocks

Northwest of most of the Laurentian resorts, and a mere 3km from Tremblant (p.426), Gray Rocks (Dec–April; ☏819/425-2771 or 1-800/567-6767; ⊛www.grayrocks.com; $33 adults, $19 juniors) is another relatively small skiing option that aims to be quite family friendly. Four lifts service a 191m vertical drop over varied terrain, with steep blacks, good greens from the summit, and blues spread throughout. Most runs are consistently groomed, perfect for novices

who can incorporate sessions at Tremblant with their ski school tuition. The
somewhat pricey slopeside accommodation consists of straightforward "heritage" rooms, florally decorated "country charm" rooms, or no-frills one- or
two-bed condos a free shuttle ride from the ski area (⑦).

Mont-Blanc

Mont-Blanc (☎819/688-2444 or 1-800/567-6715; ⓦwww.ski-mont-blanc
.com; $36 adults, $13 juniors) near Saint-Fausin-Lac-Carré, about 100km from
Montreal, follows in much the same lines as nearby Gray Rocks (see above),
with which it offers interchangeable lift tickets. It is the bigger of the two,
spread over three mountains and 36 runs, with a respectable vertical drop of
300m and plenty of choices for every level of skier, particularly intermediates
with a preference for challenging tree runs. Mont-Blanc also has one of the
best regularly maintained halppipes in the area. The affordable slopeside
accommodation and self-contained amenities let you have a bit more of a
resort experience; ski packages start at $230 per person for two nights full
board, lift tickets, and access to a pool, hot tub, sauna, and a kid's playroom (⑨).

The Canadian Rockies

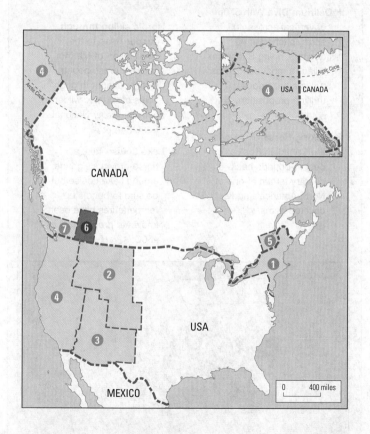

✳ **Banff** The civic heart of the Canadian Rockies is as popular for the surrounding Banff National Park as it is for its proximity to several major ski areas. See p.461

✳ **Delirium Dive** With 570m of vertical across 700 acres, pitched at 40 degrees, riding Sunshine Village's most dangerous run is a hazardous, thrilling proposition. See p.467

✳ **Kicking Horse** Ski or ride the Canadian Rockies' best in-bounds backcountry terrain at one of North America's undiscovered gems. See p.476

✳ **Rossland** The closest town to the modest resort of Red Mountain retains its nineteenth century mining image with neighborhoods full of Victorian houses. See p.486

✳ **Nordic skiing through Jasper** Head to the small resort of Marmot and rent cross-country skis for a jaunt through acres of sceniec wilderness in Jasper National Park. See p.491

✳ **Lake Louise** Take a horse-drawn sleighride around Lake Louise but be sure to bundle up, temperatures have been known to drop as low as –50C. See p.471

The Canadian Rockies

Brimming with majestic mountain views, crisp air, and reliable powder, the Canadian Rocky Mountains proffer some of the continent's most impressive ski destinations, at a cost that, more than anywhere else in North America, makes a mockery of Europe's swarming and exorbitant winter playgrounds.

The resorts of **Banff National Park**, within easy reach of the eponymous town, offer the best overall experience: the steep and taxing **Mount Norquay**; intermediate **Sunshine Village**, and the vast, varied, and hugely challenging **Lake Louise**. Outside of weekends and holidays most ski areas are less crowded than their counterparts in the United States, and all three promote themselves with a common lift-ticket system. Most visitors use the extensive, relatively inexpensive lodging and infrastructure of Banff, the region's primary hub.

North of Banff, a three-hour drive through craggy mountain scenery along the stunning Icefields Parkway lies **Marmot Basin**, a more modest, rustic ski area than those surrounding Banff, based near the quiet town of Jasper. There are many worthy, though marginally less accessible resorts further west in the British Columbia Rockies. Of these the closest to Banff is **Kicking Horse**, a couple of hours drive away; the resort is still in its infant stages of growth, but given the fabulous quality of its expert terrain, it is tipped by many to steal much of Banff's business. South of Kicking Horse is **Panorama**, a fantastic mountain for cruising and carving, with a scenic setting for its quiet resort village, also a base for heliskiing. Further south is family-oriented **Kimberley**. Multiday tickets here are interchangeable with those at **Fernie**, a mountain brimming with bowls and ridges. With all four resorts less than a couple of hours drive from their nearest neighbor, the setting is ideal for a multiresort trip tackled as a loop from Calgary. Outside of this loop, near the US border on the western fringe of the Rockies, is **Red Mountain**. Its remote location

National Park passes

Norquay, Sunshine Village, Lake Louise, and Marmot Basin are all located in National Parks; to visit them you'll need to purchase a park entry permit. These are available at park gates and park visitor centers – including those in Banff and Lake Louise. Individual daily fees are $5 for adult or $10 per vehicle. Large commercial groups pay $3 per person, per day.

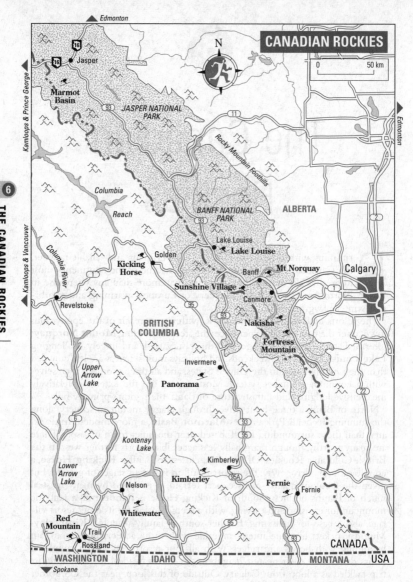

has kept development at a minimum so skiers can focus on the forested slopes and challenging steeps.

The Canadian Rockies season generally runs from mid-December until the end of May, with the **best conditions** in March. When conditions for skiing are less than optimal, explore the national parks, a perfect venue for other **outdoor activities**. A vast network of tracks for cross-country skiing, snowshoeing, dog sledding, and snowmobiling exist alongside ice climbing, skating, canyon crawling, and ice fishing.

Banff

As the major hub of the Canadian Rockies and with two ski areas in its back-yard and another nearby, **Banff** is as alluring a destination in winter as it is in summer, when thousands base themselves here for forays to the surrounding Banff National Park. Visible from town, the slopes of **Mount Norquay** are dense with expert challenges, while the well-rounded resort **Sunshine Village** is nestled in a bowl of mountains on the Continental Divide, ten miles from Banff. The snow here is dependable and dry, with some of the best early season conditions anywhere on the continent. The **temperatures**, however, can be extremely low (minus 30 degrees Celsius is not uncommon) throughout the ski season. Few lifts offer protection in the bitter cold so it's imperative to be well equipped.

Regardless, there's hardly a resort town better able to leave the vagaries of harsh mountain conditions behind than **Banff**, with its huge selection of comfortable hotels, respected restaurants, and playful nightlife. Though not exactly a slopeside base, Banff is on the doorstep of 7500 acres of skiing (including Lake Louise, see p.471) and a National Park, where cross-country skiing and snowshoeing trails cross paths with elk and long-horned sheep.

Arrival, information, and getting around

Banff is a ninety-minute drive from Calgary along the Trans-Canada Highway (Hwy 1). Several operators offer efficient **shuttle services** from Calgary Airport including Laidlaw (⊕403/762-9102 or 1-800/661-4946, ⊛www .laidlawbanff.com); Banff Airporter (⊕403/762-3330 or 1-888/449-2901, ⊛www.Banffairporter.com); Brewster Transportation (⊕403/762-6767, ⊕403/221-8242 in Calgary); and Sky Shuttle (⊕403/762-1010 or 1-888/ 220-7433, ⊛www.banffskyshuttle.com). All charge around $36 to Banff one way and around $40 to Lake Louise.

Daily **Greyhound buses** (⊕403/762-1092 or 1-800/661-8747, ⊛www .greyhound.ca) also ply the route from the center of Calgary (five daily; 1hr 40min; $20 one way), arriving in Banff's bus terminal at 100 Gopher St (7.30am–10.45pm; ⊕403/762-6767 or 1-800/661-1152). Once in Banff it's easy to **get around** on foot, though a frequent town bus service, operated by Banff Transit ($1; ⊕403/760-8294), provides transport to more outlying areas. For further **information** try the Banff and Lake Louise Tourism Bureau, 224 Banff Ave (Oct to mid-May 9am–5pm; Parks Canada information ⊕403/762-1550, town and accommodation information ⊕403/762-8421). **Taxi** services include Taxis Alpine (⊕403/762-3727), Banff Limousine (⊕403/762-5466), Banff Taxi (⊕403/762-4444), Legion (⊕403/762-3353), Mountain (⊕403 /762-3351), and Taxi-Taxi (⊕403/762-3111).

Public **transportation** to the ski hills from Banff consists of a network of shuttle buses linking Norquay, Sunshine Village, and Lake Louise. Free to Tri-Area pass holders (see p.464), rides cost between $6 and $9. It's best to confirm times and fares with hotels in the area, though you can also get information from the resorts themselves: Norquay (⊕403/760-0194), Sunshine Village (⊕403/ 762-6747), and Lake Louise (⊕403/762-4754). Note that though the service is frequent – buses run around every half an hour – the trip can take up to twice as long in either direction if several pick-ups or drop-offs are requested.

Some outlying resorts that are an easy day-trip from Banff also provide bus services as packages with a lift pass. These include Panorama (daily $49 including

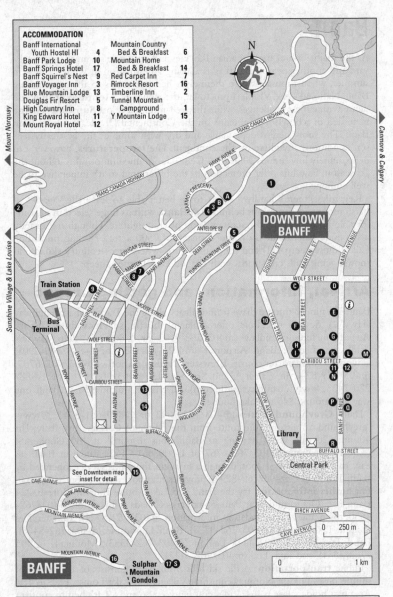

ACCOMMODATION

Banff International Youth Hostel HI	4	Mountain Country Bed & Breakfast	6
Banff Park Lodge	10	Mountain Home Bed & Breakfast	14
Banff Springs Hotel	17	Red Carpet Inn	7
Banff Squirrel's Nest	9	Rimrock Resort	16
Banff Voyager Inn	3	Timberline Inn	2
Blue Mountain Lodge	13	Tunnel Mountain Campground	1
Douglas Fir Resort	5	Y Mountain Lodge	15
High Country Inn	8		
King Edward Hotel	11		
Mount Royal Hotel	12		

N

Mount Norquay

Canmore & Calgary

Sunshine Village & Lake Louise

TRANS-CANADA HIGHWAY

HAWK AVENUE

MARMOT CRESCENT

ANTELOPE ST

COUGAR STREET

FOX STREET

DEER STREET

TUNNEL MOUNTAIN DRIVE

Train Station

Bus Terminal

RABBIT STREET

MARTEN ST

BANFF AVENUE

SQUIRREL STREET

ELK STREET

MOOSE STREET

WOLF STREET

BEAR STREET

CARIBOU STREET

BOW AVENUE

LYNX STREET

BEAVER STREET

MUSKRAT STREET

OTTER STREET

GRIZZLEY STREET

WOLVERTON STREET

ST JULIEN ROAD

BUFFALO STREET

TUNNEL MOUNTAIN ROAD

See Downtown map inset for detail

CAVE AVENUE

PARK AVENUE

RAINBOW AVENUE

MOUNTAIN AVENUE

SPRAY AVENUE

GLEN AVENUE

BUFFALO STREET

MOUNTAIN AVENUE

BANFF

Sulphar Mountain Gondola

DOWNTOWN BANFF

SQUIRREL ST

MARTEN ST

BANFF AVENUE

WOLF STREET

BEAR STREET

LYNX STREET

CARIBOU STREET

BOW AVENUE

BANFF AVENUE

Library

BUFFALO STREET

Central Park

BIRCH AVENUE

CAVE AVENUE

0   250 m

0   1 km

EATING

Aardvark	M	Evelyn's Too	C
Balkan Village	O	Joe Btfsplk's	E
Banff Springs Hotel	S	Le Beaujolais	R
Bumper's	A	Saltlik	F
Coyotes Grill	J	Sunfood Café	G
Evelyn's	I	Sukiyaki House	H

NIGHTLIFE

Aurora	Q	Rose and Crown	L
Banff Springs Hotel	S	St James Gate	D
Barbary Coast King		Voyager Inn	B
Edward Hotel	P	Wild Bill's Legendary	
Outa Bounds	N	Saloon	K

lift pass ☎403/762-8414, see p.492) and Kicking Horse (daily; $69 including lift ticket ☎403/762-4554, see p.476).

Another option is to **rent a car**. A little excessive if you plan to stay mainly at Norquay and Sunshine, a car can be worthwhile if heading to a different ski area every day. Rental options in town include Avis, Cascade Plaza, Wolf St (☎403/762-3222 or 1-800/879-2847); Banff Rent-a-Car, 230 Lynx St (☎403/762-3352), for low-priced older vehicles; Budget, 208 Caribou St (☎403/762-4546 or 1-800/268-8900); Hertz, at the *Banff Springs Hotel* (☎403/762-2027 or 1-800/263-0600); National, corner of Caribou and Lynx (☎403/762-2688 or 1-800/387-4747).

Norquay

Expert skiers have been carving the steep eastern slopes of **Mount Norquay** twenty years before the first lift was installed in 1948. In the last decade, new areas have opened with access to groomed intermediate cruising and further freestyle options, but Norquay has yet to shake its reputation as an advanced mountain, offering some of the most challenging bump runs in the region. The forested slopes offer shelter from the region's harsh winds, providing one of the few venues in the Canadian Rockies to ski or ride when others lay dormant from harsh storms. Like other resorts in the area, however, Norquay can be icy; it's best to arrive after recent snow or at least with sharpened edges. Though significantly smaller than Sunshine Village and Lake Louise, Norquay's convenient location and small liftlines are perfect for a short session on a rest day.

Mountain info

Phone ☎403/762-4421
Snow phone ☎403/762-4421
Website ☜www.banffnorquay.com
Price $47
Operating times Dec to mid-April daily 9am–4pm
No. of lifts 5, including 1 surface
Base elevation 1636m
Summit elevation 2133m
Vertical drop 503m
No. of trails 31
Acreage 190
Beginner 20%
Intermediate 36%
Expert 44%
Average snowfall 300cm
Snowmaking Yes (170 acres)
Night skiing Yes ($23; Jan–March Fri 4pm–9pm)
Nursery facilities Yes, from 19 months ☎403/760-7709

Beginner

For a first timer, Norquay is a decent place to learn turns, but after a couple of days, most will find the terrain too limited. The intermediate runs here are a big step up; the easiest is **Hoodoo** off the Spirit Quad. Many of the green trails have several awkward flat spots that force beginning boarders to unhook bindings and walk.

Intermediate

Steep and relatively narrow, the blue runs at Norquay are difficult and only consistent grooming makes intermediate cruising and carving possible. Some of the quietest and longest runs are off the **Pathfinder Express**; **Banshee** has some of the best snow conditions.

Expert

With only 400m of vertical to play with, but steep gradients available, many black runs are short and frantic. From the top of the North America chair – worth the ascent for the fine views over Banff and the Bow Valley alone –

there's a selection of expert runs, though half are frequently subject to closures from avalanche threats. Many of the runs, particularly double-diamond **Lone Pine**, are so thick with moguls that they resemble a basket of eggs from above. **Gun Run**, adjacent to Lone Pine, is a thrilling narrow chute, the resort's steepest challenge. For tree running, explore the demanding **Steep Chutes** off the Pathfinder Express.

Freestyle

Norquay has done much to attract the freestyle contingent, with its solid **halfpipe** and impressive **terrain park**. Located near the base of the Cascade lift, the park is full of tabletops with speedy approaches and kind landings. Outside the park, the slope's monster moguls can present fearsome aerial challenges; try the hits in among the trees of **Sun Chutes** and **Steep Chutes** off the **Pathfinder Express**.

Lift tickets, lessons, and rentals

Lift tickets for Norquay are pricey at $47, but you can buy tickets in hourly increments from two ($25) to five hours ($41). Beginners and freestylers can trim costs with a ticket for just the Cascade lift ($32 as this serves only green runs and the snowboard park). Skiing or riding at Norquay are also included on Tri-Area tickets and lessons are part of the Tri-Area lesson packages (see box above). Norquay's Snow Sports Center (☎403/760-7716 ⊛www.banffski school.com) provides both private and group lessons. For information on local equipment rental see p.466.

Sunshine Village

With a cold and bleak site on the Continental Divide, home to a rag-tag assemblage of only the most essential ski-resort buildings, the name **Sunshine Village** is truly a misnomer. Nevertheless, the acres of wide-open bowls, pockets of thrilling trees, and abundance of light snow – which typically ensures a 200-day season – make Sunshine Village one of the best places to ski or ride in the region.

The ski area's unconventional layout means that everyone's day begins with a gondola ride. From the base station, which harbors a restaurant and rental shop and adjoins a vast parking lot, it's a thirteen-minute ride up to the Village itself, though you can get off midway to reach the Goat's Eye area. A couple of trails run below the gondola back to the base station, but these allow a brisk return to the parking lot, more than being great trails in their own right.

Skiing here requires negotiating some bizarre links and a concentration on the confusing, five-part ski map. As the resort is flecked with flat spots and brutal traverses it pays to read the maps well – particularly if you're snowboarding

– since many can be avoided with a bit of forward thinking. Pick your line carefully on the lower portion of the mountain served by the **Continental Divide Express**: coming out of Bye Bye Bowl or off South Divide, it's difficult to carry enough speed to avoid a hike. The windswept conditions at the summit provide further problems, where poor visibility makes lines down the rocky slopes hard to pick.

Despite these inconveniences, Sunshine Village combines three fine mountains into a phenomenal ski area. Both **Lookout Mountain** and **Mount Standish** are ideal for intermediates, with many of the black runs possible for the self-assured. The former offers a selection of open trails, while the latter has varied terrain with challenging pockets for adventurous freeriders.

Beginner

Though beginner runs are scattered throughout the ski area, many are runouts for tougher runs or a means to shuttle experienced skiers between different parts of the ski area. The long, gentle, and often deserted **Meadow Park** off the **Wawa lift** is a reliably quiet run. Other decent greens on Mount Standish are **Rock Isle Road** off the **Strawberry Chair** and winding **Creek Run** off the **Standish Chair** whose consistent vertical is helpful for generating even turns. The green runs off busy **Wolverine Quad** and **Jackrabbit Express** lifts are mellow, with a choice of long cruisers off Wolverine Express and short jaunts off Jackrabbit. To progress onto blue runs try the relatively steep but extremely wide and even pistes of **Goat's Eye Mountain.**

Intermediate

If it's sunny start the day at Mount Standish, on the long sweeping runs off the Wawa lift, particularly in the **WaWa Bowl**. For smooth consistent vertical try **Big Bunkers** off the Standish Chair. When visibility is high, head to Lookout Mountain, where the best cruiser at the resort is the **World Cup Downhill**. In poor conditions it can be hard to anticipate the terrain, so head to the sheltered runs of Goat's Eye Mountain instead. Here the runs are generally wide, as are many steep blacks, including **Upper Scapegoat** and **Rolling Thunder**. Most skiers visit Goat's Eye later in the day on their way out of the ski area; come first thing for empty runs.

Expert

Nearly half of Sunshine is expert terrain, but much of the best lines are tucked away and require some searching. Hardcore riders can ski their choice of moguls, chutes, trees, and – with a bit of luck – powder, all day. The main expert area is **Goat's Eye Mountain's**, where wide open runs with varying pitch descend into narrow **glades.** Try the steep, continuous **Goatsucker**

Mountain info

Phone ☎403/762-6500 or 1-877-542-2633
Snow phone ☎403/760-7669
Website ⊕ www.skibanff.com
Price $63
Operating times Nov to late May daily 9am–4pm (gondola until 5.30pm)
No. of lifts 12, including 1 gondola and 2 surface tows
Base elevation 1658m
Summit elevation 2730m
Vertical drop 1070m
No. of trails 103
Acreage 3168
Beginner 22%
Intermediate 31%
Expert 47%
Average snowfall 1020cm
Snowmaking No
Night skiing No
Nursery facilities Yes, from 19 months ☎403/762-6563

Equipment rental in Banff

It is possible to pick up gear at either Norquay or Sunshine Village (☏403/762-6592), but both can be crowded and you're better off renting equipment the evening before at one of Banff's many outlets. These all stay open conveniently late and the competition between them keeps rates reasonable. A basic ski package – skis, boots, and poles – starts at around $25 per day, with sharp increases in price for better quality gear.

In business for over fifty years, Monod Sports, 129 Banff Ave (☏403/762-4571) in the center of town, is a good bet for skis. Boarders should try Rude Boys Snowboard Shop, 215 Banff Ave (☏403/762-8480, ⊛www.rudeboys.com), owned and operated by local riders. The largest concentration of shops is along Bear Street. Here Bactrax, no.225 (☏403/762-8177), offers packages as low as $15 per day for skis, $28 for snowboards, and offers a twenty percent discount to Hosteling International members. Other outlets on Bear Street include Banff Adventures Unlimited, no. 211 (☏403/762-4554), Performance Ski and Sport, 2nd Floor, no. 208 (☏403/762-8222), and Mountain Magic Equipment, no. 224 (☏403/762-2591), one of the best places in town for cross-country ski gear. Most shops offering rental gear also sell a good stock of equipment and accessories. If you have your own transport, consider driving east to Canmore, where Switching Gear, 718 10th St (☏403/678-1992), has an extensive selection of **secondhand** equipment with prices that can rival renting.

Glade or hike from the top of Goat's Eye Express and launch into untracked steeps. For more powder but without the hike, hit the runs beneath the **Tee Pee Town Chair** on **The Shoulder,** a short traverse on skier's right from the liftline. Along with the collection of steep chutes here you'll also find a few stretches through glades as well. For the best bump runs climb further up **Lookout Mountain** on the **Continental Divide Quad** to access the massive mogul field on **North Divide** – one to avoid in low visibility.

Freestyle

The **terrain park** off the Continental Divide Chair is full of smooth, fast hits, all labeled for difficulty but no substitute for scoping the jumps out yourself. Below the park there's a fairly average boardercross. The Silver Bullet **halfpipe** is beside the Strawberry Chair, lower down the mountain and below the natural halfpipe that runs alongside The Dell Valley. Many of Sunshine's best **natural hits** are tucked away on skier's right of the Wawa lift in an intermittently gladed area. Here a number of boulder jumps and a tricky Waterfall provide more stimulating challenges. There's also plenty of decent terrain strewn elsewhere on Mount Standish, particularly among the trees below the Standish Chair.

Lift tickets, lessons, and rentals

Adult **lift tickets** are $63 per day, children under 12 pay $21, and seniors $49. Multiday tickets are available; a two-day adult passes cost $116, five-day $275. Sunshine's Ski and Snowboard **school** charges $180 for 2-hour private lessons in peak season. Group lessons are priced at $42 per half-day or $60 per day, in a group of up to eight people. The resort's absolute beginner packages, the discovery programs, include rental equipment, an all-mountain lift ticket, and full day's lesson for $72 for the first day. For an additional $100 this offer can be extended over three days. Before committing to tickets and passes at Sunshine Village, be sure to explore the possibilities offered in the Tri-Area system (see p.464). For **rentals**, see the box above.

Delirium Dive

Closed by park services for eighteen years, the 700-acre **Delirium Dive**, with its forty-degree pitch and 570m of vertical, has recently reopened, carefully managed by the resort. The thrill of launching down the terrifying rock-strewn chutes on the steep is a risky endeavor, even for technically adept skiers, who love the run as much for the burst of adrenaline as for the access to the wonderful bowl beneath The Dive. Access to the area is through a check-in gate, where you need to be in possession of an avalanche transceiver, shovel, and a partner. Helmets are strongly recommended, though not essential for access. You can rent beacons and shovels at the base area. For information on conditions check with the Ski Patrol, on the Avalanche Info board at the Sunshine Gondola, or call ☎403/762-6511. Sunshine Village Ski and Snowboard School offer half-day guided lessons into the Dive for up to five people for $259. Avalanche equipment can be rented at Mountain Magic or Monods in Banff (see box opposite).

Accommodation

Accommodation of all manner lines the roads into town from both exits off the Trans-Canada Highway. Book in advance using the town's central reservation system, Banff Central Reservations (☎403/705-4020 or 1-877/542-2633, ⊛www.banffreservations.com). Banff Accommodation (☎403/762-0260 or 1-877/226-3348, ⊛www.banffaccommodations.com) and Ski Banff-Lake Louise (☎403/762-4561 or 1-800/754-7080, ⊛www.skibig3.com) provide package deals.

Banff International Youth Hostel HI Tunnel Mountain Rd ☎403/762-4122, ⊛www.hostelling intl.ca/alberta. Friendly, modern 216-bed hostel 3km from downtown and a $6 cab ride from the bus depot. Facilities include large kitchen, laundry, lounge with fireplace, ski workshop, and an inexpensive restaurant. Dorm beds cost $21 for members, $25 for nonmembers; add $6 per person for private double rooms. Ski packages are $192 per person for three nights. No curfew.

Banff Park Lodge 222 Lynx St ☎403/762-4433 or 1-800/661-9266, ⊛www.banffparklodge.com. Quietly sophisticated, low-slung cedar and oak hotel, a block from the town center; the best deal downtown. Scandinavian-style rooms are simple and airy; some have whirlpools and fireplaces. Hotel facilities include hot tub, steam room, indoor pool, laundry, and dry cleaning service. The ski shuttle stops at the front door. ❹

Banff Springs Hotel Spray Ave ☎403/762-2211 or 1-800/441-1414, ⊛www.fairmont.com. One of the continent's most famous hotels – built in Scottish Baronial style with turrets and cornices towering above its thick nine-story granite walls – offering luxurious service that borders on pageantry. The glut of facilities include a world-class fitness and spa complex, several stores, and restaurants. Prices are generally extravagant but extremely reasonable in winter. Bed and breakfast rates start at $210 and ski packages, priced at $350 per person for three nights – which includes use of hotel's ski shuttle – are fantastic value. ❻

Banff Squirrel's Nest 332 Squirrel St ☎403/762-4432. Pleasant rooms in quiet residential side street an easy walk from downtown. Suites have queen beds and own bathroom. Continental buffet breakfast included. ❷

Banff Voyager Inn 555 Banff Ave ☎403/762-3301 or 1-800/879-1991. Comfortable motel with chilly outdoor pool, hot tub, sauna, and the cheapest bar in town. Ski buses call at the door. ❸

Blue Mountain Lodge Corner of Caribou and Muskrat streets ☎403/762-5134 ⊛www .bluemtnlodge.com. Friendly budget lodging in town center with small rooms, all with private bathrooms and spectacular mountain views. Common facilities include a guest kitchen, lounge, and laundry facilities. ❷

Douglas Fir Resort Tunnel Mountain Rd ☎403/762-5591 or 1-800/661-9267, ⊛www.douglasfir .com. Collection of condo blocks in secluded wooded area on Tunnel Mountain, a fifteen-minute walk from town center. Best for families or groups, units have a kitchen and lounge with fireplace as well as access to leisure facilities, including squash courts and pool with waterslides. Laundromat and small convenience store onsite and ski bus pick-up at entrance. ❸

High Country Inn 419 Banff Ave ☎403/762-2236 or 1-800/661-1244, ⓦwww.banffhighcountryinn .com. Mid-range motel with some luxury suites in a central location and close to a ski bus stop. Facilities include two hot tubs and an indoor pool. ❹

King Edward Hotel 137 Banff Ave ☎403/762-2202 or 1-800/344-4232, ⓦwww.banffkingedwardhotel .com. Century-old facility in the center of town with basic, reasonably priced rooms, most over-looking Banff Avenue. ❸

Mountain Country Bed & Breakfast 427 Marten St ☎403/762-3288, ⓦwww.banffmountaincountry .com. Close to downtown Banff and a block from the ski shuttle route. The large rooms are equipped with private jacuzzi tubs, queen-size beds, and duvets. Light continental breakfast included. ❷

Mountain Home Bed & Breakfast 129 Muskrat St ☎403/762-3889, ⓦwww.mountainhomebb.com. Elegant B&B a couple of minutes walk from down-town. Spacious antique-furnished guestrooms have down comforters on king-size beds. Delicious cooked breakfasts with daily menu. ❹

Mount Royal Hotel 138 Banff Ave ☎403/762-3331 or 1-800/267-3035, ⓦwww.mountroyalho-tel.com. Bland building amid downtown shops. Most rooms have mountain views; all guests have access to a large health club with whirlpool and exercise equipment. The ski bus stops nearby. ❺

Red Carpet Inn 425 Banff Ave ☎403/762-4184 or 1-800/563-4609. Pastel shaded inside and out, this no-frills motel is a clean, central, and decent-value option for those looking for no more than a soft mattress and the most basic facilities. ❷

Rimrock Resort Mountain Ave ☎403/762-3356 or 1-800/661-1587, ⓦwww.rimrockresort.com. Elegant hotel in imposing, angular building, nestled on the lower slopes of Sulphur Mountain 3km south of town. The smart, modern rooms come with views of Bow Valley. Excellent and extensive fitness facilities are offered, as is a free shuttle into town. ❻

Sunshine Inn Sunshine Village ☎403/762-6555. The only ski-in/ski-out option in the Banff area, this modest 84-room hotel is accessed by gondola (transport is also available outside gondola operat-ing times) and remote from both the bustle of traf-fic and the diversions in Banff. Though you're guaranteed first tracks, options are more limited when the lifts close. There's a huge hot tub, sauna, exercise and game room, and a children's program every evening. Facility includes a restaurant, two bars, and small convenience store. Three-night packages start at $270 per person. ❺

Timberline Inn ☎403/762-2281 or 1-877/762-2281, ⓦwww.banfftimberline.com. Basic hotel at the base of Mount Norquay ski area. Some rooms have private balconies and many have excellent mountain views. Chalets sleep up to eight in three bedrooms. A steakhouse is on the premises, but all other services are a car or shuttle bus ride away. ❹

Y Mountain Lodge 102 Spray Ave ☎403/762-3560 or 1-800/813-4138, ⓦwww.ywca-banff.ab .ca. Clean, relaxed hostel a short walk from down-town. You can use your own sleeping bag in the dorm bunks ($21) or rent blankets and pillows ($5). There are also large, basic singles, doubles, and triples ($55–95; some with private bathroom). In addition to a huge living room with gigantic stone fireplace, the hostel also has a café with cheap food as well as a kitchen, laundry facilities, and showers ($2.50 for nonresidents).

Eating

Reflecting the origins of its many visitors, Banff has a selection of **restaurants** that's as eclectic as it is huge, from authentic sushi through hearty pub grub to delicious steakhouses. Prices vary significantly; for cheap eats you're best sticking to hostel cafés, though some of the bars in town (see "Drinking and entertainment" opposite) are decent value.

On-mountain food at Banff's two resorts is fairly tasty if a bit expensive. **Norquay**'s Cascade Lodge offers deli, cafeteria, and pub food served with good views. Over at **Sunshine**, the Eagle's Nest Dining Room in the *Sunshine Inn* caters to the upper end of the market with filet mignon and lobster. Less expensive lunch is available in the adjoining Chimney Corner Lounge, home to enormous portions of pasta. The Sunshine Day Lodge has picnic areas for brown baggers, a deli, and a cafeteria with a prime rib buffet on the third floor.

For **groceries** try the Safeway supermarket at 318 Marten St and Elk (daily 9am–10pm) or the less hectic Kellers, 122 Bear St (daily 7am–midnight).

Aardvark Pizza and Sub 304a Caribou St ☎403/762-5500. Tiny takeout joint serving subs, wings, tacos, nachos, and fantastic thick-crust pizzas until 4am.

Baker Creek Bistro Baker Creek Chalets, Bow Valley Parkway ☎403/522-2183. Romantic dining in a log cabin outfitted with antler chandeliers midway between Banff and Lake Louise on the Bow Valley Parkway. The menu has innovative steaks and pastas and good game dishes; apple cake is the house specialty.

Balkan Village 120 Banff Ave ☎403/762-3454. Cheerful restaurant best known for frantic belly dancing on Tuesdays and large portions of decent Greek cuisine with a twist. Choose from Greek versions of ribs (pork ribs in a lemon sauce) $16, chow mein, or spaghetti, or stick to the traditional favorites like souvlakia ($13) or the two-person Greek platter ($39) which includes beef souvlaki, ribs, moussaka, lamb chops, and salad.

Banff Springs Hotel 405 Spray Ave ☎403/762-6860. With fifteen dining options under one roof, the *Banff Springs* has enough variety to suit even the pickiest of diners. The *Bow Valley Grill* is the largest restaurant, its menu focused on seafood and rotisserie-grilled meats. The Sunday brunch ($25) here is legendary for its variety and value. Other eateries range from a 24-hour deli serving pizza to the luxurious *Castello Ristorante* and the *Samurai*, which serves excellent sushi and shabu-shabu – strips of beef, chicken, or fish cooked in broth and served with a selection of sauces. For snacks try *Grapes Wine Bar*'s salads, selection of pates and cheese, and excellent fondue.

Bumper's 603 Banff Ave ☎403/762-2622. Busy steakhouse with adjoining bar located just outside downtown. Entrée prices start at around $18; veg-etarians can console themselves with a decent salad bar.

Coyotes Grill 206 Caribou St ☎403/762-3963. Small, simple café off the main drag, serving tasty breakfasts. Try the cream cheese-filled French toast with fruit ($9) or the huge Mountain Man Breakfast ($9.50) which includes two eggs, two

pancakes, bacon, and roasted potatoes. For dinner the pizza, pasta, and Tex-Mex entrees are best and in the $15–25 range.

Evelyn's 201 Banff Ave ☎403/762-0352. Extensive range of coffees to wash down pastries and muffins here in a café that's popular enough to justify a second outlet, *Evelyn's Too*, at 229 Bear Ave. Both are open 7am–11pm, and both make excellent deli sandwiches (around $5).

Joe Btfsplk's Diner 221 Banff Ave ☎403/762-5529. Red vinyl seats and black-and-white tiles make this 1950s diner feel authentic, as do the giant portions of dependable, if slightly overpriced, classics like meatloaf.

Le Beaujolais 212 Banff Ave at Buffalo St ☎403/762-2712. Longstanding reputation for fine French renditions of regional cuisine. Pick from a choice of three prix-fixe menus between $55 and $90, ranging from two to six courses – though only the six-course meal includes drinks from the comprehensive wine list.

Saltlik 221 Bear St ☎403/762-2467. Swank restaurant with wacky lamps and loud art in an otherwise understated interior. The regional cuisine is fantastic; try the prime sirloin ($20). Most entrees including rotisserie chicken, smoked Alaskan black cod, and sea bass are under the $20 mark, but the price doesn't include sides (mushrooms, spinach, corn, shrimp). The selection of wines suffer little mark-up and the trendy bar is a good place for a drink before or after dinner – or with dinner as it has the best bar menu in town; don't miss the crisp shoestring fries.

Sunfood Café 215 Banff Ave ☎403/760-3933. Simple, reliable, and vaguely bohemian vegetarian eatery tucked away in a mall. Great for light meals, salads, sandwiches, and wraps, most well under $10. Hot meals include items like teriyaki tofu steak ($12) and mushroom stroganoff ($15).

Sukiyaki House 211 Banff Ave ☎403/762-2002. Chic Japanese restaurant with a broad menu; it's hard to choose, but almost impossible to go wrong. The Love Boat ($35) is a delicious, varied selection for two.

Drinking and entertainment

Banff has no shortage of **bars** – most within a short walk of one another – and several late-night clubs to stagger to afterwards. This is clearly evident during the partying that accompanies Banff's **Winter Festival**, held over a period of sixteen days at the end of January. As the town's largest winter event it involves a variety of activities including the **Lake Louise Loppet**, a Nordic competi-tion run by the Calgary Ski Club (☎403/245-9496), and an ice-sculpting competition. The town also gets fairly rowdy during regular international events like the World Cup downhill skiing competitions. The **Lux Cinema Center**, 229 Bear St (☎403/762-4629) in the center of town, runs new Hollywood releases.

Aurora 110 Banff Ave ☎403/760-5300. Loud, pricey, and popular bar and nightclub in the Clock Tower Village Mall. This pick-up joint usually gets going around midnight when a young crowd gathers to dance until 2am nightly. Live music on Friday and Saturday evenings.

Banff Springs Hotel ☎403/762-6892. The giant hotel has a selection of bars – the quaint *Waldhaus Pub*, the cigar-friendly *Ramsay Lounge*, the *Rundle Balcony* with its own pianist, and wine bar *Grapes* – and its own five-pin bowling center ($3.75 a game, $1.10 shoe rental).

Barbary Coast 119 Banff Ave ☎403/762-4616. Chaotic and occasionally rowdy bar, bulging with pool tables and sporting memorabilia. There's excellent pub grub – daily dinner specials for $7 – and a long happy hour from 4.30pm to 7.30pm; open until 2am.

King Edward Hotel 137 Banff Ave ☎403/762-4629. Hotel bar, popular for its sixteen billiard tables ($12 per hour).

Mad Trappers Sunshine Village. Once the lifts close, this rickety wooden bar at the center of the village is the place for free peanuts and satisfying beers. Don't miss the last gondola at 6pm (Fri and Sat 10pm).

Outa Bounds 137 Banff Ave ☎403/762-8434. Soulless basement bar – the main competition for

Banff's other major nightclub, the *Aurora* – that nevertheless draws in crowds of twenty-somethings for average food, pool, dancing, and occasional live music.

Rose and Crown 202 Banff Ave ☎403/762-2121. Victorian pub with restaurant serving decent bar-food and fantastic hot wings. There's a pool table and occasionally live music, particularly blues and funk.

St James Gate 205 Wolf St ☎403/762-9355. Dingy pub, originally built in Ireland then reassembled here to become hugely popular with locals and visitors alike. The thirty beers on tap include Guinness, of course, as do many of the dishes on the satisfying bar menu: Guinness, crab, and asparagus soup ($6) or Guinness, steak, and mushroom pie ($11). Occasional live Celtic music.

Voyager Inn 555 Banff Ave ☎403/762-3301. Workaday bar adjoining eponymous motel on the edge of town. Locals who appreciate the cheapest drinks in town – along with nightly specials – converge here.

Wild Bill's Legendary Saloon 203 Banff Ave ☎403/762-0333. Country-and-Western bar with live bands (country Wed–Sat; rock and blues Sun–Thurs) and weekly line-dancing lessons (Wed 8.30pm). There's also a pool hall and game room, and before 8pm good Tex-Mex and vegetarian food is available.

Other activities and attractions

With the full gamut of winter activities on offer in and around Banff, it would be a shame to visit and not go beyond the ski areas at least once. In town there's a decent collection of fitness facilities, spas, and pools. The information center (see p.461) is a good first stop for most activities, with extensive lists and contact information for guides and outfitters in the area.

To see Banff National Park, head out on either **cross-country skis** or **snowshoes**. Details of the full network are given in the *Nordic Trails in Banff National Park* pamphlet available from the town's visitor center ($1). Popular areas include Johnston Lake, Golf Course Road, Spray River, Sundance Canyon, along with several areas around Lake Louise (see opposite) An additional 300km of cross-country trails cross the Kananaskis region, many developed for Olympic competitions, radiating from Canmore Nordic Center (☎403/678-2400), south of Canmore. The Nordic Center itself maintains 70km of its own trails.

One of the best **winter walks** in the area is the hike through the scenery of Johnston Canyon, on boardwalks suspended from its limestone walls past impressive pillars of glassy ice. Occasionally icy, the boardwalks are navigable in winter with the right gear and knowledge. White Mountain Adventures (☎403/678-4099, ⓦwww.canadiannatureguides.com) offers a 3.5-hour trip down the canyon. Similar packages, down the less spectacular Grotto Canyon, are offered by Discover Banff tours (☎403/760-1299 or 1-877/565-9372) which only take an hour. For detailed **ice climbing** information visit at National Park desk in Banff's Information Center (☎403/762-1550), where climbers should also register.

Of the large selection of local commercial tours one of the best is **dogsledding**. Thrilling trips are offered for a rather steep fee (around $100 per hour) by Howling Dog Tours (☎403/678-9588) or Snowy Owl Sled Dog Tours (☎403/678-4369), while Mountain Mushers (☎403/762-3647) will take you for a shorter spin around the town's golf course. For less adrenaline-filled **sleigh rides** on the frozen Bow River, contact Holiday on Horseback (☎403/762-4551), while those who seek the positively calming experience of **ice-fishing** on surrounding lakes should contact Banff Fishing Unlimited (☎403/762-4936). For **ice-skating** or **tobogganing**, head to the Banff Springs Hotel. Ice skates can be hired from The Ski Shop (☎403/762-5333) in the hotel for $5 per hour; you can also rent sleds here ($4 per hour) for use on the unofficial run beside the rink.

If you'd rather be pampered investigate the **Upper Hot Springs**, (Mon–Thurs & Sun 10am–10pm, Fri & Sat 10am–11pm; $7 mid-May to mid-Oct, $5.50 mid-Oct to mid-May; lockers, towel, and swimming costumes rental available; ☎403/762-1515 or ☎403/762-2500 for spa bookings), 4.5km from the town center on Mountain Avenue. Originally developed in 1901, the springs have since undergone several renovations and now offer soaking at 38°C in a large outdoor pool, use of a steam room and cold plunge, and relaxing therapeutic massages ($45) and aromatherapy wraps ($32).

Another good place to give in to steaming temptation is **The Solace** (☎403 /762-2211) at the *Banff Springs Hotel*. Centered on a circular mineral pool beneath a glass ceiling, the spa offers outdoor saltwater hot tubs, steam rooms, and an extensive array – almost one hundred – of therapeutic services on offer. Rates for using the facility are steep at $50 per day, but this fee is waived if you buy a service – say thirty-minute massage ($80) – making it much better value.

Listings

Avalanche hotline ☎403/762-1460 – reports also posted at visitor centers.

Bookstore Banff Book & Art Den, Clock Tower Mall, 94 Banff Ave (daily 10am–7pm; ☎403/762-3919).

Internet The Public Library, 101 Bear St (Mon, Wed, Fri & Sat 11am–6pm, Tues & Thurs 11am–9pm, Sun 1–5pm; ☎403/762-2661), has free access but requires prior booking.

Hospital Mineral Springs Hospital, 301 Lynx St ☎403/762-2222.

Pharmacy Cascade Plaza Drug, Lower Level, Cascade Plaza, 317 Banff Ave; Gourlay's, 229 Bear St (Wolf and Bear Mall).

Post office 204 Buffalo St at the corner of Bear St (Mon–Fri 9am–5.30pm).

Road conditions ☎403/762-1450. Other weather info ☎403/762-4707 or ☎403/762-2088 (24hr recording).

Lake Louise

Lake Louise has provided the backdrop for over two decades of World Cup skiing and is second in Canada only to Whistler-Blackcomb in size. Its forty square kilometers of terrain include tricky mogul fields, challenging chutes and vast open bowls, and an abundance of gentle beginner runs and pleasant intermediate crusiers reliably covered with some of the best powder on the conti-

Mountain info

Phone ☎403/522-3555 or 1-800/258-7669

Snow phone ☎403/244-6665

Website ⊛www.skilouise.com

Price $61

Operating times Early Nov–Mid-April daily 9am–4pm; mid-April to mid-May daily 9am–4.30pm

No. of lifts 12, inc. 4 surface

Base elevation 1645m

Summit elevation 2637m

Vertical drop 1000m

No. of trails 113

Acreage 4200

Beginner 25%

Intermediate 45%

Expert 30%

Average snowfall 360cm

Snowmaking Yes (1700 acres)

Night skiing No

Nursery facilities Yes, from 6 weeks ☎403/522-3555.

nent. For most visitors, however, the resort's best assets are its tiny liftlines and the beauty of the mountains in the surrounding Banff National Park.

The functional town of Lake Louise, a short drive from the slopes, consists of several unremarkable buildings clustered around an outdoor mall. It's a fairly dull place, particularly relative to Banff, only an hour drive along the TransCanada Highway, making the latter a much better base. A more significant drawback can be the phenomenally low temperatures during January and February, with average conditions hovering at -7°C midwinter. Including wind chill, temperatures have been known to drop as low as -70°C at the summit; it's best to ski here later in the season.

Arrival, information, and getting around

Many of the **shuttle buses** providing services between Calgary and Banff (see p.461) also head to Lake Louise. The two most frequent services are the Banff Airporter (☎403/762-3330 or 1-888/449-2901, ⊛www.Banffairporter.com) and Rocky Mountain Sky Shuttle (☎403/762-5200 or 1-888/762-8754, ⊛www.rockymountainskyshuttle.com). Both travel the route at least every two hours 4am–midnight and charge around $40 from Calgary and $12 from Banff. Greyhound **buses** stop at Lake Louise on their way from Banff (4 daily; 50min; $8) at The Depot (☎403/522-2080) in the Samson Mall, location of the **Lake Louise Visitor Center** (☎403/522 3833). As many buses make the journey from the West (three from Vancouver) before heading on to Banff and Calgary.

The regular **ski shuttle** trundling between Norquay, Sunshine Village and Lake Louise ($15 return; but included in the price of a Tri-Area Pass, see p.464) is the only means of public transport. The **car rental agency** in town is National at The Depot (☎403/522-3870). In the evening Lake Louise is linked with Banff by the Rocky Mountain Sky Shuttle, and leaves at 7pm, returning from Banff at midnight. If you need a **taxi**, call Lake Louise Taxi & Tours (☎403/522-2020).

The mountain

Naturally dividing into three distinct zones, the core of the Lake Louise ski area is the **Front Side** (sometimes called the South Face). Climbing from the base area, this region is best for its groomed green and blue runs. Behind the Front Side, the **Back Bowls** are flecked with above treeline black diamonds. From the Back Bowl a long, fairly flat runout leads to the glades of the **Ptarmigan** and **Larch** area. The forested slopes here face in several directions, a combination that makes this the best region when conditions are harsh.

When temperatures are low at Lake Louise, it pays to follow the sun. Head to the Back Bowls in the morning, work Larch and Ptarmigan midday, then spend the afternoon on the Front Side. If you're new to Lake Louise try a free tour with the resort's Ski Friends (meet outside the Whiskyjack Lodge 9.30am, 10.15am, & 1.15pm), local volunteers who know the mountain.

Beginner

Accessed by the short **Sunny T-bar**, Lake Louise's learning zone is adjacent to its base area. Try the wide, gentle but occasionally busy **Wiwaxy** a little further up the mountain. Slightly harder are Deer Run and Eagle Meadows off the **Eagle Chair**. The runs in the **Back Bowl** area are really only for more confident beginners, particularly in poor visibility, and serve more as busy runouts than learning areas. Focus on the two greens in the **Larch** area instead.

Intermediate

Though blues appear all over the resort, most intermediate skiers and riders find themselves riding only two or three lifts most of the day. The bulk of the intermediate runs on the **Front Side** are groomed daily, best for cruising and carving. The longest and least busy tend to be Meadowlark and Wapta off the **Eagle Chair** and Gully and Homerun off the **Top of the World Express**. Further down the mountain, the **Men's** and **Ladies' Downhill** runs are labeled black, but are within the capabilities of confident intermediates. Boomerang is the only blue run in the **Back Bowl** area, but worth the trip for a wide open bowl; beware the black runs here which begin easy but get increasingly harder. Down valley is the sheltered **Larch** area, where a collection of varied blue runs and clusters of easy trees can keep most intermediate skiers and riders entertained for an afternoon.

Expert

When the snow is fresh the exposed **Back Bowl** is the best expert area on the mountain. Head up the Summit Platter on the Front Face and traverse or walk along a ridge to reach the best Back Bowl runs. The Whitehorn 2 Gullies, when open, offer the mountain's steepest chutes. If closed, try Ridge Run or Whitehorn 1, or head to Brown Shirt. Further down the Back Bowl, under the Paradise Chair, the **Paradise Bowl** is one of the largest and longest mogul fields in the world. The Paradise Cornice is the hardest access point, requiring navigation over ten feet of snowy overhang – a similar challenge available to those dropping down off the cornices of Eagle Ridge – to the runs ER3 to ER7, collectively known as the Diamond Mine. All steep, these rocky chutes plunge directly into the gladed Pika Trees. More forested glades are available off the **Ptarmigan Quad** and in the **Larch** area below the Larch Express lift. Also off the Larch Express, a traverse to skier's right hits the Rock Garden, a challenging obstacle course of hidden rocks, bumps, and logs. If the snow turns crusty in the Larch and Ptarmigan areas, head to the **Front Side** and carve the consistently pitched Outer Limits or the treelined fall lines of the Grizzly Bowl.

Freestyle

Lake Louise is one of the best freestyle resorts on the continent. Served by two express lifts from the base area, the gargantuan **halfpipe** on Upper Juniper has 17ft walls and a radius of 20ft. Below is the **Showtime** terrain park, packed with rails, tabletops, boxes, hips, and quarterpipe linked together by flowing berms and banked turns. There's a smaller pipe, along with some rollers and banked turns on Sunny Side, specifically for beginners. The ski area also has plenty of natural hits, with many in the Larch area among the trees and in the Rock Garden.

Lift tickets, lessons, and rentals

Adult **day passes** at Lake Louise cost $61, multiday passes are available from two ($113) to fifteen ($820) days, and Tri-Area passes (see p.464) are also valid here.

Group **lessons**, with a maximum of six participants, are available in either 2.5- or 5-hour increments and cost $64 or $83 respectively. Absolute beginners receive a half-day lesson, t-bar lift ticket, and ski rental for $44 per day. Private lessons are pricey, though three people can share a lesson: two hours runs $166. Specialist programs include women's lessons and classes for advanced skiers and snowboarders.

Lake Louise has a decent selection of **rental gear**. Basic skis cost $25 per day, high performance $47. A regular snowboard and boots combination costs $39, rising to $51 for demo equipment. A larger, cheaper selection of rental gear is available in Banff (see p.466).

Accommodation

With a fairly limited stock of beds priced at reasonable rates, **accommodation** can be difficult to come by. Consider basing yourself in Banff, but if you decide to stay at the resort book months in advance. For serviced winter **RV camping** try the *Lake Louise Trailer Site* ($23) on Lake Louise Drive under the rail bridge, and turn left on Fairview Drive.

Château Lake Louise Lake Louise Drive ☎403/522-3511 or 1-800/441-1414, ⓦwww.fairmont.com. Imposing landmark hotel, with commanding views over Lake Louise from its 511 suites. The interior is a bizarre fusion of alpine and neocolonial furnishings. Rates are reduced significantly outside of holidays and weekends with some rooms occasionally going for as little as $100. Good-value ski packages are also offered. The hotel's battery of five-star facilities includes an exercise room, pool, and several bars and restaurants (see opposite). **❼**

Deer Lodge Lake Louise Drive ☎403/522-3747 or 1-800/661-1595, ⓦwww.crmr.com. *Deer Lodge* has undergone several renovations since its first incarnation as a 1920s log teahouse – an aesthetic still partly preserved. Contrasting with the pomp of its neighbor, *Château Lake Louise*, few of the modest rooms here have phones or TV and the ambience is far more rustic. The rooftop hot tub has fantastic views, and there's a sauna too. **❸**

Lake Louise Inn 210 Village Rd ☎403/522-3791 or 1-800/661-9237, ⓦwww.lakelouiseinn.com. Five-building complex assembled into a holiday village north of the village mall, with a reliable supply of inexpensive rooms. Configurations span

from motel rooms to two-bedroom condo units with kitchen and fireplace, sleeping up to eight. Facilities include an indoor pool, whirlpool, steam room, a small ice rink, a laundromat, two restaurants, and a bar. **❹**

Lake Louise International Hostel Village Rd ☎403/522-2200. Excellent 150-bed hostel just north of the village mall, offering dorm beds (members $23; nonmembers $27) and private rooms for $28 (nonmembers $32) per person. Clean, quality facilities include communal kitchen, laundry, Internet access, a mountaineering library, and a handy restaurant (see opposite). Reservations often essential on weekends. **❷**

Post Hotel Village Rd ☎403/522-3989 or 1-800/661-1586, ⓦwww.posthotel.com. Grand log chalet a short walk from the village mall, competing with the *Château* for the top end of the market. The seventeen different room types – hotel rooms to one-bedroom condos and lofts – all have a contemporary feel, and most have a whirlpool and fireplace. Rates vary according to the view. Hotel amenities include an indoor pool, steam room, library, and use of a complimentary ski shuttle. Closed in November. **❻**

Eating and drinking

Unlike accommodations, a good meal isn't hard to come by in Lake Louise, but most **restaurants** are a little tricky to find, tucked away within the confines of various hotels. Many local **bars** are also part of hotels, so that the limited nightlife is unfocused and largely fizzles out after early-evening après. For nightlife it's better to head to **Banff** using a night shuttle bus service between the two towns (see p.472). On-mountain, four day lodges offer a selection of lunchtime options and a couple of decent spots to quaff a beer at the end of the day. The Whiskeyjack Lodge is known for their cheap, satisfying buffets (breakfast $8) at the *Northface* restaurant and hearty pub-grub in the Stizmark Lounge. The *Powderkeg Lounge* in the Lodge of the Ten Peaks is often the more sociable après spot, and pizzas are the pick of its bar menu. The Whitehorn Lodge midway up the Front Side and the Temple Lodge at the base of the Larch area largely focus on providing convenient cafeteria food. The Whitehorn does, however, host the Lake Louise Torchlight Dinner (twice weekly, ☎403/522-3555), popular for the night views and the opportunity to ski by torchlight.

Bill Peyton's Café *Lake Louise International Hostel* ☎403/522-2200. Snug hostel café doling out snacks and several full and reasonably priced meals. Menu items include sandwiches, burgers, mountainous nachos, salads, and pasta – all in the $6–10 range. The full breakfast costs $6.

Explorer's Lounge *Lake Louise Inn*, 210 Village Rd ☎403/522-3791. Family restaurant with adjacent bar offering typical diner fare, including large breakfasts under $10 and salads and burgers (around $9). Better as a nightlife venue with regular live music and a busy après scene on Fridays.

Laggan's Mountain Bakery Samson Mall ☎403/552-2017. Popular café-bakery, perfect for a quick breakfast (from 6am). Also offers basic picnic items – cookies, pies, sandwiches, quiche, and delicious sweet poppyseed bread – if you intend to brown-bag it.

Lake Louise Station Restaurant 200 Sentinel Rd ☎403/522-2600. One of the more affordable upscale options, where the quality of the Canadian cuisine is matched by the elegance of the surroundings, a restored 1909 station building 1km north of the Samson Mall. Best for steaks and grilled meats (from around $14), while a more formal section – housed in restored railway-dining carriages – serves more exotic menu items like caribou ($30) and pheasant ($27).

Post Hotel Dining Room *Post Hotel* ☎403/522-3989. Fine dining on international gourmet dishes amid cozy, low ceilings and crackling wood fire. Choose from a range of rich meat and fish preparations served with phenomenal sauces. For an appetizer try the scampi on asparagus with an orange and lemon sauce. The rack of lamb with grilled portobello mushrooms and rosemary sauce is also delectable, as is the massive duck sausage with gnocchi and mango-lime salsa. Most entrees run around $25. The extensive wine list has a strong French bias. Reservations advised. Attached *Outpost Pub* offers cheaper variations from the same kitchen.

Chateau Lake Louise Lake Louise Drive ☎403/522-3511. Several dining options located in this mammoth hotel, the least formal of which is the *Glacier Saloon*, a Western-themed bar with snacks and steaks – to be followed by billiards, live bands, or a DJ spinning chart music and country favorites. The *Poppy Room* is best for families; good value is the buffet breakfast ($13.50), the extensive Sunday brunch ($20), or the evening pizza and pasta buffet ($18). For fine dining the *Walliser Stube* offers Swiss specialties, with an excellent fondue selection (basic two-person cheese version $32) and raclette along with some local fish and game dishes; entrees run $13–20.

Other activities and attractions

Lake Louise has a phenomenal network of **cross-country** trails. Most start at the *Château Lake Louise* and head around the lake on Moraine Lake Road and in the Skoki Valley behind the ski area. The Alpine Club of Canada (☎403/678-3200, ⊛www.alpineclubofcanada.ca) operates a couple of comfortable rustic cabins for those fit enough to ski at least 11km to their door;

full board costs around $140 per night. The town visitor center (see p.472) provides free maps for all local trails.

The *Château* is also the hub for other winter activities, particularly **ice-skating** and **sleigh rides**, while several tour operations offer pick-ups here for **dogsled** or **snowmobiling** tours. Brewster Lake Louise Sleighrides (⊕403/762-5454 or ⊕403/522-3511 ext 1210, in *Château Lake Louise* ⊛www.brewsteradventures.com) provides hour-long sleigh rides daily from outside the *Château* door; $22 per person, reservations are necessary. The hotel is also the place to hire skates (at Monod Sports in the *Château* ⊕403/522-3837, $10 per day) for **ice skating** on the beautiful, floodlit lake.

Further afield, Kingmik Expeditions (⊕250/344-5298 or 1-877/919-7779) runs **dogsled tours** – from 35-minute romps ($90) to multiday adventures (around $250 per day) – while Wet 'n' Wild adventures in Golden (⊕250/344-6546 or 1-800/668-9119) offers a full day of **snowmobiling** for $180 per person.

Listings

Avalanche hotline ⊕403/762-1460.
Bookstore Woodruff and Blum, Samson Mall ⊕403/522-3842.
Internet *Lake Louise International Hostel* (see p.474).

Medical Mineral Springs Hospital, 301 Lynx St, Banff ⊕403/762-2222.
Pharmacy see Banff Listings p.471.
Post office The Samson Mall ⊕403/522-3870.

Kicking Horse

Once a modest nonprofit, club-run ski area, **Kicking Horse** represents the first major North American resort development in 25 years, having benefited from sizeable financial investment since 2000. Though the ski area's development plans are only partially complete, the results are already impressive. As you ascend the Golden Eagle Express – the resort's gondola and primary lift – you're afforded the perfect view of the area's phenomenal terrain: backcountry more familiar to heliskiers but accessible for the price of a lift ticket.

On the basis of its **terrain** alone, Kicking Horse is destined to be a celebrated resort, both a must for experts and worth consideration by beginners, who will likely find the 10km summit-to-base cruising run alone to merit a trip. Though temperatures here are milder and snowfall less than at the resort's eastern neighbors, Lake Louise and Sunshine Village, the frequent **temperature** inversions combined with Kicking Horse's northeastern aspect preserve the quality of the snow – and warmer temperatures certainly make the skiing more pleasant.

Despite the immense potential in the mountains above, the base area developments are still in their infancy. This makes visitors almost wholly reliant on the nearest town, **Golden**, 14km away. Squeezed in between train yards and plywood mills, much of this railroad town and truck stop is unattractive, but it does have all the basic hotel and restaurant amenities, and its small center, a couple of blocks away from the sprawl, is quaint enough.

Arrival, information, and getting around

If not taking the bus on a day-trip from Banff (see p.463), the only way to get to Kicking Horse is by private vehicle. From Golden, 106km from Banff and

258km from Calgary (around a 2.5-hour drive), the route to the resort is a little tricky. Follow Hwy 95 south from Hwy 1, then take either 7th Street N or 9th St N – streets in Golden are named North or South depending on which side of the river they're on – which both become Dyke Road and lead out of town to the mountain.

You can take a Greyhound **bus** (four daily) to Golden to and from Calgary ($37), Banff ($21), and Vancouver ($83 one way), stopping beside the Esso gas station, 1402 N Trans-Canada Hwy (☎250/344-6172). Options for onward travel are limited to taking a **taxi** or renting a car locally – try National, 915 11th Ave S (☎250/344-9899).

Golden's **visitor center**, 500 10th Ave (Mon–Fri 8.30am–4.30pm; ☎250 /344-7125 or 1-800/622-4653), is in an old railway station building beside the highway on the north side of town.

Mountain info

Phone ☎250/439-5400 or 1-866-754-5425

Snow phone ☎970/728-7425

Website ⊛www.kickinghorseresort.com

Price $54

Operating times Mid-Dec to mid-April 9am–3.30pm (4pm after Jan 25th)

No. of lifts 3, including 1 gondola

Base elevation 1190m

Summit elevation 2450m

Vertical drop 1260m

No. of trails 64

Acreage 2300

Beginner 26%

Intermediate 25%

Expert 49%

Average snowfall 700cm

Snowmaking No

Night skiing No

Nursery facilities No

The mountain

Navigating the mountain is simple, even though the number of possible routes from top to bottom far exceeds the 64 runs marked on the trail map. The Golden Eagle Express gondola zips over breathtaking scenery before depositing skiers and riders at the top of the ski area, leaving them with three choices: skier's left into the wide-open **Crystal Bowl**; skier's right into the steep and narrow **Bowl Over**; or straight ahead along **CPR Ridge**, to plunge down steep chutes into either bowl.

Once beyond the lip of the bowls, divisions between these three zones melt away. The trees thicken and you are thrust into the **mid-mountain** area, which is full of wild forested runs, moguls, and snow-covered rocks. Further down the mountain, once you reach the areas served by the **Pioneer** and **Catamount** lifts, the diversity of options becomes more limited, with most runs relatively gentle and groomed, perfect for the cruising and carving your legs will be begging for after the upper mountain workout. The size and lay-out of the mountain means that the run from summit to base can easily take an hour, and only doing four or five runs in a day is quite common. Should you get particularly tired on any run, consider hopping on **It's A Ten**, a green run that meanders on a gentle grade for the entire length of the mountain.

Beginner

The vast majority of the green runs are found on the groomed lower third of the mountain. Higher up, the only option is the 10km-long **It's-A-Ten** and a couple of smaller variations off it. Though tiring (and narrow in many spots – if you're still working on turns best to keep to the lower part of the mountain), this is not to be missed as it puts beginners in a position to enjoy the incredible views from the summit.

Intermediate

Intermediate skiers on the upper mountain will find a fairly limited choice of lines in both the Crystal Bowl and, to a lesser extent, **Bowl Over**. Getting into the latter can be tricky since the entrance is steep, the best bet being to traverse the short stretch down the black **Flying Dutchman** or making wide turns among the scattered trees of CPR Ridge. Choices mid-mountain are scarce, with **Show Off** below the gondola the only blue run here. Cruising down on the green It's A Ten for a while may be a more convenient alternative – particularly as it connects with each of the magnificently groomed blue runs that lead down to the base area.

Expert

This mountain was made for experts. Powder stashes are waiting for those prepared to traverse down CPR Ridge into **Bowl Over** and along the ridge below Blue Heaven in the **Crystal Bowl**. The mountain's most challenging terrain is predominantly off the CPR Ridge, where sixteen chutes lie in wait for those with enough courage to tackle them. Most are precarious, with several particularly narrow sections and occasional exposed rocks. All would be rated double black diamond elsewhere, though Kicking Horse uses only the single black diamond designation for all expert terrain. On mid-mountain, duck into any clump of trees where a huge number of lines in fresh snow lie hidden. Below here, it's tempting to cruise the bottom part of the mountain back to the gondola, but try to get out to the area around the Pioneer Chair, where some excellent **mogul runs** await.

Freestyle

Though there's **no pipe or park** at Kicking Horse, freestylers should find no shortage of natural options scattered across the mountain. You can find some of the biggest challenges on obstacles off CPR Ridge, but be sure to scope these out carefully first. For safer and more accessible hits explore Blaster and, on the opposite side of the ski area, the jumps on Bugablue.

Lift tickets, lessons, and rentals

Adult **tickets** run $54; juniors and seniors pay $44. Passes are also available in various multiday packages with only minimal savings; a five-day pass costs $255.

Group **lessons** for beginners cost $37 an hour. Strong intermediates have the choice of three different group clinics focusing on groomed terrain, powder, or freeriding. Each costs $53 and runs for two and a half hours. The resort's first-timer package is priced at $94 and includes rentals and a limited lift pass – any of the group lessons can also be taken as a package giving discounts on passes and equipment rental. Private lessons are offered for a minimum of two and a half hours and cost $177, with each additional person another $40.

Rentals at the resort are offered at basic and high-performance levels. A basic ski or snowboard package costs $30, and $40 for the high-performance gear.

Sports stores in town, like Selkirk Sports, 504 9 Ave N (☎250/344-2966), also rent gear, though expect to find a broader selection rather than lower costs.

Accommodation

Most local **accommodation** flanks the TransCanada Highway through Golden. There are more beds in the center of Golden, largely in modest B&Bs, and further afield are several lodges and holiday homes available for rent. At the mountain itself, accommodation is limited to one block of self-catering condos, although for the extravagant, the luxurious Eagle's Eye suite at the summit of the mountain beckons with its many amenities and spectacular views. Packages ($1500 per night for two) here include lift tickets with private instructor and guide, a 24-hour concierge, dinner in the restaurant below and exclusive use of the VIP gondola cabin, whose leather seats, CD player, and wine bucket lend considerable style to the twelve-minute journey. The resort also offers many far more modest ski packages through its central reservations system (call main resort number or contact via their website), with prices starting at $143 per person for two days skiing and accommodation in Golden.

Alpenrose Cabins 448 Althoff Rd ☎250/344-5549, ⊛www.alpenrosecabins.com. Scandinavian-style cabins, with kitchens and fireplaces, sleeping up to six. Located 1km west of Golden off the TransCanada Highway. ❸

Alpine Meadows Lodge 717 Elk Rd ☎250/344-5863, ⊛www.alpinemeadowslodge.com. Large chalet tucked away in a forest high above Golden, offering ten simple rooms and one four-bedroom chalet. The communal lounge is particularly relaxing thanks to the stone fireplace at its center. All rooms come with en-suite Jacuzzi tubs and there's an outdoor hot tub too. A filling breakfast is included. ❸

Country Comfort B&B 1001 10th Ave S ☎250/344-6200. Laura Ashley-style central B&B with seven floral rooms and a fireplace in the guest lounge. Hearty breakfast included. ❷

Golden Rim Motor Inn 1416 Golden View Rd ☎250/344-2216. Best of the pack among a number of bland motels, located less than a half kilometer east of Golden with sweeping views of Columbia Valley. Facilities include an indoor pool with water slides, a sauna, and hot tub. Two-night ski packages are offered from $161 per person. ❸

Kapristo Lodge 1297 Campbell Rd ☎250/344-6048, ⊛www.kapristolodge.com. Luxurious lodge overlooking the Columbia Valley 14km south of Golden. Room decor ranges from an antique aesthetic to a rustic Rocky Mountain feel – but all are very comfortable. A highlight is the communal sun room, and guests also share an outdoor hot tub and sauna. Full breakfasts included in rates. ❻

Ponderosa Motor Inn 1206 TransCanada Hwy ☎250/344-2205, ⊛www.ponderosamotorinn.bc.ca. Standard, clean, good-value motel with mountain views, some kitchenettes, and a hot tub. ❷

A Quiet Corner 607 S 14th St, ⊛www.aquietcorner.com. Central bed and breakfast in leafy residential area, with two rooms and a two-bedroom suite with sitting room sleeping four. Continental and full cooked breakfasts available. ❷

Sisters and Beans Guesthouse 1122 10th Ave ☎250/344-2443. Elegant rooms behind a restaurant (see p.480) in the center of Golden. All are en-suite and share a sauna. Extensive continental breakfast included. ❷

Whispering Pines Kicking Horse Resort ☎250/344-7188 or 1-866/355-7755, ⊛www.canadianmountainproperty.com. Swank new slopeside town homes in four designs, sleeping up to six. Units come with full kitchens, laundry facilities, gas fireplaces, and hot tubs. A three-night minimum stay is required: six people sharing pay around $400 each for a four-night stay and lift passes for three days. ❻

Eating and drinking

Eating options range from diners along the highway to more creative options in the center of Golden. On-mountain the choice is between luxurious dining in the *Eagle's Eye Restaurant* at the top of the gondola or visiting the reasonable cafeteria at its base. Nightlife is limited to **drinking** at a couple of the town's bars.

Cedar House Café and Restaurant 735 Hefti Rd ⊕250/344-4679. One of best restaurants in an area a five-minute drive south of Golden, with an open kitchen that conjures up dishes based around local fish, meat, and fowl, and offers several good vegetarian options too. The beef tenderloin with blue cheese, caramelized onions, and red wine reduction ($28) is excellent, while the baked pear, red onion, and cambozola cheese strudel in a warm cranberry sauce ($15) is the pick of the veggie dishes.

Country Garden Restaurant 1002 TransCanada Hwy ⊕250/344-5971. While the name might be a bit of a stretch for this workaday dive, you can fill up cheaply on the usual diner fare of its all-day buffets; the dinner buffet costs $17.

Dogtooth Café 1007 11th S Ave ⊕250/344-3660. Local characters and local art are the backdrop for gorging on inexpensive breakfast burritos and sandwiches.

Eagle's Eye Restaurant Kicking Horse Resort. Imposing timber-and-stone structure where unbeatable high-alpine views are complimented by a thoughtfully constructed Pacific Northwest menu. Items like local salmon, caribou, bison, and venison are particularly delectable and there's a choice of delicious veggie options too. Prices are less extraordinary than the views, with many of the lunch menu items around $11, although at dinner (available Fri & Sat) you can expect to pay around $50 a head for three courses.

Kicking Horse Grill 1105 9th St ⊕250/344-2330. Handsome log cabin furnished with Christmas light illuminations. A curiously eclectic menu supposedly brings together the food of fifteen different countries in a "taste the world" theme, with cuisine ranging from Thai to Scandinavian. But it's all much less adventurous than it sounds, with most dishes familiar to all but the most parochial: salmon pasta; Asian stir-frys; Indonesian chicken; or the house (Greek) salad – with pitas, feta, and olives – and, of course, steaks. Entrees range from around $15–20.

Mad Trapper 1203 S 9th St ⊕250/344-6661. Friendly, noisy bar that's not only the town's main drinking hole but also has some of its best bar food, as well as great piles of free peanuts. Look out for wing specials and if you're really hungry try the "awesome" burger ($10) with its steak-sized burger patties.

Sisters and Beans 1122 10th Ave ⊕250/344-2443. Trendy, faintly bohemian dining choice with local art decorating the wall. A good option for vegetarians, with several soups, curries, and pastas, though you can also find steaks and pork loin here. Fondues occasionally appear on the menu and are excellent, thanks to the restaurant's Swiss owners.

Other activities

Cross-country skiing is based around the Dawn Mountain Ski Trails (pass $15 per day; rentals available at the resort) adjacent to Kicking Horse. Here you'll find 14km of groomed track set trails, a 1.5km stretch for skating, and a warming hut with wood-burning stove. A further 5km loop of trails is available on Golden's golf course. Other outdoor activities include snowmobiling, ice-climbing, dogsledding, and ski touring, all offered by the resort's own Golden Guides (⊕250/439-5400).

Listings

Bookstore Food for Thought Books, 407 9th Ave N ⊕250/344-5600.
Internet *Jenny's Java Express*, 506 9th Ave N ⊕250/344-5057.
Medical Golden and District Hospital, 835 9th Ave S ⊕250/344-5271.

Pharmacy Gourlay's Golden Pharmacy, 826 9th Ave S ⊕250/344-8600.
Post office 525 N 9th Ave ⊕1-800/267-1177.

Heliskiing in the Rockies

The Canadian Rockies offer some of the finest backcountry skiing and boarding anywhere. Here, a pristine mountain landscape is filled with open bowls and extensive tree runs covered in legendary, untracked powder. A glut of **heliski operators** offer multiday trips, but at prices close to a $1000 per day, the experience doesn't come cheap. A more affordable option is **cat skiing** – using snow cats to transport you uphill. Though less glamorous they provide a similar experience at around a third of the price. The heli- and cat-skiing **season** runs from December through April; spaces are limited and booking well in advance is essential.

With commercial helicopters and heliskiing forbidden within the National Parks, operators are concentrated in **three major areas**: the southern Rockies around Golden (see Kicking Horse p.476) and Panorama (see p.492); at the northern end of the range west of Jasper National Park; and further into British Columbia's interior near Revelstoke.

Heliski operators

The largest operator is **CMH Heli-Skiing** (☎403/762-7100 or 1-800/661-0252 ⓦwww.cmhski.com), headquartered in Banff and operating from lodges scattered throughout the region. The variety of locations offered is second to none and the operator will pick up its guests from Calgary or accommodations in the Lake Louise and Banff area. Alternatives in the southern Rockies, particularly appealing if you're based in Banff and only looking for a day-trip, include **Purcell Helicopter Skiing** (☎250/344-5410, ⓦwww.purcellhelicopterskiing.com) in Golden. They access 2000 square kilometers of terrain and offer some of the least expensive packages around – from $444 per day. Further south, operating out of Panorama, **RK Heli-Ski** (☎403/762-3771 or 1-800/661-6060, ⓦwww.rkheliski.com) heads mostly to intermediate terrain; day-trips start at $599 per day, including rental equipment. Experienced skiers will find the terrain easy and are likely to find the operator's large groups – often five groups of eleven – unwieldy. For a week-long package try **Great Canadian Heli-skiing** (☎250/344-2326, ⓦwww.greatcanadianheliski.com), which has an exclusive licence to 2000 square kilometers of pristine terrain adjacent to Glacier National Park.

The most notable operator in the northern Rockies is **Mike Wiegele Helicopter Skiing** (☎250/673-8381 or 1-800/661-9170, ⓦwww.wiegele.com), a particularly upscale outfit based midway between Kamloops and Jasper. With 3000 square kilometers of terrain in the idyllic Monashee and Cariboo mountains, the skiing is magnificent; seats are booked up far in advance.

Revelstoke, between the Selkirk and Monashee mountains in British Columbia, is home to **Selkirk Tangiers Heliskiing** (☎250/344-5016 or 1-800/663-7080, ⓦwww.selkirk-tangiers.com) and **Cat Powder Skiing** (☎250/837-5151 or 1-800/991-4455 ⓦwww.catpowder.com). Both run trips providing up to 5000m of vertical riding per day. There are several other snowcat operations strung out south of town and a few more in the Selkirk Mountains including **Great Northern Snowcat Skiing** (☎1-800/889-0765, ⓦwww.greatnorthernsnowcat.com) and **Selkirk Wilderness Skiing** (☎604/366-4424 or 1-800/799-3499, ⓦwww.selkirkwilderness.com).

Snowcat operators

Of the region's snowcat operations, **Island Lake Lodge** (☎604/423-3700 or 1-888/422-8754, ⓦwww.islandlakelodge.com) near Fernie (see p.482) features astounding freeride terrain anywhere with an abundance of steep chutes and natural halfpipes, a favorite with boarders. Three-day packages here start at $1200.

Fernie

Given its bountiful mountain bowls and ridges among the prickly mountains of the Lizard Range, 28ft of annual powder, and recent renovations effectively doubling the resort's size, **Fernie** is rapidly outgrowing its once obscure status. Skiers from Calgary regularly make the three-hour drive to experience the wide easy cruisers, the steep glades and drops into daredevil chutes, and the open bowls filled with untracked powder, accessed via creaky lifts with nominal lines.

The resort has a modest base village, while the unpretentious mining and logging **town** of Fernie, 5km from the ski area, is slowly building into a tourist destination, adding a number of new restaurants and hotels to complement those at the resort. It's far from a major resort town, but if the number of resident snowboard bums here is anything to go by, it may just be the next Whistler.

Arrival, information, and getting around

Cranbrook, the nearest regional **airport**, is over an hour drive from Fernie, and Calgary Airport is over three hours away. Transfers between both airports are provided twice daily by Rocky Mountain Sky Shuttle (round-trip to Calgary $90; round-trip to Cranbrook $54, ☎403/762-5200 or 1-888/762-8754, ⊛www.rockymountainskyshuttle.com) and Dicken Bus Lines Ltd (☎250/423-9244 or ☎1-800/575-0405, ⊛www.thebigredbus.com). Fernie is also served by Greyhound **buses** (☎250/423-6871 or 1-800/661-8747, ⊛www.greyhound.com) plying the route between Calgary ($50 one way) and Vancouver ($90 one way) twice daily; in absence of a bus depot, tickets can be booked at the front desk of *Park Place Lodge*. The town's **visitor center** is located at the Fernie Chamber of Commerce, 102 Commerce Rd (☎250/423-6868; ⊛www.ferniechamber.com), just off the highway on the northeastern fringe of town.

Shuttle buses run by Kootenay Taxi (☎1-800/667-8770 or 250/423-4408, ⊛www.elkvalley.net/koottaxi.net) operate a half-hourly service between town and resort for $3 one way; a book of ten rides can be bought for $25. Schedules are posted at local accommodation, the guest services counter, and at the company's website.

The mountain

Navigating Fernie's five high alpine bowls is easy, but the many glades, gullies, chutes, and couloirs could literally take weeks to explore; traversing the numerous ridges and bowls requires an inquisitive attitude and considerable effort. A free **tour** with the Mountain Hosts (daily at 9.30am and 1pm) will help intermediates and below find the best runs. Experts will have to shell out $75 for a Mountain Guide if they want a tour of the more advanced terrain. Though pricey, this is the best way for riders seeking vertiginous chutes and high alpine glades to find untouched powder. Another way to find fresh powder is to join the resort's First Tracks program – two hours of guided early-morning (start at 8am) riding priced at $60 on its own or $107 when included in a day with a Mountain Guide.

Beginner

Most beginning runs are only a single chair ride from the **base area**. Higher up the mountain, however, options are far more limited. A couple of greens with excellent views stretch out from the **Great Bear Quad**, but are often busy with skiers and riders crossing from other runs. The **Timber Bowl Express Chair** has lengthy crusiers; to access all of them you'll need to brave some much harder terrain near the summit. The best options for confident novices are the relatively gentle Falling Star skirting around the limits of the ski area and Currie Powder, steeper but with comfortably wide traverses.

Intermediate

With its groomed, steep slopes and spacious bowls, Fernie is a paradise for cruisers and carvers. Concentrate on the **Timber Bowl** for some of the best snow on the mountain and a light sprinkling of trees between runs. For broad, even expanses try the **Lizard Bowl**. Elsewhere intermediates should proceed with caution, as many of the blues, particularly groomers, can be steep and challenging; most black runs are well out of reach.

Expert

Head in any direction to find impressive expert terrain. For steep **tree runs** and powder, go along the ridge below the **White Pass Quad** to **Anaconda Glades** and the rougher **Bootleg Glades**. Both empty onto the dizzyingly fast **Diamond Back** that merges with a green run at its base. The best bump runs are off the **Boomerang** lift. Fernie is best known for its **open bowls**; many of the lines within are easy enough for most intermediates and get tracked up fairly soon. If you're prepared to traverse a little you can find harder and much fresher lines from the Snake and North Ridge lines off the **Cedar Bowl.**

Freestyle

Built with consultation from local riders, the **terrain park** on Upper Falling Star, accessed from the Timber chair, is spread over two acres. Features range from easy rails to a series of gigantic tabletops. **Lower Deer**, formerly the site of the terrain park, still has three tabletops. Running parallel to Lower Deer, off the Bambi run, is the resort's odd **halfpipe** – 300ft long, 25ft-wide, and 12ft walls – where a shallow beginner pipe leads into an icy and awkward advanced pipe.

Lift tickets, lessons, and rentals

Day passes at Fernie's run $56, dropping to $45 for an afternoon pass valid from noon. Multiday passes are available, but savings are minimal; the maximum ten-day pass offers only a $30 discount.

The Winter Sports Schools group **lessons** are reasonably priced at $27 for a half-day of tuition and $43 for a full day. Private lessons are also relatively inexpensive at $58 per hour; additional students pay $22 per hour. The school's main forte is specialist clinics, with two-hour sessions ($38) focusing specifically on bumps, freeriding, powder skiing, or style and technique. Telemarking lessons are also available. Absolute beginners can purchase packages including a basic lift pass, equipment, and group lesson ($42).

A wide range of **rental gear** is available at $24–45 per day, with snowboard and boots $37–45. Minimal savings are offered in town at Gear Up, 100 Riverside Way (☎250/423-4556) – also a good source of telemark, avalanche gear, and backcountry tips. Snowboard specialists Board Stiff, 542 2nd Ave (☎250/423-3473), and Fernie Sport, 1191 7th Ave (☎250/423-3611), have a decent range of demo equipment and an efficient overnight repair service.

⑥ Accommodation

It's fairly easy to find an inexpensive bed, with several options around the base of the ski area and the town providing a slightly cheaper base better situated for most nightlife options. Purchase ski packages through the resort's reservations desk (☎403-209-3321 or 1-877/333-2339, ⓦwww.skifernie.com) or the local accommodation agency (☎1-800/622-5007, ⓦwww.ferniecentral reservations.com); the least expensive three-day packages start at around $300 for two people. Those with RVs can reserve spaces at the resort with daily ($15 per night or $20 with hookup), weekly, and monthly rates available.

Cornerstone Lodge 5339 Ski Hill Rd ☎250/423-4655 or 1-800/258-7669, ⓦwww.skifernie.com. Luxurious slopeside suites with spacious one- or two-bedroom units equipped with phone fax, Internet, kitchens, gas fireplaces, and laundry machines. There's also access to a fitness room, pool, and hot tub and underground parking. ⑥

Fernie Mountain Lodge 1622 7th Ave ☎250/423-5500 or 1-800/528-1234, ⓦwww .bestwesternfernie.com. Best Western property at the eastern end of town with varying room layouts – though all share a similar vague rustic charm, with items like wooden snowshoes nailed to their walls. Some have jacuzzi tubs and high-speed Internet access. ⑤

The Griz Inn Sport Hotel 5369 Ski Hill Rd ☎250/423-9221 or 1-800/661-0118, ⓦwww.grizinn.com. Condo block at the base of Elk lift with huge variation among the privately owned units – some sleeping up to eight – but all with kitchens and sharing hot tubs, sauna, and indoor pool. ④

Lizard Creek Lodge Fernie Alpine Resort ☎250/423-2057 or 1-877/228-1948, ⓦwww.lizardcreek .com. The resort's premier lodgings where fairly plain condo-style rooms – some with lofts – are equipped with TV and VCRs, kitchens, and fireplaces. The lodge has a spa with outdoor pool and hot tub and a vast communal room with open fire and overstuffed armchairs. Shuttles to and from Fernie are provided. ⑥

Northern Hotel 561 2nd Ave ☎250/423-4877. Basic doubles and twin rooms with minimal fur-

nishings, shared bathrooms, and an institutional feel. Located above a gritty downtown bar. ❶

Park Place Lodge 742 Highway 3 ☎250/423-6871 or 1-888/381-7275, ⓦwww.park-placelodge.bc.ca. Beige, bland, and modern hotel with large, clean, and comfortable rooms all gathered around an atrium, the location of the pool. ④

Raging Elk Hostel 892 6th Ave ☎250/423-6811, ⓦwww.ragingelk.com. Cheerful, slightly ragged hostel with kitchen and laundry facilities. Free pancake breakfasts are included. $16 dorm beds; $45 private double rooms, or $55 ski packages with lift ticket are the best value in town.

Riverside Mountain Lodge 100 Riverside Way ☎250/423-5000 or 1-877/423-5600, ⓦwww.riversidemountainlodge.com. Condo complex located beside Hwy 3 and midway between Fernie and the ski hill offering more than a dozen accommodation styles – sleeping from two to sixteen. All units share a large indoor pool with waterslide, hot tubs, and a fitness center. The lodge has its own restaurant and a pub. ❷

Royal Hotel 501 1st Ave ☎250/423-7750 ⓦwww .fernieroyalhotel.com. Authentic Victorian with highly polished bedsteads. There's a suite that sleeps six and is fantastic value at $170 per night. ❸

Snow Valley Motel 1041 7th Ave ☎250/423-4421, ⓦwww.fernieaccommodations.com. Simple motel with clean rooms and friendly staff on the town's main strip. Some rooms have kitchenettes and there's access to a hot tub. Ski packages available; shuttle. ❷

Wolf's Den Mountain Lodge 5339 Ski Hill Road ☎250/423-4655 or 1-800/258-7669, ⓦwww .skifernie.com. Comfortable, nondescript slopeside motel. Facilities include hot tubs, game room, and laundromat. There's also a pleasant, fairly small house attached to the lodge sleeping up to eight with a front door that opens onto the slopes. ❷

Eating, drinking, and entertainment

Though the selection of **restaurants** and **bars** in Fernie is limited by the town's modest size, there's a fair bit of variety available. On-mountain the only choice outside the base area is a fast-food outlet at the top of the Elk chair. The resort is at its liveliest during the annual mid-March **Griz-days festival** in celebration of Griz, a mythical man said to have grown up in the grizzly bear dens of local mountains and who fires his musket at the clouds to produce wonderful powdery snowfalls. Fernie's only cinema, the **Vogue Theatre**, 321 2nd Ave (☎250/423-7111), shows new releases and occasional indie flicks.

The Curry Bowl 931 7th Ave ☎250/423-2695. Simple and extremely popular little pan-Asian restaurant serving rice bowls, noodles, curries, and stir-frys (most around $10). Recommended starters include the *tom kah gai*, a Thai hot and sour soup ($5.25), and the sesame asparagus salad ($5.25). Arrive early for a seat as reservations aren't accepted.

Edge of the World & El Guapo Mexican Diner 902 6th Ave ☎250/423-0929, ⓦwww.edgeworld .com. Small diner and café adjoining a skate shop, catering mostly to the hostel crowd from across the road. Pick up filling nachos, tacos, veggie burgers, and burritos from around $8. Smoothies, coffee, and Internet are also available.

Eldorado 701 2 Ave ☎250/423-0009. The late-night spot in Fernie is this sports bar where DJs and regular live music fill the big floor. Free pool on Sundays.

Kelsey's Fernie Alpine Resort ☎250/423-4655. Sociable bar on the ground floor of the *Cornerstone Lodge*, dishing up the usual popular après feasts and a decent range of beers.

Lizard Creek Lodge Fernie Alpine Resort ☎250 /423-2057 or 1-877/228-1948. Small portions of savory gourmet food are served at one of Fernie's few upscale restaurants. Particularly tempting on table d'hote nights, where the set three-course menu costs $30 per person, and on Sundays where a fantastic brunch spread, including plenty of fresh seafood and tasty cakes, costs $25.

Mug Shots Bistro 592 3rd Ave ☎250/423-8018. Small counter-service café with a big selection of deli sandwiches, bagels – including a curry, lettuce, and cheddar version ($4.50) – pizza by the slice, and good-value breakfasts.

Powderhorn Fernie Alpine Resort ☎250/423-4656. Along with *Kelsey's* (see above), this cavernous slopeside bar in the *Griz Inn* is the best bet for après-ski activity, with a large stone fireplace and good pub fare.

The Pub Bar and Grill 742 Hwy-3 ☎250/423-6871 or 1-888/381-7275. Dull-looking bar which despite its isolated location away from both the resort and downtown often crowded with skiers and riders in the early evening. Try their wings and potato skins; the rest of the menu is much less memorable.

Royal Hotel 501 1st Ave ☎250/423-7743, ⓦwww.fernieroyalhotel.com. Authentic and highly polished Victorian saloon with adjoining upscale steakhouse. Good for sandwiches, burgers, and, of course, steaks; food served until midnight and the bar – haunt of a number of local characters – is open until 2am.

The Wood 701 2nd Ave ☎250/423-7749. Bistro filled with dark wood and halogen fittings serves good tapas. The imaginative mix includes tenderloin tips, mussels, fried shellfish, samosas, and thin rice rolls all around $7. For an entrée try the Alberta beef strip, the sea bass, or the rich portobello mushroom salad. Open daily from noon to 1am.

Other activities and attractions

Book **sleigh rides**, **dogsled** tours, or **snowmobiling** trips through the resort's guest services (☎250/423-4655). Pick up a complimentary map at guest services, detailing the 15km of cross-country trails maintained by the resort for free. For cross-country ski rentals ($12), snowshoes, and telemark equipment head to the slopeside Mountain Edge (☎250/423-4655) shop, in the

Cornerstone Lodge. They also organize tours (2hrs $27). In town the **Aquatics Center** (℡250/423-4466, ℗www.playinfernie.com) contains a pool, jacuzzi tub, waterslide, and steam room; perfect to wind down after a day on the slopes. Or head to Fernie Memorial Arena (℡250/423-2254) for **public skating**. Another place to skate, though on boards or blades, is at the Edge of the World 902 6th Ave (℡250/423-9292, ℗www.edgeworld.com).

Listings

Avalanche hotline ℡1-800/667-1105.
Internet Edge of the World, 902 6th Ave ℡250/423-9292, ℗www.edgeworld.com: $6 per hour; Mug Shots Bistro, 592 3rd Ave ℡250/423-8018: $5 per hour.

Medical Fernie District Hospital, 1501 5th Ave ℡250/423-4453.
Pharmacy Canada Drug Mart, 482 2nd Ave ℡250/423-6702.
Post office 491 3rd Ave ℡250/423-7555.

Red Mountain

Untamed and largely untrammeled, **Red Mountain** lies just north of the US border in a remote location midway between Vancouver and Calgary. Only a small number of skiers make it here, leaving the slopes peaceful and untracked powder plentiful. These conditions and the tucked-away setting have helped the resort develop something of a cult status, especially among experts; two-thirds of the mountain is steep, forested backcountry, a training ground for several Canadian Olympians. As befitting a favorite with those in the know, there's an unfettered feel to it all, with only basic lift services and loosely marked trails on the slopes.

Rossland, the nearest town 5km away, is a small affable place, an old mining town where Victorian houses still dominate. On first impressions, it can seem a little dowdy and limited, but within the town's gritty history lies an underlying charm unimpeded by the local ski industry. Further afield, 11km east from Rossland, the larger town of Trail is a scrappy and dreary smelter town, useful only for stocking up on supplies.

Mountain info

Phone ℡250/362-7384 or 1-800/663-0105
Snow phone ℡250/362-5500 or 509/459-6000
Website ℗www.ski-red.com
Price $48
Operating times Early Dec to early April Mon–Fri 9am–3pm; Sat & Sun 8.30am–3.30pm
No. of lifts 5, including 1 surface tow
Base elevation 1296m
Summit elevation 2266m
Vertical drop 970m
Longest run 8km
No. of trails 83
Acreage 1200
Beginner 10%
Intermediate 45%
Expert 45%
Average snowfall 760cm
Snowmaking No
Night skiing No
Nursery facilities Yes, from 18 months ℡250/362-7114.

Arrival, information, and getting around

The closest hub for air traffic is **Castlegar Municipal Airport**, thirty kilometers north of Red Mountain, and served by Air BC and Canadian Regional Airlines from Vancouver and Calgary. Shuttle buses make the trip to Red Mountain for $53 one way, $80 round-trip. The nearest international airport is in Spokane, 125 miles southwest, about a 2.5-hour drive to Red Mountain. From Spokane take Hwy 395 to Kettle Falls, Hwy-25 to the US border then Hwy-22 to Rossland. **Greyhound buses** stop at the Depot, 1355 Bay St (☎250/368-8400) in Trail, from where the best option is to take a taxi to Rossland; call ☎250/365-7222. **Shuttle buses** connect Rossland with Red Mountain, but the service is limited to trips heading out in the mornings and back after the lifts close around 3pm.

For **visitor information** contact Rossland Chamber of Commerce, 4-2185 Columbia Ave (☎250/362-5666 or 1-877/969-7669).

The mountain

The resort spreads over two distinct mountains: **Red Mountain** and **Granite Mountain**. The former was the original focus of the resort and remains popular for its incredible views over Rossland and its groomed runs, ideal for warm-ups. But Granite has supplanted it as the mainstay of the ski area, its drier, lighter snow and more extensive terrain drawing the majority of visitors.

The conical shape of Granite Mountain allows runs to spill off from almost every compass point. The dated **Motherlode** chair heads close to the summit, accessing the entire mountain. It's possible to dip off in virtually any direction without getting lost, since a cat track sweeps around the base, depositing riders back to the bottom of Motherlode. Given the huge array of possibilities on the mountain, it's worth taking a **tour** with a "snowhost." Tours are free, cater to all levels, and leave the base area at 9am and 1pm daily.

Beginner

With only around a tenth of the resort graded green there are few areas for learning. The small beginner area adjacent to the base lodge is excellent, wide, and with a trickle of traffic. More experienced beginners can ski a green run off every lift; the largest is **Ridge Road**, a narrow and often busy run that follows the course of a mountain road, good for confidence building. Beginning intermediates should try the easy blues adjacent to the green runs in the **Paradise Bowl** on Granite Mountain.

Intermediate

Most of the blue runs are clustered together in two areas: on Red Mountain and in the Paradise Area of Granite Mountain. Red Mountain is particularly good for carving – the **Face of Red** one of the best – but Paradise is the bigger of the two areas. It has the best groomers and gladed skiing among widely spaced trees. Maggie's Farm, Main Run, and Schuss are the hardest blues on the mountain; they could very well be graded expert at other resorts.

Expert

All the designated expert terrain at Red Mountain merits its rating; most black diamonds are steep, the double blacks are dangerous, and those with stars beside them on the trail map are unpatrolled and positively hazardous, with their maze of chutes, glades, and cliff bands. Some of the most challenging and enjoyable expert runs fan out from **Buffalo Ridge** (not marked on the map but skier's left off the Motherlode chair); the three Slides runs are all extremely steep, while Cambodia features a series of unavoidable 10–15ft drops. For bumps, try Gambler Towers under the Paradise chair or Centre Star beneath the Motherlode chair. Both are accessed by Links Run, one of the mountain's steepest. Untracked powder is usually available in Papoose Bowl, Beer Belly, or The Orchards.

Freestyle

A freeriders' rather than freestylers' venue, Red Mountain maintains only a modest **quarterpipe**. Try the natural hits on runs like **Cambodia**.

Lift tickets, lessons, and rentals

Lift tickets at Red Mountain cost $48 and multiday passes provide only small overall savings: three days runs $138; five days costs $220.

The mountain's Ski and Snowboard School (℡250/362-7384 ext 235) offers group **lessons** for $30 for two hours; but its $45 two-day starter package – which includes a limited lift pass, a lesson, and rentals – offers newbies the best value. Other programs offered by the ski school include weeklong ski and snowboard camps, weekend camps, powder lessons, and telemark coaching, as well as women's day, held every Sunday and Wednesday and including a two-hour lesson, discounted lift tickets, and an après party. Private lessons start at $50 per hour. Note that taking any lesson package qualifies you for a discount on rentals and lift passes.

LeRoi's Sport Shop is the slopeside source for skis and snowboards and high-performance **demo equipment**. A pair of hi-tech skis cost $32 for the day. Out in Rossland, Powder Hound, 2040 Columbia Ave (℡250/362-5311), offers demo ski rentals ($35 per day) on all models they sell and has a few snowboards for rent, while Boomtown Emporium, 2196 Columbia Ave (℡250/505-5055), is good for secondhand gear.

Accommodation

Local beds are split between smaller **chalets** and **B&Bs** within walking distance of the ski area and similar accommodations in Rossland, including a hostel, a hotel, a couple of motels, and several vacation homes. The ski area's Central Reservations (℡250/362-5666 or 1-877/969-7669) can help with bookings, or you can reserve online at the town's website (ⓦwww.rossland.com).

Angela's Bed and Breakfast 1520 Spokane St ℡250/362-7790, ⓦwww.visitred.com. Mix of accommodations in two buildings a short walk from the center of town. Options range from simple single rooms to entire apartments – all given the personal touch by the gloriously eccentric and hospitable landlady. Facilities include a hot tub, communal kitchen, laundry, and dataports. ❶

Black Bear Bed and Breakfast 1345 Spokane St ℡250/362-3398 or 1-877/362-3398, ⓦwww.blackbearbnb.com. Among the oldest properties in town, nineteenth-century country house offers rooms little changed from that era, all sharing bathrooms and an outdoor hot tub. ❸
Mountain Shadow Hostel 2125 Columbia Ave ℡250/362-7160 or 1-888/393-7160. Slightly

grungy hostel downtown. Dorms hold six beds ($17 each) and there are a couple of private rooms ($50). Kitchen facilities available.

Ram's Head Inn Red Mountain Rd ☎250/362-9577 or 1-877/267-4323, ⊛www.ramshead.bc.ca. Bed and breakfast in a large comfortable home walking distance from the lifts. The focal point for the dozen rooms is the sociable lounge area with an imposing stone fireplace and crackling fire. Facilities include an outdoor hot tub, a sauna, and game room. ❸

Red Mountain Village Red Mountain Rd ☎250/362-9000 or 1-877/362-7668, ⊛www .redmountainvillage.com. Collection of accommo-dations at the entrance to the Red Mountain Base Area, within easy walking distance of the lifts. Lodging options span from motel units through condos of various sizes, to one-, two-, and three-bedroom cabins. All are immaculately clean and well maintained with decorations kept to a mini-

mum. The friendly owners also run a rental shop specializing in cross-country gear. ❷

Red Shutter Inn Red Mountain Rd ☎250/362-5131, ⊛www.redshutter.ca. No-frills alpine-style chalet close to the lifts with sauna, hot tub, and a sociable lounge. ❷

Thriftlodge 1199 Nancy Green Hwy ☎250/362-7364 or 1-800/525-9055, ⊛www.the.travelodge .com/rossland13155. Basic chain motel on southern side of town, but with fridges and movie channels in every room, some kitchenettes, and a hot tub. Continental breakfast and ski shuttle included. ❶

Uplander Hotel 1919 Columbia Ave ☎250/362-7375 or 1-800/667-8741, ⊛www.uplanderhotel .com. Largest hotel in town with almost seventy rooms, some with kitchenettes. All sport a dingy 1970s décor. Amenities include a sauna, hot tub and fitness center, and free shuttle to the Red Mountain, and its bars are a major focal point in town. ❸

Eating, drinking, and entertainment

Rossland has an extensive dining scene for such a small town and almost all options are an easy walk from one another in the town center. **On-mountain** food is decent and reasonably priced. Try the Mid-Mountain Lodge in Paradise Basin for excellent chocolate chip cookies, but otherwise *Rafter's Lounge* is best, serving Mexican cuisine and pizza slices. Nightlife is far more modest, with one or two bars dominating. The only other entertainment is the Royal Theatre in Trail, which screens recent releases.

Amelia's Restaurant Uplander Hotel ☎250/362-7375. Dingy restaurant tucked away within a large hotel, but the food's good value, particularly the hearty, filling breakfasts.

Flying Steamshovel 2003 Second Ave ☎250/362-7323. Decent downtown bar with few preten-sions; pool and bar food such as nachos, wings, burgers, sandwiches, and pastas all around $8.

Gold Rush Books 2063 Washington St ☎250/362-5333. Laid-back bookshop and café, serving bagels, muffins, wraps, and offering Internet access ($2 for 15 mins).

Idgie's 1999 2nd Ave ☎250/363-0078. Small, tasteful restaurant, simply decorated with dim halo-gen spots illuminating warm southwestern earth-tones. Start with the wonderful homemade foccacia. Entrees include succulent baked fish in citrus sauces – salmon with lemon and dill, baked halibut in lemon caper sauce – and the more robust baked, breaded chicken with artichokes, pesto, and spinach in marinara sauce, all costing around $15 each. The menu also features lamb, seafood, and steaks, with a good range of wines to wash them down. Leave space for the mango and berry cheesecake.

Louis Blue Room Uplander Hotel ☎250/362-7375.

Rossland's stab at urban chic, this moderately enjoyable martini bar is in the town's largest hotel and good for a quiet drink or change of scene.

Mountain Gypsy 2167 Washington St ☎250/362-3342. Upscale dining option serving everything from Indian, Southeast Asian dishes, and Italian. With such a diverse array of options it's easy to be suspicious, but the execution is fantastic and the food sumptuous. With entree prices ranging between $12 and $18, it's good value too.

Powder Keg Bar Uplander Hotel ☎250/362-7375. The town's most significant and popular gathering spot with reasonable bar food, Wednesday night jazz, and live music on weekends.

Rock Cut Pub ☎250/362-5814. Cheerful sports bar beside Hwy 3 between Red Mountain and Rossland. It's ideal as an early stop for breakfast – $4 buys toast, eggs, hash browns, and meat; $8 eggs benedict – or as an après stop for pasta spe-cials; eight beers on tap.

Village Restaurant 2032 Columbia Ave ☎250/362-3390. Ordinary Chinese restaurant, where most of the best choices are filling combination meals for around $10. Good-value lunch specials and varied weekend buffets.

Other activities and attractions

Adjacent to Red Mountain, the **Blackjack Cross-Country Ski Area** (day passes $7; ☎250/362-9465, ⚲www.rossland.com/blackjack) offers 40km of maintained trails, of which 25km are regularly groomed, and a couple of trail-side shelters. Tracks climb and dip through thick woodland. Beginners are better off at the Nordic Ski Club in the Nancy Greene Provincial Park 28km north of Rossland on Hwy 3B. High Country Sports (☎250/362-9000 or 1-877/362-7668) at the *Red Mountain Village* (see p.489) has cross-country ski rentals for around $20 per day and similar prices on **snowshoes**. Another way to tour the backcountry is by **snowmobile**; High Mountain Adventures (☎250/362-5342 or 1-800/663-0105, ⚲www.highmtntours.com) offers full-day trips with fine views over the Columbia River and a barbecue lunch for $150; book through guest services in the base lodge. Rossland has facilities for **ice skating** at the Rossland Arena (☎250/362-7191), which is also used for ice hockey and curling. The nearest **recreation center**, the Aquatic & Leisure Center over in Trail (Mon–Fri 6am–10pm; Sat & Sun 8am–10pm, $4.25), offers a fitness center, racquetball and squash courts, and a pool complex with hot tubs, a steam room, and water slide.

Listings

Bookstore/Internet Gold Rush Books, 2063 Washington St ☎250/362-5333.

Medical Trail Regional Hospital, 1200 Hospital Bench, Trail ☎250/368-3311.

Pharmacy Alpine Drug Mart, 2060 Columbia Ave ☎250/362-5622 or 1-800/491-1168.

Post office 2096 Columbia Ave ☎250/362-7644.

The Best of the Rest

Fairmont Hot Springs Resort, BC

The craggy ice-capped backdrop for Fairmont Hot Springs Resort (☎250/345-6311 or 1-800/663-4979, ⚲www.fairmontresort.com; adults $26, juniors $17), and the luxurious resort itself, with its bubbling springs, belie the modest nature of this ski area. Located 20km south of Invermere along Hwy-93 and within easy striking distance of Panorama, Kimberley, and Kicking Horse, Fairmont makes an exceptional base for a family holiday. The ski area uses two lifts to access 304m of vertical, offering thirteen runs over 300 acres of predominantly intermediate terrain, though there are a few black diamond runs and some mellow greens. There's also a beginners' terrain park and pipe, and the resort maintains 14km of cross-country ski trails, an ice skating rink, and organizes snowmobile tours and sleigh rides. All facilities are gathered around the rustic but luxurious *Fairmont Lodge*, where lofts, suites, and standard rooms are available. ❹

Fortress Mountain, AB

Fortress Mountain (☎403/591-7108, ⚲www.skifortress.com; adults $34, juniors $11) contains largely untamed terrain, huddled beneath several vast, jagged outcrops. Best for skiing through trees and gullies filled with natural obstacles, the resort also maintains a decent halfpipe. Fortress Mountain offers a vertical drop of 280m and spreads over 328 acres; more than half of its 47 runs are intermediate, with the rest split evenly between beginner and expert. Approximately 630cm of light snow falls annually which, coupled with the ski area's substantial snowmaking capacity, means decent conditions are usually guaranteed. Fortress Mountain is located on Hwy-40, 15km south of the small resort of Nakiska in Kananaskis Country Provincial Park. Lift tickets are interchangeable with Nakiska (see below).

Kimberley, BC

The family-friendly resort of Kimberley (☎250/427-4881, ⓦwww.skikimberley .com; adults $49, juniors $35) lies in the squat foothills of the Purcell Mountains. Though the slopes are a far cry from their hulking cousins that surround Panorama (see p.492), the two resorts are similar in other ways, with Kimberley also known for its intermediate cruising and carving and its ideal learning terrain – good beginning package deals and extensive children's activity programs are available. There is a small collection of excellent bump runs for experts, tucked away on the edge of the ski area; a layout that helps keep different ability groups apart. It's on record as the sunniest place in British Columbia; on-mountain temperatures are rarely uncomfortable, but icy conditions along with soft snow at the low-altitude base predominate. If you decide you don't like the conditions, within an hour of issue you can exchange your ticket for a voucher for another day's skiing, either here or at Fernie (see p.482). Kimberley's dingy base village is 2km from the former mining town of Kimberley, a faintly absurd Bavarian-style village with ample facilities. The kitsch in this outpost of *dirndls* and *lederhosen* now extends to fire hydrants, painted with the town's jovial mascot "Happy Hans," and a massive cuckoo clock from which he springs at the drop of a coin – all a quirky backdrop for its friendly pedestrian core.

Marmot Basin, AB

Marmot Basin (☎780/852-3816, ⓦwww.skimarmot.com; adults $52, juniors $19) is far more modest and basic than most resorts in the Canadian Rockies, but as the only ski area in Jasper National Park it's scenically every bit as spectacular as any in the region. The quality of the 400cm of annual snow is excellent, covering 1500 acres of terrain with a vertical drop of 700m and 75 largely beginner and intermediate trails. The ski area – 362km west of Edmonton – is a day area only but is a convenient drive from the friendly, mellow town of Jasper, 19km from the ski area, also an excellent base for other winter activities. The quality of local snowshoeing and cross-country skiing, in particular, is phenomenal and, if you can afford it, there's also the prospect of spectacular heliskiing not far outside the National Park boundaries (see box p.481).

Nakiska, AB

Developed specifically for the 1988 Winter Olympics, Nakiska (☎403/591-7777, ⓦwww.skinakiska.com; adults $45, juniors $14) is located 25km south of the TransCanada Highway, around an hour's drive from either Calgary or Banff, beside Kananaskis Village. The ski area has a vertical drop of 735m, with most runs smooth and steep, making it a great intermediate mountain for cruising and beginning boarders. The lack of snow at the ski area, only 250cm annually, is rarely a problem as snowmaking covers 85 percent of the mountain. The ski area also maintains two excellent halfpipes and a terrain park.

Panorama, BC

From a deep valley in the Purcell Mountains, the Panorama (℡250/342-6941, ⓦwww.skipanorama.com; adults $52, juniors $39) ski area climbs a massive 1200m, from where it offers some of the finest views of the magnificent main spine of the Rockies. Here groomed runs stretch across a varied 2800 acres of terrain with a vertical drop of 1220m, but its popularity is limited by its remote location and, up until recently, any real investment in its lift system – upgrades which now make the expert upper mountain far more accessible. Despite the resort's vast snowmaking capacity the relatively poor snowfall record causes many slopes to ice over by the end of day. Conditions in January and February are best, but later in the season snow cover thins on the upper mountain, exposing rocks on many expert runs. The resort village, though modern and convenient, is limited, with a tiny choice of restaurants and skeletal nightlife. The alternative is staying in the nearest town, Invermere, 18km away, home to a few hotels, restaurants, and craft stores but little more. Panorama is, however, an easy day-trip from Banff (courtesy of a free bus, see p.461), Kicking Horse, or Kimberley.

Whitewater, BC

Located 10km south of Nelson along Hwy 6, the small ski area of Whitewater (℡250/354-4944, ⓦwww.skiwhitewater.com; adults $37, juniors $27) is famed for its powder, with over 1000cm of particularly feathery snow falling annually. Positioned between two distinct ridges on Ymir Peak, Whitewater offers backcountry-style skiing and steep terrain; only twenty percent of its 600 acres is graded beginner, with the rest evenly split between intermediate and expert. There are only two lifts and a surface tow, so it's easy to explore the entire mountain in a day. Intermediates should head to Joker, a blue run with some of the finest powder on the mountain, and Concentrator Trees, the mountain's best freeride area, with plenty of natural hits and smooth turns. For more challenging terrain, hike to the top of the Powder Keg Bowl off the Summit chair. Base yourself in Nelson, a classic Victorian mining town turned artsy hangout. It's a lively place – evidenced in its beatnik cafes and secondhand clothes shops – with a healthy cultural scene, thriving nightlife, and a broad selection of restaurants.

Western British Columbia

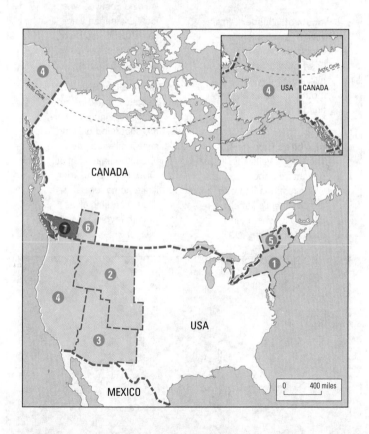

chapter 7

Highlights

✱ **Freestyling at Whistler-Blackcomb** Huck alongside the world's best riders at Canada's largest terrain park and one of North America's most prominent resorts. See p.504

✱ **Wasabi at Whistler** *Sushi Village*, a succulent Japanese bistro in the heart of Whistler Village, offers melt-in-your-mouth maki and a selection of hot sake. See p.509

✱ **Big White's tube park** The Happy Valley Adventure Park at Big White resort is home to the continent's largest tube park, where ten chutes spanning 1000 feet are graded according to difficulty and serviced by two tows. See p.518

✱ **Winter wine** Head to Sun Peaks in late-January for the resort's annual Icewine Festival, when local Okanagan vineyards display some of the "coolest" wines in Canada. See p.519

✱ **Stay at Silver Star** Because of a local ordinance requiring a colorful, decorated building style in all area structures, the base area at Silver Star seems more like a home for Santa Clause and his elves than the typical resort village. See p.524

Western British Columbia

The steep, forested slopes rising from the suburbs of Vancouver give arriving visitors only a hint of the skiing and snowboarding opportunities that **Western British Columbia** has in store. Within easy distance of the province's largest city lie major mountain ranges with rugged alpine peaks, riven by gigantic glaciers and blanketed by permanent snowfields. Given the setting, the region's consistently generous snowfalls, and the relatively large, outdoorsy local populace, it's not surprising that ski resorts have mushroomed here. Most famous among them, boasting North America's biggest vertical drop, is the much-vaunted mammoth of **Whistler-Blackcomb**, just two hours' drive from Vancouver.

Further inland, other ski resorts have firmly established themselves in the **Okanagan Valley**, an area best known for its popularity with retirees, its droves of summer vacationers, and its vineyards. The rounded mountains hugging the valley here are home to several resorts, all with ambitious expansion plans: the northernmost is the enjoyable family resort of **Sun Peaks**, near Kamloops, while further south, **Silver Star** and sprawling **Big White** are both somewhat enigmatic, requiring a little more effort to uncover their best trails.

Though Whistler-Blackcomb's sheer size makes it easy to stay put there for a week or two, it would be a shame to miss exploring the other three less crowded (and less expensive) resorts, especially when conditions are prime. If your budget can stretch to it, it's also worth adding a day's cat- or heliskiing on virgin snow far from the bustling resorts.

Before heading out to Western British Columbia, check the **weather conditions**, which are generally warmer than the Rockies. This is a mixed blessing, for although major roads are almost invariably clear, snow conditions tend to err on the damper and heavier side. At Whistler, you can always escape base level conditions, due to the resort's huge vertical, but the other resorts can quickly slide into spring conditions by early March.

Regional practicalities

Coming from overseas to Western British Columbia, you are most likely to arrive at **Vancouver International Airport** (☎604/207-7077, ⓦwww.yvr .ca), 13km south of the city on Sea Island. From there the quickest – but most expensive – option, if you are heading to a specific resort in the interior, is to

WESTERN BRITISH COLUMBIA

N

Prince George & Ski Smithers

Jasper

Red Mountain

50 km

0

CANADA
USA

WASHINGTON

BRITISH COLUMBIA

Silver Star

Vernon

Kalamalka Lake

Big White

Kelowna

Penticton

Skaha Lake

Okanagan Lake

Apex

Sun Peaks

Harper Mountain

Kamloops

Kamloops Lake

Manning Park

Lillooet

Seton Lake

Carpenter Lake

Anderson Lake

Harrison Lake

Hemlock Valley Resort

Mt Baker

Pemberton

Whistler

Whistler-Blackcomb

Squamish

Cypress Mountain

Grouse Mountain

Vancouver

Seattle

Strait of Georgia

Nanaimo

Vancouver Island

Mount Washington & Forbidden Plateau

arrange a flight from Vancouver International to one of the province's regional airports, nearer your chosen resort. If traveling overland, there's a choice of **buses**, both shuttle and public, or you can **rent a car**. Unless you plan to explore well beyond the resorts – which are all small and pedestrian friendly enough to render a car unnecessary – shuttle buses are generally the best option. If you do decide on a car, you'll find several **rental companies** operating in and around Vancouver International, including Alamo (☎604/231-1400), Avis (☎604/606-2847), Hertz (☎604/606-3700), and National (☎604/207-3730). If you don't mind an older car (and the inconvenience of getting to their downtown Vancouver location), Rent–a–Wreck (☎604/688-0001) is a good way to save money. Useful information on **road conditions** for the state can be had via (☎604/299-9000 ext 7623, ⓦwww.gov.bc.ca/tran).

Relying on **public transportation** to get around the province, while of course cheaper, is more complicated than renting a car. The main option is to use **Greyhound buses**, which leave from the Pacific Central Station bus depot (☎604/482-8747). To get to the station from the airport you can take either the Airporter bus (7am–1am; $10 single, $17 round-trip; ☎604/946-8866 or 1-800/668-3141) or a public bus operated by Translink ($2.50, or $1.75 off-peak), though both services require changing buses along the way – making taxis (approximately $25) an attractive option.

A **tourist information desk** (daily 7am–midnight; ☎604/688-5515) is located after customs and immigration at the airport and can advise on the details of public transport. A good budget alternative to using Greyhound services is to use the local backpacker-oriented bus service run by the Moose Network (☎604/944-3007 or 1-888/388-4881, ⓦwww.moosenetwork.com), which runs a number of simple shuttle services, along with more involved packages to all the region's major resorts. For **resort-specific transportation details**, see each resort's "Arrival, information, and getting around" section.

Whistler-Blackcomb

The magnificent, notoriously dangerous Sea to Sky Highway snakes its way 123km north from Vancouver, passing Howe Sound's idyllic island before pushing up into the jagged mountains of **Whistler–Blackcomb**. Frequently rated the best resort in North America by magazines and skiers alike, the two ski areas on Whistler and Blackcomb mountains are joined only at their base, where they share a common village known simply as Whistler. Though both resorts were developed in the late 1960s, much of the present-day infrastructure was built in the 1970s and 1980s; the resulting three alpine-style villages try to come off as venerable, with quarried stone and rough-hewn woodwork, but ultimately feel a little contrived and sterile. Still, the development functions efficiently enough, and is certainly a welcome departure from the strip malls, cheap motels, and gas stations that are prevalent in many of British Columbia's regional towns.

The village, of course, isn't what draws skiers and boarders here in the thousands; it's the gargantuan **ski area** above. Spread over **seven thousand acres of terrain** – including twelve mountain bowls and over 5000ft of vertical drop – it takes days for even the most advanced skiers and riders to cover a significant portion of the fantastically varied terrain. Though most visitors come here

WHISTLER-BLACKCOMB

ACCOMMODATION

Blackcomb Lodge	10
Chalet Luise	5
Chateau Whistler	8
Delta Whistler Resort	13
Edelweiss	3
Edgewater Lodge	2
Fireside Lodge	14
Glacier's Reach	7
Lost Lake Lodge	6
Pan Pacific Lodge	12
Residence Inn by Marriott	9
Shoestring Lodge	4
Southside Lodge	17
UBC Whistler Lodge	15
Whistler International Youth Hostel	11
The Whistler Resort & Club	16
Whistler Retreat	1

EATING

Araxi Restaurant & Lounge	I
Bearfoot Bistro	M
Caramba	E
Crepe Montagne	D
Gaitor's Bar & Grill	A
Gone Bakery & Soup Company	I
Ingrid's Village Café	I
La Brasserie Des Artistes	F
La Rua	I
Mogul's Coffee House	L
Monk's Grill	B
Pasta Lupino	Q
Rimrock Café	C
Splitz Grill	J
Sushi Village	K
Trattoria di Umberto	G
The Wildflower	

NIGHTLIFE

The Amsterdam Café	I
Black's pub & restaurant	O
The Boot Pub	A
Brewhouse	H
Buffalo Bill's	N
Dubh Linn Gate Old Irish Pub	P
Garfinkel's	I
Hoz's Creekside	R
Longhorn Saloon	O
Mallard Bar	G
Maxx Fish	I
Savage Beagle Club	I
Tommy Africa's	I

Alta Lake

ALTA LAKE ROAD

Nordic Estates

NORDIC DRIVE

Nita Lake

ALTA LAKE ROAD

Alpha Lake

Creekside Gondola

Whistler Creekside

Function Junction & Squamish

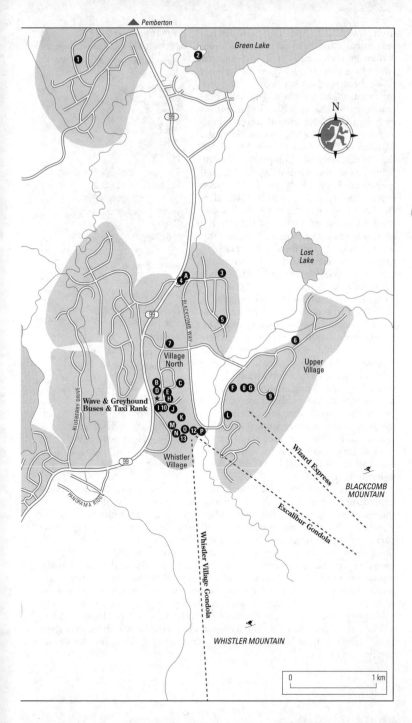

Green Lake

Pemberton

N

Lost Lake

Blackcomb Way

Village North

Upper Village

Wave & Greyhound Buses & Taxi Rank

Whistler Village

BLUEBERRY DRIVE

PANORAMA RIDGE

Wizard Express

Excalibur Gondola

BLACKCOMB MOUNTAIN

Whistler Village Gondola

WHISTLER MOUNTAIN

0   1 km

from November to April, the season can run year-round. Conditions permitting, Whistler Mountain stays open until mid-June, at which time Blackcomb reopens for summer skiing, becoming the home of training pros (many of whom are permanent local residents). Part of the attraction for professionals is the resort's **race circuit status**: it hosts a clutch of local competitions, including the Snowboard FIS World Cup in December, the World Freestyle Competition in late January, and the massive World Ski and Snowboard Festival in April – the latter such event in North America. Whistler-Blackcomb also attracts vast numbers of partying ski and snowboard bums, the majority of which make up part of the resort's 4000-strong seasonal workforce. Unsurprisingly, thanks to the sheer number of workers and visitors, the **party scene** in Whistler is in a league of its own.

Despite its fame, size, and popularity, Whistler-Blackcomb has its faults, foremost among them the often-dreary **weather**. Sitting only 80km from the sea, where warm and cold ocean currents collide, Whistler is susceptible to widely varying weather patterns. The resort's relatively low base altitude can bring rain instead of snow as well, making the usable ski area rarely as big as the resort's stats suggest. Even so, given Whistler's massive vertical drop, bad weather at the base says little about conditions at the summit, where powder prevails – though rarely in as light and fluffy a form as in the Rockies.

Mountain info

Phone ☎604/932-3434 or 1-800/766-0449; UK ☎0800/731-5983

Snow phone ☎604/932-4211 in Whistler; ☎604/687-7507 in Vancouver

Website ⊛www.whistler-blackcomb.com

Price $65

Operating times Blackcomb: late Nov to late April 8.30am–4pm; mid-June to early Aug noon–3pm. Whistler: late Nov to mid-June 8.30am–4pm

No. of lifts 33, including 3 gondolas and 12 surface lifts

Base elevation 675m

Summit elevation 2288m

Vertical drop 1609m

No. of trails 200 marked, with 12 bowls and 3 glaciers

Acreage 7071

Beginner 18%

Intermediate 55%

Expert 27%

Average snowfall 914cm

Snowmaking Yes (530 acres)

Night skiing Yes (68 acres)

Nursery facilities Yes, from 3 months ☎604/766-0449 or 1-800/766-0449

The other drawbacks of Whistler-Blackcomb – **overpricing** and **overcrowding** – suggest that the resort may be becoming a victim of its own success. Averaging more than two million visitors a year, with up to 25,000 people on the mountain at peak times, Whistler brings to mind a big theme park: impeccably organized, but with long lines for most attractions – half-hour waits for lifts are not uncommon, especially on the weekends. The crowding on the slopes continues in the evenings, too, as the town's many restaurants and far fewer bars and clubs quickly fill to capacity. Whistler is also more expensive than all other Canadian resorts, with prices for lift tickets, accommodation, and food particularly inflated (though to foreign visitors this often goes unnoticed, due to Canada's relatively weak dollar). However, when all's said and done, the resort and its world-class terrain certainly deserve their fame – even if those looking for a restful, inexpensive skiing holiday should maybe think twice.

Arrival, orientation, and getting around

Vancouver International is the closest **airport** to Whistler, and offers several easy ways of making the two-and-a-half hour trip to the resort. For a no-expense-spared approach, take the Helijet **helicopter service** (two daily; $150 one way; ☎604/273-1414 or 1-800/665-4354, ⓦwww.helijet.com) direct from the airport; it'll get you there in just under a half-hour. Otherwise, take a **shuttle bus**, from either Perimeter (Mon–Fri eight daily, Sat & Sun eleven daily; $53 one-way; reservations required one day in advance; ☎604/266-5386, ⓦwww.perimterbus.com) or Bigfoot Adventure Tours ($35 one way or $55 round-trip; ☎604/278-8224 or 1-888/244-6673, ⓦwww.bigfoottours.com); both have pick-ups at various downtown Vancouver accommodations, and Bigfoot also provides discounted lift tickets.

A cheaper alternative – just as convenient if you're staying in downtown Vancouver for a night – is a **Greyhound bus** (seven daily; three hours; $21 one way; ☎604/482-8747 in Vancouver, ☎604-932-5031 in Whistler or 1-800/ 661-TRIP, ⓦwww.whistlerbus.com). The service sets out from the Vancouver bus depot, with stops at several downtown locations, as well as Squamish and Pemberton. Bus tickets can be bought on board, but lift and ticket packages need to be purchased in the terminal. Be sure to specify that you are getting off at Whistler Creekside or Whistler Village (see below for more on this distinction).

Whistler-Blackcomb has three base areas: **Whistler Village**, **Upper Village**, and **Whistler Creekside.** The most popular is the highly polished **Whistler Village**, which blends into the adjacent **Village North** and includes a functional shopping area called Marketplace; both villages gather around plazas lined with restaurants, bars, cafés, and gear and gift shops. A five-minute walk from Whistler Village is the far smaller, duller **Upper Village** below Blackcomb Mountain, while **Whistler Creekside**, the original base area 4km back down Hwy-99, is an unremarkable collection of private homes and condos (although redevelopment is ongoing). A further 2km past Creekside toward Vancouver is **Function Junction**, a shopping area for household items that's generally visited only by local residents. Further afield, the towns of **Squamish** and **Pemberton**, located a half-hour's drive south or north, respectively, are part of "greater Whistler," serving as bedroom communities for resort staff and a less expensive ski base for visitors.

The **pedestrian-friendly** base areas and **efficient shuttle bus service** make getting around the resort easy, even without a car. Local buses are operated by WAVE (☎604/932-4020, ⓦwww.whistler.com/transit), which runs a free shuttle between Whistler Village and the Upper Village; for a fee, you can also connect to more outlying areas in the valley, including Whistler Creek (runs from around 6am to 3am; $1.50). Be sure to request a transfer if using interconnecting lines. **Taxis** pick up beside the bus stops adjacent to Village Square in the Upper Village, or you can call Whistler Taxi (☎604/932-3333).

If you do bring a car, you'll find no shortage of **parking** in the massive car park under Whistler Village and in a huge lot between Whistler Village and the Upper Village; spots cost $8–12 a day. If you're on a day-trip and want to ski Whistler Mountain only, spare yourself the final leg of the journey and take advantage of the free underground parking in Whistler Creekside. At the Blackcomb base, try lots 7 and 8, which fill up later than lot 6 and are closer to the base area.

The mountains

Both **Whistler** and **Blackcomb mountains** rise from a narrow base area and expand exponentially the higher you go. You'll need to ascend a considerable way up either mountain to get to most of the terrain, so the first journey of the day for most, regardless of skill level, is a gondola ride deep into either ski area.

Of the two peaks, Whistler is the more family oriented; it's here that **novices** will find the best terrain. **Experts** are better served at Blackcomb, where huge drops and steep couloirs are easier to find than at Whistler. **Intermediates** will find excellent runs on both mountains; differences in crowd levels may well be the decisive factor in choosing between the two. Morning bottlenecks regularly arise at both gondolas in Whistler Village; using the brisk Wizard Express from the Upper Village to access Blackcomb can cut wait times, and lines at the gondola in Whistler Creekside are often shorter. But generally, crowd levels on either mountain are unpredictable. If you find yourself stewing in liftlines in either area, consider simply switching mountains: the speedy gondolas, which are fairly empty outside the morning rush hour, will get you from one mountain to the heart of the other in around half an hour.

A good way for competent skiers and riders to get a handle on either area is to join the **free mountain tours** which set off daily at 10.30am and 11.30am from both the Guest Satisfaction Center at the top of the Whistler Village gondola and the Mountain Tour Center at the top of the Solar Coaster Express on Blackcomb. Also free (though with a $10 deposit) are **avalanche awareness tours**, run by the Whistler-Blackcomb Ski Patrol; these leave at around 9am from the Blackcomb Day Lodge, and you should register with Blackcomb Guest Relations at least a day in advance.

Beginner

Though easy trails run almost summit-to-base on both mountains, Whistler has the better learning area. **Blackcomb** has some decent terrain, but most of its greens, particularly in the upper reaches, are undemanding cat tracks that help you do little more than find your feet. The beginner runs on the bottom third of Blackcomb are better but are often undermined by poor snow conditions and rainy weather. Just head to **Whistler Mountain**: here most of the best beginner trails are on the upper mountain, where snow conditions are optimal. Warm up below the **Big Red Express**, on runs like Pony Trail, Papoose, and Bear Cub. Here the presence of easy adjacent blue terrain makes it a cinch to dabble with more taxing pistes. Similarly, the Burnt Stew Trail, high up the

Summer skiing

One of only two North American resorts offering **summer skiing**, Whistler-Blackcomb has become a place of pilgrimage for diehard skiers and boarders. It's not, however, as extensive as you might hope for: the only terrain on offer after mid-June is on Blackcomb Mountain, where, between late June and early August, a t-bar on the **Horstman Glacier** (daily, noon to 3.30pm; $38) opens up around 112 acres of terrain, with a vertical rise of 209m. Many summer visitors come for the novelty value, though several training camps for hard-core enthusiasts are available. The biggest is the Camp of Champions (☏1-888/997-CAMP, ⑩www.campofchampions.com); others include the Dave Murray Summer Ski and Snowboard Camp (☏604/932-5765, ⑩www.skiandsnowboard.com), the Smart Mogul Skiing Camp (☏604/905-4421, ⑩www.smartmogul.com), and the High North Ski Camp (☏604/905-0271, ⑩www.highnorth2002.com), which focuses on freestyle technique.

mountain off the **Harmony Express**, offers accessible, harder beginning terrain. One of the best blue runs to graduate to is the relatively easy, generally quiet **Jolly Green Giant** off the Emerald Express.

Intermediate

With over half the trails in Whistler-Blackcomb rated intermediate, those looking for carving and cruising will find as extensive and ideal a playground as anywhere in North America. Whistler's highly variable conditions cause blue runs to vary dramatically in their difficulties, depending on daily snow and grooming situation – but even in spring, when the lower half of the mountain is essentially closed, there's plenty to choose from.

When conditions are at their optimum, don't miss the speedy cruiser **Franz's Run** on **Whistler Mountain**, which twists, pitches, and rolls five miles from the treeline at the base of **Franz's chair** to Whistler Creekside. Some of the best slopes for intermediate skiers and riders are the **bowls** off the **Harmony Express**, higher up the mountain, where the snow is far more dependable. Here you'll be spoiled for choice of lines in the Symphony Bowl, while the adjoining run Boundary Piste often has decent powder even later in the day, and leads to some sweet glades further down. On the other side of Symphony Bowl, Harmony Ridge offers extensive views over both mountains and a chance to scope out the easier black runs of Harmony Bowl. But a better place for intermediates looking for **black terrain** is off Whistler's summit, accessed by the **Peak chair**. From here, there's a choice of two blue runs, The Saddle and Highway 86, which both begin as cat tracks before descending more sharply and offering access to exhilarating, yet relatively straightforward, black terrain in adjacent bowls.

Blackcomb Mountain has plenty of blues mixed among other runs throughout the slopes. **7th Heaven Express** lift, where four blue runs congregate beneath, is well worth sessioning. Their south-facing aspect gives them the mountain's best weather, and, being slightly off the beaten path, they tend to hold their powder longer than other runs. Aside from this area, hopping from chair to chair is really the most gratifying way to explore the mountain. Worth singling out is the fantastic cruising Ridge Runner, off the **Crystal chair**, and exploring **Blackcomb Glacier**. The latter is accessed via a t-bar and a brief hike to the mountain's driest and lightest snow, on varying terrain that allows even weaker intermediates to find comfortable lines. Once beyond the hiking section and the steep Blow Hole entrance to the glacier (see overleaf), a traverse leads to the main slope; the further along you travel, the shallower the angle of descent. Snowboarders beware: a long, flat runout further down is the price for the fluffy untracked carvers you'll be able to lay down on top.

Expert

Wild enough to lure filmmakers to its slopes, extreme skiers to its competitions, and pros to live at its base, the quality of Whistler-Blackcomb's expert terrain is not in doubt. The only enduring question is which mountain is better – a difficult question to answer, though most agree that Blackcomb has the lion's share of the more extreme challenges and Whistler has more empty, untracked slopes in its expansive bowls.

For immediate challenges try double black diamond **Couloir Extreme**. It is intimidating, steep, and dotted by a few jagged rocks, and several focused, precise turns are needed to get through the top section to the barely less taxing clutches of the Jersey Cream Bowl below. Another classic is **Spanky's**

Ladder, which leads to several bowls – Garnet, Diamond, Ruby, and Sapphire – all with steep entrances which soon give way to powdery bowls. Access to Spanky's is only for those prepared to hike from the **Glacier Express** – stay high on the ridge and look for signs and footprints. Another run that requires a short hike, off the Showcase t-bar, is Blow Hole, a narrow, steep, semicircular pipe made largely of hard, wind-packed snow, making it hard to slow down; fortunately, the run bottoms out at the base. Though overshadowed by the couloirs and bowls, Blackcomb also has its share of taxing **mogul runs** and **glades**. Try the bumps on the consistently steep Overbite, off the Crystal chair; for trees head to the gladed runs accessed from the Expressway, via the Solar Coaster Express chair.

On **Whistler Mountain**, head to the **powder bowls** above the treeline, particularly Glacier, Whistler, and West Bowl. Off the **Peak chair**, these black are generously dotted with steeps and cliffs. Some of the **best drops** with the freshest snow are on Cockalorum in West Bowl. Finish the day with fast black diamond carves at the Upper and Lower Dave Murray downhill, which plunges down to Whistler Creekside.

Freestyle

Whistler-Blackcomb has one of the largest and most comprehensive **freestyle parks** in North America; with the world's elite hucking next to you, the experience can be a bit intimidating. The bulk of the freestyle action centers on **Blackcomb Mountain**. Sprawling over sixteen acres below the Catskinner chair – a useful vantage point from which to first scope – the **Nintendo GameCube Terrain Park** is full of tabletops, spine jumps, rail slides, and everything else that an aspiring jibber could want. At the top of the park the terrain is best for beginners; midway down is a snowcross park where most of the twisting turns and rollers are intermediate. The park also includes a tough expert section, **The Highest Level**. Entry requires a helmet and an annual pass that's obtainable from guest services in exchange for a $15 fee and a signed waiver. Below the park is the busy, expert-level **World Cup Halfpipe**, with towering 15ft walls. If this seems a bit much, try easing yourself into the more modest halfpipe on Whistler Mountain a short walk from the Roundhouse Lodge, where the walls are a more familiar 12ft height. The Blackcomb pipe is busy with weekly competitions, for which you can register at the Blackcomb Day Lodge. In addition to the man-made terrain, it's easy to find **natural hits** on almost every black run in the ski area. After a major snowstorm explore the rocks and ridges on Surprise (under Peak chair) on Whistler Mountain as well as the various entries into the Harmony Bowl off Harmony Ridge.

Lift tickets, lessons, and rentals

Whistler-Blackcomb charges more than any other Canadian resort for **lift tickets** ($65) – though the weak Canadian dollar means it still compares favorably to major resorts in the US. Multiday passes snag only minimal savings, though those spanning over five days allow you to take a day off without penalty. The early-morning lines at ticket counters are among the worst in the resort, so it's worth purchasing tickets in advance online from Ⓦwww .whistlerblackcomb.com, or in Vancouver from Sport Mart at either 495 Eighth Ave W (☎604/873-6737) or 735 Thurlow St (☎604/683-2433). Additionally, some hotels sell tickets in advance, and most 7-11 convenience stores (except those in Squamish, Whistler, and Vancouver Airport) offer discount tickets to residents of both British Columbia and Washington State.

Backcountry options

Whistler's magnetism for North America's top skiers and riders is due not only to the gigantic amount of official terrain available on Whistler-Blackcomb mountains, but also to the fantastic opportunities beyond its resort boundaries, easily accessed on foot, by snowmobile, or by helicopter. Here, the **backcountry** is packed with vast expanses of untracked powder that can become the ski or snowboard experience of a lifetime.

On foot, the most accessible areas of backcountry start with hikes off the top of either The Peak or Harmony quads on Whistler Mountain. Options from here include the so-called **musical bowls** – Piccolo, Flute, and Oboe. **Flute Bowl** is accessed from the Burnt Stew Trail, where a serious ninety-minute, 5km hike through deep snow heads along the ridge above Symphony Bowl and past Piccolo Peak. Even though these areas are easily accessible and generally safe, venturing into the back-country should not be taken lightly. A safety course, shovel, avalanche beacons, and a partner are necessities. Be aware that in case of an accident, any rescue attempt will be your financial responsibility. The bowls mentioned above lead to the large, thickly wooded valley that separates Whistler from Blackcomb, so it's essential that you give yourself at least a couple of hours of sunlight to hike out.

If you've any hesitations, it's probably best to take some kind of **guided trip**. Once the snowpack has settled, around a dozen different areas are accessible on foot or by snowmobile from Whistler, and several companies offer tours of these areas; one experienced operator is Whistler Alpine Guides (from $200 per day; ℡604/938-3228, ⓦwww.whistlerguides.com). Another option is Callaghan Country Wilderness Adventures (℡604/938-0616, ⓦwww.callaghancounty.com), an operation based 13km from Whistler at Callaghan Backcountry Lodge. All the major guiding operations offer avalanche courses.

In addition to guided backcountry trips, the mountains dotted around the region collectively offer around a million acres of terrain accessed via several **heliski** operations in the valley. Whistler Heli-Skiing (℡604/932-4105 or 1-888/435-4754, ⓦwww.whistlerheliskiing.com) offers some of the least expensive trips, from around $650 for the most basic three-run package. Trips are tailored according to conditions and the abilities of those joining, though – as with all the overland backcountry guiding services – confident intermediate-level skills are expected.

Mirroring the size of the resort, the **ski school** at Whistler-Blackcomb is huge, with 1200 instructors. Still, personal attention comes at a steep price: private lessons cost $100 per hour; most visitors end up taking group lessons for $30 per hour. Look for the three- or four-day Ski or Ride Esprit programs, which combine instruction with a guided tour of the mountains, providing an excellent foundation for getting the most out of a vacation at Whistler. The resort's beginner package – $122 for both skiers and boarders – includes a group lesson, rentals, and a half-day lift ticket. Among the specialist programs offered are women-only clinics, free-skiing clinics, race training, and lessons for adaptive skiers.

The twenty or so **rental** stores in and around Whistler offer virtually every make and manufacturer of ski and snowboard equipment. Ski packages start at around $22 per day, while snowboard packages begin at $35. British Columbia and Washington state residents can get a discount of up to a third off rentals by buying vouchers at any 7-11 ahead of time. The resort-owned Mountain Adventure Center – with branches at the Pan Pacific Lodge (℡604/905-2295), the Blackcomb Day Lodge (℡604/938-7737), the top of Whistler Mountain (℡604/905-2325), and the top of Blackcomb Mountain (℡604/938-7425) – has some of the best high-performance equipment around, with the added benefit of being able to switch gear as often as you like during your rental period.

Accommodation

Whistler Village and its satellites collectively have around 40,000 beds – but few are cheap, and at peak times you may be scrabbling around to find a room if you haven't booked well in advance. Only the shoulder seasons of November and April really experience any let-up in the crowds and prices. During peak season, many accommodations have a thirty-day cancellation policy and have a minimum three-night stay. Most visitors arrive with accommodation already booked; the easiest way to do this is through the resort's central **reservations** (☎604/904-7060 or 1-800/403-4727, ⊛www.whistler-blackcomb.com) or the reservation service operated by Tourism Whistler (☎604/664-5625 or 1-800/944-7853, ⊛www.mywhistler.com). Both have rooms and condos in every price bracket and are equipped to put together **packages** incorporating lift tickets, lessons, activities, ground transportation, and airfare. Other, smaller players in the rental market include Powder Resort Properties (☎604/932-2882 or 1-800/777-0185, ⊛www.powder-properties.com), Crown Resort Accommodations (☎604/932-2215 or 1-800/565-1444, ⊛www.crown-resort .com), Whistler Home Holidays (☎604/938-9256 or 1-888/644-7444, ⊛www.homeholidays.com), and Affordable Holiday Homes (☎604/932-0581 or 1-800/882-6991), which is usually the cheapest option.

If a good night's rest is important to you, avoid Whistler Village, which can get noisy with nightlife. If you're looking for more character and some savings, you may want to forgo the convenience of a slopeside location entirely and consider staying in one of the moderately priced **B&Bs** scattered throughout the valley – most are only a walk or short bus ride from the lifts. The most economical option is, of course, a **hostel**: there's a decent stock in town, though at around $30 per night for a dorm bed, none are exactly shoestring options. If you have your own transport, a further money-saving option might be to stay outside Whistler in **Squamish** or **Pemberton**, thirty minutes from the slopes.

Hostels

Fireside Lodge 2117 Nordic Drive ☎604/932-4545. Ski-club lodge with basic hostel facilities, including kitchens and self-service laundry, located in Nordic Estates area off Hwy-99 between Creekside and Whistler Village. Accommodation is available to nonmembers when not busy. Dorm beds go for $30 per night; a private room with shared bathroom costs $90/night.

Shoestring Lodge 7124 Nancy Greene Drive ☎604/932-3338, ⊛www.whistler.net/boot/string.html. Rowdy, sociable, wood-clad hostel with big open fire, a ten-minute walk from Whistler Village. Shares premises with a restaurant (*Gaitor's* – see "Eating" p.508) and pub (*The Boot Pub* – see "Drinking" p.510). Dorm beds cost $30 per night and the motel-standard rooms are much pricier at $125 per night.

Southside Lodge 2121 Lake Placid Rd, Whistler Creekside ☎604/932-3644. Basic hostel occupy-

ing the top two stories of a building at the noisy main road junction at Whistler Creekside, only a short walk to the lifts and bus services into Whistler Village. The small rooms pack six people into bunk beds ($35/bed) who share an en-suite bathroom and shower. The tiny kitchen is the only other facility offered.

UBC Whistler Lodge 2124 Nordic Drive ☎604/882-5851. University-owned lodge just uphill of *Fireside Lodge* (see above), offering dorm-style accommodation for $25 per night on weekdays and $30 on weekends. Provide your own bedding or pay a $3.50 rental fee. In addition to all the usual hostel facilities, there's a sauna, jacuzzi, and some sociable wood-clad common rooms. Fills up early.

Whistler International Youth Hostel 5678 Alta Lake Rd ☎604/932-5492, ⊛www.hihostels.ca. Plush, idyllic lakeside hostel, a bit remote at ten minutes' drive from the Village; WAVE buses do serve the place, though. It's extremely well looked-after, and consequently popular, making advance booking for its 32 dorm beds ($19.50 for members, $23.50 for nonmembers) essential. Facilities include a kitchen, game room, and laundry.

Hotels, condos, and B&Bs

Blackcomb Lodge Whistler Village ☎604/932-4155. Hidden bargain in the center of Whistler Village; its motel-style units are nothing special – the studios are bigger and have kitchens – but the location couldn't be handier for skiing or the nightlife. There's use of a pool, jacuzzi, exercise room, and sauna included. ❸

Chalet Luise 7461 Ambassador Crescent ☎604 /932-4187 or 1-800/665-1998, ⓦwww.chaletluise .com. Pleasant, relaxing Alpine-style B&B within walking distance of Whistler Village. Carved pine, overstuffed sofas, and a Laura Ashley aesthetic adorn its eight rooms, most of which have fireplaces. In the absence of in-room phones and TVs, guests can putter between the sauna and hot tub in fluffy robes and slippers. Varied, filling, and healthy continental breakfasts include excellent homemade baked goods. Peak season requires a five-night minimum stay. ❺

Chateau Whistler 4599 Chateau Blvd, Upper Village ☎604/938-8000 or 1-800/441-1414, ⓦwww.chateauwhistler.com. Grand, Baronial-style building, oozing a formulaic, unconvincing rendition of Old World charm. Mismatched furnishings crowd the mad assortment of flamboyant rugs, stone paving, and gilt display cases – though its 558 country-style rooms are elegant, well-appointed, and have good mountain views. The leisure complex is top-notch and swathed in tropical foliage. A five-night minimum stay is required most of the season. ❾

Delta Whistler Resort 4050 Whistler Way, Whistler Village ☎604/932-1982 or 1-800/515-4050, ⓦwww.deltawhistler.com. Full-service resort in a dreary tower-block with fantastic lift-side location at the base of both Whistler and Blackcomb's gondolas. The interior is plush, with plenty of seasoned dark wood, though its sizeable rooms are bland. Simple suites (which sleep four comfortably) have fireplaces, whirlpool baths, kitchens, and dataports – laptops can be borrowed from reception. The fitness center is excellent and includes a pool, hot tub, exercise room, and indoor tennis courts. ❾

Edelweiss 7162 Nancy Greene Drive ☎604/932-3641 or 1-800/932-3641. Unpretentious alpine chalet with simply furnished rooms sporting window boxes and down comforters; located in a residential area a ten-minute walk from Whistler Village. The friendly innkeepers are avid skiers and offer reliable advice about current conditions. Breakfast and use of the hot tub and sauna are included. ❺

Edgewater Lodge 8841 Hwy-99 ☎604/932-0688 or 1-888/870-9065, ⓦwww.edgewater-lodge.com. Far from the bustle of Whistler Village, 5km south, this airy, modern cedar lodge has tranquil lake and mountain views from its twelve rooms and outdoor hot tub. A network of cross-country trails start from here, and the Whistler Outdoor Experience Activity Center is nearby. To get to everything else, however, you'll have to rely on either your own vehicle, the courtesy bus to the slopes, or a taxi. Breakfast included. ❼

Glacier's Reach 4388 Northland Blvd, Village North ☎604/905-4746 or 1-800/777-0185, ⓦwww.powder-resorts.com. Standard modern condo complex built with alpine-look blocks in a quiet location at the edge of the resort village, a five-minute walk from the lifts. Rates for the snug rooms, which include kitchenettes and dining area, are reasonable and include use of a heated outdoor pool and jacuzzi. Rooms with hot tubs are also offered. ❺

Lost Lake Lodge 4660 Blackcomb Way, Upper Village ☎604/905-7631 or 1-800/777-0185, ⓦwww.powder-properties.com. Rustic log and stone building outside the core of the resort, though on the free shuttle route and handy for cross-country skiing. Units are a little more spartan than building exteriors suggest, and include studios and one- and two-bedroom apartments, sleeping four to six. Communal facilities include a pool and hot tub. ❺

Pan Pacific Lodge 4320 Sundial Crescent, Whistler Village ☎604/905-2999 or 1-888/905-9995, ⓦwww.panpac.com. Luxurious lodge located in prime lift-side position. Accommodations include both cramped studios with pull-down beds and angular modern furnishings as well as far more spacious one- or two-bedroom units. All have kitchens and gas fireplaces, and some have mountain views. Plush facilities include sauna, outdoor pool, and hot tubs. ❼

Residence Inn by Marriott 4899 Painted Cliff Rd ☎604/905-3400, ⓦww.powder-properties.com. Large chalet-look hotel, located above the Upper Village and Blackcomb's base area, 3km from the center of Whistler Village. Getting to and from the base area is easy on skis or a board but requires a ten-minute walk otherwise. Available are studios (sleeping up to three) and one- and two-bedroom condos (sleeping up to six), with log beams, slate floors, and American Rocky Mountain-style furnishings. All units have a gas fireplace and share an outdoor pool, hot tub, sauna, and exercise room. A light continental breakfast is included. **❻**

The Whistler Resort and Club 2129 Lake Placid Rd, Whistler Creekside ☎604/932-2343, Ⓦwww.rainbowretreats.com. Ageing 1970s hotel with simple rooms (many without phones) – the

studios have a kitchen, living room, and fireplace, and there are some one- and two-bedroom suites. All at relatively low rates, within walking distance of lifts and bus services. Facilities include hot tub and sauna. **❸**

Whistler Retreat 8561 Drifter Way ☎604/938-9245. Smart little B&B in residential area close to cross-country skiing and a five-minute bus ride from the slopes. Most rooms share a bathroom. Facilities include an outdoor hot tub, sauna, pool table, and laundry. **❹**

Eating

Whistler's incredibly varied dining scene could keep a food critic busy for years. Most restaurants are more expensive than elsewhere in the region – still reasonably priced by international standards – and, despite the volume of possibilities, competition between diners for tables is keen; you should definitely make dinner reservations if you've got a particular place in mind.

Besides being a good way to save money, cooking your own meals in self-catering accommodation is often the most practical option if you're on vacation with the kids. Few restaurants are child-friendly, and some won't even serve those under nineteen. The main supermarket is IGA, in the Marketplace area of Whistler Village. If you're too wiped out to cook or go out, consider calling Resort Room Service (☎604/905-4711), which will deliver food from around thirty local outlets to your door for a $6 fee.

On-mountain dining facilities suffer from overcrowding, so try to have your meals outside the 11.30am–1pm peak time. The largest on-mountain facility, Whistler's Roundhouse Lodge, contains a particularly busy food court where, despite the presence of ushers to help you find space among over 2150 seats, locating a spot can be taxing. But you can't fault the vast array of reasonably priced cafeteria food, particularly the *Super Burritos* and *Roundhouse Wraps*. Whistler's several smaller on-mountain options are often less busy: these include the *Raven's Nest*, at the top of Creekside gondola, with made-to-order sandwiches and several daily soups, and *Chicpea*, at the summit of Garbanzo chairlift, known for its pizza slices and barbecue items. **Blackcomb's** biggest option is the Glacier Creek Lodge, which, like the Roundhouse, offers decent cafeteria food, including fresh sushi. Smaller alternatives include the Rendezvous Lodge for burgers, pizza, and Mexican food, and the *Cramped Crystal Hut*, which offers a variety of delicious stone-oven-cooked entrees. Despite its glorious setting, *Christine's*, the resort's elegant on-mountain restaurant at the top of the Solar Coaster chair, is best avoided in favor of the better-value options in the resort. The mountain's Fresh Tracks program ($15; ☎604/932-3434) is offered here, including a satisfying buffet breakfast for those prepared to rise early, taking lifts at 7.30am.

Inexpensive

Gaitor's Bar and Grill 7124 Nancy Greene Drive ☎604/938-5777. Tucked away in the Shoestring Lodge, a ten-minute walk from Whistler Village, *Gaitor's* has unexciting good-value food. Choose from a filling range of pastas, soups, burgers, and

decent Mexican eats, or graze from the well-priced lunch buffet on Saturdays and Sundays.
Gone Bakery and Soup Company 4205 Village Square, Whistler Village ☎604/892-5560. Small bakery with limited seating in an easily overlooked

location behind a bookshop. Excellent selection of fresh-baked breads and daily choice of homemade soups, sandwiches, and salads. Bargain prices by local standards, and a good place to stock up on picnic items.

La Brasserie des Artistes 4232 Village Stroll, Whistler Village ☎604/932-3569. Cheery spot serving what many think is the best breakfast in town. Try the eggs benedict with fluffy buttermilk pancakes or the decent omeletes. Service can be a bit hit or miss.

Ingrid's Village Café 4305 Skiers Approach, Whistler Village ☎604/932-7000. Drop in for good light breakfasts and lunches at reasonable prices. Sandwiches start at $4, burgers

(including veggie) around $6. Save time by grabbing items for later on the mountain. Open until 5pm.

Mogul's Coffee House 203-4204 Whistler Village Square ☎604/932-4845. One of several quiet coffeehouses in town that challenges *Starbucks'* dominance, this laid-back refueling spot has oversized muffins, cookies, and a selection of soups and wraps.

Splitz Grill 4369 Main St, Whistler Village ☎604/938-9300. Packed, tiny bistro dishing up unbeatable 5oz burgers, served with house-cut fries for $9. There's also lamb, chicken, Italian sausage, and veggie burgers, and, unusually for Whistler, a good kids' menu for $6.

Moderate

Caramba 4314 Main St, Whistler Village ☎604/938-1879. Unadventurous but cheerful, this family-oriented dining option has decent prices, including a two-person rotisserie platter for $33. The rest of the menu is mostly Italian-oriented, with pizzas, pastas, and grilled calamari.

Crepe Montagne 116-4368 Main St, Whistler Village ☎604/905-4444. Bustling family-owned restaurant based around imaginative crepes, from simple, sweet affairs to vegetable, meat, or salmon-filled offerings. Excellent raclettes and fondues also available. Open for breakfast, lunch, and dinner.

Monk's Grill 4555 Blackcomb Way, Upper Village ☎604/932-9677. Decent moderately priced steak-

house; the best place in town to placate carnivorous hankerings. Try the premium Alberta prime rib.

Pasta Lupino 4368 Main St ☎604/938-2040. Intimate, plainly decorated trattoria with a limited but excellent selection of homemade pastas, soups, and salads.

Trattoria di Umberto 4417 Sundial Place ☎604/932-5858. Casual but classy Italian restaurant where local seafood and veggies are crafted into fine Tuscan dishes, like the roast chicken with oregano and lemon, with stewed peppers, eggplant, zucchini, and tomatoes. Pastas cost around $11, meat and fish entrees $22–30. It's also a good choice for a more refined lunch, with dishes priced $7–14.

Expensive

Araxi's Restaurant and Lounge 4222 Village Square, Whistler Village ☎604/932-4540. Dependable upscale dining choice in a large, dimly lit restaurant at the center of Whistler Village. Ignore the slightly stiff atmosphere and enjoy delicious West Coast food like salmon, scallops, Atlantic char, braised rabbit, rack of lamb, and tenderloin. The Pemberton sheep cheese, veggies and herbs, and Okanagan tomatoes come from nearby farms and are well worth trying, as are the mussels in chili, vermouth, and lemon grass.

Bearfoot Bistro 4121 Village Green, Whistler Village ☎604/932-3433. Rather showy, pretentious playground for the decadent in the *Listel Whistler Hotel*. The menu is a maze of exclusive items such as duck foie gras and beluga caviar, where wild game entrees – like wild mushroom-stuffed pheasant breast – hit the $30 mark. The wine selection is vast, but expensive; reservations are essential.

La Rua 4557 Whistler Way ☎604/932-5011. Unassuming place where understated décor – red flagstone floors, modern oils on the walls – belies the quality and presentation of the food and the excellent service. You'll find all the local upscale favorites here, and some elegant renditions of Italian fare.

Rimrock Café 2117 Whistler Rd ☎604/932-5565. One of the oldest restaurants in town, with a small wood and stone dining room, 3.5km from Whistler Village toward Whistler Creek along Hwy-99. Worth the journey not only for its renowned seafood, but also for the racks of lamb and steak, as well as for a break from the bustle at the center of the resort.

Sushi Village 4272 Mountain Square, Whistler Village ☎604/932-3330. The best of five Japanese restaurants in Whistler suffers from its popularity, affecting service. Expect to wait at least 45 minutes to be seated for the first-class sushi. The combination plate is the best, and a relatively inexpensive choice for those unfamiliar with the cuisine. **The Wildflower** 4599 Chateau Blvd, North Village ☎6024/938-8000. Elegant dining option overlooking the ski slopes of Blackcomb, tucked away inside the ostentatious *Chateau Whistler* (see review p.507). Against a backdrop of cluttered décor, the menu offers a spread of Pacific Northwest cuisine. Sunday's brunch buffet ($40) is particularly appealing, and it's hard not to overindulge on the battery of superb options, which range from fresh fruits, yogurts, and cold cuts to waffles, omelets, seafood platters, and dim sum.

Drinking, nightlife, and entertainment

Considering its reputation as one of the continent's most exciting hotbeds of après-ski, the **nightlife** in Whistler is, though undoubtedly thriving, quite cliquey and ultimately rather bland. While some bars try to distinguish themselves with various gimmicks, the beer-swilling frat-crowd atmosphere is ubiquitous in most, with seasonal workers dictating where's cool and temporary visitors relentlessly bar-hopping in search of a better time. But despite the sorry state of the local scene, at least the resort's reputation always ensures a large volume of people bent on enjoying it.

As the slopes begin to empty out, the **slopeside bars** attract the brunt of the early evening action, with the *Garibaldi Lift Co.* at Whistler Village Gondola, *Merlin's Bar* in the Upper Village at the base of Blackcomb, and *Dusty's* at Whistler Creekside filling up quickly. After a brief ebb in the activity, the heaving masses reassemble in a select number of clubs in the center of Whistler Village. Last call is around 2am, but it pays to arrive early: covers ($5–10) aren't usually charged before 9pm, while after 10pm you can expect long lines to get into the most popular places. The situation is compounded during major competitions and **festivals**, including the early February Gay Ski Week. The larger celebrations, like the April World Ski and Snowboard Festival, come with their own events, particularly outdoor concerts. **Event information** is listed in the free local newspapers *Pique* and *Whistler This Week*, available from dispensers dotted around the resort. The local Sea and Sky radio station is another good source of entertainment information. Whistler also has two **cinemas**, the Rainbow Theatre, in the Whistler Conference Center (☎604/932-2422), and the Village 8 Cinema, in Whistler Village (☎604/932-5833).

The Amsterdam Café 4234 Village Stroll, Whistler Village ☎604/932-8334. Busy bar in a central location. Good place to people-watch and limber up for a night out, while chowing down on the usual range of bar food.

Black's Pub and Restaurant 4270 Mountain Square, Whistler Village ☎604/932-6408. Popular gathering-place for immediate après in view of lower-mountain runs at the base of Whistler. The pub has nine local microbrews, a massive selection of imports, and the town's most definitive whiskey collection. Pizzas are the best accompaniment here and, though only $13, are large enough for two. **The Boot Pub** 7124 Nancy Green Way ☎604/932-3338. Neighborhood pub in the Shoestring Lodge with regular live entertainment: rock bands and a twice-weekly strip show by the Boot Ballet. Play darts or shoot pool (free on Sundays). **Brewhouse** 4355 Blackcomb Way ☎604/905-2739. Lively microbrewery dotted with TVs and billiard tables. Food goes beyond standard bar grub with its decent Chinese noodles and stir-frys. Wash it all down with a choice of six of the *Brewhouse's* own beers: four ales including Frank's Nut Brown, a smooth and malty local offering, and two lagers, with Northern Light a particularly refreshing option. Great pre-club venue.

Buffalo Bill's 4122 Village Green, Timberline Lodge ☎604/932-6613. Mainstream bar and club that can be hit-or-miss. Clientele are mainly thirtysomethings, lured here by popular comedy nights, hypnosis shows, a dozen video screens, huge dance floor, and dated party music. **Dubh Linn Gate Old Irish Pub** 170-4320 Sundial Crescent, Whistler Village ☎604/905-4047. Sociable, Irish-style pub beneath the Pan Pacific Lodge, with a huge range of beers on tap (including Guinness) and regular live music. Food – mostly soups, sandwiches, and meat pies – is also good, and moderately priced.

Garfinkel's 1-4308 Main St, Whistler Village ☎604/932-2323, ⊛www.garfswhistler.com. Largest club in town, universally known as *Garf's* and a hopping, reliable venue for a good night out. Regular bands attract mostly college kids who blend preppy with grungy.

Hoz's Creekside 2129 Lake Placid Rd, Whistler Creekside ☎604/932-5940. Escape the resort scene at this off-the-beaten-path neighborhood bar, with reasonable prices and a down-to-earth atmosphere. An adjoining restaurant has a large menu of moderately priced pizzas, pasta, burgers, and more sophisticated entrees, including salmon, schnitzel, and steaks, plus reasonably priced daily specials.

Longhorn Saloon 4290 Mountain Square, Carleton Lodge, Whistler Village ☎604/932-5999. Cornerstone of post-slope boozing activities and also a good first stop on a night out, with mainstream tunes blasting out onto a large dance floor. Some of the best bar food in town, too, including an excellent burnt onion soup.

Mallard Bar 4599 Chateau Blvd ☎604/938-8000. Peaceful, relaxing spot in *Chateau Whistler*, for subdued, classy après ski, with fireside piano music and views over the base of Blackcomb Mountain.

Maxx Fish 4232 Village Stroll ☎604/932-1904. Self-consciously hip basement club with pounding hip-hop, house, and R&B from internationally known DJs and occasional live bands. Wednesday is a big locals' night, so get here early if you want to get in at all.

Savage Beagle Club 4222 Village Square, Whistler Village ☎604/938-3337. Stylish split-level club with cocktail and martini bar at ground level above a basement dance floor, where you'll hear anything from classic rock to salsa or hip-hop, depending on the night. The crowd here is slightly older and significantly less boisterous than at surrounding bars.

Tommy Africa's 4222 Village Square, Whistler Village ☎604/932-6090. Dingy club sporting an African theme – zebra-striped walls and thatched bars – where a big attraction is the wannabe go-go dancers, here to lure a disproportionate number of men into a mediocre night out.

Other activities and attractions

As one of North America's most highly commercialized resorts Whistler-Blackcomb offers almost every possible winter activity, most by several competing companies. The **Whistler Activity and Information Center**, just off Hwy-99 near Whistler Village, 4040 Whistler Way (daily 9am–5pm; ☎604/938-2769, ⊛www.mywhistler.com), does a useful job of summarizing all the opportunities; you can also book activities through them. The Chamber of Commerce, in Whistler Creek at 2097 Lake Placid Rd (daily 9am–5pm; ☎604/932-5528), is also a good source of fliers and contacts.

Despite suffering from unreliable low-altitude snow conditions, there's a reasonable web of local **cross-country skiing** trails around Whistler. The most convenient radiates from the Lost Lake ski area, next to the Blackcomb Mountain parking lot. Here, 28km of trails, from beginner to expert, fan out beyond the Whistler Nordic Center in the Nicklaus North Golf Clubhouse, where you can pick up trail day-passes for $10 and book **lessons**. Before you head out, be sure to pick up a local **trail map** from the Whistler Activity and Information Center, who can advise on where to go further afield and provide a list of companies offering backcountry ski trips.

Another way to explore the backcountry is by **snowshoeing**. Several companies in town offer equipment and guide service, including Whistler Outdoor Adventures (☎604/932-0647, ⊛www.adventureswhistler.com) who run trips from $40–65 for a four-hour trip that tours a local ghost town and includes lunch; they also rent snowshoes for $15 per day. Whistler Backcountry Adventures, 36-4312 Main St (☎604/932-4086 or 1-888/297-2222, ⊛www.whistlerbackcountry.com), specializes in **dogsledding** ($135 for two and a half hours) and **snowmobiling** trips (from $90 for two hours), with training on offer for complete novices. Other operators that run snowmobiling trips, at similar prices, include Canadian Snowmobile Adventures, located in the Carlton Lodge at 4290 Mountain Square, Whistler Village (☏604/938-1616, ⓦwww.canadiansnowmobile.com), and Blackcomb Snowmobile (☏604/905-7002, ⓦwww.snowmobiling.bc.ca).

For an old-fashioned **sleigh ride** around Whistler-Blackcomb visitors have plenty of choices, many including hot chocolate, bonfires, and a good deal of contrived joviality, often in the form of singalongs. One reliable company is Blackcomb Horse-drawn Sleigh Rides, 103-4338 Main St, Whistler (☏604/932-7631), which offers night tours up a wooded trail with fine views over Whistler's twinkling lights ($45 per adult).

For **ice-climbing** try Whistler Alpine Guides (☏604/938-3228, ⓦwww.whistleralpineguides.com) for regular guided trips. The Great Wall Underground, 4340 Sundial Crescent (daily 10am–10pm; ☏604/905-7625, ⓦwww.greatwallclimbing.com), is an indoor **climbing** facility located under the *Westbrook Hotel* in Upper Whistler Village. Day passes are $15, and the basic equipment package adds an extra $8; first-time climbers should take advantage of the $35 introductory lesson. The Great Wall is also one of the few local **kid-friendly activities** in town, with a program that lets kids be dropped off for a meal and climbing session, nightly between 6pm and 9pm.

Another good choice for **indoor recreation** is the municipal Meadow Park Sports Center, 8107 Camino Drive (☏604/938-3133), located 6km north of Whistler Village and served by the Alpine Meadows bus service. Here you'll find a pool, skating rink, hot tub, sauna, steam room, exercise room, and two squash courts. A useful alternative to hotel facilities are the pampering options offered by Whistler Body Wrap, St Andres House, Whistler Village (☏604/932-4710). A variety of **spa treatments** and salon services are offered, in addition to basic **massages** (thirty minutes for $50), including body wraps. A full-day herbal wrap with lunch costs $250.

Listings

Avalanche hotline ☏604/938-7676.
Bookstore Armchair Books, Whistler Village ☏604/932-5557.
Car rental Budget, *Holiday Inn Sunspree*, 4295 Blackcomb Way ☏604/932-1236; Thrifty, *Listel Whistler Hotel*, 4121 Village Green ☏604/938-0302.
Internet Electric Daisy Internet, Whistler Village ☏604/938-9961, and *Hotbox Coffee & Internet* ☏604/935-8648 – both charge around 20 cents per minute. There's also a free on-mountain

Internet service at Telus Telecommunication Center, on the first floor of Roundhouse Lodge (9am–2pm).
Medical emergencies Whistler Health Care Center, 4380 Lorimer Rd ☏604/932-4911, or The Town Plaza Medical Clinic, 40-4314 Main St ☏604/905-7089.
Pharmacy Nesters Market, 7019 Nesters Rd ☏604/932-3545.
Post office 106-4360 Lorimer Rd ☏604/932-5012.

Big White

A modern, characterless resort 54km southeast of Kelowna, **Big White** is often overlooked, even though it's Canada's fourth-largest ski area and has a very dependable supply of dry snow. In fact, snow often falls so thick and fast here that poor visibility, together with the ski area's predisposition for freezing fog, has led sniping locals to dub the resort "Big White-out." On a clear day, however, visitors will find a ski area that's both varied and easily explored, with short lines and a speedy lift system. The beginner and intermediate terrain is particularly diverse, with expansive groomed cruisers rolling downhill between ribbons of fantastic glade. Just be forewarned that some of Big White's trail classifications are misleading; in particular, the difficulty of the black and double black diamond terrain is vastly exaggerated.

Big White's sprawling **base village** focuses primarily on serving the family ski holiday. All accommodation has ski-in and ski-out convenience, and children are excellently catered for by the resort's Kids' Center, an extensive daycare facility. Yet for adults, the selection of restaurants and bars is lacking; those looking for nightlife will find the resort pretty dull, even though it's often packed with upbeat Australians who not only own and largely run the resort, but also visit in droves. Come prepared to entertain yourself or rent a car for forays to Kelowna.

Mountain info

Phone ☎250/765-3101 or 1-800/663-2772

Snow phone ☎250/765-7669 or 1-888/663-6882

Website ⊛www.bigwhite.com

Price $55

Operating times mid-Nov to mid-April daily 8.30am–3.30pm

No. of lifts 11, including 1 gondola and 3 surface lifts

Base elevation 1755m

Summit elevation 2319m

Vertical drop 77m

No. of trails 112

Acreage 7155

Beginner 18%

Intermediate 56%

Expert 26%

Average snowfall 750cm

Snowmaking No

Night skiing Yes (38 acres; late Dec to late April Tues–Sat 3.30–9pm; $19)

Nursery facilities Yes, from 18 months ☎250/765-3101

Arrival, information, and getting around

Kelowna International Airport (☎250/765-5125) is served by several daily flights from Vancouver, Calgary, and Seattle, each around an hour's flight away. The airport even receives direct flights from Toronto. Try Air Canada (☎1-888/247-2262), Westjet (☎1-800/538-5696), or Horizon Air (☎1-800/547-9308), which in particular goes out of its way to entice skiers, often offering good-value ski packages for $100 per person per night for three days skiing and lodging, with ground transport included.

Most flights to Kelowna International Airport are met by the **resort shuttle** (twelve daily; $60 round-trip; ☎250/765-888 or 1-800/663-2772; reserve three days in advance), which makes the 54km trip to Big White in 45 minutes. **Helicopters** from Big White (☎250/491-4244) can also pick you up from the airport for $450 one way for up to six passengers. Both transport options are also available for transfers to Silver Star Mountain. You can also rent a car, and of the companies based at the airport, Budget (☎250/765-8888 or 1-800/663-2772) is particularly convenient, since it offers one-way rentals between the airport and the resort. Thrifty (℡250/765-6655) and Rent-a-Wreck (℡250/763-6632) also have local offices.

Kelowna itself is served by Greyhound bus service from Vancouver (six daily; six hours; $58 one-way), Banff, and Calgary. The **bus terminal** at 2366 Leckie (℡250/860-3835) is 3km north of the town center, while the town's Infocenter, operated by the Chamber of Commerce, is on Hwy-97 as it travels through town, at 544 Harvey (8am–5pm; ℡250/861-1515 or 1-800/663-4345, Ⓦwww.kelownachamber.org).

The mountain

Spread out over three peaks, Big White offers a huge quantity of terrain, though much of it is tucked away, requiring some perseverance to find. There are good **beginner** and **intermediate** runs off every lift in the resort, and the Black Forest and Bullet Express lifts, which rise conveniently from the fringes of the base village, are the most popular. This area is particularly attractive when the weather's less favorable, with trees offering a break against wind and fog. But the runs here are really just the beginning of the available terrain: most of the mountain's best cruising and carving, along with the bulk of the **expert challenges**, are further from the base area at the opposite and markedly quieter end of the resort. Getting there's not hard – you just have to take a few overlapping lifts – but take a trail map to get back.

Beginner

The training ground for beginners is beside the **Plaza chair**, which runs beneath the base village. The runs here can be unnervingly busy, with better skiers moving between different areas of the ski hill. So once you've got the basics down, it's best to head over to the **Bullet** and **Black Forest chairs** for a good selection of less-crowded green runs and a few easy blues. And, despite the absence of a dense network of green runs elsewhere, make a point of exploring the rest of the ski area, as those that do exist are pleasant long cruises. Don't miss heading up the **Alpine t-bar** to explore the empty, gentle, summit plateau runs.

Intermediate

A glance at the trail map suggests that intermediates should head straight to the dense tangle of blues accessed from the **Ridge Rocket Express**. And many do, making this area of typically narrow cuts through trees the busiest on the mountain. But despite the quality and variety of runs here, a far better option, particularly if you're looking for fresh snow and fewer skiers, is to head to the fringes of the resort around the **Gem Lake Express**. Here the sweeping blue Kalina's Rainbow heads out into the Sun-Rype Bowl, an expansive magnet for fresh wind-blown snow that funnels into the relatively easy Black Bear Glades. From the base of the glades, Blue Ribbon heads down to the base of the lift, following a fast and varied fall line with rollers, steeps, and dips providing some of the most playful cruising on the mountain. During stormy weather, this area gets windswept, making it best to leave in favor of the sheltered and frequently groomed slopes served by the **Black Forest Express** at the opposite end of the resort.

Expert

Big White is short on expert terrain, with many of the designated black runs here equivalent to trickier blues in other resorts. Nevertheless, the Parachute

Heliskiing at Mount Arthur

Available to both skiers and riders based at either Big White or Silver Star (see pp.513 and 523), **heliskiing** on Mount Arthur is the best way to find fresh powder on untracked slopes. Only a ten-minute helicopter ride from Big White (a helicopter transfer is available from Silver Star), with fine views of the surrounding Monashee Mountains, a package of three runs and a picnic lunch costs around $800; it's possible to pay extra for additional runs.

Bowl, off the top of the desolate wind-blown plateau that's reached by the **Alpine t-bar**, is steep and powdery with a huge selection of difficult lines. Other than the Parachute Bowl, most of the resort's best expert terrain is hidden among trees. One area to repeatedly session is the glades below the **Gem Lake Express lift**, home to Blackjack, one of the best fall line runs on the mountain and ideal for high-speed carving. Other exhilarating tree runs can be found below Grizzly off the **Falcon chair**.

Freestyle

Big White is the regular site of notable freestyle **competitions**, including the Canadian National Snowboarding Championships. The main **terrain park** is between the Bullet and Black Forest Express lifts and contains a comprehensive collection of jumps and hits, as well as a strong boarder cross course – though the banks built for sweeping S-turns are a little low. Still, the nearby 450ft **halfpipe** is one of the finest in North America, with 12ft-high walls and 5ft transitions. A dedicated **beginner pipe** and **obstacle course** are located away from the more gung-ho freestylers in the main park, below the Ridge Rocket Express on Speculation.

Lift tickets, lessons, and rentals

Lift tickets at Big White cost $55 for the full day and $19 for night skiing. A ticket covering both is $60, while an afternoon pass costs $42, or $55 when combined with the night ticket. For **lessons** at Big White visitors have the choice of joining the sociable Mountain Adventure Club, a group lesson program that allows you to drop in for one ($39), three ($99), or five ($149) mornings for a two-hour lesson on each day. Private lessons cost $79 per hour for one and $30 for each additional person. If it's your first time on skis or a board, take advantage of the resort's Discover Programs; a good value at $49 for skiers and $59 for snowboarders, the package includes a two-hour lesson, rentals, and a lift ticket for the Plaza lift.

Virtually all the **equipment rental** at Big White is organized via a giant store in the Village Center. Basic ski rental packages cost $34 for the first day and around $20 for each additional day. Prices for snowboard packages are slightly more expensive, while high-performance ski packages cost an extra $10 per day.

Accommodation

With Kelowna a bit too far away to be a practical base, many skiers stay at Big White. Most lodging options here are self-catering **condo units**, though **hotels** and **hostels** are also present. Pretty much everything is available only through Central Reservations (☎250/765-8888 or 1-800/663-2772); try to get a place near the village plaza, location of all services, to avoid cold trudges back and forth around the sprawling resort.

Additional accommodation in the area – ideal for groups of four or more – is offered by Rent Chalets at Big White (☎250/765-9131 or ☎1-877/397-0956, ⊛www.rentchalets.com). Those with RVs can camp ($30 per night for full hook-up) near the base of the Black Forest Express lift; hot tubs and showers are conveniently adjacent. Should you need to stay in Kelowna, its Infocenter (see "Arrival, information, and getting around," p.513) can provide a list of the town's many accommodation options.

Chateau Big White Big White Resort ☎250/765-8888 or 1-800/663-2772. One of the resort's premier hotels, in a very central location, with a choice of 55 sleek units with comfy couches and warm lighting, ranging from studios with wood-clad kitchenettes to lofts and one-bedroom suites. Gas fireplaces, microwaves, and mini-fridges are standard; there's also a spa and an outdoor hot tub. ❺

Eagles Resort Big White Resort ☎250/765-8888 or 1-800/663-2772. Large modern condo complex that's a good family choice for its proximity to beginner areas; the simply furnished three-bedroom condos sleep up to twelve people. Units have well-equipped kitchens and gas fireplaces, and share a vast hot tub, sauna, and laundry with the other units. ❻

Graystokes Inn Big White Resort ☎250/765-8888 or 1-800/663-2772. Drab building just above the village center, with comfortable, inexpensive one- and two-bedroom condos filled with mismatched, dated furnishings. Some rooms have woodburning fireplaces, and facilities include an outdoor hot tub, sauna, and laundry. ❸

The Inn at Big White Big White Resort ☎250/765-8888 or 1-800/663-2772. Central, full-service hotel located just below the village plaza. Both the simply furnished rooms and one-bedroom suites are equipped with kitchenettes and gas fireplaces; the larger deluxe rooms have better views.

Facilities include the only outdoor pool in the resort, as well as a hot tub, fitness area, and laundry. ❺

SameSun Hostel Big White Resort ☎1-877/562-2783 or 250/765-2100, ⊛www.samesun.com. Huge, sociable hostel spread over two locations: the Alpine Center, on the upper fringes of the resort, and the SameSun Ski Lodge, a short walk above the center. The latter is reserved mainly for long-term guests, in private rooms with few communal facilities, while the Alpine Center has pool tables, TV rooms, laundry, Internet access, and several poorly maintained outdoor hot tubs. Dorm beds cost $20, while private rooms are $49 for a single, $59 for a double, or $79 for a room sleeping four, with kitchen and bathroom. A pancake breakfast is included in the rates.

White Crystal Inn Big White Resort ☎250/765-8888 or 1-800/663-2772. Smart hotel at the base of the Bullet Express lift, with panoramic views over surrounding mountains. On offer are spacious doubles, loft suites, and some two-bedroom suites for up to six people. Facilities include sauna, hot tub, and laundry. ❺

Whitefoot Lodge Big White Resort ☎250/765-8888 or 1-800/663-2772. Budget accommodation located above several stores at the lower end of the resort. Most rooms are simple, though there are some plusher one- and two-bedroom apartments. Guests share a hot tub, sauna, cold plunge, and laundry. ❸

Eating and drinking

There aren't many **places to eat** at Big White, and the choice of **nightlife** venues is even more limited. Still, almost all the options are decent, although limited capacity makes it wise to book ahead at all restaurants. The Mountain Mart and Deli (☎250/765-7666), a small supermarket in the Whitefoot Lodge, is the only place to stock up – so if you're considering **cooking for yourself**, head to a supermarket in Kelowna before journeying up to the resort. The cafeteria with outdoor barbecue in the Ridge Day Lodge, at the base of the Ridge Rocket Express, is the only **on-mountain option**, although choices in the village are convenient enough.

Beano's Big White Resort ☎250/765-3101 ext 291. Small café in a corner of the huge lobby of the Village Center. The coffee here is excellent, and for lunch, if the lines aren't too long, it's a good place to pick up a sandwich ($6) or a cup of hearty homemade soup ($7).

Big White Bakery Big White Resort ☎250/765-3101 ext 289. Hidden in the basement of the Village Center, this bakery is usually a bit quieter than *Beano's*, on the floor above; it's a good lunch option for a pizza slice, hot wraps, or rotisserie chicken ($7).

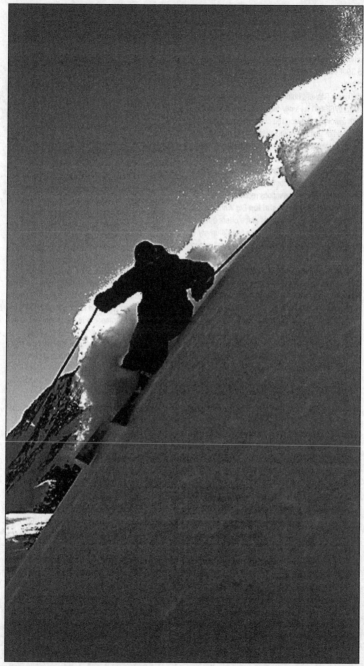

517

△ Skier carving through powder, Whistler, BC

China White Big White Resort ☎250/491-7780. Chinese restaurant with a huge, mostly Cantonese, menu. Pick from with a variety of chow meins (around $12) and chop sueys ($14), or try the satisfying, hugely varied buffet (11.30am–2pm and 5.30–8pm), on offer for $12 at lunch or $18 at dinner.

Coltino's Raakel's Hofbrauhaus, Big White Resort ☎250/765-5611. Family-friendly Italian restaurant with awful pastel décor. The crab and prawn cakes on a bed of linguini are the pick of the appetizers, while pasta, pizza, and meat entrees ($13–17) form the core of the main menu. Particularly tasty is the chicken parmigiana and the perfectly marinated lamb osso buco. Leave room for the outstanding tiramisu. Open daily 5–9pm; reservations recommended.

de Montreuil White Crystal Inn Big White Resort ☎250/491-9690. Small, quiet place offers a frequently changing menu with items like Cajun-style Alberta beef ($24) and local chicken breast braised with fennel, apple, carrot, onion, and white wine ($20). Put together your own multicourse meals for $32 for two courses or $44 for four. Adjacent to the restaurant is a subdued bar where the free pool and darts are the main attraction.

Kettle Valley Steak House Happy Valley Day Lodge, Big White Resort ☎250/491-0130. Moderately expensive steakhouse at the base of the Happy Valley gondola, where tasty Black Angus steaks are the cornerstone of a changing menu. Good wine selection.

The Powder Keg in the *Inn at Big White*, Big White Resort ☎250/491-2009. Bistro serving a range of pub food – wings, dips, and sandwiches – with the welcome addition of several Greek and vegetarian choices.

Raakel's Ridge Pub Big White Resort ☎250/765-5611. Dingy, sociable bar removed from most of the other evening hangouts in the resort, below the Village Plaza in the Hofbrauhaus. Pick up enormous and inexpensive portions of après fare, including burgers, pizzas, fries, wings, salads, and Quebecois-style *poutine*.

Snowshoe Sam's Big White Resort ☎250/765-1416. Split-level establishment with a decent, moderately priced restaurant on the first floor, and a cavernous, neighborhood-style bar – frequently the busiest drinking hole in town – filling the basement. Upstairs, choose from great steaks (from $20), chops, and seafood, or veggie options like tofu and bean penne ($13), peppercorn basil fettuccini ($16), and coconut cream curry ($18). Downstairs, gorge yourself on big portions of inexpensive pub food like nachos and burgers. Look out for live bands and DJs here, although the most flamboyant performance is in the restaurant: order a gunbarrel coffee and watch flaming Grand Marnier poured down the barrel of a shotgun into a glass of brandy cacao and whipped cream.

Other activities and attractions

Big White offers several **family activities** off the slopes. The main hub for organizing these is the Big White Activities Desk in the Village Center (☎250/491-4244), where you can book everything from snowshoeing, dogsledding, and horse-drawn wagon rides to snowmobiling and scenic helicopter flights. The helicopter flights cost around $200 for four people sharing a twenty-minute ride.

The best activity area, though, is the **Happy Valley Adventure Park**, linked by the eponymous gondola to the main village. Happy Valley is home to North America's largest **tube park**, where ten chutes spanning 1000ft are graded according to difficulty and serviced by two tows; two hours' tubing costs $13. The park also offers a free **ice-skating rink** (rentals from the Happy Valley Day Lodge) and a kids' snowmobiling track; it's also the start of the **cross-country** area, which encompasses 25km of trails. Cross-country skiers can use the Plaza Quad chair for free access to different parts of the trail system, but must purchase a $10 trail pass. Rental skis are available from the Village Center for $20 per day.

Listings

Bookstore Coles the Book People, 3151 Lakeshore Rd, Kelowna ☎250/868-3158.
Internet *China White* restaurant (see review above) has wireless access for $10 per hour.
Medical Whitefoot Medical Clinic ☎250/765-

0544. Walk-in clinic daily 3–6pm. Also massages.
Pharmacy Pharmasave, 3155 Lakeshore Rd, Kelowna ☎250/717-5331.
Post office Card Corner Misson Park, PO 28-3155, Lakeshore Rd, Kelowna ☎1-800/267-1177.

Sun Peaks

Wrapped around a snug base village at the northern end of the Okanagan Valley, **Sun Peaks** excels as a family destination. In the last decade a massive injection of capital, significant terrain expansions, and improvements and additions in both slope-side accommodation and on-mountain facilities have only fueled this reputation.

The slopes are ideal for intermediate cruising and strong beginners, with acres of impeccable grooming across a swath of wide runs. A few challenging bowls, chutes, and plenty of interesting glades do exist, and the resort provides more expert terrain than any other ski area in the Okanagan region, but difficult black diamonds are in short supply. Freestylers, however, have one of North America's biggest **terrain parks** and huge halfpipes at their disposal.

Because Sun Peaks is 50km from **Kamloops**, the closest functional city, most visitors base themselves in the self-contained village at the base of the lifts. Hotels, chalets, and B&Bs are dotted within walking distance of most amenities including a broad selection of restaurants and pubs, but visitors looking for nightlife beyond après have relatively few options.

Mountain info

Phone ☎250/578-7842 or 1-800/807-3257

Snow phone ☎250/578-7332

Website ⊛www.sunpeaksresort.com

Price $56

Operating times Mid-Nov to mid-April daily 8.30am–3.30pm

No. of lifts 10, including 5 surface lifts

Base elevation 1199m

Summit elevation 2080m

Vertical drop 881m

Number of trails 114 (including 12 gladed areas)

Acreage 3491

Beginner 20%

Intermediate 61%

Expert 19%

Average snowfall 559cm

Snowmaking Yes (80 acres)

Night skiing No

Nursery facilities Yes, from 18 months ☎250/578-5433.

Arrival, information, and getting around

A regional transport hub, **Kamloops** is well connected to the rest of western Canada. Both Air Canada and Canadian Airlines serve Kamloops airport from Calgary and Vancouver. From Vancouver **Via Rail** stops in Kamloops (three weekly; $75 one way; ☎250/372-5858 or 1-800/561-8630, ⊛www .viarail.com) en route to Edmonton. The resort is a four-hour drive along the TransCanada Highway from Vancouver; try Sun Peaks' own **shuttle bus** (Wed & Sat; $91 round-trip; $53 one way; 6hrs; ☎250/578-5467 or 1-800/807-3257) or the **Greyhound** bus (5 daily; $53 one way; ☎250/374-1212, ⊛www.greyhound.ca), which leaves its passengers at the Kamloops bus station at 725 Notre Dame Dr. The station is close to Hwy 1, location of the **Kamloops Visitor Information Center** (Mon–Fri 8.30am–4pm; ☎250/374-3377 or 1-800/662-1994, ⊛www.city.kamloops.bc.ca).

From Kamloops airport, train station, bus depot, or the town itself, take the Sun Star Shuttle (Six daily; $30 one way; ☎250/377-8481; 48 hours advance booking required) or the pricier option of taking a cab; try Sun Peaks Taxi (☎250/371-1665). A number of regular shuttle bus services operate between Sun Peaks and other regional resorts. The **Cahilty Lodge** in Sun Peaks runs a service to Whistler (Mon, Wed & Sat; 5hrs; $117 one way; ☎250/578-694 or

1-800/224-8424), while the resort (☎250/578-5467 or 1-800/807-3257) organizes buses to Silver Star ($85 one way; 3.25hrs) and Big White ($106 one way; 4hrs) on Wednesdays and Saturdays.

The mountain

First impressions of Sun Peaks, where a glance up at the hunched surrounding mountains suggests short runs and little vertical, can be deceiving. Only when you actually reach the summit and start heading in various directions does the ski area really open up; you can ski all day here and never do the same run twice.

Sun Peaks divides into four distinct areas, each accessed by a major lift; the **Sunburst Express** leaves the village to the majority of the resort's intermediate and expert runs. Climbing the flanks of Mount Tod is the extraordinarily slow **Burfield Quad**, which serves mostly expert terrain, while the nearby **Sundance Express** accesses a fine assortment of beginner runs, intermediate cruisers, and rolling trails as well as the resort's terrain park and halfpipe. The **Morrisey Express**, on the opposite side of the valley and connected to the Sundance area by a trail, boasts a cluster of consistent fall line intermediate runs.

The ski area divides naturally into terrain suitable for different abilities, and its layout is so easy to follow that the **mountain tours** offered from the top of the Sunburst chair (daily: 10am & 1pm) are almost redundant – though they do remain a useful way of discovering a couple of hidden treasures and finding companions with similar ability. For an informal skiing session with Olympic champion and director of skiing Nancy Greene – one of the resort's unique selling points – look for signs at the top of the Sunburst lifts indicating what times she'll be meeting guests here.

Beginner

With green options off every major lift, **beginners** have the run of the mountain, but will probably find themselves focusing on the learning terrain around the Sundance Express. The Platter lift at the base of this area serves the wide, uncongested runs snaking down gentle grades. By virtue of their width, the blue runs here are fairly easy; **Sundance**, below the lift, is the best place to start. Off Sunburst Express try the long, broad **Five Mile** trail and **The Sticks**, a secluded run off Mount Morrisey.

Intermediate

Strong **intermediates** should head to the broad, empty groomers off Sunburst Express, staying close to the liftline for the most consistent vertical drop. When the runs get choppier later in the day, head to the **Mount Morrissey** via the platter lift on the other side of the valley. Less confident intermediates, along with those in search of easy glades, should try the Sundance area.

Expert

Several adjacent black diamonds start from Sunburst Express; working down along the ridge line, each is generally harder than the one before, and the last two are challenging bump runs. If the Sunburst lift is too busy press on via the **Crystal chair** to the Crystal Bowl for enticing powder lines through steep, narrow chutes. Also off this chair is Spillway, perhaps the steepest groomed run in western Canada, and Head Walls, location of the annual Canadian Speed Skiing Championships on the last weekend of February. Yet much of the resort's best expert terrain is further from the base village, off the **Burfield Quad**. The lift is renowned not only for the tricky terrain below, but also the

Independent backcountry options

Freeriders should head to the **Gils**, an area accessed by a fifteen-minute hike from the top of Burfield Quad. Several unnamed and unmarked backcountry routes are located here. Almost all the lines descend to join the **five-mile** run back within the resort boundary – or at least hook up with an ungroomed cat track leading to this run. Discuss plans with the ski patrol before setting out. A safer backcountry option is to cat ski on the adjacent Mount Tod, an activity offered by the resort for $140 per day including lunch and a guide.

cold, slow ride up mountain. The base-to-summit trip takes over twenty minutes; consider using the mid-station to session one half of the mountain at a time. Most of the easier blacks are located in the top of the area, and the double blacks nearer the base. Try the steeps of **Freddy's Nightmare** and the wide, ungroomed **Challenger.** Hunt for powder stashes in the trees between **Father Toms** and **Mid Mountain.** Another dozen glade runs are scattered around the resort; the fastest tend to be off the Sundance chair, while the gladed areas between the black runs off the **Sunburst chair** are steeper and much more technical.

Freestyle

With approximately twenty acres beneath the Sundance Express lift, Sun Peaks has one of North America's biggest **terrain parks** and its huge halfpipes, array of jumps, and relaxed transitions should satisfy any **freestyler**. The banked slalom run here is particularly smooth, with riders easily flowing between the seven banked turns. The maintenance of the park is excellent and the halfpipes – which include a novice pipe – are dug into the ground, in good form even in poorer snow conditions. For a satisfying array of natural hits explore **Sunrise Glades**, just above the terrain park. Those looking for high-speed hits should head to Roller Coaster at the other end of the resort, beneath the Burfield Quad, where a series of rollers is large enough to huck.

Lift tickets, lessons and rentals

An adult ticket runs $56, with only small savings on multiday purchases, and half-day passes are slightly cheaper (around $10). Never-evers can save more by buying a $16 ticket only good for the Platter lift – useful only for your first day on the snow.

The resort's program of group **lessons** is divided into four categories based on ability level and is available for both skiers and boarders. The most basic, the Discover package ($65), includes a three-hour lesson, rental equipment, a lift pass for the Sundance lift, and lunch. If you've already grasped the basics, try the Breakthrough package ($74 with a two-hour lesson, full lift pass, and rental equipment included) or the Explorer program ($37), which includes a two-hour lesson. Experts have access to a range of two-hour Top of the World clinics ($42), specializing in bumps, powder, steeps, or park and pipe. Multiday lesson packages are available for three or five days ($117 and $203). The resort's private lessons, priced at $75 per hour, are costly and only worth it if you don't respond well to groups.

For rental gear, the resort shop at the base of the Sunburst lift offers competitive prices; basic ski packages come in at $28 for skis and $35 for snowboards. High-end equipment, telemark skis, and ski boards are also available. McSporties (☏250/578-6930), in the center of the village, are specialists in high-end demos and repairs; Oronge (☎250/578-8685) is the local snowboard rental and servicing authority.

Accommodation

Sun Peak's compact base village is filled with ski-in and ski-out accommodation and since all properties, with the exception of the hostel, have been developed in the last few years they are modern and furnished with the latest amenities. Central Reservations can book almost everything on the mountain (☎250/578-7710 or 1-800/807-3257). A short walk from the base village a large number of privately owned condos are available for rent, many managed by Peak Accommodations (☎250/578-2002 or 1-800/337-3257, ⓦwww.sunpeakshomes.com). If arriving with an RV you can **camp** in a lot located opposite the Sports Center for $20 per night with electric hookup; pre-register with Central Reservations.

Cahilty Lodge 3220 Village Way ☎250/578-6941 or 1-800/244-8424, ⓦwww.cahiltylodge.com. Comfortable slopeside lodge under management of Canada's Olympic champion Nancy Greene – whose medals are on display in the foyer. There's a dozen accommodations, from hotel rooms through studios with kitchenettes up to three-bedroom suites. Facilities include fitness center, hot tubs, and a laundry. ❸

Heffley Inn 3185 Creekside Way ☎250/578-8343. Central village hotel with decent, nondescript rooms and all the usual amenities – including kitchenettes – but the lodge's main draw is its number of room configurations, suiting anywhere from two to ten people. ❹

Horie Sun Lodge 2232 Sunburst Dr ☎250/578-0250, ⓦwww.sunlodge.com. Friendly, simply furnished bed and breakfast run by a hospitable elderly Japanese couple. A short walk from most village amenities, located at the base of two of the resort's signature runs. Most of the five rooms come with two queen beds, TV, and fireplace, though rooms with bunkbeds are also available. ❷

Pinnacle Lodge 2503 Eagle Court ☎250/578-7850 or 1-866/578-7850, ⓦwww.pinnaclelodgesunpeaks.com. Spacious Scandinavian-style hotel rooms in a fairly secluded spot a five-minute walk from the slopes. Premium rooms have a fireplace and oversized tubs. All guests have access to the hot tub and sauna. Continental breakfast included. ❺

Sun Peaks International Hostel 1140 Sun Peaks Road ☎250/578-0057, ⓦwww.sunpeakshostel.com. Friendly but cramped digs at the base of the Burfield Quad a ten-minute walk from the village. Beds are offered in dorms ($20 per night; $120 per week) as well as private double and twin rooms (all windowless and $50 per night). The hostel offers a communal kitchen, Internet access, storage lockers, a free pancake breakfast, and pick-up service from Kamloops. Guests can also pick up cheaper lift tickets (day tickets reduced by $6) and use the sports center for half price.

Sun Peaks Lodge 3180 Creekside Way ☎250/578-7878 or 1-800/333-9112. Simple hotel in the main village offering the most competitive ski packages in the resort; accommodation, lift pass, and buffet breakfast from $90 per person. Facilities include sauna and steam room. ❸

Sundance Lodge 3160 Creekside Way ☎250/578-0200 or 1-800/483-2888, ⓦwww.sundancelodge.com. Ski-in ski-out property at the center of the resort offering a choice of eight different room types, from generic hotel rooms to two-bedroom apartments sleeping up to six. All options are spacious, immaculately clean, simply furnished, and come with fridges and microwaves; some also have a kitchen and gas fire. The hotel's small fitness center has an outdoor hot tub overlooking the base of the ski hill. ❹

Eating and drinking

With Kamloops out of convenient range for a night out, most visitors head to one of the generally reliable village restaurants. The limited number of bars are popular for après; look for the two-for-one offers listed in the simple sheet of *Weekly Activities* produced by the resort. This also details a number of other evening events, like casino nights, that are laid-back, sociable, and ultimately quite enjoyable. The resort's premier event is its late-January annual Icewine Festival (ⓦwww.owfs.com), when a dozen of the local Okanagan vineyards converge on village hotels and restaurants with their wares every evening. If the base village isn't convenient enough for lunch, try the Sunburst Day Lodge at the top of the eponymous lift, which also serves breakfast – including a First Trax buffet ($14) which includes the run of pristine slopes afterward – and dinner to those torchlight skiing ($43). Book either event with the Resort Activity and Information Center (see "Other activities" below).

Bottom's Bar & Grill Sundance Lodge ☎250/578-0013. Boisterous bar with filling pub food and a good range of local beers on tap. Popular when the lifts close, especially when you can soak up rays on the deck outside.

Horie Sun Lodge 2232 Sunburst Dr ☎250/578-0250. Small, simply furnished restaurant in a slopeside location. The array of light food – sushi rolls (about $5 for eight pieces), udon soup ($8.50), and several spicy curries – make it an ideal lunch (noon–1pm) stop. Dinner is served 6–9pm, when you can bring your own alcohol.

Macker's Bistro & Bar 3220 Village Way ☎250/578-7894. Neighborhood bar in the Cahilty Lodge popular with locals. A range of delicious options from sumptuous egg breakfasts and traditional bar favorites to the dinner menu which includes Thai Gado Salad ($14), escargot ($15), pheasant ($19), or the succulent sea bass ($23). There's also a kids' menu, and food is served here later than anywhere else in the village. For a light, refreshingly tangy pint, try the Laughing Leprechaun.

Masa's Bar & Grill Village Day Lodge ☎250/578-5434. Sun Peaks social hub with great bar food – wings, soups, salads, sandwiches – and a good kids' menu. A lively crowd, the only dance floor in the resort, and live bands on weekends.

Mountain High Pizza 3170 Creekside Way ☎250/578-7272. Good range of takeout pizzas, subs, and pitas delivered free around Sun Peaks.

Powder Hounds 3170 Creekside Way ☎250/578-0014. Friendly, upscale restaurant with a wide selection of wines by the glass but a more limited menu. Choose from items like lamb shank osso buco braised with root vegetables, saffron, and red wine ($19), Chianti tenderloin ($27), or a range of excellent gourmet pastas ($14) for vegetarians.

Servus 3170 Creekside Way, Hearthstone Lodge ☎250/578-7383. Small Austrian restaurant with a range of carefully prepared dishes. When available, the chowder soup is a superb start to any meal, but leave room for entrees like the rich seared duck breast, squash gnocchi, or the delicious two-person raclette Walliser. Entrees start at $17.

Val Senales 3180 Creekside Way, Sun Peaks Lodge ☎250/578-7878. Plain restaurant whose décor is far outdone by the enticing menu; even old standbys get a new spin, like pork loin cured in raspberry tea. Evenly split between seafood and meat, most entrees run from $20 to $25. The international seafood sampler is a good starter for two. The restaurant is also open daily for a buffet breakfast which, priced at $12, is great value.

Other activities and attractions

The **Resort Activity and Information Center** (☎250/578-5542) in Village Day Lodge can book dogsled rides, sleigh rides (from $21), and snowmobile tours (from $117 for two hours). Snowshoeing tours are also offered (from $24). Snowshoes and cross-country ski rentals are available at the Village Day Lodge. Explore the free network of trails in the area, including 10km of track-set trails and an additional 40km of trails – around half are groomed. For more cross-country skiing, try the Stake Lake Trails (☎250/372-5514), a web of 45km of groomed trails a 25-minute drive from Kamloops. Back in the village, visit the **Sports Center** ($6 daily noon–10pm; ☎250/578-7843) for its outdoor pool and hot tub and to ice skate or play drop-in hockey ($4 for skate and stick rentals).

Listings

Bookstore Several in Kamloops including Chapters Inc 1395 Hillside Drive #4 ☎250/377-8468.
Internet Java Net Café, Fireside Lodge ☎250/578-2085; Alpine Images, *Heffley Inn* ☎250/578-0424.
Medical On-call medical services in resort

☎250/319-8111; Royal Inland Hospital, ☎311 Columbia St, Kamloops ☎250/374-5111.
Pharmacy None in resort; Pratt's Pharmacy, 321 Nicola St ☎250/374-7226, is in downtown Kamloops.
Post office 301 Seymour St, Kamloops.

Heliskiing around the Okanagan Valley

Heliskiing in the Okanagan region is dominated by TLH Heli-skiing (☎ 250/558-5379 or 1-800/667-4854, ⊛ www.tlhheliskiing) operating from Tyax Mountain Lake Resort on the shore of Tyaughton Lake. They service an enormous 1200-square-mile stomping ground of a bewildering matrix of valleys in the remote and heavily glaciated Chilcotin Mountains. In contrast to many heliski operations elsewhere, the snow pack is significantly more stable here, opening up more lines and steeps than normally available to heliskiers. TLH also arranges ice fishing, snowmobiling, snowshoeing, and sleigh-riding trips. Packages include lodging, skiing, equipment rental, and all meals; a three-day high-season package costs around $3000 per person. Overland transfers are offered from Whistler, a resort with which combined packages are offered.

TLH's sister company is **Last Frontier Heli-Skiing** (☎ 250/558-7980 or 1-888/655-5566, ⊛ www.tlhheliskiing.com/lfh), which offers the most remote commercial heliskiing in North America – flying from a lodge in northern British Columbia, near the Alaskan Panhandle. Not for the initiated, this region is full of huge powder bowls, tight tree runs, and vast glaciers. Many slopes are unnamed and unexplored, so there's a good chance of being the first ever to ski some areas. Packages start at $5300 and include meals, accommodation, and transfers.

Silver Star

Just northeast of Okanagan Lake, **Silver Star**'s base village is a disarmingly kitsch, faintly absurd, technicolor town straight out of a Disney movie, done up in multi-hued gingerbread style to comply with local building codes. The adjacent ski area, however, doesn't appear nearly as frivolous, with plenty of variety, an abundance of untracked powder, and a natural division of terrain, even if the layout is fairly unusual: many runs either begin or end with long traverses from the lifts, a headache for snowboarders.

Silver Star is only partway through an ambitious ten-year master plan set to double the acreage and triple the accommodation. Now owned by Big White (see p.513), the two are bound together, most visibly through the development of frequent bus and helicopter shuttle services and the development of a common lift pass. Yet Silver Star remains a relatively small operation; choices of hotels and restaurants are limited, so it's better to head to the nearest town of **Vernon** some 22km southwest.

Mountain info

Phone ☎ 250/542-0224
Snow phone ☎ 250/542-1745
Website ⊛ www.skisilverstar.com
Price $59
Operating times Mid-Nov to mid April daily 8.30am–3.30pm; night skiing Thurs & Sat 3.30pm–8pm; Fri 3.30–9pm.
No. of lifts 12, including 7 surface
Base elevation 1155m
Summit elevation 1915m
Vertical drop 760m
Number of trails 107
Acreage 2725
Beginner 20%
Intermediate 50%
Expert 30%
Average snowfall 700cm
Snowmaking No
Night skiing Yes (8 runs; $21)
Nursery facilities Yes, from newborn ☎ 250/558-6028

Arrival, information, and getting around

The closest **airport** to Silver Star is Kelowna Regional Airport, a short flight from Vancouver, Calgary, and Seattle and a little over an hour's drive (64km) from the resort. Airport **shuttles** are operated by Country Coachways ($60 round-trip; ℡250/542-7574, Ⓦwww.vernonairporter.com) and require advance booking.

Silver Star is a 545km, six-hour **drive** from Vancouver following the route along TransCanada Hwy 1. The **Greyhound** bus from Vancouver drops passengers at Vernon's depot, 3102 30th St (five daily 8hrs; $63 one way ℡250/545-0527) and heads to and from Calgary. Around 4km south of the Greyhound station along Hwy 97 is Vernon's Chamber of Commerce (Mon–Fri 9am–5pm; ℡250/545-0771 or 1-800/665-0795, Ⓦwww.vernontourism.com), the local source of **visitor information**. Transport from Vernon to the resort requires a cab (Vernon Taxi ℡250/545-3337), except during weekends and holidays when a shuttle ($4) operated by BC Transit runs along the route.

Once at the **resort** walking is the best option, though a shuttle bus ($1 per ride 8am–4.30pm) loops around the area's peripheral developments until 10pm, with a couple of daily runs to the Sovereign Lakes Cross-Country Area and a weekly trip to Vernon as well.

An intermountain shuttle service transports guests between Silver Star and Big White (see p.513) every Wednesday, Thursday, and Saturday ($30; ℡250/558-6093).

The mountain

The mellow runs near the base village contrast dramatically with Silver Star's overall terrain. Far from being carpeted by the broad, relatively gentle pistes here, many runs are narrow, challenging cuts through forested slopes. Finding quality novice and intermediate terrain is simply a matter of shuffling beyond the base village, but the expert challenges are further afield and require some hunting down. The free mountain tours that leave from the village plaza at 10am and 1pm are particularly recommended for better skiers.

Aside from the tiny **Silver Queen** beginner zone, Silver Star divides into two distinct areas linked together via a couple of green runs at the summit. Adjacent to the resort village, the **Vance Creek** region is largely beginner and inter-mediate terrain. **Putnam Creek** is the expert area with runs filtering down to a single high-speed quad. The shallow pitches that link the two areas can be tiresome – particularly for snowboarders; most visitors tend to settle into one area or the other. Additionally, the long traverses to and from the Putnam Creek Express can also be exhausting for snowboarders; many stay in the Vance Creek zone, missing the best powder in Putnam Creek's deep sheltered bowls and chutes.

Beginner

Segregated from speedy skiers, newbies should head to the gentle, relatively quiet hill accessed by the **Silver Queen**. With some practice all the greens on the main mountain should be within a beginner's grasp. Some greens are clut-tered by fast skiers and boarders shuttling themselves to different parts of the ski area. It's best for novices to stick to **Far Out**, the quietest of beginning runs, or head to Eldorado, graded blue – and for a short stretch even black – but for-givingly wide and extremely quiet.

Intermediate

Despite a smattering of blue runs – most notably Gypsy Queen and Sunny Ridge – Putnam Creek is beyond the grasp of all but the most confident intermediates. Stick to the **Vance Creek** area where a group of relatively wide blue runs offer fine cruising on rolling terrain. **Whiskey Jack** has the best fall lines and, given a series of smooth transitions between rollers, is deservedly popular.

Expert

Arrive early enough at Putnam Creek and you should be able to get fresh tracks down for at least three or four runs. Warm up on **Caliper Ridge** below the lift and preview the narrower and steeper trails nearby, including **Holy Smoke** and **Bon Diablo,** both black diamonds that develop bumps later in the day, lined by occasional natural hits and short drops. Far more difficult is the precipitous gully run of **Spirit Bowl** between the two. Other gully runs worth exploring are the forested piste of **Stardust** and ungroomed **Valhalla Ridge**, labeled a backcountry area by the resort but still within bounds. On the Vance Creek side, all the moguls and steeps are clustered around the **Attridge Area**. The ultimate quest for powder locally, however, is to go **heli-skiing** – an activity run in conjunction with Big White (see p.523), to which shuttles are provided.

Freestyle

In the Vance Creek area Silver Star offers **freestylers** a variety of features in two terrain parks, including an Olympic standard halfpipe and a speedy boardercross run. The rest of the park resembles an old-school skate park, where dips and lips provide limited airtime and appealing lines. For **natural hits** head to the gullies on the Putnam Creek side, particularly **Three Wise Men** for obstacles scattered at its base or the series of drops along a creekbed in the trees between **Cat Man Do** and **Gong Show**.

Lift tickets, lessons, and rentals

Day tickets cost $59 per day or $67 with night skiing ($21) included. Multiday passes include night skiing, are available for any number of days, and allow savings of $20 for a five-day pass.

The resort's ski school (℡250/558-6056) offers private **lessons** for $85 per hour. Group lessons cost $44 for two hours and can be bought as a bundle of five in a "ski week" for $170. The resorts beginners' package includes ticket, lesson, and rentals at $53 for skiers or $64 for snowboarders.

The resort rental shop charges $36 per day for skis, boots, and poles (an extra $10 for high-performance versions) and $44 for snowboard and boots. Also at the resort, Geo's Rental Shop (℡250/558-6007) has ski packages for $37 per day and snowboards for $39. Weekly rates are available.

Accommodation

There's plenty of reasonably priced and varied accommodation in and around Silver Star's small, tacky resort village. Contact the resort's central reservations (℡1-800/663-4431), where pass and lodging packages are offered from around $100 per person. If you have an RV, you can hook it up in the lot at the resort; full hook-up costs $23 per day. The only reason to stay outside the resort is if you're looking for a cosy **B&B** or the marginally lower accommodation prices in Vernon.

Castle on the Mountain 8227 Silver Star Rd ℡250/542-4593 or 1-800/667-2229. Faux-Tudor B&B 10km east of Silver Star set back from Hwy 97. Rooms vary in size and price but all are spacious and have glitzy, somewhat tacky interior furnishings. The friendly owners also run a commercial art gallery on the premises. ❸

Creekside Condominums Silver Star Mountain Resort ℡250/558-7825 or 1-877/630-7827, Ⓦwww.staraccommodation.com. Group of centrally located condominiums in blocks containing studio, one- and two-bedroom units. Kitchens and gas fireplaces are standard, though facilities and decor do vary. All units have individual photos on the management company's website. ❹

Highwayman Motel 3500 32nd St ℡250/545-2148 or 1-877/667-0599. In downtown Vernon – one of many on 32nd Street – with clean standard rooms and weekly rates available. ❷

Lord Aberdeen Apartment Hotel ℡250/542-1992 or 1-800/553-5885, Ⓦwww.lordaberdeen.com. Small, central apartment block with bland but comfortable one- and two-bedroom units equipped with full kitchens (stove, fridge, dishwasher, microwave, and coffeemaker) and with access to a sauna. ❺

Putnam Station Inn Silver Star Mountain Resort ℡250/542-2459 or 1-800/489-0599, Ⓦwww.putnamstation.com. Cozy hotel at the center of the resort, built in the style of a nineteenth-century railway station and filled with appropriate curios. Rooms span from regular hotel rooms (with refrigerators) to one- and two-bedroom suites with kitchenettes. An outdoor hot tub overlooks the resort's central plaza. ❺

Samesum Ski Hostel 9898 Pinnacles Rd, Silver Star Mountain Resort ℡250/545-8933, Ⓦwww.samesun.com. Clean, spacious hostel with dorm beds ($20) and private rooms with shared bathroom ($59 for two people). A large kitchen adjoins a sprawling social area and TV room. Linen and a pancake breakfast are included.

Silver Lode Inn Silver Star Mountain Resort ℡250-549-5105 or 1-800/554-4881, Ⓦwww.silverlode.com. The resort's least expensive hotel with simple, brightly decorated rooms, some with fireplaces and kitchenettes. Amenities include an indoor hot tub. ❹

Silver Star B&B 7981 Silver Star Rd ℡250/558-1688, Ⓦwww.ingenius.bc.ca/silverstar. The closest of several B&Bs near the resort – on the road between Silver Star (7km away) and Vernon – this large, modern family home offers three snug, florally decorated rooms that share a guest kitchen and living room. ❷

Silver Star Club Resort Silver Star Mountain Resort, ℡250/549-5191 or 1-800/610-0805, Ⓦwww.silverstarclubresort.com. The hub of Silver Star village, this three-building complex offers a selection of accommodations, from standard hotel rooms to suites sleeping up to six people. Larger units have full kitchen and fireplace and all guests have access to the rooftop hot tubs and a small fitness center. ❹

Eating, drinking, and entertainment

Finding lively places to **eat**, **drink**, or **party** after dark in Silver Star can be a bit of a struggle. Almost all the restaurants are open and convenient for lunch; on-mountain dining is limited to Paradise Camp at the midstation of the Putnam Creek Express. For a rundown of resort activities, seek out the *Entertainment Weekly* flyer in foyers of most hotels. There's the occasional movie at the National Altitude Training Center (see overleaf), and live bands play on weekends. **Vernon** is better for evening activity, with movie theaters, a bowling alley, and restaurants. If you're traveling through Vernon by car and intend to cook for yourself be sure to stock up in the large supermarkets here, as the small grocery and liquor shore at the Aberdeen Deli Company (see below) has only a small selection of items. All the places below are located in the resort.

Aberdeen Deli Company ℡250/260-4904. Small deli with a few tables offering picnic foods including soups, pizza, bruschetta, spanakopita, samosas, and salads.

Cellar Lounge ℡250/542-2459. Basement bar in the *Putnam Station Inn* and the best place for mulled wine and Tapas in front of a roaring fire. Always cozy, but blows hot and cold as a nightlife venue.

Clementines ℡250/549-5191. Popular but unspectacular family dining option above the Vance Creek Saloon featuring good-value prime rib, sushi, and buffet nights.

Craigellachie Dining Room ℡250/542-2459. Snug, wood-clad dining room in *Putnam Station Inn* offering pastas ($13), seafood, and steaks ($16) along with a few more interesting options like the chicken cordon bleu ($16) served alongside a decent selection of local wines. Pick up gargantu-an burgers for lunch here.

Italian Garden ⊤250/549-5191. Simple bistro dishing up quality pasta and pizza at very reasonable prices. Try the delicious gourmet slices for a quick lunch.

Long John's ⊤250/542-1992. The resort's busiest pub due in part to the tasty bar food, especially the huge portion of nachos ($8). There's a selection of entrees (around $10) including pastas, sandwiches, fish and chips, mussels, and burgers, including a mouthwatering portabello mushroom incarnation soaked in garlic oil and red wine.

The Silver Lode Inn ⊤250/549-5105. Swiss-style restaurant specializing in expensive alpine dishes. The raclette ($43) and cheese fondue ($43) are excellent, as is the seafood, including the pan-fried halibut with baby prawns ($20) or the seafood linguini ($20). The *Silver Lode* serves the best steaks on the mountain and offers a Thursday night buffet.

Vance Creek Saloon ⊤250/549-5191. The largest bar in town is usually empty, with its few patrons dotted around the pool and fussball tables. But on Wednesday and Saturday nights it gets livelier, with bands bringing in the crowds. Light meals are available until midnight.

Other activities and attractions

Most winter activities on offer are conveniently located beside Brewer's Pond at the base of the Silver Queen area, adjacent to the center of the resort. Brewer's Pond is open for ice-skating (daily 9am–9pm), with skate rentals available at the Silver Queen Day Lodge. Next door, **Tube Town** (Mon–Wed 3.30–9pm; Thurs–Sat 10am–9pm, ⊤250/269-5302; 2hrs $14) offers three groomed runs included in the price of any lift ticket. There's also a mini **snowmobile** park here, run by Silver Star **Snowmobile Adventures** (⊤250/558-5575 or 1-800/416-5794), designed for children to explore local forest trails on mini snowmobiles for $3 per lap. Adults can take snowmobile tours of a local provincial park, lasting from one to four hours. **Dogsled rides** (⊤250/545-3901) and **sleigh rides** (daily 9am–10pm, ⊤250/558-6039) can be arranged from Brewer's Pond. If you'd rather rely on your own legs to explore the area you can **snowshoe** with Valhalla Pure (⊤250/558-4292, ⓦwww.valhalla-pure.com); afternoon, evening, and night walks cost $25 per adult.

The main attraction is the 105km of groomed and track-set **cross-country** skiing trails, many around Soverign Lake where 4km are lit for night skiing, along with three warming huts around the network. Unlike most resorts, the cross-country trails cross the downhill ski area, with trails stretching from top to bottom, connecting and merging in several places, including some strenuous climbs. The popularity of these trails is increased by the presence of the **National Altitude Training Center** (⊤250/549-6722), which attracts an international clientele of cross-country athletes and has two biathlon ranges. Day passes ($14) to use the network can be picked up here, and lessons are also available. A package including a pass, lesson, and rental equipment costs $37, or you can pick up rentals at Geo's Rental Shop (⊤250/558-6007) in the village center for $18 per day. The National Altitude Training Center also has its own fitness room, swimming pool, and **climbing wall** (lessons and rentals available). **Yoga classes** and massages (half-hour for $70) are available. For a quick soak head to **Doc Simmon's Soak and Swim** (2.30pm–8pm) at the center of the resort village. It's a no-frills pool and hot tub facility, free to all those staying at the resort.

Listings

Bookstore Bookland, 3400 30th Ave, Vernon ⊤250/545-1885.
Internet *Samesun Ski Hostel* (see overleaf); Oakanagan Regional Library ⊤250/542-7610.
Medical Vernon Jubilee Hospital, 2101 32nd St,

Vernon ⊤250/545-2211 or 1-800/456-6622.
Pharmacy Nolan's Pharmasave, 3101 30th Ave, Vernon ⊤250/542-2929.
Post office Vernon Stn Main, 3101 32nd Ave ⊤1-800/267-1177.

The Best of the Rest

Apex

Deep in British Columbia's interior, Apex (☎250/292-8222, ⓦwww .apexresort.com; $35 adults, $25 juniors) is one of the smaller resorts in the Okanagan region. Located 7km from Penticton, it packs sixty runs into only 550 acres of terrain, with a vertical drop of 605m, all serviced by four, uncrowded lifts (two are surface tows). The majority of the terrain is for inter-mediates and experts; its skiing ranges from comfortable cruising on wide groomers to long intimidating mogul fields, steep chutes, and huge powder bowls. But for expert skiers, one of the main attractions here is Apex Peak, locally referred to as Proper, a fearsome, enticing backcountry area. Six runs are lit for night skiing and around 60km of cross-country trails, half groomed and trackset, are nearby. Snowmobiling, sleigh rides, and ice-skating are also offered through the resort.

Cypress Mountain

Cypress Mountain (☎604/419-7669, ⓦwww.cypressmountain.com; $36 adults, $17 juniors) doesn't provide the spectacular views over Vancouver as does Grouse (see below), but overall it's the most challenging mountain in the city's vicinity (around 15km from downtown) with forty percent of the runs graded expert. Advanced skiers will appreciate over 500m of vertical drop, though with little more than 200 acres many skiers will bore quickly. The area's 25 runs are open for night skiing, usually until 11pm, though hours can vary - call ahead. Shuttle buses to the resort are provided from Park Royal in west Vancouver for $10 round-trip. (☎604/878-9229).

Forbidden Plateau

Forbidden Plateau (☎250/334-4744, ⓦwww.forbidden.bc.ca; $28 adults, jun-iors $22) is much smaller than its Vancouver Island neighbor Mount Washington (see p.530), with only 340 acres served by three t-bars and a tow rope. But it's generally a cheaper, quieter option better suited for beginners, with half the terrain rated novice and few expert runs available. The 350m of vertical drop, 22 runs, and small terrain park are enough to attract local freerid-ers, particularly at night, when a third of the runs are open for night skiing. Access to Mount Washington and Forbidden Plateau from the mainland requires a ferry ride from Horseshoe Bay – just north of Vancouver – to Nanaimo on Vancouver Island.

Grouse Mountain

The terrain at Grouse Mountain (☎604/980-9311, ⓦwww.grousemountain .com; $25 adults, $15 juniors) is largely unexceptional, but the resort has made a lot out of what little they have. Particularly notable are the magnificent views over nearby Vancouver – especially spectacular during the night – and worth-while if you're in the mood for a short burst of winter activity. A twenty-minute drive from downtown, the resort is served by local buses every half-hour (#236 from Lonsdale Quay or #232 from Phibbs Exchange). Once at the ski area an aerial tram takes you to the summit from where the 369m vertical runs through 202 acres of terrain harbouring 22 runs – 13 of which are open for night skiing, daily until 10pm. Eighty percent of the terrain is evenly split between novice and intermediate runs, and fairly decent snow quality is ensured with 75 percent snowmaking capacity.

Harper Mountain

Beyond the upper reaches of the Okanagan Valley, on the fringes of Kamloops, Harper Mountain (℡250/573-5115; $25 adults, $18 juniors) is a tiny local alternative to Sun Peaks (see p.518). With only 400 acres and a vertical drop of only 427m, Harper is substantially smaller than its neighbor, though Harper is cheaper and offers night skiing not available at Sun Peaks. The terrain – half of which is intermediate, the rest equally divided between beginner and advanced – is decent enough to justify dropping in if you're in the area. All its fifteen trails are below treeline and funnel back to the day lodge. Novices should try smooth Big Bend, while intermediates should head to mellow Spillway for its mix of pitches.

Hemlock Valley

Sleepy Hemlock Valley (℡604/797-4411; ⓦwww.hemlockvalley.com; $30 adults, $16 juniors), with its 300 acres of terrain and vertical drop of 366m, is the largest of the interior resorts and the closest to Vancouver 144km to the east. Its dry snow covers 34 predominantly intermediate, fairly bland runs – most above treeline – and a couple of bowls. Hemlock does, however, have its share of hardcore devotees, here for the uncrowded slopes and puny liftlines. The resort, folded 1000m into the mountains near Harrison Hot Springs, the nearest town, offers condominiums, chalets, and townhouses in addition to tobogganing, cross-country skiing, and snowshoeing.

Manning Park

East of Vancouver, 264km into British Columbia's interior, Manning Park (℡250/840-8822, ⓦwww.manningparkresort.com; $31 adults $19 juniors) is a small, family-oriented resort with only 180 acres of varied terrain. Lifts are all fairly basic, but the resort uses its 430m of vertical well, keeping the varied runs in great shape. The bonus here is the fabulous scenery of the surrounding Manning Provincial Park, an area that lures cross-country skiers with its 190km of backcountry trails. You can also toboggan and ice skate and use designated snowshoe trails around the resort for free (rentals available).

Mount Washington

Mount Washington (℡250/338-1386, ⓦwww.mtwashington.bc.ca; adults $44, juniors $23) benefits from its location on Vancouver Island's mountainous spine, against which Pacific storms barrel, resulting in vast amounts – around 975cm annually – of heavy, wet snow. Located near the quaint town of Courtney, Mount Washington has a small resort village and a sizeable 500m vertical drop. The ski area spreads over 1500 acres and has an exceptional variety in both terrain and conditions; on the same run you can move from light powder to heavy corn snow via rock-hard moguls and smooth corduroy. The bulk of the terrain is typified by sweeping runs with rollers and intermittent steeps; the presence of gladed areas and two terrain parks with a halfpipe offer trickier alternatives for freestylers. The resort also maintains a 40km cross-country network.

Ski Smithers

The largest ski area in northern British Columbia, Ski Smithers (☎250/847-2058, ⓦwww.skismithers.com; $31 adults, $18 juniors) is near its eponymous town, a 1430km drive from Vancouver. This may seem like a long way to go for a resort with four lifts, of which three are surface tows, but if you absolutely need slopes to yourself and are jaded by the crowds around Vancouver and Whistler, it may be worth it. The ski area consists of only around 300 acres of terrain and 534m of vertical, but the snow is fantastic. Another 900m of vertical are available further up the mountain, reserved for those willing to hike. Another possibility for the independent is to ski the 24km back to town – though you'll want to find a local guide for this. Smithers has a decent quantity of backcountry cross-country trails and a fair array of accommodation, restaurants, and pubs.

Glossary

Glossary

Après-ski Also just known as *après*; post-ski entertainment, usually involving drinking, dancing, and eating.

Avalanche-control The triggering of avalanches through artificial means – usually with controlled explosions – to make a slope safe for skiers and riders.

Backcountry skiing Used to describe skiing **off-piste**, either in-bounds or out of bounds, and frequently describes cross-country skiing away from track-set trails.

Berm Snowbank, often used to provide stability on the outside of a turn.

Black diamond Expert trail denoted on maps and trail signs by a black diamond.

Boardercross Course designed for snowboarders to race against each other; typically involving bank turns and jumps. Skiercross competitions exist, but are less common.

Bowl Mountain basin.

Bumps Large rounded masses of snow, also called moguls, caused by skiers turning.

Bunny slope Slope used by absolute beginners.

Burton's Learn-to-Ride A snowboard instruction program offered at a handful of top resorts, run by Burton snowboard company. The program includes specially designed boards with deep sidecuts that allow for easier turns and help prevent bone-jarring falls.

Carving Series of clean turns made using the edge of a ski or snowboard.

Cat skiing or boarding Using a snowcat rather than lifts to reach a summit.

Cat track Track used by snowcats, typically a mountain road connecting two runs; also called **catwalk**.

Catwalk See **cat track**.

Chute Steep, narrow gully.

Cirque Steep-walled semicircular mountain basin, its sides generally steeper than those of a **bowl**.

Corduroy Freshly groomed snow, perfect for **carving**.

Corn snow Granular snow generally occurring in spring.

Cornice Overhanging mass of snow or ice formed by wind on the downwind side of a ridge.

Couloirs See **chute**.

Cross-country skiing Using skis longer and thinner than downhill counterparts to explore flat trails typically limited to following track-set trails – parallel grooves made by grooming machinery. Also called Nordic skiing.

Crust An icy top layer on snow that intermittently supports the weight of a skier or boarder.

Edge The sharpened part of a ski or board on either side of the base, usually made of carbon steel, that bites into the snow on turning. **Edging** a ski or board is to tilt so that you balance on the edge; in motion this becomes **carving**.

Face shots Action of snow blowing against face on turning because of its light, fluffy, and deep nature.

Fall line Most direct route downhill; in line with gravity and the route water naturally takes.

First tracks Applied to those skiers who are the first to ride and carve the slopes in the morning.

Freeriding or freeskiing Snowboarding or skiing that embraces the whole possible spectrum of terrain, from smooth carving to awkward off-piste jumps.

Freestyle Skiing or snowboarding that primarily focuses on tricks performed on the pipe or terrain park.

Fun box Box made to enable a variety of tricks in a terrain park.

Glade skiing Skiing through woodland; frequently where gaps between trees have been widened through off-season grooming.

Goofy Stance on snowboard where right foot is at the front.

Granular/frozen granular A harder, icier version of corn snow – typically found early morning.

Grooming Smoothing of trails using mechanical equipment, typically snowcats, to prevent formation of moguls.

Halfpipe U-shaped ditch with sides made of smooth, compacted snow used by freestylers for aerial tricks. They are groomed by a pipe dragon, a form of snowcat, the more frequently groomed the better. The larger superpipes, with walls 17ft and higher, are competition standard.

Herring-bone Climb uphill on skis, using them in a spread-eagled fashion so as not to slide backward.

Huck Launch from a jump.

In-bounds Within the limits of a maintained and patrolled ski area.

Jib Riding a snowboard or skis on a surface other than snow, particularly rails. Used as both noun and verb.

Kicker Jump with ramp that launches the skier or rider into the air suddenly and steeply.

Lifties Seasonal workers who operate and oversee all mountain lifts.

Magic carpet Conveyor-belt surface lift, designed for absolute beginners.

Mailbox An extended mailbox rail used as an obstacle in terrain parks.

Moguls See bumps.

Never-evers First-time skier or riders also known as newbies.

Nordic skiing See cross-country skiing.

Off-piste Terrain that is not groomed as a run, either within or outside ski area boundaries, though the latter is more usually termed backcountry.

Packed powder Snow that has hardened thanks to grooming and skier or rider traffic.

Pipe Common way of referring to a halfpipe of any size.

Piste Maintained ski run; more commonly called trail in North America.

Poma Type of gondola made by the French Poma corporation.

Powder Fresh, dry, and lightweight snow; also used to describe new snowfall.

Quarterpipe Halfpipe divided lengthways and used for single aerial maneuvers.

Rail slide Metal rail built as an obstacle for airborne skis and snowboards to slide down.

Regular Stance on snowboard where left foot is at the front.

Ride Ride is to snowboarders what skiing is to skiers, though terms can be used interchangeably.

Rollers Series of natural mounds or ridges on a slope which result in a motion similar to that on a rollercoaster; temporary weightlessness, alternating with high-speed plummeting.

Runouts Horizontally pitched area that allows skiers to slow down from a fast section above or a term for a fairly flat run to link harder runs with the base of a lift.

Schussing Skiing straight down without turning.

Session To repeatedly do the same run or part thereof.

Shaped ski Ski that is far wider at the tip and tail than at the center and generally far wider than traditional skis. Also known as carving skis and similar to powder skis which tend to be a little wider all over.

Sixpack High-speed lift carrying up to six skiers up the mountain at a time.

Skate-skiing Type of cross-country skiing that uses skating technique and shorter skis.

Skier's left The area to the left of a skier or boarder traveling downhill.

Skier's right The area to the right of a skier or boarder traveling downhill.

Ski-in Accommodation that can be skied to from the ski area.

Ski-out Accommodation located where you can ski from the door to the lifts.

Snowboard park See terrain park.

Snowcat Caterpillar vehicle used on snow, typically for grooming resorts or cat skiing.

Snowplow Method of slowing and turning in skiing; done by bringing tips together, pushing tails apart, and putting most of the weight on the inside **edges**.

Snowskate park Area set aside with small jumps and jibs, for the use of snowskates – a skate and snowboard hybrid.

Straightlining Skiing or riding straight down; like **schussing**.

Superpipe A large version of a **halfpipe** (usually with 15–18ft walls).

Surface lift Lift that requires skiers or boarders to be pulled or towed along the surface of the snow, rather than sitting on a chairlift or gondola.

T-bar Ski lift, usually for beginners, that tows one or two riders up a hill.

Telemark skiing An early form of skiing, now a hybrid of cross-country and downhill skiing; best for **backcountry skiing**.

Terrain park Assemblage of jumps and obstacles typically cordoned off from the rest of the ski area and designed for freestyle skiing or riding; often contains a **halfpipe**.

Tracked-up Fresh or freshly groomed snow that has seen a fair bit of traffic.

Transitions or trannies Section of halfpipe that links the floor with the vertical walls.

Traverse Descending a run in a zigzag pattern using its full width to ease the gradient.

Tree well Dangerous hollow spaces formed around the base of trees after substantial snow build up.

Vertical Consistent and fairly steep slope angle down a run or set of runs.

Wedge-turn See **snowplow**.

Wind-hold Temporary closure of lifts due to high wind.

Index

and small print

Index

Map entries are in color

INDEX

A Rough Guide to Rough Guides

In the summer of 1981, Mark Ellingham, a recent graduate from Bristol University, was traveling round Greece and couldn't find a guidebook that really met his needs. On the one hand there were the student guides, insistent on saving every last cent, and on the other the heavyweight cultural tomes whose authors seemed to have spent more time in a research library than lounging away the afternoon at a taverna or on the beach.

In a bid to avoid getting a job, Mark and a small group of writers set about creating their own guidebook. It was a guide to Greece that aimed to combine a journalistic approach to description with a thoroughly practical approach to travelers' needs – a guide that would incorporate culture, history, and contemporary insights with a critical edge, together with up-to-date, value-for-money listings. Back in London, Mark and the team finished their Rough Guide, as they called it, and talked Routledge into publishing the book.

That first *Rough Guide to Greece*, published in 1982, was a student scheme that became a publishing phenomenon. The immediate success of the book – with numerous reprints and a Thomas Cook prize shortlisting – spawned a series that rapidly covered dozens of destinations. Rough Guides had a ready market among low-budget backpackers, but soon also acquired a much broader and older readership that relished Rough Guides' wit and inquisitiveness as much as their enthusiastic, critical approach. Everyone wants value for money, but not at any price.

Rough Guides soon began supplementing the "rougher" information about hostels and low-budget listings with the kind of detail on restaurants and quality hotels that independent-minded visitors on any budget might expect, whether on business in New York or trekking in Thailand.

These days the guides – distributed worldwide by the Penguin Group – offer recommendations from shoestring to luxury and cover more than 200 destinations around the globe, including almost every country in the Americas and Europe, more than half of Africa and most of Asia and Australasia. Our ever-growing team of authors and photographers is spread all over the world, particularly in Europe, the USA, and Australia.

In 1994, we published the *Rough Guide to World Music* and *Rough Guide to Classical Music*; and a year later the *Rough Guide to the Internet*. All three books have become benchmark titles in their fields – which encouraged us to expand into other areas of publishing, mainly around popular culture. Rough Guides now publish:

- Travel guides to more than 200 worldwide destinations
- Dictionary phrasebooks to 22 major languages
- History guides ranging from Ireland to Islam
- Maps printed on rip-proof and waterproof Polyart™ paper
- Music guides running the gamut from Opera to Elvis
- Restaurant guides to London, New York, and San Francisco
- Reference books on topics as diverse as the Weather and Shakespeare
- Sports guides from Formula 1 to Man Utd
- Pop culture books from Lord of the Rings to Cult TV
- World Music CDs in association with World Music Network

Visit **www.roughguides.com** to see our latest publications.

Rough Guide Credits

Text editor: Glenn Kaplan
Managing Director: Kevin Fitzgerald
Series editor: Mark Ellingham
Editorial: Martin Dunford, Jonathan Buckley, Kate Berens, Ann-Marie Shaw, Helena Smith, Olivia Swift, Ruth Blackmore, Geoff Howard, Claire Saunders, Gavin Thomas, Alexander Mark Rogers, Polly Thomas, Joe Staines, Richard Lim, Duncan Clark, Peter Buckley, Lucy Ratcliffe, Clifton Wilkinson, Alison Murchie, Andrew Dickson, Fran Sandham, Sally Schafer, Matthew Milton, Karoline Densley (UK); Andrew Rosenberg, Yuki Takagaki, Richard Koss, Hunter Slaton, Chris Barsanti (US)
Design & layout: Link Hall, Helen Prior, Julia Bovis, Katie Pringle, Rachel Holmes, Andy Turner, Dan May, Tanya Hall, John McKay, Sophie Hewat (UK); Madhulita Mohapatra,

Umesh Aggarwal, Sunil Sharma (India)
Cartography: Maxine Repath, Ed Wright, Katie Lloyd-Jones (UK); Manish Chandra, Rajesh Chhibber, Jai Prakesh Mishra (India)
Cover art direction: Louise Boulton
Picture research: Sharon Martins, Mark Thomas
Online: Anja Mutic-Blessing, Jennifer Gold, Suzanne Welles, Cree Lawson (US); Manik Chauhan, Amarjyoti Dutta, Narender Kumar (India)
Finance: Gary Singh
Marketing & publicity: Richard Trillo, Niki Smith, David Wearn, Chloë Roberts, Demelza Dallow, Claire Southern (UK); Geoff Colquitt, David Wechsler, Megan Kennedy (US)
Administration: Julie Sanderson
RG India: Punita Singh

Publishing Information

This first edition published September 2003 by **Rough Guides Ltd**,
80 Strand, London WC2R 0RL.
345 Hudson St, 4th Floor,
New York, NY 10014, USA.
Distributed by the Penguin Group
Penguin Books Ltd,
80 Strand, London WC2R 0RL
Penguin Putnam, Inc.
375 Hudson Street, NY 10014, USA
Penguin Books Australia Ltd,
487 Maroondah Highway, PO Box 257,
Ringwood, Victoria 3134, Australia
Penguin Books Canada Ltd,
10 Alcorn Avenue, Toronto, Ontario,
Canada M4V 1E4
Penguin Books (NZ) Ltd,
182–190 Wairau Road, Auckland 10,
New Zealand
Typeset in Bembo and Helvetica to an original design by Henry Iles.
Printed in Italy by LegoPrint S.p.A

560pp includes index
A catalogue record for this book is available from the British Library

ISBN 1-84353-079-1

1   3   5   7   9   8   6   4   2

Help us update

We've gone to a lot of effort to ensure that the first edition of **The Rough Guide to Skiing & Snowboarding in North America** is accurate and up-to-date. However, things change – places get "discovered", opening hours are notoriously fickle, restaurants and rooms raise prices or lower standards. If you feel we've got it wrong or left something out, we'd like to know, and if you can remember the address, the price, the time, the phone number, so much the better.

We'll credit all contributions and send a copy of the next edition (or any other Rough

Guide if you prefer) for the best letters. Everyone who writes to us and isn't already a subscriber will receive a copy of our full-color thrice-yearly newsletter. Please mark letters: **"Skiing & Snowboarding in North America Update"** and send to: Rough Guides, 80 Strand, London WC2R 0RL, or Rough Guides, 4th Floor, 345 Hudson St, New York, NY 10014. Or send an email to **mail@roughguides.com**
Have your questions answered and tell others about your trip at **www.roughguides.atinfopop.com**

Acknowledgments

The authors would like to collectively thank: Glenn Kaplan for his patient, persistent and quality editing, along with Julie Feiner who helped get this guide off the ground and Hunter Slaton for additional editing (and driving) assistance; Martin Dunford and Andrew Rosenberg for giving us the opportunity to write the guide and for overall guidance, support, and the occasional re-write; Katie Lloyd-Jones and Maxine Repath for their map-making genius; Andy Turner and Katie Pringle for the lovely layout; Stephen Lipuma and Louise Boulton for their fine photo-researching; and Margaret Doyle for eagle-eyed proofreading.

Stephen would like to thank all of the invaluable people who helped out during both the researching and writing stages of this guide, including but certainly not limited to: Karl Stone; Cheryl Fullerton; Susan Duplessis; Ken Kraus; Nathan Rafferty; Dan Malstrom; Connie Marshall; Dave Fields; Melissa Mabe; Katie Eldridge; Kristen Case; Susie Barnett Bushong; Anna Olson; Kim Jackson; Grizzly; Pam Cruickshank; Andrew Rubenstein; Kirt Zimmer; Jeanne McKenna; Myra Foster; Andrew Lafrenz; Chris Johnston; Sarah Romish; Ann "KMA" Yuhas; the entire RG posse, who I miss greatly; Tamsin and Christian for their help and hard work; Ted and the rest of the Coyle clan for ice-riding in Maine; Justin, Randy, John and Jon for all the good days; Michael, Lino and Dee for all the love; and my wonderful parents, for continued support and rent-free use of the office. Finally, thanks to Sandra for keeping me sane and in love with life: you are the greatest.

Christian: thanks all those at the ski resorts of Canada and Washington State who helped with this guide. In Canada special thanks to Justin Downes at Kicking Horse; Jikke Stegeman at Kimberley; Eric Ommundsen at Panorama; Melody Kultgen at Fernie; Christine Grimble at Lake Louise; Andrè-Anne Lèonard at Tremblant; Maude Bedard at Mont Sainte-Anne; Cathy Owen and Christopher Nicolson at Whistler; Don Beaulieu at Sunshine Village; Rob Ellen at Marmot Basin; and Jenny Rutherfurd-Drasdo at Big White. And an extra special thanks to those who went well out of their way to assist me: Lucie Fortier and Lynn Russell at Red Mountain; and Vince Accardi and Leah McFarlan at Sun Peaks; in Washington thanks to Tiana Enger at Crystal Mountain

and Lori Vandenbrink at Stevens Pass; Jocelyn Byfield in Vancouver ("Jocelyn?" "No!"). Thanks also to Raymond for appreciating the fluffiness of powder and pancakes and to Nabby for running illegal *fromage* over international borders (sorry about the knee). At Rough Guides thanks goes to Andrew Rosenberg for deciding I was the right man for the job and to Glenn Kaplan for sticking with us during editing despite almost losing his sanity and probably beginning to gray in the process.

Tamsin: Kudos to all the local tourist board and resort staff who helped out, skied and drank with me, and answered endless questions, often at the last minute; and to SIA (Snowsports Industries of America) for being an invaluable resource. Thanks to all who kept me company and let me crash on their floors, particularly Shea, Pezz and John, Beth, Brad and Maya, the Vail Polar crew, and Bubba and co in CO; Kyle and Kelsey in NM; Alison, Charlotte, Doug, Bryan, Timmy, Talla and Munky in SF; Chuck Mass, Boddeker, Sylvia, Lisa and Halo in Tahoe; Martha and Gary, Jake Randazzo, Sean Dog and the crew at Outward Bound in AK; Jason, Natalie, Document Snowboard Magazine and the Winter Mission jokers; and Rebecca and Shem, bdub, Mags and Wig. Special thanks for helping to maintain my sanity while writing up goes to Leka, Rusty, Kaia and Ruby, Bod and Theresa, and to Sara; thanks to Fos for the confectionary, Gin for the tunes, and Tyler for living near the best skateparks in the country. For flow, champions include Dan Johnston at Volvo and the good people at Salomon, K2, Slam City Skates, Giant, Bonfire, Bakoda, Local Motion and GMC. Respect is due to all the ski patrols of North America, particularly those at Monarch Mountain. In addition to appreciation for the tireless work of all at the Rough Guide offices, I'm extremely grateful to Stephen Timblin for constant support and backup. Finally, my most indebted thanks go to the NHS and staff at the Middlesex Hospital, who put me back together in order that I might go and hurt myself again.

The **editor** would also like to thank Andy Turner, Katie Pringle, Katie Lloyd-Jones, and Margaret Doyle; Hunter Slaton for his last-minute editorial support; all the editors at Rough Guides for their good humor; and Andrew Rosenberg for his invaluable editorial assistance and direction.

Photo Credits

Rough Guides travel

key: 🌍 map   🖹 phrasebook   ⊙ cd

Rough Guides publishes new books every month

Rough Guides music & reference

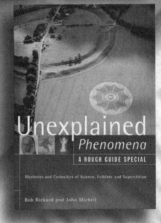

NOTES

NOTES

NOTES

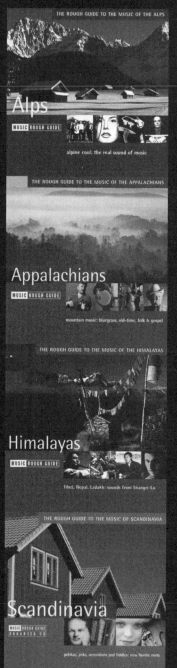